Double coincidence three times

On December 5, 1664, a ship with 81 passengers sank in the Menai Strait off the coast of Wales, leaving only one survivor, a man named Hugh Williams. On December 5, 1785, 121 years later, another ship sank in the Menai Strait and, again, all of the passengers perished except one – named Hugh Williams. On December 5, 1860, yet another ship, a small, 25-passenger vessel, sank in the Menai Strait. And once again there was only one survivor – and once again his name was Hugh Williams . . .

Human Combustion Survivor

Although there are many recorded instances of people bursting into flames for no apparent reason, sceptics contend that human spontaneous combustion is impossible. But you won't convince Jack Angel of Atlanta, Georgia. Some believe Angel to be the only victim of the phenomenon who has lived to tell the tale . . .

CHARLES BERLITZ'S
World of
STRANGE PHENOMENA

Mysterious and Incredible Facts
Strange People and Amazing Stories
The Odd and the Awesome

WARNER BOOKS

A *Warner* Book

First published in Great Britain in 1995
in three volumes: *Mysterious and Incredible Facts, Strange People and Amazing Stories* and *The Odd and the Awesome* by Sphere Books 1989, 1990 and 1991

Copyright © Charles Berlitz and Stonesong Press, Inc 1988, 1990, 1991

This omnibus edition published by Warner Books 1995

The moral right of the author has been asserted.

A CIP catalogue record for this book
is available from the British Library.

ISBN 0 7515 1482 9

Printed in England by Clays Ltd, St Ives plc

Warner
A Division of
Little, Brown and Company (UK)
Brettenham House
Lancaster Place
London WC2E 7EN

Beneath the tides of time and space—
strange fish are swimming!

Volume One Contents

Volume Two Contents

Volume Three Contents

CHARLES BERLITZ'S

World of

STRANGE PHENOMENA

■■■ VOLUME 1: ■■■

Mysterious and Incredible Facts

Foreword

The fascination that mystery exerts on the human mind has been the reason for the extension of our knowledge of the world around us and the development of modern science. Our continuing desire to solve the mysteries of space has pushed us toward exploration of our solar system, the stars and planets of our universe, and then to the other universes beyond.

During the last five hundred years we have nearly exhausted our exploration of the world's geographic mysteries. We have mapped or photographed most of the earth's surface, and, since the 1940s, have been able to record the approximate position of the mountains, gulfs, plains, and abysses on the sea bottom. Hunters and zoologists have alternately exterminated or catalogued most of the world's animal life, although the depths of the sea may have reserved some surprises. Modern and ancient man have been exhaustively studied and classified. Even remote and uncivilized populations have been made familiar to everyone via television, which itself only a few centuries ago would have been considered a breathtaking manifestation of magic.

In a world of computers, robots, guided missiles, space travel, manipulative genetics, and the first steps in the artificial creation of life, one wonders if there are any further mysteries to be solved, or, considering the dangers of the atomic age and the development of scientific warfare, whether there will be time to discover further secrets of the universe—before mankind is destroyed.

Certainly much still remains clouded in mystery. Even today, at the apogee of our scientific expertise, the mysteries of space, time, coincidence, paranormal manifestations, and exceptions to what we consider natural law remain elusive. As our search for the unknown has progressed, our formerly separate concepts of science and the paranormal have begun to merge. We now classify a whole range of paranormal potentialities.

The power of the human mind, for one thing, is proving to be much more powerful than previously thought. Quasi-physical manifestations of the mind now being extensively studied include telepathy, teleportation, telekinesis, and the ability to see what is happening in far places and in other times.

Ghosts are paranormal phenomena that have overstepped the boundaries of fiction and are making their way into serious scientific studies. What are ghosts? The Indians of the Amazon and the natives of New Guinea have no difficulty accepting the visual actuality of ghosts when they see films of tribesmen who they know have died. It is difficult to explain to them that the movie camera has reproduced scenes from the past. To them it is much more simple: The camera has captured the departed spirit. To ourselves, we can explain the camera; but how can we explain the multitude of "haunted" places—houses, castles, battlefields, and ships—so often reported in our modern scientific world? Do there exist residues of personalities or events that can be captured and reconstructed?

Thought transference through telepathy is on the verge of becoming an accepted theory. It is believed that animals, within the pack or herd, employ this ability for warnings and hunting, and it is probable that human beings made use of this faculty as well before they became civilized. Even now, cloaked in our veneer of civilization, we often experience moments of unlearned prescience, which seem to indicate that we possess some powers of telepathy. The power to foresee future events, however, is still a mystery, one that may be linked to the final secrets of space and time.

Are all future prophecies simply lucky guesses? Jules Verne, in writing of a trip to the moon by rocket 150 years before such an event happened, imagined and then described the length and shape of the rocket accurately. His fictional rocket missed the arrival time of the real rocket by only fourteen minutes.

Verne's prediction may have been just a lucky guess, but as far as prescience in prophecy is concerned it is extremely difficult to discredit Nostradamus, who, during his lifetime in the sixteenth century, accurately foretold the duration of the not-yet-existent British Empire, details of the French Revolution two hundred years before it happened, the two World Wars of modern times, complete with air raids and city evacuations and a German Führer with the slightly garbled name of "Hister." Nostradamus foretold earthquakes on the west coast of the New World and even some of the most recent events in Libya and Iran.

We have no acceptable explanation for the accuracy of detailed prophecies from the far past. Time, as we understand it, is a road from the past to the future through the present. But perhaps it is a two-way street, a theory of some who believe that time, like space, may be circular.

Perhaps the most striking example of prophecy comes from ancient India, from descriptions in the *Mahabarata* and other records composed thousands of years ago. These books described projectiles that would burst with the force and heat of "ten thousand suns," obliterating the opposing army, sweeping war elephants, chariots, and men up into the vortex, destroying cities, poisoning food supplies, and forcing even the victorious soldiers to preserve themselves by washing their bodies, clothing, and equipment in rivers to avoid the fatal aftereffects. These bombs whose explosions caused great "umbrella-like" clouds to spread out from the core were called "the Iron Thunderbolt[s]."

Coincidentally, when the ancient measurements and modern coordinates are compared, the findings indicate that the Iron Thunderbolt was a projectile of approximately the same shape and size as the atom bomb dropped on Hiroshima, marking the beginning of the end of World War II.

Not until 1945, when the first atom bomb was exploded in combat, were the descriptions in the *Mahabarata* considered anything but fervid dreams. And now that we have begun to consider the *Mahabarata* seriously, we must examine the possibility that these predictions were perhaps not visions of the future but of the past and that the writings referred to incidents of warfare that actually happened, perhaps over ten thousand years ago, between civilizations that no longer exist.

Perhaps the most inexplicable and mysterious incidents taking place in today's world purportedly occur in the night skies over the Earth. In the United States alone, it is estimated that more than 20 million persons claim to have seen unidentified flying objects (UFOs or OVNIs in Latin countries) and half of the total population believe in their reality.

Although objects in the skies have been seen since ancient times and have been randomly interpreted as divine lessons, signs, tests, and omens, UFO sighting has only gripped the general attention of the world's nations since 1947, when pilot Kenneth Arnold encountered and pursued a group of unknown objects spinning over the Cascade Mountains of Washington, which, he observed, resembled "flying saucers." It is notable that these unexpected visitors have, from the first wave, been seen over the southwestern United States, especially in Arizona, at times that concurred with government experiments concerning the elemental forces of the universe, as if the occupants of the craft, whether from Earth or space, were especially interested in them.

Today UFOs receive worldwide notice and press coverage. They are reported by people all over the world and regularly over the Bermuda Triangle, which, because of its magnetic anomalies and sudden climatic aberrations, has been considered by some a cosmic gateway for visitors from space.

UFOs have been reported to be of different shapes, although they are usually said to be round. They have been observed and photographed from planes, merchant ships, and naval craft. They buzz planes and seem to interfere with tracking radar. They also seem to be capable of inconceivable speeds and are able to vanish at will.

Suppose they *are* real; why are they flying through the skies of Earth? Do they come for new materials, water, exploration, conquest, or, more altruistically, have they come to warn us about our blowing up our planet? (If this last is true, such a benign approach has rarely been evident in our own historical records of human invaders.)

Mankind is approaching maturity and is preparing to face mysteries not only concerned with the exploration of the earth but also with that of the solar system, the stars (and planets?) of the galaxy, and the universes beyond and the possible entities that we may meet there, as well as those which, in our airspace, appear to be investigating *us*.

The great mysteries of our time, those which affect us most deeply, do not deal, as in an earlier age, with the unknown parts of the Earth but with the cosmos, our planetary system, the galaxy, and the universe beyond. The mysteries of today also concern the human mind, its communicative powers, and even its physical powers, of which we are just beginning to be aware. We are becoming more serious in our study of such things as prescience, coincidence, dreams, reincarnation, inherited memories from ancestors, psychic manifestations, and UFOs. The witchcraft of former times is now the object of scientific inquiry.

We have long embarked on the study of life and how to prolong it, but now we are developing functional forms of invented life, namely robotics, and soon we may be able to create life itself, which the magicians of former centuries tried unsuccessfully to do. We are now able to control or destroy large sections of the Earth. But even the ancient magicians did not contemplate the destruction by man of the Earth itself.

To protect what we have and to further our capabilities, we still possess a potent shield—the largely untapped potential and the positive power of the human mind in its search for the solution to the mysteries that surround us.

CHARLES BERLITZ'S
World of
Strange
Phenomena

Murdered and Reincarnated

⬤
___

Dr. Ian Stevenson is the world's foremost expert on reincarnation, a specialist in tracking down cases of children who seem to remember past lives. Particularly striking are those cases in which the child is born with birthmarks seemingly inherited from his or her past existence. One of his most dramatic cases is that of Ravi Shankar, who was born in Kanauj in Uttar Pradesh, India, in 1951.

From his earliest years, Ravi claimed that he was really the son of a man named Jageshwar, a barber who lived in a nearby district. He also claimed that he had been murdered. His present-life father did not believe a word and started beating him to make him stop talking such nonsense. The beatings did little to suppress Ravi's memories, and he became more obsessed with his past-life revivifications the older he grew. He even developed the strange delusion that his former murderers were still out to get him. While the entire story was fantastic, Ravi had, in fact, been born with a bizarre birthmark. It was a two-inch long serrated mark under his chin that resembled some sort of knife wound.

Ravi's memories and obsession were eventually traced to a murder that took place in the local region six months before his birth. On July 19, 1951, the young son of Jageshwar Prasad—a local barber—was murdered by two men, who decapitated him. The men, actually relatives, wanted to inherit the father's estate. Even though the murderers were taken into custody, they had to be released because of a legal technicality.

When Jageshwar Prasad learned of Ravi's claims, he decided to visit the Shankar family to check out the reports personally. The barber conversed with Ravi for an extended period of time and Ravi gradually recognized him as his former father. Ravi even offered him detailed information about his murder, information known only to Jageshwar and the police. And to this day, Ravi still shows that strange birthmark under his chin, a remnant of his past-life murder in India.

The Self-Propelled Coffin

Many critics contend that coincidence is nothing more than an artifact of human consciousness. Separate incidents simply float to the surface of our awareness, goes the argument, where they are noticed and turned into coincidences. In other words, we remember the so-called coincidence but forget a myriad of other occurrences that have no obvious connection.

What is one to make, then, of the curious coffin of Charles Coughlan? Coughlan was born in the Canadian province of Prince Edward Island, on the northeastern seaboard. But the end of the nineteenth century found him in Galveston, jewel of the Texas Gulf Coast, performing in a traveling actors' troupe for his daily bread. The year was 1899; Coughlan collapsed and died, perhaps from one of the tropical fevers rampant in the era before autopsies.

Coughlan was laid to what was supposed to be perpetual rest in a lead-lined coffin and buried in the community cemetery. Galveston itself, then Texas's most populous and prosperous city, was built on what amounted to a big sandbar, a precarious position that left it vulnerable to hurricane and high sea alike.

On September 8, 1900, hundred-mile-an-hour winds pushed a twenty-foot wall of water into the town, submerging all but the highest structures. The town was totally destroyed. Somewhere between six and eight thousand Galvestonians perished, drowned in their shoes, their bodies washed out to the open sea by the returning swell.

The dead were disturbed, too. The cemeteries were churned open by battering waves, coffins left their graves and floated away with the tide. For eight years, Coughlan's lead-encased corpse bobbed in the warm waters of the Gulf Stream. Eventually, it made its way around the tip of the Florida Keys and into the Atlantic, where the prevailing currents carried it north along the Carolinas and the New England coast.

In October 1908, a small fishing vessel off Prince Edward Island spotted the battered box awash in the tide. Attaching a grappling hook, the crew hauled it aboard. A copper nameplate revealed the weatherworn coffin's contents.

The coffin was washed ashore less than a mile from the small church were Coughlan had originally been christened. His remains were removed and buried again, right where his journey had started so many years and miles before.

Musical Mystery

Rosemary Brown, a London widow, owned a piano but was not very accomplished at playing it. She knew only one musician—a former church organist who was trying to teach her to play. The music world and the rest of London was hard-pressed to explain then, how, in 1964, she began writing pieces of music that seemed to come from the masters themselves.

Indeed, Brown was a self-proclaimed clairvoyant, whose mother and grandmother were also alleged to be psychic. She said that Franz Liszt, who had "visited" her once before in a vision when she was a child, appeared to her and began bringing music from the likes of Beethoven, Bach, Chopin and others. Each dictated his own music. Sometimes, she said, they controlled her hands, moving them to the proper keys; sometimes they only dictated the notes. But among the works she produced were the completion of Beethoven's Tenth and Eleventh Symphonies, which had been incomplete at the time of his death; a forty-page sonata by Schubert; and numerous works by Liszt and the others.

Musicians and psychologists alike examined the material and investigated every line of music and every line of Brown's testimony. Although some music critics dismissed the work as copied, and not copied well, others were amazed at the quality of the work. All agreed that each piece she produced was definitely written in the style of the composer to which it was attributed. No one has found evidence that she was lying, and most investigators pronounced her to be sincere. Quality music or not, it was music well beyond Brown's capability.

Liszt, however, had failed Brown in one respect. In his first visit to her, the clairvoyant claimed, Liszt had promised to make her a great musician one day. Yet she remained an unaccomplished pianist. Perhaps that is why, Mrs. Brown's story goes, the composers, who dictated to her in English, would often raise their hands and yell "Mein Gott!"

I Came Back for My Dog

Joe Benson of Wendover, Utah, was a spiritual leader of the Goshute Indians. His constant companion was a magnificent German shepherd he called Sky.

As Benson grew old and his vision failed, Sky guarded his steps and kept him from harm. Benson's health continued to decline and one day in late 1962 he told his wife Mable that he was about to die. She notified the relatives and soon they and their children had come to his bedside. But because they no longer followed the Indian traditions, they insisted that he be taken to the hospital in nearby Owyhee, Nevada. They ignored his protests and Sky's deep-throated growls and carried him away.

Benson stayed at the hospital for only a short time. When the doctors saw there was nothing to be done, they sent him back home, where soon afterwards, in January 1963, he died.

After the funeral ceremonies several of the mourners asked if they could have Sky. Mrs. Benson, who saw that the dog seemed to be grieving even more than she was, sensed that this would be wrong, so she kept him.

Ten days later she happened to look out the window to see someone coming up the road to the house. She built a fire in the cookstove and put on some fresh coffee. When she looked up, she saw someone she recognized in the doorway: her late husband.

True to her people's traditions, she gently told him he was dead and had no business in this world. Joe Benson nodded and said only, "I am going. I came back for my dog."

He whistled and Sky, his tail wagging furiously, came running into the kitchen.

"I want his leash," Benson said. His wife took it down from a hook on the wall and handed it to him, taking care not to touch him. He snapped the leash on Sky's collar and the old man and his dog went out the door, down the steps, and on to the path that wound around the hill.

After hesitating for a few moments, Mrs. Benson ran outside to the other side of the hill. Joe and Sky were nowhere to be seen.

As it happened, Joe and Mable's next-door neighbor, their daughter Arvilla Benson Urban, witnessed this strange visitation and swore to it in an affidavit. She said, "I saw my father enter the house and not more than a few minutes later I saw him leave with his dog on a leash. I saw my mother go after him and I, after I could think, went after her.

"When I reached the top of the hill, my father and his dog were gone."

For the next several days the young men of the family searched for the dog without success. It appeared that Sky had vanished, with his beloved master, into another world.

A Vengeful Ghost

The strange story began on February 21, 1977, when the body of Teresita Basa was found by police. The forty-eight-year-old woman was lying on the floor of her high-rise Chicago apartment, stabbed to death and partially burned.

Like so many other hopeful immigrants, Basa had come to the United States from the Philippines seeking employment and a better quality of life. She had been working as a respiratory therapist at Edgewater Hospital, and the police didn't have a clue toward solving the crime. Their initial impression was that perhaps she had been killed by a boyfriend. The real solution to the case, however, would eventually come from Basa's ghost.

Dr. José Chua and his wife also worked at the hospital, though they hadn't been particularly close to Teresita. But one evening while home together in Skokie, a small city just outside Chicago, Mrs. Chua unexpectedly entered a strange sort of trance. She got up and walked into the bedroom, where she lay down. Then a strange voice, speaking in Tagalog (a Philippine language) issued from her mouth: "I am Teresita Basa." After the strange voice accused a hospital orderly of the murder, Mrs. Chua emerged from the spell. But she suffered similar spells during the next several days, declaring in the murdered woman's voice, that the orderly, a black youth named Allen Showery, had taken her jewelry and given her pearl cocktail ring to his common-law wife.

Dr. Chua, terrified by the claims, was left with no alternative but to contact the local police. His call was turned over to Joseph Stachula and Lee Epplen, two veteran detectives.

The detectives were naturally skeptical of Dr. Chua's story, but with no other leads in the case, decided to follow it up. When they met with the Chuas, they questioned them minutely about the deceased Teresita Basa's claims. They especially asked the couple if Teresita claimed that she was raped as well as murdered. No rape had actually taken place and the detectives asked this question to see if the couple would follow the spurious lead. But the Chuas didn't take the bait. The investigators were also impressed by how much the Chuas seemed to know about the murder.

"To this day," Detective Stachula wrote some time later, "I'm not quite sure that I believe how the information was obtained. Nonetheless, everything [was] completely true."

Working with these clues, the Evanston police searched Showery's apartment and found Teresita's jewels. They even found her pearl cocktail ring in the possession of his girlfriend. When confronted with the evidence, Showery confessed to the murder and was later convicted of the crime. The case was officially closed in August, apparently solved by the ghost of Teresita.

The Slow but Sure Bullet

Henry Ziegland of Honey Grove, Texas, walked out on his girlfriend one day in 1893. Her brother did his "heroic" duty and shot Ziegland. Ziegland, however, was barely injured by the bullet, which only left a small scar on his face before embedding itself in the trunk of the tree in front of which Ziegland was standing. The brother, thinking himself avenged, ended his own life with the same weapon.

Twenty years later, in 1913, Ziegland decided to remove the tree from his property. Unable to perform the task manually, he decided to use dynamite. In the explosion, the bullet, which had originally been intended for Ziegland, became dislodged with such a catapulting jolt that it was shot violently into Ziegland's head, killing him at last.

The Strange Moons of Mars

It was not until 1877 that the astronomer Asaph Hall, while observing the night sky through instruments, first saw two moons circling Mars, moons that no other astronomers had previously reported seeing.

But Jonathan Swift, the author of the pre-science fiction fantasy *Gulliver's Travels*, wrote about them long before Hall, even nonchalantly giving their proportions and orbits. But this was in a fictional narrative, written in 1726, some 151 years before Asaph Hall "officially" discovered them.

Swift wrote of "two lesser stars or satellites, which revolve about Mars. The innermost is distant from the center of the primary planet exactly three of its diameters, and the outermost five; the former revolves in the space of ten hours, and the latter in twenty-one and a half."

How did Swift know? Had he read about it somewhere in some ancient commentary unknown to science or literature? Or if he imagined it, how did he get it right? He never said.

The moons are now an accepted truth of astronomy. Asaph Hall, in a graceful tribute to antiquity, called them Phoebus (Terror) and Deimos (Rout), which were the ancient names of the *horses* of Mars, the god of war, for whom the red planet was named several thousand years ago.

But an even greater mystery, suggested by the form and eccentric behavior of the moons, is yet to be solved. It has been theorized by some observers that they may be controlled or artificial space stations. This question may be cleared up within the next few years, if space exploration continues its rate of development.

James Chaffin's
Second Will

James L. Chaffin was a North Carolina farmer who died in 1921. His family was no doubt surprised and depressed when they learned the terms of his will. The elderly man left his entire property to his third son Marshall, disinheriting his wife and three other sons completely. The will had been written and properly witnessed in 1905.

Four years later, however, son James P. Chaffin began dreaming that his deceased father wanted to talk to him. He would see the farmer by his bedside, dressed in his old black overcoat; and one day the figure finally said, "You will find my will in my overcoat pocket," and disappeared.

Chaffin was puzzled by the experience, but felt that he should check out the ghost's strange claim. It turned out that the overcoat was in the possession of another brother, so he made the trip to his brother's residence where he found the coat and ripped open its seams. There, hidden in the lining of a pocket, was a piece of paper upon which was written, "Read the twenty-seventh chapter of Genesis." Chaffin realized he was onto something, and so he went to his mother's house accompanied by several witnesses—to whom he eagerly told his story. The Bible wasn't easily found but eventually turned up. The book was so dilapidated that it fell to the floor in three pieces when handled. Thomas Blackwelder was one of the witnesses, and he picked up the portion of the Bible containing the Book of Genesis. He immediately discovered that two pages had been folded together to make a pocket. When he opened it, the surprised witnesses found a handwritten will dated 1919. It appeared that the deceased farmer had reconsidered, for this new document stated in part, "I want, after giving my body a decent burial, my little property equally divided between my four children, if they are living at my death, and the personal and real estate divided equal and if not living, give share to their children. And if she is living, you must take care of your mammy. Now this is my last will and testament.''

By this time, Marshall Chaffin had died and his property was controlled by his widow, so James P. Chaffin took the will to court. Several witnesses testified that the 1919 will was truly in the handwriting of the deceased farmer. Marshall's widow didn't try to fight the case and the small estate was properly redistributed.

Occupants
of a Different Kind

UFO occupants commonly fall into two broad, but distinct categories—extraterrestrial beings virtually indistinguishable from humans in appearance and size, and "humanoid" entities that are typically gray-skinned, thin-limbed and short, with large fetal heads and dark, wrap-around eyes.

But there may be a third category as well. Consider the bizarre beings seen near a Kelly, Kentucky, farmhouse the night of August 21, 1955, by eight adults and three children. This scary episode began when the house's owner, Billy Ray Taylor, rushed inside saying he had seen a flying saucer with a rainbow-colored exhaust land in a nearby forty-foot deep gully. The others laughed at first. Then the dog began barking.

Taylor and Lucky Sutton went to the back door, where they watched in awe as a hideously strange, glowing figure approached across the fields. Only three-and-a-half feet tall, the silvery entity supported a bulbous head with huge, flared ears and long arms ending in sharp talons reaching nearly to the ground. Sutton and Taylor both grabbed guns and fired, knocking the creature backwards, head over heels. Instead of falling to the ground, however, it scurried away.

Back in the living room a few minutes later, the men said they saw a similar creature and fired again. Apparently, they were now under siege, for when Taylor walked out onto the front porch to survey the damage, another one of the entities clawed at him from the roof.

Shortly before midnight, both families piled into two cars and hurtled into nearby Hopkinsville. The police returned to the farmhouse, but could not substantiate the story. One of the searchers stepped on a cat's tail in the dark, however, and nearly ignited a fatal panic. Finally, around 2 A.M., the police left.

The creatures came back once more, the group claims. But when the sun finally came up, they were gone for good.

We Interrupt This Program for a Special Premonition

Disasters are sometimes preceded by visions, dreams, or nightmares that foretell the event. Most of these premonitions come during sleep, but Mrs. Lesley Brennan's incredible vision came over the telly, as it is called in England.

On the morning of Saturday, June 1, 1974, the movie she was watching was interrupted by a special bulletin announcing that an explosion had ripped through the Flixborough Nypro plant, a nearby chemical plant that produced materials used in nylon, and that several people had died. About noon that day, two friends paid her a visit, and she asked them if they had heard about the accident. They hadn't.

And neither had anybody else, because the explosion actually took place at 4:53 P.M. The death toll was twenty-eight, and many were injured. When they heard later newscasts about the explosion, the three women at first thought the newscasters were stating the details incorrectly. But a check of the paper the next day showed the actual time of the explosion.

Brennan could offer no explanation. Perhaps she had fallen asleep and actually dreamed the telecast. Whatever happened, she had relayed the story of the event to two friends almost five hours before it actually occurred.

A Human Lightning Rod

Roy Cleveland Sullivan, a retired forest ranger from Waynesboro, Virginia, was known as the Human Lightning Rod because he had been struck by lightning *seven* times in the course of his thirty-six-year career.

The first strike, in 1942, caused the loss of a big toenail. Twenty-seven years later a second bolt of lightning burned his eyebrows off. The following year, in 1970, a third bolt seared his left shoulder.

After Sullivan's hair was set afire by a fourth strike in 1972, he began hauling a bucket of water around with him in his car. He was driving on August 7, 1973, as a bolt came out of a small, low-lying cloud, hit him on the head through his hat, set his hair on fire again, knocked him ten feet out of his car, went through both legs and knocked his shoe off. Sullivan poured the bucket of water over his head to cool off.

Sullivan was struck for the sixth time on June 5, 1976, hurting his ankle. The seventh blow from above hit Sullivan on June 25, 1977, while he was fishing. He required hospitalization for stomach and chest burns on that occasion.

Though he was never able to explain his peculiar attraction for lightning, Sullivan once said that he could actually see the bolts as they headed for him.

At 3 A.M. on the morning of September 28, 1983, Sullivan, aged seventy-one, took his own life with a bullet. Two of his Ranger hats, burned through the crown by lightning blasts, now reside in Guinness World Exhibit Halls in New York City and Myrtle Beach, South Carolina.

A Chilling Escape

The winter of 1984-85 set numerous cold-wave records across the continental United States from Michigan to Texas. It also saw one of the most remarkable survivals in the annals of modern medicine.

By the morning of January 19, 1985, the temperature in Milwaukee, Wisconsin, had dropped to a bone-numbing sixty degrees below zero. While his parents slept, two-year-old Michael Troche, dressed in light pajamas, wandered outside into the snow.

Found by his frantic father several hours later, Michael had quite literally frozen stiff. He had stopped breathing; ice crystals had formed both on and beneath his skin; and his limbs were rigid as sticks.

Rushed to Milwaukee's Children's Hospital, Michael was treated by a team of twenty nurses and eighteen doctors, including Dr. Kevin Kelly, a specialist in hypothermia. When Michael arrived at the hospital, Kelly pronounced him "dead, extremely dead." Physicians could actually hear his poor, frozen body cracking as they lifted it on to the operating table. And Michael's inner core temperature had fallen to sixteen degrees Centigrade; a precipice from which no one had ever returned alive.

The team set to work immediately, hooking Michael up to a heart-lung machine to warm his blood, injecting drugs to prevent his brain from swelling, thawing his body, and making incisions along his limbs as tissue filled with water from frozen cells and threatened to burst.

For three days the boy lay in a semiconscious state, hovering between life and death. Then, miraculously, Michael recovered almost as quickly as he had been frozen. He suffered some minor muscle damage to one hand and had to undergo skin grafts to patch the long incisions made in his arms and legs, but other than that was remarkably unaffected by his ordeal.

And at last report, the amazing Michael Troche failed to display any evidence of the feared brain damage that would have turned him into a vegetable. Ironically, doctors said he probably survived *because* he was so young and small; he had literally been flash-frozen by the wind-chill factor. His tiny brain and reduced metabolism required little oxygen to operate. A little older and larger, and Michael would have been another winter statistic.

Target: Tunguska!

Shortly after sunrise on June 30, 1908, something from space struck central Soviet Siberia. The eruption, detected on seismographs as far away as the United States and central Europe, was one of the largest explosions the world has ever known. For weeks afterwards, dust and debris thrown up by the gigantic conflagration colored skies and sunsets around the globe. Magnets were affected throughout the world at the moment of impact and horses stumbled and fell in cities thousands of miles distant.

The immediate area, that of the stony Tunguska River basin, was largely devastated. Acres of permafrost instantly turned to steam. Trees were flattened for twenty-five miles, and at ground zero their trunks were sheared of limbs and bark. The forest itself burst into flames. Herds of animals and a few scattered human settlements were incinerated where they stood. The Tungus tribesmen who returned home "found only charred corpses." That night in Europe no night fell. In London a paper could be read at midnight; in Holland pictures could be taken of ships sailing the Zuider Zee.

Because of Tunguska's remoteness, the first scientific investigator did not arrive at the scene of the tragedy until Dr. Leonid A. Kulik, a meteorite specialist from Petrograd, led an expedition there in 1927. Sixty years later the origin of the gigantic Tunguska explosion is still hotly debated.

Was it a wayward comet? A tiny mass of anti-matter that hit

and possibly passed *through* the Earth? Or the nuclear generator of a crippled spaceship, swerving to miss the Earth's population centers? Each theory has its proponents and its problems. Some witnesses interviewed by Kulik and later investigators reported a fiery ball trailing a tail, an image conceivably consistent with either a meteorite or comet. But if the Tunguska object was a meteorite, what happened to the crater, and more importantly, the meteorite itself? None was found. And if it was a comet, why was not it seen sooner on approach? Moreover, since comets are mostly gaseous, "dirty snowballs," where did the immense energy, estimated at thirty megatons, come *from*?

Particle physicists have long prophesied the presence of what they call anti-matter, mirror images of ordinary matter, but negatively charged. Anti-matter as we know it, however, is extremely short-lived. A small body of anti-matter coming into contact with normal matter would indeed result in a sudden, tremendous release of energy. Unfortunately for the hypothesis, no one expects to find lumps of anti-matter floating through this part of the universe.

The Tunguska event *could* have been caused by an extraterrestrial spaceship, but again the evidence is largely inconclusive. Some Soviet researchers have found anomalous radioactivity readings at the devastated site, others have not detected any. A craft would also have to have been completely vaporized in the explosion, because no unusual metal fragments were ever found.

The Bleeding Walls

Atlanta homicide detectives are accustomed to blood. It comes with the territory, along with shot, stabbed and battered bodies. But they weren't prepared for blood *without* a body, especially blood that poured from walls and pooled on the floors of an elderly Georgia couple, William Winston, seventy-nine, and wife Minnie, seventy-seven.

Minnie Winston first noticed the blood spouting from the bathroom floor "like a sprinkler," when she went to take a bath in their three-bedroom brick house of twenty-two years in September of 1987. The couple called the police shortly after midnight on the ninth, when they found more blood oozing from walls and floors in five separate rooms.

"I'm not bleeding," said William Winston. "My wife's not bleeding. And no one else is here." Winston had gone to bed about 9:30 that evening, after locking the doors and activating a security alarm system. Neither of the Winstons heard any intruders, nor did the alarm go off.

Steve Cartwright, an Atlanta homicide detective, admitted the police found "copious amounts of blood" splattered throughout the house, but no corpse, animal or human, that would have accounted for it. The Georgia State Crime Laboratory confirmed the blood as human the following day.

Cal Jackson, Atlanta police spokesman, said the department was treating the incident "as an unusual circumstance because we don't have a body or a cause for the blood."

Spontaneous Human Combustion

Some people say the kitchen is the deadliest room in the house. But on January 8, 1985, seventeen-year-old Jacqueline Fitzsimons, a cookery student at Halton Technical College in Widnes, Cheshire, England, had left the kitchen and was talking to classmates in the corridor when she abruptly burst into flames.

Jacqueline first complained of a burning sensation in her back while talking to a girlfriend, Karen Glenholmes. "Suddenly, Jacqueline said she did not feel well," Karen said. "There was a smell of smouldering and we saw her shirt burning. She screamed to us for help and said she was burning all over. In a moment even her hair was on fire."

Staff members and other students in the hallway ripped away Jacqueline's apron, then beat her burning clothing in an effort to stifle the flames. She was then rushed to hospital, where the devastating damage of her injuries became evident: 18 percent of her skin was burned away. After fifteen days in intensive care, she died.

Cheshire fire prevention officer Bert Gilles admitted he was as baffled as anyone. "I have interviewed seven eyewitnesses," he said. "So far, there is no clear explanation of the fire, though spontaneous combustion is a possibility that should be examined."

A jury in the subsequent coroner's inquest later ruled that Jacqueline Fitzsimons had died of "misadventure," which was certainly true enough.

Cosmic Nemesis

Sixty-five million years ago the dinosaurs disappeared from the earth in the comparative twinkling of a geological eye. Some 165 million years before that, the dinosaurs had been the ruling species of the land, sea, and air.

Paleontologists have long pondered their disappearance, proposing abrupt changes in the earth's climate as the most likely suspect. But what caused those catastrophic changes in the first place? A gradual alteration of the atmosphere or environment should have allowed the dinosaurs ample time to adapt.

The first clue of a cosmic culprit came from the collaboration of a scientific father-and-son team at the University of California Berkeley campus. Geologist Walter Alvarez had been studying deposits near Gubbio, Italy, in 1977, when he discovered a layer of sediment rich in the rare element iridium, not usually found in the Earth's crust. His father, Luis Alvarez, a Nobel laureate in physics, suggested an explanation: A huge, extraterrestrial object, perhaps a comet or asteroid, could have struck the Earth and thrown up a massive amount of debris, raining down a layer of iridium. Fossils in the clay in which the younger Alvarez found iridium dated the deposit to 65 million years ago, the exact time of the great dinosaur extinction.

Other mass extinctions, moreover, seem to occur periodically every 26 million years, give or take a few thousand millennia. Could some recurring cosmic cycle account for such widespread extinctions, including the one that wiped out Tyrannosaurus Rex and his kin?

Some scientists think so. In 1984, Berkeley astrophysicist Richard Muller and astronomer Marc Davis, along with another astronomer, Piet Hut, of Princeton's Institute for Advance Study, proposed the existence of a solar companion known as the Death Star, or Nemesis, circling our sun every 26 to 30 million years. As it nears the solar system, Nemesis' gravitational field might dislodge asteroids in their orbit or drag comets in its wake, sending them crashing into the Earth's surface.

If real, our sun and Nemesis would be bound together in a binary system. In fact, most stars in our galaxy *are* binary, but none are known to have such long periods of revolution. Their orbits are usually measured in weeks or months. Moreover, any such companion star should be readily visible. Muller believes Nemesis may be a small red star, which would render it much harder to detect. Longer periods of revolution among binary systems might be common, too, says Muller. We just haven't recognized them for what they are *because* of their extreme orbits.

A team of astronomers lead by Muller has already eliminated all but three thousand candidate stars visible from the Northern Hemisphere. If Nemesis is not found among those, says Muller, they will turn their attention toward Southern Hemisphere stars.

We needn't worry about the Death Star sneaking up on us in the meantime. Present calculations put Nemesis at the far side of its orbit, meaning it won't return for another 10 to 13 million years.

Firestarter

⬤━━━━━━━━━━━━━━━━━━━━━━━━━━━━━━━

Nothing is more terrifying than a fire on the rampage, especially if—in the true tradition of Stephen King's *Firestarter*—the arsonist lurks subconsciously within the mind. That's the problem the Willey family faced on their Macomb, Illinois, farm in 1948. Mr. Willey operated the farm with his brother-in-law and two children. Rounding out the household was his little niece Wanet. Nothing seemed out-of-the-ordinary there until curious brown spots began appearing on the wallpaper in the house. These spots would become incredibly hot, often reaching 450 degrees Fahrenheit before breaking into flames. The fires were so frequent that the Willeys' neighbors would stay in the house with buckets filled with water, waiting to douse each fire as it erupted. Several of these blazes broke out each day.

Nobody could figure out the cause of the blazes, not even the local fire department. "The whole thing is so screwy and fantastic that I'm almost ashamed to talk about it," admitted local fire chief Fred Wilson to reporters.

As the days rolled by, the fires became more frequent and bizarre. Soon they began to blaze from the porch, curtains, and other places in the house. And explanations began flying about. Representatives from a nearby Air Force base thought that high-frequency radio waves were causing the problem, while fire officials suggested that combustible gas was building up in the farmhouse walls. Despite these clever explanations, no practical answer to the Willeys' problem emerged.

Finally, after witnessing the fires for days, the tired and frustrated fire department badgered a confession from little Wanet. She had started the fires, the department told news reporters, by flicking lighted matches when no one was looking.

Nobody believed that explanation. The best evaluation came from Vincent Gaddis, who studied the case in 1962. Writing in his book *Mysterious Lights and Fires*, he stated that little Wanet must have had "incredible persistence, an unlimited supply of matches, and exceptionally nearsighted relatives and neighbors." In other words, like the heroine of *Firestarter*, he suggested she might have caused the fires through paranormal means, in a way far beyond the comprehension of the local officials.

Life at Stake

Humans have at one time or another survived almost every catastrophe imaginable, from falling out of an airplane without a parachute to impalement by an assortment of sharp instruments. Among the latter category consider the case of English motorcyclist Richard Topps, twenty-one, of Derbyshire, who survived an unwanted encounter with a fence post.

In August of 1985, Topps's motorcycle was involved in a collision with a car, seriously injuring his passenger. Richard himself hurled over the handlebars and into a fence, where he was impaled diagonally from chest to hip on a wooden post four feet long.

Because of the confusion Richard was left hanging for more than an hour, completely conscious but unable to help himself, until he was found by his brother. To free the stake piercing his torso required a two-hour operation, during which surgeons found that all his internal vital organs had escaped damage. Topps quickly recuperated from the surgery and went his way.

Eighteen-year-old Kimberly Lotti of Quincy, Massachusetts, suffered a similar impalement in December 1983 while driving her pickup home from work, and also lived to talk about it. Her truck swerved and cut into a chain-link aluminum fence. One of the two-inch diameter posts broke loose and shattered her windshield, passing all the way through her left upper chest.

"It was eerie," Kimberly said later. "I didn't feel any pain at all. I thought the pipe was just pressing against my arm. I guess I was in shock."

Rescue workers cut the pipe off about five inches from the front and back of her body and hauled her to the hospital, where the rest of the aluminum stake was safely removed.

Lady in Blue

The canon of Catholic miracles bulges with documented historical reports that are of peculiar interest to parapsychologists. For sheer quantity, however, few spiritual careers can match that of the humble Lady in Blue, Suor María Coronel de Agreda. By her own account Suor María bilocated, or appeared in two places at the same time, on some five hundred occasions between the years of 1620 and 1631.

Born in Spain in 1602 to a religious middle-class family, Suor María experienced intense visions while still a child. As a teenager she lapsed easily into ecstatic trances. As a young woman she joined the Franciscan convent of the Immaculate Conception at Agreda.

There she opted for a self-imposed regimen that included long periods of fasting, sleeplessness, and self-flagellation. Among the miracles attributed to her during this time was the uncanny ability to respond to the unspoken thoughts of others and to levitate her frail body above the convent floor.

But it was for her astounding facility of bilocation that Suor María is known. Her ghostly projections, it is said, hurled her across the Atlantic Ocean and into the desert environment of seventeenth-century west Texas, where she ministered to the physical and spiritual needs of a red-skinned, nearly naked people.

Of all the native Indian tribes that inhabited the American Southwest before the coming of the conquistadors, the least is known about the poor Jumanos, who lived along the Rio Grande River near what is modern-day Presidio, Texas. Early in the Spanish migration from Mexico they were encountered by Father Alonzo de Benavides, a Franciscan priest. To his great surprise, he found the mostly hunting-and-gathering Jumanos already converted to Christianity. What's more, they claimed that they had been directed to the meeting by a mysterious "woman in blue," the same gentle soul who had given them rosaries, nursed their wounds, and originally introduced them to the message of Jesus Christ.

Almost as perturbed as he was startled, Father Benavides fired off letters to both Pope Urban VIII and King Philip IV of Spain, demanding to know who had preceded him in his ministry? He did not receive an answer until 1630, on his own return to Spain, when he heard of Suor María's miracles, visited her convent in person, and learned that the habit of her order was blue.

Inside a Tornado

Nature presents numerous violent spectacles, but few compare with the destructiveness and intensity of the tornado, in which centrifugal winds can reach two hundred miles per hour.

Despite a plethora of still and video pictures of tornadoes, however, upclose eyewitness accounts are scarce. But an extremely rare observation of the *interior* of a tornado comes from a storm that blew through McKinney, Texas, north of Dallas, on May 3, 1943. "The bottom of the rim was about twenty feet off the ground," said a startled Roy Hall, whose house the tornado had just destroyed. "The interior of the funnel was hollow; the rim itself appeared to be not over ten feet in thickness and, owing possibly to the light within the funnel, appeared perfectly opaque. Its inside was so slick and even that it resembled the interior of a glazed pipe." The outer rim rotated in front of Hall's eyes with dazzling rapidity.

"I lay back on my left elbow, to afford the baby better protection, and looked up," he continued. "It is possible that in that upward glance my stricken eyes beheld something few have ever seen before and lived to tell about. I was looking far up the interior of a great tornado funnel.

"It extended upward for over a thousand feet, and was swaying gently, bending slowly toward the southeast. Down at the bottom the funnel was about one hundred and fifty yards across. Higher up it was larger, and seemed to be partly filled with a bright cloud, which shimmered like a fluorescent light. This brilliant cloud was in the middle of the funnel, not touching the sides."

Only one other account of the inside of a tornado is known, and that comes from a Greensburg, Kansas, farmer, Will Keller, who watched in awe as one of the terrible twisters skipped over the storm shelter in which he stood on June 22, 1928. The surrounding air, said Keller, was as still as death. The interior of his tornado was lit up, with lightning crackling from side to side. From the ragged rim at the bottom of the funnel, smaller tornadoes formed and whirled away, like an aerial Moby Dick giving birth to a litter of baby whales. The interior also contained a solitary cloud like the one Hall witnessed.

Neither man had anything to gain from fabrication. If true, however, their stories should result in a revision of what we know about tornadoes, particularly since present theory fails to account for such a complicated internal structure, especially one containing clouds and lightning.

A UFO at Socorro

The afternoon of April 24, 1964, found police officer Lonnie Zamora of Socorro, New Mexico, behind the wheel of his white Pontiac patrol car. A black Chevrolet whizzed past the small town courthouse and Zamora took off in chase. Instead of issuing a simple speeding ticket, the five-year veteran policeman took a detour through the Twilight Zone.

He was heading south on Old Rodeo Street in hot pursuit of the offender, when he "heard a roar and saw a flame in the sky to the southwest some distance away." Now outside the city limits, Zamora turned off paved streets onto a rough gravel road leading into the hills and toward the roaring flame.

Zamora slid and swerved up the steep hill. Then he "suddenly noted a shiny type object to the south about one hundred fifty to two hundred yards away." At the bottom of an arroyo, Zamora saw what he first thought was an overturned car "standing on radiator or on trunk." Beside it were "two people in white coveralls. One of these persons seemed to turn and look straight at my car."

Hoping to help, Zamora drove ahead, radioing headquarters about a possible accident. But when he heard the loud roar again, he dove for cover behind his car, knocking his glasses off in the process. Zamora said he could now see that the oval-shaped object was not an automobile at all, but an aluminum-white craft balanced on four landing legs. Its surface was smooth, with no visible doors or windows. Centered on one side was a red insignia, a bisected triangle two-and-a-half feet high and two feet wide. The thing rose out of the arroyo on a tail of fire, Zamora said, as the roar turned to a high-pitched whine.

When he went back to investigate the sighting sometime later, Zamora found some charred greasewood bushes and, more importantly, four podmarks indicating, he believed, the spot where the thing had landed.

Zamora's sighting was later investigated by several military and government officials, including Dr. J. Allen Hynek, then an astronomy consultant for the Air Force's Project Blue Book (a compendium of UFO sightings). Hynek tried to char the bushes with matches and create podlike impressions with a shovel, but found he couldn't satisfactorily reproduce the physical evidence himself. He also interviewed Zamora's old schoolteacher and a number of townsfolk, concluding that Zamora was a "solid, unimaginative cop."

The landing at Socorro, Hynek maintained until the day he died, was one of the most compelling pieces of evidence ever to fit into the puzzle of UFOs. Even more skeptical colleagues at Blue Book were swayed; some Air Force personnel spent years trying to prove Zamora's experience was the result of a secret government weapon gone dangerously awry.

Tucson's
Rock-Throwing Phantom

●──

A nightmare began for Mr. and Mrs. Berkbigler and their five children early in September, 1983. They had just moved into their large, but only half-finished desert home when large rocks started smashing into the structure every night. The rocks seemed to come out of nowhere and even the police couldn't find who was responsible. In short, the Berkbiglers were suffering from a rock-throwing poltergeist, a particularly bothersome sort of spook that likes to pelt houses with stones. The family members invariably ran outside to catch the culprit responsible, but there was never anyone in sight. The attacks would usually start between 5:30 and 7:00 P.M. when the family arrived home from their jobs or school. The stones would come in brief flurries and then stop, only to resume. Sometimes the family heard a mysterious knocking on the doors and windows as well.

The Berkbiglers originally felt that a vagrant was responsible for the mischief, but Mrs. Berkbigler was less sure of the cause. "Maybe it's a spirit," she finally told reporters from the *Arizona Daily Star*. "Maybe we've built over some sacred burial grounds or something."

Soon the local press was calling the Berkbiglers' problem the "phantom stone-thrower." During the following weeks, the local sheriff's department visited the house and called in helicopter surveillance to solve the mystery. They ended up being struck by the rocks themselves, often in broad daylight, and became reluctant to visit the property.

The most frightening episode of the case occurred on Sunday,

December 4. The rocks had been active but sporadic all that day, so two reporters from the *Star* visited the house to interview the family. By 6:10 that evening, rocks were being hurled against the side door of the house with such viciousness that the reporters couldn't leave. The siege lasted for two hours until the family finally called in the police, who escorted the reporters away.

What was so bizarre was that, to hit the side door, the rocks had to travel through the house's open garage. Since a van was parked there that evening, the rocks had to be thrown with uncanny accuracy through a slim, two-foot opening between the garage's ceiling and the roof of the van. Yet the phantom stone-thrower accomplished this superhuman feat without any difficulty.

The case came to its climax on December 6 and 7, when scores of people began showing up at the house to help the family trap the culprit. Despite the constant patrols of the property, the rocks were thrown as usual, picking off people in the pitch black desert with astonishing skill. The self-styled posse succeeded in chasing an intruder from the property, but he turned out to be from the sheriff's office.

But then the rock-throwing simply stopped. The daily sieges ended after the second night of the search, and the case of Tucson's mysterious stone-thrower was left unsolved. It remains so to this day.

From Dream to Reality

One of the worst disasters in aviation history struck Chicago's O'Hare Airport on May 25, 1979. That was the terrible day an American Airlines DC-10 crashed on take-off, killing all of its crew and passengers. The accident stunned the entire country, but came as little surprise to a middle-aged manager in Cincinnati,

Ohio. Beginning on May 16, Dave Booth, who worked with a car rental agency, had dreamt of a terrible airline crash every night.

"The dream would start," he later stated in writing, "with me looking out onto a field from the corner of a one-story building. The building was made of yellow tile bricks and had a gravel roof. The windows facing the field appeared to have paper cutouts pasted in. The impression I received of the building was that it was a school. However, I also associated a factory of some kind with the building. Behind the building was a gravel parking lot with a driveway coming around in front of the building then going back around to the main road behind me. As I'm looking out over the field I see a tree line running from northwest to southeast. All the trees and the grass are green. It is afternoon because the sun is in the west and it is setting, as opposed to rising. Looking over the tree line in a northeasterly direction I see this big airplane in the air. The first impression I get is that for being so close to the airplane it should be making a whole lot more noise than it is making. I keep sensing that something is wrong with the engine. The plane then starts to bank off to the right in an easterly direction, the left wing is going up in the air, very slowly, not in slow motion, the plane rolls over on its back and goes straight down into the ground. As I see the plane hit, it is as though I'm looking at the plane from straight ahead, not a side or rear view of the plane. When the plane hits the ground, there is a huge explosion. I can't think of any words to describe the explosion except that it was awesome. . . . As the sound of the explosion is dying out, I would wake up. The airplane I saw was an American Airlines three-engine jet."

This disaster struck nine days after Booth's dreams began, when an American Airlines DC-10 crashed after taking off at 3:03 P.M. in Chicago. The plane lost an engine just after takeoff, then lost altitude and crashed into an abandoned airport adjacent to O'Hare. Bystanders reported the plane's uncanny silence, as though its remaining engines had failed. The plane also rotated perpendicularly to the ground and hit with its left wing first. Next it struck a hangar and exploded, billowing flames 400 feet into the sky.

Luckily, evidence for Mr. Booth's prediction doesn't rest solely on his personal word. When the dreams began recurring, he became so upset that he contacted both American Airlines and the Cincinnati Aviation Administration. They didn't know what to make of his call, so Booth next called the FAA, where representatives took detailed notes of his call and dreams. Their detailed notes were turned over the Institute for Parapsychology in Durham, North Carolina, where researchers investigated the case.

Booth's disturbing dreams ended on the day of the crash.

Some Dramatic Deaths

The Greek playwright Aeschylus is known as the Father of Tragedy. History so honored him because of his plays, but the same honorific might equally have been bestowed because of the dramatic manner of his demise. According to legend, he was killed when an eagle mistook his bald pate for a rock and let drop a tortoise shell, cracking both open.

Modern victims of fate have suffered similarly ironic demises. Consider the case of the Prague, Czechoslovakia, woman who leapt out a third-floor window after learning of her husband's unfaithfulness. The husband, entering the building just as she jumped, broke her fall. She survived. He died on the spot.

Then there's the thirty-six-year-old San Diego woman who, in 1977, plotted to kill her twenty-three-year-old Marine drill instructor husband for his $20,000 insurance policy. She dropped the venom sac from a tarantula in a blackberry pie she baked, but he only ate a few bites. Next she tried electrocuting him in their shower, but that failed, too. So did attempts to kill him with lye, run him down in a car, inject an air bubble into his veins, and slip amphetamines in his beer while driving in hopes he would hallucinate and crash.

Exasperated, she enlisted a twenty-six-year-old female companion in crime. Together, they beat the husband over the head with metal weights as he slept. It was only at that point that he finally succumbed.

Finally on Memorial Day, 1987, a forty-year-old Louisiana lawyer stood up in his boat as a thunderstorm approached. "Here I am,'' he taunted the skies, raising his hands over his head. A bolt of lightning struck, killing him instantly. The lawyer's first name was Graves.

Falling Frogs

In May of 1981, residents in the southern Greece city of Naphlion woke up to a rain of green frogs. Thousands of the little amphibious creatures, weighing only a few ounces each, plopped out of the sky and flopped in the streets.

Scientists at the Greek Meteorological Institute, Athens, trotted out the usual explanation. A whirlwind out of North Africa had sucked the frogs from a marsh and wafted them some six hundred miles across the Mediterranean to drop them at Naphlion's doorstep.

Remarkably, few of the frogs died from the violent journey. In fact, they adapted quite well to their new surroundings. Some of the local citizens, however, report trouble sleeping at night: Their amphibious immigrants make too much noise.

Languages Reincarnated

What would happen if you hypnotized somebody and they started talking in ancient Norsk? That's just what happened to Dr. Joel Whitton, a prominent Canadian psychiatrist and skeptic exploring the issue of reincarnation.

Ever since the famous Bridey Murphy case back in the 1950s, New Age psychologists have tried regressing their subjects back to their previous lives. Few of them ever seem to come up with anything of interest, but that didn't prevent Whitton from trying, too. The psychiatrist's star subject was a professional psychologist who, during their hypnotic work together, began remembering and hearing foreign languages he apparently spoke during two past lives. What gradually emerged were memories of a Viking existence about A.D. 1000, and an earlier incarnation in Mesopotamia.

Reporting the case to the Toronto Society for Psychical Research, Whitton said his subject successfully recalled some twenty two words of Norsk, the precursor of modern Icelandic and the language used by the ancient Vikings. Many of these words, including those that concerned the sea, have been identified and translated by two experts conversant in Norsk.

Whitton's subject, whose identity has not been revealed, never successfully spoke in seventh-century Mesopotamian, but he did write out some scattered scripts that resemble Sassanid Pahlavi, a dead language common to Persia between the third and seventh centuries A.D.

Whitton is not certain that this unique case proves the existence of reincarnation. It's possible, he concedes, but not likely, that his subject picked up the words and scripts from some normal source.

Sugar, the Homing Cat

Science is far from certain that it understands just how animals "home." Navigation by the position of the sun or by the earth's magnetic field represent two possibilities. But what about lost animals who find their way to their owners through unfamiliar territory? The case of Sugar, the homing cat, represents just such a mystery.

Sugar, a cream-colored Persian cat, was the pride and joy of Mr. and Mrs. Stacy Woods of Anderson, California. The couple decided to leave the area in 1951, but since Sugar was frightened by cars, they reluctantly decided to leave her behind with neighbors. Driving to their new residence on a farm in Oklahoma would be difficult enough without a troublesome cat to contend with. The Woods set out for the town of Gage and probably thought little more of Sugar while setting up their new house. But one day fourteen months later, Mrs. Woods was standing near the barn when a cat leapt through the window, landing right on her shoulder. Mrs. Woods was naturally startled and brushed the cat aside. But in taking a more careful look, she saw that it uncannily resembled Sugar. Both she and her husband soon adopted the feline and often commented on the resemblance.

Despite the coincidence, neither Mr. nor Mrs. Woods really believed the cat *was* Sugar until several days later. Mr. Woods was petting the feline when he noticed the cat's deformed hipbone. This was the exact same defect from which Sugar suffered. When they finally contacted their former neighbors in California, the Woods learned that Sugar had disappeared a few weeks after their departure. The neighbors had not told the couple about the disappearance, fearing they would be upset by the news.

The Bélmez Faces

One of the craziest hauntings on record was originally reported from Spain in 1971, when strange faces began appearing in a small house in Bélmez.

The case first came to wide public attention in August, when Maria Pereira, a housewife in the small village, discovered that a female face had "formed" on the hearthstone of her kitchen fireplace. She tried to scrub the face from the stone but it seemed to emerge directly from the concrete. She even had the face covered by a second layer of cement, but it showed through that. Then faces began appearing on the kitchen floor, sometimes disappearing later in the day or changing expressions.

The house soon became a local tourist stop and Mrs. Pereira began charging an admission fee to see the faces. Hundreds of people began flocking to the house, until local political and religious authorities ordered the sightseeing to stop.

Luckily, by this time Dr. Hans Bender of the University of Freiburg in Germany had learned of the case. Germany's leading parapsychologist, Bender decided to investigate the cause célèbre in collaboration with Spain's own Dr. German de Argumosa. In order to test the faces, the two investigators fastened a plastic plate over the kitchen floor. It was left there for several weeks and removed only when water condensed under it. The faces continued to form even under these controlled conditions. They consistently appeared through 1974, and although Mrs. Pereira had a new kitchen built onto the house, it didn't take long before the faces began appearing there, too.

Professor Argumosa personally witnessed the materialization of a face on April 9, 1974, and photographed it, which was fortunate, since it later disappeared. The use of photographic documentation rules out any suggestion that the faces were hallucinations or chance configurations in the concrete.

In order to test further for fraud, Argumosa and his colleagues checked to see whether the faces were fashioned from artificial coloring. The results of this chemical study were published in November 1976 in the *Schweizerisches Bulletin für Parapsychologie* and it showed nothing suspicious.

The cause of the curious haunting has never been firmly established. Some of the local townsfolk dug up Mrs. Pereira's kitchen and found some old bones buried there. Rumor has it that the house was built over an ancient cemetery, a resting site for Christian martyrs killed by eleventh century Moors.

The Ghost Wore Blue

Today, Dr. Julian Burton works in Los Angeles as a psychotherapist helping people with their problems. His dissertation for his graduate work, however, dealt more with the supernatural than the pathological, since it was devoted to the subject of spontaneous contact with the dead. Burton surveyed hundreds of people during his research, only to learn that communing with deceased friends and relatives is not unusual at all. This came as little surprise to the psychologist, since the idea for the project emerged from his own personal experience.

Burton's mother died in 1973 at the age of sixty-seven after suffering a massive stroke. He took the death hard but recovered by the following September, though the bond between them was to continue long after her death.

"One evening that September," recounts Burton, "my wife and I were entertaining relatives. I was in the kitchen cutting a pineapple when I heard what I thought were my wife's footsteps behind me to the right. I turned to ask the whereabouts of a bowl but realized that she had crossed to the left side outside my field of vision. I turned in that direction to repeat my question and saw my mother standing there. She was fully visible, looking years younger than at the time of her death. She was wearing a diaphanous pale-blue gown trimmed in marabou, which I had never seen before."

As Burton looked on, the figure simply dissolved, and the next morning he phoned his sister to report his experience.

"She was upset," continued the psychologist, "and began to sob, asking why our mother had not come to *her*. I felt bad about this and asked her if she believed what I had told her."

It turned out that, two weeks before her stroke, the two women had gone shopping and their mother had seen that same pale-blue gown. She had wanted to buy it, but didn't want to spend the two hundred dollar price for it.

The experience profoundly influenced Burton, who at the age

of forty-two decided to go back to school to finish his doctorate. "I felt," he said, "that many people probably had similar experiences to tell."

A Miraculous Cure

Leo Perras can walk today even though he was a hopeless cripple for years. The story of his miraculous healing begins with a modern miracle worker, Father Ralph Di Orio, whose ministry is still going strong.

Father Di Orio was born in Providence, Rhode Island, in 1930 and was ordained a Roman Catholic priest in 1957. A linguist as well as an educator, Di Orio was quite conventional in his theological views and practices until 1972. That's when his predominantly Spanish-speaking congregation decided to become charismatic, a form of worship that emphasizes personal religious expression and spontaneous experience. Father Di Orio was resistant to the change and modified his services only with the approval of his bishop. Finally getting into the swing of things himself, the middle-aged priest began to practice laying-on-of-hands during the services and soon discovered that he possessed the power to heal. He was conducting his healing services at St. John's Church in Worcester, Massachusetts, when he first met Leo Perras.

Perras, from the nearby community of Easthampton, had been crippled in an industrial accident years before when he was only eighteen. Surgery failed, leaving him paralyzed from the waist down and confined to a wheelchair. Muscular atrophy eventually set into his legs, which damaged them even further and left Perras in considerable pain. He was taking pain medication daily when he sought out the New England priest.

When he first met Father Di Orio, Perras had been confined to his wheelchair for twenty-one years. The priest prayed over his visitor during the service, and the results were nearly instanta-neous. The paralyzed man simply got up from his wheelchair and walked out of the church. The muscles of his legs apparently strengthened spontaneously and his long-endured pain vanished.

The story sounds too good to be true, but it is particularly well documented. The man's own physician, Mitchell Tenerowicz, chief-of-staff at Cooley Dickinson Hospital in Northampton exam-ined the patient shortly after the healing and found that his legs were still atrophied, making it physically impossible for Perras to walk. But walk he did. Perras's legs strengthened over the next several weeks and on September 29, 1980, NBC-TV's *That's Incred-ible* interviewed him and broadcast his story nationwide.

The Thirteenth Print

Nobody knew his real name. He called himself Cheiro the Great, and by the time he came to New York City from London in 1893 he had already established himself as the best-known, best-paid fortune-teller in the world.

Several years earlier he had made the headlines in English newspapers by deducing the identity of a murderer after studying a bloody handprint on a grimy wall. Now, the cynical New York reporters demanded proof of Cheiro's skills. They invited him to look at thirteen palm prints, then to describe the various people who had made these prints.

Within ten minutes, he had correctly described the donors of twelve of the prints, including that of the celebrated performer Lillian Russell, whom he correctly identified as a child of fate with great talent and ambition, but with great unhappiness as well.

But what about the thirteenth palm print? Why did he hesitate before getting to it?

Finally, he explained. "I refuse to identify this print to anyone but the owner," he said, "because it is the mark of a murderer.

He'll give himself away through his own self-confidence and he will die in prison."

The thirteenth print was that of Dr. Henry Meyer, who was then in Tombs prison charged with murder. Meyer was convicted, and died a few months later in an institution for the criminally insane.

A Psychic Nightmare

Sometimes a psychic experience will take the edge off an otherwise shattering tragedy. When nineteen-year-old Wendy Finkel was killed in a car accident near Point Mugu on the southern California coast, her mother didn't need to hear about it from the police. She already knew. The date was Thursday, November 19, 1987.

It was the day before Wendy's birthday. The college coed and three of her friends had driven in from Santa Barbara to take someone to the Los Angeles airport. Two of the students planned to attend a rock concert. They took Wendy out for dinner and dancing, and then visited her sister, who lived near UCLA. The Finkels were looking forward to Wendy's birthday that Friday and especially to having their children home for Thanksgiving. The tragedy struck sometime early in the morning, when the car carrying the students apparently drove off the Pacific Coast Highway, and plunged down the embankment into the sea. A fisherman happened to see the 1986 Honda Civic floating in the water upside down the next morning, and the bodies of Wendy's three friends were soon recovered.

At the same time as the accident, Mrs. Finkel had awakened suddenly in her Woodland Hills home gasping for air. "I felt like I was drowning," she later told reporters. "I couldn't get any air in my lungs. I looked at the clock and it said two something. I'm assuming that's when the car got to Point Mugu and went off the cliff."

Wendy's body has not yet been recovered, though her mother has little doubt about her fate.

The Ghosts of the
S.S. *Watertown*

Tragedy struck the oil tanker S.S. *Watertown* when it sailed from New York City to the Panama Canal early in December 1924. Two seamen, James Courtney and Michael Meehan, were cleaning a cargo tank when they were accidentally killed by gas fumes. Their bodies were buried at sea in proper maritime tradition on December 4.

The ghosts of the S.S. *Watertown* appeared the next day, but not in the form of sheet-clad phantoms stalking the ship's decks: The faces of the two unfortunate men were seen following the ship in the water. The disconcerting phantoms seen day after day by the ship's captain, Keith Tracy, and by the entire crew, seemed determined to follow the ship right through the canal.

Captain Tracy reported these eerie events to his head office when the ship docked in New Orleans, and officials from the company suggested that he try photographing them. He eventually delivered a roll of film with six exposures to the Cities Service Company, which had it commercially developed. While five of the shots revealed nothing unusual, the sixth exposure clearly showed the two faces lugubriously following the ship.

Interestingly enough, the Cities Service Company didn't try to play down the fascinating story or hide it from the public. They reported it openly in their own company magazine, *Service*, in 1934, and even displayed a blowup of the photograph in the main lobby of the Cities Service Company in New York.

Viewing the Future

Every student of the paranormal knows that ESP is not constrained by distance. Considerable research has shown that it can travel between two rooms as easily as halfway around the world. Even more amazing is the power of ESP to transcend the fabric of time itself. Some research conducted at Mundelein College in Chicago in 1978 certainly demonstrated this eerie fact.

The researcher in charge of the program was John Bisaha, who has long been interested in *remote viewing*, during which a subject tries to "see" what is taking place miles away. The experimental procedure is really quite simple. The subject merely sits with the experimenter while a target person (called the outbound experimenter) drives to some location either in the vicinity or even miles from where the subject is being tested. The subject is then asked to make contact with, or visualize, the outbound experimenter, and describe where he is. Bisaha used this procedure but added a significant revision. He asked his subject to describe the place the outbound experimenter would visit *the next day*.

For the most important part of his tightly controlled tests, Bisaha suggested that his star subject describe his upcoming sightseeing adventures in eastern Europe. For five consecutive days, Brenda Dunne—back in Chicago—tried to see where Bisaha would be visiting twenty-four hours later. At no time were the two participants in contact during the experiment.

The results were truly remarkable. When the sightseeing expedition took Bisaha to a circular restaurant built on some pillars rising from the Danube River, Brenda Dunne had already seen him "near water . . . a very large expanse of water." She also envisioned "vertical lines like poles . . . a circular shape like a merry-go-round." Similar successes were reported for the other days as well.

When the researcher returned to the United States, he took the records of the five sessions and turned them over to an independent judge, who was also provided with photographs of the target cities. His job was to match each of the reports given by Dunne to the correct photograph—and he didn't have any difficulty doing it.

Seagoing Pleisiosaur

In April of 1977, the nets of the Japanese fishing vessel *Zuiyo Maru* reeled in a strange haul off the coast of New Zealand—a forty-four-foot long, unknown marine animal that looked for all the world like a primordial monster of the deep. The crew hoisted the carcass out of the water and took color pictures of the bizarre catch before the captain, fearing a contaminated cargo, ordered it dropped overboard.

Professor Tokio Shikama, a student of ancient animals at Yokohama National University, studied the pictures and declared that the corpse was neither that of a known mammal nor of a fish. In fact, he compared its body to that of an ocean-dwelling *pleisiosaurus*, thought to be extinct for more than 100 million years.

Several other vessels in the area searched for the creature's remains after it was dumped by the Japanese, but without success. The tragedy is that even a single specimen of a pleisiosaur would have been worth far more than the captain's catch of normal fish.

Hog-Tied and Died

UFO occupants have reportedly demonstrated more than a passing interest in cattle and equines over the years. If Norway, South Carolina, farmer Richard Fanning is to be believed, their activities may extend to pork-on-the-hoof, too.

On the evening of December 6, 1978, the twenty-one-year-old Fanning, his wife and two other companions, spotted a ten-foot-diameter, white circle of light hovering over their hog pen. Beneath this object were two pairs of red and green lights, each about the size of automobile headlights.

"That doesn't look right," Fanning told his companions. "Let's leave." As he drove away, the silent lights followed, the white circle skimming the road at car-height and keeping fifty yards away, while the red and green lights pulled alongside.

Fanning headed for his house, where he kept a gun. But, he said, "All of a sudden the big white light made a U-turn behind my car and went back above the hog pen." The smaller, accompanying lights turned around as well. Fanning and the others watched the display until "after three or four minutes, all the lights went out." Fanning said, "I was scared, and I'm not scared of many things." He was so scared, in fact, that he and his wife stayed with relatives for the next two nights.

Three days later they went back to feed their stock and Fanning found one animal lying dead on its side. Another hog was "standing up dead." said Fanning. "I kicked him and he fell over."

An examination of the hog on its side revealed a missing jaw bone and a carcass "sort of like a sponge, with all the weight gone, kind of like jelly." Fanning said the animal alive had tipped the scales at 250 pounds, but that its remains weighed only about 50 pounds. "It was," he added "the weirdest thing I've ever seen in my life."

Holes in the Head

●
———————

Some strange rituals evolved out of the Flower Power of the sixties, but few were as bizarre as the practice of drilling a hole in one's head in order to achieve an expanded state of awareness.

Trepanation, the artificial opening of the skull, was common among some primitive societies for reasons not completely understood. Rationale for the risky, but survivable operation was probably both medical and religious in nature. Today's trepanners generally hold the same opinion.

The modern movement began in 1962, when a Dutch doctor, Bart Huges, claimed that the degree and state of one's consciousness depended foremost on the brain's blood volume. Things were different when we walked around on all fours, according to Huges, before we evolved the upright stance that separates us from most of nature. Problem was, the brain became encased in a confining, rigid structure; worse, gravity reduced the flow of oxygen and nutrients to the brain.

Huges's solution to the dilemma was to take an electrical drill and remove a small circle of bone from his cranium. The result, he said, was an increased blood flow and the ability of the now-freed brain to palpitate in rhythm with the heart. His consciousness returned to the childlike state he sought, in which the unfettered mind remained in touch with its primal dreams, imagination, and intense sensations. Adults lost this ability, Huges thought, as their skulls slowly solidified.

Trepanation as a solution to the human condition, however, did not set well with the local Dutch authorities, who promptly sentenced Huges to an insane asylum for observation. His ideas fared a little better, though, among the emerging hippies, for whom any kind of new "awareness" seemed worth the risk.

Huges's hole through the cranium directly into the brain promised a permanent mental stimulation. The trouble, of course, was finding someone to perform the operation, ancient witch doctors and shaman priests being in short supply. The answer was every handyman's dream: do-it-yourself.

Huges's foremost disciple was Joseph Mellen, a London accountant who had graduated from Oxford and met the Dutchman in Ibiza in 1965. Huges turned him on to the idea of trepanation. (Huges's own philosphy by this time had been encapsulated in a single word: "Brainbloodvolume.")

Mellen's own self-inflicted trepanation, following three aborted tries, was so "successful" that he later wrote a book about it, *Bore Hole*, the first sentence of which nicely sums up its contents: "This is the story of how I came to drill a hole in my skull to get permanently high."

Mellen reported a newfound sense of well-being from the trepanation that he claims remains with him today. His girlfriend, Amanda Fielding, subsequently undertook the cure, too, though instead of writing a book about her ordeal, she filmed it, calling her small movie *Heartbeat in the Brain*. Together, the two modern-day trepanners presently operate a London art gallery.

Power of Prayer

Many people think that science is the enemy of religion, but the tools of experimental research have sometimes documented the power of faith. Just such a project was recently undertaken by Dr. Randy Byrd, a cardiologist and a devout Christian. Byrd was so intrigued by the possible power of prayer that he decided to conduct an experiment to test it.

Since he was working at San Francisco General Hospital at the time, he certainly had enough patients to choose from. He began by programming a computer to choose 192 cardiac patients while an additional 201 similar patients were chosen to serve as his control group. Byrd wanted to see if those patients who were prayed for would recover from cardiac surgery better than the controls. He didn't perform the praying himself, but asked selected people and prayer groups across the country to participate in the study. The participants came from several different denominations and were provided with the names of the patients, but never met or otherwise contacted them. Nor did any of the patients ever know that the study was in progress.

The experiment took a year to complete and fully supported the belief that prayer really works. Byrd reported the amazing results of his study to the 1985 meeting of the American Heart Association, which convened that year in Miami. To a statistically significant degree, he told the group, prayed-for subjects required less postoperative antibiotic treatment and developed less pulmonary edema (the formation of water in the folds of the lungs). He also found that fewer prayed-for patients died during the study, although this trend wasn't statistically significant.

The reaction to this study by other physicians was surprising, to say the least. Many of them loved it. Probably the most surprising reaction came from Dr. William Nolan, the author of *The Making of a Surgeon* and an outspoken skeptic and critic of unorthodox medicine—and especially religious healing. Even he was impressed by the Byrd study.

"If it works, it works," he said of the power of prayer, when asked to comment on Dr. Byrd's study by the *Medical Tribune*.

The Real Dracula

The most famous horror novel of all time, Bram Stoker's *Dracula*, was based on the bloodthirsty career of a real person, Wallachian Prince Vlad IV, or Vlad the Impaler, who ruled fifteenth-century Rumania with an iron fist and sharpened stake.

Also known as Dracula, or "son of the devil," Vlad was one of the most ruthless rulers the world has known. A survey conducted in 1981, in fact, ranked him with only Idi Amin, Hitler, and Caligula in terms of total disregard for human life and suffering. He earned the soubriquet of Impaler because of his penchant for the wooden stake as a favorite tool of torture. Thousands of Turkish soldiers and civilians, thrust on poles staked in the ground, died in agony at his hands.

Vlad would dine among his writhing victims, supping or bathing in their life-fluid. So tightly did his terrible reputation grip the countryside that when he died in 1477, rumors surfaced that he rose from the dead in search of even more blood. Such stories may have contributed to the popular notion that the only way in which to stop a vampire's deadly depredations was to plunge a wooden stake through its still-living corpse. In an often overlooked tidbit of trivia, however, Stoker's original Count Dracula was only killed after his head was severed and a Bowie knife plunged in his chest—by a Texan. An almost incredible coincidence came to light in modern times.

A blood descendent of the real Dracula was located in Communist Rumania—working in a blood bank.

A Historical Female Vampire

History hints at other suspected vampires hidden among European royalty, too. The beautiful Elizabeth Bathory, born in 1560, and married to the Carpathian Count, Ferencz Nadasdy, at the age of fifteen, is a prime example. A wily wizard known only as Thorke reputedly tutored the young Elizabeth in the black arts. When the count was called off to war, his bride eloped with a stranger who had pointed white teeth and pale countenance, dressed in black. Elizabeth returned alone, sunk in savagery and given to torturing her servants. Back from battle, the count's protestations were of no avail.

Faced with her fading beauty, Elizabeth's mind became unhinged. She ordered a young housemaid murdered, her blood drained in a vat. The bath rejuvenated Elizabeth, temporarily. Now the need for youthful victims and their restorative bloodbath drove her beyond all bounds of humanity. With her own stock of servants exhausted, Elizabeth lured other prospects to the castle with the prospect of employment. Finally, she resorted to kidnappings, but one would-be victim escaped and alerted authorities.

Her confreres confessed to their crimes and were summarily executed. Elizabeth herself was judged insane and walled up in her rooms for life, dying in 1614.

Hypnotic ESP

Back in the days of Franz Anton Mesmer, it was widely believed that hypnotized people automatically became psychic. The mesmerists claimed they could prompt their subject to see into the future, envision distant places, and diagnose the sufferings of people standing before them. These claims died out, however, as hypnosis became better understood.

But that doesn't mean these claims have disappeared.

While a doctoral student in psychology at Cambridge University, Carl Sargent decided to see whether there was any truth behind these fantastic eighteenth-century claims. To implement his experiment, the young experimental psychologist recruited forty subjects, mostly college students. One half of them were hypnotized and tested for ESP with standard ESP cards. The other subjects were tested with the same cards while totally awake.

The results of the experiment indicated that good old Dr. Mesmer may have been right. The hypnotized subjects scored well above chance, which would normally be five hits per run of twenty-five cards. They averaged a whopping 11.9 hits. The control subjects scored right at chance.

Sargent says his experiment shows something important about the nature of ESP. It is obviously enhanced by a relaxed, perhaps altered, state of mind.

The Buttercup Mammoth

Mammoths appear to have vanished from the face of the earth some ten thousand years ago, victims of climatic change wrought by the last great Ice Age and growing bands of aboriginal hunters who slaughtered them for their meat, tusks, and hide. Since the turn of the century literally hundreds of their frozen carcasses have been found in the frigid tundras of Alaska, Canada, and Soviet Siberia.

At least one of these finds, on the banks of the Beresovka River, Siberia, threatens to overturn the conventional wisdom of how mammoths became extinct. Half-kneeling and half-standing, the Beresovka mammoth was in an almost complete state of preservation. So solidly was its flesh frozen that investigating scientists actually feasted on its flanks. Even more amazing, however, was the fact that buttercups were discovered in the creature's mouth.

The great mammoth had itself been feeding on temperate temperature plants at the time of its death. What froze it to the bone in mid-bite, as suddenly as if it had been dipped in liquid nitrogen? The prevailing notion of a gradual climatic change to which mammoths could not adapt won't wash in this case.

Slow freezing would have formed ice crystals and subsequently resulted in putrefaction of the thawing flesh. But the Beresovka mammoth was fresh enough to eat without ill effect. The temperatures necessary to achieve such a flash-freeze have been estimated at minus 150 degrees Fahrenheit, readings never even recorded in the natural icebox of the nearby Arctic.

What could have accounted for such a catastrophic drop in the temperature of the surrounding air? In the absence of a nuclear winter brought on by atomic bombs, we must look for an alternative scenario. Forest fires and volcanic eruptions also throw huge amounts of heat and light-blocking debris into the atmosphere, as recent studies have shown.

One theory suggests that a mighty earthquake, the largest Earth had ever known, rent the world ten thousand years ago. Occurring along the junction of two tectonic plates, the quake resulted in the massive release of lava and accompanying volcanic gases. These gases rose high in the atmosphere and circulated toward the poles. Super-chilled, they plummeted back toward the earth, losing even more ambient heat in their rapid descent. Finally, they pierced the warmer air below, flash-freezing the Beresovka mammoth and others of its kind as they dined on a meal of flowers.

Psychic Archaeology

Jeffrey Goodman began his career as an executive with a small oil company in Tucson. With a degree in business, he wasn't particularly prone to wild flights of fancy. That's why it's so surprising to find him, these days, championing the new field of psychic archaeology, in which gifted psychics help find promising dig sites.

Goodman's psychic odyssey began in 1971, when he learned that conventional anthropologists believed mankind first appeared in the Americas sixteen thousand years ago. Goodman felt the date to be too recent. In fact, he felt sure he could find evidence of an earlier civilization right in Arizona if only he knew where to look. So in order to explore his hunch further, Goodman consulted with Aron Abrahamsen, a well-known psychic from Oregon. Working from his home there, the psychic offered several clairvoyant descriptions that helped Goodman locate a dry river bed in the San Francisco Peaks outside of Flagstaff. It was an unlikely place to look for a lost civilization, since no archaeological finds had ever been unearthed there. But not only did Goodman simply ignore that inconvenient fact, he even asked his psychic to predict the geological formations they would find while digging.

By digging just where the psychic directed, Goodman unearthed man-made artifacts dating back at least twenty thousand years. What was even more surprising was that 75 percent of Abrahamson's geological predictions were completely correct, even though two local geologists had originally scoffed at them. The Oregon psychic predicted, for instance, that the excavators would hit one-hundred-thousand-year-old strata at the twenty-two-foot level. And that's just what they did.

Precognition and the Races

Skeptics like to scoff at psychics, saying that if ESP really works, why haven't they made a killing at the races? In fact, there is good evidence that some of them really have.

The British Broadcasting Company aired a series of talks on psychical research in 1934. Among the participants was Dame Edith Lyttleton, a former delegate to the League of Nations, who was herself a gifted psychic. Lyttleton devoted her presentation to the subject of precognition, ending the broadcast by urging her listeners to report their own experiences to her. She then systematically followed up the more promising cases, especially those for which outside documentation could be found. Surprisingly, an extraordinary number of cases were submitted by people whose precognitive experiences focused on horse races. Many of the witnesses had even used the information to place bets.

For example, one of Lyttleton's correspondents was a Mrs. Phyliss Richards, whose experience had occurred the year before.

"I crossed from Belfast to Liverpool on the night of Thursday, March 23, 1933, in order to see the Grand National which was being run the next day," Richards said. "On the boat I discovered that I had forgotten my mackintosh and felt a little worried. I went to sleep and dreamt that I was at the race, that it was pouring with rain and that a horse whose name began with 'k' and ended with 'jack' had won the race, although he was not the first horse past the winning post."

Richards ultimately placed a small bet on Kellesboro Jack, who ended up passing the winning post only after a riderless horse. And she won.

After hearing this account, Lyttleton and a colleague tracked down one of the people to whom Richards had told the dream before the race took place. He fully corroborated the incident and verified the winnings, too. Lyttleton published several similar cases in 1937, concluding that perhaps some people really can profit (in every sense of the word) by paying attention to their dreams.

A Phone Call From the Dead

Karl Uphoff, onetime rock musician, today believes in life after death. The reason: a phone call from his deceased grandmother, received in 1969.

Karl was eighteen years old when his maternal grandmother died. There had been a special bond between them, and when the old woman grew deaf in her later years, she often wanted Karl's help. Since Karl wasn't always home, she had a habit of calling his friends to find him. And because she couldn't even hear if anyone picked up the receiver, she would simply dial a number, wait a few moments and then say, "Is Karl there? Tell him to come home now." She would repeat the message a few times and then terminate the call, proceding on to the next number on her list. These calls had ceased, however, two years before her death in 1969, when Karl's sister began taking care of her.

Two days after the woman's death, Karl decided to pay an impromptu visit to the home of Mr. and Mrs. Sam D'Alessio in Montclair, New Jersey, whose son, Peter, was a friend of his. Peter and Karl were downstairs in the basement talking when the upstairs phone rang. The two boys could hear Mrs. D'Alessio talking impatiently with the caller and becoming rather miffed. Karl was stunned when she called down to him.

"There's an old woman on the phone," she yelled. "She says she's your grandmother and she says she needs you. She just keeps saying it over and over."

Karl dashed up the stairs to grab the receiver, but by the time he reached the phone, no was on the line. But that night, back home, Karl received a series of phone calls. Nobody was ever on the line when he picked up the receiver.

Was the call a hoax of some sort? This possibility seems extremely doubtful. When questioned by an investigator, Karl claimed that none of his current friends knew of the calls his grandmother used to make, and the D'Alessios were recent acquaintances. He also added that he had gone to visit them spontaneously, and that nobody could have known his whereabouts when the call was received.

Psychic Vision

When a housewife in Watts, a predominately black inner-city part of Los Angeles, had a vision that a body was buried in her yard, the coroner's office became interested.

The story began on July 17, 1986, when the woman, who was studying to be a minister, told police about the body. She had been having psychic visions for some time, and she had finally decided to act. When she and a friend began digging, they soon found part of a human skull and some other bone fragments. These finds were so provocative that the L.A. Police Department and some Explorer Scouts continued the dig and found even more.

Where did the bones come from? Police authorities aren't yet sure. From the scattered remains, it isn't possible to determine the sex of the person buried, or the cause of death, or how long the bones have been there. Dr. Judy Suchy, a forensic anthropologist with the coroner's office, is in charge of running experiments on the fragments in hopes of answering some of these questions.

Pitchforked Witch

The police were perplexed by the brutality of the murder. Charles Watson, a harmless old man, had been pinned to the ground by the two-prong pitchfork thrust through his throat. From his chest protruded a hedge-slashing hook, another familiar tool of Warwickshire farmers.

Locals bruited darkly of a ritual witch murder, but there weren't supposed to be any witches in February of 1945, not even in war-ravaged England. Since the Bobbies had few clues to go on, they called in the famous Superintendent Fabian of Scotland Yard. Although Fabian spent months on the case, he was never able to bring a suspect to justice.

Who killed old man Watson, then, remains a mystery. But, Scotland Yard finally figured that he had been perceived as a witch. Certainly Watson's eccentric behavior aroused the suspicions of his neighbors. He kept mostly to himself, sharing a thatched cottage with his niece. Spurning the camaraderie of pubmates, be bought his cider by the gallon jug and drank alone.

Gossip, however, centered around Watson's other peculiar habits. He was given to solitary wanderings in the wilds of Warwickshire, where he was frequently seen and heard communing with the birds of the air. Watson said he had his own understanding with them.

He also raised toads in a small garden. Rumor had it that he hitched them to miniature plows and followed them across the fields at night.

Rumors and innuendos were one thing, but what about reality? Could Watson really have been a witch, practicing his craft openly and holding his neighbors in fearful thrall? Regardless of one's beliefs, on a cold winter's day Watson was brutally murdered beneath a willow tree. The only motive Scotland Yard could uncover was that of witchcraft in the first degree.

The Headless Ghost

An early settler in the small Illinois town of McLeansboro, a man named Lakey, was found dead. His body was discovered by a passerby, his head chopped off, apparently by the ax that was still stuck in the stump next to his body. No one could understand the crime since Lakey appeared to have no enemies at all.

One day after his funeral, two men were riding horseback near the Lakey cabin site, along what is now known as Lakey's Creek. They had probably gone fishing on the Wabash River and were passing the cabin just as night fell, when they were joined by another, a headless horseman on a large black steed. Unable to speak, the men rode on fearfully, down the bank and into the creek. Suddenly the mysterious rider turned off, moved downstream and seemed to disappear into a pool of water below the crossing.

At first afraid to tell their story, the men soon found that others had seen the same apparition. The ghostly rider's trail was always the same. He joined riders coming from the east, turned near the center of the creek, and then disappeared.

Today, a concrete bridge carries automobiles over the same spot where riders once forded Lakey's Creek, and motorists have yet to see the restless ghost. The mystery of Lakey's death has never been solved.

Lost and Found

As a girl growing up in Yorkshire, England, Kate dreamed that she would marry "an army officer who wore gray flannels and tweed jackets, had a mustache, smoked a pipe and drove a sports car."

In her young adult life she moved to Toronto, where she met a man fitting that description. He was John Tidswell, an officer in the Canadian army and an amateur race-car driver. He divorced his first wife and married Kate on November 24, 1956. In due course the couple had three children—two boys and a girl. Their marriage seemed to be a happy one.

One day during the last week of July 1970, though, John took his sloop for a cruise on Lake Simcoe, thirty-five miles from the couple's home. He did not return. Searchers eventually found the disabled craft. There was no sign of John Tidswell, and on October 8, 1971, a court declared him legally dead.

And so matters remained until a few years later, when Kate Tidswell suddenly began having vivid dreams about her late husband. They were so disturbing that in 1979 she went to visit a psychic, seeking an explanation. The psychic told her that John was still alive, living elsewhere and using the name "Halfyard."

Kate began a search that took her across thirteen states. She did not find her husband, but her dreams and the psychic's words left her convinced he was out there somewhere.

Meanwhile, a Denver man named Robert Halfyard was having legal troubles. He had won a trip to Europe but when he applied for a passport, authorities checked into his background and found out who he really was: John Tidswell. He had faked his death and abandoned his Canadian family to start a new life in the United States.

His "widow" promptly lost her pension from her husband's military career. Just as promptly she sued him for $100,000 in alimony and child support.

She told reporters she was trying hard to "see the humor" in the situation.

Proving Near-Death Experience

Opinion is certainly divided when it comes to the near-death experience. Some experts believe that it's a genuine preview of the afterworld, while others dismiss it as an hallucination. Can the reality of the near-death experience ever be proved? A recent attempt has been made by Kimberly Clark, a social worker at Harborview Medical Center in Seattle, Washington.

Clark's first encounter with the NDE came while she was working with a patient named Maria. Maria was a migrant worker visiting relatives in the city when she suffered a heart attack. She survived the crisis but suffered a second close call with death while recuperating in the hospital. Since so much medical technology was close by, she was easily and expertly revived.

The social worker saw the patient later that day. She was taken aback when the woman suddenly said, "The strangest thing happened while the doctors and nurses were working on me. I found myself looking down from the ceiling at them working on my body." Not impressed by the story, Clark assumed Maria was

confused by her ordeal. But the social worker grew more interested when Maria said that while functioning out-of-body she
"flew" up to the third-floor ledge on the northern side of the
building, where she spotted a tennis shoe.

"She needed someone else to know that the tennis shoe was
really there to validate her out-of-body vision," said Clark, who
went upstairs to hunt for the tennis shoe with mixed emotions.

"Finally," she reported, "I found a room where I pressed my
face to the glass and looked down and saw the tennis shoe. My
vantage point was very different from what Maria's had to have
been for her to notice that the little toe had worn a place in the
shoe and that the lace was stuck under the heel and other details
about the side of the shoe not visible to me. The only way she
would have had such a perspective was if she had been floating
right outside and at very close range to the tennis shoe. I retrieved
the shoe and brought it back to Maria. It was very concrete
evidence for me."

The Money Hole

Off the coast of Nova Scotia lies tiny, irregular-shaped
Oak Island. Far out of proportion to its size, however, is the
awesome enigma of what lies hidden beneath the deceptively
innocent surface. Rumors hint of a fabulous pirate treasure of
almost unimaginable wealth. Exploratory findings speak of a potential for tragedy and an engineering feat by whoever hid the
treasure unrivaled in its almost supernatural ingenuity.

Whatever the eventual outcome, for almost two hundred years
Oak Island has frustrated every single attempt to pry loose its
secret. The first to try was sixteen-year-old Daniel McGinnis and
two companions who rowed across Mahone Bay from the Canadian mainland in 1795. In a clearing on the wooded eastern end of
the island they discovered an old ship's tackle block hanging from

a single tree above a filled-in depression. Intrigued, they dug
down, uncovering the opening of a thirteen-foot-wide circular
shaft. At a depth of ten feet, the boys encountered the first of the
thick oak platforms. Twenty feet down, they found a second
platform, and at thirty feet, a third.

Digging through the flinty clay exhausted the young treasure
hunters, both physically and spiritually. But there would be others to take their place. Work next resumed in 1804, financed by
Simeon Lynds, a well-to-do Nova Scotian. Lynds's diggers found
five more oak platforms, each at depths of ten-foot increments,
three of which had been sealed over with ship's putty and a layer
of coconut fibers. At ninety feet, they found what became known
as the "cipher stone," inscribed with obscure symbols that one
source interpreted to mean "ten feet below, $10 million are
buried." The amount would be exponentially greater in today's
dollars.

Eight feet under the cipher stone a miner's crowbar struck
something solid, thought to be a treasure chest. Lynds's men
broke off for the day. The following morning the pit had filled
with water to a depth of sixty feet.

The Money Pit broke Lynds, as it broke the back of any number
of similar expeditions since. Over the years just enough tantalizing evidence has been pulled out of the pit to keep treasure
hunters coming back, including bits of gold chain and indications
of chambers containing wooden chests.

The mystery of what the Money Pit holds deepened when two
channels connected to the pit were discovered at the 111- and
150-foot levels. Filled with coconut fibers, both led to the island's
beaches, where they seem to serve as sponges, soaking up the
sea, and forever flooding the shaft with water. The coconut fibers
hint of a South Pacific origin for the hidden treasure.

Treasure hunters continue to sink money into the frustrating
hole, risking their lives in the process. Daniel Blankenship, a
former Miami contractor, is director of Oak Island excavations
from Triton Alliance Ltd., a forty-eight-member consortium of
wealthy Canadian and U.S. backers. Blankenship was once deep
in the pit when steel casings holding back the sides fifty feet
above his head began collapsing. Workers winched him out of the
hole only seconds before the shaft gave way.

Having already sunk $3 million in the site, Blankenship and
Triton vow to fight on. Now in the works is what Triton president

David Tobias calls "in all probability the deepest and most expensive archaeological dig ever made in North America." The new plan calls for sinking an immense steel and concrete shaft, sixty to seventy feet wide and two hundred feet deep, that will reveal, once and for all, what lies at the bottom of the Money Pit. Estimated cost? Ten million dollars.

Haunting the
Rich and Famous

Ghosts don't haunt just broken-down old houses. Even the superchic of Hollywood sometimes get stuck with them. That sad situation was a constant nuisance to German-born actress Elke Sommer and her husband, writer Joe Hyams, back in the 1960s.

The couple came to realize that their house was haunted shortly after buying it in 1964. The first witness was a German newspaperwoman who was lying by the pool when she saw a stranger in the yard. Apparently in his fifties, he was neatly dressed in a white shirt, tie, and black suit. The guest reported the stranger to her hosts, who were baffled by the incident since they knew of no such person matching the description. But two weeks later the stranger appeared a second time when Elke Sommer's mother woke up to see the same figure. The elderly woman was getting ready to scream when the figure simply vanished.

The two visitations only represented the beginning of the couple's problems. From that time forward, strange noises were often heard in the house late at night. There was an odd rustling, and sometimes it even sounded as if the dining room chairs were being shuffled about.

At first, Hyams didn't think the problem was caused by the supernatural, so he cut back the trees and bushes to stop the rustling. But his efforts did little to eliminate the problem. Every night before retiring, he would carefully lock the doors and windows, only to find one particular window downstairs unlocked in the morning. Often, Hyams would hear the front door open and shut throughout the night, only to find it bolted in the morning. The frustrated writer finally planted three miniature radio transmitters around the property, but failed to catch any prowler responsible for the disturbances.

Finally, in the spring of 1965, the couple left the house in the care of a friend during a trip to Europe. No matter how carefully this caretaker locked the front door, it would be standing wide open the next day. And that August, the ghost made a repeat visit when the couple's poolman saw a stranger lurking in the dining room. The intruder was six feet tall, heavily built and wore a white shirt and tie. The poolman thought the stranger was a prowler until the man disappeared before his eyes.

With no end to the problem in sight, Joe Hyams finally contacted the Southern California Society for Psychical Research, which turned the case over to Dr. Thelma Moss. Then a psychologist at the UCLA Neuropsychiatric Institute, Moss took several psychics to the house, including such well-known local sensitives as the late Lotte van Strahl and Branda Crenshaw. Some of the psychics immediately sensed the ghost's presence, and their combined descriptions tallied with the reports of the eyewitnesses. Since all information concerning the case had been kept from them, Moss felt these correlations were extremely significant. The sensitives described the ghost as a gentleman in his fifties who had died of a heart attack. He was somehow attached to the house, they felt, and didn't want to leave.

While the investigation was still in progress, Hyams checked with the house's previous owners. It seems that they, too, had experienced similar trouble while they lived there. The house seemed to be permanently haunted, but the California writer wasn't intimidated by the discovery.

"Whoever or whatever the ghost is," he stated in a report published in the *Saturday Evening Post*, "we do not intend to be frightened out of our house."

But leave the house they ultimately did. After Moss completed her investigation, Sommer and Hyams brought in yet another psychic to explore the situation. Jacqueline Eastlund toured the residence in 1966 and then warned her hosts, "I see your dining room in flames next year. Be careful." The exhausted couple finally decided to sell the house in 1967, but a mysterious fire broke out in the dining room before they could leave. The cause of the blaze, like the haunting itself, has never been explained.

The Blue-Eyed Indians Who Spoke Welsh

Shortly after the American Revolution, when the lands west of the Mississippi were still claimed by Spain or England, an English surveying party visited a camp of Mandan Indians in what is now Missouri. When the officer in charge spoke to his orderly in Welsh (they were both Welshmen), they were astonished when a nearby Indian suddenly joined in the conversation. Apparently the two palefaces were speaking the Indian's language. They started to compare words and found that the Mandan language was about 50 percent Welsh. (*English:* bread, paddle, great, head, etc. *Mandan:* bara, ree, ma, pan, etc. *Welsh:* barra, ree/rhwyf, mawr, pen, etc.)

In addition, many of the Mandans did not resemble the other Indian tribes. They had blue eyes and their skin was of a lighter color than that of other Indians. The Mandan women, found to be "exceeding fair," were especially pleasing to the British explorers.

Then the English officer remembered that a Prince Madoc of Wales in A.D. 1170 sailed with his retinue to the west into the unknown ocean. Could he and his followers have sailed into the Gulf of Mexico and up the Mississippi and then stayed there?

Some time later most of the Mandans including the elderly "storytellers" and "rememberers" were wiped out by a plague brought by the whites. The few who survived were absorbed by other tribes. The chances for ever finding out why the Mandan Indians spoke Welsh are very slim, since all pure-blooded Mandans have now disappeared.

It All Depends
on How You Look at It

A mysterious stone carved with letters in an unknown alphabet was excavated in Bat Creek, Tennessee, in the late 1800s. A report and reproduction of the inscription was sent to the Smithsonian Institution in Washington, attributing its origin to the Cherokee tribe. However, after fifty years of mystery as to what it meant, Joseph Maker of Georgia observed upon viewing it, "It's upside down. Turn it rightside up. It's Canaanite Hebrew." It turned out to mean "Year one of the Golden Age of the Jews," thereby solving one mystery and initiating another. A message from ancient Israel? In Bat Creek, Tennessee?

Guided by a Voice

Romer Troxell, a 42-year-old resident of Levittown, Pennsylvania, was devastated by his son's murder. Charlie Troxell's body had been found by a roadside in Portage, Indiana. All identification had been removed from it, and robbery had been the probable motive for the crime. But the murdered youth was now seeking revenge.

While driving through Portage to claim the body, Troxell kept hearing his son's voice inside his mind, and he kept his eyes open hoping to spot someone driving his son's stolen car. The voice, he said, started telling him where to look and Troxell finally found the vehicle.

"I made a U-turn and followed the car about a block behind," Troxell said. "I wanted to crash into the car but Charlie warned me against it."

So instead, Troxell merely trailed the vehicle until its driver stopped and stepped out. He then engaged the suspect in conversation while another relative driving with Troxell summoned the police. The officers later arrested the man, whom they quickly recognized as a suspect in the crime based on their own confidential information.

After the suspect was taken into custody and charged, Charlie's voice no longer echoed in his father's head.

"Charlie's in peace now," Troxell stated. "The police were onto the killer, though. I came to realize that when they later showed me what they had uncovered in their investigation. But when I heard my son guiding me, I acted. Maybe the Lord wanted it that way."

Swallowed by a Sperm Whale

The case of James Bartley, a seaman on board the whaler *Star of the East*, is a fairly convincing answer to doubters of the biblical text concerning Jonah.

According to British Admiralty records, in February 1891 Bartley left the ship as part of a longboat crew during a whale hunt. The sea was rough. The harpooner made a strike, the whale dove and suddenly came up under the longboat wrecking it and scattering the crew. All of the sailors were picked up except Bartley. The whale then died and its body floated. It was cut and sectioned with the long flensing knives of the crew. A shoe attached to a foot and leg appeared during the flensing. Then Bartley was extracted from the whale's stomach, alive but unconscious. He regained consciousness but could not speak for several weeks. He remembered little except the opening of enormous jaws and sliding down a long tube on his way to the whale's stomach, where he remained for fifteen hours, as attested to by the signed declaration of the ship's doctor and all hands.

Bartley's sight was affected by his experience and his skin was bleached. He spent his remaining years on land and died at the age of thirty-nine.

Previews of the Hereafter

All over the world, people have long noted and taken seriously the visions of those who approached death. During World War II, supplemental records were kept in at least one field hospital in the U.S.S.R. concerning seriously wounded soldiers who had literally been brought back to life from the edge of death. According to one study of numerous cases concerning those who had "returned" from being very close to the "other side," most individuals received a quick vision of a religious nature according to their individual religions. Among the principal groups, the Orthodox Catholics glimpsed visions of ancient saints and heard hymns, the Moslems found themselves at the edge of a verdant and promising paradise, whereas the dedicated Communists remembered nothing. Many persons also remembered seeing family members who were already dead.

The case of Thomas Edison is especially interesting since, as a scientist, he would be likely to report his last impression with a certain detachment. As he lay dying he seemed to be in a coma. Suddenly he raised himself up and said in a clear but wondering tone, "I *am* surprised. It's very beautiful over there." He made no further comment about what he had seen and died shortly thereafter.

Voltaire, the famous French philosopher and critic of the established church lay in a semicoma, dying. During his productive and contentious life, his enemies had frequently threatened that he would receive a just punishment after his death, presumably in hell. Just before he died the smouldering logs in the fireplace of his chamber burst into vigorous flames. He looked up and, with his accustomed wit, observed to his friends: *"Quoi! Les flammes déjà?"* ("What! The flames already?")

A Tale of Three Titans

The greatest maritime disaster of all time befell the greatest man-made behemoth of all time—the White Star Line's tragically ill-fated *Titanic*. The real-life tragedy was matched only by that of the *Titan*, a fictional luxury liner that also went down with a terrible loss of life in April 1898, fourteen years before the *Titanic* struck the iceberg that sent her to a watery grave, also on an evening in April.

The *Titan* sailed only in the pages of Morgan Robertson's novel, aptly named *Futility*. But the parallels between the two gigantic passenger ships stagger the imagination. Robertson's prophetic *Titan* departed Southampton, England, on her maiden voyage, as did the "unsinkable" *Titanic* herself. Both ships were the same length, 800 feet and 828½ feet long, and of comparable tonnage—70,000 and 66,000 tons respectively. Each had three propellers and carried 3000 passengers apiece.

Each ship was jammed to the gunwales with wealthy citizens. Both struck an iceberg at the same spot and sank. And both boats suffered terrible casualties because neither carried enough lifeboats. In the case of the *Titanic*, 1,513 passengers died, most from exposure in the frigid Atlantic.

One of those who died aboard the *Titanic* was famous spiritualist and journalist W. T. Stead, who had written his own short story foretelling a similar sinking in 1892. But neither *Futility* nor Stead's story could save the doomed *Titanic*. Another premonition, however, *did* avoid a tragedy. In April 1935, seaman William Reeves was standing the bow watch aboard the tramp steamer *Titanian*, bound for Canada from England. The similarities and memories of the *Titanic* tragedy preyed on young Reeves's mind and sent a shiver up his spine. His boat's bow was cutting through the same still waters the *Titanic* had. And as midnight, the hour of the great ocean liner's end, approached, Reeves remembered that the date the great ocean liner sank—April 14, 1912—was his own birthday.

Overwhelmed by coincidence, Reeves called out, and the *Titanian* hove to, stopping just short of a looming iceberg. Soon after, other crystal mountains rose out of the night. The *Titanian* sat still, but safe, for nine days, until icebreakers from Newfoundland finally cut a swath through the deadly ice.

The Eels of Atlantis

The instinctive memory of animals causes them to gather in great numbers and to cross thousands and thousands of miles of earth and sea. The underwater migration of eels to a section of the mid-Atlantic Ocean is an outstanding and very curious example of this.

About every two years the eels from the lakes and rivers of Europe swim westward to the Atlantic where, in great living banks, they cross the ocean to the Sargasso Sea. There they meet with the great mass of eels from the American continent, which in turn have been swimming eastward to the same sea within the ocean. Aristotle, the ancient Greek philosopher and naturalist of the fourth century B.C., noted the eel migration from Europe but did not know about the west-to-east migration from the still unknown Americas. It is thought that the concentration of seaweed in the Sargasso Sea is the reason both eel populations make their pilgrimage to it, as the plentiful underwater seaweed would tend to protect their eggs. After spawning, the eels die and the young American eels, when sufficiently developed, return westward to the Americas, while the young European eels swim eastward to Europe. Both species are helped by the Atlantic current that flows clockwise.

Why is there so much seaweed in the Sargasso Sea? Is it perhaps possible that a mid-Atlantic continent, such as Atlantis, once existed there?

If it is true that Atlantis sank relatively quickly beneath the ocean, part of its vegetation may have adapted itself into seaweed still growing over what is now an underwater continent, the original spawning ground of the eels still alive in their ancestral and instinctive memory.

Possessed by a Murdered Man

Giuseppe Verardi was nineteen years old when his body was found under a bridge separating Siano and Catanzano, two small towns in Italy. His body was clothed only in undergarments, and the rest of his clothing was strewn nearby. The date was February 13, 1936, and the town authorities of Siano ruled that Giuseppe had killed himself. This pronouncement was greeted with skepticism by the boy's friends and family, who couldn't believe that a mere thirty-foot fall could explain the youth's injuries.

Giuseppe's death was history by January 5, 1939, when a strange drama unfolded in town. The prime player in the story was seventeen-year-old Maria Talarico, who had never known Giuseppe or his family. She was crossing the bridge with her grandmother when she suffered a strange spell, fell to her knees and became delirious. With the help of her grandmother and a kind passerby, she was taken back home. But when she recovered from the fit, she was no longer Maria. A strange masculine voice issued from her mouth, claiming to be Giuseppe Verardi himself.

The restless ghost of Giuseppe took complete control of Maria and even wrote a letter to his mother in his own, earthly, calligraphy. That same evening, the entity forced Maria to engage in a curious pantomime, in which "he" relived his last night in Siano. The spirit pretended to be drinking and playing cards, just as Giuseppe had done the night he died. The entity kept gulping down more and more wine, even though Maria never drank more than one glass with her meals. Then the entity began to reenact a fight with his fellow cardplayers, which presumably took place on the bridge.

Giuseppe's mother came to visit Maria the next day, and the possessing entity immediately recognized her and described the injuries found on his body. He also named his murderers, even though few of them still lived in Siano. Mrs. Verardi later returned home and prayed that her son's spirit would leave Maria. Later that day, Maria walked to the fateful bridge while still possessed by the murdered youth. She then took off her clothes and lay under the bridge in the exact position in which Giuseppe's body had been found. Within a few minutes Maria woke up with no memory of what had happened.

The psychic return of Giuseppe Verardi received a great deal of press coverage in 1939. Ernesto Bozzano, then probably Italy's leading psychical researcher, studied the case and issued a report of the occurrence in 1940.

Electrical Emission From the Brain

Hans Berger is best remembered today as the father of encephalography, the scientific study of brain waves. Few people realize, though, that Berger's interest in the brain's electrical emissions stemmed from his desire to explain ESP.

The scientist's interest in the paranormal stemmed from an experience he had when he was nineteen years old. A soldier taking part in some military exercises in Würzberg, Germany, Berger was riding his horse when it stumbled. He was nearly crushed by the wheels of a cart, but the horses were stopped just in time.

That same evening, Berger received a telegram from his father asking him if he were all right. It was the only time the youth had ever received such an inquiry. He later learned the reason for the communication. At the same time as the mishap, his eldest sister had a sudden presentiment that something was wrong with her brother, and she urged her parents to send the telegram.

"The incident was a clear example of the spontaneous transmission of thought," wrote Berger. "At the time of grave danger, I acted as some sort of transmitter and my sister became a receiver." Berger delved into the study of the brain in hopes of finding a physical explanation for telepathy. He failed, but his research helped scientists to better understand the brain's electrical rhythms.

The Clock
That Stopped at Death

Every schoolchild learns to sing "My Grandfather's Clock," that wonderful German folk song about the clock that "stopped short, never to run again when the old man died." What few people realize is that this song is based on a genuine phenomenon. Clocks often stop when their owners die.

Several such cases were collected by the Duke University Parapsychology Laboratory, where Dr. Louisa Rhine worked for many years classifying reports of psychic phenomena sent in from the general public. Several of these cases concerned mysterious clock stoppings. For example, one gentleman from Canada explained to Dr. Rhine how he had helped his sister-in-law during his brother's last illness. When the patient died at 6:25 in the morning, he called the family and the doctor before helping to prepare a quick breakfast for everybody. The corpse had to be at the undertaker's by 9:30, so they had to watch the time carefully. When someone asked for the time during the meal, the witness took out a gold pocket watch. It had been a gift from his brother, and it had stopped at the exact time of his death.

"I called the attention of those gathered around the table to the phenomenon," wrote the witness, "and in order to show that it was no common occurrence, asked my [other] brother to wind the watch to make sure it had not run down. It was three-quarters wound."

The Too-Dangerous Machine Gun

It is rare in history when one finds that a new or suggested weapon has been considered by the controlling authority to be too cruel or destructive to use. Nevertheless, this is what happened when the inventor of a multiple firing weapon—or a sort of machine gun—was offered to Louis XVI of France in 1755 by an engineer named Du Peron. Louis and his ministers refused it as being too deadly because it would kill too many people at one time. Considering the opinion of Dr. Edward Teller, the so-called "father of the H-bomb," one realizes that Louis XVI would be considerably out of date in the world of modern warfare. Dr. Teller has estimated that an exploding H-bomb in a large metropolitan area would cause the death of about 10 million people, while a "bad nuclear war could kill a couple of billion."

A Real Ghostwriter

Sports figures and other public personalities frequently seek assistance for their autobiographies in the form of "ghost" writers, professional authors hired to whip their prose into shape. But real ghostwriters have plied their ethereal trade, too, as evidenced by the career of Mrs. J. H. Curran and her spiritual scribe, "Patience Worth."

Curran, of St. Louis, was originally distrustful of mediums and spiritualism, but on July 8, 1913, she attended a seance in which a Ouija board was employed. Placing her hands on the board, Curran spelled out the name Patience Worth. Patience revealed herself as a seventeenth-century English woman from Dorset, whose parents had emigrated to America, where she was killed in an Indian attack.

Intrigued, Curran continued her conversations with Patience. Over the next several years, and in the course of countless sittings, a remarkable sequence of poems, stories, and treatises poured from Patience, through Curran, and into print. A series of historical novels included *The Sorry Tale*, set in the first century, and the nineteenth-century *Hope Trueblood*. Her most celebrated spirit novel, *Telka*, was set in medieval England and penned in the language of the day, an archaic style Curran never studied.

Patience could "dictate" two or more novels simultaneously, shifting from one to another by chapter while never losing her train of thought. And Curran proved the perfect collaborator, dutifully recording Patience Worth's remarkable stories of days long gone by.

Angels in the Sky?

People who say they see angels are usually considered crazy. But it's hard to pin such a label on Dr. S. Ralph Harlow, a highly respected religion professor at Smith College in Massachusetts. His encounter of the angelic kind took place while he and his wife were walking in a wooded glen in Ballarvade, Massachusetts.

Harlow first heard some muted voices, the story goes, then declared, "We have company in the woods this morning." No source for the sounds could be found, so the couple proceeded with their walk. The voices seemed to grow closer, and finally emanated from just above. The perplexed couple looked up to behold an incredible sight: "About ten feet above us, and slightly to our left, was a floating group of spirits, of angels, of glorious, beautiful creatures that glowed with spiritual beauty," reported Harlow. "We stopped and stared as they passed above us.

"There were six of them, beautiful young women dressed in flowing white garments and engaged in earnest conversation. If they were aware of our existence they gave no indication of it. Their faces were perfectly clear to us, and one woman, slightly older than the rest, was especially beautiful. Her dark hair was pulled back in what today we would call a ponytail, and although I cannot say it was bound at the back of her head it appeared to be. She was talking intently to a younger spirit whose back was toward us and who looked up into the face of the woman who was talking."

Neither Dr. Harlow nor his wife could decipher what the beings were saying, though they both say they clearly saw and heard the beautiful phantoms. They watched in awe and exasperation as the "angels" passed by. Dr. Harlow, a careful observer, then asked his wife to tell him exactly what she had seen. Her description of the encounter matched his own.

Resurrection Roses

Dr. Nandor Fodor was both a psychoanalyst and psychical researcher, a man dearly loved by those who knew him. When he died on May 17, 1964, objects in his apartment mysteriously started to move, as if the deceased researcher was trying to demonstrate his continued existence to the world. But it was the behavior of the terrace flowers that most impressed his wife.

"On our terrace there are flowers," she explained. "The climbing roses usually last four days, then lose their petals and new buds form. But after my husband's death the roses, about one hundred and fifty of them, bloomed at once and lasted for several weeks." The more Amaya Fodor observed the roses, the more her interest grew.

"For that period of time, no rose dropped a petal," she reported. "Then one day they all withered together. I cut them off and as I did so I asked for just one rose. I got it one week later—just one rose, which also lasted for several weeks."

Could these mysterious roses have bloomed by coincidence? That's a possibility, but for the fact that Fodor's case isn't unique. The well-known novelist Taylor Caldwell reports a similar experience in the October 1972 issue of *Ladies' Home Journal*. Ms. Caldwell and her husband, Marcus Rebak, had a shrub of resurrection lilies that never bloomed—not once in twenty-one years. Rebak used to quip to his wife, in fact, that "you can't prove the resurrection by these lilies." Yet when he died in April 1970, the lilies finally bloomed—on the day of his funeral.

Mark Twain's Premonition

Mark Twain, born Samuel Clemens, remains America's best-loved writer. Born in the little town of Florida, Missouri, and raised in nearby Hannibal, he was able to pen true Americana in such books as *Huckleberry Finn*. But few people know that beneath the humor and cynicism, Mark Twain was a serious student of the paranormal. His interest in the subject stemmed from personal experience, including the day in 1858 when he precognized his brother's death.

The writer was then working as a steersman on a packet traveling between New Orleans and St. Louis. One night while remaining ashore for a few days, he dreamt that his brother Henry was lying in a metal coffin dressed in one of Twain's own suits. The coffin was suspended between two chairs, and a bouquet of flowers—with a red rose in the center—rested on his chest. The dream was so vivid that when he awoke, Twain didn't realize that he had been sleeping and thought he was at home.

The dream had a tragic denouement two days later. While Twain remained in New Orleans, the packet on which he worked continued down the Mississippi. His brother also worked the boat and was continuing the journey when a boiler exploded. Henry was severely injured and taken to Memphis, where he died when the doctor accidentally injected him with too much morphine.

When Henry was prepared for burial, some kind ladies raised the money to procure a metal casket for him. His body was dressed in one of Twain's suits. While the writer was mourning his brother's death, a lady entered the room and placed a bouquet of white roses—with a red rose in the center—on the chest of the deceased. Later the casket was sent to St. Louis, where it was placed upstairs in his brother-in-law's home. When Mark Twain visited the room housing the body, he saw that the coffin had been placed on two chairs, just as he had seen in his dream.

A Shared Vision

Carl Jung, the famous Swiss psychiatrist, was equally well known for his interest in the occult. No subject within the realms of the paranormal bypassed his interest. He followed the burgeoning field of parapsychology, became a student of both astrology and alchemy, and carefully recorded his personal paranormal experiences. Many of these encounters are fully reported in his autobiographical *Memories, Dreams, Reflections*.

He had what was probably his strangest experience in 1913, while visiting the tomb of Galla Placidia in Ravenna with a friend. The psychiatrist was particularly impressed by a mosaic of Christ holding his hand out to Peter sinking beneath the waves. Jung and his woman friend examined the mosaic for twenty minutes and discussed the original rite of baptism in some depth. Jung never forgot that work of art. He had wanted to buy a photograph of it, but couldn't find one.

When Jung returned to his home in Zurich, he asked another friend, who was going to Ravenna, to obtain a picture of the mosaic. The upshot was both surprising and mystifying: The mosaic Jung and his friend had seen didn't exist. Jung reported this discovery to his former companion, who refused to believe that they had shared some sort of hallucination or vision. But the truth of the matter couldn't be countered: No such mosaic had ever been located on the baptistry wall.

"As we know," wrote Jung, "it is very difficult to determine whether, and to what extent, two persons simultaneously see the same thing. In this case, however, I was able to ascertain that at least the main feature of what we both saw had been the same."

Jung later characterized his experience in Ravenna as "the most curious of my life."

The Night Visitor

Dr. Michael Grosso was teaching a course in parapsychology at Jersey City State College in 1976 when he met Elizabeth Sebben, a bright anthropology major who had experienced many psychic encounters and was glad to find someone she could talk to. Grosso was especially interested in her out-of-body experiences. He suggested that she try to visit him should she find herself traveling out-of-body anytime soon. The visitation came in the autumn of 1976. Living by himself in a six-room apartment, he often passed his time practicing the flute. His musical exercises were usually placed on a music stand, which always stood near a particular bookcase. Grosso realized that something was peculiar one morning when, upon waking, he found the music stand in the middle of the room, even though he had never placed it there.

Grosso didn't think much of the incident until later that day, when Elizabeth called. She had tried to contact him the night before while out-of-body and wanted to tell him what she perceived. Without prompting from her friend, she told the following story: She had been studying the night before when she started feeling that she was leaving the body. She recalled that she wanted to visit Grosso, so she concentrated on him and soon found herself in his kitchen. She saw him seated at a table studying some papers and sipping tea. She tried to attract his attention, but failed, and she then began searching for a way to prove her presence. She examined the residence until she spotted the music stand. She focused on the object and then, inexplicably, perceived that her intent had moved the stand to the middle of the room. Seconds later, she found herself back in the body.

Grosso doesn't believe that the experience can be explained away as some sort of illusion. "When a lady visits a man at night, especially under such curious circumstances," he says, "it would be the height of unchivalry to dismiss her as an insignificant illusion."

Cross Correspondences

Three famous founders of the British Society for Psychical Research—Henry Sidgwick, Frederic Myers, and Edmund Gurney—figure prominently in one of the most compelling cases of spirit correspondence ever recorded. More miraculously, the three distinguished gentlemen figured not as receivers, but *senders*.

The story of the Cross Correspondences, as they came to be known, started in 1901, when five different women who had no previous knowledge of one another began receiving messages from departed spirits. All five employed a technique known as automatic writing, entering into a trance state in which the communicating entity takes over and conveys its message by writing.

The first woman to be contacted—by a spirit identifying itself as Myers—was Mrs. A. W. Verrall. A little later, Lenora Piper of the United States also began receiving messages from Myers. Unbeknown to each other, Alice Fleming, Rudyard Kipling's sister, and her daughter, Helen, started receiving similar communications from beyond the veil while in India. These four were soon joined by another Englishwoman, a Mrs. Willet. But the breakthrough came in 1903, when Helen Holland (née Fleming) received a request from Myers, asking her to contact some of his old friends. Helen's hand wrote out the name of the friend: "Mrs. Verrall, 5 Selwyn Gardens, Cambridge."

Mrs. Fleming turned her script over to the Society for Psychical Research and slowly the separate strands came together. In America, Lenora Piper was tested by G. B. Dorr, who asked what "lethe" meant to her. "Myers," the spirit that guided her hand, responded with a string of classical allusions, befitting his earthly profession as classical scholar. The same query was put to Mrs. Willet in England by the reknowned physicist Oliver Lodge. Her spirit on the other side gave essentially the same answer, as well as the name of the American interrogator—Dorr.

Eventually, Mrs. Willet was able to communicate with all three "targets"—Myers, Sidgwick, and Gurney, classical scholars all. Through her, the Prime Minister's brother, Lord Balfour, questioned the esteemed Sidgwick on the relation of the body to the mind. Gurney, or the spirit who claimed to be him, addressed the origins of the soul.

Myers himself was asked what it was like to communicate from beyond the grave. "I appear to be standing behind a sheet of frosted glass," he replied, "which blurs sight and deadens sound, dictating feebly to a reluctant and obtuse secretary. A feeling of terrible impotence burdens me."

The Pearl Tiepin

Next to good old-fashioned Monopoly, the Ouija board is probably one of the most popular games in the world. Even though many people don't take the board seriously, claims are that sometimes it leads to genuine contact with the beyond.

Hester Travers-Smith was a British psychic and an expert at working the board. One of her most famous cases involved a curious incident she shared with Geraldine Cummins, an Irishwoman and a gifted psychic herself. They were working with the board in London during the terrible years of World War I when a cousin of Cummins, recently killed in France, took control of the board. The entity spelled out his name and then wrote, "Do you know who I am?"

The communicator next wrote the following message: "Tell mother to give my pearl tiepin to the girl I intended to marry. I think she should have it." The lady's full name, totally unfamiliar to the psychics, was then spelled out. The entity also offered the lady's London address, but when the psychics sent her a letter, it was returned to them. Since the address was either wrong or fictitious, the psychics lost interest in the case.

Six months later, however, Cummins learned that her cousin *had* been secretly engaged, a fact unknown even to his immediate family. His fiancée's name was the same as that spelled through the board, and when the War Office sent the youth's effects back to England, the family found the pearl tiepin mentioned in a will he had written while in France. It instructed his family to send the tiepin to his fiancée if he failed to return.

The entire case was later certified by Sir William Barrett, a noted physicist of his day, who examined the original records.

Lifesaving Telepathy

Some critics claim that even if ESP exists, it has no practical value. John H. Sullivan would disagree with that sentiment, since telepathy probably saved his life.

The incident took place on June 14, 1955, when Sullivan was welding a water pipe in the West Roxbury section of Boston. When his trench suddenly caved in, Sullivan was buried by dirt and only his hand could be seen sticking out. At roughly the same time, Sullivan's friend and fellow welder, Thomas Whittaker, was working at a different site. But something kept preying on his mind. He finally stopped work early and told another employee that something was wrong at the Roxbury site. Whittaker found himself driving to the location, taking several roads he usually specifically avoided. When he reached the trench, he saw one of his company's trucks unattended, its generator running.

"I walked over and looked into the fourteen-foot trench," he later testified. "At first I could see only dirt. Then I realized it was a cave-in, and then I saw a hand."

Whittaker began digging out the buried man, and some firemen arrived in short order to help. Sullivan was badly injured and probably would have died had the rescue been delayed.

The Angels of Mons

On August 26, 1914, the defeated British Expeditionary Force at Mons, France, found itself outnumbered by Germans three-to-one, and in full retreat. Disaster loomed on the horizon as a unit of Emperor Frederick Wilhelm's cavalry blocked their path.

But the coup de grace never fell. Suddenly, the German horses panicked, rearing on their hind hooves, nostrils flaring. The German cavalry fled the scene and the retreating British poured through to safety.

What stayed the German swords and panicked their horses? An article published in London's *Evening News* a month after their miraculous survival said the English soldiers had been spared by the sight of a squadron of angels hovering over their heads. The author of the article was one Arthur Machen, a writer of occult horror tales who rubbed shoulders with Yeats and Aleister Crowley as members of the Hermetic Order of the Golden Dawn, the twentieth-century's most infamous magical society.

According to Machen's article, "The Bowmen: The Angels of Mons," when the Germans deployed their forces for the final kill they beheld a vision in the heavens of a ghostly army arrayed on the British side. Even more remarkable, the angels were in the form of British bowmen of yore, their long bows drawn and aimed directly in the face of the enemy.

The story caused such a sensation in England that Machen finally admitted the angels were totally a figment of his own active imagination. But the account of celestial saviors aiding the Tommies in the trenches refused to die. When the survivors of Mons began returning home, many told tales that corroborated the angelic bowmen. A flood of articles and pamphlets subsequently supported the story. The Reverend C. M. Chavasse, an army chaplain, said he had it firsthand from both a brigadier general and two of his fellow officers who had been at the battle.

Despite Machen's denials, the Angels of Mons took on a life of their own. Unaware of his own actions, perhaps Machen had tapped into the collective consciousness of war-torn England. Undoubtedly the angels boosted spirits in the darkest days of the war, when England's finest were being slaughtered pell-mell in the fields of France. And in the end the ruse, if it was one, worked. The English and their allies did emerge victorious. The angels had been on the winning side after all.

Jungle Visions

Some travelers along the Amazon have reported that the natives there sometimes become psychic when they ingest certain plant distillates.

Dr. William McGovern was an assistant curator of South American ethnography at the Field Museum of Natural History when he made his observations in the 1920s. He was exploring the native settlements of the Amazon River, where he watched the

Indians concoct a psychedelic brew from an hallucinogenic chemical called harmaline, found in the *Banisteriopsis caapi* vine.

"Certain of the Indians," he said, "fell into a particularly deep state of trance in which they possessed what appeared to be telepathic powers. Two or three of the men described what was going on in *malokas* [settlements] hundreds of miles away, many of which they had never visited, and the inhabitants of which they had never seen, but which seemed to tally exactly with what I knew of the places and people concerned. More extraordinary still, on this particular evening, the local medicine man told me that the chief of a certain tribe in far away Pira Panama had suddenly died. I entered this statement in my diary, and many weeks later, when we came to the tribe in question, I found that the witch doctor's statements had been true in every detail."

Harmaline was later imported to Europe, where researchers at the Pasteur Institute in France experimented with it. They reported that their subjects became so psychic after taking it that they renamed the drug "telepathine."

The Thompson-Gifford Case

The scene was New Bedford, a coastal town in Massachusetts where two very different people liked to take long exploratory walks. The first was a rather unremarkable craftsman and Sunday painter of sorts named Frederic Thompson, and the other was the internationally acclaimed artist Robert Swain Gifford. Frederic Thompson liked to hunt for game along the coast and on rare occasions met Gifford, who liked to paint scenes suggested by the local landscape.

Frederic Thompson's strange psychic odyssey began in the summer of 1905 when he suddenly developed the urge to paint and sketch. He was continually haunted by landscape scenes that invaded his mind, and even believed that part of his personality was somehow linked to R. Swain Gifford. He didn't know that the celebrated painter had died and it was only sometime later that he discovered this fact while working in New York. Walking down a street on his lunch break, Thompson discovered an art gallery where the *late* R. Swain Gifford's paintings were on display. The shock was so great that he blacked out. His last memory before entering this short-lived fugue was of a voice saying, "You see what I have done. Go on with the work."

By the end of the year, Thompson's personality had begun to disintegrate, and he could no longer perform his job. He still felt compelled to paint and sketch, and the results often mimicked Gifford's style. He finally sought out Professor James H. Hyslop, then in charge of the American Society for Psychical Research in New York.

Hyslop, well trained in the psychology of his time, wasn't impressed with Thompson's tale. He felt that the man was probably heading for a breakdown and little else; but the professor did feel that a simple experiment might be in order. Since he was scheduled to visit a psychic shortly after this interview, Hyslop decided to take Thompson with him. Perhaps, he reasoned, the psychic could help diagnose the man's problems. This sitting proved productive since the psychic immediately sensed an artist at the séance and even described a landscape that had been haunting Thompson's mind.

The mystery deepened in July 1907, when Frederic Thompson gave Hyslop a series of his sketches revolving around two different scenes: a group of five isolated trees, and two gnarled oaks by a wild shoreline. Hoping to investigate the case on his own, Thompson then went to visit Gifford's widow in Nonquitt, a small Massachusetts town. There he found that his sketch of the five trees exactly matched an unfinished painting in Mrs. Gifford's possession. Her husband had been working on it at the time of his death. The following October, Thompson discovered the scene that had inspired his sketch of the oak trees and shoreline just off the New Bedford coast.

James H. Hyslop published his study of the case in the *Proceedings* of the American Society for Psychical Research in 1909. Frederic Thompson himself later became a successful artist, exhibiting his work for nearly two decades in the well-known galleries of New York.

The Imaginary Ghost

A thought-form is a physical object materialized through the power of the human mind. But do thought-forms exist? In the summer of 1972, several members of the Toronto Society for Psychical Research decided to search for so-called thought-forms by conjuring up a ghost. After several false starts, the group finally worked out a procedure that looked promising: recreating the atmosphere of a typical Victorian séance. To facilitate the experiments, the group decided to establish contact with a totally fictitious entity. So one of the members created a biography for the spook. Named Philip, he was a Catholic nobleman in seventeeth-century England who had killed himself when his wife exposed his mistress as a supposed witch.

The group met weekly and, while sitting around the table, would exhort Philip to reveal himself. When they placed their hands on the table, Philip would often respond by tilting it. The table eventually began moving about, emitting mysterious raps from its surface.

"I wonder if by chance Philip is doing it," one of the sitters finally asked. When a clear rap responded, the group became tremendously excited and began to converse regularly with the ghost by code.

As might be expected, the raps—for which no normal explanation could be found—would reply in complete accordance with Philip's fictitious biography. If the entity were asked a question for which the group had never created a proper response, the table would emit only weird sawing sounds.

The sound and movement grew stronger the longer the group sat. Members reported that the table raised upon one leg and even levitated. They also said it displayed a raucous sense of humor. If anyone tried to sit on the table to stabilize it, a sudden force would throw him or her to the floor. The raps would also sometimes leave the confines of the table and sound from elsewhere in the room.

Because of the spectacular nature of these experiments, the Toronto group began to doubt the existence of bona fide *spirits*. Instead, it declared, spiritlike behavior could be traced to thought-forms created solely through the powers of the mind.

Spontaneous Regeneration

Pierre de Rudder was a Belgian peasant who lived in Jabbeke, near the city of Bruges. His strange story began in 1869, when he fell from a tree and shattered his leg. The damage was so extensive that the leg couldn't be reset, and when the bone fragments were removed, over an inch separated the upper and lower parts of the limb. Dangling freely, de Rudder's lower leg was held in place only by muscle tissue and skin. His physician wanted to amputate the limb, but despite the pain de Rudder steadfastly refused. He suffered from the pain for eight years before he decided to visit the city of Oostacker, the site of a shrine in honor of Lourdes.

Riding to Ghent by train caused de Rudder intolerable pain. He was even lifted onto the train by three helpers, and the discharge from his injury was so objectionable that he was nearly thrown off.

Needless to say, de Rudder was in a terrible state when he finally arrived in Oostacker, but he made his way to the shrine and began to pray. That's when a sudden ecstasy overcame him and, according to reports, he stood up and walked without the help of his crutches.

De Rudder died in 1898 and Dr. van Hoestenbergh had his body exhumed two years after so that he could more closely examine his former patient's legs and their primary bones. Photographs of the bones clearly showed, the doctor declared, that new bone was used to fuse the irreparably broken leg.

Damascus Steel

Among the numerous magical methods that seemed to work in earlier days was the damascene process of hardening steel swords by thrusting a superheated blade into the body of a prisoner or slave and then into cold water. In the Middle Ages Christian knights learned, to their dismay, that swords made of Damascus steel were more resilient and also harder than those of European manufacture.

Five hundred years after the Crusades, however, experiments in Europe indicated that the process was not magic after all. The Europeans found that thrusting a red-hot sword into a mass of animal skins soaking in water had a similar effect to the Damascus method. The organic nitrogen given off by the skins in the water produces a chemical reaction in the steel.

Map Dowsing

Dowsers usually work by holding twigs or rods in their hands, waiting for them to bend near water or precious ores. But dowsing can be used to discover more than just substances alone. J. Scott Elliot, a retired British military officer and expert dowser, uses his skill to help uncover archeological sites. Sometimes he doesn't even visit the locations he wants to probe, but merely holds a pendulum over a map.

One of his typical successes was reported in 1969, when he used map dowsing to predict that a large structure would be unearthed under a cottage in the town of Swinebrook. Local excavators were skeptical, since Scott Elliot had designated a town in which no buried ruins had ever been found. It was six months before a trial dig was made there, and sure enough, the structure pinpointed by the dowser was readily discovered.

By making a five by ten foot trial cut, the local excavators found postholes, bones, and some pottery. When the site was more thoroughly exhumed in 1970, they found the floors of a structure and even its hearth. Two highly polished Bronze Age tools capped the sensational find.

A Double Nightmare

Like the young George Washington, Steven Linscott, a twenty-six-year-old Bible student from Illinois, felt compelled to tell the truth—but Linscott ended up in jail for it.

The events leading to his incarceration began on October 4, 1980, when Oak Park, Illinois, police were searching for leads in the murder of Karen Ann Phillips. The twenty-four-year-old nurse had been killed the previous morning and the police were visiting the Good Neighbor Mission—a halfway house for ex-convicts—in hopes of finding some relevant information. That's when they met Linscott.

A highly respected Bible student at a nearby college, Linscott happened to work at the mission. And when the police explained their purpose, he began thinking about his recent nightmare—in which he saw a blonde young woman beaten to death. It was only after considerable thought that he finally told the police about his dream.

"I suddenly became intrigued by the possibility of my dream being an inspired experience," he later said. "If nothing else, going to the police seemed like an interesting diversion from memorizing two chapters of Romans."

Linscott's dream certainly did prompt the interest of detectives Robert Scianna and Robert Grego, who questioned their informant in detail. Linscott apparently knew so much about the murder that he was taken into custody as a suspect. He was formally arrested and charged with the murder in November.

Even though the prosecution's case was wholly circumstantial, the jury found him guilty, despite the fact that he had no motive and the fingerprints found at the crime scene weren't his. Linscott was shattered by the verdict. "Everybody trusts the system," he later explained. "Everybody trusts the fact-finding process. Nobody realizes that it's a slick pole once you start sliding on it and you can't get off."

Steven Linscott served three years of his forty-year sentence before the Illinois Court of Appeals released him. The state's Supreme Court reinstated the conviction later, but the Bible student is currently free on bond pending another appeal.

Food
for Spanish Horses

When the Spanish conquistadors first reached Peru, center of the great empire of the Incas, the Peruvian Indians thought that the Spanish war horses were ferocious and deadly monsters, quite unlike their own gentle llamas, especially when the horses stamped their hooves, snorted, and shook their heads.

The Peruvians nervously asked the Spanish calvarymen through an interpreter, "What do these fierce animals eat?" The Spanish knew what to reply. Pointing to the gold jewelry and gold ornaments of the Peruvians they said, "They eat those things of yellow metal. They are hungry now but do not wish to be seen eating. Leave the food in front of them and go away." At this point the Indians would gather a pile of gold objects that the Spaniards would pocket and then, calling back the Indians, would say, "These fierce animals are still hungry. Bring more food."

Psychic Mind Control

Wolf Messing, who died in 1974, was undoubtedly the Soviet Union's most celebrated psychic performer. He was best known for his stage performances during which he would carry out telepathic commands suggested by members of the audience. Those who became his close friends, however, had more spectacular stories to tell, including tales of his power to control another person's mind—even from miles away.

One such story has been told by Dr. Alexander Lungin, whose mother was Messing's unofficial secretary for several years. The incident took place while Lungin was in medical school in Moscow. His anatomy instructor, a Professor Gravilov, had taken a fierce dislike to him, and continually warned the youth that he planned to fail him, regardless of the work he did. The day of reckoning came when Lungin had to take his final examination. Each student had to take an oral test by approaching a table at which several examiners sat. One of them would then proceed with the questions. Just before the test, Gravilov gleefully told Lungin that he would be personally examining him. Terror-stricken by the news, Lungin conveyed his fears to his mother who phoned Messing and asked him to intercede. The psychic, who lived miles from the school, called back later and made it clear that he would.

When the time finally came, Lungin walked up to the examiners to take his orals and Gravilov didn't say a word. Instead, he merely looked on while Lungin was examined by another professor. The vindictive teacher even watched as the other professor signed Lungin's record book to show he had taken the test.

Needless to say, the student was delighted by these events, but what happened next was even more bizarre.

Lungin left the classroom and went outside to talk to some of the other students. Professor Gravilov came stalking out imperiously a few minutes later to ask if everyone had taken the examination. When the students replied that they had, Gravilov glared at the student he despised.

"Lungin hasn't taken it yet," he growled.

When the students explained that he had taken it and passed, Gravilov became enraged. "How did he pass?" he demanded sternly. "It can't be. Who gave him the exam?"

When the professor checked the records, he became livid and scurried off. Alexander Lungin had somehow outwitted him—probably with a little help from his famous friend Wolf.

Dadaji's Strange Visit

Can a person be physically present in two places at the same time? The idea sounds totally preposterous, but just such a case was reported by two respected parapsychologists in 1975. Dr. Karlis Osis and Dr. Erlendur Haraldsson, visiting India in 1970 to study that country's holy men, were especially interested in Dadaji, a businessman-turned-saint. He had a large mass of followers in southern India, and while looking into his purported miracles, the two researchers uncovered the following story:

Sometime in the early part of 1970, Dadaji visited Allahabad, some four hundred miles from his home, and stayed with a local family. During that stay, he went out to meditate and later told his followers that he had bilocated to Calcutta. He even told his hostess that she could substantiate his story by contacting her sister-in-law, who lived there. The holy man also gave her the address of the residence where he projected himself.

According to the family who lived in the house, they did in fact verify Dadaji's unbelievable story. Roma Mukherjee, a disciple of the holy man, explained that she was reading a book in the study when Dadaji appeared before her. His figure was transparent at first, she explained, but then more fully materialized. The phantom's sudden appearance so frightened her that she screamed, summoning her brother and mother to her side. Dadaji, in the meantime, did little but motion to the girl to bring him some tea.

"When she returned to the study with the tea," report the two researchers, "Roma was followed by her mother and physician brother. She reached in through the partly opened door and gave Dadaji the tea and a biscuit. The mother, through a crack in the door, saw Dadaji. The brother, standing in a different position, only saw Roma's hand reach in through the opening and come back without the tea. There was no place she could have set the cup without entering the room. Then the father, a bank director, came home from morning shopping at the bazaar. He didn't believe what they told him and, brushing away their objections, peeked in through the crack in the door, where he saw a man's figure sitting on a chair."

When the family finally entered the room, Dadaji had disappeared, but a half-burned cigarette was left on the study table. It was Dadaji's favorite brand.

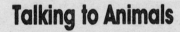

Talking to Animals

Vladimir Durov was an exceptional circus performer and extraordinary animal trainer. Capable of making his show animals perform whatever stunts he wanted, he claimed that part of his success came from the ability to establish psychic contact with his beasts. This claim eventually came to the attention of Professor W. Bechterev, head of the Institute for the Investigation of the Brain in St. Petersburg.

Intrigued, Bechterev tested Durov's claims with the help of a fox terrier. The usual procedure was for Bechterev to choose a series of commands, then tell them to Durov, who would take little Pikki's head into his hands, stare into the dog's eyes, and impress the instructions onto his brain.

For the first trial, Bechterev suggested that Durov make his pet jump on a specific chair, climb over to a table right next to it, then scratch the painting positioned over it. Durov complied by impressing the signals onto Pikki's brain, a procedure that took several minutes, and the little dog went to work.

"Pikki, after a few seconds, jumped from his chair, quickly ran to one at the wall, then equally quickly jumped on a little round table," reported Bechterev. "Rising on his hind legs, he reached the portrait with his right paw, scratching it a little with his claws." Taking instructions from Durov, Bechterev even found he could communicate instructions to Pikki himself.

The celebrated scientist could not, however, rule out the possibility that he and Durov were unintentionally cuing the dog with eye movements, so he later sent two of his colleagues to work with Durov and Pikki in Moscow. Durov explained his procedure for impressing commands on the dog, and the scientists performed their experiments while wearing blindfolds or metal screens over their faces. Pikki was able to respond to their psychic commands despite the controls.

But one especially provocative puzzle remains. Could Durov really communicate with his pet by psychically impressing instructions to the dog's brain, or was Pikki merely an especially psychic dog?

Search for Sasquatch

Grover Krantz claims his chosen field of research has torpedoed his academic career and brought him nothing but ridicule from colleagues. An anthropologist at Washington State University, Krantz specializes in the study of the world's most elusive primate, the so-called Bigfoot, or Sasquatch, often reported as inhabiting the dense forests of the Pacific Northwest.

Stories of huge, hairy, apelike animals in the Blue Mountains of Washington and Oregon date back to the nineteenth century. Orthodox anthropologists tend to dismiss such tales as fanciful folklore, but not Krantz, who believes the Sasquatch may be our nearest living relative. Humans, in fact, may be directly descended from the shy interloper, remains of which have never been found.

The controversial primate draws its name from the gigantic footprints it leaves behind, prints two feet long in some cases, separated by a six-foot stride. According to eyewitnesses, Sasquatch stands as much as eight feet tall and may weigh as much as eight hundred pounds. The body is completely covered in dark-brown hair, save for the flat face, and the palms and soles of its hands and feet. The face is characterized by a receding forehead and prominent brow ridge. Sasquatch's proportions are roughly those of a human, except for its dangling long arms. For food it seems to prefer roots, berries, and an occasional rodent.

Serious interest in Sasquatch was revived in the spring of 1987, with the discovery of four new sets of prints and the published analysis of another set of prints made by U.S. Forest Service rangers in 1982. The latter set of tracks measured seventeen inches long. Moreover, said Krantz, they showed evidence of dermal, or skin, ridges on the soles of the feet, along with sweat pores and wear patterns, anatomical details almost impossible to duplicate, even by the cleverest of hoaxters.

Pointing to the bone impressions in the plaster casts, Krantz also noted that the ankle seemed to be moved further forward on the foot than that of any other known primate, man and gorilla included. Such an evolutionary shift forward, Krantz added, would be necessary to support the creature's immense weight, another key detail fake prints would probably overlook.

Krantz himself isn't taking any more chances with the evidence or his reputation. He has vowed to shoot Sasquatch on sight, believing the scientific value to be gained should outweigh any squeamishness at the act. "The only way to convince anyone is with a real specimen," Krantz said. Short of shooting a Sasquatch, he hopes to use a helicopter and infrared detector to try to locate the decomposing remains of one.

New Zealand UFO

Movies and still photographs of UFOs are relatively rare. The ones that stand up to scrutiny are scarcer still. But some of the best and most thoroughly analyzed UFO pictures ever were taken by an Australian network TV crew on the night of December 30, 1978, near Kaikoura, New Zealand.

UFOs had been repeatedly reported during the previous weeks, primarily in the area of Cook Straight, which divides New Zealand's North and South Islands. Smelling a story, reporter Quentin Fogarty and cameraman David Crockett flew to Wellington. From there, they boarded the freight plane *Argosy*, piloted by Captain Bill Startup, and bound for Christchurch, on the south of New Zealand's two largest islands. Also accompanying the crew were co-pilot Bob Guard and sound engineer Ngaire Crockett, David's wife.

Fogarty and Crockett were filming introductory material from the plane just before landing when the cockpit came alive. Startup and Guard spotted several UFOs and contacted air-traffic control in Wellington. Wellington, in turn confirmed the sightings on radar. By the time Fogarty reached the flight deck, five pulsating lights were visible, varying from a pinpoint to what looked like a large balloon filled with light.

At this juncture Wellington informed the plane that "you have a target in formation with you." Startup banked the *Argosy* in a 360-degree turn but nothing immediate could be seen until he finally switched off the navigation lights. Then everyone could make out a single, bright light hovering in the night sky. Crockett switched seats with Guard, his TV camera running all the while. On the return flight from Christchurch, more UFOs were seen.

The videotape of the "Kaikoura Lights" is probably the single most heavily analyzed photo in UFO history. Even so, the results are largely inconclusive. Several potential light sources, such as the planets Venus and Jupiter, and brightly-lit squid boats on the ocean's surface can be eliminated as candidates. But what the tape does show may never be known, except that it clearly portrays an unidentified flying object.

Young Dante's Dream

The Divine Comedy of Dante Alighieri is rightly regarded as one of the world's great spiritual masterpieces. But for the dream of the dead poet's son, Jacopo, however, the complete manuscript might have been lost forever.

When Dante died in 1321, Jacopo and his brother, Pietro, despaired, not only for the loss of their father, but for the incomplete manuscript of the *Comedy* he left behind. The two turned the house upside down and rummaged through his papers, but the elder Dante's missing papers were not to be found.

In the depths of their mourning, Jacopo had a dream. His father entered his room, arrayed in blazing white garments. When Jacopo asked if he had finished his masterpiece, Dante nodded yes, and indicated where the missing sections could be found.

With a lawyer friend of his father bearing witness, Jacopo entered Dante's chambers. Behind a small blind attached to the wall they found a tiny window. In the cubicle on which it opened they beheld the poet's final pages, covered in mold. *The Divine Comedy* was again whole, thanks to a faithful son's dream.

A Ghost With a Message

Early in the morning of December 6, 1955, Lucian Landau, a London businessman, had an unusual drama. He was sleeping in the home of Constantine Antoniadès in Geneva when he felt someone entering his room. When he turned over in bed, he saw a faint pool of light in which he gradually perceived the figure of his host's late wife. Next to her figure stood an Alsatian dog with an unusual brown coat. The apparition soon began to disappear, but while desolving, Landau heard it say, "Tell him."

The London businessman didn't hesitate to impart the information to his host when they met later in the day. But he didn't explain exactly what had occurred. Instead, he merely asked whether his host's wife had ever had an Alsatian dog.

"Oh, yes," responded Mr. Antoniadès. "He is still alive."

This response puzzled Landau, since there was no evidence of a dog in the house. Antoniadès then explained that he boarded the dog at a kennel when his wife became ill, since he couldn't look after it. When Landau finally told his host about the ghostly visitation, Antoniadès called the kennel, only to learn that the dog had been destroyed a few days earlier.

The words "tell him" were finally beginning to make sense.

When an investigator from the Society for Psychical Research in Great Britain looked into the case, Antoniadès corroborated the remarkable episode. "I affirm," he testified, "that there was not any photograph of my wife with the dog or the dog alone anywhere in the house where Landau could have seen it before the incident occurred."

Psychic Stock Market Tips

Beverly Jaegers isn't your typical psychic. She doesn't conduct séances. And she would probably wince if you gave her some Tarot cards. But she does live in a lovely St. Louis home, bought with the money she's made by using her sixth sense. In fact, Jaegers views psi with all the rigor of a Wall Street executive. It isn't a fleeting and unreliable capability, she says, but something we can use productively every day of our lives.

In order to prove her point, Jaegers helped the *St. Louis Business*

Journal perform an unusual experiment in 1982. The paper wanted to see just how reliable Jaeger's powers really were, so they pitted her against the stock market. The experiment began when the *Journal* asked each of nineteen prominent stockbrokers to choose five stocks they believed would increase in value. These stocks were subsequently monitored for six months. Even though Jaegers had no business experience or training, she was asked to pick five stocks based purely on her sixth sense.

The result?

The stock market entered into a downtrend during the period of the test, and by the time the experiment was completed, the Dow-Jones industrial average had fallen by eighty points. Because of this unfortunate trend, sixteen of the stockbrokers lost their shirts. They were undoubtedly surprised to learn that, during this same period, the stocks intuitively chosen by Jaegers increased in value by 17.2 percent. Only one of the stockbrokers matched her uncanny success.

Corn From the Sky

Since 1982 kernels of corn have been falling on houses along Pleasant Acres Drive in Evans, Colorado, just south of Greeley. Gary Bryan, who lives there, says, "I'd probably have a ton of it if I picked it all up." Once in a while a pinto bean appears amid the corn.

The problem is that there are no cornfields near the houses, and the nearest grain elevator is five miles away. Nobody can figure out where the corn could be coming from. All the witnesses can say is that from time to time it is seen descending from the sky.

When the press heard the story in September 1986, reporters from area newspapers and television channels came to the site and saw the bizarre phenomenon for themselves. As the corn was falling, they searched for a prankster with a slingshot but found none.

People who hadn't seen the fall with their own eyes didn't believe it—until they saw it themselves. As one convert, Eldred McClintock, told the *Rocky Mountain News*, "It really came down. I've seen it now and I believe it."

Kangaroo Monster

"It was as fast as lightning and looked like a giant kangaroo running and leaping across the field," the Reverend W. J. Hancock said. Frank Cobb, who also saw it, said it didn't look like anything he'd ever seen, although in some ways it resembled a kangaroo.

Kangaroos, which are not native to Tennessee, are unaggressive, herbivorous animals. But this beast was a killer. In January 1934 the creature was terrorizing the tiny community of Hamburg, Tennessee, and had already killed and partially devoured several German shepherd dogs.

When the creature visited the Henry Ashmore farm on January 12, it left five-clawed tracks the size of a big man's hand. Will Patten saw the thing and chased it away. The next day he found a partially-eaten dog in his yard.

The creature was also killing geese and chickens and as armed parties searched for it without success, panic set in. A. B. Russell, chief of police of nearby South Pittsburg, Tennessee, tried to defuse the hysteria, calling it "superstition started by a mad dog." But those who had seen it knew better. They said it was huge—weighing at least 150 pounds—and incredibly agile, able to leap fences and other hurdles with ease. It ranged between South Pittsburg and Signal Mountain, which meant that to get around it had to cross two mountain ranges and two rivers.

Finally a bobcat was shot and killed on Signal Mountain on January 29, thirteen days after the creature's last appearance. The authorities and the newspapers declared that the mystery had been solved, but witnesses resolutely rejected that explanation. What they had seen, they said, was large and kangaroolike.

The monster was never seen again and it has never been satisfactorily identified or explained.

The Dover Demon

For more than twenty-five hours in April 1977 a strange creature from another world made its presence known in the wealthy Boston suburb of Dover.

The Dover demon first appeared at 10:30 on the evening of April 21, when three seventeen-year-olds were driving north on Farm Street. The driver, Bill Bartlett, thought he saw something creeping along a low wall of loose stones to his left. Then his headlights illuminated something he had never imagined even in his wildest dreams.

The creature slowly turned its head and stared into the light, revealing two large, lidless eyes shining "like two orange marbles" and an otherwise featureless face with no apparent nose. It had a head shaped like an upright watermelon and nearly the size of the rest of its body, which was thin and spindly. The hairless skin had the apparent consistency of "wet sandpaper." About four feet tall, it had been making its way uncertainly along the wall, wrapping its long fingers around the rocks as it moved.

The sight struck Bartlett speechless and a few seconds later, when he found his voice, his headlights had passed the creature. His two companions, their attentions elsewhere, had not seen it at all.

Not long afterward, fifteen-year-old John Baxter was walking home up Millers High Road after dropping his girlfriend off at midnight. A mile later he saw a short figure approaching and assumed it was a friend who lived on the street. Baxter called out to him but got no response.

The two continued to approach each other until the short figure stopped. Baxter stopped too and asked, "Who is that?" The sky was overcast and he could see only a shadowy form. When he took one step forward, the form shot off to the left, ran down a shallow gully, and dashed up the opposite bank.

Perplexed, Baxter followed the stranger until he got to the gully. He looked across and thirty feet away saw something with a monkey-shaped body, a "figure-eight-shaped" watermelonlike head, and glowing eyes. Its long fingers were entwined around a tree.

Baxter felt suddenly uneasy and left the scene.

The next person to see the Dover demon was Bill Bartlett's friend, Will Taintor, eighteen. Taintor knew about the creature from Bartlett. Still, he was shocked when he and his friend Abby Brabham, fifteen, saw the thing along Springdale Avenue. Their description matched Bartlett's except that where he described glowing orange eyes, they swore the eyes were green.

When investigators interviewed the witnesses, they were impressed with the consistency of their testimony. They were also impressed when the police chief, the high school principal, schoolteachers, and the youths' parents all said the young people were honest and reliable.

As one of the investigators, Walter Webb, observed at the conclusion of his probe into the case, "None of the four was on drugs or drinking at the time of his or her sighting so far as we were able to determine. . . . None of the principals in this affair made any attempt to go to the newspapers or police to publicize their claims. Instead the sightings gradually leaked out. As for the idea the witnesses were victims of somebody else's stunt, this seems most unlikely, chiefly due to the virtual impossibility of creating an animated, lifelike 'demon' of the sort described."

What was the Dover demon? Some have suggested it was an extraterrestrial. Others say it may be something known to the Cree Indians of eastern Canada as the Mannegishi. Little people with round heads, no noses, long spidery legs, and six-fingered hands, the Mannegishi legend goes, live between rocks in the rapids of streams and rivers.

Hotel in
Another Dimension

It all began innocently enough in October 1979, when two couples in Dover, England, set off on a vacation together intending to travel through France and Spain. It ended in a journey that took them to another world.

Geoff and Pauline Simpson and their friends, Len and Cynthia Gisby, boarded a boat that took them across the English Channel to the coast of France. There they rented a car and proceeded to drive north. Around 9:30 that first evening, October 3, they began to tire and looked for a place to stay. They pulled off the autoroute when they saw a plush-looking motel.

Len went inside and in the lobby encountered a man dressed in an odd plum-colored uniform. The man said there was no room in the motel but there was a small motel south along the road. Len thanked him and he and his companions went on.

Along the way they were struck by the oldness of the cobbled, narrow road and the buildings they passed. They also saw posters advertising a circus. "It was a very old-fashioned circus," Pauline would remember. "That's why we took so much interest."

Finally the travelers saw a long, low building with a row of brightly lit windows. Some men were standing in front of it and when Cynthia spoke with them, they told her the place was an inn, not a hotel. They drove further down the road until they saw two buildings, one a police station, the other an old-fashioned, two-story building bearing a sign marked "Hotel." Inside, everything was made of heavy wood. There were no tablecloths on the tables, nor was there any evidence of such modern conveniences as telephones or elevators.

The rooms were no less strange. The beds had heavy sheets and no pillows. There were no locks on the doors, only wooden catches. The bathroom the couples had to share had old-fashioned plumbing.

After they ate, they returned to their rooms and fell asleep. They were awakened when sunlight filtered through the windows, which consisted only of wooden shutters, no glass. They went back to the dining room and ate a simple breakfast with "black and horrible" coffee, Geoff recalled.

As they were sitting there, a woman wearing a silk evening gown and carrying a dog under her arm sat opposite them. "It was strange," Pauline said. "It looked like she had just come in from a ball but it was seven in the morning. I couldn't take my eyes off her."

At that point two gendarmes entered the room. "They were nothing like the gendarmes we saw anywhere else in France," according to Geoff. "Their uniforms seemed to be very old." The uniforms were deep blue and the officers were wearing capes over their shoulders. Their hats were large and peaked.

Despite the oddities, the couples enjoyed themselves and, when they returned to their rooms, the two husbands separately took pictures of their wives standing by the shuttered windows.

On their way out Len and Geoff talked with the gendarmes about the best way to take the autoroute to Avignon and the Spanish border. The officers didn't seem to understand the word "autoroute," and the travelers assumed they hadn't pronounced the French word properly. The directions they were given were quite poor; they took the friends to an old road some miles out of the way. They decided to use the map instead and take a more direct route along the highway.

After the car was packed, Len went to pay his bill and was astonished when the manager asked for only nineteen francs. Assuming there was some misunderstanding, Len explained that there were four of them and they had eaten a meal. The manager only nodded. Len showed the bill to the gendarmes, who smilingly indicated there was nothing amiss. He paid in cash and left before they could change their minds.

On their way back from two weeks in Spain, the two couples decided to stop at the hotel again. They had had a pleasant, interesting time there and the prices certainly couldn't be beat. The night was rainy and cold and visibility poor, but they found the turnoff and noticed the circus signs they had seen before.

"This is definitely the right road," Pauline declared.

It was, but there was no hotel alongside it. Thinking that somehow they had missed it, they went back to the motel where the man in the plum-colored suit had given them directions. That motel was there, but there was no man in the unusual suit and the clerk denied such an individual worked there.

The couples drove three times up and down the road looking for something that, they were now beginning to realize, was no longer there. It had vanished without a trace.

They drove north and spent the night in a hotel in Lyons. Room with modern facilities, breakfast and dinner cost them 247 francs.

Upon their return to Dover, Geoff and Len had their respective rolls of film processed. In each case the pictures of the hotel (one by Geoff, two by Len) were in the middle of the roll. But when they got the pictures back, the ones taken inside the hotel were missing. There were no spoiled negatives. Each film had its full quota of pictures. It was as if the pictures had never been taken—except for one small detail that a reporter for Yorkshire television would notice: "There was evidence that the camera had tried to wind on in the middle of the film. Sprocket holes on the negatives showed damage."

The couples kept quiet about their experience for three years, telling it only to friends and family. One friend found a book in which it was revealed that gendarmes wore the uniforms described prior to 1905. Eventually a reporter for the Dover newspaper heard it and published an account. Later a television dramatization of the experience was produced by a local station.

In 1985 Manchester psychiatrist Albert Keller hypnotized Geoff Simpson to see if he could recall any more of the peculiar event. Under hypnosis he added nothing new to what he consciously remembered.

Jenny Randles, a British writer who investigated this bizarre episode, wonders, "What really happened to the four travelers in rural France? Was this a time slip? If so, one wonders why the hotel manager was apparently not surprised by their futuristic vehicle and clothing and why he accepted their 1979 currency, which certainly would have appeared odd to anybody living that far back in the past."

The travelers—perhaps time-travelers—have no explanation. "We only know what happened," says Geoff.

African Alarm Clock

Many people can wake themselves up at any time of night, just by giving themselves the proper suggestion before falling asleep. During the 1960s, a researcher in Cape Town, South Africa, proved that he could wake up given the correct *psychic* suggestion.

Mr. W. van Vuurde was the subject of these experiments, which were conducted in collaboration with Professor A.E.H. Bleksley of the University of Witwatersrand. Mr. van Vuurde had discovered that he could wake up to match the time set on a broken clock, even if he didn't look when he manipulated the hands while setting it. When he explained his peculiar talent to Dr. Bleksley, the professor was eager to test the subject under more stringent conditions.

For a series of 284 nonconsecutive nights, W. van Vuurde kept a careful record of each time he woke during the night. Meanwhile, elsewhere in the city, Professor A. E. H. Bleksley randomly set a clock to a different time each night the experiment was conducted. A trial was considered a success when van Vuurde woke on any experimental night within sixty seconds of the appropriate time. Since he typically slept for eight hours, the chances for any given night's success was 160-to-1.

Out of the 284 experiments, the subject woke to the correct time on eleven occasions. That may not seem like much, but because of the low odds, the chances of this success rate resulting from chance is 250,000-to-1.

Psychic Detective

No subject raises the skeptic's hackles like police who rely on psychics—especially when the officials go public with the news.

On Sunday morning, August 4, 1982, Tommy Kennedy went on a picnic near Empire Lake in New York and disappeared. Soon everyone was called in to help locate the missing five-year-old, from the lake's casual visitors to the Tioga County Sheriff's Department. Nobody could find a trace of the boy, and Tommy's mother grew increasingly frantic. By six o'clock that evening, nearly 100 people were exploring the nearby woods. Finally, Richard Clark, a fireman who was taking part in the work, suggested they call Phillip Jordan, a prominent local psychic, who happened to be the firefighter's tenant. Nobody thought much of the idea, except for Deputy David Redsicker, who had seen the psychic at work.

That evening, Phil Jordan visited the Clarks at their home in Spenser, New York. Without telling him anything, the fireman handed the psychic a T-shirt the lost boy had worn. After fingering it for several minutes, Jordan asked for a pencil and some paper. Then he began sketching a lake, some overturned boats, and a house by a rock.

"That's where they'll find the boy," he explained. "I can see him lying under a tree with his head in his arms. He's sound asleep."

This information was immediately forwarded to the sheriff's office. The next day, Richard Clark and Phil Jordan went to Empire Lake to continue the search. Tommy's mother was naturally present and cooperative, and this time the psychic gathered his impressions from a pair of the boy's sneakers. His second series of impressions matched the first, so the search party was directed into the woods to find the tree and house he had seen.

Tommy Kennedy was found within the hour, in the exact place identified by the psychic on his map. The boy had wandered off the day before, and subsequently walked in the wrong direction until he became hopelessly lost in the woods. He had spent the night crying and sleeping under a tree.

Phil Jordan was given an honorary deputy sheriff's badge from the Tioga County Sheriff's Department for his help on the case. "The boy had lain and slept under that tree for most of the twenty hours and we missed him," said Sheriff Raymond Ayres. "Phil Jordan simply used some kind of paranormal talent that the rest of us don't have. I would not hesitate to call on him again if I thought he could help."

Death Clicks

The Samoans believe that when death hovers near, paranormal raps will break out in the victim's home. This strange phenomenon has been called the death click or death rattle, and its existence represents more than mere folklore.

Genevieve B. Miller, for instance, often heard these strange sounds, particularly as a small girl. She first heard the raps during the summer of 1924 in Woronoco, Massachusetts, when her sister, Stephanie, was bedridden with a mysterious illness. While the girl remained in bed, knocking sounds, which sounded like knuckles cracking, echoed through the house. They would come in sets of three, with one drawn-out click followed by two shorter raps. Once, Mrs. Miller's father became so irritated by the sounds that he ripped out every window screen in the house, blaming them for the ruckus. But his little rampage did nothing to stop the noise.

By October 4, it was clear that Stephanie was dying. When the doctor arrived, he heard the noises too.

"What on earth is that?" he said while turning to find the source of the sound. When he turned back to his small patient, she uttered her last words and died.

The raps decreased their activity after the death, but never completely stopped. They erupted now and then when the family moved to a new home. Then, in 1928, Stephanie's brother broke through the ice while walking over a frozen river and drowned.

From that day forward, the death clicks were never heard again.

The Man With the Photographic Mind

Ted Serios has been called "the man with the photographic mind"—not because of his memory, but because of his ability to impress pictures on Polaroid film by pure concentration.

Most of what we know about the case comes from Denver psychiatrist Jule Eisenbud, who worked with Serios in the sixties. A former Chicago bellhop, Serios lived in Eisenbud's home for the duration of the experiments. His usual procedure was to stare into the camera lens, often through a black paper cylinder, and tell the experimenters when to snap the shutter. A blurry scene would often be found printed on the resulting snapshot.

Of course, skeptics howled that it was a fraud from start to finish, claiming the strange cylinder Serios liked to work with contained a hidden lens. But such criticisms can't explain all of Serios' successes by any means.

An especially provocative experiment was designed by Dr. Eisenbud in 1965. Several witnesses gathered at his home and each wrote a target theme on a slip of paper. Serios, not told of the suggestions, was simply asked to imprint one of the suggested targets onto Polaroid film. This meant that some part of Serios' mind had clairvoyantly to receive the slips, choose one of the targets, and then imprint it onto the photographic paper.

Serios began his part of the experiment by drinking a few beers and then got to work by focusing into the Polaroid camera. The image that subsequently resulted looked like a blurry close-up of a spider. It didn't seem to match any of the suggestions offered by the guests. The only one that came close was a slip with the words "staggerwing airplane" written on it. Two years later, however, Dr. Eisenbud was looking through a copy of *The American Heritage of Flight*, where, to his surprise, he found a series of photographs of staggerwing planes—and Serios' previous photograph was identical to one of them.

Fire and Faith

The Free Pentacostal Holiness Church is a fundamentalist sect with branches scattered throughout the South. Its members take the Bible literally and seriously believe the Bible when it states that true believers can defy serpents, poison, and fire. So as part of the religious services, the congregation will whip itself into a frenzy, at the height of which they will handle rattlesnakes, drink strychnine and touch fire, without any discomfort or ill effect.

A scientific study of the Free Pentacostal Holiness Church was undertaken by New Jersey psychiatrist Berthold Schwarz in 1959. He visited Tennessee several times to observe the church meetings, and watched while the parishioners held kerosene lamps to their hands and feet without getting burned. "On three occasions," reports Schwarz, "three different women held the blaze to their chests, so that the flames were in intimate contact with their cotton dresses, exposed necks, faces, and hair. This lasted for longer than a few seconds. At one point, a congregation member picked up a flaming coal the size of a hen's egg and held it in the palms of his hands for sixty-five seconds while he walked among the congregation." Schwarz, on the other hand, could not touch a piece of burning charcoal for more than a second without developing a painful blister.

Dr. Schwarz believes that these worshipers probably enter some sort of trance during the proceedings. But what power prevents their clothing from burning remains a scientific enigma.

The Handprint
in Cell 17

In the 1860s and 1870s, the United States was wracked by violent labor unrest. Working conditions in the Pennsylvania coal mines were terrible—one long, hazardous day's work paid an average of fifty cents—and the mostly Irish-immigrant miners were frequently at odds with their bosses, most of whom were of English and Welsh descent.

To fight the mine owners, a secret society called the Mollie Maguires was formed. The Mollie Maguires directed the first strike against mining companies in America. But their resistance went further: They incited riots and killed about 150 persons.

The owners bought the services of the Pinkerton Detective Agency, which placed undercover agent James McParlen in the ranks of the Mollies. McParlen's subsequent testimony would send twelve members of the group to the gallows. In 1877 "Yellow Jack" Donohue was convicted of the murder of a foreman of the Lehigh Coal and Navigation Company. Three other men were sentenced to hang as well for the murder of another mine foreman. Two of these men went stoically to their deaths. But one—Alexander Campbell—swore he was innocent.

As he was being dragged from his first-floor cell, number 17, Campbell rubbed his left hand in dust from the floor and pressed his palm against the plaster wall. "This handprint will remain here for all time as proof of my innocence," he shouted. He repeated this vow over and over again as he was led struggling to the gallows, where after the trap was sprung he took fourteen minutes to die by strangulation.

Campbell was gone but his handprint remained, just as he had said it would.

In 1930, when Robert L. Bowman was elected sheriff of Carbon County, he vowed to remove the handprint, which was being taken as proof of a terrible injustice in the county's history. In December 1931 a work crew came to cell 17 and removed the section of plaster wall containing the handprint, replacing it with a new wall of fresh plaster.

The following morning the sheriff entered the cell, where he was horrified to see the faint outline of a hand in the still-moist plaster. By evening a black handprint was fully visible.

Although the cell is now kept locked and is opened only to an occasional visitor, the handprint remains there to this day.

As late as 1978 a private citizen who sneaked into the cell tried to paint over it, only to have the print reappear minutes later in the fresh paint.

The Lifesaving Dolphin

One day in early August 1982, eleven-year-old Nick Christides was surfing in the Indian Ocean off the Cocos Islands when he was swept out to sea. For the next four hours he drifted helplessly in shark-infested waters as boats and airplanes searched for him in vain.

Fortunately Nick had a friend: a dolphin that joined him early in his ordeal and protected him from the sharks that were stalking him. The dolphin stayed at his side, fending off the would-be attackers and making sure he did not lose his strength and sink to the bottom of the ocean.

Eventually Christides was spotted from the air and rescued. His father told reporters, "The dolphin just stuck with him, either swimming beside him or going around in circles. He must have realized Nick was in trouble and being pulled out by the northerly current."

Dreams of the Dead

Many technologically unsophisticated cultures believe that we can contact the dead through our dreams. In fact, some anthropologists suggest that belief in a life beyond death stems from the fact that we commonly dream about our deceased friends and relatives. Some new research, however, suggests that some of these peculiar dreams could be literally true.

Several cases pointing in this direction have been collected by Helen Solen of Portland, Oregon, who has been particularly interested in the dream experiences of a housewife she calls Gwen. Gwen's postmorten dreams began in 1959, soon after her mother died. "I don't specifically remember if I ever dreamed of anyone dead or not," she explained to Solen. "However, I was very distraught over my mother's death at the early age of forty-nine. Many times after that she came to me in my dreams, especially when I was perplexed or disturbed."

Gwen soon learned that she could ask her mother for help in a crisis, and the phantom would reply in her dreams. One night, for example, Gwen dreamed of a room filled with coffins. The eerie dream suggestion: that her father was about to die as well. Her mother appeared in her dreams that night to comfort her, and to explain that she would personally help the elderly man make the transition. Gwen's father entered the hospital suddenly, two days later, and physicians advised that bypass surgery be performed. Gwen gave her permission for the surgery, but the denouement came two days after that.

Gwen's mother appeared in an early-morning dream to say the crisis was over at last. Gwen woke right after the dream and saw that it was 7 o'clock. Later in the morning, the hospital called to say that her father had died—at precisely 7:10 A.M..

ESP vs. Bombs

German-born anthropologist Ruth-Inge Heinze, a renowned student of religion and shamanism, today teaches at the California Institute of Integral Studies in San Francisco. But had it not been for her sixth sense, she would have lost her life in World War II.

The incident occurred during an air raid, when Dr. Heinze often had to scurry to bomb shelters during the Allied raids over Germany. During one raid, however, the bombing was so intense that she couldn't make it to a shelter. She sought safety in the entrance to a public building instead.

"Shrapnel fragments from the antiaircraft cannon fell like rain everywhere," she later explained. "Hundreds of guns, big and small, kept shooting at the multitude of planes. The entrance niche barely offered any cover. Suddenly, however, I felt compelled to go out on the street and run to the next house, approximately one hundred yards away. It was a miracle that I was not hit by any of the shrapnel pieces, which were falling all around me. The moment I reached the next building, the first house where I had been standing was hit by a bomb and completely demolished. I had somehow sensed the course of the oncoming bomb."

Today, Heinze simply scoffs when skeptics try to tell her that ESP doesn't exist.

The Little People

Stories of so-called "little people" who share space with us on this planet are so pervasive that we must conclude one of two things: Either earlier societies had a peculiar penchant for amusing themselves with similar fairy tales, despite vast differences in geography and culture, or some little-understood stimulus gave rise to the stories.

In Central America, for instance, diminutive, dwarflike humanoids are known as the *ikals* and *wendis*. In the Tzeltal Indian language, the ikals are hairy, three-foot-tall beings said to live in caves like bats. In fact, according to contemporary accounts collected by Berkeley anthropologist Brian Stoss, "about twenty years ago or less, there were many sightings of this creature or creatures, and several people apparently tried to fight it with machetes. One man also saw a small sphere following him from about five feet. After many attempts he finally hit it with his machete and it disintegrated, leaving only an ashlike substance."

Stoss was also told that the *ikal* paralyzed and kidnapped Indian women, who were then taken back to their caves and impregnated as often as once a week, giving birth to black offspring who were taught to fly.

These tales raise several curious comparisons with modern-day experiences reported by UFO abductees, who report small, humanoid entities that paralyze, probe, and impregnate their victims. Could the little people of yore be the forerunners of today's UFO occupants? If so, perhaps we should be looking to *inner*, as opposed to outer, space for their origins.

Carried Off
by a Giant Bird

At 8:10 P.M. on July 25, 1977, ten-year-old Marlon Lowe of Lawndale, Illinois, had an experience that science says is impossible: He was snatched off the ground and carried through the air by an immense bird.

The first Lawndale resident to notice something unusual in the air was a man named Cox, who saw two large condorlike birds descending out of the southwest. At the time Marlon Lowe was running with some friends, unaware that just behind him the two large birds, unlike any known to exist in Illinois, were flying level at about eight feet above the ground. Marlon was still running when one of them snatched him with its claws and carried him into the air.

His mother Ruth Lowe, who watched this happen, screamed in terror and ran off after the birds. After carrying him for about thirty-five feet, the creature dropped Marlon, who fell unharmed to the ground. It and its companion then flew off to the northeast. In all, six persons witnessed the incredible event.

Mrs. Lowe thought the birds looked like enormous condors, with six-inch beaks and necks one-and-a-half feet long with a white ring in the middle. Except for the ring the birds were black. Each wing was, by the most conservative estimate, four feet long.

Even with six witnesses the story was so incredible that, though it attracted nationwide publicity, hardly anyone believed it and the Lowe family was subjected to vicious persecution. The local game warden called Mrs. Lowe a liar. Pranksters began leaving dead birds, including on one occasion "a big, beautiful eagle," on the Lowes' doorstep. Local youngsters teased Marlon and called him "Bird Boy."

The stress of the original attack and its aftermath was such that Marlon's hair turned from red to gray. For more than a year afterwards he refused to go outside after dark.

Two years later, looking back, Mrs. Lowe told investigators

Loren and Jerry Coleman, "I'll always remember how that huge thing was bending its white-ringed neck and seemed to be trying to peck at Marlon as it was flying away.

"I was standing at the door and all I saw was Marlon's feet dangling in the air. There just aren't any birds around here that could lift him up like that."

John Lennon's Death Foreseen

Psychic Alex Tanous was being interviewed by Lee Speigel for NBC radio's "Unexplained Phenomena" show. The two were sitting in the office of the American Society for Psychical Research, located on West 73rd Street in New York City, just across the street from the Dakota Apartments.

Speigel asked for a prediction that would be of special interest to the station's listening audience, eighteen to thirty-four-year-old rock enthusiasts.

"The prediction that I will make," Tanous said, "is that a very famous rock star will have an untimely death and this can happen from this moment on. I say untimely death because there is something strange about this death, but it will affect the consciousness of many people because of his fame." Without mentioning a name, he added that the star might be foreign-born but living in the United States.

The show was aired on September 8, 1980. Three months later, John Lennon, the English-born rock star living in New York City, was shot and killed outside the Dakota Apartments, visible through the windows of the office in which Alex Tanous had been sitting when he foresaw the tragic event to come.

James Dean's Porsche

Sometimes it is the thing itself, a fabulous jewel or ill-fated ship, that seems to harbor and perpetuate a curse. Other times, a public figure may become inexplicably intertwined with a particular object, provoking the hand of fate.

This could be the case with the Porsche in which teen legend James Dean crashed and died in 1955, tragically ending what many considered one of the most brilliant and promising Hollywood careers of all time.

Whatever its previous pedigree, from the moment Dean died behind the wheel, the Porsche took on a jinx of its own. After Dean's death, car enthusiast George Barris bought it first, but as it was being removed from the tow truck it slipped and broke a mechanic's leg. Barris sold the engine to a doctor and amateur racer, who installed it in his car. The car subsequently went out of control during competition and killed its owner. Another driver in the same race was injured when his racer crashed while using the drive-shaft from Dean's Porsche.

The body and chassis of the Porsche had been so badly damaged during Dean's original accident that it wound up on display in a traveling road-safety campaign. In Sacramento it fell off its mounting, breaking a teenage viewer's hip. Then it was moved to the next stop aboard a trailer truck that was hit by another car from behind. The driver of the colliding car was thrown out, run over, and killed by the cursed Porsche.

Another race driver almost died after using two tires from Dean's death car. The tires blew out at the same time. Meanwhile, the touring display continued to suffer its indignities. In Oregon, the truck's emergency brake failed, sending it slamming into a storefront. While mounted on supports in New Orleans, the Porsche itself literally disintegrated breaking into eleven parts.

The sports car—and Dean's accompanying curse—disappeared while being shipped back to Los Angeles by train.

A Cathar Priest

He should have been a poor parish priest. Instead, François-Berenger Saunière kept company with a beautiful Parisian opera star and secreted away four bank accounts, with which he financed the restoration of an obscure French chapel at Rennes-le-Chateau. The church was decorated with a statue of the devil, causing people to ask whether Saunière's newfound wealth came from God or Satan.

The answer may be found among the legends of a heretical thirteenth-century sect known as the Cathars, which once controlled the French province of Languedoc, on the Mediterranean. The Cathars (Greek for "purified") believed that the world had been created by the Demiurge, God's competitor, so to speak. The Demiurge, an evil that had to be overcome in order to achieve salvation, was said to be as capable of bestowing favors on his servants as the Christian God.

On March 2, 1244, the last Cathar stronghold at Montségur was overcome by orthodox forces. But rumor had it that Cathar treasure had been smuggled out before the final fall. Whispered gossip said it was the same treasure Saunière discovered shortly after he took charge of the small church of Sainte-Madelaine, in Rennes-le-Chateau, in 1885.

Soon after his arrival at Rennes-le-Chateau, Saunière visited Paris, and life was never the same for the poor country priest. His fellow parishioners were startled when the humble Saunière was subsequently visited in Rennes-le-Chateau by Emma Calve, the world-renowned soprano. She continued to see the priest, in fact, until her marriage to the tenor Gasbarri in 1914.

Whatever his unknown expenditures, Saunière spent more than a million francs restoring and transforming the previously obscure church of Sainte Madelaine, including the demons in stone. Over the front portico he had inscribed these words: "This is a fearful place."

Kirlian Photography

Serendipity plays an inescapable role in scientific discovery. As one example, consider Russian engineer Semyon Kirlian, who was repairing an electrotherapy device in 1939 when his hand brushed too near a live electrode. The resulting flash and shock piqued Kirlian's curiosity: What would happen if he used the electrical charge itself as a sort of flash photography aid?

To Kirlian's surprise, his first picture—of his own hand—revealed an auralike discharge streaming from the appendage. Kirlian photography had been born, and its chance discoverer would devote the next forty years of his life to plumbing its depths.

He soon found that, among other applications, his machine could apparently determine the health of a particular specimen. This came about when a colleague tried to trick Kirlian by submitting two supposedly identical leaves for analysis. When their photographs showed dramatically different "auras," Kirlian checked his equipment closely, but to no avail. The trickster finally admitted that the sample with the weaker aura had been taken from a diseased tree, whereas the other leaf came from a perfectly heathly one.

Many theories have been propounded to explain the Kirlian effect, from electromagnetic fields surrounding the body to electrical charges coursing through a layer of sweat to the ethereal "life force" itself.

Human Batteries

In ways still unknown, the electricity in a wall socket seems intimately linked with the human nervous system, although science seems reluctant to acknowledge the biological equivalent. But there have been people whose "batteries" were of an unusual and supercharged nature, like that of Angelique Cottin, a fourteen-year-old French girl whose amazing electromagnetic properties were the subject of a study by the Academy of Sciences.

Beginning on January 15, 1846, and for the next ten weeks, Angelique drove compasses wild. Objects, including heavy furniture, would retreat from her touch and vibrate in her presence. Whatever her strange power was, the Academy equated it with "electromagnetism." The force seemed to stem from her left side, the experts said, particularly at the elbow and wrist, and to increase in intensity in the evening. During a seizure, Angelique herself would often go into convulsions, her heart pulsing at 120 beats per minute.

Another supercharged human was American teenager Jennie Morgan of Sedalia, Missouri, who allegedly sent charged sparks between herself and anyone who approached, sometimes knocking them unconscious. Animals became unfriendly and fled from her presence.

A London, Ontario, teenager named Caroline Clare exhibited similar symptoms following an undiagnosed illness during which she described places she had never actually visited. The illness lingered for a year and a half. When it disappeared, Caroline was so magnetized that cutlery stuck to her skin and had to be pulled off by another party. She, too, was the subject of a study, this one conducted by the Ontario Medical Association.

The most powerful human battery, however, may well have been Frank McKinstry of Joplin, Missouri, who became so energized he supposedly stuck to the earth. If McKinstry stopped walking, for example, he was unable to take another step unless others lifted his feet off the ground, breaking the circuit.

Nazi UFOs

Some theorists have long sought an earthly explanation for the elusive UFO. The similarities between the advent of the modern flying saucer in the summer of 1947, and the subsequent abrupt advances in both Soviet and Western aerospace technology, they argue, are simply too striking for coincidence.

In fact, scattered sources indicate that Hitler's *Luftwaffe*, which deployed the world's first jet fighter, was hard at work developing a range of supersecret aerial weaponry during the closing days of World War II. According to a report issued on December 13, 1944, by Marshall Yarrow, a Reuters correspondent, "the Germans have produced a 'secret' weapon in keeping with the Christmas season. The new device, which is apparently an air defense weapon, resembles the glass balls that adorn Christmas trees. They have been seen hanging in the air over German territory, sometimes singly, sometimes in clusters. They are colored silver and are apparently transparent."

Were the flying Christmas balls the "Foo Fighters" of World War II fame, or had Nazi engineers developed something even more sophisticated? Italian author Renato Velasco alleges that the Germans produced a low-profile, disc-shaped flying machine they dubbed the *Feuerball*, or "Fire Ball," used both as an antiradar device and psychological warfare weapon against the Allied forces.

An improved version, the *Kugelblitz*, or "Ball Lightning" fighter, replaced the earlier gas turbine engine of the *Feuerball* with one employing jet propulsion. According to Velasco, the *Kugelblitz* was the first aircraft capable of "jet lift," vertical takeoff and landing. Its designer was Rudolph Scriever, and it was reportedly manufactured at the BMW plant near Prague in 1944. The craft was first flown in February 1945, over the vast underground research complex of Kahla, Thuringia, Germany. It was also in this same area of the Harz Mountains that Hitler reportedly intended making his last stand, fortified by the awesome array of new "secret weapons" *Luftwaffe* commander Goering had been repeatedly promising.

Time ran out for the secret Nazi armory. But if the Soviets or some other power managed to capture flying disc technology, it may have led to experimentation and development of something that gave rise to the frequent reports of early UFOs, starting in 1947.

Apocalypse Soon

Above all else, ancient myths around the world address two major matters: beginnings and endings. Concern with how the world and human life as we know it began, and, more importantly, how it will end, or what catastrophes it will have to suffer through to survive, is universal.

Prophets, both religious and secular, have likewise found themselves preoccupied with the approach of a global apocalypse. The sixteenth-century French sage, Nostradamus, customarily cryptic as to specific dates, chose to be uncharacteristically precise when it came to the following prediction:

> The year one thousand nine hundred ninety-nine, the
> seventh month
> A great frightening king will come from the sky.

We don't have to wait too long to learn what Nostradamus had in mind. What's more, other sources suggest that a terrible judgment or trial of sorts is at hand. Islamic theology prophesied that the Muslim religion would last until sometime after man walked the moon. A Tibetan tradition holds that Buddhism would end with the dethronement of the thirteenth Dalai Lama, and that, too, has come to pass. An Old Testament prophecy says the Messiah's second coming will be marked within a generation of the Jew's reestablishment in their homeland.

And that most magnificent creation of Mesoamerican civilization, the Mayan calendar, comes to a crashing halt on December 24, 2011, signifying the end of the present fifth age. The fifth cycle, called *Tonatiuh*, is scheduled to end in massive cataclysms or earthquakes.

The significance of these various myths and traditions of impending doom is not that they vary in date, but that they all converge so remarkably at the close of the present second millennium, 2000 A.D., the astrological Age of Pisces Whether the ancients will be proven right remains to be seen.

Nostradamus

Of all prophets past and present, few have captured the public imagination like Michel de Nostredame, or Nostradamus, a Jewish physician born in Saint Remy, France, in 1503. In 1555, he published his *Centuries*, a series of prophecies written in three groupings of one hundred stanzas each, and almost immediately became what we today would call an overnight media success.

The prophecy that made his reputation went like this: "The young lion shall overcome the old on the field of battle in single combat; in a cage of gold he will pierce his eyes, two wounds in one, then he dies a cruel death."

Shortly after publication, Henry II of England, during wedding festivities, jousted with the younger Montgomery, whose lance shattered and pierced Henry's golden helmet, striking him in the eye. Ten days later, the king, who used a lion as his emblem, died an agonizing death.

The reputation of Nostradamus was assured. One might argue that the interpretation was made to fit the fact, especially as it related to events in his own time. However, Nostradamus' predictions anticipated people, places, and events centuries in the future, including the French Revolution, the ill-fated flight of

Louis XVI and Marie Antoinette, ending at the guillotine, the rise of Napoleon, World War II (he made puns on the names of both Hitler and Roosevelt), air raids on England, and even the use of atomic weapons. What mystery is there today in this couplet, for example?

> A Libyan prince shall become powerful in the West.
> France shall be preoccupied with the Arabs.

No imagination is needed to supply the name of the Libyan prince, only a copy of the latest headline. And the reemergence of the Ayatollah Khomeini, as well as the downfall of the Shah of Iran, is eerily foreshadowed in this stanza:

> Rain, hunger, and unceasing war in Persia.
> Excessive faith will betray the king.
> Finishing there—begun in France.

One remembers that it was during his exile in France that the Ayatollah laid the foundations for the revolution against the Shah and his own return to Iran.

Modern Prophecies

Prophecy is a long esteemed tradition. Thus, there is no reason to believe that there are not equally adept prophets practicing their prescient craft among us today. In fact, there could be even more than during the Middle Ages, given the simple increase in the human population.

H. G. Wells missed the predicted outbreak of World War II by a year and the location, a Danzig railroad station, although he had the correct country, Poland. (The Germans, in fact, used a radio transmitter as the excuse for their attack.) Homer Lee, a military commentator, accurately foresaw that the Japanese would use a pincer movement launched from the Lingayen Gulf to invade the Philippines and cut off the Americans at Corregidor thirty-two years before it came to pass.

The problem, of course, is that prophecies can be right but still have no effect on subsequent events if they are not acted upon. A case in point is the prediction told to Lord Kitchener, who was warned by the professional psychic, Cheiro, not to travel by sea in the year 1916. Kitchener ignored the warning by embarking for Russia aboard the H.M.S. *Hampshire* in the year foretold. The ship struck a mine and went to the bottom, taking Lord Kitchener with it.

Convulsions and Cataclysms

Geologists will be the first to admit that the planet Earth appears primed for an apocalyptic catastrophe of a global nature. The crust itself is under immense stress and strain as continent-sized tectonic plates collide with one another in a dangerous, immemorial dance accompanied by drums and torches, the grinding earthquakes, and volcanic fires that rim the deceptively "Pacific" Ocean.

In 1883, the world recorded its most powerful explosion in this area when Krakatoa erupted, literally vaporizing itself, and sending tidal waves around the globe. So much ash and dust were thrown into the upper atmosphere that sunsets changed color and climatic conditions were drastically altered for years to come.

Because of our vast low-lying population, an explosion today would no doubt extract a toll of lives measured in the hundreds of thousands. Even the coastal regions of faraway Japan and Hawaii would be threatened.

The coastline of California stands perched on the edge of disaster, with an earthquake on the order of the one that destroyed San Francisco in 1906 expected at any moment. Pressure is also building up beneath Great Britain and Scandinavia. If released, it could flood portions of Scotland and turn London into a North Sea port.

Psychics have long warned of a global convulsion of nature that threatens the future of humanity on this planet. Now they are being joined by the scientists themselves, whose own predictions are just as dire. Beyond earthquakes and volcanoes, they see a rising "greenhouse effect" that could raise the world's ocean levels to encompass most present-day ports. This decrease in the protective ozone layer overhead could dramatically increase the incidence of cancer in the population. Some even predict a sudden reversal of the Earth's magnetic poles.

In fact, nearly all of these potential geographical catastrophes are in the natural order of things, including advancing and retreating ice ages, and bombardment by celestial bodies the size of a small country. What has changed most on a planetary scale is that there are immensely more people around now to suffer the consequences. The question is no longer whether the scientists or psychics are right, but whose crystal ball will shatter first?

Lost Continents
Under Two Oceans

Atlantis is not the only ancient land purported to have sunk beneath the sea. Scholars and fabulists alike speak of two other sunken continents, the legendary lands of Lemuria and Mu.

The name Lemuria comes from the ancient family of lemurs, and was coined by nineteenth-century English zoologist P. L. Sclater to account for the similarity of lemur fossils found in the southern tip of India and the Natal province of South Africa. Sclater postulated the existence of Lemuria, a drowned continent that formerly spanned the Indian Ocean connecting Southern Africa and Southern Asia.

The notion of a tropical bridge once connecting the existing land masses captured the fancy and support of no less an evolutionary authority than Thomas Huxley. In Germany, biologist Ernst Haeckel went so far as to speculate that ancient Lemuria might have been the long lost Garden of Eden, the cradle of the human race.

The missing land mass of Mu has also been long sought by students of the unexplained. It first surfaced in a series of books authored by James Churchward, a retired British colonel who once served with the Bengal Lancers in India. While assigned to famine relief, said Churchward, he became acquainted with a rishi, or Indian high priest, who had in his possession a library of stone tablets written in Naacal, the native tongue of Mu.

According to Churchward's theory, based on the Naacal tablets and the oral traditions of the Pacific islands and parts of South and Central America, the first humans originated in Mu some 200 million years ago. Their science, including the ability to manipulate gravity, had advanced far beyond what we know today. But approximately twelve thousand years ago, tragedy struck in the form of a cataclysmic gas explosion. Undermined, the continent of Mu collapsed into the Pacific Ocean. All that remained of the five-thousand-mile-long by three-thousand-mile-wide land mass were a few scattered islands surviving above the waves. The huge and unexplained remains on a number of Pacific Islands and the great head statues on Easter Island could not have been constructed by the manpower available on islands limited in population by their present size. It is also to be noted that the native Hawaiians still call this lost continent Mu.

Of the people of ancient Mu, 64 million are supposed to have perished in the cosmic explosion. Those who survived eventually colonized the other continents. Churchward died in 1936, aged eighty-six, after having written five books on the subject of Mu. Other written references to Mu are supposed still to exist in certain monasteries in the high mountains of Central Asia.

The Palatine Lights

More things sail the sea than Horatio ever imagined. Consider the story of the unfortunate brig *Palatine*, immortalized in John Greenleaf Whittier's stirring poem of the same name. In 1752, the story goes, the *Palatine* sailed from Holland with a load of immigrants bound for Philadelphia. According to the poem by Whittier, the crew mutinied off New England's Block Island after the ship ran aground. There they burned her, the cries of one poor woman passenger who remained behind rising above the crashing waves.

According to legend, the baleful brig periodically reappears as a blazing ball of fire out at sea. Whittier described it thus:

> Behold! again, with shimmer and shine,
> Over the rocks and seething brine,
> The flaming wreck of the *Palatine*.

Unfortunately, no register shows the *Palatine* ever sailing from Holland, or any other port of call. But in this instance, at least, the facts are as compelling as poetic legend. Records do show that a *Princess Augusta* weighed anchor at Rotterdam in 1738, destination Philadelphia, with a contingent of 350 German passengers from the districts of Lower and Upper Palatinate. The voyage was ill-starred from the start.

A tainted water supply soon killed half the crew and a third of the passengers in their bunks, including Captain George Long, who died from a deadly draught. Then the *Augusta* hit cold weather and rough seas that blew her off track. The crew added to her troubles by extorting money and possessions from the remaining passengers. Almost mercifully, she ran aground on December 27, on Block Island's north end. The islanders saved many of the passengers, but could not salvage any luggage due to the activities of the crew, who cut the *Augusta* loose, leaving her to crash and sink. Mary Van der Line, having lost her senses by now, went down with the ship, guarding to the end her chests of silver plate. Of the 364 who had set sail from Rotterdam, only 227 survived.

But what of the fire, "the shimmer and shine," of which Whittier wrote? Shortly after the *Augusta* went down, another captain passing through Block Island Sound reported a blazing ship at sea. According to his log, "I was so distressed by the sight that we followed the burning ship to her watery grave, but failed to find any survivors or flotsam."

What observers have seen ever since, however, became known as the "Palatine Light," a ghostly glow that manuevers in and around the waters near Block Island, whose residents take it almost for granted. Local physician Aaron C. Willey, writing in 1811, noted, "Sometimes it is small, resembling the light through a distant window, at others expanding to the highness of a ship with all her canvas spread. The blaze actually emits luminous rays.

"The cause of this 'roving brightness' " Willey added, "is a curious subject for philosophical speculation." And also for those who believe life imitates art, in all its ramifications.

The Crystal Skull

Crystal quartz is enjoying an immense revival in popularity today because of its alleged spiritual properties. But the same material fascinated our ancestors. The Greeks called it *crystallos*, or "clear ice." In Egypt, as early as 4000 B.C., foreheads of the dead were adorned with "third eye" quartz crystals thought to enable a soul to see its way to eternity. Traditionally, the preferred medium for the crystal balls used by seers and psychics has always been the highest-grade rock quartz.

But the single most compelling quartz object known is the so-called Mitchell-Hodges Crystal Skull, variously thought to be Aztec, Mayan, or Atlantean in origin. Even its original discovery is much disputed. It was reportedly found by eighteen-year-old Anna, the adopted daughter of vagabond adventurer F.A. Mitchell-Hodges, in 1927, while excavating the ruins of Lubaantun, "City of Fallen Stones," in the jungles of British Honduras. After three years of digging at the ancient Mayan site, Anna uncovered the life-size, rock-crystal skull in the debris of a collapsed altar and adjoining wall. A matching jawbone was found twenty-five feet distant three months later.

The Mitchell-Hodges team excavated extensively in the area. In fact, it contributed heavily to our present store of artifacts and knowledge about pre-Columbian civilization in the New World. But Mitchell-Hodges himself was also known to be a devout believer in the legend of Atlantis. Indeed, it was the faith that a link between Atlantis and the Maya could be confirmed that drove him to dare the jungles of Central America in the first place.

Rock crystal, unfortunately, cannot be dated by conventional means. However, the Hewlett-Packard laboratories, which studied the eerie skull, estimated that its completion would have required a minimum of 300 years' work by a series of extremely gifted artisans. On the hardness scale, rock crystal ranks only slightly below diamonds. Why was it so valued by whoever wrought it that they spent three centuries patiently polishing a piece of non-native stone?

The mystery of the crystal skull deepened when the two pieces were attached, and it was learned that the clear cranium rocked on the jawbone base, giving the appearance of a human skull opening and closing its mouth. It could have been manipulated by temple priests as a divinatory oracle.

Other properties attached to the crystal skull are even more peculiar. The frontal lobe, for example, is said to cloud over sometimes, turning milky white. At other times it emits an almost ghastly aura, "strong with a faint trace of the color of hay, similar to a ring around the moon." Whether the product of an over-wrought imagination, or stimulated from within the skull itself, those who keep company with it for long periods of time report unnerving experiences that affect all five senses, including ethereal sounds, smells, and even ghosts. The skull's visual impact is hypnotic, even on the skeptical.

Whatever its powers, though, a fatal curse on its owner does not seem to be part of the parcel. Mitchell-Hodges himself hardly let the skull out of his sight for more than thirty years, during which time he survived three knife attacks and eight bullet wounds. At his death on June 12, 1949, aged seventy-seven, he bequeathed the crystal skull and its mysterious heritage to his adopted daughter, who first found it buried beneath an ancient altar in the Honduran jungle. The skull, with an estimated value of $250,000, has remained in private hands.

Flames From the Sky

Legend has it that the Great Chicago Fire of 1871 began when Mrs. O'Leary's cow kicked over a lantern, igniting her straw. The flames then allegedly consumed her barn, jumping from one wooden structure to another until virtually the whole city lay under flame. Before the flames were through, more than seventeen thousand buildings were destroyed, a hundred thousand people were left homeless, and at least two hundred fifty had died.

Less well known is that the whole of the American Midwest fell victim to disastrous fires the night of October 8, 1871, from Indiana to the Dakotas, and from Iowa to Minnesota. All told, they represent the most mysterious and deadly conflagration in national memory. Eclipsed in history by the Chicago cauldron, little Peshtigo, a small community of two thousand near Green Bay, Wisconsin, fared far worse in terms of lives lost. Half the town— 1,000 people—died that terrible night, suffocated where they stood, or consumed by flames whose origins remain unknown. Not a single structure was left standing.

Where did the fires come from, and why so suddenly, without any warning? "In one awful instant a great flame shot up in the western heavens," wrote one Peshtigo survivor. "Countless fiery tongues struck down into the village, piercing every object that stood in town like a red-hot bolt. A deafening roar, mingled with blasts of electric flame, filled the air and paralyzed every soul in the place. There was no beginning to the work of ruin; the flaming whirlwind swirled in an instant through town." Other survivors referred to the phenomenon as a tornado of fire, reporting burning buildings lifted whole in the air before they exploded into glowing cinders.

What eyewitnesses described was more like a holocaust from heaven than an accidental fire started by the nervous cow. And in fact, according to a theory propounded by Minnesota Congressman Ignatius Donnelly, the devastating fires of 1871 *did* fall from above, in the form of a wayward cometary tail. During its 1846 passage, Biela's comet had inexplicably split in two; it was supposed to return in 1866, but failed to appear. Biela's fragmented head finally showed up in 1872 as a meteor shower.

Donnelly suggested the separated tail appeared the year before, in 1871, and was the prime cause of the widespread firestorm that swept the Midwest, damaging or destroying a total of twenty-four towns and leaving 2,000 or more dead in its wake. Drought conditions that fall no doubt contributed to the extent of the conflagration.

History today concentrates on the Chicago Fire alone and largely overlooks the Peshtigo Horror, as it was then called. It ignores altogether Biela's comet and its unaccounted-for tail.

Lincoln's
Precognitive Dream

Some premonitions come true and some do not, no matter how real and terrible the events they portray. Take, for instance, the case of the sixteenth president of the United States, Abraham Lincoln, who foretold his own assassination in a dream.

Lincoln recounted his nocturnal warning to a close friend, Ward Hill Lamon, who left a written account for posterity. In his dream, said Lincoln, "there seemed to be a deathlike stillness about me. Then I heard subdued sobs, as if a number of people were weeping. I thought I left my bed and wandered downstairs.

"No living person was in sight, but the same mournful sounds of distress met me as I passed along. I kept on until I arrived at the East Room and there I met a sickening surprise.

"Before me was a catafalque, on which rested a corpse wrapped in funeral vestments. Around it were stationed soldiers who were acting as guards. 'Who is dead in the White House?' I demanded of one of the soldiers. 'The President,' was his answer. 'He was killed by an assassin.' "

Within a few days of this dream, the president was dead, felled by the derringer of John Wilkes Booth. Mortally stricken, Lincoln was carried from Ford's Theater to a private house across the street. After his death, his body lay in state in the White House's East Room, just as it had in Lincoln's dream.

Phantom Hitchhikers

On a winter's eve in 1965, Mae Doria of Tulsa, Oklahoma, set out alone on the forty-three-mile drive to her sister's house in Pryor. "While driving on Highway 20," Doria remembered, "a few miles east of the town of Claremore, I passed a schoolhouse and saw this boy who appeared to be around eleven or twelve years old hitchhiking by the side of the road."

Concerned about someone so young on such a cold night, Doria pulled over and offered him a ride. "He got in the car, sat down next to me on the front seat," she said, "and we chatted about things that people who don't know each other usually talk about." Doria asked him what he was doing in the area, and he said, "Playing basketball at the school." Her passenger appeared to be about five feet tall and well built, "like a boy would look if he played sports and used his muscles." He was a Caucasian, with light-brown hair and bluish-gray eyes. But unbeknown to Mae Doria, she had just picked up a phantom hitchhiker.

The young man eventually pointed at a culvert outside Pryor and said, "Let me out over there." Not seeing any houses or lights, Doria asked where he lived, to which he replied, "Over there." She was trying to determine where that might be when her passenger simply disappeared. Doria stopped the car immediately and jumped out. "I ran all around the automobile, almost hysterical," she said. "I looked everywhere, up and down the highway and to the right and left, but to no avail. He was gone." Later, Doria remembered the hitchhiker had not been wearing a jacket, despite the winter chill. A chance conversation with a utility employee two years after the event revealed that the phantom figure had first been picked up at the same spot in 1936.

An even eerier encounter involved an accidental death for which a phantom hitchhiker was at least partially responsible. In February 1951, Charles Bordeaux, of Miami, was an officer in the Air Force's Office of Special Investigations in England. An American airman had been shot and killed under mysterious circumstances, and Bordeaux was ordered to investigate.

He learned that a security guard had spotted a man running between two parked B-36 bombers. He shouted "Halt!" three times, and when the figure refused to stop, shot at him. "I could have sworn that I hit him, but when I got to that area of the airfield, no one was there. He had disappeared." Instead, the guard's errant bullet struck and killed another airman.

Continuing his investigation, Bordeaux spoke to an officer who had also been on the flight line that fatal night. He had been driving by prior to the incident when he saw a man in a Royal Air Force uniform hitchhiking. After he climbed in, the officer said, he asked if he could spare one of his Camel cigarettes. Then the figure asked for a lighter. The officer saw the flash of flint out the corner of his eye, but when he turned his head the passenger had vanished into thin air, leaving his lighter lying on the empty seat.

The Castle of Unrequited Love

The lonely little Latvian toiled mostly at night, working in the humid air of Florida to erect a monument to a love that would never be his. From 1920 to 1940, diminutive Edward Leedskilnin (he stood only five feet tall and weighed 100 pounds) labored at massive coral blocks weighing as much as thirty tons, using techniques only he knew. The results, which look more cast or poured than carved, continue to amaze architects and engineers, as well as the one hundred thousand tourists who flock here every year.

The object of Leedskilnin's love and labor was a teenage bride he forever referred to as "Sweet 16." Spurned the day before the wedding, he left Latvia and settled in Florida. Using the native building blocks at hand, Leedskilnin began constructing Coral Castle on ten acres of land, presumably hoping to lure his reluctant love to America.

She never came, but Leedskilnin kept doggedly at work, weaving an impenetrable aura of mystery and majesty around his solo project. No one knew how he lifted the gigantic coral blocks off the ground and onto his flatbed truck, or how he shaped and maneuvered them into place, in one case balancing a nine-ton slab so delicately that it swung open at the touch of a single finger. If visitors called, Leedskilnin broke off work; when they left, he resumed.

When Leedskilnin died in 1951, his secrets died with him, though he intimated that they related to the same techniques used to build the Great Pyramid of Cheops. All he would ever say for certain is that he had conquered the natural laws of weight and balance.

Leedskilnin was less lucky at love. Several years ago Sweet 16 was contacted and asked if she would like to visit Coral Castle. "I wasn't interested in him at sixteen," she retorted, "and I'm not interested in him at eighty."

Approximately eight thousand visitors now tour his handiwork every month, marveling at wonders like an eighteen-ton model of Saturn, complete with rings, perched atop three-foot-thick walls. Mars, also represented by an eighteen-ton coral globe, squats frozen in orbit nearby.

A monument built for love is reminiscent of the Taj Mahal, at Agra, India, a tomb that is considered the world's most beautiful building. It was built by the Mogul Emperor Shah Jehan, for his favorite wife Mumtaz Mahal. But the Taj Mahal was built by hundreds of skilled workers, assisted by the specialized hoists and derricks used to build the marvelous Mogul palaces, aided by unlimited funds and an army of suppliers and long lines of oxen for hauling, whereas the Coral Castle was built at night— by one single man.

Toads Sealed in Stone

Stories of living or mummified animals found encased in stone abound. An inordinate number of these involve
frogs and toads. During construction of the Hartlepool Water-
works near Leeds, England, in April of 1865, for instance,
quarry workers supposedly found a living toad entombed in
200-million-year-old magnesian limestone. The toad, at a depth
of twenty-five feet, had left the form of a perfect mold in the
limestone. According to newspaper accounts, the toad was
quite lively, but unable to croak because its mouth was sealed
shut. Instead, barking noises issued from its nostrils. Aside
from the "extraordinary length" of its rear claws, it appeared to
be a normal specimen, though it died within a few days of
being freed.

About the same time, the magazine *Scientific American* reported
how silver miner Moses Gaines split open a two-foot-square boulder to find a toad perfectly concealed inside, again as if the rock
had almost been poured around it. The animal was described as
"three inches long and very plump and fat. Its eyes were about
the size of a silver cent piece, being much larger than those of
toads of the same size such as we see every day." Gaines's toad
was alive, too, albeit sluggish. "They tried to make him hop or
jump by touching him with a stick," the magazine reported, "but
he paid no attention."

These stories and others opened a scientific Pandora's box that
has yet to be satisfactorily shut. A Dr. Frank Buckland tried replicating the feat by sealing six test toads in limestone and sandstone blocks, and burying them a yard deep in his garden. The
following year, when dug up, the sandstone toads had all died.
The limestone toads fared better; two were alive and had actually
put on weight. But when Buckland repeated the experiment to be
sure, all the toads died.

Undaunted, a Frenchman known as Monsieur Séguin went
Buckland one better. In 1862, he encased twenty toads in plaster

of Paris and allowed the block to set. Then he buried it. When Séguin opened the block twelve years later, the story goes, four of the toads were still alive.

What the Petrified Hand Held

In the summer of 1889, farmer J. R. Mote of Phelps County, near Kearney, Nebraska, was excavating a cave when he came across a "large brown stone weighing over twenty pounds. When the clay was removed from it," according to an article in the August 7 issue of the *San Francisco Examiner*, "a large fossil, representing a clenched human hand, was revealed. The specimen had been broken from the arm just above the wrist, and the imprint of a coarse cloth or some woven material was plainly outlined on the back of the hand. At the time of the discovery nothing was said of it," the article continued, since "Mr. Mote does not belong to the curious class of people."

That soon changed, however. "A small boy in the family, whose faculty for smashing things was just beginning to develop, conceived the idea of opening the hand. When broken, to his astonishment, there rolled out eleven brilliant transparent stones."

Mr. Mote did have enough curiosity over this unusual turn of events to seek out a jeweler, who proclaimed them genuine first-water diamonds, without a speck to flaw or mar their beauty.

"The jewels," the article continued, "are nearly all uniform in shape and are about the shape of lima beans. They have the appearance of being water worn, but are still beautiful stones."

Lincoln and Kennedy

Shortly before he departed for Dallas in November 1963, President John Fitzgerald Kennedy's secretary, Evelyn Lincoln, warned him not to go. Kennedy dismissed her premonition of tragic consequences. On November 22, he was slain when Lee Harvey Oswald fired a bolt-action, Italian carbine from a window on the sixth floor of the Texas School Book Depository.

The number of curious parallels between the American Presidents John Kennedy and Abraham Lincoln, also assassinated after a premonition warning of his death, strain the bounds of coincidence. Lincoln, for example, had been elected president on November 6, 1860, Kennedy on November 8, 1960. Both had also been first elected to Congress a hundred years apart, Lincoln in 1846, Kennedy in 1946. The two men who succeeded them as president were also born a century apart, Andrew Johnson in 1808 and Lyndon Baines Johnson in 1908. Their assassins, John Wilkes Booth and Oswald, were born 101 years apart.

Booth shot Lincoln in the head from behind, in a theater, and fled to a barn: Oswald struck Kennedy in the head from the rear, from a warehouse, and fled to a theater. Both assassins in turn were killed before they could come to trial. Both Kennedy and Lincoln were shot on a Friday, in the presence of their wives. Lincoln had been shot in Ford's Theater, Kennedy in a Lincoln made by the Ford Motor Company.

And both presidents foresaw their own deaths. Lincoln told a guard on the day he was assassinated that there were "men who want to take my life. . . . And I have no doubt they will do it. . . . If it is to be done, it is impossible to prevent it."

A few hours before he was felled by Oswald's bullets, Kennedy said to his wife, Jacqueline, and Ken O'Donnell, his personal adviser: "If somebody wants to shoot me from a window with a rifle, nobody can stop it, so why worry about it?"

The Coffins That Would Not Stay Still

Dead persons may not talk, but that doesn't mean they don't get around. The most moving case on record belongs to a burial vault on the island of Barbados, a former British colony of the Lesser Antilles, just off the coast of Venezuela.

The scene of the macabre happenings was the family burial vault of the Walronds, wealthy plantation owners who laid their dead to rest, or what they thought was rest, in a tomb hewn out of rock in Christ Church cemetery. Family member Thomasina Goddard was first buried there in 1807, but within a year the vault's ownership had been taken over by another generation of slave-owners, the Chases. Two of their daughters were buried in the tomb in the years 1808 and 1812.

Thomas Chase, their father, also passed away in 1812. When the massive marble slab covering the underground vault was drawn back for his burial, the workers recoiled in horror. The leaded coffins of both girls stood on their ends, upside down. No sign of a break-in or human tampering could be found. Somehow the coffins had moved themselves, but how?

A male relative died in 1816, causing the tomb to be opened again. And again, the coffins inside were found in a state of total disarray; that of Thomas Chase, which had required eight men to carry, was leaning upright against one wall.

Eight weeks later yet another intended interment drew a curious crowd. Though the vault had been sealed after the last discovered disturbance, the Chase coffins had *again* been moved around. Lord Combermere, the governor of Barbados, was called in. In 1819, he had the coffins stacked and seals placed around the covering marble slab. But the government proved no match for ghosts. When noises were heard issuing from the haunted tomb the following year, Lord Combermere ordered the vault opened for inspection. The expected ensued. After the governor's intact seals were removed, inspectors entered the damp darkness and found the lead caskets had done their deathly dance yet again. Only Thomasina Goddard's original wood coffin remained untouched.

Finally, the bodies were removed and reburied in a more restful corner of the cemetery. Today, the Christ Church vault remains open and abandoned, the dead driven out by powerful forces unknown.

The Powers of Uri Geller

The most widely celebrated psychic in the world today is Israel's Uri Geller, a former army paratrooper who continues to amaze audiences while amassing a considerable personal fortune, estimated in the millions, from private displays of his incredible powers.

Born in Tel Aviv in 1946, Geller demonstrated his psychic abilities as early as age three by reading his mother's mind. More tangible events emerged at age six, when he learned he could move the hands of a watch without touching them. Years later, similar demonstrations would bring him fame and fortune.

Geller first came to widespread attention in the early seventies, when public performances in Munich, Germany, resulted in a wealth of bent silverware and keys, two of Geller's favorite mental targets. He also caused watch hands to stop and start running again. Two of his more spectacular feats occurred when he drove through Munich's cobblestoned streets blindfolded, and stopped a cable car dead in its tracks in the Chiemagu Mountains.

Geller soon came to the attention of psychical researcher and author Andrija Puharich, who sponsored a visit to America so the Israeli psychic could be examined in a scientific setting. The results of experiments Geller did at the Stanford Research Institute under the guidance of physicists Hal Puthoff and Russell Targ seemed to confirm his paranormal abilities without doubt. He not only passed the carefully controlled protocol the scientists had set up, registering high scores in remote viewing, clairvoyance, and psychokinesis, but apparently was also able to affect a wide range of sensitive electronic instruments.

Another stellar Geller performance took place on November 23, 1973, during an appearance on BBC-TV's "David Dimbleby Talk-In" program. Following the show, hundreds of startled viewers called in to say their silverware and other metal objects at home had begun bending as they watched Geller. When the former paratrooper returned to America, he was an overnight celebrity.

Geller critics like professional stage magician James ("The Amazing") Randi, of course, contend that these purported psychic powers are nothing more than standard, stock-in-trade conjurer's tricks. And admittedly, Randi has shown himself adept at recreating several so-called "Geller phenomena," like the bending of spoons and keys, by sleight of hand and other techniques.

But Geller may have the last laugh, all the way to the bank. After a period of a few years, during which he dropped largely out of public view, Geller recently returned to the world stage with a new book and greatly enlarged bank account, including a palatial estate with helicopter pad outside London. Geller's latest gimmick, reportedly, is locating petroleum reserves and precious metal deposits from the air, simply by flying over the site in a small plane, with his hand held out. His earnings from these and other psychic activities over the past decade have been estimated at $40 million.

The Levitations of Peter Sugleris

Twenty-two-year-old Peter Sugleris has much in common with the famous Israeli psychic Uri Geller, including the ability to bend metal objects such as keys and coins, affect electromagnetic instruments at a distance, and start and stop the hands of watches. Sugleris also says he can levitate like the venerable Joseph of Copertino and the nineteenth-century medium D. D. Home.

Even as a boy, Sugleris' Greek mother, who thinks his ability to levitate may be inherited, referred to him as "Hercules" because of his peculiar powers. Her own maternal uncle was known to have levitated on at least two occasions while he was sixteen and eighteen years of age.

Sugleris says he most frequently levitates in the presence of family members in the course of ordinary life. But, he adds, he can levitate at will, though not on demand, for others as well. The feat involves immense concentration, he says, and he frequently prepares several months ahead by adhering to a vegetarian diet.

On the most recent occasion, videotaped by his wife Esther in late February 1986, Sugleris rose off his kitchen floor a distance of approximately eighteen inches, and remained suspended in space for forty-seven seconds. During the levitation, his face took on such a grimace that he frightened his wife. "I thought he would burst," she said, "he was so inflated."

Afterward, Sugleris described the experience, saying he broke into a profuse sweat accompanied by dizziness and drowsiness. "It took me ten to fifteen seconds to recover my consciousness," he noted. "I was confused and dizzy, and I felt that I would black out. This was done out of anger. I wanted to prove that I could do it."

The frightening grimace during levitation is at least partially reminiscent of the circumstances of St. Joseph of Copertino, the most frequent flier of all, who, witnesses agreed, would begin and end his flights with a shrill, piercing cry.

The Dreams and Premonitions of Chris Sizemore

People who suffer from multiple personalities have enough problems. But like Chris Sizemore, the real-life protagonist of *The Three Faces of Eve*, many multiples report being haunted by psychic images and dreams.

Sizemore says she had her most vivid psychic experience as a child, when her sister fell sick with pneumonia. At least everybody thought it was pneumonia, except for Chris, who reported a curious dream. She saw herself running down a green hill in a pasture. When she turned to climb up the slope, again, Jesus appeared before her and said, "My child, your sister has diphtheria, not pneumonia. Go and tell your mother."

When Chris told her parents the story, they remained skeptical but finally summoned their physician. He reexamined the girl briefly before diagnosing the problem as diphtheria. Chris's dream probably saved her sister's life.

Even when this experience took place, Chris was already suffering from the competing personalities within her. She was never cured by her psychiatrists, despite the uplifting ending to both the book and movie made about her. She went through years during which her personality constantly changed, living at one period of her troubled life in Roanoke, Virginia, where her psychic experiences repeatedly occurred.

These incidents usually took the form of premonitions and invariably focused on her family. On one occasion, for instance, she had a vision in which her husband was electrocuted. She begged him not to go to work that day, and his replacement was sent to repair some power lines and was electrocuted on the job. Later, she became fearful when her daughter was scheduled to receive the Salk polio vaccine. Her husband refused to take the premonition seriously and the girl was later injected with spoiled vaccine, and became seriously ill, almost dying from the injection.

A UFO Landed at the
Stonehenge Apartments, Jersey City

UFO landings are generally assumed to be furtive affairs, conducted in relatively isolated areas, far from prying eyes. No UFO, for example, has ever turned up on the White House lawn, or touched down in Red Square.

Nevertheless, UFOs have frequently been sighted in populated cities. A number of people claim to have seen one landing in the Stonehenge Apartments, in Jersey City, the night of January 12, 1975. The spherical object was seen by at least nine observers, including the doorman, both in and outside the apartment building.

According to published reports, after the UFO settled to the ground in the park, a hatch opened, and small humanoid occupants, dressed like "kids in snowsuits," descended a ladder. They then dug around in the grass with what looked to be shovel-like instruments. After dumping their soil samples into the equivalent of extraterrestrial pails, the tiny humanoids reboarded the UFO. It then lifted off with a bright flash of light and vanished in the night sky. The "dark, almost black" sphere made a droning noise, like a "refrigerator motor."

A year later, in January and February 1976, the UFO seemingly revisited the scene of its earlier excavations. It was seen on three separate occasions by Stonehenge Apartment tenants and pedestrians simply passing by. An improbable coincidence exists in the name of the apartments. For in England, on the Salisbury Plain, the strange and unidentified ruins of Stonehenge have often been supposed to have been constructed by or received visits from extraterrestrials.

Cannibalistic Coincidence

Fact often follows fiction. Take the uncanny case of the two Richard Parkers. The first was a cabin boy in Edgar Allan Poe's uncompleted adventure novel, *Narrative of Arthur Gordon Pym*, published in 1837. In the course of the story, four sailors are shipwrecked at sea and escape in a small lifeboat. Facing starvation, the four finally decide to draw straws to see who will be sacrificed and cannibalized by the other three. Parker draws the short stick and is promptly stabbed and eaten by the surviving trio.

More than forty years later, Poe's unfinished tale was repeated in amazingly accurate and grim detail. Four survivors of a shipwreck, adrift in an open boat, *did* draw straws to see who would survive and who would be eaten. And the loser was Richard Parker, the ship's cabin boy. His mates stood trial for his murder in England in 1884.

The macabre event might not have come to light at all but for a contest sponsored by the *London Sunday Times* seeking remarkable coincidences. Twelve-year-old Nigel Parker won the competition. The unfortunate cabin boy eaten by his comrades had been Nigel's great-grandfather's cousin.

Saving Dream

Great calamities have been foretold by dreams. But nocturnal visions have saved lives, too, including that of Captain Thomas Shubrick, whose ship set sail from Charleston, South Carolina, for London in 1740. Shubrick had barely cleared port when a terrible storm hit. The wind blew so viciously that friends and relatives in Charleston could only pray for the crew's survival. There was no hope that the vessel itself would emerge unscathed.

But that night, the wife of one of Shubrick's closest friends, a Mrs. Wragg, had a dream in which she saw the captain alive and clinging to floating flotsam. The vision so moved her she insisted her husband lead a search party. A small boat was sent out, but returned empty-handed.

The dream repeated itself a second time and so did the unsuccessful search. When the dream appeared yet again, Mrs. Wragg begged her husband to search one last time. On the final voyage, Captain Shubrick and another exhausted sailor were rescued from a piece of the ship's wreckage. Persistence paid off, and so did Mrs. Wragg's dream.

Caught by a Ghost

Frederick Fisher was drunk on the night of June 26, 1826, when he stumbled from a pub in Campbelltown, New South Wales. He had already led a checkered career that had seen his fortunes swing from prisoner to prosperous farmer. Only a few months before, in fact, he had been locked up for bad debts, leaving his estate in the hands of an ex-convict named George Worrall.

Local suspicions were aroused when Fisher disappeared after his night at the pub and Worrall was seen wearing a pair of his pants. According to the story told by Worrall, Fisher had sailed for England aboard the *Lady Vincent*. The police, however, were unconvinced and posted a $100 reward for information leading to the discovery of Fisher's body. Questioned again, Worrall admitted that four of his friends had killed Fisher. Still skeptical, the police arrested Worrall instead. But without a corpse they stood little chance of conviction.

The standoff between Worrall and the authorities persisted

until that winter. One night James Farley, a well-respected farmer in the community, chanced to walk by Fisher's house. A sinister figure was sitting on the railing, pointing at a spot in Fisher's paddock. Convinced he had seen a ghost, Farley fled.

Farley contacted Constable Newland and the officer, in the company of an aborigine tracker, visited Fisher's property. The two turned up traces of human blood on the railing. At the spot the ghost had indicated, they dug down and found Fisher's badly shattered body. Worrall was sent to the gallows, convicted by the ghost of the friend he had murdered.

The Prophecies of Mother Shipton

Visitors to Knaresborough on the River Nidd, Yorkshire, are still shown the old well and cave where Ursula Sontheil once held court. Deformed at birth in July 1488, Sontheil became better known as Mother Shipton, the prophetess who foretold the deaths of kings, as well as the coming of the automobile, the telephone, and submarine.

Despite her physical deformities, young Ursula had an agile mind, learning to read and write far more easily than her peers. At the age of twenty-four, she married Toby Shipton of Shipton, York. Her reputation as a local psychic soon spread to encompass all of England and Europe, as hundreds of the curious flocked to her side to receive her often cryptic couplets.

Some pronouncements, though, were not so obscure, as when Mother Shipton predicted, "Carriages without horses shall go, and accidents shall fill the world with woe." The telephone and satellite television she prophesied with this refrain: "Around the world thoughts shall fly, In the twinkling of an eye."

Her contemporaries would have been equally confused when

/enned this couplet: "Men shall walk over rivers and under
.rs, Iron in the water shall float." Today, of course, we take
.bmarines and iron battleships for granted.

Mother Shipton foresaw many of the historical events that
shaped the modern world, including the defeat of the Spanish
Armada in 1588: "And the Western Monarch's wooden horses,"
she said, "Shall be destroyed by Drake's forces." In longer lines
she anticipated Sir Walter Raleigh's opening of the New World to
English commerce:

> Over a wild and stormy sea
> Shall a noble sail
> Who to find will not fail
> A new and fair countree
> From whence he shall bring
> A herb and a root.

The herb, of course, was tobacco, the root, the potato.

Mother Shipton died in 1561, at age seventy-three, having precisely predicted the day and hour of her own death years before.

Spirit Voices on Tape

When Friedrich Jürgenson died in 1987, the Swedish
psychic and filmmaker left behind a most unusual library. It
contained thousands of tape recordings on which mysterious
voices were imprinted—voices Jürgenson claimed had been produced by the dead.

Jürgenson began his research into the psychic world in the
1950s when he became interested in establishing contact with the
dead. Wondering whether the dead could imprint their voices on
magnetic tape, Jürgenson started sitting by his tape machine,
invoking spirit presences to speak to him through the recordings.
Nothing happened for months, until he tried to tape some bird

songs near his house. Some strange interference came over the playback, suggesting to the filmmaker some otherworldly sounds.

"A few weeks later I went to a small forest hut and attempted another experiment," he explained. In an interview with London's *Psychic News*, "I had no idea, of course, what I was looking for. I put the microphone in the window. The recording I made passed without incident. On playback I first heard some twittering of birds in the distance, then silence. Suddenly, from nowhere, a voice, a woman's voice in German: 'Friedel, my little Friedel, can you hear me?'"

At the time, Jürgenson didn't know he had embarked on a long-lived search to contact the dead. Even a few parapsychologists became interested in the project. William G. Roll of the Psychical Research Foundation then based in Durham, North Carolina, visited the filmmaker in 1964 to conduct some experiments. For these sessions Jürgenson would load his tape recorder with a blank cartridge, and then everyone in the room would engage in some casual conversation. When the recording was played back extra voices could clearly be heard darting in between the rest of the talk. An unusually conservative parapsychologist, Roll was impressed enough to issue a special report on his Scandinavian trip. Jürgenson and his "spirit" voices, he declared, certainly seemed for real.

The Archduke's Fatal Car

Environmentalists frequently assail the modern automobile as the curse of the twentieth century. Some cars have been indisputably cursed, but hardly in ways foreseen by the Sierra Club.

The open limousine in which Archduke Franz Ferdinand, heir to the Austrian and Hungarian thrones, was assassinated seems to have been such a car. His wife died with him in the assassination, which led to the outbreak of World War I.

Shortly after the opening of hostilities, the car was taken over by Austria's General Potiorek, who was subsequently disgraced at the battle of Valjevo and died insane. A captain on his staff next assumed ownership. Nine days later the officer struck and killed two peasants, swerving into a tree and breaking his neck.

The governor of Yugoslavia acquired the cursed convertible after the end of the war, but fared little better, suffering four wrecks in four months. In one of the accidents, he actually lost an arm. The car was then passed on to a doctor, who six months later overturned in a ditch and was crushed to death. A wealthy jeweler then purchased it—and committed suicide.

The disasters continued when another owner, a Swiss race-car driver, crashed in the Italian Alps and was hurtled over a wall to his death. A Serbian farmer who forgot to turn off the ignition while the car was being towed became the next victim as the vehicle lurched into motion and ran off the road. The last driver was garage owner Tibor Hirshfield, who was returning from a wedding with four companions. Hirschfield's friends were killed when he tried to pass another automobile at high speed.

The car was subsequently installed in a Vienna museum, where its blood lust seems to be satiated, at least temporarily.

Tulpas

We know that the mind can create its own phantasms, but what about its ability to project these images into the exterior world outside the brain's boundaries? Where does one end and the other begin? More importantly, what happens when the mental projection takes on a life of its own?

The strange experience of Madame Alexandra David-Neel supplies a cautious answer and warning. David-Neel, who lived to the ripe old age of 101, was one of many adventurous women of the English Empire who braved the mysterious East alone and often left written records of their travels.

David-Neel not only traveled widely in primitive nineteenth-century Tibet, she studiously followed the religion and teachings of the Buddhist lamas with whom she lived. Her most trying ritual involved the creation of what the Tibetans called a *tulpa*, or phantom being generated by the mind. The lamas warned her that these "children of our mind" could sometimes turn dangerous and uncontrollable, but David-Neel persisted.

She shut herself away and began coalescing her concentration, having targeted for her *tulpa* the image of a fat, short monk "of an innocent and jolly type." Surprisingly successful, she was soon treating her new "companion" like any human guest in her apartments.

When David-Neel went on her next horseback adventure, the ethereal monk went along. From her saddle she would turn and look over her shoulder at the *tulpa*, engaged in "various actions of the kind that are natural to travelers, and that I had not commanded."

As testament to her success, others in her train began seeing the monk and mistaking him for a living being. At that point, her *tulpa* took a turn for the worse. His features took on a malignant, mocking countenance. Once the decision was made to banish the monk, however, his eradication proved almost as difficult as his original creation. In *Magic and Mystery in Tibet*, David-Neel recounts the six months of hard struggle that followed before her wayward *tulpa* finally vanished.

"There's nothing strange in the fact that I may have created my own hallucination," David-Neel concluded. "The interesting point is that in these cases of materialization, others see the thought-forms that have been created."

From Manila to Mexico City

On October 25, 1593, the fabric of space and time warped, depositing a Spanish soldier from the Philippine capital of Manila into the main plaza of Mexico City, nine thousand miles away. The soldier, dressed in a different uniform than those around him, quickly drew a crowd, and was forced to surrender his arms.

Asked for an explanation, the startled soldier could only stammer, "I know very well this is not the governor's palace in Manila," he managed, "but here I am and this is a palace of some kind, so I am doing my duty as nearly as possible." Pressed for additional details, he said that the governor of the Philippines had been killed the night before, and hence the need for additional guards.

Needless to say, the confused sentry was quickly thrown into prison, where he remained until a Spanish brig from the Philippines confirmed his account of the governor's assassination.

The teleported soldier, moreover, fared better than the man with a similar story arrested by Portuguese authorities in 1655. According to John Aubrey's *Miscellanies*, the man had been in the Portuguese colony of Goa, in India, when he found himself suddenly whisked through the air, back to Portugal.

Charged with witchcraft, because everyone knew only witches could fly, officials of the local Inquisition gave him a fair trial and expeditiously then ordered him burned at the stake.

Psychic Warfare

The days of casual interest in psychic phenomena are long departed, and the reason is not hard to fathom. If clairvoyance, remote viewing of targets, and psychokinesis are repeatable, controllable human faculties, as they appear, neither superpower can afford to let the other open a potential gap in the ability to wage psychic war.

According to Charlie Rose, a member of the United States House Select Committee on Intelligence, psychic sensing "would be a hell of a cheap radar system. And if the Russians have it and we don't, we're in trouble."

Rose also expressed concern about the discrepancies in levels of psychic research funding between the two competing superpowers. *Known* U.S. spending is between $500,000 and $1 million, whereas the Soviet budget is estimated to be at least ten, and perhaps as much as a hundred times that.

Nor do the Soviet studies concentrate solely on passive perception. For instance, a Defense Intelligence Agency document on "Soviet and Czechoslovak Parapsychology Research" detailed Russian experiments in which a gifted psychic was able to stop a targeted animal heart from beating.

According to the DIA report, the frog heart was placed in a glass 2½ feet from the psychic. As she concentrated on controlling its beat, the electrocardiogram showed, the rate of contraction actually decreased. "Five minutes after the experiment began," according to the report, "she stopped its beat entirely."

Using the mind to wage war opens a Pandora's box of possibilities. Not only would an individual leader be subject to remote assassination, but thermonuclear weapons could be held hostage to psychic threat, or even exploded. According to Ron Robertson, a security officer at the Lawrence Livermore Laboratory, "all that it takes is the ability to move one-eighth of an ounce a quarter of an inch." A similar scenario is painted by Texas A&M University military historian Robert A. Beaumont in *Signal*, the journal of the

U.S. Armed Forces and Electronics Association. "An effective ESP system," said Beaumont, "would, depending on the nature of the phenomena, offer potential to the executor of a surprise attack, from the psychic influencing of targets through precognition and remote sensing, to message transmission below the detection and countermeasure threshold of a potential victim."

The Scientist Who Knew the Ultimate Secret

Robert Sarbacher, an American physicist who died in July 1986, claimed to have been privy to a secret that is "the most highly classified subject in the United States government, rating higher even than the H-bomb," as he described it to a group of Canadian scientists who met with him in his office at the Department of Defense on September 15, 1950.

What was this extraordinary secret? It was that the U.S. government possesses the remains of crashed extraterrestrial spaceships and the bodies of alien beings. Dr. Sarbacher told the scientists that the matter was being studied by a super-secret group headed by Dr. Vannevar Bush, who was President Truman's chief science adviser.

Sarbacher was not the sort of man given to wild exaggerations. His entry in *Who's Who in America* consists of three inches of tiny print, attesting to a richly successful scientific, academic, and business career. During World War II and after, he volunteered his services as a "dollar-a-year man" to the government and specialized in issues relating to guided-missile control.

The Canadians, who regularly met with Sarbacher to discuss matters of mutual interest to the national securities of the two countries, had asked their American colleague if there was any truth to persistent rumors of this kind of direct physical evidence of the reality of UFOs. Sarbacher confirmed there was but would provide no further details because of the subject's extreme sensitivity.

One of the Canadians, radio engineer W. B. Smith, was so impressed that when he returned to Ottawa he urged his government to begin its own UFO project. Soon afterwards such a project, code-named "Magnet," was put into operation, with Smith in charge. But he was unable to learn any more about the American government's alleged UFO secrets.

In 1983 UFO investigator William Steinman located Sarbacher, who was then living in Florida, and asked him about what he had told the Canadian scientists. Sarbacher replied that, while he had not been involved directly in the UFO-recovery project, he did recall that "certain materials reported to have come from flying saucer crashes were extremely light and very tough. There were reports that instruments or people operating these machines were also of very light weight, sufficient to withstand the tremendous deceleration and acceleration associated with their machinery. In talking with some of the people at the office," he said, "I got the impression these 'aliens' were constructed like certain insects we have observed on earth."

In a later interview with another investigator, Sarbacher said the craft were believed to be from another solar system. He said that he was invited to a conference at Wright-Patterson Air Force Base in Dayton, Ohio, where scientists and military officers were to report what they had learned from their analyses of the material and the bodies. Unfortunately, because of pressing other commitments, Sarbacher was unable to attend, though he later talked with those who did go.

Those who spoke with Sarbacher were struck by his obvious sincerity and his consistent refusal to embellish or elaborate on his story. His testimony may well represent a rare glimpse behind the curtain of secrecy covering the U.S. government's knowledge of what UFOs are.

Nova Scotia's
Sea Serpents

For at least a century and a half the seagoing folk of Nova Scotia, on Canada's far eastern coast, have been encountering some very strange—and very large—creatures.

One of the first known sightings occurred in 1845, when fishermen John Bockner and James Wilson saw a 100-foot-long "serpent" in St. Margaret's Bay. They reported their sighting to the Reverend John Ambrose, who not long afterwards had his own run-in with the monster.

In 1855 residents of Green Harbour were terrified to see, in one citizen's words, "a hideous length of undulating terror" pursue local fishing boats, apparently intent on bodily harm. As the fishermen raced desperately for shore, their families watched on helplessly. One observer described the creature in an issue of the nineteenth-century American magazine *Ballou's:* "Near what might be the head rose a hump or crest crowned with a waving mass of long, pendulous hair like a mane, while behind, for forty or fifty feet, slowly moved, or rolled, the spirals of his immense snakelike body. The movement was in vertical curves, the contortions of the back alternately rising and falling from the head to the tail, leaving behind a wake, like that of a screw-steamer, upon the glassy surface of the ocean."

As the creature got closer to shore, observers could hear a sound like escaping steam emanating from the beast. They could now see glistening teeth, protruding ridges over evil-looking eyes, dark-blue scales on the head and back, and dirty yellow on the bottom. The head they saw was six feet long.

The creature finally gave up the chase and the exhausted fishermen arrived safely on land. But it was seen again by three men in a boat the next day. They rowed away as fast as they could and were not pursued.

Then, in 1883, six military men fishing in Mahone Bay were startled to see what looked like an immense version of a "common snake" with a head six-feet long sticking out of the water. The rapidly moving creature had a neck as thick as a tree and was dark brown or black with irregular white streaks. Although they couldn't see all of its body, the witnesses agreed it must have been something like eighty feet long.

In 1894 a man named Barry observed a similar beast as he was relaxing on a wharf in the coastal town of Arisaig. About 120 feet away and approximately 60 feet long, the creature was moving with an "undulating" motion. A tail "like half of a mackerel's tail" was visible as well.

Reports of these giant "lunkers," as the Nova Scotians call them, have continued well into our own time.

On July 5, 1976, Eisner Penney of Nova Scotia's Cape Sable Island saw an enormous something and told some friends about it. They scoffed at him but a few days later one of them, Keith Ross, along with his son Rodney, had an encounter of their own. "It had eyes as big around as saucers and bright red-looking," he said. "I mean, you could see the red in its eyes like they were bloodshot. It had its mouth wide open and there were two big tusks—I call them tusks—that hung down from its upper jaw. It passed astern of us, so close. And we could see its body, about forty or fifty feet long with grayish, snakelike looking skin, full of lumps and bumps and barnacles. And it appeared to us to have a fish's tail, an up-and-down tail, not a flat tail like a whale's"

Ross's boat roared away and soon lost the creature in a fog. He detected another boat on shipboard radar and made his way toward it. Ironically, Eisner Penney was on that boat. As Ross told him what he'd just seen, they heard the creature passing by not far away. The creature was seen again a few days later by fisherman Edgar Nickerson.

No one has any idea what these creatures are, although similar beasts have been reported around the world. In the 1800s they were called "sea serpents" and were the object of a spirited controversy among zoologists. Whatever the Nova Scotia lunkers may be, it seems safe to say they are not serpents, even oversized ones: Snakes cannot undulate vertically. Nor, of course, do they have fishlike tails.

Foo Fighters

Popular history dates the beginning of the modern UFO phenomenon to the summer of 1947, when Idaho businessman Kenneth Arnold saw nine silvery, crescent-shaped objects flying in formation like "a saucer skipping over water" near Mount Rainier, in Washington State. Several years earlier, however, at the height of World War II, similar flying saucers were reported by both Allied and Axis air crews in the European and Pacific campaigns.

On the Allied side, at least, such nocturnal lights and daylight discs were known as *Foo Fighters*, after a popular Smokey Stover cartoon character who was forever mumbling, "Where there's foo, there's fire." Foo itself, of course, was a play on the French word, *feu*, for fire.

The best-documented Foo Fighter encounter occurred on Black Thursday—October 14, 1943—when B-17 Flying Fortresses of the American Eighth Air Force suffered disastrous casualties during a daylight bombing raid on Schweinfurt's heavily defended ball-bearing factories. Historian Martin Caidin called it "one of the most baffling incidents of World War II, and an enigma that to this day defies explanation."

As the 384th Bombardment Group completed its run over the target, numerous pilots and top-turret gunners in the staggered formation reported a cluster of small silver discs straight ahead. Plane Number 026, in an effort to avoid a head-on collision, took immediate evasive action, but too late: According to the debriefing report, the bomber's "right wing went directly through a cluster with absolutely no effect on engines or plane surface." The pilot did add that one of the discs was heard to strike his tail assembly, but that no explosion or damage followed.

Accompanying the discs at a distance of about twenty feet were several clumps of black debris measuring three by four feet in size; this, too, seemed to have no harmful effect on the Flying Fortresses. The debriefing report also noted that two other aircraft flew through the discs with no apparent damage.

Foo Fighters were also seen as nocturnal lights of an orange red, or white hue. On the night of November 23, 1944, for instance, a three-man crew assigned to the 415th Night Fighter Squadron encountered eight to ten of the mysterious globes over the Rhine River, north of Strasbourg. They looked at first like distant twinkling stars, said intelligence officer Lieutenant Fred Ringwald, but within minutes appeared as orange balls "moving through the air at a terrific speed."

Another B-17 pilot, Charles Odom of Houston, recalled his daytime Foo Fighter experience after the war. The saucers "looked like crystal balls about the size of basketballs," he said. They seemed to "become magnetized to our formation and fly alongside. After a while, they would peel off like a plane and leave."

Crisis Telepathy

Much evidence suggests that telepathy often takes place between people who know each other. But according to a case reported by parapsychologist Lyall Watson, this isn't an irrefutable fact.

The incident studied by Watson concerned a Cajun shipman named Shep, who had just joined a fishing crew off the Hawaiian Islands. At one point during the expedition the crewman decided to go to his quarters. He grabbed the hatch rail and swung himself down the forecastle, but slipped and landed right on his back. Paralyzed by the fall and in intense pain, Shep was convinced he would die. And at 9:12 that evening, his thoughts turned to a friend.

The friend, a woman named Milly, had been visiting the home of the boat's captain that evening, socializing with his wife. The captain's wife, a full-blooded Samoan, kept to her needlework during the visit until she suddenly felt a staggering blow to her head. She fell to the floor in sort of a trance, saying, "Something very bad has happened on the boat." She knew that her impression didn't refer to her husband, but couldn't say anything more. Milly checked the time and saw that it was 9:14 P.M.

It wasn't until the next morning, though, that the women heard from the Coast Guard. They had taken Shep to Kauai with a broken back.

But why did the captain's wife experience the telepathy instead of Milly, Shep's good friend? "The sender was a man from a culture that, at least unconsciously, allows for the existence of telepathy," he explains. "The message was intended for a woman whose upbringing made her less receptive and, when she proved unresponsive, it appeared to have been rerouted to another person nearby, someone who was only indirectly involved but whose cultural background and perceptual set made it easier for her to respond."

Abducted Cop

The morning of December 3, 1967, turned out to be unlike any other in the life of Ashland, Nebraska, police patrolman Herbert Schirmer. Schirmer's logbook for that day contained this bizarre entry: "Saw a FLYING SAUCER at the junction of Highway 6 and 63. Believe it or not!"

At 2:30 A.M., while on routine patrol, Schirmer had seen what looked like a large football encircled by red flashing lights near the intersection of the two highways on Ashland's outskirts. Alone in his patrol car, the trooper watched in silence as the UFO lifted off the ground, trailing a red-orange flame and emitting a shrill siren-like sound.

Filling out his log report thirty minutes later, Schirmer checked the time and suddenly stopped short. He was sure no more than ten minutes had elapsed before his sighting of the object, but now his watch showed 3 A.M. Where had the missing twenty minutes gone?

Under hypnosis conducted by Dr. Leo Sprinkle, a University of Wyoming psychologist, Schirmer was able to recall the additional details of his seemingly innocent UFO encounter. The experience began, Schirmer said, when "the craft actually pulled me and my car up the hill." The car stopped, he claimed, and two humanoids emerged from the bottom of the UFO. Dressed in uniforms, they had high foreheads, long noses, gray complexions, and round, catlike eyes.

One alien carried a boxlike instrument that flashed a green light around the patrol car Schirmer said. The other reached in through the open window and touched his neck, inflicting a sharp pain. The humanoid who had touched him asked, "Are you the watchman of this town?" Schirmer replied, "Yes, I am." In a deep voice, without moving his slit of a mouth, the "leader" of the two then intoned, "Watchman, come with me."

Inside the craft, the humanoid showed Schirmer their power source, a spinning contraption that resembled "half of a cocoon, giving off bright colors like the rainbow." He informed Schirmer that the ship employed "reversible electrical-magnetism." They had come to Earth, Schirmer added, "to get electricity."

The guided tour of the craft also included a second level above the power room, where Schirmer saw "all kinds of panels and computers . . . a map on the wall, and . . . this large screen." The map portrayed a sun with six circling planets in a nearby galaxy. Said the patrolman, "They were observing us and *had* been observing us for a long time."

The humanoid leader again said, "Watchman, come with me," and Schirmer was led out of the craft. "What you have seen and what you have heard," he was told, "you will not remember."

Schirmer was eventually interviewed by the University of Colorado Condon Committee, then conducting an Air Force-sponsored UFO investigation. The project staff concluded that "the trooper's reported UFO experience was not physically real." But Sprinkle, who hypnotically regressed Schirmer, disagreed. "The trooper," Sprinkle declared, "believed in the reality of the events he described."

Presidential UFO

"I am convinced that UFOs exist because I have seen one." The speaker? No less a personage than James Earl Carter, a former submarine officer with a degree in nuclear physics and president of the United States.

Carter's sighting took place during his term as governor of Georgia, on January 6, 1969, while in the company of a dozen members of the Leary Lions Club. The group was standing outside, waiting for a speech to begin, when one member noticed a brilliant object low in the western sky.

"It was the darndest thing I've ever seen," and Carter. "It was big; it was very bright; it changed colors; and it was about the size of the moon. We watched it for about ten minutes, but none of us could figure out what it was.

"One thing's for sure," Carter added. "I'll never make fun of people who say they've seen unidentified objects in the sky."

Six months after his election as president, in response to public pressure and a campaign promise, Carter had his science adviser, Dr. Frank Press, ask NASA about the possibility of reevaluating the UFO phenomenon. While declining to open a new investigation, NASA's administrator, Dr. Robert Frosch, did say that "if some new element of hard evidence is brought to our attention in the future, it would be entirely appropriate for a NASA laboratory to analyze and report upon an otherwise unexplained organic or inorganic sample. We stand ready to respond to any bona fide physical evidence from credible sources. We intend to leave the door clearly open for such a possibility."

Underwater Dead Who Seemed Alive

Visitors to the Topkapi Museum in Istanbul, Turkey, are often told of the cruelties and dangers of the times when the Topkapi, built on a cliff high over the Bosphoros, was the imperial palace of the Turkish sultans. The sultans of Turkey, like the Roman emperors, possessed the power of life and death over their subjects. One of the more unnerving legends concerns the disposal of imperial concubines who, through unfaithfulness or petulance, had displeased the sultan.

"Abdul the Damned" was an especially notorious ruler. The penalty for his unhappy concubines was to be sewn, alive, into a weighted sack and dropped down a chute into the waters of the Bosphoros. But they did not quite disappear. Years later divers operating in deep water near the palace sometimes encountered these weighted sacks standing up on the sea floor, swaying back and forth as if alive in the cold waters of the current.

In 1957 an even more frightening underwater incident was experienced by scuba divers in Czechoslovakia in a body of water called Devil's Lake. The divers were searching for the body of a young man presumed drowned while boating on the lake. What they found, however, in deep waters was not one corpse but many, and not all of them were human beings. What they found were soldiers in full combat uniform, some sitting in trucks or on caissons, and many of the horses still standing upright in their harnesses. These were all the remains of a German artillery unit which, while crossing the ice during the fighting German retreat of World War II, had cracked through, probably under bombardment, and settled on the bottom of the lake. The extremely cold and deep water had preserved them for twelve years and would have preserved them for many more, positioned and ready for combat—but dead.

The Nun's Ghost
at Borley

The Borley Rectory, in Essex, England, was troubled from the beginning of its existence in the early 1860s. Perhaps its haunting appearance—it was often called a monstrosity and had thirty rooms—had something to do with it. Its first inhabitants, the Reverend Henry Dawson Ellis Bull, his wife, and his fourteen children, told many tales of strange noises and the frequent sighting of the ghost of a nun. After Henry's death, the oldest son, Harry Bull, took over the rectory from 1892 until 1927, and the unusual events continued. So frequently was the nun seen that the area she appeared in was known as the Nun's Walk. Some people even reported a headless coachman driving a coach pulled by fire-breathing horses.

The next inhabitants, the Reverend and Mrs. G. Eric Smith, stayed only a few months, citing the strange events in the house as their reason for leaving.

Finally, the Reverend Lionel Foyster, his wife Marianne, and their daughter arrived. The stories continued, with Marianne insisting a ghost had slapped her in the face and shaken her out of her bed.

In an effort to investigate, the British National Laboratory of Psychical Research intervened. Its founder, Harry Price, advertised in the London *Times* for people to join him in a vigil of the haunted rectory. The ad called for unbiased, critical, and intelligent observers, and Price took forty of them to the house. Again, there were reports of moving objects and unexplained noises. Commander A. B. Campbell said he was hit by a flying piece of soap, for instance, and another man, philosopher C. E. M. Joad, reported seeing a thermometer plummet ten degrees for no apparent reason.

Again controversy ensued. When the Foysters vacated, Price himself moved in and reported a wide variety of phenomena, enough for a book. After his death, however, critics said that

Price fabricated some of the phenomena and exaggerated others.

The story becomes more interesting, though, after a fire razed the building in 1939. The Reverend W. J. Phythian-Adams, canon of Carlisle, in Canada, suggested that the nun so often seen was not English, as had always been assumed, but French. A woman named Marie Lurie, it seemed, had left her convent to elope with her lover in the eighteenth century. They went to England, but the scoundrel turned on her and murdered her. In fact, he strangled her and reportedly buried her in the basement of the building that occupied the Borley land before the rectory was built. After the fire, diggers actually uncovered a grave containing only some religious medals and the skull of a woman.

The destruction of the building seems to have eliminated the ghostly walks by the nun, but the story does not end there. A group trying to conduct a recent scientific study of the premises heard strange, inexplicable noises in the night, recorded sudden temperature variations, saw lights of unknown origin, and detected strange smells.

The Battle
Heard Ten Years Later

In early August 1951, two English sisters-in-law were vacationing in France when their sleep was disrupted by gunfire. It wasn't long before they realized they were hearing the sounds of war, and the noise continued off and on for the next three hours.

The next day, when the shaken women tried to find out what had happened, they were shocked by the news that no battle had taken place. In fact, no one else had heard a thing.

Upon investigation, however, they learned that they were vacationing in Puys, on the beach near Dieppe, an occupied and heavily fortified area during World War II. There, almost nine years to the day earlier, the Allies had launched an invasion that was to be a rehearsal for the D-Day attack. Sadly, the invasion was a very costly and bloody one. More than half of the 6,086 men who hit the beach on August 19, 1942, were killed, wounded, or captured.

The women soon learned that the sounds they had heard were an almost exact audio reproduction of that battle, as if they had been lodging there the moment it took place. They heard shelling and shouting in the early morning, "about 4 A.M.," and the noise stopped abruptly fifty minutes later. The actual shelling began at 3:47 A.M. and stopped, according to military records, at 4:50 A.M. They heard bombers and the cries of the men, and silence again, and again the military records confirmed the bombing stopped at about that same time, between 5:07 A.M. and 5:40 A.M.

Every sound they had heard matched military records of the battle. Interestingly, the battle had stopped at 6:00 A.M., the same time all the battle noises stopped for the women as well. Yet the sisters-in-law heard the pained cries of wounded and dying men for the next hour, growing fainter and fainter as time passed.

What Happened at Roanoke?

The first British child born in America was named Virginia Dare. Her parents had sailed to the New World with a group of settlers who landed on Roanoke Island, off the coast of North Carolina, and Virginia arrived shortly after, on August 18, 1587.

The vessel that brought the Dares and others to the new land eventually returned to England with all but ten men aboard. Those men were left behind to begin a settlement. But when the next ship arrived, the men could not be found. The second ship, too, returned to England, this time leaving a hundred people to begin the settlement. Some time later, the next ship arrived, and its passengers again found the island empty. There was no trace of violence, struggle, or even a grave, only the word "CRO" carved in one tree and "CROATAN" carved in another. Croatan, another island off North Carolina, was apparently the place the group had settled. But the ship's captain, fearing a lack of food and the approaching winter, decided to set sail for the West Indies and winter there. By the time the next ship reached the island of Croatan, there again was no sign of the abandoned settlers. There was no sign of or story about an Indian massacre. There were no graves or markers, and save for an occasional tale of an Indian child with "yellow" hair or blue eyes, not a single one of the original 110 was ever found. Although a subject of countless rumors and legends, the mystery has never been explained.

The Long Voyage Home

Whether the homing ability of animals comes from a superior sense of direction or a sixth sense unknown to science, the homing ability of the dog has continually astounded his best friends. In at least three documented cases, dogs have traveled thousands of miles, and there are many instances of dogs finding their way over shorter distances as well.

Doug Simpson's dog Nick, for instance, disappeared during a camping trip they took together in southern Arizona in November 1979. Simpson spent two weeks frantically searching for the German shepherd, but she was not to be found, so he returned to his home in Pennsylvania. Four months later, with cuts still bleeding and fur torn, Nick showed up at the home of Simpson's parents in Selah, Washington. The dog had apparently crossed the Arizona desert, the Grand Canyon, the treacherous mountains of the Rockies, frozen streams, snow-covered mountains, and countless highways. When she arrived in the driveway where

Simpson's old car was parked, she promptly collapsed from exhaustion. Simpson's mother found the dog, who was rewarded when her master came to take her back home.

A year later, Jessie, another shepherd, was living at his new home in Aspen, Colorado, where he found himself when his master, Dexter Gardiner, moved from East Greenwich, Rhode Island. The rest of the Gardiner family had remained behind, and so had the dog next door. Jessie, apparently feeling abandoned, left Aspen and showed up at the Gardiners' six months later, only to find his loved ones gone for the summer. After a brief stay in the pound, he was adopted by Mrs. Linda Babcock, but he again took off for his old home, which this time was not nearly so far. This time, the Gardiners were there, and welcomed him back, although they were mystified by his sudden appearance. An investigation of Jessie's long journey eventually led the Gardiners to Mrs. Babcock, who, after friendly negotiations, ended up keeping the dog.

The longest homing effort on record, however, was achieved in 1923 by Bobbie, a collie who belonged to a family in Silverton, Oregon. He was lost on a family vacation in Walcott, Indiana. But six months later, he had made it back home, a distance of more than 2,000 miles. Details of the dog's trek were later supplied by the families that cared for him along the way, and his route was traced through Illinois, Iowa, Nebraska, Colorado, Wyoming, and Idaho. Bobbie had crossed the Rockies in the middle of winter.

JAL Flight 1628

Despite the popularity of the phrase "flying saucers," UFO shapes and sizes actually fall into several categories, including discs hundreds of feet in diameter, and objects that resemble triangles, cigars, and even teapots. UFOs of immense size, frequently accompanied by smaller flying craft, are known as "mother ships."

One such mother ship was reported by the pilot of Japanese Air Lines flight 1628, a Boeing 747 bound from Iceland to Anchorage, Alaska, on November 17, 1986. Flying over Alaska just after 6 P.M. Captain Kenju Terauchi reported bright white and yellow lights ahead, darting about "like two bear cubs playing with each other." Terauchi radioed Anchorage and the air controller confirmed he had a target on radar. The Japanese pilot switched on his own onboard digital color radar, and though it was designed to pick up weather systems and not solid objects, also registered a reading.

Then Terauchi noticed his 747 was being shadowed by a single, gigantic walnut-shaped UFO the size of two aircraft carriers. He asked Anchorage for permission to execute a 360-degree turn and descend to 31,000 feet, which was granted. The mother ship remained on his tail throughout the maneuver. Anchorage directed two other aircraft in the area to Terauchi's immediate vicinity, but by the time they arrived the UFO had disappeared, having been in sight and pursuit of the 747 for fifty minutes.

Boy From Nowhere

Caspar Hauser might as well have dropped out of the sky. He appeared on the streets of Nuremberg, Germany, in 1828, barely able to walk and speak his name. According to a crudely scrawled letter on his person, Caspar was sixteen years old. But the letter, addressed to the captain of the Sixth Cavalry Regiment stationed in Nuremberg, offered few other details of the boy's life. "If you do not want to keep him," it offered, "kill him or hang him up a chimney."

The local jailer took pity and installed Caspar in his own quarters, slowly teaching him to talk. All he could remember was that he had been raised in darkness in a room barely larger than a closet, fed on a diet of bread and water. He seemed unfamiliar with the most ordinary items. One observer noted that when confronted with a candle, he kept trying to pick the flame off with his fingers. But his sense of sight was so acute that he could reportedly read in the dark and see stars during the day. Caspar was also ambidextrous, with a marked aversion for meat.

Because of his plight, the whole of Nuremberg adopted Caspar, treating him as its own. He was placed under the personal care of a Professor Daumer, and even attracted the attention of both German and European society.

Then on October 17, 1829, Caspar was found in Daumer's home, his forehead bleeding from a knife wound, delivered by a man in a black mask who had suddenly appeared and stabbed him. In 1831, he was wounded in the forehead again, when a pistol accidentally discharged. On December 14, 1833, Caspar Hauser ran from a park, mortally wounded by yet another knife-stab. A search of the park failed to find the weapon. More mysteriously, only Caspar's footprints could be seen in the fresh snow. He died three days later.

Von Feurbach, one of his biographers, had this to say about the enigma of Nuremberg: "Caspar Hauser showed such an utter deficiency of words and ideas, such perfect ignorance of the commonest things and appearances of nature, and such horror of all customs, conveniences, and necessities of civilized life, and, withal, such extraordinary peculiarities in his social, mental, and physical disposition, that one might feel oneself driven to the alternative of believing him to be a citizen of another planet, transferred by some miracle to our own."

Spring-Heel Jack

Had Charles Dickens a perverted sense of humor he might have created a character the likes of Spring-Heel Jack. That this phantasm apparently sprang full-blown from the bowels of London shows that reality continues to outstrip the artist's imagination.

Spring-Heel Jack first turned up in the 1830s, haunting Barnes Common in southwest London by leaping out at people, physically assaulting them, and bounding away with impossible jumping ability. A typical victim was eighteen-year-old Lucy Sales, attacked on her way home in Green Dragon Alley, Limehouse. The cloaked figure jumped out of the darkness, spat flames that temporarily blinded Lucy, then bounded away.

Another victim was Jane Alsop of Bearhind Lane. Answering a knock at the door, Jane confronted a dark figure cloaked in a cape who said, "I am a policeman. For God's sake bring me a light. We have caught Spring-Heel Jack here in the lane!"

She returned with a candle, but the "policeman" threw back his clothes, revealing a terrible vision dressed in a skin-tight, horned helmet and a form-fitting, white uniform. He immediately grabbed Alsop and began pawing her body. Of her attacker Alsop said, "His face was hideous, his eyes like balls of fire. His hands had icy-cold great claws, and he spewed forth blue and white flames."

Hysteria swept the neighborhood. Vigilante posses were organized, but Spring-Heel Jack stayed a jump ahead of his would-be captors. One of his last known appearances was at the Aldershot Barracks in 1877, where three sentries were attacked and rifles fired at their assailant—to no effect.

One theory said Spring-Heel was actually the wastrel nobleman Henry, Marquis of Waterford, who supposedly managed the athletic agility attributed to Jack by means of carriage-springs strapped to his ankles. Such a hypothesis seems almost as far-fetched as the fire-belching Spring-Heel Jack himself. The Marquis of Waterford would have had to have kept his astounding act up for more than four decades, no mean feat for a man who would have by then been in his sixties.

The above theory seems even less likely in light of the fact that German paratroopers during World War II experimented with similar springs designed to soften their landing. The experiments resulted in a rash of broken ankles instead.

Missie, the Dog That Foretold the Future

When Mildred Probert, a retired pet store manager from Denver, inherited Missie, she hoped to restore the brown Boston terrier puppy to health. It took five years, but finally the extraordinary talents of the little terrier emerged: One day, as Probert was walking down the street with Missie, they passed a woman and her young child. Probert asked the child his age, but the youngster was obviously too shy to respond. The mother answered by saying the boy was three. As she tried to coax the boy into saying "three," Missie spontaneously barked three times. Everyone laughed at the coincidence, but the incident turned out to be more than merely a lark. It turned out that Missie could respond to many questions by barking in response, especially mathematical problems. It also soon appeared that the dog could even predict the future.

But the canine's real breakthrough came on New Year's Eve in 1965, when she was "interviewed" on KTLN radio. New York was undergoing a crippling transit strike at the time, and negotiations were at a standstill, so the talk-show host asked Missie when the strike would be over, phrasing questions that could be answered by the number of times that Missie barked. Missie barked to signify that the critical date would be January 13—

which was indeed the exact date the transit strike ended. The little dog also successfully predicted the outcome of that year's World Series.

Sometimes Missie would come up with highly unexpected information. On September 10, 1965, Probert received a visit from a pregnant woman she knew. Since Missie had often predicted delivery dates for babies in the past, the couple decided to consult the dog. Missie responded to the inquiry by signifying September 18. The pregnant woman had to chuckle since, she explained to her hostess, she was scheduled for a Caesarian on October 6. She became even more skeptical when Missie declared that the baby would be born at 9:00 P.M., since her physician didn't work in the evening.

But it all came to pass just as Missie predicted. The visitor went into labor unexpectedly on the 18th and was rushed to the hospital, where her baby was born precisely at 9:00 P.M.

Missie's career as a psychic celebrity didn't last very long. She choked on a piece of candy and died in May 1966. At the time, Walt Disney was planning to make a movie about her extraordinary life.

The Flying Humanoid

At about 8:30 on the quiet evening of July 12, 1977, Adrián de Olmos Ordóñez, forty-two, was resting on the balcony of his home in Quebradillas, Puerto Rico, when he saw something crawl under a barbed-wire fence on a farm not far away. In the dusk De Olmos could see it was a small figure, apparently a child.

A closer look, though, revealed that this was no normal child at all. The creature wore a bulbous green garment and a metallic helmet, at the top of which was an antenna "with a bright light or flame at its tip."

De Olmos called his daughter Irasema to bring him a pencil and paper so that he could sketch the figure as he watched it. As he would tell Puerto Rican ufologist Sebastián Robiou Lamarche, "I told her to turn on the light in the living room, but she made a mistake and she turned on the outside balcony light instead," De Olmos said. The creature took fright and fled.

"The minute the balcony light went on, I saw the creature run back instantly toward the barbed-wire fence. It passed under the wire and then stopped," he explained. "It placed its hands on the front part of its belt and then a thing that it had on its back, resembling a knapsack, lit up and emitted a sound like the noise of an electric drill. And then it rose up into the air and made off toward the trees." At that point the witness's daughter, wife, and two sons came out of the house to see the lights from the flying device on the being's back as it sailed through the air.

For the next ten minutes they watched the lights moving from tree to tree, sometimes descending briefly to ground level. Meanwhile, a group of neighbors joined them and they too saw the strange spectacle. Eventually, a second group of lights, presumably from a second humanoid, joined the first—perhaps, De Olmos thought, to help its companion because "the apparatus on the creature's back was not working quite right."

Soon the lights were out, leaving only a badly frightened collection of people who wasted no time in notifying the police. The police conducted an extensive investigation, as did well-known Puerto Rican ufologist Robiou Lamarche. Reporting on his investigation in Britain's *Flying Saucer Review*, Lamarche wrote, "In the course of our inquiries we ascertained that Sr. Adrián is a serious and well-respected and hard-working person, held in high regard by all the neighbors. He is a businessman, engaged in the distribution of cattle feed throughout the northwestern area of the island. He had never before taken the slightest interest in the UFO phenomenon, or in any related subjects. But, he told us, 'Now I believe in these things.' "

Red Light Over Ithaca

Rita Malley, a young mother of two, was driving home to Ithaca, New York, on the evening of December 12, 1967, when she noticed a red light in pursuit. At first she thought she was being followed by a police car. She was about to pull over to the side of the road when she took another look and this time saw that the light was attached to a strange flying object traveling just above the power lines to her left.

That was startling enough, but nothing compared to her sudden realization that she could no longer control her car. She shouted to her son, who was traveling with her, to brace himself for an accident. But strangely, he did not respond or even move. "It was as if he were in some kind of a trance," she said later. "The car pulled over to the shoulder of the road by itself, ran over an embankment into an alfalfa field, and stopped.

"A white twirling beam of light flashed down from the object," Malley said, "and I heard a humming sound. Then I began to hear voices. The words were broken and jerky, like the way a translator sounds when he is repeating a speech at the United Nations."

As Malley recalls it, she became hysterical when the voices told her a friend was involved in a terrible accident miles away. After a while, though, her car began to move again. She pushed down hard on the accelerator and sped home.

"I knew something was wrong the moment she walked into the house," her husband John told a reporter for the *Syracuse Herald-Journal*. "I thought maybe she had had an accident with the car or something." The next day she learned that a friend indeed had experienced a serious car accident the night before.

For days afterwards, according to reporters and UFO investigators who interviewed her, Mrs. Malley could not discuss the bizarre experience without bursting into tears.

UFOs in Mexico

On May 3, 1975, Carlos Antonio de los Santos Montiel was flying to Mexico City when his Piper PA-24 aircraft began shaking for no apparent reason. Moments later the young pilot spotted a dark gray disc-shaped object, about ten or twelve feet in diameter, just beyond the plane's right wingtip. A similar craft was pacing him on the left.

Most frightening of all, however, was a third object coming straight at him. The UFO passed just under his plane, so close, in fact, that it scraped the underpart of the fuselage.

De los Santos was nearly beside himself with fear, and his terror was intensified when he discovered that the controls seemed frozen. He could not operate them yet, strangely, the plane continued flying at a steady 120 miles per hour.

When the UFOs were no longer visible, de los Santos regained control of the plane. He instantly radioed the airport at Mexico City, and wept as he reported the incident.

The control tower took his report seriously because personnel there had tracked the objects on radar. As air traffic controller Emilio Estañol told reporters, the objects made a 270-degree turn at 518 miles per hour in an arc of only three miles. "Normally a plane moving at that speed needs eight to ten miles to make a turn like that," he said. "In my seventeen years as an air traffic controller I've never seen anything like that."

After he landed safely, de los Santos was given a medical examination and pronounced fit. But as he would soon learn, his ordeal was not over.

His sighting got headline treatment in the Mexican press and two weeks later de los Santos, a retiring twenty-three-year-old man whose ambition in life was to become an airline pilot, was asked to appear on a television talk show to discuss his experience. He reluctantly agreed.

On the day he was to appear, he drove his car down the freeway on the way to the television station. Along the way he saw a large black automobile—he thought it looked like a diplomat's limousine—pull up in front of him. When he looked through the rearview mirror, he saw an identical car behind him. The two cars, which looked so new that to all appearances they were being driven for the first time, were crowding him and soon forced him to the side of the road.

No sooner had he stopped than so did the other cars. De los Santos was about to get out when four tall, broad-shouldered men hopped out of their vehicles. One put his hands on Carlos's door as if to ensure that he would not be able to leave his car. He spoke quickly, speaking an oddly "mechanical" Spanish: "Look, boy, if you value your life and your family's too, don't talk any more about this sighting of yours."

De los Santos, too stunned to respond, watched the four men, who were "Scandinavian" looking, with unusually pale skin and black suits, return to their cars and drive away. For his part Carlos turned around and went back home.

Two days later he told his story to Pedro Ferriz, the host of the television show on which he had been scheduled to appear. Ferriz, a UFO buff, said he had heard other reports of strange "men in black" who threatened UFO witnesses. He assured the young pilot that despite the threats he would not be hurt. In due course he persuaded Carlos to do another interview, which went off without incident.

A month later, Carlos met Dr. J. Allen Hynek, the Northwestern University astronomer who had served as the U.S. Air Force's chief scientific consultant on UFO matters. The two talked and before they parted, Hynek invited him to have breakfast with him the next morning.

At 6:00 A.M. de los Santos left his house and went to the Mexicana Airlines office, where he had applied for a job. Then he went to Hynek's hotel.

As he walked up the steps, he was surprised to see one of the men in black who had forced him off the freeway four weeks earlier. "You were already warned once," the strange man said. "You are not to talk about your experience." As if to underline the seriousness of the threat, he pushed Carlos back several feet.

"Look," he continued, "I don't want you to make problems for yourself. And why did you leave your house at six o'clock this morning? Do you work for Mexicana Airlines? Get out of here—and don't come back!"

De los Santos left immediately without meeting Hynek.

Recalling the bizarre events two years later, de los Santos told two American UFO investigators, "They were very strange. They were huge, taller than Mexicans are, and their skin was deathly white."

Marchers From the Ancient Past

Late one evening in September 1974, writer A. C. McKerracher decided to take a break from work and step outside for a breath of fresh air.

McKerracher and his family had recently moved into a new housing estate on a hill above the small country town of Dunblane in Perthshire, Scotland. It was a clear, frosty night, and the town below was covered in mist. Suddenly, the quiet was disturbed by what sounded like the movement of a large group of people streaming across the fields.

Certain that he was suffering from overwork, McKerracher decided to go inside. But twenty minutes later, puzzled by the occurrence, he went outside again only to find that the sounds were louder, and closer, than ever. This time it sounded as if a mighty legion was marching on the other side of the houses across the street.

"I stood rooted to the spot as the unearthly, unseen cavalcade passed by," he remembered. "The marchers must have numbered in the thousands, for the noise went on and on."

By now fearing for his sanity, he forced himself to go back inside and straight to bed. A week later, however, McKerracher was visiting an older couple who lived nearby when he heard a strange story. Late one night a week earlier, the couple said, their cat and dog had abruptly awakened and stood bolt upright, the hair bristling on their backs. They seemed to watch something crossing the lounge for about twenty minutes," the couple said. "They were terrified."

McKerracher had said nothing about his own experience. But the animals' curious behavior occurred at exactly the same time he had heard the invisible legion a week before. Seeking an explanation, he soon found that an ancient Roman road ran north directly behind the houses on the other side of the street. Moreover, in A.D. 117 an elite IX Hispania Legion had been dispatched to the area to subdue a tribal uprising in Scotland. It had consisted of four thousand men.

The legion was known as the "Unlucky Ninth" since in A.D. 60 men of the IX had flogged Queen Boadicea of England's Iceni tribe and raped her daughters. Boadicea swore an eternal curse against them and later led a revolt that left the Ninth with severe casualties.

The legion regrouped but was never the same. Its march into Scotland came to a mysterious end: It vanished without a trace shortly after it passed through what centuries later would be Dunblane.

In October 1984 McKerracher, who did not hear the sound again and later moved to the older section of Dunblane, gave a lecture on local history to a ladies' club. Afterwards Cecilia Moore, a member, came up to say she might have heard the ghost of a Roman army herself.

It turned out that she had lived across the street from his former house. "I was putting the cat out one night when I heard what sounded like an army passing right through my back garden," she said. The incident, McKerracher determined, took place the same night and at the same time as his own.

"I am convinced, " he wrote, "that what she and I heard—and what my neighbors' animals saw—was the doomed Ninth Legion marching to its terrible unknown fate nearly two thousand years before."

Deathbed Visions

Most of us have heard of the near-death experience in which those who have clinically died report "leaving the body" and journeying to heaven. More rarely discussed, however, are deathbed vision cases in which the patients see welcoming figures, usually friends and relatives, coming to greet them and help them through death. Recently, some important research suggests that these experiences can't be explained away as hallucinations.

For several years now, Dr. Karlis Osis, formerly the director of Reseach for the American Society for Psychical Research, has been conducting computer studies analyzing hundreds of deathbed vision cases collected from the United States. By checking the pertinent medical records for each patient, Osis has been able to determine that their experiences weren't caused by toxic effects of either their illnesses or medications. Working with psychologist Dr. Erlendur Haraldsson of the University of Reykjavik in Iceland, Osis also traveled to India to conduct an identical study and to see whether these curious visions occurred there as well. The researchers especially wanted to determine if the Indian visions conformed to different cultural patterns, a clear sign that they were psychological in nature instead of real.

The finding? Terminal patients in India describe the same range of experiences the dying report in the West, say Osis and Haraldsson. While psychological reactions to the experiences may differ from East to West, the contents do not. These findings have led Osis and Haraldsson to conclude that deathbed visions really do represent a peak beyond death.

A Big Bird?

It was 10:30 on the evening of January 14, 1976, and Armando Grimaldo was sitting in the backyard of his mother-in-law's house on the north side of Raymondville, Texas. He had come to visit his estranged wife Christina, who was now asleep inside. Grimaldo was about to have an all-too-close encounter with a creature from another world.

"As I was turning to go look over on the other side of the house," he went on, "I felt something grab me, something with big claws. I looked back and saw it and started running. I've never been scared of nothing before but this time I really was. That was the most scared I've ever been in my whole life."

Something had dived out of the sky—and it was something Grimaldo had never seen before or wanted to see again. It was as tall as he—five feet, eight inches—and it had a wingspread of from ten to twelve feet. Its skin was "blackish-brown," leathery and featherless, and its face had huge red eyes.

Grimaldo screamed and tried to run but in his panic tripped over his feet, falling face-first into the dirt. As he struggled back up, he could hear his clothes being ripped by the beast's claws. He managed to dash under a tree as his attacker, now breathing heavily, flew off into the night.

Christina was awakened by his shouting and was on her way downstairs when she heard him crash into the house "in some kind of shock." Unable to speak coherently, he kept muttering *pájaro* (Spanish for "bird") over and over again. He was taken to the Willacy County Hospital and released after half an hour when doctors determined that he had suffered no physical injuries.

Armando Grimaldo may have been luckier than Joe Suárez's goat. Something ripped it to pieces in the early hours of December 26. The animal had been left tied up in a corral behind Suárez's barn in Raymondville. There were no footprints around the body and the police could not explain how it had been killed.

Something had invaded the Rio Grande Valley. Before it was

gone a month or so later, local wits had dubbed it "Big Bird" after the "Sesame Street" character. To most people it was an object of amusement. Those who saw it considered it no laughing matter.

A similar creature slammed into Alverico Guajardo's trailer in nearby Brownsville. When Guajardo went outside, he got into his station wagon and turned on the lights to see what he described as "something from another planet." As soon as the lights hit it, the thing rose up and glared at him with blazing red eyes. Guajardo, paralyzed with fear, could only stare back at the creature, whose long, batlike wings were wrapped around its shoulders. All the while it was making a "horrible-sounding noise" in its throat. Finally, after two or three minutes, it backed away to a dirt road three feet behind it and disappeared in the darkness.

Yet another sighting of the creature occurred on February 24, far to the north, in San Antonio, when three elementary school-teachers driving to work on an isolated road southwest of the city spotted an enormous bird with a wingspan of "fifteen or twenty feet, if not more." It was flying so low that when it swooped over the cars its shadow covered the entire road.

As the three watched this unlikely creature, they saw another flying creature off in the distance circling a herd of cattle. It looked, they thought, like an "oversized seagull."

Later, when the teachers searched through books trying to identify the first bird they had seen, they were able to identify it. The only trouble was, that the bird closely resembled the pteranodon, a flying dinosaur that had not existed for 150 million years.

They were not the only south Texans to think they had seen a prehistoric winged reptile. Just a month before, two Brownsville sisters, Libby and Deany Ford, sighted a "big black bird" near a pond. The creature was as tall as they were and had a "face like a bat." Later, when they came upon a picture of a pteranodon in a book, they concluded that was what they had seen.

The Big Bird scare subsided in early 1976, but that was not the last the Rio Grande Valley was to see of the creature. On September 14, 1982, James Thompson, an ambulance technician from Harlingen, saw a "large birdlike object" pass over Highway 100 at a distance of 150 feet. The time was 3:55 A.M.

"I expected him to land like a model airplane," Thompson told the *Valley Morning Star*. "That's what I thought he was, but he flapped his wings enough to get above the grass. It had a black or grayish rough texture. It wasn't feathers. I'm quite sure it was a hide-type covering. I just watched him fly away." It was, he would later realize, a "pterodactyl-like bird."

The International Society of Cryptozoology, a scientific organization that investigates reports of unknown or allegedly extinct animals, noted that the sighting "occurred only 200 miles east—as the pterodactyl flies—of Mexico's Sierra Madre Oriental, one of the least explored regions of North America."

The Persistent Hitchhiker

As he was driving from Mayagüez, Puerto Rico, to his home in Arecibo late in the evening of November 20, 1982, Abel Haiz Rassen, an Arab merchant who lives in Puerto Rico, passed through a section known as "The Chain." A balding man was standing on the side of the road hitchhiking. Haiz Rassen glanced at the man, who was about thirty-five years old and dressed in a gray shirt and brown jeans, and drove on.

But when he stopped for a red light at the next intersection, his car stalled. As Haiz Rassen struggled to start it again, he did not notice that the hitchhiker was opening the passenger door and getting inside.

"I'm Roberto," the man said to the startled Haiz Rassen. "Could you please take me to my home in the housing project, Alturas de Aguada? I have not seen my son and my wife Esperanza for almost two months."

Haiz Rassen declined the request, saying his wife was waiting for him in Arecibo. But Roberto pleaded with him. The driver went back to trying to start the car, which suddenly began running again.

He agreed to take Roberto as far as the El Nido Restaurant. In the course of the short journey his unwelcome passenger cautioned him to drive carefully and not to drink. He asked that Haiz Rassen pray for him.

It was with some relief that Haiz Rassen pulled up to the restaurant parking lot. Observers nearby saw him talking animatedly, apparently to himself. One asked if he needed help.

"No," Haiz Rassen replied, "but this gentleman wants me to take him home." He turned to his right to indicate his passenger—but there was no one there.

He was so shaken that he nearly became ill. The police were summoned and two officers, Alfredo Vega and Gilberto Castro, took him to a local hospital, where he related his bizarre story.

Skeptical but still intrigued, the officers went to the housing project and knocked at the door with the address the driver said he had gotten from Roberto. A woman carrying a small boy answered. To the officers' questions she replied that her name was Esperanza. She was the widow of Roberto Valentín Carbo.

Her husband, who was partially bald, had been wearing a gray shirt and brown jeans on October 6, 1982, when he was killed in a car accident—at the exact spot along the roadside where six weeks later Abel Haiz Rassen first spotted him.

Out-of-Body Travelers

Parapsychologists have spent a great deal of time studying the phenomenon of out-of-body experiences, or astral projection.

In one case, recorded by a physician, a man named Wilson fell asleep and dreamed that he had visited a woman friend who lived forty miles from him. A maid answered the door and told him she was not at home, but he asked to come in and have a glass of water. The maid obliged. Wilson thought nothing more of it, until another friend of his received a letter from the woman in the dream, and the letter spoke of Wilson's visit, and even mentioned his coming in for water. This caused Wilson to take some friends along to that house to investigate. When he got there, two maids identified Wilson as the man who had been there and had come in.

A more celebrated projector is a man named Blue Haray, who claims the power of leaving his body at will, and has put his claims to the test at the Psychical Research Foundation in Durham, North Carolina. In these experiments, Haray's eye movements, respiration, and other bodily functions were monitored by a maze of instruments, and all monitors showed significant changes when he reported an out-of-body experience. On one occasion, he visited a doctor who was not expecting the visit. The doctor reported seeing a "red orb" flash across his room at 3:15 A.M., exactly the time Haray said he had been there. Pets kept in separate, sealed rooms were used as the targets in another series of experiments. In one test, a cat stopped meowing and sat motionless when Haray reported his visit; in another test, a hostile snake that had been acting normally suddenly tried to strike at something unseen by the cameras, again at the same time Haray said he was "visiting" the target room.

Yet another out-of-body journey was reported by a young lieutenant on duty in Panama in 1943. He was worried about his mother, who had just undergone major surgery in New York. Leave to visit her was not possible. But during a training break at a quarter past one he fell asleep for a few moments and dreamed he was standing in front of the Memorial Hospital near the East River Drive. He entered and asked the receptionist for permission to visit his mother. The receptionist checked a list and signed him in as a visitor. Another nurse told him that she recognized him from the photograph in his mother's room. The picture showed him wearing a winter uniform, the same as he was wearing in the hospital. He got into the elevator and a nurse saw him push the button. On the way up in the elevator the lieutenant felt everything become hazy and dreamlike. He woke up, still in Panama, at 1:15 P.M. Some days later he received a letter from his mother telling about an odd unexplained incident. She had been told that her son had come to visit her, but he never arrived. Although the receptionist and another nurse had seen him enter the elevator, no one saw him get out. The time: 12:15 P.M. in New York and 1:15 P.M. in the Panama time zone. The name of the officer who wanted to visit his mother had been written in the register. It was my own name, Charles Berlitz.

A Massacre in Flight

Something terrifying happened in the air one day in the late summer of 1939—and to this day the incident is shrouded in secrecy.

All that is known is that a military transport plane left the Marine Naval Air Station in San Diego at 3:30 one afternoon. It and its thirteen-man crew were making a routine flight to Honolulu. Three hours later, as the plane was over the Pacific Ocean, a frantic distress signal was sounded. Then the radio signal died.

A little later the plane limped back to base and made an emergency landing. Ground crew members rushed to the craft and when they boarded, they were horrified to see twelve dead men. The only survivor was the copilot, who, though badly injured, had stayed alive long enough to bring the plane back. A few minutes later he was dead, too.

All of the bodies had large, gaping wounds. Even weirder, the pilot and copilot had emptied their .45 Colt automatic pistols at something. The empty shells were found lying on the floor of the cockpit. A foul, sulfuric odor pervaded the interior of the craft.

The exterior of the airplane was badly damaged, looking as if it had been struck by missiles. The personnel who boarded the craft came down with an odd skin infection.

Strict security measures were quickly put into effect and the emergency ground crew was ordered to leave the plane. The job of removing the bodies and investigating the incident was left to three medical officers.

The incident was successfully hushed up and did not come to light for fifteen years, when investigator Robert Coe Gardner learned of it from someone who was there. The mystery of what the crew encountered in midair that afternoon in 1939 has never been solved.

Lightning Strikes
More Than Twice

In 1899 a bolt of lightning killed a man as he stood in his backyard in Taranto, Italy. Thirty years later his son was killed in the same way and in the same place. On October 8, 1949, Rolla Primarda, the grandson of the first victim and the son of the second, became the third.

Just as strange was the fate of a British officer, Major Summerford, who while fighting in the fields of Flanders in February 1918 was knocked off his horse by a flash of lightning and paralyzed from the waist down.

Summerford retired and moved to Vancouver. One day in 1924, as he fished alongside a river, lightning hit the tree he was sitting under and paralyzed his right side.

Two years later Summerford was sufficiently recovered that he was able to take walks in a local park. He was walking there one summer day in 1930 when a lightning bolt smashed into him, permanently paralyzing him. He died two years later.

But lightning sought him out one more time. Four years later, during a storm, lightning struck a cemetery and destroyed a tombstone. It was Major Summerford's.

K-19

For years Thomas Wolfe, the famous American writer, had an idea for a novel. It was to be titled *K-19* and it would be about a Pullman car bearing that designation. The lives of all the characters in the story would in some way be affected by that car. He discussed *K-19* with his editor, Maxwell Perkins, but he could never put the story together in a satisfactory manner. Perkins suggested he concentrate on other writings until he was sure he had a plot that worked. Wolfe agreed, but as fate would have it, he was unable to return to his *K-19* idea. He died suddenly of a heart attack in 1938.

Perkins took responsibility for shipping Wolfe's body back to his native Asheville, North Carolina, where it would be buried. As the train was pulling out of the station, Perkins was watching the car bearing Wolfe's casket. As it passed out of sight, he suddenly realized what its number was: K-19.

The Crash That Never Happened

On October 10, 1931, America's newest dirigible, the U.S.S. *Akron,* was scheduled to circle the Fairfield Stadium in honor of the Washington and Jefferson-Marshall football game in Huntington, West Virginia.

The first person to see the dirigible en route was Harold Mac-Kenzie, who watched it making its way over the nearby town of

Gallipolis, Ohio. He called to friends at the Foster Dairy plant to come watch it with him.

Two of them, Mr. and Mrs. Robert Henke, went to First Avenue with their friend Mrs. Claude Parker. The three watched the craft through binoculars and were soon joined by other observers, who saw the *Akron* sail over the river.

On the other side, in Point Pleasant, West Virginia, other watchers followed the ship's progress. The ship, about 100 to 150 feet long, was flying at the altitude of about 300 feet when, at 2:50 P.M., something unexpected and terrifying happened.

As Mrs. Henke told the *Gallipolis Daily Tribune* on October 12, "When we caught sight of the ship, it seemed to buckle and fall. Some who saw it said that four persons jumped with parachutes. There seemed to be smoke surrounding the object but it may have been clouds that we saw."

Horrified observers saw the blimp erupt into flames and crash into the hills south of Gallipolis Ferry, West Virginia.

Half a dozen witnesses reported the incident to Dr. Holzer, owner of the Gallipolis Airport. At dawn the next day searchers set out for the site. All that day they went over the site from both ground and air—and found no trace of the ship or its doomed crew.

There was a simple reason: They did not exist.

By evening the day of the alleged disaster, spokesmen from the Akron Airport were denying that any such tragedy had occurred. The *Akron* was safe in its hangar, as were the three blimps of the Goodyear Zeppelin Company. The *Akron* had flown over northern Ohio earlier that day but had not gone south to the Huntington stadium because the navy had turned down Senator H. D. Hatfield's request that it do so.

All eastern and midwestern airports asserted that none of their craft were missing. Nor were there any foreign dirigibles operating in that area of the United States.

The witnesses, however, adamantly rejected theories that they had seen a flock of birds or simply dreamed the sighting. To this day this peculiar episode remains unexplained.

Psychic Control
of the Weather?

⚫━━━━━━━━━━━━━━━━━━━━━━━━━━━━━━━━━━━

The place was the Indian city of Dharamsala, home to many Tibetan refugees. The date was March 10, 1973, time for the refugees to mourn the flight of the Dalai Lama from Tibet. But with storms rolling down the Himalayan slopes for weeks, the proceedings seemed doomed. With no letup in sight, the local residents finally sought help from Gunsang Rinzing, an elderly lama both feared and renowned for his power to control the weather. The lama's work was later described by David Read Barker, an anthropologist conducting field work in India at the time. It was 8:00 P.M., Dr. Barker explains, and Rinzing began by building a fire in the rain.

"He was in a state of concentration," reported Barker, "and recited mantras and a sadhana, frequently blowing on a trumpet fashioned from a human thighbone and beating the two-headed drum of a shaman. After several hours of watching him from a respectful distance, we retired to bed, certain that the weather would be as miserable the next day as it had been for the preceding days. Early the following morning the rain had diminished to a drizzle, and by ten o'clock it had become only a cold fog over a circle with a radius of about one-hundred and fifty meters. Everywhere else in the area it continued to pour, but the several thousand refugees were never rained on during the six hours they were assembled. At one point during the Dalai Lama's speech, a huge hailstorm swept past, causing a tremendous clatter on the tin-roofed houses adjoining the festival grounds, but only a few dozen hailstones fell on the crowd."

Fourteen years before, at the time of the Chinese Communist invasion of Tibet and the Dalai Lama's escape to India, unexpected atmospheric conditions assured his safe arrival across the Himalayas into India. While Chinese aircraft tried to find him and his party, a thick fog providentially cloaked the area he was traversing, making the travelers completely invisible from the air.

To Tibetans, of course, this sudden zero visibility was simply a proof of the Dalai Lama's divine power over the weather.

Saved by a Dead Boy

At 10 o'clock one night early in 1978, seventy-two-year-old retired farmer Henry Sims returned from a Florida hospital, where his eighteen-year-old daughter was staying. His wife Idellar remained at the hospital. Another daughter, five grandchildren, and a family friend were sleeping in the house when Sims returned. He went to bed and soon fell asleep.

"The next thing I remember," he would recall, "is the dream. I could see my brother-in-law's two children—Paul and his eight-month-old baby sister—coming toward me. They were both burned to death in 1932 when fire swept through their home in Live Oak, Florida. In my dream Paul, whom I remember clearly, was walking toward me saying, 'Uncle Henry, Uncle Henry.' I had never had a dream like this before and I awoke suddenly with the smell of smoke in my nostrils. My first thought was my grandchildren—to get those kids out of the place. So I began shouting and yelling."

His cries awoke the other sleepers, who fled the burning house just in time to save their lives.

Fire inspector Lieutenant Frederick Lowe of Hialeah Heights, Florida, said, "Miraculously, this man managed to wake up at the vital moment. Another two minutes and everyone would have been dead."

"God wasn't ready for me to die," Henry Sims concluded. "It was He who sent young Paul to warn of the danger and to pluck us all from that burning building."

The Deadly Number—191

In May 1979 an American Airlines DC-10 crashed near O'Hare Airport in Chicago shortly after taking off for a flight to California. Among the victims was author Judy Wax, whose book, *Starting in the Middle*, had just been published.

The flight number of the doomed plane was 191. On page 191 of her book Mrs. Wax had discussed her fear of flying.

The May 1979 issue of *Chicago* reviewed her book and ran a picture of her with it. Readers who held up the page to the light could see on the reverse side a full-page advertisement for an American Airlines DC-10 flight to California.

Disappearance of the S.S. *Iron Mountain*

Nothing seemed out of the ordinary in June 1872 when the steamship *Iron Mountain* chugged off from Vicksburg, its crew intact, its cargo of baled cotton and barrels of molasses stacked on the deck and a line of barges in tow.

A few minutes later it rounded a bend, making its way northward toward the steel town of Pittsburgh. The ship was never seen again.

The *Iroquois Chief*, another steamer, was traveling on the river late that morning when its crew spotted a line of barges churning downriver. The ship managed to steer clear of the barges and then, assuming they had been separated from their towship, caught up to the barges, secured them, and waited for the towing steamer. It never came.

The tow line for the barges had been cut, indicating that the crew of *Iron Mountain* had sensed a problem: Perhaps the boilers were about to explode, perhaps the ship was about to sink. But, there was, however, no trace of the ship anywhere along the river, nor was there any trace of its cargo, which would have dotted the river for miles had the steamer gone down.

The mystery of the *Iron Mountain* has never been solved.

Annemarie's Poltergeist

It was a paranormal version of the bull in the china shop when the events struck a lawyer's office in Rosenheim, Germany, in 1967. While the town is usually quiet and uneventful, something began running amok in the office by making phones go haywire, blowing fuses, and causing other electrical malfunctions. Soon the phenomenon accelerated: Lights began to flash on and off; light bulbs exploded for absolutely no reason; and the phones rang without apparent cause.

The staff didn't know what to do, so they began with the obvious: They called in experts from the local power company. The investigators who came checked every conceivable fuse, wire, and power source, but failed to find any natural cause for the problem. They even cut off the building's power supply and hooked up an emergency unit to feed juice into the office. These procedures didn't phase the spook and the disturbances went on.

Finally, renowned German parapsychologist Hans Bender was called in. The country's chief ghost-hunter, he quickly diagnosed the problem as a poltergeist—a type of ghost likely to throw household items, move furniture, pelt houses with stones, and start fires. Unlike conventional ghosts, who infest a particular place, poltergeists usually focus on a person. And it didn't take long for Bender to find the individual human target: Annemarie Schnabel, a teenager who worked in the office. Sometimes the disturbances would occur as soon as she showed up.

"When this young girl walked through the gangways [halls], the lamps behind her began to swing," reported Bender. "If bulbs exploded, the fragments flew towards her. Soon," he added, "paintings began to swing and to turn, drawers came out by themselves, documents were displaced. But when Annemarie was sent on leave, nothing happened. And when she left the offices for a new position, no more disturbances occurred, though similar, less obvious events happened for some time in the new office where she was working."

Once Schnabel left, the lawyer's office seemed to be haunted by more conventional ghosts. When a news team arrived at the office, for instance, several witnesses saw a vapory materialization, resembling a human arm, appear by a floor vent. The materialization flew to a nearby wall, where it crashed into a painting, which reeled on its wire. Luckily, the shouts of the bystanders alerted the crew, and they successfully filmed the movements of the painting.

What was the cause of the Rosenheim poltergeist? According to Bender, it was Annemarie herself. She was an unhappy girl possessed by pent-up frustrations over her job and romantic life, he said. No doubt, he added, her repressed hostility seethed within her unconscious mind until it erupted in the form of the poltergeist.

A Hymn for the *Titanic*

One Sunday morning the Reverend Charles Morgan, minister of the Rosedale Methodist Church in Winnipeg, Manitoba, Canada, arrived early to prepare for the evening service. Before entering his study, he posted on the hymn board the choirmaster's choice of hymns, then went on to other preparations.

This done, he retired to his office and decided to nap until it was time for the service. Soon he fell asleep, and no sooner had he begun to doze than he had a vivid dream of darkness and the sounds of huge, crashing waves. Above the din a choir sang an old hymn Reverend Morgan hadn't thought of in years.

The dream was so disturbing that the minister awoke, the hymn still ringing in his ears. He checked his watch and saw that he had time to resume his nap, which he did—assuming, incorrectly, that his brief waking period had cleared his mind of the unsettling vision.

As soon as he fell back asleep, the dream returned: the crashing waters, the deep darkness, the old hymn. He woke up with a start, strangely upset. Finally he got up, walked out into the empty church, and posted a new hymn number on the board.

When the service began, the congregation sang the hymn that had haunted Morgan's dreams—an odd hymn to sing in a church thousands of miles from the ocean: "Hear, Father, while we pray to Thee, for those in peril on the sea." Hearing the words, Morgan felt tears fill his eyes.

Not long afterward the minister was to learn that at the time he and his flock were singing the hymn, a great tragedy was occurring on the ocean. It was April 14, 1912, and far out on the North Atlantic the *Titanic* was sinking.

The Fourth Death of Musyoka Mututa

Musyoka Mututa of Kitui, Kenya, was lowered into the ground in September 1985. His brother Timothy said the body had been left out for two days—just in case, even though "we had no expectation of another miracle. He told me the fourth time would be for good."

Although only a humble shepherd, Mututa was a legend in Kenya. He was known as the "man who cheated death."

His first "death" occurred when he was three years old. As he was being lowered into the ground, he cried out and was quickly brought back to the surface.

When he was nineteen, he disappeared. Six days later searchers found his apparently lifeless body in a field. A funeral was held and as his coffin was being lowered, mourners were startled to see the lid start to rise. Mututa had "come back to life."

He "died" again in May 1985 after a short illness. A surgeon pronounced him dead. His body lay in state for a day, at the end of which he rose and demanded a glass of water.

Mututa claimed that during each of his three "deaths" his soul left his body and ascended to heaven, where angels explained it was a "case of mistaken identity" and returned him to earth.

Apparently on the fourth try they got the right man.

Dowsing With a Peach-Tree Stick

Officials at Gates Rubber Company in Jefferson, North Carolina, were frantic when they learned that leaks in the town's water system threatened to drain the plant's water supply. Desperately seeking new water sources, they hired professional well-drillers, who brought $350,000 worth of equipment to the search. They couldn't find water.

Then in September 1983, an eighty-year-old retired stonemason named Don Witherspoon came on the scene, a Y-shaped peach-tree branch in hand. He said he had been dowsing for thirty-eight years and was sure he could find what everyone was looking for.

He walked up and down the company's grounds until his branch suddenly tugged and pointed to the ground. Some distance away the branch repeated this strange performance.

The company found water at both sites—so much, in fact, that soon it was drawing up to seventy gallons a minute, nearly eliminating the plant's need to draw on the town's water supply.

"It may be 'witching' but it apparently works," plant manager Richard Thurston said. "All I know is we've got water and we're thankful."

Witherspoon said he could not explain his ability. He called it a "gift. To tell you the truth," he said, "I didn't believe in the water fork myself until I tried it."

A Temporal Lobe Apparition

Brain dysfunctions can cause people to report all sorts of strange experiences. Small seizures in the brain's temporal lobes, for instance, can cause a person to smell strange odors, hear bizarre sounds, be overwhelmed by mystical feelings, and even see phantoms.

A fascinating temporal lobe apparition was reported by Scottish psychiatrist James McHarg in 1976. He reported that a patient suffering from temporal lobe epilepsy was visiting a friend in 1969 when she experienced a sudden attack. First she smelled a foul milky odor, then her surroundings seemed to become "unreal," and finally she saw a phantom. The figure appeared to be a woman with soft brown hair standing by a cooker on the far side of the kitchen. The figure lingered only temporarily and faded from view when the seizure subsided.

The patient reported what she had seen to her hostess, who was fascinated by the story. Though the friend's kitchen currently lacked a cooker, there once *had* been one placed in the kitchen exactly where the patient reported seeing it. By researching the history of the house, moreover, the hostess discovered that the figure probably represented one of two sisters who had previously lived there. When the patient was shown a photograph of the sisters, she immediately recognized the lady she had seen.

So did this patient see a genuine ghost? Not likely, according to Dr. McHarg, since the woman in the vision was still alive. Nonetheless, he concluded, the seizure probably rendered his patient open to extrasensory influences, which came into play and influenced what she saw.

"Come Find Me"

Mary L. Cousett, twenty-seven, of Peoria, Illinois, vanished one day in April 1983. The police soon concluded that she had been murdered and they arrested her boyfriend, Stanley Holliday, Jr. But because her body was nowhere to be found, they feared they would be unable to mount a successful prosecution.

Finally, all other means having failed, Madison County authorities took their problem to Greta Alexander of Delavan, Illinois. Alexander, a psychic, provided a detailed description of where the body lay. It would be found, she said, near an embankment, a river, and a bridge. A church and salt would have something to do with the discovery. The body would have leaves around it. Part of a leg would be missing. The head would be recovered some distance away.

A man "with a bad hand" would find the body. The initial "S" would be involved. The body would be found near a main road.

On November 12 auxilary policeman Steve Trew, who had an injured hand, uncovered Cousett's remains near an embankment close to a bridge over the Mackinaw River, half a mile from a church camp and across the river from a highway salt-storage area. The body lay in a shallow grave covered by leaves. The left foot was missing and the skull, apparently removed by animals, lay five or ten feet from the rest of the body.

Detective William Fitzgerald of Alton told reporters that twenty-two of Alexander's psychic impressions had hit the mark.

"This young woman was really wanting to be found," Alexander said. "The spirit never dies; it lives on. She was saying, 'Here I am. Come find me.' "

Two Snowbanks

Warren Felty and William Miller of Harrisburg, Pennsylvania, got together on Veterans Day 1986 to celebrate an unlikely series of events that had taken place more than four decades before.

One night in February 1940 Felty was driving home to Middletown, Pennsylvania, when he saw the taillights of the car in front of him begin to sway. The car was skidding into an embankment near Camp Hill.

Felty pulled over and ran to the scene of the accident. When he got to the car, he saw that the driver had been thrown through the windshield into a four-foot snowbank and was now unconscious and covered with blood. Felty lifted him up, carried him back to his own car, and drove him to the Harrisburg Hospital.

Four days later the accident victim, William Miller, recovered consciousness. Later he learned the name of the man who saved him. After he left the hospital, his path crossed Felty's a few times but the two men did not really become acquainted.

They could not know when America entered World War II, that each had signed on with the Army Air Force and become a B-17 pilot. They did not know, either, that the other had been shot down over Germany and herded with four thousand other prisoners toward Nuremberg, just ahead of the advancing Russian army.

The prisoners were weak from hunger and ill-clad for marching in the bitter winter of 1944, the coldest Germany had experienced in eighty years. Many didn't make it, falling to the ground and freezing to death in the snow.

As Warren Felty was marching along, he saw a body in the snowbank along the road. Hoping to revive the fallen fellow marcher, he kicked the man and, as Felty would recall years later, "there he was, Bill Miller. Unbelievable."

Miller, who was only barely conscious, had to be dragged and tugged all the way to the march's destination. Felty, Miller, and the other prisoners eventually ended up at a detention camp at Moosburg, from which Patton's Third Army freed them on April 29, 1945.

The two men still remember how on two occasions, in places five years and four thousand miles apart, one carried the other to safety by lifting him out of a snowbank.

Blue Man on Studham Common

At 1:45 in the afternoon of a rainy day, January 28, 1967, on Studham Common in England's Chiltern Hills, seven boys were walking to school through a shallow valley called the Dell. One of them, ten-year-old Alex Butler, happened to be looking south over the Dell when he saw what he later described as a "little blue man with a tall hat and a beard."

He quickly pointed it out to a friend who was walking next to him, and the two decided to get a better look at the curious looking figure. They ran toward it but when they were about twenty yards from it, it "disappeared in a puff of smoke."

The boys alerted their companions, who began looking for the little man, hoping he would reappear. Soon he was back, this time on the opposite side of the bush from where he had been when first observed. As the boys approached him, he vanished again, then reappeared at the bottom of the Dell. About this time the boys heard "voices" speaking in a "foreign-sounding babble" in nearby bushes and for the first time they felt slightly afraid.

When they got to school that rainy afternoon of January 28, 1967, their teacher, Miss Newcomb, could tell they were excited about *something*. At first they wouldn't give her the reason. All they would say was, "You'll never believe us." Finally she separated all seven and got each to write his own independent account of the strange event. The accounts were remarkably similar, enough so that Miss Newcomb was persuaded that something decidedly out of the ordinary had taken place that afternoon.

The accounts were eventually published in a booklet called *The Little Blue Man on Studham Common*.

In due course the report came to the attention of British investigators Bryan Winder and Charles Bowen, who learned that in recent months a number of local people had reported seeing UFOs. Two landings had been reported at the spot where the little blue man was seen. The connection with UFOs, however, remained conjectural, since the boys had claimed no sighting of one.

The investigators interviewed the boys in the presence of their teacher. As Winder wrote, "They estimate the little man as three feet tall, with an additional two feet accounted for by a hat or helmet best described as a tall brimless bowler. They could discern a line that was either a fringe of hair or the lower edge of the hat, two round eyes, a small seemingly flat triangle in place of a nose, and a one-piece vestment extending down to a broad black belt carrying a black box at the front about six inches square."

The Teleported Coin

Raymond Bayless has confronted the paranormal many times during his career as a psychic investigator. His strangest encounter, however, involves a phenomenon known as teleportation in which matter travels mysteriously from one location to the next.

The incident took place in 1957, when Bayless was walking down Hollywood Boulevard with psychic Attila von Szalay. The two men entered a leather-goods store and Bayless, an enthusiastic coin collector, saw a curious British coin on the proprietor's desk. One side depicted one of England's royal princesses, and the reverse side was marred by a long scratch. Intrigued, Bayless asked to buy the coin, but his offer was refused.

As the two men walked from the store, Bayless glanced at the coin one last time and continued on his way. "We had walked perhaps one hundred feet down the block," he said, "when I suddenly felt something strike my elbow and then my pants leg. I looked down in surprise and found on the sidewalk by my feet the identical penny. To make sure it was indeed the same coin, I looked on the reverse side, and there was the scratch I had noticed on its surface in the leather store.

"Mr. von Szalay was on my other side and was surprised when I picked up the penny and showed it to him, explaining that the last time I had seen it, it was lying on the storekeeper's desk. Without going into any more details and lengthy explanations, I will rest content in stating that there was no way that the coin could have reached me normally, and its strange transportation provided a remarkable mystery."

It probably didn't seem too mysterious to the shop owner, who no doubt figured his customer had pocketed the coin.

Mr. Wilson's 1897 Airship

The deepest mystery of American aviation is a mostly forgotten but still unexplained episode that began in November 1896 and ended in May of the following year.

From California to Maine thousands of Americans reported seeing large, piloted "airships" unlike anything that could have flown in those years, several years before the Wright Brothers invented heavier-than-air flight and forever changed history. The "airships" sparked wonder and speculation about who their inventor or inventors were, but to this day nobody knows. All we have are some tantalyzing clues, none more intriguing than those concerning a very strange man named Mr. Wilson.

On April 19, 1897, Mr. Wilson made his presence known. A young man from Lake Charles, Louisiana, was driving a team of horses when he saw an enormous airship pass overhead, frightening the animals so badly that they bolted and threw the driver to the ground. At that point the airship stopped and hovered nearby—the ability to hover was just one of the unlikely capabilities of these mysterious craft—while a rope ladder dropped down. Two of the airship occupants climbed down and helped the witness to his feet. "It was decidedly gratifying to find that they were plain, everyday Americans like myself," the young man would report. The aeronauts apologized for the trouble they had caused. To make up for it, they invited him aboard the ship, introducing themselves as Scott Warren and "Mr. Wilson." Wilson said he was the ship's owner. Aboard the craft Wilson and Warren explained the vehicle's propulsion system, but the account was so technical that the young man did not understand what they were talking about.

A day later, near Uvalde, Texas, an airship landed and was discovered by Sheriff H. W. Bayler, who conversed with members of the crew. One identified himself as Wilson and said he was a native of Goshen, New York. Wilson then asked about Captain C. C. Akers, a local man.

Later, when asked about Wilson, Akers told a reporter, "I can say that while living in Fort Worth in seventy-six and seventy-seven I was well acquainted with a man by the name of Wilson from New York State and was on very friendly terms with him. He was of a mechanical turn of mind and was then working on aerial navigation and something that would astonish the world. He was a finely educated man, then twenty-four years of age, and seemed to have money with which to pursue his inventions, devoting his whole time to them. From conversations we had while in Fort Worth, I think that Mr. Wilson, having succeeded in constructing a practical airship, would probably hunt me up to show me that he was not so wild in his claims as I then supposed."

The airship next appeared a day or two later, when it came down for repairs at Kountze, Texas. Witnesses talked with the pilots, who said their names were "Wilson and Jackson." On the twenty-fifth, between midnight and 1:00 A.M., the *San Antonio Daily Express* reported the next day, "The sky was heavily clouded and not a star was visible. This brought out all the stronger the keen white light of the airship headlights together with the shimmer that the strong illumination cast about it. It prevented, however, anything like a view of the structure itself, but as the strange object wheeled about and came nearer, a dozen or more dim lights, among them a cluster of green lights on the side of the ship toward the city, and another immense cluster of red lights at the stern, plainly indicated its artificial nature."

The paper goes on to say, without explaining how it knows this, that the "inventors were Hiram Wilson, a native of New York and son of Willard B. Wilson, assistant master mechanic of the New York Central Railroad, and electrical engineer C. J. Walsh of San Francisco. The men had labored on their project several years, and when their plans had matured they had the parts of the ship constructed to order in different sections of the country, whence they were shipped to the rendezvous at San Francisco and put together on the island."

The Daily Express claimed that after being tested in California, the ship flew to Utah and was hidden "in some out-of-the-way section of the West" while defects were corrected. Then it resumed its eastward flight across the United States.

And then no more was heard of Wilson and his remarkable machine.

Who was he? Inquiries in recent years have come up with a blank. And a study of airship reports from 1897 gives us reason to suspect Mr. Wilson was even more mysterious than first appearances suggest. According to writer Daniel Cohen, author of The Great Airship Mystery, "There is a great deal about this Wilson episode that is confusing and contradictory. Any attempt to trace the path of 'Wilson's airship' across south Texas during the last week or two of April 1897 is hopeless. Airships seemed to pop up all over the place. There would have to be at least two or perhaps three different airships all pursuing highly erratic paths in order to account for all of the sightings and encounters. Aside from the name Wilson, which appears in at least five separate accounts, the names of the other crewmen vary. So does the size of the crew, from two to eight. And though many stories quote the inventor as saying that he soon will make his airship public, he never did."

Another researcher, Jerome Clark, noticed something even odder: "We have one simple 'impossible' fact, which by itself is sufficient to raise some profound questions about Wilson's purported role," Clark said. "Namely, Captain Akers says that twenty years prior to Wilson's appearance at Uvalde, he was twenty-four years old. At Lake Charles, in 1897, he is described as 'apparently a young man.' Even today, with our longer life spans, a forty-five-year-old man is never called young except in the most relative sense; eighty years ago he would have been well into middle age."

Some researchers have speculated that the episode was not what it seemed. The airships and their mostly human-looking occupants were not American inventors who inexplicably never came forward to claim the rewards their creations would have brought them, but instead the products of an enigmatic alien intelligence, that sought to disguise itself by donning a garb that American culture of that period could accept.

That is a fantastic explanation and there is no way for us, nearly a century later, to know whether it is true or not. We can only be certain that the mysterious Mr. Wilson—and the strange airships associated with his appearance—will remain an enigma.

Teleported Through the Fourth Dimension

The strange story began routinely enough on June 3, 1968.

Dr. and Mrs. Gerardo Vidal of Maipú, Argentina, had gone to Chascomus to attend a family reunion. Another couple from Maipù, also relatives of the family, went as well.

The neighbors traveled in separate cars and later that evening, both couples set out toward home. When the Vidals did not arrive, however, their neighbors got back into their car and retraced the route, fearing an accident had occurred. They drove eighty miles back to Chascomus but saw no sign of the Vidals or their car. Back in Maipù they began calling hospitals and still no information emerged.

Forty-eight hours later Señor Rapallini, at whose home the reunion had been held, got a long-distance call from Mexico City.

The caller was Dr. Vidal, who said he and his wife were well and would be flying back to Buenos Aires. He asked his relative to pick them up at the airport.

Friends and relatives were waiting when the couple got off the plane, wearing the same clothes they had on when they left the party. Mrs. Vidal, who appeared greatly shaken, was immediately taken to a private hospital, suffering from what a press account called a "violent nervous crisis."

Dr. Vidal told an incredible story about what had happened to him and his wife in the previous two days. He said that on their drive home they had entered a bank of fog. The fog was so intense that everything went black. And then, suddenly, it was daylight.

They were on an unfamiliar road. And when the doctor got out of his car, he discovered that all the paint had been scorched off the automobile's surface.

When he flagged down a motorist to ask where they were, the man told him they were outside Mexico City. Later, when the couple went to the Argentine consulate, they learned two days had passed since they had entered the fog.

The incident caused a sensation in Argentina.

"In spite of the halo of fantasy that the story of the Vidals seems to wear," the publication *La Razón* remarked, "there are certain details that do not cease to preoccupy even the most unbelieving: The entrance of Vidal's wife into a Buenos Aires clinic; the proved arrival of the couple on an airplane that arrived nonstop from Mexico; the disappearance of the car; the intervention of the consulate; the serious attitude of the police in Maipú in regard to the event; and the telephone call from Mexico to the Rapallini family." All this makes the account one people must strive to understand.

Death of an Alien

One of the most peculiar—and tragic—close encounters ever reported occurred in May 1913, on a Farmersville, Texas, farm.

Three brothers, Silbie, Sid, and Clyde Latham, were chopping cotton when they heard their two dogs, Bob and Fox, barking, Silbie would recall, "just like they was in terrible distress." When the "deathly howl" continued, Clyde, the oldest, said "Let's go up and see what them dogs treed. Must be somethin' pretty bad."

The dogs were about fifty to seventy-five feet away on the other side of a picket fence. Clyde, the first to get there, would be the first to see what had upset the dogs. "It's a little man!" he shouted.

According to Silbie Latham, who related the story to Larry Sessions of the Fort Worth Museum of Science and History, "He looked like he was resting on something. He was looking toward the north. He was no more than eighteen inches high and kind of dark green. He didn't have on any clothes. Everything looked like a rubber suit including the hat."

Right after the brothers arrived, Silbie said, the dogs jumped the entity and tore him to bits, leaving red blood and human-looking internal organs on the grass.

"We were all just country as hell and didn't know what to do about it," Silbie Latham would say to explain why he and his brothers had done nothing to stop the slaughter. "I guess we were just too dumb."

The boys went back to their hoeing, occasionally returning to the spot to view the remains. The dogs huddled by them, as if afraid. The next day when the three returned to the site, there were no traces of any kind. All evidence of the little man was gone.

"My grandfather has a most solid reputation for truth and honesty but has never told this story outside the family for fear of ridicule," Lawrence Jones, Silbie Latham's grandson, recently told the Center for UFO Studies in Chicago. "He has agreed to tell this only after much prompting and encouragement from me, his history-oriented grandson. He would take a polygraph or be hypnotized or whatever you need. There is no question in my mind that he is telling the truth."

Gilbert Murray's Games

Gilbert Murray, an esteemed professor of Greek at Oxford University, was also a psychic and a keen student of the paranormal. Most of his experiments weren't conducted in a laboratory, but in a gamelike setting at his home. In a typical demonstration, one of his two daughters, Agnes Murray, and Mrs. Arnold Toynbee would choose a subject and sometimes communicate it to the other guests after their father had left the room. He would then return, concentrate for a moment, and reveal his impressions. Dozens of these tests were completed with outstanding success.

For example, in one session Mrs. Toynbee thought of a scene from a play by Gustav Strindberg: A gentleman sitting by a tower has fainted and his wife wishes he were dead.

When Professor Murray came back into the room, he immediately sensed the literary theme of the target. "This is a book and a book I haven't read," he began. "No, not Russian, not Italian. It's somebody lying in a faint. It's very horrible. I think somebody is fainting and his wife or some woman is hoping he is dead. It can't be Maeterlinck—I think I have read them all. Oh, it's Strindberg!"

During the course of another experiment, Mrs. Toynbee thought of two mutual friends drinking beer in a Berlin cafe. Professor Murray not only immediately felt that the target concerned a public house, but eventually named both people chosen by his daughter.

These informal but impressive experiments were conducted in the Murray household for many years, from 1910 through 1946. Some skeptics believe that Professor Murray probably had an acute sense of hearing and simply overheard his daughters talking about the targets to the other guests. But this theory can't explain Professor Murray's success when the targets were mentally created and never explained to the other spectators at all.

Exorcising
the Loch Ness Demon

The late Reverend Dr. Donald Omand, an Anglican priest and exorcist, had no doubt that the fabled monster of Loch Ness, known affectionately to some as "Nessie," existed. But he had serious reservations about the notion that it was some kind of prehistoric animal or, for that matter, any living creature at all.

Writer F. W. (Ted) Holiday, who had spent years on the shores of Loch Ness, tended to agree. In a 1973 book, *The Dragon and the Disc*, he rejected biological theories about the creature and urged investigators to consider the notion of visitors from the paranormal realm.

So when Holiday heard of Dr. Omand's belief, he wrote a letter, and in due course the two men met. One thing they talked about was the strange tale of Swedish writer Jan-Ove Sundberg, who had been at Ness on August 16, 1971. That evening Sundberg had tried to take a shortcut through the woods near the lake and somehow got lost. As he wandered through the trees, he came upon an "extremely strange machine": a 35-foot-long gray-black cigar resting on the ground about 200 or 250 feet away from where he stood.

Sundberg claimed to have seen three figures come out of the bushes each wearing a diving suit and a helmet over his head. At first Sundberg thought they were technical workers from a nearby power plant. After a while the figures entered the craft through a hatch in the top. The craft then rose forty or fifty feet into the air, then shot off.

When Sundberg returned to Sweden, he was, he said, trailed by mysterious figures in dark suits—the fabled "men in black" who are reported to intimidate some UFO witnesses—and eventually suffered a nervous collapse.

Holiday would normally have dismissed the story as "psychotic bunk" (his words), if he had not heard of other UFO sightings at the loch that same week in August 1971. But there was one problem: At the site of the incident, investigators found a forest so dense that "nowhere could a UFO bigger than a matchbox land." Sundberg's photograph had shown only trees.

Sundberg believed he had had a UFO encounter. But there also seemed no question that it had not happened as he thought it did. Had he been swept up in some kind of supernatural event?

Acting on that theory, Omand, accompanied by Holiday, went to Loch Ness to exorcise its demon on June 2, 1973. Omand performed the rite of exorcism at five locations around the lake.

"Grant that by the power entrusted to Thy unworthy servant," he prayed at each site, "this highland loch and the land adjoining it may be delivered from all evil spirits; all vain imaginations; projections and phantasms; and all deceits of the Evil One. O Lord, subject them to Thy servant's commands that, at his bidding, they will harm neither man nor beast, but depart to the place appointed them, there to remain forever."

"I am not formally religious," Holiday would write of the experience, "yet I felt a distinct tension creep into the atmosphere at this point. It was as if we had shifted some invisible levers, and were awaiting the result."

The following Monday, Omand reenacted the exorcism for a crew from the BBC. On Tuesday, Holiday set out to investigate the Sundberg UFO report. First, however, he called on Winifred Cary, a psychic who lived nearby. When he told her about Sundberg's reported encounter, she replied that she and her husband, a Royal Air Force commander, had seen UFOs in the area as well. She urged Holiday not to go to the site. "One reads of people being whisked away," she said. "It may be nonsense but I shouldn't go." Dr. Omand had told Holiday the same thing.

"At that precise moment," Holiday wrote in his book *The Goblin Universe*, "there was a tremendous rushing sound like a tornado outside the window, and the garden seemed to be filled with indefinable frantic movement. A series of violent thuds sounded as if from a heavy object striking either the wall or the sun-lounge door. Through the window behind Mrs. Cary I suddenly saw what looked like a pyramid-shaped column of blackish smoke about eight feet high revolving in a frenzy. Part of it was involved in a rosebush, which looked as if it were being ripped out of the ground. Mrs. Cary shrieked and turned her face to the window. The episode lasted ten or fifteen seconds, and then was instantly finished."

Cary also heard the sound. "I saw a beam of white light that shot across the room from the window on my left," she said. "I saw a white circle of light on Ted Holiday's forehead. I got a terrible fright."

Holiday decided not to go to the site of the Sundberg sighting. But early the next morning, as he stepped outside on a small errand, he was surprised to see an odd-looking figure standing thirty yards away. It was a man dressed entirely in black.

He recalls, "I felt a strange sensation of malevolence, cold and passionless. He was about six feet tall and appeared to be dressed in black leather or plastic. He wore a helmet and gloves and was masked, even to the nose, mouth and chin."

Holiday approached the figure and walked a few feet beyond him, then gazed at the lake for several seconds. He then turned his head in the direction of the mysterious man in black. At that moment he heard a "curious whispering or whistling sound." He turned to see nothing at all.

Holiday immediately dashed to the nearby road. "There was about half a mile of empty road visible to the right and about a hundred yards to the left," he wrote. "No living person could have gotten out of sight so quickly. Yet he had undoubtedly gone."

The next day Dr. Omand left, saying he would try to exorcise the long-lived phantom when he visited the loch again.

Holiday, meanwhile, returned to Loch Ness in 1974. A few days into his trip, he was felled by a nonfatal heart attack while on the lake shore. As a stretcher carried him up the side of the loch, it passed directly over the spot where the man in black had stood.

A second heart attack killed Ted Holiday in 1979.

Visions of Aberfan

One of the worst disasters in British history struck in Wales on October 21, 1966, when a huge stockpile of coal refuse collapsed and buried a school in the small mining town of Aberfan. More than 140 people, including 128 school children, were killed.

During the weeks that followed, it became increasingly clear that some of the children, as well as other people throughout England, had foreseen the tragedy. Thirty-five such cases, in fact, were collected by British psychiatrist J. C. Barker. One of his informants was the mother of a child killed in the slide. She told Barker that the day before the disaster, her daughter suddenly started talking about death, explaining that she wasn't afraid to die. Her mother was perplexed by the strange conversation, but didn't realize the significance of the child's subsequent remarks, which concerned an odd dream she'd just had.

"I dreamt I went to school," she told her mother, "and there was no school there. Something black had come down all over it."

Even the child failed to recognize that the dream was a warning, and skipped off to school the next day, only to be killed two hours later.

A middle-aged woman from Plymouth, England, had experienced precognitions of the tragedy, too.

"I actually 'saw' the disaster the night before it happened," she related, "and the next day I had already told my next-door neighbor about it before the news was broadcast. First, I 'saw' an old schoolhouse nestling in a valley, then a Welsh miner, then an avalanche of coal hurtling down a mountainside. At the bottom of this mountain of hurtling coal was a little boy with a long fringe looking absolutely terrified to death. Then for a while I 'saw' rescue operations taking place. I had an impression that the little boy was left behind and saved."

Of the many cases collected by Dr. Barker, the majority were symbolic dreams that tended to occur the week before the slide.

Falling Alligators

Accounts of living things falling from clear skies are as old as recorded history and have never been explained in any satisfactory way. Most reports describe falls of small animals—frogs, fish, and insects—but sometimes larger creatures come plummeting out of nowhere, too. Alligators, for instance.

On December 26, 1877, no less than *The New York Times* reported the following: "Dr. J. L. Smith of Silverton Township, South Carolina, while opening up a new turpentine farm, noticed something fall to the ground and commence to crawl toward the tent where he was sitting. On examining the object he found it to be an alligator. In the course of a few moments a second one made its appearance. This so excited the curiosity of the doctor that he looked around to see if he could discover any more, and found six others within a space of two hundred yards. The animals were all quite lively, and about twelve inches in length. The place whereon they fell is situated on high sandy ground about six miles north of the Savannah River."

A similar story emerged in 1957, courtesy of writer John Toland, who told the story of the U.S. Navy airship *Macon*. In 1934 the *Macon* had participated in maneuvers in the Caribbean and was sailing westward on its return trip. As it was entering the sky over California on the afternoon of May 17, the commander, Robert Davis, heard a loud splashing over his head from one of the ballast bags.

Concerned, he climbed into the rigging as the splashing grew louder and louder. He opened the ballast bag and looked in. Swimming around excitedly was a two-foot alligator.

No one had any idea where it came from. They had been in the air for several days and it seemed highly improbable that this big, noisy creature could have been with them all that time without making its presence known. Moreover, Davis, a restless fellow by nature, had been up and around the ship ever since their departure and he had seen nothing so out of the ordinary as an alligator.

The only possible explanation—though it made no sense at all—was that the reptile had fallen on the ballast bag from above.

Yet another tale comes from Mr. and Mrs. Trucker of Long Beach, California, who heard a loud thump in their backyard in 1960. Immediately following that, they heard a loud grunt. When the couple stepped outside, they were astonished to encounter a five-foot alligator. They could only conclude it had dropped from the sky.

The Man Who Shot a UFO Traveler

One of the strangest close encounters ever took place on a cold November night in 1961. The witnesses were four North Dakota men driving home from a hunting trip as freezing rain beat down on the windshield of their car. The heating system had nearly given out and the rain turned to ice on the windows. Three of the travelers were asleep when the only one who was awake, the driver, saw a blazing object descending out of the sky.

It came down half a mile away, on the right side of the highway. The driver, alarmed, nudged the sleeping man on the passenger side and he revived quickly enough to see the object, too. So did one of the sleepers in the backseat. All were certain they were witnessing a plane crash.

They sped to the scene, where they found a silo-shaped object sticking at about an eighty-five-degree angle from the ground and 150 yards away. Four figures stood around it. Trying to make all this out on a dark night and at some distance made for serious eyestrain, so the men in the car plugged a hand spotlight into the cigarette lighter and shined it on the craft and its occupants. At this point, as one of the hunters later told an investigator for the National Investigations Committee on Aerial Phenomena, "there was an explosion and everything went out."

The men were horrified. They thought the plane had blown up and began driving into the field. But as they approached the site, the craft was nowhere to be found.

Now they awoke the fourth man, a medic at a local Air Force base, and told him that once they found the "accident" site they would need his help. The medic urged them to go back to where they had been when they first saw the object. That way, he said, they could retrace their steps and make another guess as to where the plane had gone down.

Soon after they returned to the highway, they saw the object and its occupants again. The medic turned on the spotlight and ran it up and down the silvery, silo-shaped vehicle. Then his light hit one of the figures, a human-shaped form about 5½ feet tall and dressed in white coveralls. Strangely, he was waving his arm in a get-out-of-here gesture. If there had been a plane crash, the witnesses wondered, why was this man signaling them to leave?

The hunters drove a short distance, arguing all the while about what they should do next. Someone thought the object was an Air Force test device that they weren't supposed to see. One argued that the figure was a farmer and the "plane" was a silo. Eventually they resumed their journey home. They drove two more miles when the object returned and gently landed less than 150 yards away. Suddenly two figures were visible in front of the ship.

One of the hunters got down to a prone position with a rifle and squeezed off a shot. The closer figure was hit in the shoulder. He spun around and fell to his knees. As his companion helped him up, he hollered, "Now what the hell did you do that for?"

The four men later tried to reconstruct what happened next, and realized their memories were hazy at best. Two of them would deny that a rifle had been taken out of the car at all. The man who remembered shooting the figure said his behavior seemed irrational and bizarre. The only clear memory they had was that of arriving home just as it was becoming daylight, their worried wives sitting in wait.

The next day the medic—the man who had fired the shot—was surprised to find some strange men waiting for him at work. Addressing him by name, they said they had "received a report" about his experience the night before. They asked if he had gotten out of the car during the first part of the experience, and they also wanted to know what he had been wearing. When he answered hunting gear and boots, they asked him to take them to his home to examine the clothes.

After examining the gear, they got up to leave. The one who had done most of the talking thanked him for his cooperation, then warned, "You'd better not say anything about this to anyone from now on." The men got into their car and drove off, leaving the medic stranded. He had to call a cab to get back to the base.

"They never asked anything about the shooting and all their questions were concerned entirely with the first part of the sighting," the medic remembered. "I think they probably knew more than they said, but I don't know."

He never saw them again and to this day he has no idea who they were and exactly what they wanted from him.

The Little People of Iceland

There is hardly a place in the world where people did not at one time believe in the existence of a hidden race of little people with supernatural powers. As it happens, belief in a hidden race of little people persists even in modern Europe, especially in Iceland, a nation with an excellent educational system and a high literacy rate.

"Those who tell me these stories," says Helgi Hallgrimsson,

manager of the Museum of Natural History in Akureyri, "are honest people and many of them did not believe in such creatures until they saw them themselves."

The fairies are supposed to be protective of their territory and no end of trouble to those who try to invade it. In 1962, when the new harbor at Akureyri was being constructed, for instance, workers tried to blast some rocks with no success. No matter what they did, the equipment would not function at the critical moment. Workers were continually suffering injuries or falling suddenly ill.

Finally a young man named Olafur Baldursson stepped forward to declare that the fairies were unhappy because they lived at the site of the blasts. He offered his services as a mediator, saying that if the city authorities wanted, he would work things out with the little people. The magistrates agreed and in due course the fairies were satisfied. At least it was so assumed, because after Baldursson reported as much the work went ahead with no further problem.

This wasn't the last time the fairies apparently acted to protect their land. In 1984, when the Icelandic Road Department tried to build a new road near Akureyri, construction workers suffered strange illnesses and excavators broke down without apparent reason.

Not all Icelanders are prepared to believe in the hidden folk, of course. The Custodian of Antiquities, Thor Magnusson, dismisses the many sightings, saying, "Personally, I think that those who see fairies and little people should have their eyes examined."

But believers disagree. Helgi Hallgrimsson retorts, "There are many things in nature that science cannot yet explain."

Phantom Landscape

Is time travel possible? Incredible as it may seem, a number of seemingly sane, reputable individuals have reported traversing the years to visit centuries before.

One such case was investigated by Mary Rose Barrington of London's Society for Psychical Research. According to Barrington, the participants, who went by the names of Mr. and Mrs. George Benson, took a trip to the hills of Surrey one Sunday in July 1954. The day had begun oddly when the two woke up feeling inexplicably depressed. Neither told the other about this feeling, which seemed irrational in view of the pleasant diversion of the day.

Arriving in Surrey by bus, the couple decided to visit the Evelyn family church at Wotton. They had a long-standing interest in John Evelyn, a seventeenth-century diarist, and were curious to see which of his relatives were buried in the graveyard. The visit proved so interesting that the Bensons spent more time there than they had intended.

When they finally left the churchyard, they turned right and discovered an overgrown path with high bushes on either side. Climbing up the path, they soon came to a wide clearing with a wooden bench. An expanse of grass stretched from the left of the bench to trees about twenty-five yards away. To the right of the bench the land fell sharply down into a valley, from which they could hear the sounds of chopping wood and a dog's steady bark.

At that point Mr. Benson looked at his watch, saw it was noon, and unpacked the sandwiches the couple had brought along. Too depressed to eat, however, Mrs. Benson crumbled up the bread for the birds. Suddenly everything became silent, and no birds could be heard.

A feeling of sheer terror overcame Mrs. Benson, she reported, as she literally sensed three menacing figures in black clerical garb standing behind her. When she attempted to turn around, she couldn't.

Mr. Benson saw nothing, but he touched his wife. Her body

was so icy that it could have been a corpse. Eventually Mrs. Benson felt better and the two agreed to move on.

They walked down the hill and a short time later crossed a railway line. Then, though they had planned to take a walk, they suddenly lay down and fell asleep. Everything after that was a blur, and the next thing they knew they were in Dorking getting on the train that would take them home to Battersea.

For the next two years Mrs. Benson lived in almost constant fear. She remembered vividly the terror that had gripped her when the three oddly garbed strangers appeared. Finally, feeling that only by confronting the experience head-on could she leave it behind, she went off by herself to retrace the path she and her husband had taken that fateful day.

But as soon as she got to the church, she realized something was wrong. First of all, there was no path to the hill—because there was no hill. In fact, the area was flat. There was no abundance of overgrown bushes and there were no woods for half a mile.

She talked with a local man who said he knew the area well and knew of nothing in any way comparable to what she was describing. He also said that there was no wooden bench along any local path of which he was aware.

On her return to Battersea Mrs. Benson told her husband what she had learned. He did not believe her, but when he came to the church the following Sunday, he quickly discovered that she was speaking the truth.

Some years later Mary Rose Barrington and John Stiles of the Society for Psychical Research went to the area hoping to find the landscape the Bensons had entered. They found nothing, to Mrs. Benson's disappointment, that could provide a conventional explanation, and they concluded that some kind of extraordinary psychic experience had taken place.

Barrington read through John Evelyn's diaries hoping to find some clues. She noticed that Evelyn's description of the landscape of his youth was very similar to the one the Bensons observed. In a later entry, dated March 16, 1696, Evelyn mentioned the execution of "three unhappy wretches, whereof one a priest," who were part of a Catholic plot to assassinate King William.

Barrington theorized that in some way the Bensons had entered a "deviant reality" and that their fascination with John Evelyn had caused them in some unknown fashion to enter his world— a world that had not existed for 250 years.

UFOs Over
the White House

●─────────────────────────────────

   One criticism leveled at UFOs asks why, if they exist, haven't they landed on the White House lawn and made themselves known? Aside from the fact that their occupants might not have found a presidential administration to their liking, UFOs *have* appeared in close proximity to Pennsylvania Avenue on more than one instance.

Late on the night of July 26, 1952, for example, unidentified flying objects peppered radar screens in the nation's capital. At one point as many as twelve separate targets were picked up: four, spaced a mile and a half apart, proceeded in an orderly pace at a speed of a hundred miles per hour, while eight others moved randomly about at higher speeds. At least two military personnel and a commercial pilot bound for Washington National Airport reported visual contact with white and orange-white lights in the night sky.

On January 11, 1965, UFOs were again reported over the White House by both military and civilian personnel. Immediately prior to that, on December 29, 1964, three unknown targets had been tracked on radar at speeds established at almost five thousand miles per hour. The Air Force later discounted the incident as due to mechanical malfunction.

Eight days before, one Horace Burns said his car stalled on U.S. Highway 250 while in the presence of a large, cone-shaped UFO. Measuring 125 feet wide and 75 feet high, the UFO sat in an adjoining field for more than a minute and a half before leaving "at a square angle." Professor Ernest Gehman and two DuPont engineers subsequently examined the site for radiation and found levels much above normal.

In fact, five other sightings of UFOs over or near Washington were reported between October 1964 and January 1965 alone. On January 25, policemen in Marion, Virginia, saw a glowing, hovering object that departed in a shower of sparks. Twenty minutes later, nine people in Fredericksburg, 300 miles away, also reported a bright light trailing sparks.

Sea Serpent Sunk

May 1917 found the *Hilary*, a 6,000-ton, armed merchantman, traversing calm waters near Iceland, when the lookout spotted "something large on the surface." Fearing a sneak attack by a German submarine, Captain F. W. Dean alerted his gun crews and sailed straight for the target.

But Dean and crew encountered no enemy U-boat. What they found instead was a marine mystery. From a distance of thirty yards, the captain stared in wonder as a "head . . . about the shape but somewhat larger than that of a cow" broke surface. No visible protrusions, such as horns or ears, were evident. The head itself was described as "black, except for the front of the face, which could clearly be seen to have a strip of whitish flesh very like a cow has between its nostrils." A four-foot high "thin and flabby" dorsal fin was also visible. The entire creature was estimated to be some sixty feet long, twenty feet of which consisted of a sinewy neck.

Then in one of the more unfortunate bungles of maritime and zoological history, Dean decided his gun crews could use practice. Withdrawing to a distance of 1,200 yards he ordered them to open fire. A direct hit struck the creature. Its death throes roiling the water, the living submarine sank from view.

Two days later, on May 25, 1917, the *Hilary* itself sailed into the sights of a real U-boat. Still, she fared better than the sea serpent she had sunk: Most of her crew survived to fight again.

Vanishing Regiment

War not only tries the soul, it tries the senses as well. Who knows what can happen in the crash of conflict. Perhaps one world can open and swallow another, as seems to have happened with an entire British regiment during the Turkish campaign of World War I.

The date was August 28, 1915. The Turks occupied high ground near Sulva Bay, and the fighting between them and attacking British, New Zealand, and Australian troops was fierce, with many casualties suffered on both sides.

Weather that morning was clear and sunny, marred only by six to eight bread-loaf-shaped clouds surrounding a contested mound of earth known as Hill 60, from which the Turkish forces unleashed a withering fire. Curiously, despite a five-mile-an-hour breeze from the south, the strange clouds held their ground.

The First Fourth Norfolk regiment drew the dirty job of mounting a charge on the Turkish position. They moved forward and straight into one of the clouds straddling a dry creek, Kaiajak Dere. It took almost an hour for the file of one to four thousand men to disappear into the cloud, according to New Zealand sappers dug in 2,500 yards away.

Then the incredible happened. The low-lying cloud, described as eight hundred feet long and two hundred feet wide, rose slowly in the sky and disappeared in the direction of Bulgaria.

With the cloud went the men of the British First Fourth regiment. No earthly crosses mark their graves today. If they were annihilated in battle, then their obliteration was more abrupt and complete than any in military history. But if they were lifted in the clouds and carried away, as the New Zealand sappers said, they could well be anywhere, perhaps even in a world without war.

Doorway to the Beyond

Suspected, but never seen, black holes may be the gateway to universes beyond our own. Such sinkholes in the fabric of space were first postulated by the German astronomer Karl Schwarzschild in 1916. Schwarzschild suggested the existence of a mass so dense that nothing, not even light, would be able to escape its gravity.

Everything within the black hole's immediate vicinity is inexorably sucked toward its center, what physicists call a "singularity," the point of infinite density where the laws of space and time as we know them break down and fall apart. The point of no return for energy and objects being drawn toward the singularity is known as the "event horizon."

Although a black hole has never been directly detected, astronomers think they are formed when the matter in immense stars suddenly collapses on itself. Black holes may lie at the center of our own galaxy, at the heart of quasars (highly active, quasi-stellar energy sources) and even in some binary star systems.

Theoreticians like Cambridge mathematician Roger Penrose have formulated a potentially unique use for black holes. An astronaut, for example, might be able to plunge below the event horizon of a particularly massive, rotating black hole and emerge in another universe altogether, or reemerge in our own universe, vast distances away, at the same instant. A third alternative is that our adventurous astronaut could enter into a negative universe where nature is upside down. Gravity, for instance, might appear more like a repelling than an attracting force.

To accomplish such a feat requires the existence of the black hole's opposite, the "white hole," which spews matter and energy *out* of its singularity and beyond the event horizon.

Presently the search for both supermassive objects goes on, especially for possible black holes among the star clusters. One of the leading candidates in the search is the Star Cygnus X-1 in the constellation Cygnus. The search is of considerable import, since if our earth or solar system came too close to a large enough black hole, it could theoretically be sucked into it, totally modifying, compressing, or destroying all matter with which we are familiar and perhaps spewing it out again in a different form.

It seems incredible that the astronomy of our time, after only several hundred years of practice and research, has been able to identify the secrets—and dangers—present in the distant stars. But has our cosmic knowledge been so recent? Clay tablets kept by the Sumerian's 5,000 years old refer to a danger star, called by them the "demon bird of Nergal." Nergal was the powerful and sinister lord of the underworld. And the dangerous "demon bird," when translated and located on their star-charts, turns out to be *our* Cygnus X-1.

Pierced Brain

On September 11, 1874, Phineas P. Gage, twenty-five, was using an iron tamping rod three feet seven inches long to pack explosives in holes prior to their detonation. For some reason, one of the loads exploded prematurely, blasting the rod back in Gage's face. The thirteen-pound tamping tool, one and a quarter inches in diameter, penetrated his left cheek just above the jaw line. The force of the explosion drove the rod completely through and out his brain, dislodging a large frontal chunk of his skull in the process.

A few hours after the accident Gage was said to have asked about his work! For the next several days he spat out bits of bone and brain through his mouth. Then he fell into a delirium and eventually lost sight in his left eye. After that, Gage recovered physically, though acquaintances said he had deteriorated into an untrustworthy brute.

Gage's miraculous survival was written up at length in both the *American Journal of Medical Science* and the *British Medical Journal* of the day. His story, sad as its outcome was, causes us to ponder how much of our brain is really necessary for survival? A 1982 Swedish TV documentary on the subject showed several patients functioning normally with just a fraction of their gray matter. One subject, a young man named Roger, had only 5 percent of his brain intact yet managed to earn a degree in mathematics.

Curse of the Hope Diamond

According to legend, the fabulous jewel now known as the Hope Diamond once decorated the forehead of an Indian idol, from whence it was stolen by a Hindu priest. The poor priest, so the story goes, was captured and tortured for his troubles.

The remarkable gem, said to carry a deadly curse, first surfaced in Europe in 1642, in the possession of French trader and smuggler Jean Baptiste Tefernier. He reaped a sizable profit from its sale, but allowed his wastrel son to squander much of the money. Traveling to India to recoup his fortune, Tefernier was attacked by a pack of rabid dogs and torn to pieces.

The gem passed next to France's fabled King Louis XIV, who reduced its staggering size from 112.5 carats to 67.5. This reduction, however, did not affect the curse. After Nicholas Fouquet, a government official, borrowed the diamond for a state ball, he was convicted of embezzlement and sentenced to life in prison, where he died. Princess de Lambelle, who wore the diamond regularly, was beaten to death by a Parisian mob. The King himself died broke and scorned, his empire in ruins. Louis XVI and Queen Marie Antoinette died beneath the blade of the guillotine.

In 1830, the now historic treasure was purchased by London banker Henry Thomas Hope for $150,000. It proved a mixed blessing. Family fortunes declined rapidly, and one grandson died penniless before another heir finally sold the tainted stone. Over the next sixteen years, the Hope Diamond went from owner to owner, including Frenchman Jacques Colet, who committed suicide, and Russian Prince Ivan Kanitovitsky, a murder victim. In 1908, Turkish Sultan Abdul Hamid paid $400,000 for the Hope and promptly bestowed it on his favorite concubine, Subaya. But within a year Hamid had stabbed Subaya to death and had been dethroned himself. Simon Montharides had it next, until his carriage overturned, killing him, along with his wife and infant daughter.

Diamond and accompanying curse next made their way to American financial tycoon Ned McLean, who payed the bargain price of $154,000. Vincent, his son, soon succumbed in a car crash, and a daughter died from a drug overdose. McLean's wife became addicted to morphine, and McLean himself died in an insane asylum. Mrs. McLean passed away in 1947, leaving the hazardous heritage to six grandchildren, including then five-year-old Miss Evalyn.

Two years later, the McLean family sold the diamond to Harry Winston, a dealer in precious stones. Winston, in turn, deeded it to the Smithsonian Institution, where it now remains. Perhaps the curse can't work its misery on institutions the way it did on individuals. Or perhaps the terrible disenchantment finally died with Evalyn McLean, one of the six McLean grandchildren, found dead of unapparent cause in her Dallas apartment on December 13, 1967, at the age of twenty-five.

Sailing to Oblivion

She was a fine brig she was, firm of timber and square of sail, when first christened the *Amazon* at Spencer Island, Nova Scotia, in 1861. But there were forebodings even then when her first captain died within forty-eight hours of taking command.

A series of smaller disasters ensued. On her maiden voyage the *Amazon* struck a fishing weir, gashing her hull. A fire broke out during repairs, resulting in the firing of her second captain. Under her third master she undertook her third Atlantic crossing—and collided with another ship in the straits of Dover.

Then in 1867, the *Amazon* was wrecked in Glace Bay, Newfoundland, where she was left for the salvagers. A company of Americans eventually raised her, restored her, and sailed her south. There they registered the ship under the U.S. flag and rechristened her the *Marie Celeste.*

Captain Benjamin S. Briggs bought the *Celeste* in 1872. On November 7 of that year he set sail from New York for the Mediterranean with his wife, daughter, a crew of seven, and seventeen hundred barrels of commercial alcohol valued at $38,000.

On December 4, a British brigantine found the *Celeste* 600 miles west of Portugal. Crewmen boarded her, but found no one alive above or below decks. The cargo was in good order with one exception—a single cask of alcohol had been opened. The crew's sea chests, still packed with their belongings, including pipes and tobacco pouches, remained behind. The last entry in the log, dated November 24, gave no hint of impending disaster. The only clue was a section of railing, which lay on the deck where the lifeboat had been.

The fate of Captain Briggs, his family and crew, remains one of the more endurable of the open sea's many mysteries. What seems clear is that everyone abandoned ship in the single lifeboat in great hurry. Perhaps they feared an immediate explosion. The alcohol, loaded under cold conditions, *could* have begun giving off fumes in the heat of the tropics. Briggs, unfamiliar with his cargo, *could* have sounded the alarm to abandon ship. A wind *may* have come up and blown the *Celeste* away.

The one thing for certain is that we will never know.

Fire From Above

Furnacelike blasts of heat from the heavens have occurred on several occasions. Ask anyone near Lake Whitney, Texas, on the otherwise uneventful night of June 15, 1960.

At first, witnesses report, the sky overhead was clear, stars sparkled and temperatures hovered around seventy-five degrees Fahrenheit. Then lightning flickered on the horizon and a light breeze blew off the lake. Without warning a roaring wind tore away the roof of the Mooney Village Store, sprawling bread and canned goods in the aisles.

And with the winds came a lung-searing heat. The thermometer outside the Charley Riddle Bait and Tackle Shop shot from a midnight reading of near 70 degrees to 100 in a matter of minutes, then peaked at 140 degrees Fahrenheit.

Car radiators boiled over, sprinkler systems went off, and frightened mothers in the small town of Kopperl literally swathed their babies in wet sheets. When rancher Pete Burns turned in earlier that night, his newly plowed cotton crop had been in the best of health. The morning found it charred black. Cornfields in the same area were wilted and scorched.

Even so, the strangest storm ever to hit Texas probably would have gone unrecorded if veteran TV cameraman Floyd Bright had not photographed evidence of the destruction the following day. Weather forecaster Harold Taft of Channel Five in Forth Worth theorized that the downdraft from a roaming thunderstorm might have been responsible. "Descending air heats at the rate of five point five degrees Fahrenheit for every one thousand feet of fall," Taft said. If the downdraft began at the top of a 20,000-foot tall thunderhead, at 25 degrees temperature, it would have heated an additional 110 degrees by the time it reached ground level.

But hot air also tends to rise. Taft admitted "the downward force must have been fierce," which would help explain the eighty to one-hundred-mile-an-hour winds recorded that night.

One is still left in awe at the force and fury of the heavens, wondering if what incinerated a cotton field in central Texas might not have caused, on other nights, some of the great unexplained fires that occasionally appear around the world.

Bligh Bond's
Amazing Archaeology

The site of Glastonbury in Somerset, England, figures prominently in ancient traditions and lore. Arthurians hold that King Arthur was buried beneath the Glastonbury Abbey. Christian legend says that Saint Joseph of Arimathea brought the Holy Grail to Glastonbury and planted a thorn tree that can still be seen on the grounds. Moreover, Glastonbury is said to be the site where those in the field of "psychic archaeology" made perhaps their strongest mark.

In 1907, Glastonbury Abbey, a pile of neglected and overgrown ruins, was bought by the state and placed in the care of a Diocesan Trust anxious to excavate the site. The trust handed the work over to the Somerset Archaeological Society, which selected as its director of excavations a promising ecclesiastical architect from Bristol named Frederick Bligh Bond.

Unbeknown to the clerics and other officials involved, Bond was a member of the Society for Psychical Research, as was his friend, Captain John Bartlett. The two agreed to employ Bartlett's automatic writing ability, in which spirits supposedly communicated through the captain's pen, to excavate Glastonbury.

At 4:30 P.M., on November 7, 1907, the experiment began. "Can you tell us anything about Glastonbury?" Bond asked. Bartlett responded by tracing out plan drawings of the abbey, including measurements, followed by messages in a mixture of bad Latin and what appeared to be early English, seemingly dictated by long departed monks. Much of what he learned went against Bond's educated knowledge, but he pressed ahead.

The discoveries began pouring in, first an unsuspected chapel at the eastern end of the abbey, next an unknown doorway, then a polygonal apse and a crypt. Bond's genius was celebrated in both archaeological and ecclesiastical circles—until 1918, when he revealed in *The Gate of Remembrance* how monkish spirits had led him to his finds. The horrified authorities began a movement to strip Bond of his position, and they succeeded. They then removed or altered many of the archaeological inscriptions he had erected at the site, and even forbade the sale of his scholarly books at the abbey.

Despite Bligh Bond's record of amazing psychic discoveries at the abbey, and his personal love for the site, he was hounded from Glastonbury by narrow minds solely because he employed unconventional techniques to reveal its wonders.

Ghost of the *Great Eastern*

The *Great Eastern* was undoubtedly one of the grandest ships ever to sail the seven seas. She was also one of the most ill-starred, cursed from the start by the ghost of a worker walled up in her double hull.

Her creator, Isambard Kingdom Brunel, was already a successful bridge and railroad contractor when he conceived the idea of a floating city connecting London and the rest of the world. Naval architects had already designed and built transatlantic passenger liners that displaced nearly three thousand tons. But Brunel's *Great Eastern* dwarfed all ships that had come before. In fact, with an estimated displacement of one hundred thousand tons, it shamed anything afloat. Ten big boilers driven by 115 furnaces powered her two 58-foot paddle wheels and a backup 28-foot propeller. Five funnels shoveled her coal smoke skyward. The *Great Eastern* had enough auxiliary systems to support a small navy, including ten anchors of five tons each, six towering masts and sails, and her own gas plant for lighting.

Yet the ship proved haunted from the start. For the world's largest boat launch, Brunel invited the army of workers who had built her. One who failed to show was a quiet master shipwright who had labored on the double hull.

The christening ceremony didn't quite go according to plan as the *Great Eastern*'s bulk and weight caused the launching mechanism to jam. She probably wouldn't have been launched at all, if record high tides hadn't floated her into the Thames. But soon after that small success Brunel's Great Eastern Steam Navigation Company went broke—and Brunel himself was dead. On the day of his death, in fact, the captain complained to his chief engineer that his sleep had been "rudely disturbed by constant hammering from below."

On the heels of that ghostly incident, one of the *Great Eastern*'s stacks exploded, killing six and wrecking the grand saloon. Though her fortunes improved momentarily, on the luxury liner's fourth Atlantic crossing a vicious gale wrecked her paddle wheels and blew her lifeboats overboard. Again, even in the high winds, a phantom hammering was heard below decks.

The *Great Eastern* was able to make port, but as a passenger ship she was finished. Her last owners even had a difficult time selling her for scrap. In 1885, as she was finally being broken up, the welders made a ghastly find. Beside a carpetbag of rusting tools lay the skeleton of the missing shipwright, lodged between the iron walls of the *Great Eastern*'s double hull.

Spacebase Baalbek?

Near the devastated plains where Sodom and Gomorrah once stood lie the magnificent ruins of Baalbek, named after the god worshipped by the ancient Phoenicians. Baalbek's most prominent remnant of times past is a gigantic stone acropolis unmatched in antiquity for the massive building blocks used in its construction.

In fact, the Baalbek blocks are unmatched in modern times as well, leaving some to speculate that they may have served as a platform for visiting spaceships. What else could blocks of stone sixty-four feet long, thirteen feet high, ten feet thick, and weighing as much as 2 *million* pounds be expected to support? The huge monoliths of Baalbek were hand-quarried, laboriously transported a half mile, and then raised twenty feet off the ground to provide a virtually immovable base for—what?

A clue may be found in the biblical account of the former inhabitants of Baalbek rendered in Numbers. While wandering in the wilderness, it was written, Moses sent spies into Canaan to determine the odds of an invasion.

"We be not able to go up against the people," they reported, "for they are stronger than we. . . . The land, through which we have gone . . . is [one] that eateth up the inhabitants thereof; and all the people that we saw in it are men of a great stature. And there we saw the giants, the sons of Anak . . . and we were in our own sight as grasshoppers, and so were we in their sight."

It boggles the mind to ponder the possibilities of ancient giants working to colossal ends at which we can only guess. But the fact that the monumental stones of Baalbek rose so near to the obliterated cities of Sodom and Gomorrah may be more than just a curious coincidence.

Tektites From Above

No scientist has ever sufficiently explained the existence of tektites, strange globules of glasslike, radioactive rocks found in, among other places, Lebanon. According to a theory put forward by Dr. Ralph Stair of the U.S. National Bureau of Standards, tektites might have come from a destroyed planet, fragments of which now orbit between Mars and Jupiter as the asteroid belt.

Another even more startling proposal has been put forth by a Soviet mathematician known as Professor Agrest. Agrest reasoned that tektite composition called for high temperature as well as nuclear radiation. He knew that no nuclear devices had *recently* been exploded in Lebanon, but what about during Biblical times? There was, after all, *this* curious account of the destruction of Sodom and Gomorrah recorded in the *Dead Sea Scrolls*:

"A column of smoke and dust rose into the air like a column of smoke issuing from the bowels of the Earth. It rained sulphur and fire on Sodom and Gomorrah, and destroyed the town and the whole plain and all the inhabitants and every growing plant. And Lot's wife looked back and was turned into a pillar of salt."

The column of smoke and soot sounds suspiciously like an atomic mushroom cloud, Agrest says. But who in Biblical times could possibly have possessed nuclear weapons? For Agrest there was only one inescapable conclusion: Weapons capable of wreaking such havoc could only have come from above. Perhaps we have been visited by extraterrestrials in the remote past, he suggests, though we will never know for sure until the violent secrets of tektite structure have been revealed.

The Ship With a Mind of Its Own

Even while she was under construction, the Nazi dreadnought *Scharnhorst* had a mind of her own. When she was only half-built, she suddenly groaned and rolled over, crushing 60 men to death and seriously injuring 110 more.

On the night before her scheduled launching, the *Scharnhorst* broke from her bounds and ground up a pair of huge barges as she proceeded, unmanned, from the docks into the water. Then, in one of her first engagements, a turret exploded, killing twelve.

Near war's end the battle cruiser was dispatched to destroy British convoys off the northern tip of Norway. One British commander, sensing a Nazi ship nearby, ordered a salvo fired at random. The *Scharnhorst* sailed squarely into it, and was subsequently ripped apart by explosions. She rolled over and plunged to the bottom of the sea, about sixty miles off the coast of Norway.

Most of her crewmen died immediately, but a few survivors were picked up by the British. Two others managed to reach a tiny island on a life raft. Their bodies were only found years later, when the war was just a cruel memory. Apparently their emergency oil stove had exploded, killing them instantly.

The curse of the deadly *Scharnhorst* had reached out again.

Trans en Provence Case

These days, France is the only country with a government-sponsored UFO agency. GEPAN, the unidentified aerial phenomena research group, is a separate department within the French national space agency. All UFO reports originating in France go directly to GEPAN, which then determines the merits of the case.

Because of the transient nature of UFO phenomena, GEPAN has come up with few extraordinary or even conclusive results. But one French case stands out. On January 8, 1981, at about 5 P.M., a Monsieur Renato Nicolai, age fifty-five, was working in his garden in Trans en Provence when he heard a whistling noise. He turned around, he claimed, to see a spacecraft descending toward the ground.

Nicolai said the craft "was in the form of two saucers upside down, one against the other. It must have been just about 1.5 meters high and the color of lead." According to Nicolai, the craft remained on the ground for about a minute. Then, he said, "it took off rapidly in the direction of the forest, which is to say toward the northeast."

GEPAN investigators took soil and plant samples at the landing site the following day, and again three days later. The agency also collected samples thirty-nine days after the incident, and once more two years later.

According to GEPAN, physical traces of a landing were found. The soil, the agency says, included small quantities of phosphate and zinc, and seemed to have been heated to a temperature between three and six hundred degrees Centigrade. But perhaps the most important finding was a subsequent 30- to 50-percent decrease in the amount of chlorophyll and carotenoid pigments produced by plants in the immediate vicinity of the landed craft. Moreover, according to GEPAN, "there was a significant correlation between the disturbances observed and the distance from the center of the phenomenon." The trauma, GEPAN noted, *might* have been induced by an electromagnetic field.

Although hesitant to conclude that an actual extraterrestrial spaceship had touched down in Nicolai's garden, French scientist Alain Esterle, former head of GEPAN, concluded that "for the first time we have found a combination of factors suggesting that something similar to what the eyewitness has described actually did take place."

No Hand at the Helm

Ships sometimes do the strangest things, even without a human hand at the helm. In 1884, while on the return run to Rouen from Spain, for instance, the French boat *Frigorifique* collided in dense fog with another steamer, the British-registered *Rumney*. When the *Frigorifique*'s sides split open, the French captain gave the order to abandon ship. Fortunately, the crew and passengers were picked up by the *Rumney*, whose captain called for a course that steered her away from the sinking *Frigorifique*.

The soaking French sailors and their rescuers were celebrating their success when the watch again cried out. Looming momentarily out of the fog was the ghost of the *Frigorifique*, which just as quickly vanished from view. The two crews heaved a sigh of relief.

But the damaged *Frigorifique* hove into sight once more. This time she rammed the *Rumney*, forcing both crews to lower their lifeboats. As they pulled away from the fatally stricken ship, the survivors spied the supposedly doomed *Frigorifique* through the thick mists. Her screw was still turning as one of her funnels belched thick black smoke.

Rendlesham Forest Encounter

The pine trees of Rendlesham Forest in Suffolk, England, separate a Royal Air Force Base at Bentwaters from its American counterpart at Woodbridge, two miles distant. In the early morning hours of December 27, 1980, according to U.S. deputy base commander Lieutenant Colonel Charles I. Halt, Woodbridge security patrolmen spied unusual lights outside the base's back gate.

Thinking that an aircraft might have gone down in the forest, they asked permission to investigate. Three patrolmen soon reported a strange glowing object in the forest. They claimed it was metallic in appearance and triangular in shape, approximately two to three meters across the base and two meters high. It illuminated the entire forest with a white light.

"The object itself had a pulsing red light on top and a bank of blue lights underneath," Halt reported in his signed statement. It was either hovering or on legs. As the security force approached the object, it maneuvered through the trees and disappeared. At this time the animals on a nearby farm went into a frenzy. The object was briefly sighted approximately an hour later near the back gate.

"The next day," Halt continued, "three depressions one and a half inches deep and seven inches in diameter were found where the object had been sighted on the ground. The following night the area was checked for radiation. Beta/gamma readings of 0.1 milliroentgens were recorded, with peak readings in the three depressions.

"Later in the night a red sunlike light was seen through the trees," Halt's bizarre statement read. "It moved about and pulsed. At one point it appeared to throw off glowing particles and then broke into five separate white objects and then disappeared. Immediately thereafter, three starlike objects were noticed in the sky, two objects to the north and one to the south, all of which were about ten degrees off the horizon. The objects moved rapidly in sharp, angular movements and displayed red, green, and blue lights."

When queried about the Rendlesham Forest incident, the British Ministry of Defense denied any knowledge. Later, a copy of Halt's signed statement was acquired in the United States through the Freedom of Information Act. A voice recording made by Halt was also obtained.

Authorities from both governments have subsequently declined to comment further, except to say that their "defense security was never in danger." Skeptics have claimed that the whole incident was caused by the revolving beam of a nearby lighthouse!

1897 Airship Flap

Human conquest of the skies supposedly began on a December's day in 1903, when two bicycle mechanics, the brothers Orville and Wilbur Wright, first flew their flimsy biplane a few scant yards above the sand dunes at Kitty Hawk. But seven years before that brief but monumental flight, in November 1896, *some-*

thing apparently manmade was seen in the skies over San Francisco. By April of the following year, when reports peaked, the Great Airship of 1897 had been sighted on both coasts and throughout the heartland of the nation, from Chicago to Texas.

Hardly a community was spared. Yet the ubiquitous 1897 airship has never been satisfactorily explained. Historians of "official" aviation dismiss it as beneath contempt. But the moldering pages of the newspapers of the day headlined the mystery airship in terms surprisingly reminiscent of latter-day UFOs. Even folklorists and sociologists are hard pressed to explain the prevalence of the reports.

Typically, the sightings fell into two categories: Some people described only nocturnal lights and beams of bright illumination. Others reported a magnificent flying machine crewed by an odd assortment of individuals. The ship was often reported stranded in the countryside, usually in need of simple repairs, before continuing on its way.

There was so much speculation about the airship's origins that famous inventors like Thomas Alva Edison regularly called press conferences to deny the contrivance was theirs. Other, less honorable, inventors did claim the airship as their own, though they were never able to produce a working model on demand. By the fall of 1897, however, airship reports dropped off dramatically and by the turn of the century they were virtually gone.

Nevertheless, students of anomalous phenomena continue to debate the significance of the Great Airship to this day. Charles Fort, America's greatest cataloguer of the odd and unusual, suggested that the flying machine was simply an idea whose time had come. Others believe that the Great Airship of 1897 somehow spurred the subsequent advances in aviation technology. The Wright brothers may not have been innocent innovators, these pundits argue, but rather the unwitting tools of an unconscious evolutionary urge. This outward impulse, some even suggest, is mirrored in the prevalence of today's UFO reports.

Scandinavian Ghost Rockets

In the aftermath of World War II, before the modern era of ufology had really begun, people from Norway to Finland were terrified by ghostly, rocketlike objects in the sky.

The first sightings, made over northern Finland near the Arctic Circle on February 26, 1946, were initially described as meteors. However, it soon became apparent that meteor activity could hardly account for the hundreds of hurtling daylight objects that were variously compared to a football, cigar, bullet, or silver torpedo.

Such silhouettes, in fact, seemed more in keeping with the Nazi V-1 and V-2 rockets that rained death and destruction on London and other wartime targets. But the German guided-missile bases on the European mainland had either been captured or bombed into submission. Besides, their maximum range was barely a fourth of that required to reach northern Finland, Norway and Sweden, where the ghost rocket reports proliferated. Even if the Soviets had captured a contingent of working V-2s, as the Swedes and others feared, why would they waste them over the Scandinavian countries for no apparent purpose?

What is known is that the Scandinavians themselves took the ghost rockets seriously. Proscriptions against publishing such reports in public, so as not to aid "the power making the experiments," were first taken by Sweden on July 17, 1946. Norway followed suit two days later, and Denmark enacted similar strictures on August 16. The Swedish news blackout came in the wake of a single 24-hour period, during which 250 individuals across the country reported a streaking, silvery, teardrop-shaped object high in the heavens. The following day, the Defense Staff named a committee of both civilian and military specialists to look into the matter. Altogether, more than a thousand reports were collected.

Meanwhile, the ghost rockets had attracted international attention. On August 20, 1946, an RCA vice-president and former general, David Sarnoff, landed at Stockholm's Bromma Airport. He was joined the same day by Douglas Rader, a former colonel in the RAF, and American war hero James Doolittle. On August 21, the distinguished trio met with Sweden's top Air Force brass.

What transpired remains shrouded in secrecy. Doolittle, who served on several U.S. intelligence operations after the war, declined to publicly discuss the Swedish mission. Sarnoff supposedly reported directly to President Truman on his return to the United States. He also told a group of electronic experts he thought the ghost rockets were real and not imaginary.

History has tended to ignore the significance of the Scandinavian mystery missiles because they were never as widely publicized as the flying saucers that followed in their wake. Many curious questions remain. Were the rockets part of a ghostly phenomenon that somehow assumes different shapes in response to the anxieties and preoccupations of a particular culture? Or did the Soviets, or some other power, unbeknown to the world at large, vastly improve the range and performance of Nazi Germany's most advanced weapons? And if that's the case, could the same phantom perpetrators be responsible for today's UFOs?

Wilhelm Reich: UFO Buster

The career of pioneer Freudian analyst Wilhelm Reich was so scarred with controversy that his most controversial work, his battle against invading UFOs, was hardly noticed at all.

Born in Austria in 1897, Reich quickly displayed a temperamental genius for human psychology, becoming a Freudian convert while still at the university. In fact, he might have succeeded the master psychoanalyst had he not out-Freuded

Freud, so to speak, with his insistence that free-flowing libido energy, otherwise known as the uninhibited orgasm, was an unmistakable sign of physical and mental health. That philosophy promptly got its author thrown out of the International Psychoanalytic Association as well as the fledgling Communist Party.

Reich retreated to Scandinavia, where he claimed to have discovered the "bion," a microscopic blue cell that was the basic building unit of all living matter, and "orgone," the organizing energy of life itself. Subsequently hounded out of Scandinavia, Reich eventually settled at an estate in Maine that he called Orgonon in honor of his discovery. From here he waged war on UFOs with his "cloudbuster," a device designed to drain negative orgone energy from clouds.

Reich became convinced that UFOs were interplanetary life forms spying on his work, and also that they were accumulators of what he called "deadly orgone" that caused desertification of the planet. He wondered what would happen if he trained the hollow tubes of his cloudbuster on the UFOs. The answer came on the evening of October 10, 1954, as a series of red and yellow UFOs (beneficial ones, according to Reich, would have been blue) converged over Orgonon. Reich declared that aiming the cloudbuster at the lights caused them to dim in intensity and take evasive action.

Writing in his log book of the experiment, witnessed by several co-workers, Reich noted that, "Tonight for the first time in the history of man, the war waged from outer space upon this earth . . . was reciprocated . . . with positive results."

But Reich would not live to see the war won. He died in November 1957, while confined to a federal penitentiary for having refused to stop selling "orgone boxes," which he claimed could cure cancer.

King of the World

According to the beliefs of many Mongolians and Tibetans (and attested to by numerous Buddhist monks who claim to have visited it), a vast underground country called Arghati lies beneath the high plateau of Central Asia. From within the tunnels of Arghati, the prophecy goes, will one day emerge the mystical King of the World and his subjects.

Before the king comes forth, sometime around the close of the present millennium, the Buddhist teaching says, "men will increasingly neglect their souls. The greatest corruption will reign on earth. Men will become like bloodthirsty animals, thirsting for the blood of their brothers. . . . The crowns of kings will fall. . . . There will be a terrible war between all the earth's peoples . . . entire nations will die . . . hunger . . . crimes unknown to law . . . formerly unthinkable to the world will be committed."

During this period of lawlessness, the prophecy continues, families will be dispersed and multitudes will flood the escape routes as the world's "greatest and most beautiful cities . . . perish by fire.

"Within fifty years there will be only three great nations . . . and, within the next fifty years there will be eighteen years of war and cataclysms. . . . then the people of Agharti will leave their subterranean caverns and will appear on the surface of the earth."

The Men in Black

Perhaps the strangest wrinkle in the already perplexing UFO phenomenon are the semidemonic figures known as MIB, or Men in Black. The first MIB report in modern ufology came from Albert K. Bender, a teenage UFO buff who directed the International Flying Saucer Bureau and published the bureau's news bulletin, *Space Review*. In September 1953, Bender claimed, he was approached by three men clad in black suits, who told him he must abandon his UFO research if he wanted to stay safe. Bender did indeed abandon his career in ufology, but the MIB phenomenon went on. UFO investigator and author John Keel, for instance, has talked to numerous eyewitnesses who claimed to have been confronted by similar MIB entities.

Some unusual aspects of the MIB phenomenon emerged when the reports were studied by folklorist Peter Rojcewicz. For instance, Rojcewicz notes, MIB "often dress in black clothing that may appear soiled and generally unkempt or unrealistically neat and wrinkle-free. On occasion they display a very unusual walking motion, moving about as if their hips were on swivel joints, their torso and legs at odds with one another. Some display a penchant for black Cadillacs or other large, dark sedans. Some MIB show an unusual growth of hair, suggesting that their hair had grown back unevenly after having recently been shaved." Nearly all races and complexions, he says, have been reported, with Asian features predominating.

The motives of MIB remain murky, though they are frequently bent on retrieving UFO data and warning witnesses away from any further involvement with the subject. "They may show up at the home or workplace," says Rojcewicz, "demanding photographs or negatives of UFOs *before* the witness has even let it be known publicly that he possesses any." On several such occasions, the MIB posed as military intelligence officers.

Where MIB come from and where they disappear to after their mischief is accomplished is an enigma. What is known, however, is that their presence further clouds the waters already made murky by the UFO.

Mokele-Mbembe

●

Most scientists maintain that dinosaurs have been extinct for millions of years. But people in the Cameroons, along the western curve of Africa, continue to report a huge, four-footed creature that bears every resemblance to the brontosaurus itself. In fact, when shown a drawing of a brontosauruslike dinosaur and asked to name it, the local inhabitants inevitably refer to it as *mokele-mbembe*.

The earliest authenticated accounts of mokele-mbembe were collected by Captain Freiherr von Stein zu Lausnitz in 1913. According to his report, the elephant-sized animal was brownish-gray in color, with smooth skin and a long, flexible neck. This unusual behemoth was said to live in underwater caves washed out by the river, and that any canoe that dared approach was doomed. On at least one occasion, however, a band of pygmies allegedly killed one of the creatures and feasted on its carcass. Those who actually ate the flesh were said to have sickened and died.

In recent years, Westerners such as University of Chicago biologist Roy Mackal have mounted four expeditions to the relatively isolated lakes and rivers of the Cameroons in search of the elusive beast. Although no specimen has been captured, unidentified animals resembling the native accounts have been seen, photographed, and even recorded on videotape.

Unfortunately, the local political situation and turgid terrain is hardly conducive to "drop in" explorations. Most Western observers agree that if a dinosaur *wanted* to hide out, it could hardly have chosen a better locale. But perhaps one day soon even these impediments will be overcome and the world will learn whether it harbors a surviving remnant of its fantastically remote past.

Miracle Man Sai Baba

The modern tendency, hardly well-founded, is to dismiss religious miracles as a thing of the past. That way they can be safely disregarded as the product of a more gullible age.

But disciples of numerous religious leaders continue to bear witness to a panoply of paranormal events that hark back to the prophets and messiahs of other ages. Most accomplished of these contemporary divines is India's Sai Baba, a yogi who claims to be a reincarnation of his namesake, Sai Baba of Shirdi, who died in 1918, eight years before his own birth in provincial Puttaparti.

The second Sai Baba had a relatively normal life until the age of fourteen, when he suffered a debilitating seizure, during which he periodically broke into song and recited poetic passages of Vedantic philosophy. Emerging from the trancelike illness, he suddenly announced to his surprised parents that he was an avatar, or divine reincarnation, of the celebrated holy man who had died almost a decade before his own birth.

Other yogis from the mysterious East have claimed to have mastered a psychic trick or two in the course of their public careers. Sai Baba, by contrast, demonstrates miracles in a businesslike way as most of us would balance a checkbook or write a letter.

Among the feats of faith Sai Baba is alleged to have accomplished are teleportation, levitation, psychokinesis, and the manifestation of material objects—he seems to have a distinct preference for rose petals—out of thin air. He has also supposedly resurrected the dead and multiplied a store of food a hundred times.

Fish Falls

Back in the 1800s, the French Academy of Sciences declared that meteors do not exist. The peasants who claimed they saw stones falling from the sky, said the experts, were simply imagining the whole thing. Cuvier, the French scientist who was the founder of comparative anatomy and vertebrate paleontology, categorically stated that stones "cannot fall from the sky because there *are* no stones in the sky."

Science responds in similar fashion today to widespread reports of falling fish. Since there aren't fish overhead, runs the orthodox objection, how can they possibly come splashing down? If such stories are true, the fish must have been plucked out of water by a whirlwind, transported distances great and small, and then deposited in someone's backyard.

The fish, nevertheless, do fall. The city of Singapore, for instance, was rocked by an earthquake on February 16, 1861, and for the following six days rain poured in buckets. After the sun came out on the twenty-second, French naturalist Francois de Castlenau looked out his window to see "a large number of Malays and Chinese filling baskets with fishes which they picked up in the pools of water that covered the ground." When asked where the fish had come from, they simply pointed overhead. The fall, involving a species of local catfish, covered an area of fifty acres.

Almost a century later, on October 23, 1947, marine biologist D. A. Bajkov was eating breakfast with his wife at a Marksville, Louisiana, cafe when it started to rain. Before long fish filled the streets outside. Bajkov identified them as "sunfish, goggle-eyed minnows, and black bass up to nine inches long." They were also found on rooftops, stone cold dead, but still fit to eat.

Nor are fish the only animate matter to have fallen from the sky. Those chronicling this sort of anomaly have also reported deluges of birds, toads, yellow mice, snakes, blood, and even chunks of raw meat, suggesting that the heavens may harbor more varieties of food than the manna that reportedly fell down on the Israelites.

How Long Did Dinosaurs Survive?

According to prevailing scientific opinion, dinosaurs died out 65 million years ago, never to be seen again. But comparatively modern artifacts from five widely separated sites all bear eerie likenesses of animals that can only be described as dinosaurlike. Are they hoaxes or racial memories of living creatures, perhaps buried in the collective subconscious of ancient artisans? Or did the dinosaurs themselves survive significantly longer than once thought?

The first indication that dinosaurs may have been a relatively recent phenomenon emerged in 1920, when ranch hands digging on the property of William M. Chalmers near Granby, Colorado, discovered a granite statuette weighing sixty-six pounds and standing fourteen inches high. The stone, found at a depth of six feet, portrays a stylized human with what purports to be a Chinese inscription dating to approximately 1000 B.C. More intriguing are two inscribed animals on the sides and back that appear to be a brontosaurus and a mammoth. Although clear pictures were made of the object from several angles, the Granby Stone itself has long since vanished. Even the site where it was found has disappeared, submerged by the waters of the Granby reservoir.

An unusual piece of evidence came to light in 1925, when University of Arizona archaeologists working in a lime kiln outside of Tucson unearthed a short, heavy broadsword inscribed with a brontosaurus. Other artifacts found at the site bore both Hebrew lettering and a form of Latin used between A.D. 560 and 900. Even though many of the Tucson artifacts were unearthed by professionals, controversy continues to rage over their authenticity. Common sense, however, suggests that the last thing any hoaxter hoping to be taken seriously would inscribe on a sword blade would be an extinct dinosaur.

Another curious collection of indeterminate artifacts can be found in the church of María Auxiliadora in Cuenca, Ecuador, under the protection of Father Carlo Crespi. The pieces, mostly plaques, number in the hundreds and have been brought in by the Jivaro Indians from outlying jungle caves. Some have been fashioned from gold; others are obviously modern fakes, made out of olive oil cans. A bewildering variety of forms and styles are present, including dinosaur portraits and motifs that appear to be Assyrian and Egyptian in origin. Ancient Phoenician, Libyan, and Celt-Iberian inscriptions have also been identified.

While mastodons are not to be included in the dinosaur era, they are generally supposed to have become extinct before man developed any recognizable civilization. But an interesting find of a mastodon's skeleton was made in Blue Lick Springs in Kentucky at a dig that had reached twelve feet below the surface, and as the excavating team dug deeper, looking for more bones, they came across a set-stone pavement, three feet *under* where they had found the mastodon.

Finally, an Ica, Peru, museum owned by Dr. Javier Cabrera presently houses almost twenty thousand riverbed stones, all intricately inscribed with curlicued pictographs portraying several dinosaur species and other long extinct animals. Again, the brontosaurus seems to be an artistic favorite. The Ica stones, moreover, are characterized by an artistry casual hoaxters would find hard, if not impossible, to emulate. Precise anatomical details abound. And the sheer numbers raise the question of why anyone would go to such trouble for little or no reward. More importantly, similar stones have been dug out of pre-Columbian graves nearby.

The Levelland Egg

A series of sightings reported in the small Texas Panhandle town of Levelland on the night of November 2, 1957, qualify as one of the strongest cases in UFO annals.

First to call in was a "terrified" farmhand named Pedro Saucedo. Saucedo and a friend had been driving on Route 116, four miles west of Levelland, at about 10:30 P.M. when "lightning" flashed off to one side. "We didn't think much about it," Saucedo said later, "but then it rose up out of the field and started toward us, picking up speed. When it got nearer, the lights of my truck went out and the motor died. I jumped out and hit the deck as the thing passed directly over the truck with a great sound and a rush of wind. It sounded like thunder, and my truck rocked from the blast. I felt a lot of heat."

What Saucedo called "it" was a torpedo-shaped object approximately two hundred feet long. Patrolman A. J. Fowler, who handled his call, thought Saucedo was drunk and dismissed it. But less than an hour later, "it" was back. This time the caller was Jim Wheeler. He, too, had been on Route 116 when he came upon a two-hundred-foot, egg-shaped UFO blocking the highway. As Wheeler approached the object, his headlights and engine died.

Before morning's end, five other motorists in the immediate vicinity of Levelland would report a similar experience: a large glowing egglike object straddling the highway or squatting nearby, and a failure of their vehicle's electrical system, which returned to normal when the UFO departed.

The most amazing thing about the legendary Levelland sightings, however, is the fact that the Air Force's Project Blue Book, following a cursory examination, "solved" them by attributing the phenomenon to ball lightning!

Nina Kulagina and Psychokinesis

Nina Kulagina is proably the leading psychic in the U.S.S.R. She is best known for her psychokinetic skills, which she reportedly uses to move objects mentally from one spot to the next. Indeed, films smuggled out to the West show the famous psychic using hand or eye motions to deflect a variety of things: Matchsticks, compasses, small boxes, cigarettes, and plexiglass tubes were all grist for her psychic mill.

The best of these films was taken by Zdenek Rejdak, a Prague Military Institute researcher who visited the U.S.S.R. in 1968 specifically to study Kulagina and test her PK. "After we sat down around the table," Rejdak explains, "I required Mrs. Kulagina to leave the position at which she had decided to sit, and to sit at the opposite side of the table. The first test was to endeavor to turn a compass needle first to the right and then to the left. Mrs. Kulagina held her hands approximately five to ten centimeters over the compass, and after an interval of concentration, the compass-needle turned more than ten times. Thereafter, the entire compass turned on the table, then a matchbox, some separate matches, and a group of about twenty matches at once."

When the display was over, Dr. Rejdak placed a gold ring on the table and, he said, Kulagina had little difficulty moving it as well. Finally the Czech scientist said, he watched her use PK to move some glassware and some plates.

Despite the seemingly effortless nature of these powers, Rejdak reported that Kulagina's PK seemed guided by several standard principles. For instance, it was easier for her to move cylindrical objects and more difficult to move angular ones. Objects with which she was unfamiliar tended to move *away* from her. And when she exerted herself to make objects move, they tended to move in exact coincidence with her body, sometimes continuing to move even when she had stopped.

Beginning in the late 1960s, a few Western researchers visited the Soviet Union to study Kulagina for themselves. Dr. J.C. Pratt and Champe Ransom from the University of Virginia were the first, and their observations corroborated Rejdak's. In his book, *ESP Research Today*, for instance, the late Dr. Pratt recounted how he watched Kulagina "practice" her PK from his position behind a slightly opened door.

"I could see Kulagina through the open door," he recalled. "She was sitting on the far side of a small round table facing me and the matchbox and compass were lying in front of her on the table. After a time I noticed that while she held her hands stretched out toward the matchbox, it moved several inches across the table in her direction. She put the box back near the center of the table and it moved again in the same way."

Because of the publicity Soviet parapsychology received in the late 1960s, Kulagina was soon placed off-limits to Western researchers, but this dictum was relaxed around 1972. Today, Kulagina still gives occasional demonstrations to foreign parapsychologists, and her name was mentioned in many a Western newspaper when she was called in to help doctors deal with Khrushchev's ailing health.

The Highway of Remembrance

Déjà vu translates literally from the French as "already seen." It manifests itself in the form of an intense feeling of familiarity with a situation or place, even though the person has never experienced it before. Many experts say such incidents could be caused by small seizures in the brain, but some cases stretch beyond psychology, suggesting that the paranormal is at work.

A fascinating case reported by parapsychologist D. Scott Rogo serves as a case in point. In 1985, a New Jersey woman wrote to tell him about a trip she had taken along the New Jersey Turnpike. The landscape was strangely familiar, and the woman finally turned to her traveling companion and said, "You know, I have never been here before, but I believe about a mile or so down the road is a house I used to live in.

"Approximately three miles or so passed," the woman related "and I told my friend that around the bend we would come to a small town set very close to the turnpike. I told her that the houses would be white-frame, two-story homes, rather close together. I felt I had lived there when I was six years old or so, and that I used to sit with my granny on the front porch. The memories overwhelmed me, and I could remember sitting on the swing on the front porch as my grandmother buttoned up my high-topped shoes."

When the woman got to town, she recognized the house immediately, even though the front porch swing was gone. She also recalled walking two blocks down the street to a drugstore with a high marble counter, white, and ordering lemonade. Driving down the street, the women found the building, boarded up and run-down, but still there.

As the two friends continued driving out of town, the woman had her next experience of déjà-vu. "In about three blocks there will be a small hill, rolling, and a cemetery is *there*, and that is where they buried me." The cemetery *was* there, but the woman's friend, by now totally panicked, refused to stop and search for the grave.

Suicide Hotel

Can a person "tune in" to past events? Yes, according to psychic Joan Grant, who was convinced by an experience she had in 1929.

Vacationing with her husband on the Continent, Grant had spent the night in a Brussels hotel room. For some inexplicable reason, the room made her uneasy, but since no other accommodations were available, she remained. Her husband thought her fears were nonsensical and soon left to do some errands.

Grant finally decided that taking a hot bath would calm her nerves, but when that didn't help, she read and then went to bed. That's when the shock came. For while lying on the bed, she experienced a frightful vision: A young man seemed to run from the bathroom and hurl himself out the window. She expected to hear the thud of this body striking the ground, but it never came. The perplexed psychic tried to pray, but later on she experienced the vision again.

It was then that Grant concluded her uncomfortable feelings about the room stemmed from an event in the past. A suicide victim, she reasoned, had once rented the room, and was now communicating his discomfort to her. She also decided she could free the suicide's spirit, or whatever was haunting the room, by merging with it. Her greatest fear, however, was that she would merge with the suicide too completely and would plunge out the window herself.

Taking a chance, she went to the window and said, "Your fear has entered into me and you are free." She repeated this message several times before she felt the room suddenly become clear.

When her husband returned later that evening, Grant was annoyed. "You monster," she said. "Going off like that and deliberately leaving your wife to deal with a suicide. No thanks to you that I didn't fall out the window and break my neck."

"What's the matter?" he replied. "What happened?"

"This room's been haunted," Mrs. Grant informed him. "I told you something was wrong with it. A fellow kept running out of the bathroom and jumping out the window. I had to shift level and release him and I practically went over the edge myself."

The next day, Mr. Grant checked out the story with the hotel manager. It turned out that a suicide *had* actually occurred in the room only five days earlier, when the occupant jumped from the window.

Death Flight at Godman

Captain Thomas Mantell, a highly experienced Air Force pilot, died in a controversial plane crash on January 7, 1948. According to the official report, the plane continued upward until a loss of power caused it to level out, then dip to one side and dive in a fatal spiral. Mantell himself, officials said, lost consciousness due to oxygen starvation and never revived.

In truth, Mantell's death flight began when the tower at Godman Field in Kentucky sighted a large, bright, disc-shaped object in the sky. The tower crew decided the object was not a weather balloon and, unable to identify it, finally sent Flight Commander Mantell, along with a group of planes, to see what was going on. Mantell climbed to 15,000 feet, at which point the other planes turned back because a higher altitude required different oxygen equipment. But Mantell went on. Finally he issued his last known radio contact: "It looks metallic and it's tremendous in size. It's above me and I'm gaining on it." Sections of Mantell's plane were later recovered permeated with hundreds of small holes.

Despite these facts, Air Force officials denied the possibility of a UFO, and later determined that Mantell saw either the planet Venus or one of a series of large Navy weather balloons supposedly in the vicinity at that time.

Ufologists, however, were quick to respond: The sun would have been too bright to allow people standing on the ground to see Venus that clearly. Indeed, the sightings were simply too widespread for all to have seen Venus, or even Venus and a balloon.

Air Force officials finally countered that witnesses saw Venus and *two* balloons, seemingly attached together to form one massive UFO. But they could never explain the rumors surrounding Mantell's body: It was apparently removed by the police and immediately enclosed in a coffin, convincing some investigators that Mantell had been covered with strange wounds or that no body was ever found at all.

Tears of Joy

Newspapers frequently report on cases of paintings or statues that show either tears or blood flowing. These cases usually come from members of the Roman Catholic faith, where belief in the miraculous abounds. Sometimes, however, such reports come from Protestant sources as well.

Just such a case was reported by the Reverend William Rauscher, rector of Christ Episcopal Church in Woodbury, New Jersey, who was attending seminary school in 1975. Rauscher was visiting the room of his friend, Bob Lewis, when the conversation turned to Bob's grandmother. The first to introduce young Lewis to the joys of religion, she had cried for joy when she learned he was embarking on a religious career. But she died before seeing her grandson graduate from the seminary.

While relating this tale, Lewis noticed that a picture of the elderly woman, kept on his dresser, was crying. "The photograph of Bob's grandmother was soaking wet, dripping, with a small pool of water spreading onto the dresser from it," Rauscher explains. "Examining the picture, we found that it was wet *inside* the glass. That was genuinely puzzling. The back of the picture, made of dyed imitation velvet, had streaked and faded.

"Removed from its frame, the photograph didn't dry quickly. And when it did, the area around the face remained puffed, as though the water had originated there and run downward, from the eyes."

In short, Rauscher could never find a normal explanation for the incident. And as for Bob Lewis, he graduated from the seminary content in knowing that his beloved grandmother had again wept for joy.

The Ganzfield Effect

Some experts believe that everyone is psychic. The problem, they point out, is tapping this sixth sense in the secret vaults of the mind.

One of the most successful procedures to help people learn to use ESP is the Ganzfield technique, in which the volunteer subject is seated in a sealed, soundproof booth and told to relax while halved Ping-Pong balls are taped over his eyes. Since the translucent spheres diffuse the light, the subject sees nothing but an undifferentiated red visual field. Headphones placed over his ears emit a gentle hissing sound, and the subject is now cut off from most sources of sensory input.

Now the experimenter, sitting in a separate room, looks at randomly selected pictures and tries to send them to the subject via ESP. When the experiment is over thirty-five minutes or so later, the subject is then asked to separate copies of the target pictures from several dummies.

In Ganzfield's experiments, first reported by Charles Honorton of the Maimonides Medical Center's division of parapsychology and psychophysics in 1973, close to half the subjects chose the correct target. When the target theme for one session was "Birds of the World," for instance, the subject reported "a large hawk's head" and "the sense of sleek feathers."

You can't get much more telepathic than that.

Since the Maimonides workers first reported their success, the Ganzfield Effect has been replicated by several other parapsychology laboratories. It remains one of the field's most reliable tools for ESP testing to this day.

The Strange Visit of Mary Roff

In the long-debated issue of reincarnation, one of the earliest cases on record is also the most startling. It is the story of Mary Lurancy Vennum, who as a thirteen-year-old in 1877 suffered some epileptic fits with strange results.

The first evidence of Vennum's reincarnation emerged following a seizure that rendered her unconscious for five days. When she woke up, she told her parents she had visited heaven and talked to a brother and sister who had died. Mary Vennum had no brothers or sisters; and to her parents she seemed destined to wind up not in heaven but in an asylum, particularly after she started speaking in the voices of a strange woman and man.

But Asa Roff, a friend of the family, intervened. Roff's daughter had died sixteen years earlier during an epileptic seizure, and he knew of a doctor who could help. Dr. E.W. Stevens arrived to find Mary Vennum in a trance, taking on the character of the man and then the woman. Stevens quickly hypnotized the girl, who told him she had been taken over by evil spirits. When the doctor suggested *another* spirit from beyond was needed to help her sort out the personalities, Mary herself offered a suggestion: She proposed summoning Mary Roff, Asa Roff's deceased daughter. The startled Asa vigorously agreed.

Whatever psychological disorders the girl may have been suffering from, the science of psychology can hardly offer an explanation for what followed. The next day, Mary Vennum seemed to become Mary Roff, and when Mrs. Roff and a daughter visited, she called the sister by name, though they had never met, and hugged them both and cried. She went back home with the Roffs and seemed to recognize everything and everyone in the neighborhood, constantly recalling incidents from Mary Roff's childhood. Questioning her at length, Stevens himself was convinced that the girl knew all about the life of Mary Roff.

After a short time, the girl told the Roff family that she could only stay a few months. Later she announced the exact day she was departing, and finally said goodbye. After that, she returned to the Vennum home, where Mr. and Mrs. Vennum were happy to find Mary Lurancy Vennum back for good—and cured of her epilepsy in the bargain.

Catching Shoplifters With ESP

If you have a penchant for petty theft, don't try it at the Shoppers Drug Mart in Canada. Instead of using an elaborate security system, the chain employs a psychic to spot shoplifters, and officials there claim he's worth every cent.

In fact, Reginald McHugh, psychic watchdog, has had a long and distinguished career. One day, while waiting to speak with reporters from Mediavision, a film company making a documentary about him, McHugh suddenly became excited. Even though he was sitting in a windowless room toward the back of the store, he exclaimed, "Wait. I feel vibes. Soon a dark woman in a long orange dress will come in and steal a blue box with yellow stripes on it." The psychic immediately relayed his impressions to the store detective.

Ten minutes later, in walked an East Indian lady wearing an orange sari. The store detective watched her slip a small box into her purse and promptly apprehended her when she tried to leave. The blue and yellow box contained throat lozenges.

The film crew was disappointed that they hadn't caught the episode on film, so they came better prepared the next day. This time McHugh wore a microphone under his collar and correctly predicted and pointed out several shoplifters.

"Shoplifting takes place so quickly," says associate producer Tony Bond, "that unless you know who's going to do it, there's no way to film it. It would be an absolute fluke, with all the aisles and displays, if you were to catch someone in the act. And we did that several times."

Psychic Plant Growth

It was the craze of the sixties: Talk to your plants and help them grow. Now, it seems, there was a method to the madness. Scientific evidence gathered by McGill University morphologist Bernard Grad shows that some people *can* use psychic power to help plants thrive.

To perform his experiment, Grad planted barley seeds in several separate plots, where they were watered with a salt solution to stunt their growth. The catch was that some of the beakers containing the solution were "treated" by Hungarian-born psychic Oskar Estebany, who held them and embued them with his healing powers. Needless to say, the plots watered with the specially treated solution gave richer yields than those given the straight saline.

Grad soon replicated the experiment, but this time used two mental patients suffering from depression for his healers. He wanted to see if a person's mood could influence plant growth. The patients were instructed merely to hold the beakers of water before the plants were fed. The yield of their plots was later compared to those of a lab assistant, who had taken part in the original work with Estebany. The results were partially consistent with the earlier research. The lab worker's plots grew better than that of one of the mental patients. But the other subject's plots grew rather well. Dr. Grad was confused by the results, until he discovered that taking part in the experiment had so excited the patient that she had been roused from her depression.

Therapeutic Touch

Therapeutic touch is the most recent name for what was previously called the "laying-on of hands." The practitioner runs his or her hands over the patient, trying to infuse or redistribute energy throughout the body. People receiving therapeutic touch report feeling better and often find their pain gone. But is there any objective evidence that it really works? Yes, according to a report published by Dr. Janet Quinn in 1984.

To determine whether therapists were actually transmitting energy, Quinn first had them enter a state of inwardly focused consciousness, supposedly necessary before the treatment can work. Then she had them administer treatment by moving their hands above the patients' bodies. Each patient rated his or her level of anxiety both before and after receiving the treatment. Just as predicted, the patients reported a significant reduction in their anxiety after receiving therapeutic touch.

Quinn also tried to rule out the placebo effect, which some skeptics believe can explain the effectiveness of therapeutic touch. To do that, she made sure that *some* patients received "mock" therapy, administered by nurses not skilled in the technique. These practitioners were told how to mimic therapeutic touch, but didn't know how to enter the special state of consciousness that helps it work. Those subjects receiving the bogus treatment reported no effects at all. Quinn also videotaped the nurses performing both the real and the fake procedure, and showed the tapes to judges who were asked to differentiate between the two groups. The judges couldn't tell the difference, indicating that the patients couldn't have either.

The Ghost of Washington Irving

Would the author of one of the most famous American ghost stories ever return from the dead to play a prank? Washington Irving, author of *The Legend of Sleepy Hollow*, was a witty man who liked to have fun, sometimes at the expense of others. Shortly after Irving's death, one of the author's old friends, a Dr. J.G. Cogswell, was working in the library when he saw a man shelve a book and disappear. Cogswell felt certain the man was Irving—until he saw another ghostly figure, the image of a second deceased friend, return a book as well.

That was not the end of it. Irving's nephew, Pierre, reportedly saw the ghost of his uncle in the Irving home in Tarrytown, New York. There, Pierre and his two daughters said they clearly saw the famed author walk through the parlor and into the library, where he used to do his work.

While alive, Irving professed no belief in ghosts. The headless horseman of his writing, after all, was really a mortal dressed to scare away a rival. It's likely his nephew shared that belief—until Irving himself proved them both wrong.

Floating Fakir

Transcendental meditation gained great notoriety in the 1970s, when leaders of the movement claimed that practitioners could levitate. But despite all the assertions, not a single meditator was ever seen to float above the ground.

This doesn't mean, however, that the powers of the mind can't help a person defy gravity. Eyewitness reports of human levitations dot the history of cultures both East and West. One of the most impressive of these eyewitness reports was made in the 1860s by Louis Jacolliot, a French judge who traveled extensively in the East. According to Jacolliot, his interest in yoga was piqued when he befriended a fakir named Covindasamy in 1866. The two men began conducting psychic experiments together, and one day before lunch Covindasamy decided to give his friend a startling demonstration.

The yogi was walking toward the door to Jacolliot's veranda, the judge wrote in his book, *Occult Science in India and Among the Ancients*, when he obviously had second thoughts. "The fakir stopped in the doorway from the terrace into the backstairs, and folding his arms, he was lifted—or so it seemed to me—gradually without visible support, about one foot above the ground. I could determine the exact height, thanks to a landing marker upon which I fixed my eyes during the short time the phenomenon lasted. Behind the fakir hung a silk curtain with red, golden, and white stripes of equal breadth, and I noticed that the fakir's feet were as high as the sixth stripe. When I saw the rising begin, I took my watch out."

According to Jacolliot, the fakir remained suspended for about ten minutes; for five of those minutes, he appeared not to move at all.

Psychic Stream

Some experts believe that we receive psychic impressions continually during the day, even if these messages never enter into waking consciousness. This idea was merely a theory until the 1960s, when New Jersey electrical engineer E. Douglas Dean decided to demonstrate it.

Drawing upon some earlier research done in Czechoslovakia, Dean used two subjects for his experiments. The first subject, the "receiver," was placed alone in a room, his finger hooked up to a plethysmograph, a device that monitors blood flow in the body. Meanwhile, in a different room, the "sender" went to work. He or she would study a series of cards, each one either blank or labeled with a random name, a name emotionally significant to the sender, or a name significant to the receiver. Dean hoped that when the sender became aroused by seeing an emotionally significant name, the subject would also respond. Such a reaction would show up on the plethysmograph chart, which would show a sudden increase in little dips.

The experiment was successful, but not in the way the experimenter had expected. What happened was that the subject's blood flow responded when the sender looked at names significant to his experimental partner. It seemed as though the subject's unconscious mind was constantly vigilant during the experiment, looking out for any messages that might be important. While subjects were not consciously aware when the ESP signals were received, their bodies subtly responded to them.

Child Finder

A woman desperate to find her missing children will do almost anything. Take New Yorker Joanne Tomchik, who lost her children, aged three and five, when they were kidnapped by her former husband in 1972.

Frantic, Tomchik enlisted the help of police and even hired private detectives. But one year and six thousand dollars in fees later, there was still no clue as to the whereabouts of her husband or children.

Then she heard a radio broadcast about ESP and decided to enlist the aid of a psychic. The group involved in the broadcast referred her to Mrs. Millie Cotant, who focused on photographs of the Tomchik children and finally came up with a vision. She saw a trailer and a light-blue pickup truck with Carolina plates.

That was enough for Mrs. Tomchik. She notified the police in both North and South Carolina, furnishing them with photos of her children and their father. One month later, in Wilson, North Carolina, Andrew Tomchik was located, living with the children in a trailer park. He had been using a light-blue pickup truck. Tomchik was found guilty of violating his visitation rights, and Mrs. Tomchik was happily reunited with her children.

Papal Prophecies

One of the Middle Ages' more obscure prophets was Saint Malachy, an Irish monk who became Archbishop of Armagh. He died in 1148, but his prophecies, found in note form, were collected and published by Vatican officials in or about 1595.

Saint Malachy's prophecies were couched in the form of a papal register, or list, projected from the twelfth century forward, with a comment about each of the new popes or the character of his reign, many of which have proven surprisingly apt. The register ends with "Peter the Roman," at a time calculated as roughly the end of this century, or the coming of the millennium.

Between Peter and who appears to be Pope Pius XI will be six other Vatican rulers. During Peter's reign, "the city of the Seven Hills will be destroyed, and the Awful Judge will judge his people."

The prophetic history of the papacy has often been referred to among Catholic theologians. Knowledge of it may have even contributed to the vision reported by Pope Pius in 1909. Emerging from a trance, he said, "What I see is terrifying. Will it be myself . . . or my successor . . . the pope will quit Rome and after leaving the Vatican he will have to walk over the dead bodies of his priests."

Time, of course, will tell whether Saint Malachy's terrifying prophecies come to pass.

Bodily Elongation

The most prolific performer of modern miracles was unquestionably the nineteenth-century spirit medium, Daniel Douglas Home (1833–86), who once floated out a second-story window and back again in broad daylight, in full view of witnesses.

Among Home's stable of miraculous secular feats were the ability to levitate heavy objects, converse with spirits of the long departed, and wash his face in burning embers without suffering apparent harm. The physically frail Scotsman could also elongate his body dramatically, adding as much as six inches to his height.

On one occasion this feat was witnessed by no less a personage than Lord Adare, son of the third Earl of Dunraven. Standing between the Lord and a Mr. Jencken, Home entered into the familiar trance state in which the majority of his miracles were accomplished. "The guardian spirit is very tall and strong," he intoned. Without notice, Home suddenly sprouted an additional six inches, his head rising above those of the two dumbfounded men who stood to either side.

To their inquiries, Home responded, "Daniel will show you how it is," and unbuttoned his coat. (He always referred to himself in third person while in a trance.) The elongation appears to have taken place from the waist upwards, Lord Adare noting that four inches of new flesh now showed between Home's waistcoat and the waistband of his trousers.

Home shrunk back to his original size, then said, "Daniel will grow tall again." And to Lord Adare's obvious amazement, he did.

Dressed in slippers, Home stalked the room, stamping his feet

to show they were planted firmly on the floor, and slowly returning to his normal height. As with most of his startling feats, Home
could apparently perform the height "trick" almost at will.

Mystery on Mitchell Flat

Ghost lights that haunt the same locale year after year
are hardly an isolated phenomenon. At least thirty-five such sites
are known in the U.S. and Canada alone. But few ghost lights can
match the lore and lure of those that are said to hover over
Mitchell Flat, outside the present-day town of Marfa in west
Texas.

Reports of dancing globes of luminosity above the desert floor
here date back at least to the time of the Mescalero Apache. One
of the first white settlers in the area, Robert Ellison, saw them as
early as 1883, and thought they were Indian campfires. More
recently, James Dean, while filming *Giant* in Marfa in the 1950s,
kept a telescope perched on a barbed-wire fence in hopes of
spotting the lights.

Nowadays, when conditions are right, the lights can be seen
like glowing Mexican jumping beans from a vantage point on
Highway 90, about eight miles east of town. Usually they dance
in the distance, midway between the highway and the Chinati
Mountains, but on rare occasions they venture close enough for
accurate observation.

Charles Cude, a San Antonio funeral director, was parked at
the roadside pullover one night when he saw two lights that
"looked like an automobile racing across, going from east to
west." At the same time that Cude realized there weren't any
roads out there, one of the lights suddenly shot straight up.

A few moments later, another light shot between Cude's car
and the one adjacent, disappearing across the desert floor. Cude
said the light appeared to be between eighteen and twenty-four

inches in diameter. Its surface reminded him of pictures of the earth taken from outer space, a glowing globe covered with swirling clouds.

The False (or Real) UFOs in the Hudson Valley

The largest mass-sighting incident in UFO history began on New Year's Eve 1982, inundating the Hudson Valley in New York, and particularly Westchester and Putnam counties. By the summer of 1987, more than five thousand people had seen (and in many cases photographed and videotaped) a huge, triangular-shaped UFO outlined in lights that became known as the "Hudson Valley Boomerang."

Most of the sightings fell within the years 1983 and 1984. Motorists on the Taconic Parkway would frequently pull their cars to the side of the road staring up at a gigantic, slow-moving, silent object that many described in terms of football fields rather than feet. One stunned witness said it was as large as an aircraft carrier. Another compared it to a "flying city."

In spite of the number of authentic photographs, and reliable witnesses that included pilots, engineers, and corporate executives, skeptics rashly declared the case "solved." The culprits were supposedly a group of private pilots who, in direct violation of FAA regulations, gathered together in the evenings to scare the living daylights out of local residents. The "Martians," as they called themselves, reportedly flew their Cessnas in tight, night formations to give the illusion of a large, lighted object maneuvering overhead.

The only problem with the skeptical "solution" was that several witnesses filmed both the "Martians" and UFO in flight, and the difference was easily distinguishable. Other witnesses said the

Cessnas could plainly be heard, whereas the UFO was eerily quiet. Moreover, the huge, illuminated boomerang *hovered* over the local nuclear power plant, an acrobatic achievement that civilian Cessnas, no matter how accomplished their pilots, have yet to manage.

Finally, if the skeptics feel they've really solved the case of the Hudson Valley UFO, they are morally obligated to turn the offenders over to the authorities for proper punishment. Otherwise, we're forced to conclude that giant, unidentified flying objects lie outside the present jurisdiction of the Federal Aviation Administration.

Psychophysics and Silver Futures

Can psychic powers help predict the movement of the commodities market? That's the question recently asked by psychologist and psychic Keith Harary and physicist Russell Targ. To conduct their experiment, the researchers focused on the silver market, which is notoriously unstable and fluctuates rapidly from day to day. Several investors were willing to bet sizable sums of money on Harary's predictions.

In order to smooth the experiment and keep Harary from feeling too strained while making his predictions, the prognostications were made in a second-hand way. Every Thursday beginning September 16, 1982, Targ asked Harary to describe the object—chosen from a group of objects—that he would see the following Monday. Each of the four objects designated a particular flux in the silver market, from up a lot to down a lot.

After the psychic had given his responses, Targ would look over the target pool and decide which object Harary had described. The corresponding flux in the silver market would then be communicated to investors, who would use the information to either buy or sell.

The experiment was a striking success. Seven consecutive transactions were made based on the seven correct predictions, and the investors made $120,000 on the gamble.

Shirley MacLaine
Conquers Stage Fright

In an up-and-down acting career that suddenly began to rocket, Shirley MacLaine has become a major star, a multi-talented one who sings and dances as well as acts. She even won an Oscar for her performance in the hit movie, *Terms of Endearment*, but then, she knew she would. While preparing for the movie, she says, she envisioned the future events as they occurred: The movie was a hit, she won the Oscar, and then wrote a book about her psychic experiences entitled *Out on a Limb*.

Throughout her long career, MacLaine said, she had suffered from stage fright, not uncommon for actors. But she found a cure. It came after visiting an acupuncturist in the New Mexican desert. After undergoing treatment, MacLaine, like many of his clients, recalled past lives. In fact, she said, one life had been lived as an eighteenth-century court jester beheaded after one particular performance before the king. She said that in her recall experience, she could actually see the jester's head rolling on the floor.

"No wonder I had stage fright," she noted. The vision helped her work through the problem, she noted, and contributed to her future success.

Haunted TV

Many gifted psychics claim they can project images onto sealed film. But there are a few who say they can actually transmit pictures to the screen of a TV.

One of the most unusual such cases was reported by the Travis family of Blue Point, New York. The three Travis children were up early one morning watching television when they saw a face appear on the screen, obscuring the program they were trying to watch. Mrs. Travis didn't believe the story when it was reported to her, but she stopped dead in her tracks when she saw it for herself. The face seemed to be female, and it looked like a profile in silhouette. Even when the set was turned off, the silhouette remained clearly visible.

News of the "haunted" TV spread quickly throughout Blue Point. And for the next two days, dozens of people, including news reporters, photographers and TV repairmen, flocked to the house. Everyone had a theory as to how the face came to be there. Some of the witnesses, for instance, thought the profile was an electronic residue of singer Francy Lane, who had appeared on TV the day before. But this suggestion and others never panned out.

The picture finally faded fifty-one hours later, as mysteriously as it had materialized, though several photographs remain to prove the image was actually there.

Hazelnuts From the Sky

Alfred Wilson Osborne and his wife like to tell the tale of a day in March 1977 when they were showered with objects from the sky.

Osborne, a newspaper chess correspondent from Bristol, England, says he and his wife were on their way back home from church on a Sunday morning when they were barraged by several hundred hazelnuts plummeting to the ground. Over the next few minutes, the nuts banged and pinged on passing cars, the parked cars of a nearby car dealer, and passersby.

The incident was reported in the Bristol paper with no explanation. It was a nearly cloudless day, there were no nut trees on the road where the event occurred, and the objects clearly seemed to be falling from the sky.

Osborne was amazed at what he saw, but said the most amazing thing of all was that the hazelnuts, not in season until September or October, were fresh and ripe. "I have thought that it might be a vortex that sucked them up," he said, "but I don't know where you suck up hazelnuts in March."

Is the Dutchman Still Flying?

Of all the tales of the sea, none is ghostlier than that of *The Flying Dutchman*. The legend is based on an actual vessel, captained by a skilled but boastful seaman named Hendrik Vanderdecken, a Dutch East Indian who set sail from Amsterdam to Batavia, then a port in Dutch East India, in 1680. Though he was commissioned by a trading company to sail the company's boat and bring back a full load of cargo, Vanderdecken was certain he would bring back enough of his *own* loot to make himself rich as well.

When Vanderdecken's ship was battered by a tropical storm, legend has it, he tried every maneuver he knew to advance the ship. The safe course would have been to wait out the storm, but prodded by a challenge from the devil in a dream one night, he decided to ignore the Lord's warnings and try to steer the ship around the Cape. It soon foundered, and the crew died. For his penance, it is said, Vanderdecken was cursed to sail his ship until Judgment Day.

An exciting and romantic legend it is, but witness after witness swears it is more. In 1835 the captain and crew of a British ship saw a phantom ship approaching through a heavy storm with all sails set, which suddenly disappeared as it came dangerously close. In 1881, sailors on the British ship H.M.S. *Bacchante,* said a crew member fell from the rigging to his death the day after another midshipman saw the ghostly vision.

A more recent and highly acclaimed sighting of the *Dutchman* reportedly took place in March 1939, on Glencairn Beach in South Africa. The day following the sighting, a newspaper carried the story of dozens of bathers watching the ship, discussing details of the vision, and noting that it was full-sailed and moving steadily, despite the lack of any wind at the time.

Some scientists explained the group sighting as a mirage. But witnesses protested that it would have been difficult for them to envision a seventeenth-century sailing vessel in such detail, since most had never even seen one.

The Staircase Ghosts

The National Maritime Museum, located in Geenwich, England, is toured by thousands of visitors each year. Many preserve their memories with photographs.

That's what the Reverend R. W. Hardy had in mind when he and his wife, touring the facility in 1966, tried to photograph one of the museum's most popular exhibits—the Tulip Staircase, originally built for Queen Anne of Denmark. Hardy waited until the rest of his tour group passed upstairs so he could get a clear shot of the staircase's metal bannister, featuring tulip designs sculpted into the ironwork.

Hardy, his wife, and officials at the museum all declared that the staircase was empty when the photo was taken. Yet when Hardy returned to his native Canada and had the film developed, two figures appeared on the stairs. Shrouded in white, they were clearly not normal humans, but ghostly apparitions. Both appeared to be walking up the stairs, one hand on the bannister, and taking no notice of the camera. A large ring was discernible on the hand of one of them.

The Reverend Hardy did not believe in ghosts, but seeking an explanation, he eventually contacted the London Ghost Club. The club had Hardy's negatives analyzed by Kodak, where it was found the film had not been tampered with in any way. Club members also interviewed the Hardys at great length and determined they were honest and in no way trying to perpetrate a fraud or a hoax.

Eager to pursue this event, the organization soon sponsored an overnight ghost watch at the staircase, employing cameras, electronic sensors, temperature gauges, and devices to measure wind and atmospheric conditions. The investigators soon recorded a number of strange sounds, which they identified as footsteps and weeping, but collected no images on film. The apparitions, the club members concluded, were ghosts that appeared only during the daytime; the identity of the figures in the photo, they added, could not be determined.

D. D. Home:
Fakir or Faker?

Daniel Douglas Home, an American who died in 1886, kept the company of princes and kings. His claim to fame? He could put himself in a trance, becoming immune to fire or intense heat. Not only could he pick up red-hot coals, but he could transfer his immunity at will to spectators, handing the coals to them with no harm done.

Sir William Crookes, then director of the British Society for Psychical Research, witnessed his feats and reported that Home took a hot coal as "big as an orange" and held it with both hands. Then he blew on the coal until it got white hot and a flame flickered above it around the man's fingers. Crookes inspected Home's hands before and after, but could find no evidence of any kind of ointment or other treatment. And he was amazed to find Home's hands soft and delicate, "like a woman's."

Lord Adare of Ireland, a frequent companion of Home's and the author of a book on his life, wrote that he once saw him put his entire face into a fire and shake it back and forth. Home also put a scalding hot coal in Adare's hand; Adare claimed he held the coal for several moments, and, he added, it barely felt warm.

Home professed other spiritual powers as well. He held countless séances and was said to be able to make objects move. Once, before three witnesses, he allegedly floated out of a second-floor window and then floated back in. Closer scrutiny showed a number of flaws in the story, including the possibility of a hidden rope or even the blackmailing of Lord Adare by threats of uncovering Adare's homosexuality.

No one, however, has ever explained Home's immunity to fire, which was witnessed by countless others time and again.

The Ghosts of Flight 401

Next to the ghosts in the White House, one of the most acclaimed and popular ghost stories of recent times is known as the Ghosts of Flight 401. Bob Loft was captain of Eastern Airlines Flight 401 the day it took off from New York to Miami on Friday, December 29, 1972. That night, the plane crashed in the Everglades, and more than 100 were killed, including Loft and Dan Repo, the flight engineer. An investigation was launched and the cause of the crash was officially listed as a combination of equipment failure and pilot error. After the investigation, salvageable parts were collected for use on other Eastern planes.

Soon after, the rumors began: Pilots and flight crews on various Eastern flights reportedly saw the ghosts of Loft and Repo, who seemed to appear most often aboard Plane Number 318. In early incidents, some flight atttendants found the lower galley where food was prepared to be abnormally cold. Others had the strong feeling of someone else in the room with them when no one was there. Then, a flight engineer arrived to make his preflight inspection and saw a man in an Eastern second officer's uniform. He immediately recognized his old acquaintance, Dan Repo, who told him not to worry about the inspection because he had already taken care of it. On yet another flight, the ghost of Captain Loft was seen by a pilot and two flight attendants. Occasionally Repo or unidentified flight attendants would be seen through the glass panel on the elevator from the lower galley—and then vanish before the door opened.

An informal investigation into the stories was hampered both by an unwillingness of employees to talk, and by a reported series of missing log sheets from the plane. But investigators did eventually learn one striking fact: Many parts salvaged from Flight 401 were later used on Plane Number 318.

Photographing the Yeti

March 6, 1986, was the date when Bigfoot hunters finally got the "hard" evidence for which they had been patiently waiting. While traveling in the Himalayas, an explorer caught the yeti—Tibet's counterpart of our indigenous Bigfoot—with his camera.

Anthony Wooldridge, a British traveler, was mountain climbing near Nepal in order to study village life when he spotted the creature. He was jogging in the snow by some trees when he chanced upon some tracks "I wondered what was sharing the wood with me," he said, "but could think of no satisfactory explanation. I took two quick photographs of the tracks and pressed on knowing that time was precious if I was to reach my destination before the snow became too soft. Perhaps half an hour later, as I emerged above the tree line, there was a sudden bang followed by protracted rumbling."

The explorer was continuing up the slopes to better evaluate the risk when he spied the Abominable Snowman by some shrubbery. "Standing behind the shrubs," explains Wooldridge, "was a large, erect shape up to two meters tall." Convinced that whatever it was it would disappear quickly, Wooldridge took several photographs. It didn't take long, he said, "to the realization that the only animal remotely resembling the one in front of me was the yeti."

Wooldridge later submitted the photos to the International Society for Cryptozoology, which investigates reports of strange or unknown animals. Since that time, his best photograph has been published in *BBC Wildlife*, causing more than a little controversy. *BBC Wildlife* first sent the photograph to Dr. Robert D. Martin, a physical anthropologist at University College, University of London. Martin noted that the creature *could* have been a Hanuman langur, though langurs are generally smaller than the creature in the photograph, and they have tails. Similar observations have been puzzling anthropologist John Napier, a well-known Bigfoot skeptic who also examined the photograph. The possibility that Wooldridge really did photograph a previously unknown life form, says Dr. Napier, "is remarkable but quite logical."

Remembrance of a Former Life and Death

Hypnotists often take adult subjects back to childhood. Many mesmerists have also taken the regression further, using hypnotism to help subjects trace former lives.

English hypnotist Henry Blythe, for instance, began experimenting with a woman named Naomi Henry, from Exeter. Under hypnosis, Henry claimed she was an eighteenth-century Irish farm woman named Mary Cohen. Cohen described her entire life, including her youth, her stressful marriage to a violent farmer, and even her death.

Blythe's subject described her last moment, a point past pain, when suddenly she became silent. Blythe watched in panic as the color left the woman's face. Soon she had stopped breathing and he could find no pulse. "You are safe," he kept repeating. Finally, after several seconds, her pulse returned and she began breathing again. Slowly, she returned to normal.

Everyone was relieved, and Blythe later reported that Henry had told him of another life as an English girl in the early 1900s.

The Unhappy Times
of Black Gold

A famous thoroughbred named Black Gold won many a dollar for bettors, owners, and jockeys, but a trail of misfortune followed the colt from its first day of life. Born "under the light" of a comet, the horse was branded a bad omen by owner H. M. Hoots, who caught pneumonia that very night and then died.

Black Gold himself nonetheless became a winner, overcoming the pain of a weak left foreleg to be an entrant in the 1924 Kentucky Derby. The horse won at ten-to-one odds, but the bookies made off with the betting money and no one got paid. Some time later, J. D. Mooney, Black Gold's jockey, gained so much weight that he was dismissed, and the trainer was also fired for allowing the horse to overwork his bad leg. The stable agent, Waldo Freeman, thought he had beaten the curse when he won bets in three big races, but he died of a heart attack before the day was over. Perhaps the worst fate hit Black Gold himself when he was put out to stud late in 1924. He was found to be sterile.

The Unlucky Sevens
of Captain McLoed

Captain Hugh McDonald McLoed became a captain when he was nineteen years old, but it was the sinister number "7" that seemed to figure prominently in his life. And well it should, for he was the seventh son of a seventh son.

Hailing from a sailing family, McLoed had two brothers who were also captains. In fact, on December 7, 1909, his siblings set sail as captain and first mate on the steamer *Marquette & Bessemer No. 2*, bound for Port Stanley, Ontario. But the steamer never made it. The ship and its entire crew disappeared. Four months later, on April 7, Hugh was notified that his brother, John, had been found, his body encased in ice in the Niagara River. On October 7, 1910, his other brother's body was washed up onto shore at Long Point.

Four years later on April 7, 1914, Captain McLoed, then skipper of a whaleback steamer named the *John Ericsson*, was towing a barge down Lake Huron. The fog was so thick he couldn't see the ship being towed—the *Alexander Holly*—at all. But he finally caught sight of the *Holly*'s flag flying at half-mast. He slowed his ship down and pulled in the tow line, only to learn that the barge's captain had been washed overboard—the day before.

It should be no surprise that McLoed finally retired from his command on December 6, 1941, at the same time the Japanese were bombing Pearl Harbor, on December 7, across the International Date Line.

Curse of King Tut's Tomb

Though the great pyramids of Egypt stood intact and untouched for centuries, by the early 1920s many of the structures and tombs of the pharaohs had been plundered by looting archaeologists and treasure-seekers.

One tomb, however, remained intact: that of the now famous Tutankhamen, or "King Tut." Legend had it that the tomb was guarded by a curse dooming anyone who entered to death. But that didn't stop George E. S. M. Herbert, fifth Earl of Carnarvon, who first went to Egypt hoping that the dry climate would ease his troubled breathing.

Though Herbert had no background in archaeology, he had the money to sponsor expeditions. And before long, he and archaeologist Howard Carter had set out to find the fabled tomb.

After several digs over many years, they finally found some fragments of pieces bearing the name of Tutankhamen. And the pieces led them to the gold-laden, treasure-filled room housing the long-sought Tutankhamen.

A party of twenty stood witness as Carter made his way into that room on February 17, 1923, but Lord Carnarvon hardly lived to relish the find. He died in April in the Hotel Continental in Cairo, after suddenly contracting an undiagnosed high fever that racked his body off and on for twelve days. Within minutes of his death, there was a power failure in Cairo. And Carnarvon's dog, at home in London, died that same day.

Before the year was out, twelve others out of the original party of twenty were dead. But others would die, too. George Jay Gould, son of financier Jay Gould and a friend of Carnarvon's, came to Egypt after his friend's death to see the site for himself. He died of bubonic plague within twenty-four hours of visiting the tomb.

By 1929, sixteen others who somehow came in contact with the mummy had died as well. Victims included radiologist Archibald Reid, who had prepared the Tutankhamen remains for x-raying; the wife of Lord Carnarvon; and Richard Bethell, his personal secretary. Even Bethell's father died, taking his life by his own hand.

The mystique of this famous mummy, renowned in grade-B horror films, was probably a large factor in the overwhelming success of the United States tour of the Treasures of King Tutankhamen. But as the tens of thousands who saw the mummy can attest, the curse seems ended, at least for now.

But the others who entered the tomb certainly had occasion to remember, while they lived, the hieroglyphics written on the seal at the entrance: "Death will come on swift wings to he who violates the tomb of the Pharaoh."

Miracle at Remiremont

Remiremont, a small French town close to the German border, contained a statue of the Virgin Mary called *Notre Dame du Trésor*. Presented to Remiremont in the eighth century, the statue had long been considered the town's protector and every year since 1682 it had been paraded through the streets during a special ceremony in its honor.

But in 1907 the statue became the center of a heated dispute: When the Pope gave the ceremony his official sanction, anti-Catholic forces within the town gave vent to violent protest. City officials were so intimidated by the threats that the ceremony was canceled and no public procession took place for the first time in centuries.

It seemed like divine retribution when a fierce and sudden hailstorm struck Remiremont on May 16, shortly after the procession was to have been held. Some of the stones were the size of tomatoes and didn't break upon hitting the ground. Others, according to reports, were actually impressed with the likeness of the *Notre Dame du Trésor*.

A detailed description of the stones was even placed on record by the Abbe Gueniot, a local priest: "I saw very distinctly on the front of the hailstones, which were slightly convex in the center, although the edges were somewhat worn, the bust of a woman, with a robe that was turned up at the bottom, like a priest's cope," he wrote. "The outline of the images was slightly hollow, but very boldly drawn."

The figure found on the stones, however, represented only one miraculous outcome of the storm. Those special hailstones, townsfolk reported, fell at the same time that other, normal ones plunged to the ground. But they seemed to fall slowly, as though floating to earth, and did no damage to anything at all.

The Case of Renata

Czech psychiatrist Stanislov Grof, an expert on hallu-cinogens, currently works at America's famous Esalen Institute in Big Sur. But before he left his homeland, he treated a self-destructive young housewife named Renata.

Grof asked his patient to recall her painful past with the help of LSD, and before long, she began to report scenes from seven-teenth-century Prague. She correctly described the architecture, dress, and weaponry of the period. She had vivid memories of Bohemia's invasion by the Austrian Empire of the Hapsburgs. And she even described the beheading of a young nobleman by the Hapsburgs.

Grof tried to understand the visions with every therapeutic tool at his disposal, but could find no psychological explanation at all. He left for the United States before the case could be resolved. But two years later he received a letter from his former patient. It turned out that Renata had encountered her estranged father, whom she hadn't seen since early childhood. During their talks, she learned that her father had traced their family line back to the seventeenth century—to a nobleman beheaded by the Hapsburgs during their occupation of what is now Czechoslovakia.

Just how Renata came to "recall" this information remains a mystery, since her father apparently made these discoveries after leaving his family. Renata believes her impressions emerged from some form of "inherited" memory. Grof himself contends that Renata's memories stem from a past life in Prague.

Gypsy Curse

For years, legend has it, the Epsom Derby was plagued by a curse, courtesy of a gypsy woman named Gypsy Lee. One year, it seems, the gypsy had predicted that a horse named Blew Gown would win the derby, and she wrote her prediction down on a piece of paper for all to see. One of the owners at the track, however, haughtily pointed out that the horse was named Blue Gown, not spelled with a "w" at all. Bristling at the thought of looking foolish, Gypsy Lee issued a curse: No horse with a "w" in its name would win the Epsom Derby, she decreed, as long as she lived. And none ever did. But when Gypsy died in 1934, her mourning family bet all they could on Windsor Lad, and the horse won, paying seven-to-one.

Rasputin's Murder Foretold

"Count" Louis Harmon was best known by his stage name of Cheiro. A celebrated clairvoyant and palm reader, he was widely courted by royalty and other notables earlier this century for his amazingly accurate readings.

In 1905, for example, in the course of a meeting with the controversial Mad Monk of Russia, Cheiro warned Rasputin of the fate that awaited him. "I foresee for you a violent end within the palace," he said. "You will be menaced by poison, by knife, and by bullet. Finally, I see the icy waters of the Neva closing above you."

Rasputin's subsequent checkered career as spiritual guide for

Tsar Nicholas II and his family certainly earned him enemies in Russia's royal court. Still, he was not suspicious when Prince Felix Yusupov invited him to his palace for dinner the night of December 29, 1916, promising him an assignation with a lady of the court who wished to meet him. Refusing wine and tea, Rasputin munched instead on pieces of cake the prince had laced with cyanide. Yusupov was startled to see the monk consume several pieces without ill effect.

The prince then drew a pistol and shot Rasputin in the back. While he was leaning over the body, Rasputin's eyes flew open and a desperate struggle ensued. Other plotters came to the prince's rescue, a conspirator named Purishkevich pumping two more bullets into Rasputin's body. Yusupov then battered the fallen "monk" with a steel bar.

Prince and helpers tied Rasputin's arms and carried his seemingly lifeless body down to the Neva. Breaking a hole in the ice, they pushed his body into the river, but Rasputin came to life again. His last act was to make the sign of the cross with one hand. Then he slipped beneath the icy waters, fulfilling Cheiro's prophecy and one of his own.

Before his murder Rasputin had warned the royal family: "If I am killed by common assassins you have nothing to fear. But if I am murdered by nobles, and if they shed my blood, their hands will remain soiled. Brothers will kill brothers and there will be no nobles in the country."

Within the year the Bolsheviks mounted the Russian Revolution. On July 16, 1917, the Tsar and his family were murdered at Ekaterinburg. And the nobles found that to remain in Russia was highly dangerous to one's health.

Lightning Balls

At five minutes after midnight, Eastern Airlines Flight 539 was over New York City, bound for Washington, D.C. The night was moonless and dark, with thunderstorms roaming the eastern seaboard. Suddenly the plane was enveloped by an electrical discharge.

Passenger Roger Jennison, a professor of electronics from Kent University, was even more startled to see "a glowing sphere a little more than twenty centimeters in diameter emerge from the pilot's cabin and pass down the aisle of the aircraft." Jennison described the light ball as blue-white in color and seemingly solid. It moved at about the same pace as a person would walk, at a height of about seventy-five centimeters off the floor.

Fortunately, no one was injured in the incident, and the plane mananged to land safely at its destination. Such balls of light *have* been known to explode on occasion, frequently with devastating results.

Scientists call the elusive phenomenon "ball lightning," but that hardly explains it since lightning itself still holds so many mysteries for physicists. One curious theory, however, was put forward by researchers M. D. Altschuler, L. House, and E. Hildner of the National Center for Atmospheric Research at Boulder, Colorado. The trio theorized that thunderstorms might act like giant natural particle accelerators capable of emitting protons charged with enormous energy. When the charged protons collide with atomic nuclei in the atmosphere, a mini-nuclear reaction generates highly charged atoms of oxygen and fluorine. In turn, these decaying atoms would emit both positrons and gamma rays—plenty of energy, in other words, to power ball lightning.

If the theory is correct, it means that close encounter victims of ball lightning may have another problem to worry about: namely, a lethal dose of radiation.

Seven Times Seven

When the late Arthur Koestler published *The Roots of Coincidence*, a study of curious synchronicities in time and place, he was bombarded by letters from people who had had similar experiences.

The most consistently coincidental of all probably came from Anthony S. Clancy of Dublin, Ireland, who was born on the seventh day of the seventh month of the seventh year of the century, which also happened to be the seventh day of the week. "I was the seventh child of a seventh child," he wrote, "and I have seven brothers; that makes seven sevens."

Actually, it makes eight sevens if one counts the number of letters in his first name, but to continue: On his twenty-seventh birthday, according to Clancy, he went to the track. The seventh numbered horse in the seventh race was named Seventh Heaven, and was handicapped seven stone. The odds against Seventh Heaven were seven-to-one, but Clancy bet seven shillings anyway.

Seventh Heaven finished seventh.

Vice Versa

Allan Falby was a motorcycle captain with the El Paso, Texas, County Highway Patrol in the 1930s when a collision with a speeding truck almost ended his career. His life was slowly seeping out a severed artery in his leg when a passerby, Alfred Smith, stopped to render aid. Smith tied off the bleeding leg and

Falby survived, although it was several months before he was fully recovered and able to resume his duties.

Five years later it was Falby who arrived at the scene of another accident in the area. A man had crashed his car into a tree and was bleeding profusely from a severed artery in his right leg. Before the ambulance arrived Falby was able to tie off a tourniquet and save the man's life. Only then did he realize that the victim was his own savior of five years before—Alfred Smith.

Falby took the incident in professional stride. "It all goes to prove," he said, "that one good tourniquet deserves another."

Fireflies

The Victorians, known for their sense of adventure, often encountered things in their world travels that still remain unexplained. In 1895, for example, while exploring the Niger Protectorate and Gabon region of Africa, Mary Kingsley camped on Lake Ncovi between the Ogowe and Rembwe rivers.

In her book, *Travels in West Africa*, Kingsley told how she set out alone in her canoe one night to take a bath. "Down through the forest on the lake bank opposite," she wrote, "came a violet ball the size of a small orange. When it reached the sand beach it hovered along it to and fro close to the ground."

Within a matter of minutes the violet ball of light was joined by a similarly colored companion that approached from behind one of the islets. The two small globes of light then proceeded to play a game of tag, darting at and circling around one another.

Kingsley beached her boat nearby, but one of the lights vanished in the bushes and the other set out across the lake. Following in her canoe, Kingsley was amazed when the violet apparition suddenly sank beneath the surface of the lake. "I could see it glowing," she said, "until it vanished in the depths."

The intrepid Kingsley thought the phenomenon might be a rare species of luminous insect. But the natives she interviewed referred to it as an *aku*, or devil. Whether devil or insect or even swamp gas, the phenomenon remains unexplained.

The Man Wouldn't Hang

Standing on the steps of the scaffold erected for his execution, John Lee was asked by the hangman if he had any last words. "No," he said. "Drop away."

The date was February 23, 1885, and Lee was about to hang for the murder of his employer, Emma Ann Keyes of Exeter, England, who had been found with her throat cut and head battered with a hatchet. Now justice was about to be served. The hangman slipped a sack over Lee's head and tightened the noose around his neck. Then he gave the signal to drop the trapdoor. Nothing happened.

The noose was removed from Lee's neck, and the trapdoor mechanism examined for defects. Nothing wrong could be found, so the prisoner was put in place again. Again the order was given, and again the trapdoor failed to release. This time the edges of the door were planed to assure a loose fit. But for a third and finally a fourth time, the trapdoor refused to drop.

Baffled, the sheriff returned Lee to his cell. His case quickly made the headlines and even the House of Commons joined in the debate about what to do with "the man they couldn't hang." Eventually, Lee's sentence was commuted to life in prison. After twenty-two years behind bars, the luckiest man alive was released on parole in December 1907.

Lee lived at least another thirty-five years, and is thought to have died in London about 1943. Although his miraculous escape from the hangman's noose was frequently resurrected by reporters of the odd and unusual, no satisfactory explanation for the faulty trapdoor was ever found.

The Learjet to Jeddah?

Most mysteries fall into clear-cut categories, whether it is UFOs, lake monsters, Bigfoot, or puckish poltergeists. On occasion, however, something so strange and bizarre occurs that it establishes a new category all its own. This certainly seems to be the case with the disappearance—and discovery—of a Learjet that was lost over the Egyptian Desert southwest of Cairo.

The jet was presumed missing on August 11, 1979, when it left Athens, bound for Jeddah, but failed to arrive. Aboard were the jet's owner, Lebanese shipbuilder Ali El-din al-Bahri, Swedish oil expert Peter Seime, Theresa Drake, and two pilots. The plane was tracked on several radars, and had an estimated four hours flying time left in its tanks when it was last contacted by Cairo air controllers. No distress call was heard.

But the Lear never arrived at Jeddah. Egyptian and Saudi Arabian air forces both mounted an extensive search along the plane's flight path, but no wreckage was spotted. Al-Bahri's family spent an additional $1.5 million hiring private searchers who roamed as far afield as Kenya. Still, no Learjet was found.

In February 1987, however, a team of archaeologists stumbled across the lost plane, 270 miles southwest of Cairo. The fuselage was intact, and there was no sign of fire, though one wing was a mile from the main site. Bedouins had apparently found the jet a couple of years earlier and stripped its interior.

At first glance there were no human remains aboard. Closer inspection, however, revealed crushed, almost powdered, human bones piled on the aircraft's floor. The largest, said Theresa Drake's father, Tom, was "no bigger than a thumb."

Professor Michael Day, an osteologist at London's Saint Thomas Hospital, thought the bones should have been almost intact. "In eight years they would certainly not have begun to disintegrate. Even wild animals would not have left such tiny fragments," Day said.

Australia's Yowie

The Himalayas have their yeti. And in Australia, shaggy ape-like creatures are known as yowie. In fact, according to local naturalist Rex Gilroy, the Blue Mountain area west of Sydney is home to more than 3,000 historical sightings of such creatures.

In December 1979, Lec and Patricia George ventured into the region, located in eastern Australia, in search of a quiet picnic spot. Their Sunday soiree was suddenly shattered when they came across the carcass of a mutilated kangaroo. Moreover, said the couple, the apparent perpetrator of the mutilation was only a scant forty feet away. They described a creature covered with hair, and "at least ten feet tall," that stopped to stare back at them before finally lumbering off into the brush.

The picnic was quickly canceled, but Gilroy still has plans to mount an expedition of his own in search of the legendary beast.

Plague of Defense Deaths

Between March and June 1987, the British press reverberated with a series of seemingly unrelated deaths that struck individual scientists involved in the defense industry. There were ten incidents in all, including eight suspicious suicides, a disappearance, and one case in which the victim survived a sixty-foot fall. Five of the victims were employees of Marconi, an electronics company with many government defense contracts, and several others had ties to programs involving the Stingray torpedo and nuclear submarine countermeasures.

The first incident actually occurred on August 5, 1986, when a Stingray software specialist jumped to his death from the Clifton suspension bridge in Bristol. Vimal Dajibhai was only twenty-four, and had no apparent motive for driving from London to Bristol to commit suicide. Press reports said that small puncture marks were found on his buttocks.

On October 28, 1986, another Marconi employee, Ashad Sharif, twenty-six, reportedly killed himself on Siston Commons, Bristol, by tying a rope to a tree, looping it around his neck, and driving off. He, too, had driven up from London. On January 8, 1987, a friend of Dajibhai's, working for the Ministry of Defense on a sonar project, disappeared while on an outing at a Derbyshire reservoir.

Four days earlier, a Marconi computer consultant, Richard Pugh, had been found with a plastic bag over his head. The same month a Royal Armaments computer consultant died of carbon monoxide poisoning. Carbon monoxide also took the life of Peter Peapell, forty-six, on February 22, 1987. Peapell had been a specialist in Soviet beryllium technology, a metal crucial to nuclear reactors.

On March 30, 1987, David Sands committed suicide by loading cans of gasoline into his sports car and driving it at high speed into an abandoned restaurant. Wife and colleagues reported that Sands had been "acting strangely" prior to his successful suicide.

On April 24 of the same year, Mark Wisner, a twenty-five-year-old Royal Air Force software designer, was also found dead with a plastic bag wrapped over his head. He was wearing a woman's corset and boots at the time of his death. Another defense-related scientist, Victor Moore, is said to have killed himself with a drug overdose. Robert Greenhaigh, forty-six, a Marconi employee, survived a sixty-foot leap from a Maidenhead railway bridge when he landed in soft grass. Greenhaigh had been a friend of alleged double agent Dennis Skinner, with whom he worked for fifteen years. Skinner was said to have been pushed from a Moscow flat to his death in 1983.

Such a string of suicides and defense-industry related deaths seems to stretch the definition of coincidence. Now that man has brought hostilities into the heavens, via Star Wars, perhaps the heavens have decided to fight back.

The Min Min Lights

        For more than a century a ghostly luminous phenomenon has haunted the remote outback east of Boulia, in southwest Queensland, Australia. The lights are named after a combination post office and pub called Min Min, which has long since crumbled to dust. But the lights continue to perplex the casual and curious alike.

One of the first written accounts, published in March 1941, tells of a stockman who was traveling between Boulia and Warenda Station one cloudy night. About 10 P.M., as he passed the old cemetery left over from Min Min's wilder days, he spied a strange glow emanating from the middle of the graveyard. The light swelled to the size of a watermelon, hovered momentarily above the tombstones, then moved off in the direction of Boulia. According to the stockman, the light followed him all the way into town.

Earlier reports subsequently surfaced, however. In *Walkabout*, Henry Lamond recounted his own childhood experience with the Min Min lights in 1912. At first he thought it was the headlights of an approaching automobile. "Cars," he said, "though they were not common, were not rare." But it quickly became evident that this was no normal light. "It remained in one bulbous ball," Lamond noted, "instead of dividing into two headlights as it should have done. And it floated too high for any car. There was something eerie about it."

The light floated gradually toward Lamond, who was on horseback, until it passed by him, about 200 yards away. "Suddenly," he said, "it just faded and died away. It did not go out with a snap. Its vanishing was more like the gradual fading of the wires in an electric bulb."

The Min Min light—whatever it is—still startles people who travel along on lonely stretches of road in the Australian outback.

Ghost Lights

The Welsh called them "corpse candles," and associated the ghostly globules of dancing light with impending death. They have also been called ghost lights, jack-o'-lanterns, and will-o'-the-wisps.

In his book, *British Goblins*, Wirt Sikes, a former U.S. consul to Wales, collected several eyewitness accounts of such mystery lights, including one in which the passengers of a coach between Llandilo and Carmathen saw three pale lights as they crossed a river bridge at Golden Grove. Three men drowned at the same spot a few days later, when their small boat capsized.

John Aubrey, author of *Miscellanies*, recounted the tale of a woman who said she saw five lights hovering in the newly plastered room of the house in which she worked. A fire was lit to dry the walls, she said, and five other workers subsequently died from fumes.

Other first-hand stories of ghost lights can be found in William Corliss' encyclopedic collection, *Lightning, Auroras and Nocturnal Lights*. One particularly haunting tale comes from a Lincoln, England, man who was riding horseback in the spring of 1913. In the course of his outing, he said, "a jack-o'-lantern caught my attention, proceeding in the same direction as I was traveling. Its motion was irregular, sometimes near the surface, and then suddenly, rising to the height of five or six feet.

"I followed very cautiously for some distance, being determined, if possible, to obtain a near view of my luminous guide. As the night was rather dark, I had everything favorable for observation.

"At length it rested just at an angle in the road. I dismounted in hope of capturing it. But by this time I was disappointed. For, on my near approach, whether from the noise I made, or some other cause, it suddenly rose from its resting place, about two feet from the ground, cleared a high bank, and pursued its course in a direct line over the adjoining fields.

"The broad and deep dikes rendered pursuit fruitless. But my eyes followed its almost butterfly motion till the glimmering taper was lost in the distance."

The Sheep
With the Golden Teeth

George Veripoulos, a Greek orthodox priest living in Athens, was in for a surprise in 1985 when he sat down to eat a dish of kefalaki—boiled sheep head. He was just about to enjoy his repast, given to him by his sister, when he noticed something strange. The sheep's bottom teeth were filled with gold.

The priest took the head to a jeweler, who confirmed that the teeth were filled with gold worth about $4,500. The priest next reported the strange find to his brother-in-law, Nicos Kotsovos, who immediately checked the rest of the flock—all four hundred sheep. None of them had similar teeth. A local veterinarian was consulted, but he, too, remained baffled by the golden teeth. Finally even the Greek Ministry of Agriculture was called in to the bizarre case. A veterinarian/spokesman for the ministry later told reporters, "There is also gold in the jawbone. How do you explain that? I can't. I'm completely baffled."

Everyone else was baffled, too. But in Athens, the local farmers have begun checking their sheep's mouths very carefully.

This Is Where We Came In

After the first atomic bomb was tested in Alamogordo in 1945, the site of the explosion was found to be covered with a floor of fused green glass, sand transformed into glass by the blast.

Several years after the end of World War II, scientists happened to be digging in the vicinity of Babylon, the once great metropolis of Mesopotamia and presumed site of the Tower of Babel. For the purpose of ascertaining how far down the layers of ruins and artifacts extended, archaeologists dug an experimental mine shaft straight down to catalog their discoveries by epochs.

They dug below the era of great ancient ruins, and through an earlier city buried under layers of flood loess. Then farther down, they found villages indicating an agrarian culture. Still farther down, they discovered settlements of a hunting and herding culture with even more primitive artifacts. The excavation came to an end when, underneath the preceding layers, a solid floor of fused glass was encountered.

CHARLES BERLITZ'S

World of

STRANGE PHENOMENA

◼◼ VOLUME 2: ◼◼

Strange People and Amazing Stories

Foreword

People generally find it hard to accept concepts and things they've never before considered or seen. Many of the objects and machines that today are everyday necessities were once regarded as frauds or dreams.

How could it have been regarded except as wild imagination or magic to speak of flying through the air or speeding across the landscape borne by a machine? Did it not once sound absurd to suggest that one could travel under the sea without getting wet, or speak to friends in distant cities throughout the world from one's home, or see events happening in far places at the very moment of their occurrence? And finally, was it not a simple reversion to ancient mythology to contemplate flying through space to the moon, other planets, and even further?

Not only were they not believed but many of today's scientific miracles were opposed and disdained during their experimental phases. In 1868, newspapers ran editorials claiming that telephones were pure trickery, designed to delude and fleece the public. For five years after the Wright brothers' successful airplane flight, *Scientific American* steadfastly refused to print a report of or comment on it. In fact, Simon Newcomb of the Smithsonian proved mathematically that the flight of a heavier-than-air machine was impossible. The famous eighteenth-century French scientist Antoine-Laurent Lavoisier stated that meteorites did not exist. He said, "It is impossible for stones to fall from the sky because there are no rocks in the sky." Prior to 1914 the French army command staff decided that airplanes might be useful for military observation but for no other military purpose whatsoever. When the phonograph was first tested at the Paris Academy of Science, the permanent secretary suddenly grasped the demonstrator by the throat, shouting that the sound was the demonstrator practicing ventriloquism, but of course the record continued to play.

Even the atomic theory remained only a convenient theory until August 1945, when it proved itself to be indisputable fact.

There are other imaginative suppositions and themes that science has yet to accept but that in recent decades have achieved a measure of respectability and become the objects of experimental study. Some of these are telepathy, teleportation, telekinesis, precognition, transmigration, foresight, and the existence of a *psyche* (Greek for "soul"). The notion of the existence of a psyche, which implies that the brain has a spiritual component separate from its physicality, is still as mysterious as it was in the Middle Ages. Could this separate entity be an intelligence that can survive death and sometimes even separate from the body during life? There are increasing indications that the psyche is not simply a behavioristic pattern within one's intelligence but something more, perhaps possessing motive and mobile force.

With the new methods of research and experimentation currently available, this mystery, along with the other arcane mysteries of the world and the universe, is now the subject of scientific investigation.

The lines separating the paranormal from the accepted sciences are beginning to fade, and the two in some cases are beginning to blend. What we thought was the ultimate in fantasy may be another fact. As J. B. Haldane observed, "We are living at a time when history is holding its breath and the present is detaching itself from the past like an iceberg that has broken away from its moorings."

The Future of the Face

For prehistoric man, teeth were both powerful weapons and necessary tools for eating unprocessed foods. But as the human race evolved, developing arsenals of armaments and the ability to produce soft, refined foods, the hard appendages of the jaw have become increasingly less important to survival. The eventual result of all this, according to one tooth expert, is the evolution of a sleek, toothless, hairless version of man.

According to orthodontist David Marshall, "Human jaws have already begun to get smaller and the brain cage has begun to grow. Meanwhile, teeth are losing cusps and tooth roots have started to shrink." Marshall, who has studied the human skull for thirty-five years and established an anatomical museum in Syracuse, New York, now says his research points to definitive changes in man. Indeed, Marshall has found, if evolution is left to its own devices, a few million years from now man will have a bald pate, squeezed, prominent features, and a small jaw.

Unlike prehistoric *Homo sapiens*, however, *we* have greater control over our environment, Marshall asserts. And, he adds, "such things as genetic engineering could very well change the projections."

Underwater Living Dead

The sultans of ancient Turkey, like the Roman emperors, possessed the power of life and death over their subjects. Concubines were particularly susceptible to the whims of an affronted ruler. Under Abdul the Damned, for example, unfaithful or petulant mistresses were sealed inside a weighted sack and dropped from the walls of the palace, which perched on a cliff high above the Bosporos. Although they plummeted to their deaths in the deep water, they didn't quite disappear: Years later, exploring the deep strait that cuts through European Turkey and Asian Turkey, divers found the women still packaged in their sacks but standing upright on the seafloor and swaying in the current as if they were alive.

Scuba divers discovered an even more astounding sight at the bottom of Czechoslovakia's Devil's Lake. In 1957, searching for a young man who presumably drowned while boating, they discovered not one body, but an entire German artillery unit—soldiers in full combat uniform, some sitting in trucks or on caissons, as well as horses standing upright, still in their harnesses. During World War II, the army attempted to cross the frozen lake during a winter retreat from the Russian forces. Under the pressure of such heavy weight, the ice cracked, sending humans and horses to their watery deaths. The extremely cold and deep water, however, preserved them until their discovery twelve years later, seemingly positioned and ready for combat.

Deadly Alibi

On the clear, sunny afternoon of April 4, 1953, a man was observed by several people as he tried to break open the door of a plush Chicago apartment. Not only did the witnesses note the exact time of the incident, but they also recognized the perpetrator—thirty-two-year-old William Brooks.

If ever the Chicago police thought they had an open-and-shut case, it was this one. But they would soon learn that all the clues pointed to a man who had a strange, but perfect, alibi.

When they investigated Brooks, Chicago detectives learned he was a penniless parolee. The case seemed cinched when a search of Brooks's automobile revealed a screwdriver hidden in the upholstery. The tip of the instrument fit exactly into the marks left on the apartment door by the would-be intruder.

But at his trial, Brooks said he couldn't be guilty because he had been dead at the time. His court-appointed attorney checked out his claim and found, bizarre as it sounded, that it was true.

Brooks's tale went like this: After he was discharged from a veterans hospital where he'd been treated for ulcers, in March 1953, his records had been switched with those of another man who had the same name. The problem was, the other man had died in the hospital. On the day of the attempted break-in, Brooks had been at the Veterans Administration office attempting to straighten out this mix-up, so he could receive military disability payments.

Records showed he was sitting in the VA office at the time the crime was committed, awaiting a telegram proving his identity. That telegram finally arrived at 1:44 P.M.

The court quickly found Brooks innocent, thanks to what may be the most unique alibi in history. When the burglary was attempted at 1:30 P.M., William Brooks was, legally, a dead man.

Asteroid Aliens

Space aliens may have found the perfect place to set up a colony—the asteroid belt between Jupiter and Mars.

Astronomer Michael Papagiannis of Boston University points out several reasons why this band of rocks might appeal to space travelers. Not only are the asteroids rich in the raw materials a space colony would need, they are also close enough to the sun to harness solar energy. In addition, the asteroids have gaps that would make convenient parking lots for spaceships.

Papagiannis says the asteroids' rocky terrain would also offer another advantage—natural camouflage for the aliens' activities. But why would extraterrestrials want to hide their space colony from Earth's prying telescopes? "We've made tremendous technological progress," Papagiannis answers. "The aliens may be deciding whether to help us or wipe us out."

A Rain of Birds

"Raining cats and dogs" is simply a description for a hard, driving rain. But there have been several recorded instances of dead birds literally raining down from the sky.

In the fall of 1846, according to one respected source, for instance, parts of France were covered with dead or dying birds that fell from the sky along with strange red rain. Scientists in Lyons and Grenoble were unable to figure out what had killed the hundreds of larks, ducks, robins, and quails that dropped from the sky—nor could they decipher what the red "rain" was made of.

Fifty years later, in July 1896, hundreds of dead woodpeckers, catbirds, thrushes, blackbirds, wild ducks, and other birds plummeted to the ground around Baton Rouge, Louisiana. Curiously, some of the ill-fated birds were not even native to that part of the country.

In the summer of 1960, the strange phenomenon occurred again, this time in Capitola, California. Police officer Ed Cunningham first noticed the deluge of dead birds around 2:30 A.M. when large dead birds started crashing around his patrol car. "They were falling so fast and hard they could have knocked me senseless," he recalled. "I thought I had better stay in the car and that's just what I did."

Eventually driving from Capitola for about five miles to West Cliff Drive, however, Cunningham found the shore highway and beach also covered with dead birds. At sunrise, the carnage was even more dramatic—bird carcasses covered power lines, fence posts, shrubbery, and TV antennas.

Authorities identified the large birds as a type of petrel known as the sooty shearing. A few of the creatures survived their plunge to earth and eventually flew away.

But what caused the birds to drop to earth in the first place? Was it smog, weather conditions, disease, poison? Experts who examined the dead birds confirmed they were killed by the fall. But why they stopped flying in the first place and fell like rain from the sky remains a mystery to this day.

Ancient Blonde Mummy

Chinese archaeologists have unearthed the oldest, most complete mummy ever found in China—but the well-preserved woman, who died when she was about forty, isn't Chinese. Instead, the mysterious lady is a blonde Caucasian who perished in China almost four thousand years ago.

The newspaper *China Daily* reported that the woman was about five feet tall, had reddish brown skin and long blonde hair. Because the desert where she was buried is so dry, her skin was well preserved and elastic and her internal organs were found to be virtually intact.

Researchers concluded that the woman was most likely a member of a nomadic group called the Uigurs, who were forerunners of modern Turks. According to Boston Museum of Fine Arts curator Wu Tung, the Uigurs were influenced by the Greeks, Indians, and Chinese.

Physicians in Shanghai who studied the preserved corpse came up with some baffling new information about the blonde mummy of China. Whoever she was, she died with high levels of cholesterol in her muscles—and inexplicable traces of the silvery white metalloid element antimony in her lungs.

Human Combustion Survivor

Although there are many recorded instances of people bursting into flames for no apparent reason, skeptics contend that human spontaneous combustion is impossible. But you won't convince Jack Angel, of Atlanta, Georgia. Some believe Angel to be the only victim of the phenomenon who has lived to tell the tale.

Once a perfectly healthy salesman who earned $70,000 a year, Angel is today disabled and confined to his home—all because of a bizarre incident that happened when he was in Savannah on a business trip. While taking a nap in his mobile trailer, Angel was jolted awake by searing pain as his body erupted in flames. When physician David Fern arrived at the scene to help the badly burned man, he found that Angel had a hole in his chest, fused vertebrae, and an arm so badly charred it could not be saved.

According to Fern, since no objects in the trailer were even singed, the only explanation for Angel's injuries is spontaneous combustion—an unexplained molecular reaction that literally causes people to burn up.

Computerized Evolution

Has man stopped evolving? Not according to scientist Hans Moravec. But his vision of tomorrow's human is a bit different from the large-skulled, slit-mouthed, hairless humanoid so popular in the science fiction literature of today. Instead, Moravec, an artificial intelligence researcher at the Carnegie-Mellon Robotics Institute, predicts that the path of human evolution is heading straight toward a merger with machines.

Within thirty years, Moravec contends, people will be substituting their weak mortal limbs for more durable robotic parts and the relatively slow human brain will be aided by superintelligent computers. He also believes we'll be able to transfer exact copies of our brain patterns to computer programs that will enable us to think thousands of times faster than ever before possible.

Another giant evolutionary step will take place, Moravec explains, when superhuman robots lose their desire to be individuals and begin to share their programs. For example, an architect who knows nothing about cooking will be able to prepare a gourmet dinner by simply borrowing the memory of a talented chef. And scientists will be able to access brilliant minds and spend their time collectively pondering the mysteries of the universe.

Even further down the evolutionary man/machine trail, Moravec sees the concept of "self" blurring. Eventually, he predicts, all human brains will merge with the brains of both earthly and extraterrestrial life forms. "After years of exchange," he notes, "we might wind up with a single conscious entity whose memory is stored in a vast bank spanning the universe."

Moravec's theory, however, has been held by Hindu philosophers for thousands of years. In the very old Sanskritic records mention is made of the eventual return of all life and all things produced by human brain power to Brahma, the original force, or godhead.

The Devil's Sea

The Bermuda Triangle isn't the only place where ships seem to disappear with alarming regularity. An area in the Pacific Ocean off the coast of central Japan has inexplicably swallowed up so many vessels that the Japanese government has officially designated it a danger zone.

The perilous spot has been known as the Devil's Sea, or the Demon Sea, ever since nine ships disappeared there in 1955; a government expedition ship (the *Kaiō Maru #5*) sent to find them vanished after about ten days. Over the next fifteen years, more than a dozen boats were lost in the Devil's Sea.

Japanese researchers suggest that severe winter weather conditions and huge waves could be the cause of some of the disappearances. They also point out that the Demon Sea has a peculiar trait—true north and magnetic north are aligned there, making it impossible to get an accurate compass reading in the area.

In hopes of unraveling the mystery of the treacherous waters, the Japanese Transport Ministry has launched another on-site investigation of the area. But instead of risking a crew of men, the government is installing a robot-buoy in the Devil's Sea, where for several years it will analyze the wind, weather, and wave conditions in the Japanese equivalent of the Bermuda Triangle.

The Hollow Earth

●
───

Belief in a hollow earth surfaces in many cultures around the world. In classical Greece, for example, it was believed that some volcanoes served as entrances to Hades deep within the planet. According to Japanese mythology, an underworld dragon moved beneath Japan, causing the earth to quake. And in Central Asia, the Mahayana Buddhist legend of Arghati depicts the world below Mongolia and Tibet where the King of Earth and his retainers reside.

Some Americans, however, have taken such tales literally. Cyrus Read, for example, founded the Hollow Earth Society in 1870 and succeeded in attracting thousands of members. Even earlier, in 1832, navy Captain John Symmes took his hollow-earth theory to the United States Congress. Within our world, he said, was a "rich, warm land stocked with thrifty vegetables and animals, if not men." To find them, Symmes wanted to sail to the North Pole in search of what he called the "Symmes Hole," enter it, and explore the inner planet. With congressional approval, the secretaries of the Navy and Treasury ordered three ships to be outfitted for the venture but President Andrew Jackson intervened to stop the effort.

Believers in a hollow earth continue to publish books on the subject, some even showing aerial photographs of the North Pole's purported "hole." Adherents of the theory point out that many things in nature—bones, pits, fruits, and animals, for example—are structured around an inner cavity. Therefore, it's logical to assume that the earth is as well.

Hitler and the Hollow Earth

Captured by the Allies during World War II and later released, a German air force pilot named Bender intrigued his countrymen with an exceptional theory. The land, water, and everything else we see on earth are really on the planet's inner shell, he asserted. Smaller than we think they are, the sun and moon actually lie between us and an outer dome that we can't see because of vapor.

Attracted to Bender's theory, Adolf Hitler approved a government-sponsored expedition that might help him win the war. Believing that a hollow earth would facilitate tracking of the British fleet, German scientists as well as air force and navy officers assembled on the Baltic island of Rügen. According to G. S. Kniper, later of the Mount Palomar Observatory, they thought "the concave curvature of the earth would facilitate long-distance observation by means of infrared rays, which are less curved than visible rays."

Their belief in the hollow-earth theory, however, worked against them. Conducted in April 1945, at considerable expense, the elaborate Rügen experiment distracted the attention of key scientific and military personnel from the war effort. It also diverted radar equipment needed for the protection of German cities from Allied air attacks.

The Lasting Legend of Loch Ness

Accounts of Scotland's celebrated Loch Ness monster have emphasized the animal's 40- to 60-foot length, its four short legs or flippers, and the carriage of its reptilian head. The description resembles that of the plesiosaur, which has been extinct for fifty million years.

Records of the Loch Ness monster go as far back as the sixth century, when it was described as a "noted demon . . . a source of terror in the neighborhood." St. Colomba is said to have stopped it from eating a swimmer. Another story relates how Nessie, as the beast is called, dragged two children under the water at a section of the lake now known as Children's Pool. A century ago, hundreds of people reportedly watched as it swam on the water's surface.

In the twentieth century, an increasing number of people have seen the monster in the lake. Perhaps encouraged by the Black and White Whiskey Company's offer of $2.5 million for proof of Nessie's existence, survey teams, for example, have scoured the lake. In 1967, a local politician witnessed the monster and was disqualified as the neutral chairman of a debate on the existence of Nessie. A skeptical Loch Ness hotel owner, Johnny Macdonald, was ranting about it being nothing but myth when the monster reared its head out of the water and cruised past the hotel.

Nessie has been photographed by numerous people, and clocked as it traveled through the water at 30 to 40 miles per hour, creating breaking waves on the shore. At least one underwater flash photograph showed what appears to be an unfriendly horned head looking directly at the camera. And electronic detectors have revealed a 25- to 35-foot-long shape swimming 40 feet below the surface of Loch Ness.

Nessie, however, seems only indirectly dangerous. In 1952, for example, John Cobb was racing across the calm water when his speed boat was struck by powerful waves. The sudden disturbance in the water may have been caused by the surprised monster diving to escape the boat.

Indeed, strangers may not be welcome at all. During the filming of a movie, shot on location at the lake, a model was used for the role of Nessie. During one of the scenes, "something" snapped the tow rope and carried the imitation monster to the bottom of the lake. It was never recovered.

Australian Ice-Age Painting

Rock paintings of the Ice-Age creature diprotodon, a rhinoceros-sized animal that became extinct about six thousand years ago, have been discovered in Europe. But researchers were surprised when they found a similar painting in Australia, home of pouch-bearing, or marsupial, mammals such as the kangaroo. Discovered at a rock shelter north of Cairns, in Queensland, the picture shows the diprotodon with a rope around its neck, suggesting not only that it had lived on the Australian continent but that it had been domesticated as well.

Ezekiel's Vision

When Josef Blumrich, the German space and rocket designer who later became chief of NASA's systems layout branch, read Erich von Däniken's *Chariots of the Gods*, he became annoyed. Von Däniken argued that the biblical Book of Ezekiel contains obvious references to space rockets and ancient astronauts. Blumrich, who had developed Skylab and Saturn V, was irked by the author's ridiculous theory and set out to prove von Däniken was wrong.

Just the opposite happened, however. Blumrich discovered that Ezekiel describes possible spacecraft landing gear and gives a detailed account of what a rocket ship would have looked like to an observer who couldn't have recognized it as such. For example, Ezekiel's reference to the "whirlwind . . . out of the north, a great cloud, and a fire infolding itself" could describe a rocket landing. The "sole of their feet . . . like the sole of a calf's foot" would be landing struts.

The likeness of winged creatures on each of the four sides,

according to Ezekiel, interpreted as the faces of a man, a lion, an ox, and an eagle, was probably suggested as the machine turned, offering a different viewing angle. Interestingly, the Gemini capsule of the modern space age, with its port windows, looks like a long ox face.

The sentence "They had the hands of a man under their wings," moreover, seems to indicate the mechanical arms attached to cylinders. The phrases "burning coals" and "out of the fire went forth lightning" are apt descriptions of a landing. Ezekiel also mentioned changing colors that he compared to the color of jewels, and wheels that touched the earth. Chapter 1 closes with his mention of "the likeness of a throne," and upon the likeness of the throne, a man. Ezekiel added, of course, that "this was the appearance of the likeness of the glory of the Lord."

As a result of his study of the von Däniken book, Blumrich was convinced that Ezekiel had seen a vehicle from space. Instead of disproving von Däniken, Blumrich turned around and wrote his own book, *The Spaceship of Ezekiel*.

Beware the Nuclear Winter

Despite predictions that an atomic war would cause millions, even billions, of deaths, many people have been optimistic that survivors would somehow be able to resume their lives and repair the damage. Some scientists, however, have challenged that supposition.

According to the "nuclear winter" theory of astronomer Carl Sagan and others, a large-scale atomic war would spread dust, soot, and smoke into the atmosphere. With the sun's rays blocked out, lakes, rivers, and parts of the oceans would freeze and the earth's temperatures would drop by at least 75°F. Most of the world's food crops would die off, causing starvation and battles over whatever stored food remained. This, combined with continuing fires ravaging the earth's forests and urban centers, would make the victors no better off than the losers.

Out-of-Place Animals

Claims of kangaroos hopping around North Carolina may sound about as plausible to most folks as sightings of pink elephants. But Loren Coleman, a psychiatric social worker who pursues cryptozoology in his spare time, says there's an explanation other than hallucination for reports of out-of-place animals. Coleman, who has studied dozens of these cases, thinks the animals may have somehow mysteriously "teleported" from one location to another.

"There's a random pattern to these things," Coleman notes. "Sometimes these animals literally come out of the blue." For example, in the early 1980s, kangaroos were spotted in North Carolina, Oklahoma, and Utah, and a penguin was found on a New Jersey beach. Several Florida residents were startled when they came across six-foot-long Nile monitor lizards—creatures that are supposedly found only in their native Africa.

Coleman admits that some scientists would argue these animals were brought into the country, perhaps as babies. "But it's not that simple," he asserts. He points out that he has investigated hundreds of sightings of strange animals, talking to game wardens, police, and ordinary citizens. And while a logical explanation is found in more than half of the cases, at least 20 percent of the sightings remain enigmas.

Touching a Lake Monster

Hundreds of people over several centuries have reported seeing dinosaurlike lake monsters, including Loch Ness's famous Nessie. But a British Columbian woman has gained the distinction of being the only human reported to have actually *touched* one of the creatures.

Barbara Clark's adventure began on a sunny bright morning in July 1974, at Okanagan Lake. She was taking a swim toward a diving platform about a quarter mile offshore when, suddenly, she felt something huge and rough pass her in the water, scratching her legs. Quickly, Barbara threw herself upward, reached out for the raft, and climbed aboard. When she turned around, she saw it—a dark gray, serpentine animal about thirty feet long and four feet wide, swimming five yards away. The creature's head was underwater but its fluked tail was clearly visible.

J. Richard Greenwell, secretary of the International Society of Cryptozoology, an organization that researches reports of unexplained or long-thought-extinct life forms, investigated Barbara Clark's claim and found her a highly credible witness. "She did not come forward until recently," he notes. "She was afraid no one would believe her."

Greenwell points out that even before Europeans settled in the area, local Indians related tales of a monster that dwelled in Okanagan Lake. Over two hundred eyewitness reports of the creature, called Ogopogo by local residents, have been collected over the years—most of them, Greenwell says, describe an animal that sounds strikingly similar to the one Barbara Clark encountered.

Whatever it was that slithered through the dark waters of the lake toward Barbara, it did not seem to be interested in attacking her. Greenwell says its tail may explain why. "The creature's fluked tail points to [its being] a mammal," he notes. "Mammals are very curious. It may have come to Barbara just to see what was splashing in the water."

The Mystery of Oliver

Oliver was discovered in the Congo more than a decade ago, and no one is sure whether he's a mutant, a hybrid, or part of a new species of chimp. He looks like a bald chimpanzee, but his ears are at the top of his head rather than at the center. His nose protrudes much like that of humans, and unlike apes, who prefer walking on their knuckles, Oliver seems to naturally walk upright.

Studied extensively by Ralph Helfer, an animal behaviorist who heads Gentle Jungle, a Burbank, California, organization that trains animal actors, Oliver apparently has forty-seven chromosomes, falling between an ape's forty-eight and a human's forty-six, and suggesting a crossbreed or possibly Down's syndrome. His intelligence, however, rules out a simian form of Down's syndrome. He watches television Westerns and action programs for hours, unlike chimps, which become bored after a few minutes.

Everyone, from Sasquatch hunters to anthropologists, is baffled. "No one thinks he's a chimp, and no one has suggested he's an infant bigfoot," Helfer says. Everyone, however, admits that Oliver is an unusual primate.

Teen Wolf

In 1976, a local village chief found a human child frolicking with three wolf cubs in a forest in the Sultanpur district near Lucknow, India. According to later reports by the Press Trust of India domestic news agency, the boy's nails had grown into claws. Estimated to be about eight years old, he had thick body hair with tangled, matted hair on his head.

Because the boy resembled a bear, the chief called him Bhaloo. Although the name was later changed to Bhaskar, many people simply referred to him as the "wolf boy" because they believed he had been reared by a wolf.

The chief had hoped to civilize the wolf boy but his efforts were unsuccessful. Eventually Bhaskar entered Prem Nivas, a home for the destitute and poor operated by the Missionaries for Charity in Lucknow, 270 miles southeast of New Delhi. He remained there until he died in 1985.

Lost River Found

●
───────────────────────────────────────

As most of the world cooled and entered the Ice Age about two million years ago, the area near the borders of Egypt, the Sudan, and Libya drastically changed from grassland to desert. Prehistoric man was probably the last to see the great rivers, valleys, channels, and flood plains that once predominated there. The region has since been hostile to almost all living things; rain is believed to fall only every forty years or even less frequently.

Since ancient times, however, explorers have journeyed into this hostile environment seeking the remnants of *Bahr-bela-ma*, a mammoth river system believed to have existed beneath the sands of the Sahara Desert. In fact, the legend of the "great rivers without water" persisted even though no trace of the supposed river systems was ever found—until 1982.

Studying the earth's terrain, scientists on board the space shuttle captured radar images of an extensive river topography beneath the Saharan sands. According to the U.S. Geological Survey's John McCauley, a leader of the team that conducted the shuttle experiments, it is unlikely that the buried river valleys link to the Nile. The rivers veer to the south and west, the opposite of the Nile's present-day movement. It is possible, he conjectured, that the buried rivers and the Nile once joined in the interior in a basin as large as the Caspian Sea.

Baby Mammoth

●
───────────────────────────────────────

Huge prehistoric mammoths once roamed what is now Siberia. During one herd's travels across the frozen tundra about forty thousand years ago, a seven-month-old animal became trapped in silt. The frightened infant probably fought to escape but soon exhausted itself and was drowned in the sedimentary material. The carcass was completely covered and protected from carnivorous animals; the site itself was eventually buried under snowslides that never thawed.

The burial site lay untouched until 1977, when a bulldozer operator uncovered the baby mammoth in a layer of ice, broken stone, and silt in the northern Magadan region. The fully preserved corpse was removed to a deep-freeze chamber, where excited Russian scientists weighed, measured, described, and preserved everything. Previous mammoth finds have been considerably damaged, according to Nikolai Vereschagin, chairman of the Committee for Mammoth Studies of the USSR Academy of Sciences.

The baby mammoth, the first completely preserved specimen ever discovered, offers a fuller idea of the mammoth's external appearance as well as the structure of the animal's internal organs. Soviet researchers were able to study its brain, skeleton, and muscles. They removed the heart, lungs, kidney, stomach, and other internal organs. They may also be able to determine the reasons for the extinction of the behemoths, which were seemingly well adapted to severe climate.

Bikini

Nowadays the name Bikini is more noted as a brief bathing attire rather than the Bikini Island atoll in the Pacific Ocean where the hydrogen bomb was tested from 1946 to 1958. The association of names may stem from the obvious fact that there is so little of either of them, Bikini being only two miles square.

Nevertheless, the island of Bikini formerly contained a number of inhabitants who were quite satisfied with their place in the sea. They were all removed by U.S. authorities as were the native dwellers of Eniwetok, a nearby island that was the site of a series of nuclear blasts in the 1950s.

In 1968 the original inhabitants of both islands were permitted to return, but when the Bikini islanders farmed crops, the yield was found to be radioactive and the confused islanders were shipped out again. Eniwetok, a somewhat larger island, was decontaminated and new palm trees were planted since all vegetation had been blown away by the bomb. The authorities, however, forbade the islanders to eat the coconuts that grew on the newly planted trees.

The natives were disappointed and puzzled, but most of them were familiar with the Bible as a result of the untiring efforts of generations of missionaries, and many of them recalled the mention of an earlier and more pleasant garden where the Supreme Authority had forbidden the dwellers in the garden to eat another apparently harmless fruit: "the fruit of the tree which is in the midst of the garden."

Sunken City

Once the Monte Carlo of the Roman Empire, the ancient city of Baiae boasted luxurious villas and pavilions that were built right into the sea. Possibly encompassing an area four miles long and a quarter mile wide, it was larger than its neighbor Pompeii. Even the emperor Augustus Caesar and the orator, statesman, and philosopher Cicero, among others, kept homes at the resort on the west coast of Naples.

During the second century, Romans constructed a seawall to protect the area from the onslaught of storms. The wall, however, proved insufficient against other natural forces. Eventually, earthquakes and volcanic eruptions caused the coastal resort to descend into the sea.

Today, the great villas and their treasures and other artifacts still lay at the bottom of Italy's Bay of Pozzuoli, but only divers can enjoy the thrill of exploring the well-preserved underwater community. German archaeologist Bernard Andreae, however, has proposed the construction of an airtight plastic bubble to be placed at least over the imperial villa. Andreae, who has taken part in excavations of Baiae, would lay a tube from the shoreline to the bubble, drawing the water out and replacing it with air. Visitors would find not only the remains of the elegant structure, but also reconstructions of the statuary that have been recovered placed where it was during Roman times.

The Kiss of Death

Retreating from the festivities of their wedding reception in northeast China, a young Chinese bride and groom secluded themselves in the nearby bridal suite. There, the newly married lovers would consummate their union, as the groom began to kiss his wife passionately on the neck.

Before long, however, their guests heard a scream. Rushing into the bedroom, they found the newly married lovers unconscious. They rushed the couple to the hospital, but the bride was declared dead on arrival.

The intensity of their passion and the length of the groom's kiss, the doctors determined, had caused heart palpitations. The bride had died from cardiac arrest.

A Recent Disappearance in the Bermuda Triangle

After thirty years as a top pilot in the Ford Motor Company's fleet, having flown such officials as Henry Ford and former Ford executive Lee Iacocca, Dick Yerex retired in 1986. He and his wife left their Gibraltar, Michigan, home and moved to North Palm

Beach, Florida, where Yerex took a job with a local commuter service.

On May 27, 1987, Yerex was on a routine commuter flight en route to pick up passengers on Abaco Island in Bermuda. His twin-engine Cessna was in excellent condition, with no history of mechanical problems. The weather was clear except for occasional light rain. And Yerex had an outstanding record as a pilot. All in all, everything was going well.

Just forty minutes after takeoff, however, Yerex radioed another pilot to inform him of the location of a government satellite balloon. It was the last time anyone heard from him. He was last seen heading into the Bermuda Triangle, the infamous area formed by imaginary lines drawn from Melbourne, Florida, to Bermuda to Puerto Rico and back to Florida.

"The only factual thing we know is that the aircraft took off," said Ron Bird, an air safety investigator with the National Traffic Safety Board in Miami. "Beyond that, anything is possible."

After an extensive but fruitless search, Yerex was listed as missing and presumed dead; his twin-engine Cessna, presumed destroyed.

Mystery Manuscript

In 1912 British book dealer Wilfrid Voynich purchased a 204-page manuscript from a Jesuit college in Italy. Illustrated with multicolored drawings, the mysterious volume was handwritten in an unknown alphabet, and Voynich gave copies to anyone interested in trying to translate it.

There were many attempts to decipher the language, but no one was successful until April 1921, when the University of Pennsylvania's William Romaine Newbold claimed to have broken the code. According to Newbold, Voynich's manuscript was the work of Roger Bacon, the thirteenth-century English Franciscan friar and inventor. The translation indicated that Bacon had built and used microscopes and telescopes four hundred years before they were believed to have been invented.

Not long after Newbold's death, however, his diligent translation was disproved, although no one else came up with a more substantial theory. The manuscript eventually was donated to Yale University, where it remains today—still a mystery to researchers and scholars.

Extraterrestrial Bigfoot

⬤
_____

The sounds outside her home late one night in February 1974 startled the Pennsylvania woman. Not taking any chances, she went to the front door armed with a gun and cautiously stepped out onto the porch. Suddenly, she was confronted by a flesh-and-blood bigfoot-like creature six feet away. When she shot the gun, aiming for his middle, she was astonished to see it disappear in a burst of light.

Having heard the shot, the woman's son-in-law rushed to her aid. Once outside, he saw other bigfoot creatures at the edge of the nearby woods. Hovering overhead was a bright red flashing light.

There have been a number of cases in which both UFOs and Bigfoot have been sighted at the same time and in the same area. Another case involving the humanoid creatures and UFOs took place on a farm near Gettysburg, Pennsylvania. A twenty-two-year-old farmer's son named Stephen went to investigate a large, bright red luminous ball sighted one night in October 1973. He and the two ten-year-old boys who accompanied him saw the object hovering close to the ground. Nearby, there were two tall, apelike creatures with green glowing eyes and long, dark hair. When they began to approach the threesome, Stephen fired a shot over their heads. When the creatures continued moving forward, Stephen fired three more times, hitting the largest creature. The UFO suddenly disappeared, and the hairy creatures turned around and walked into the woods.

A Future American Triangle?

The Bermuda Triangle is formed by imaginary lines that run from a point near Melbourne, Florida, to Bermuda to Puerto Rico and back to Florida. It's long been infamous because of the dozens of ships and planes that have disappeared within its boundaries. According to Hugh Cochrane, an authority on deadly triangles throughout the world, such zones are created by energy originating at the bottom of the ocean.

Triangle zones can move, however, just as earthquake zones do, says Cochrane, author of *Gateway to Oblivion*. In fact, that is exactly what the Bermuda Triangle is doing, he claims. And it is moving westward—toward the United States. As a result of the shift inland, he adds, passenger vehicles may not disappear, but there will be more train wrecks and airplane crashes.

Bermuda Triangle's Power Source

Tom Gary, author of *Adventures of an Amateur Psychic*, claims that the Bermuda Triangle's destructive force comes from energy emanating from beneath the sea. "There is speculation that a power structure is still underwater in the Bermuda area," Gary says. The structure, he adds, rests atop a large core that extends down through the crust of the earth. "When conditions are right the power structure works intermittently, causing ship and plane captains to lose control of their crafts."

According to Gary, streaming ions form an electric current that produces a magnetic field and this causes instrument failure in craft in the vicinity. Magnetic compasses, fuel gauges, altitude indicators, and all electrically operated instruments are affected. Adds

Gary, pilots who have survived such activity have reported battery drainage as well.

Strange Theft

One day, a would-be shoplifter walked into a store, tried on a sports jacket, and began to walk out of the store. Before he reached the door, however, the coat exploded. It seems a terrorist group had been planting incendiary devices in department stores and placed one of them in the coat's pocket. The unharmed but embarrassed shoplifter had a rough time convincing the Federal Bureau of Investigation that he wasn't a terrorist.

In another FBI case involving theft and terrorists, Croatian hijackers forced a commercial pilot to land in Paris, where they were apprehended. The passengers were flown home to the United States on another plane, while the crew returned with the hijacked plane to Chicago. No one, however, seemed to know what happened to the terrorists' bomb—until the plane's captain and flight attendants finally admitted they had whisked it away, thinking it would be a great souvenir.

The FBI's files are filled with unusual cases. People, it seems, will steal anything—a North Carolina-bound beer truck filled with nothing but empty bottles, a shipment of ox lips, and even horse manure. Then, there was the case of the talking parrot with a vocabulary of 250 words who could even bark like a dog. With such talent, the bird was a strong enticement to the burglar who nabbed it and then found a family to buy it from him. Police soon learned the whereabouts of the valuable parrot as word of its talents spread through its new neighborhood.

Anything of value, of course, is subject to theft, like 3.13 ounces of frozen bull semen from the world's greatest dairy stud. The semen was stolen from a storage tank at a breeders association in Waupun, Wisconsin, and probably steered toward Canada. Worth $90,000 in the United States, its value would be tripled across the border.

Another bird—actually a store mannequin dressed as a chicken—gained the interest of a passerby. Finding the display irresistible, the man broke the window and ran off with the pseudobird, but he was apprehended a few blocks away.

Bursting into Flames

Incidents of spontaneous human combustion usually seem to occur behind closed doors and without any observers. For instance, the night that Cornelia di Bandi, an eighteenth-century Italian countess, died, some people noticed yellowish smoke coming from her bedroom. A maid rushed into the room, but found just a heap of ashes next to the bed. Only the countess's legs seemed to have been untouched by the flames. And in America, a twenty-seven-year-old Pontiac, Michigan, welder was apparently in the process of committing suicide by inhaling carbon monoxide when he combusted—of course, nobody saw.

According to the experts, in fact, the first case with a bona fide witness occurred in 1982, when a Chicago man sitting in his car casually noticed a woman crossing the street. When he turned back for a second glance, she was on fire. Examination by bomb and arson investigators found no foul play involved.

The Dark Star of the Hopi

Hopi tradition, which goes back farther than the tradition of other Indian tribes residing today in the United States of America, preserves accounts of the various world catastrophes that have almost annihilated mankind. Like the Aztecs, the Hopis divided the periods between the catastrophes by "Suns" (the Sun of Water, the Sun of Earth, the Sun of Wind, and the present one, the Sun of Fire).

According to the Hopis, the Sun of Fire is due to end shortly after the year 2000 and will be heralded by the appearance of a dark star, even now approaching Earth. The end of the Sun of Fire will also be indicated by an unusual blue flower that will bloom in the desert. According to tribal reports, a strange blue flower, hitherto unknown, has been found in the desert regions of New Mexico.

Although the Aztecs counted five suns, they agree with the Hopi that the present Sun, the Sun of Fire, will be the last.

Ralph Waldo Emerson and Mrs. Luther

Incidents of spontaneous extrasensory perception occur when people least expect them. Therefore, they're often dismissed as mere coincidence, like the experience of the wife of the nineteenth-century Trinity College mathematician F. S. Luther.

Once a friend asked Mrs. Luther if she had any books about poet Ralph Waldo Emerson. No, she didn't, she replied, and thought no more about it. That night, however, she dreamed she had given such a book to a friend; the friend, in turn, dreamed she had received the text. The next day, the mathematician reported, his wife suddenly and inexplicably turned to the bookshelves. She pulled out a copy of *Century Magazine* and immediately opened to an article entitled "The Homes and Haunts of Emerson."

The Destruction of Mary Reeser

When investigators arrived at Mary Reeser's home in 1951, the front door was too hot to handle. Eventually getting the door opened, they were then confronted by a gust of hot air. They were too late, however, to save Reeser. All they found were her remains in the chair where she had burned to death during the night.

The overstuffed chair was burned down to its springs. The carpet around the chair was charred. Directly above, a patch of ceiling was covered with soot. Unlike other fire deaths in which the skull swells or explodes, Reeser's skull had been shrunken by intense heat. Given the extent of her cremation, according to forensic scientist Wilton Krogman, the entire apartment should have been rightfully consumed. Nothing else in the house had been damaged by the fire, however, not even a pile of papers near the chair.

Numerous theories were proposed to explain Reeser's death, including ignition of methane gas in her body, murder by flamethrower, napalm, even a "ball of fire" that one letter writer claimed to have seen. Krogman himself suggested that Reeser had been burned elsewhere by someone with access to crematorium-type equipment who then returned her remains to the apartment. There, her murderer added such touches as heat-buckled objects and a doorknob that was still hot in the morning.

The coroner, meanwhile, accepted the FBI's theory that Reeser had fallen asleep while smoking and the lit cigarette set her on fire. But the case was never *officially* resolved.

Russian Telepathy

Though paranormal research in the Soviet Union has long been classified as top secret, Russian physiologist Leonid Vasiliev revealed a while back that he and other researchers have been able to give telepathic orders to hypnotized patients. They were, he said, even able to induce hypnosis telepathically.

In one experiment recounted by Vasiliev, for instance, a partially paralyzed woman, whose condition had been diagnosed as psychosomatic, was able to move her left arm and leg with ease while under hypnosis. More important, Vasiliev discovered, when he sent her telepathic directives she would use her limbs—without the use of hypnosis at all.

Demonstrating the ability before an audience of other researchers, Vasiliev blindfolded the woman. Each directive was written down and handed to the group before Vasiliev or his assistant mentally focused on it. Not only was the patient able to pick up the message and obey, but she could even indicate who actually sent the message.

In more recent studies, a committee of Soviet scientists supervised a session using biophysicist Yuri Kamensky in Siberia and actor and journalist Karl Nikolaiev in Moscow. In one test, Nikolaiev correctly described six objects given to Kamensky and identified twelve out of twenty ESP cards.

Interestingly, moreover, the scientists were able to produce independent evidence of the results by connecting Nikolaiev to an electroencephalogram (EEG) machine: As soon as Kamensky began to mentally image the objects, Nikolaiev's brain waves altered.

Based on the EEG results, the scientists devised a technique for sending messages in Morse code. When they instructed Kamensky to imagine he was fighting Nikolaiev, the EEG indicated distinct changes in Nikolaiev's brain waves. Kamensky was able to transmit Morse "dots" and "dashes" by imagining fighting bouts of various lengths: a forty-five-second bout produced a flurry of brain wave activity, interpreted as a dash; a fifteen-second bout was read as a dot. The scientists, two thousand miles away in Moscow, were then able to identify the Russian word *mig* (instant).

The Vultures of Gettysburg

The battle of Gettysburg was one of the bloodiest of the Civil War. After three days of fighting, thousands of slaughtered horses lay among some fifty thousand dead and mortally wounded men strewn across the field. And Plum Run, the stream passing through what is now a national military park, flowed red with blood. It was a smorgasbord for vultures, symbolic sentinels of death.

Today, the carrion-eating birds annually return to Gettysburg, as they have for at least a century, according to park resource specialist Harold J. Greenlee. Virginia Polytechnic Institute and Pennsylvania State University students, working with Greenlee, have been studying the vultures, including their migration patterns. They are also researching Civil War history, looking for mention of the avian scavengers.

"The birds roost on Little Round Top and Big Round Top, hills where some of the heaviest battles took place," Greenlee says. "It's not unreasonable that the vultures could have been attracted to the bodies; they might have scavenged, stayed on for the winter, and then gotten into the habit of coming here." As a result of their investigations, Greenlee and the students hope to explain why nine hundred vultures continue to roost in a national park.

Telepathic Morse Code

Telepathy is an elusive phenomenon, one that tends to occur at unpredictable times and places. Electrochemist and psychic researcher Douglas Dean, however, has found one constant measure of the phenomenon: the volume of blood flowing through the brain changes measurably when people receive messages about a family member or intimate friend. For example, if the communicator concentrated on an image of a person's mother, Dean would be able to tell exactly when the person tuned in to the sender's mind by measuring the movement of his blood.

Using the blood volume measuring instrument called the plethysmograph, Dean went on to develop a Morse Code technique based on his recordings. He interpreted a measurable response to the subject's mental activity as a Morse dot; no response during a specified time was read as a dash. In this manner, Dean has been able to transmit telepathic Morse messages over both short and long distances. In one case, he was able to send such a message from New York to Florida—a distance of twelve hundred miles.

The Mind of an English Clergyman

The nineteenth-century English clergyman Canon Warburton saw his brother catch his foot on the edge of a landing's top stair and fall headfirst to the bottom. Using his hands and elbows, his brother just barely managed to break his fall and prevent serious injury.

Warburton suddenly woke, finding himself in an armchair in his brother's home. The scene he had witnessed had been only a dream. Arriving in London from Oxford to visit his brother, Canon

Warburton had dozed off while awaiting his brother, who had left a note indicating that he had gone to a dance and would return around one o'clock in the morning.

"I have just had as narrow an escape of breaking my neck as I ever had in my life," his brother told him when he returned about half an hour later. "Coming out of the ballroom, I caught my foot and tumbled full length down the stairs."

India's Gravitational Anomaly

Sriharikota, located off the southeast coast of India, is that country's main spacecraft-launching facility. The launch site, however, is notorious for the large number of crashes that occur. Now comes an explanation from Professor Ram S. Srivasta, one of India's most respected space researchers. The disasters occur, Srivasta declares, because the facility is in the middle of "the greatest gravitational anomaly in the world." Srivasta can offer no explanation for the great gravitational swings he has detected at the site. He nonetheless believes that these major variations in gravitational force cause rockets to deviate from course and fall helter-skelter from the Indian sky.

Were the Pyramids Built of Cement Blocks?

Motion pictures like *The Ten Commandments* have left images of thousands of slaves forced to drag huge stones from quarries miles away to the site of pharaohs' tombs, the great pyramids. Barry University chemist Joseph Davidovits, however, presents a different theory: The ancient Egyptians, he says, used concrete, made up of more than two dozen natural ingredients, including limestone and shells. Although the modern Egyptian government denied him permission to verify his theory with on-site sampling, Davidovits believes pouring the stones as the pyramids were built explains their perfect fit.

The Pharos of Alexandria

The highest tower of historical antiquity was most probably the Pharos of Alexandria, an enormous lighthouse guiding ships to and from Alexandria, the Greco-Egyptian metropolis in ancient Egypt. During the night, a great fire burned from its lofty top, and during the day a giant mirror reflected the sun's rays, reputedly visible from thirty miles out over the Mediterranean sea. Its height has been estimated at five hundred to six hundred feet.

To get up and down the towering structure, the lighthouse personnel and garrison had the use of carts, pulled by surefooted asses, which constantly ascended and descended the tower on a series of ramps. The ramps followed a zigzag from level to level, and riders in the carts, soldiers or custodians, could get on or off at the various levels, much like entering or leaving a modern elevator.

This primitive elevator system stopped functioning in the early Middle Ages when Alexandria was captured by the Arabs. Then the Caliph Al-Walid had the Pharos partially dismantled in a search of suspected hidden treasure. Part of the ruined structure was converted into a mosque, but even that was destroyed by an earthquake, and the ruins were carted away for use in other buildings.

About forty years ago divers discovered a large marble column on the sea bottom. It was identified as the *finger* of one of the huge statues that adorned the corners of the great Pharos.

Sucked into the Air by a UFO

In early 1988, forty-eight-year-old Fay Knowles and her three sons were driving near the small village of Mundrabilla on the remote Eyre Highway in the vast desert of southern Australia. Suddenly, their car veered in an unexpected direction—straight up.

The Australian family told police they were pursued by a "huge bright glowing object" that sucked their auto and its shocked passengers into the air. During their bizarre ride, Fay Knowles and her sons noticed that their voices became strangely slurred and abnormally slow. Then the UFO dropped the car back onto the highway, causing a rear tire to blow out. And eerily, three other people in southern Australia saw the unidentified flying object as well.

"The sightings took place hundreds of kilometers apart and these people had no reason to conspire," says police sergeant James Fennell of Ceduna, a town about 370 miles away. Beyond that, he added, an investigation of the Knowles's car showed that it was covered in a thick coating of black ash inside and out. The roof was damaged, too.

"The family members were extremely distraught," Fennell declared. "Something happened out there."

The 1897 Spaceman

On April 19, 1897, something so extraordinary happened in the tiny farming community of Aurora, Texas, that townsfolk talk about it still. According to accounts published in the Dallas and Fort Worth newspapers of the time, on that fateful spring day, a cigar-shaped spaceship roared out of the sky and slammed into Judge J. S. Proctor's home, destroying a window, a water trough, and a flower garden in the process.

S. E. Hayden, a local cotton buyer and newspaper correspondent, reported that the little man who piloted the craft was dismembered by the crash. "However, enough remains were picked up to determine it was not an inhabitant of this world," Hayden wrote in a newspaper article describing the strange event. "The men of the community gathered it up, and it was given a Christian burial in the Aurora cemetery."

The alien's grave marker disappeared several years ago. Residents of Aurora claim they are no longer sure where the grave is and they doubt much could remain in it. But, periodically, areas of the cemetery are dug up—most likely by people hoping to find the remains of the only extraterrestrial said to be buried on planet Earth.

Reward for a UFO: £1,000,000

Kenneth Arnold, an experienced pilot, flying his plane over the Cascade Mountains of Washington in 1947, suddenly saw nine unidentified circular metal objects flying at an estimated speed of 1,300 miles per hour. Since then, many thousands of UFO sightings have been reported over the plains, mountains, deserts, lakes, oceans, and cities of Earth. Although strange objects have been noted in the skies through the centuries, the Arnold sighting seemed to launch an avalanche of reports, which has continued ever since.

Many UFOs have been photographed, but not one has been produced for public inspection. Their landing tracks in the earth have been tested for traces of minerals or chemicals, for geometric signs or mathematical indications, and flight and takeoff patterns have been compared with other international reports.

According to the *People's Almanac* (Bantam, 1981), the Cutty Sark Company of 3 St. James Street, London SW1, has posted a bona fide reward of £1,000,000 to anyone able to capture a "spaceship or other vehicle" that is verified by the Science Museum of London as having "come from outer space." The Cutty Sark Company, makers of Scotch whisky, claims that the reward for a provable UFO is a serious offer, and the company has taken out insurance to cover the possible expense.

Although no one has yet claimed this prize money, a possible candidate is rumored to exist in the form of a crashed flying saucer or spaceship found on July 2, 1947, near Socorro, New Mexico (*The Roswell Incident*: Ace Books, 1988). The saucerlike spaceship was first taken to Roswell Air Force Base and then shipped for further examination, along with its dead humanoid crew, to Muroc Air Force Base in California for inspection by President Eisenhower and others, who maintained regulation military security with the press. After that it was sent to Wright-Patterson Air Force Base, Ohio, where it was held in Building 18A, Area B. Eventually it was sent to Langley Field, Virginia, headquarters of the CIA. Other parts of the wreck are rumored to be at McDill Air Force Base in Florida, and photographs are alleged to be on file or exhibit in the "Blue Room" at Wright-Patterson, where a top-secret exhibit of UFO activity is displayed.

It is unlikely that Cutty Sark will have to make good the reward in the case of the Roswell incident because all corroborative reports concerning it are now classified. Nevertheless, when the incident first occurred, the press gave it wide coverage in interviews with civilians as well as military personnel.

These reports, however, do not qualify for the Cutty Sark award. Cutty Sark will keep its £1,000,000, and its whisky label will continue to feature a sailing ship and not an interplanetary spacecraft. If there is any concrete proof of captured or crashed UFOs held by other nations, it will probably remain secret. During the present world situation, knowledge of the construction and operation of UFOs from space or from Earth itself would represent an extraordinary advantage to the country possessing it.

Giant South Pole Crater

Imagine a hole so huge it would nearly fill the space between Chicago and Indianapolis. An Indiana University–Purdue University scientist John G. Weihaupt says he has proof that such an enormous crater exists, still undiscovered, near the South Pole—the result of the largest meteorite ever to strike the earth.

"We now have evidence that a crater comparable to the largest craters that exist on the moon exists on Earth," Weihaupt contends. He estimates that beneath the ice of northern Antarctica lies a crater a half mile deep and 150 miles wide—four times larger than any other meteorite crater found so far on this planet.

What could have made such an enormous hole? According to Weihaupt, the answer is a mammoth meteorite. Weighing in at around 13 billion tons and measuring 2.5 to 3.75 miles across, the meteorite is believed to have smashed into the earth between 600,000 and 700,000 years ago, at a speed of 44,000 miles per hour.

Although the impact was enormous, when the meteorite hit it spared the earth a greater catastrophe. Weihaupt says his calculations show that the crash lacked enough force to change the planet's axis or rotation.

Ancient Electricity

In 1936, while excavating an ancient Parthian settlement in what is now Iran, Austrian scientist Wilhelm König came across a puzzling object. Although it dated from about 250 B.C., the instrument seemed to have technical workings. In fact, König suspected it was an electricity-producing battery.

Encased in a terra-cotta pot, the tubular object was 2.5 centimeters wide. Made of copper sheeting soldered with a tin-lead alloy, it stood about 12 centimeters high. A tight-fitting copper cap, insulated with pitch, covered one end while the other was sealed with a pitch stopper. Poking out of this was an iron rod insulated with copper. When the contraption was filled with an acid solution (like vinegar, wine, or lemon juice) or with an alkali (for example, lye), König deduced that a working galvanistic element would be produced.

Two experiments—one conducted in the United States in 1957 and another repeated recently by Egyptologist Arne Eggebrecht of the Hildesheimer Museum in Germany—used copies of the object (the original is housed in the Iraq Museum of Baghdad) to prove that it *can* create an electric current. With the help of a copper sulfate solution, the battery designed by so-called barbarian nomads emitted .5 volts of electricity.

There are clues that the ancient Egyptians also knew how to produce electrical power. Many monuments built during the time of the pharaohs are filled with rooms and passageways that have no apparent light source. No trace of soot from torches, candles, or petroleum lamps has ever been found, according to Professor Helmuth Satzinger of the Kunsthistorisches Museum in Vienna. Could the builders of the great Egyptian edifices have worked by the glow of electric lights?

Located on the shore of the Nile opposite the city of Qena, the ancient Egyptian temple of Dendera may hold the answer to that question. Inside, strange wall reliefs show human figures beside objects that look like giant light bulbs with serpents—or symbols of filaments—undulating inside. Perhaps it is more than coincidence that Thoth, the Egyptian god of science who illuminated the night with his light, is shown nearby.

The walls of the temple are covered with other illustrations and hieroglyphs that Egyptologists have been unable to fully decipher. But Dr. John Harris, a British scientist at Oxford, who studied the reliefs, concluded that they appear to be the ancient equivalent of technical writing used by today's scientists. Austrian scientist Walter Garn, who has extensive experience as an electrical engineer, agrees that the temple of Dendera holds technical information—specifically, directions on how to produce electricity.

Garn interprets the "serpents" in the bulblike pictographs as electrical arcs; he suggests that the men shown kneeling opposite each other beneath the bubble are symbolic of opposing electrical currents. He also notes that a fluted column that seems to support the "bulb" looks remarkably like a modern high-voltage insulator.

Death Star

When scientists from the University of California analyzed the ages of the earth's largest impact craters, a startling pattern emerged. The craters, created when comets slammed into the planet, appear to have been formed every 28 million years—a time frame that coincides exactly with the mysterious mass extinctions of animals that once roamed the planet.

But what could bring comets into the earth's path at such precise intervals? The researchers say the earth is at the mercy of an uncharted "death star" that brings comets—and catastrophic destruction—to the earth as it regularly passes by this part of the solar system.

Physicist Richard Muller, working with Princeton physicist Piet Hut and Berkeley astronomer Marc Davis, has come up with a theory that explains how the "killer star" operates. A small, cool dwarf, it has an elliptical orbit that takes it as far as 2.4 light years away from the sun—right into a part of space where a comet cloud containing 100 billion comets is located. Whizzing through the cloud, the star picks up some of the comets and later, as it soars past the solar system every 28 million years, it tosses some of the asteroids toward the earth.

"The earth is a small enough target that you'd expect about two dozen of those to hit it," Muller points out. "But they would do it in a relatively short period."

When the meterorites smashed into the planet in the past, Muller theorizes, they created a cloud of dust that blocked sunlight and prevented photosynthesis. That, he says, would explain why dinosaurs were suddenly wiped out about 65 million years ago, after ruling the earth for 140 million years—dust storms plunged the planet into months of cold and darkness and caused the creatures to die of cold and hunger.

The scientists say there's every reason to believe that the "death star" will pay the earth another terrifying visit. But this time, we'll know when it's headed our way: It's due back in about 15 million years.

Ancient Greek Use of Solar Energy

Around 214 B.C., the story goes, Greek mathematician and inventor Archimedes figured out a novel way to stop the Roman forces who were attacking the Sicilian port city of Syracuse—he used solar energy to roast them alive.

Archimedes reportedly instilled a giant concave mirror on the shore. The reflective surface magnified the sun's rays and focused them back on the Roman ships, which caught fire in seconds.

To find out if this tale is simply a myth or if it could be historical fact, a present-day Greek engineer, Ioannis Sakkas, reenacted the event in 1973. Theorizing that Archimedes actually used hundreds of soldiers' mirrored shields instead of one huge curved mirror, Sakkas linked up seventy Greek sailors along the seashore, each holding a five-by-three-foot bronze-coated mirror. Then he signaled the group to angle their mirrored shields in the direction of a plywood boat that floated about 160 feet out in the ocean. The result? The boat burst into flames within a few minutes.

Sakkas noted that Archimedes probably had even greater success with his solar energy assault—the Romans' ships were more flammable than his model, and, while the men participating in the experiment stood at sea level, the Syracusans probably had the advantage of being elevated on a wall. "Archimedes," Sakkas concluded, "would have operated under better conditions."

The Balloonists of Nazca

History books say that the first manned hot-air balloons didn't get off the ground until the eighteenth century. But there's evidence that an ancient people living in what is now Nazca Valley soared above the bleak Peruvian plains centuries earlier. In fact, their aerial talents could explain how the Indians were able to draw giant abstract designs and figures that stretch in straight lines for miles—creations that are visible only from the sky.

In 1975, a travel-oriented organization called the International Explorers Society, based in Coral Gables, Florida, began studying the possibility that the Nazcas were balloonists. The group's members theorized that while Nazca workmen laid out gigantic linear designs on the ground, they were guided from above by observers who hovered over them in hot-air balloons.

Their research came up with a picture on a Nazca ceramic pot that appears to illustrate a hot-air bag. They also learned that textiles recovered from desert graves proved that the Nazcas had the materials needed to make a balloon's envelope.

In addition, they discovered a reference in a document at the University of Coimbra in Portugal that could be an important clue. According to this source, a Brazilian-born Jesuit missionary named Bartholomeu de Gusamão visited Lisbon in 1709. There he demonstrated a model of a balloon that, when filled with smoke and hot air from glowing coals contained in a clay pot, lifted off his hand and drifted upwards. This event was surprising not only because it occurred nearly seventy-five years before France's balloon pioneers, the Montgolfier brothers, flew their first balloon over Paris but also because it is believed that de Gusamão's balloon was modeled after one used by South American Indians.

The International Explorers Society tested their flying Nazcas theory by building the Condor I, a replica of what they believe a Nazca balloon may have looked like. The contraption featured an eighty-eight-foot-high envelope made from fabrics similar to the materials recovered from Nazca graves, as well as lines and fastenings woven from native fibers and a gondola made from the reeds that grow in Peru's Lake Titicaca.

On its maiden flight, the Condor soared to an altitude of 600 feet in just thirty seconds. But, caught up in strong winds, it crashed back to the ground briefly, dumping its two pilots. Then it was off again, rising to 1,200 feet and flying over two miles in eighteen minutes before it gently landed on the desert plain.

Although the experiment got off to a bumpy start, Michael DeBakey (son of the famed heart surgeon and a director of the International Explorers Society) insisted that the flight of the Condor had achieved its goal. "We set out to prove that the Nazcas had the skill, the materials and the need for flight," he stated. "I think we have succeeded."

Monkey See, Monkey Communicate

Animals have long been known to communicate with one another—sounds and body movements, perhaps instinctive, are used as warnings, as aids in pack hunting, and as a means of meeting other basic needs. In recent years, scientists have found that some animals can be taught to communicate directly with humans. For example, the famous gorilla Coco has learned to recognize and react to human words and even to construct her own sentences through the use of sign language.

One incident, however, has caused some to wonder if a group of monkeys could use their own *spoken* language to tell each other about a tragic event and to seek revenge.

After a youth cruelly stoned a baby monkey to death at the Penang Botanical Gardens in Malaysia, about sixty monkeys began attacking joggers and visitors in the area. "Several of us saw a large group of monkeys coming toward us," one jogger was quoted as saying in the *New Straits Times*. "Initially, we thought they were just coming for food and tried to chase them away. We had to run away when they started charging at us."

What was most remarkable about the monkey-human confrontation was that the animals went after only the people who were wearing the same color clothes as the youth who killed the baby monkey—yellow.

Krause, the Miracle Mule

Everybody knows that the mule, which is a cross between a female horse and a male donkey, is incapable of reproduction. It's a scientific fact. But obviously no one ever informed a mule named Krause.

Krause's owners, Bill and Oneta Silvester of Champion, Nebraska, noticed that their mule was gaining weight. "Her mother was a Welsh pony and they have big stomachs," Oneta comments. "So we just thought she was getting fat." It wasn't until Krause delivered a foal that the Silvesters realized they had a very unusual mule on their hands.

According to geneticist Oliver Ryder of the Zoological Society of San Diego's Center for the Reproduction of Endangered Species, there have been other reports of mules apparently giving birth. But in the past, whenever researchers were able to investigate, the claims always turned out to be inaccurate. "The supposedly fertile mule would sometimes prove to be a mulish-looking horse," Ryder notes. "Or she was indeed a mule, but the foal wasn't her own; she had 'adopted' the foal of another horse or donkey."

However, when Ryder investigated Krause and her offspring, named Blue Moon, he found that chromosome testing and a blood analysis showed the mule had definitely given birth to the foal.

"Based on the available evidence, it has always been safe to conclude that mules of both sexes were completely sterile," Ryder explains. "Horses have sixty-four chromosomes and donkeys have sixty-two. Mules inherit sixty-three chromosomes that 'get along' with each other quite well as far as forming a mule; it is only when the mule tries to produce reproductive cells that the incompatibilities are manifest."

But, inexplicably, Krause was somehow able to do what is scientifically impossible for mules to do—reproduce. "To my knowledge, this is the first case of alleged mule fertility that has stood up to complete scientific analysis," Ryder concludes.

Modern-Day Neanderthals

The hairy, low-browed Neanderthal became extinct thousands of years ago. Or did he? According to archaeologist Myra Shackley of Britain's University of Leicester, numerous eyewitness reports suggest that a small band of Neanderthals is still living in caves, high in the mountains of Outer Mongolia. The wild men are called Almas by other residents of the desolate area that stretches between the southern USSR and China.

Shackley, who published her research in the prestigious archaeology journal *Antiquity*, states that "the idea that modern man can be the only surviving hominid species is outmoded biological arrogance. It seems impossible to deny the existence of the Almas."

Shackley notes that responsible citizens, including scientists, have reported spotting the living Neanderthals. While doing fieldwork in Outer Mongolia, Shackley came across possible traces of the Almas herself—stone tools that looked like those known to have been made by Neanderthals. Hoping to discover the origin of the artifacts, she traveled along the edge of the Gobi Desert and the Altai Mountains, asking local herders who made the objects. The answer was always the same, she says—they were made "by people who used to live in the area." These people, the archaeologist was told, now live in mountain caves and hunt for food.

The Mongolians expressed surprise that Shackley was interested in the Almas. "To the Mongols, they were common knowledge," she notes.

The Woman Who Attracts Lightning

Does the thought of lightning striking from out of the blue scare you? Then you'd be wise to steer clear of Betty Jo Hudson of Winburn Chapel, Mississippi—a woman who seems to attract the flashing bolts of electricity.

It all started when she was a child and lightning struck her head and face. Then her parents' house was repeatedly hit by lightning. In 1957, a jolt finally destroyed the home.

In recent years, Betty Jo and her husband, Ernest, have witnessed lightning strike all around their residence in the rural community of Winburn Chapel. Not only was their house hit three years in a row, but their neighbor's home was also damaged by lightning. Other bolts from the blue killed the Hudson's dog, zapped a tree and a pump, and carved out deep ruts in their yard.

So far, Betty Jo has escaped serious injury, but she has had several close calls. For instance, one summer the Hudsons were shelling butter beans on their porch when dark clouds gathered and a summer storm erupted. The couple retreated to their front bedroom only minutes before a bolt of lightning crashed through a window in another bedroom. "If we had been in there," says Betty Jo, "we would have been hit."

UFO Snapshot

Dave and Hannah McRoberts were driving on British Columbia's Vancouver Island when they decided, at about noon, to pull over into the Eve River Rest Area. Off in the distance the couple could see a rugged mountaintop set off against the sky by a white cloud—just the scenic view that Hannah thought would make a pretty snapshot.

Hannah focused her camera and took a single photo. A few weeks later, in October 1981, the film was developed. The mountain scene came out clear and scenic. But there was something odd about the photo, something the McRobertses didn't remember seeing when the picture was taken—a silvery disc flying through the sky.

The McRobertses quickly contacted the Canadian National Defense office at Comox about the UFO they had inadvertently captured on film. The army wasn't interested. However, friends and neighbors were fascinated by the photo, and the McRobertses were soon having copies of the picture made and distributing them to anyone who wanted one.

A copy of the snapshot came to the attention of psychologist Richard Haines in Pasadena, California. Haines, president of the North American UFO Federation, decided to find out more about the photo. He visited the McRobertses at their Campbell River home, examined and tested their camera, and then investigated the area where the photograph had been taken.

In July 1984, Haines told an audience at the Rocky Mountain UFO Conference at the University of Wyoming that, based on his investigation and a computer analysis of the photo, he had come to believe that the saucer-shaped object was real.

He noted that a blowup of the UFO revealed a clear dome on top of the disc. But there's still no explanation of exactly *what* Hannah McRoberts accidentally caught on film. "It remains unidentified," Haines concludes.

Out-of-Body Poll

With all the attention paid to the out-of-body experience (OBE) in recent years, psychiatrist Fowler Jones and two colleagues from the University of Kansas have set out to see whether the phenomenon is real. Toward that end, they questioned 420 randomly selected people from thirty-eight states and three foreign countries. Their findings? A large majority of those polled said they had experienced at least one out-of-body excursion—and some said they had taken a mind-over-matter trip *hundreds* of times.

"Healthy, intelligent people, many of whom attend church on a regular basis, reported these experiences," Jones noted. He points out that OBEs are not drug-altered states of consciousness, nor are they simply dreams.

Whatever the experiences are, Jones adds, they are described as pleasant by 85 percent of those surveyed. "People who have such experiences feel they're quite real. They describe them in various ways, but the common denominator is that the mind, the *I* part of the personality, the thinking-feeling part, is no longer located inside the physical body but is deposited somewhere else in the environment," Jones relates. "It is as if they have a mobile center of consciousness located just a few feet, or several miles, from the physical body."

When the mind leaves the body, it can apparently glimpse events that later turn out to have actually taken place. For example, one man interviewed for Jones's research pointed out that an OBE saved his life. When his mind left his body, it traveled to a room filled with co-workers who were planning to murder him. After returning to his body, Jones relates, the man confronted one of the plotters. She was so frightened by his knowledge of the planned assassination that she confessed on the spot.

UFO-Caused Automobile Accidents

In the summer of 1979, two teenaged boys watched unexplained lights pass over their car. Then some sort of energy pinned them to their seats. When the youngsters were finally able to drive away, they found their car racing out of control as if it had a mind of its own.

A couple of weeks later, at 1:40 A.M., a Minnesota policeman saw an unusual light in the sky and felt his car being blown across the road by an unseen force. Then he blacked out. When he came to, the officer found that his windshield had been shattered and his antenna bent; his clock was inexplicably fourteen minutes slow.

According to the Center for UFO Studies in Evanston, Illinois, these incidents are not unique—there have been 440 cases reported around the world of UFOs provoking car accidents or near accidents. The UFOs appear to initiate "electrochemical events" that can stall engines and break or block radios with static.

Most of the incidents have no scientific explanation, says astrophysicist Mark Rodenghier, who has studied the reports. He points out that the Ford LTD driven by the Minnesota policeman was examined by Ford engineers, who insisted that no known phenomenon could cause the automobile to behave in such a strange way.

Elvis Makes a Comeback

In late 1980, about a hundred miles from Memphis, a truck driver noticed a strange glow coming from some nearby woods. Then he saw a hitchhiker walk in front of the light and turn toward the highway. Stopping to offer the traveler a ride, the trucker noticed that something about the polite young man seemed familiar. But it wasn't until they reached the bright lights outside Memphis that the truck driver recognized his passenger as someone who had died three years earlier—Elvis Presley.

According to psychiatrist Raymond Moody, the trucker's experience isn't unique. As he documents in his book *Elvis After Life* (Peachtree, 1987), since the King of Rock 'n' Roll's death, reports of his ghostly appearances have popped up all around the country. "A psychotherapist, who met Elvis when she was a youngster, claims he unexpectedly stopped by her office one day—after his death—and counseled her on the emptiness of her life," Moody says. "Another woman told me that Elvis materialized in the delivery room to help her with a difficult childbirth."

Moody notes that in addition to ghostly visits, Elvis has also been linked to other paranormal experiences. One fan had a precognitive dream the night before Presley's death in which the singer announced "this is my last concert." Another repeatedly witnessed one sleeve of a jacket once owned by Elvis move up and down by itself.

Goose Falls

Hundreds of geese were swarming over Norfolk county in England in early January 1978 when these masters of flight began falling from the sky. Before long, 136 dead pink-footed geese were found in an area forty-five kilometers long. Another 105 fell near Wicken Farm, Castleacre. Others were discovered in various areas, in groups of two to as many as fourteen.

The goose deaths were not the result of hunters shooting for the sport of it; there were no signs of gunshot wounds. Autopsies also ruled out the possibility of the birds being struck by lightning. Instead, some birds had lungs with blood clots and signs of hemorrhaging, while others had ruptured livers.

Some researchers finally speculated that the geese, traveling across the area, met with an advancing meteorological cold front that carried strong tornadoes. The unsuspecting geese apparently were caught in the vacuum cleaner-like winds and were swept up into higher atmosphere. At such great heights, the birds' lungs then hemorrhaged, causing their sudden death in the air, and they fell to earth over a long strip of land.

Cobweb Storms

Anyone who's seen *The Wizard of Oz* is familiar with the image of a tornado picking up everything in its path and carrying it for miles. But while tornadoes and whirlwinds leave grave damage in their wake, people are often amazed at what they find in the aftermath.

Even small whirlwinds, for instance, have deposited hay on telephone and electrical wires. And ordinary air currents have transported and then dropped cobwebs to Earth. Charles Darwin, for instance, observed a rain of cobwebs while on board the *Beagle*, sixty miles from land. After landing, Darwin reported, many of the spiders formed another web and took off once again.

Today scientists know that some spiders migrate by clinging to an airborne strand of cobweb. In fact, floating cobwebs have on occasion deluged an area as they fell to the ground. In Milwaukee, Wisconsin, during October 1881, for example, webs well over two feet long came in from over a lake, descending from a great height. In a similar case in Green Bay, Wisconsin, webs floated in off the bay; this time, though, strands were up to sixty feet in length and could be seen high in the sky. No one in either of these instances saw any spiders at all.

Yet other cobweb sightings include wads and patches of white material known as "angel hair." Soaring through the sky, reflecting sunlight, a mass of such material might easily resemble a fleet of UFOs.

Manna from Heaven

The biblical story of the Israelites' exodus from Egypt tells the tale of manna that fell to earth in great quantities and prevented the people from starving during their long trek. Scientists have always disagreed on the nature and source of that food.

There have been other reports of manna from heaven, however, occurring in more recent times. In 1890, for example, a shower of manna fell in Turkey, covering an area approximately ten kilometers in circumference. Composed of small spheres that were yellow on the outside and white within, the "manna" was examined by botanists, who determined that it was a member of the lichen family. A plant made up of alga and fungus, desert lichen grows on such solid surfaces as rocks and pebbles; some have suggested it as the source of the Israelites' heavenly food.

Manna, however, has more than one possible source. In a 1927 research expedition organized by Jerusalem's Hebrew University, scientists determined that the manna phenomenon is well known around the world. In many cases, the food source is a clear, sweet excretion from a plant known as the *Tamarix nilotica*. The fluid is ingested by the plant lice and other insects that live on the desert shrub. The dry desert climate causes the syrup to crystalize, producing whitish grains that cover the branches or fall to the ground.

The Lost Fleet of Alexander the Great

The appearance of Greek words in American Indian and Pacific island languages is an intriguing mystery. The first white men who came to Delaware and Maryland found a river that the

Indians called *Potomac*," a soundalike for the Greek word *potomos*, meaning "river."

When the Spanish conquistadores invaded the Aztec Empire of Mexico, they noted that the pyramid temples (where the Aztec priests tore out the hearts of sacrificial victims and threw the bodies down the pyramid steps) were called *Teocalli*. This is a combination of two Greek words, *theos* and *kalias*, meaning "dwelling (of the) god." The meaning in Nahuatl (Aztec) is identical.

While it is possible that ancient mariners of different nationalities reached the Americas through the southern Gulf Stream, Greek words in Hawaiian and related Tahitian are even more striking. Here are a few:

English	Hawaiian	Ancient Greek
eagle	aeto	aetos
come/arrive	hiki	hikano
think/learn	manao	manthano
sing/melody	mele	melodia
thought/intelligence	noo-noo	nous

Where did the Hawaiians get these Greek words? Could it have been from Greek metal-and-horsehair war helmets that the Hawaiians copied in wood and feathers? But where could the Hawaiians have seen the helmets? Could the Greeks have crossed the Atlantic eighteen hundred years before Columbus and *then* crossed the Pacific as well?

There may be a simpler, though equally intriguing, explanation. This concerns Alexander the Great, the conquerer of most of the ancient world. Alexander, after conquering the Persian Empire, pushed eastward into the Indian peninsula, and northward into what is now the USSR, looking for new worlds to conquer. Meanwhile, his fleet of eight hundred vessels, under Admiral Nearchus, explored the coast of India. Most of this fleet was recalled to the entrance of the Persian Gulf in 324 B.C. to take part of his now tired and disaffected troops back to Greece.

But part of the fleet never returned. Had it gone beyond the coast of India, the Malay peninsula, and then continued out into the currents of the Pacific? Perhaps some of the ships reached islands like Tahiti and Hawaii, where life was pleasant, the maidens attractive, and strangers from the sea, with their superior armor and weapons, would probably be treated like visiting gods.

Earthquake Hair

The earthquake roared through eastern Siam, wreaking havoc. The rivers rippled and bubbled, turning white. During the shock, the earth split open, throwing out everywhere what seemed to be human hairs. Long and upright, they remained firmly planted in the ground. Burned, they even smelled like human hair. Reporting on the 1848 quake, the *Singapore Free Press* suggested the hairs were produced by electric currents. Later explanations theorized that some natural material, perhaps tar, shot out through the earth's pores into fine strings. Congealing as it encountered cooler temperatures, the substance resembled hairs.

The appearance in Siam of earthly hairs is not a solitary incident. Chinese who have collected such hairs after earthquakes for thousands of years believe they may belong to a subterranenan animal whose sudden movement causes the earth to shake and the rivers to bubble.

Breathing Earth

For three weeks the islands that constitute the Moluccas were covered by a sulphurous fog. Then on November 1, 1835, a violent and destructive earthquake shook the tiny region to its roots.

Incidents of sulphur released into the atmosphere—along with water, sand, and other material—are not uncommon in early earthquake reports. Indeed, modern scientists have detected an increased emission of gases contained within the earth. The discharge of radon by hot springs and in mines, for example, has been linked to subsequent earthquakes. A significant amount of helium was also discovered along the fault line formed by the 1966 Matsuhiro quake in Japan. In this case, it was suggested that molten rock deep in the earth released the helium that then rose upward and through the earth's crust.

In a 1978 paper published by the prestigious magazine *Nature*, West German biologist Helmut Tributsch proposed that gases forced out of the earth prior to an earthquake are electrically charged, forming ion clouds. The flow of ions, he suggested, would explain the animal agitation, human physiological effects, and atmospheric phenomena that have been reported prior to many big quakes.

Indeed, earthquake lore throughout history is filled with stories of bizarre animal behavior that may have forewarned people of the impending destruction. Five days before the great earthquake that destroyed the Greek city of Helice in 373 B.C., for example, citizens observed mice, weasels, snakes, and other subterranean creatures vacating their underground abodes and making a mass exodus.

Long before humans detect anything, birds, fish, and mammals all seem to sense something unusual is afoot. Cows have been seen bracing themselves by setting their forelegs apart, sheep continually bleat, dogs howl, wolves bark, and cats run frantically about.

During the 1930s, the Japanese studied catfish and found that they showed signs of unrest up to a full six hours before an earthquake registered on seismic instruments. Placed in an aquarium, the normally placid catfish were unresponsive during normal periods when scientists knocked on the glass or on the table. When a quake was impending, however, the same action caused the fish to jump or swim around in a highly agitated state.

Scientists have often tried to tie this mysterious phenomenon to subaudible sound or electromagnetic field changes. Now, thanks to Tributsch, ionized air has also made the list.

Solitary Monster Waves

The Italian ship *Michelangelo* sailed westward through gale winds on April 12, 1966. Proceeding at a cautious, steady speed, six hundred miles southeast of Newfoundland, it headed toward New York—through twenty-five- to thirty-foot waves. Suddenly, a wall of water rose from the sea, towering above all the other waves, and smashed into the ship. Steel superstructures collapsed, heavy steel on the bow was torn off, bridge windows were crushed, and the bulkhead under the bridge was bent back at least ten feet. Three people were killed and twelve injured.

Almost every sailor has a tale of a monstrous wave that appeared suddenly out of nowhere. Measurements vary: In 1921, a giant wave in the North Pacific was estimated to be seventy feet high; a later one about one hundred miles off Cape Hatteras, Virginia, was about one hundred feet high. As far back as 1826, French scientist and naval officer Captain Dumont d'Urville encountered sudden waves eighty to one hundred feet high, an estimate supported by three colleagues. Admiral FitzRoy, first director of the Meteorological Office, reported that he himself had measured waves as high as sixty feet, adding that bigger waves were not unknown.

The cause of these giant waves is still unclear. Some scientists say they are caused by severe storms that generate large waves that then reinforce each other and create an even bigger wave. Yet many giant solitary waves appear in calm seas and can't be attributed to the winds at the time. Could they be the result of underwater earthquakes or volcanic eruptions? Oceanographers continue to study the phenomenon, but the mystery is still there.

Fog Guns

W. S. Cooper was sailing on the Gulf of Mexico, about twenty miles southeast of Cedar Keys, Florida. The water was calm, the sky cloudless. There was a light fog and no breeze. Shortly after sunrise, however, he heard the sound of a gun or distant cannon repeated in five-minute intervals. His companion, who lives on the coast, told Cooper that on still mornings the sounds were often heard.

In a similar account, one A. Cancani reported that in Italy the sound is longer than that of a cannon shot, and not unlike distant thunder, although more prolonged, and comes at various intervals. In the East Indies, another report adds that several noises, sounding like a foghorn, occur every few seconds, lasting one or two seconds each.

Modern investigators of such mysterious explosive sounds along the coasts of North America and Europe have generally dismissed them as sonic booms. The problem with this explanation is that the foghorn bleats have been reported throughout the world in areas near seacoasts for at least a century.

According to another hypothesis, the shots are caused by the eruptions of natural gas beneath the sea. The discovery of pockmarks in many of the continental shelves at the oceans' bottoms supports the idea of natural gas frequently being released.

Holistic Healing

Some religions teach that we can send a healing force over considerable distances. This belief, which pervades many world cultures, was recently put to a scientific test.

The experiment was designed by Dr. Robert Miller, a well-known scientist, engineer, and inventor. Working with the Holmes Center for Research in Holistic Healing in Los Angeles, California, Dr. Miller wanted to see if people could be healed of their afflictions even if they didn't know a psychic healing effort was going on.

Working on the project from 1976 to 1979, Miller began by recruiting eight healers: four were Science of Mind practitioners, two were psychic healers, and the others were Protestant ministers. The healers were asked to treat high blood pressure patients, who were not told they were part of the experiment.

The patients were secretly selected by several physicians known to Dr. Miller. The healers never met the patients but were provided with their locations, initials, and a few other personal facts. Each healer treated six patients located randomly in the United States. Forty-eight patients were treated during the course of the project, while another forty-eight patients served as the control group. Not even the physicians knew which patients were selected for the psychic treatment and which weren't. The doctors were asked merely to monitor their patients' diastolic and systolic blood pressure readings, heart rate, and weight.

The healers were instructed to treat the patients in any manner they wished, and most of them "healed" by visualizing the subjects in perfect health.

According to the researchers, the experiment was a modest success. More than 92 percent of those receiving distant healing showed a reduction in their blood pressure readings, though 75 percent of those in the control group improved as well.

Children and the Near-Death Experience

Rushed to a hospital emergency room after nearly drowning in a community swimming pool, a seven-year-old girl sank into a deep coma. "I was dead," she related after regaining consciousness three days later. "I was in a dark tunnel. It was dark and I was scared. I couldn't walk."

A woman named Elizabeth materialized to escort her to heaven, the small girl said. Once there, she encountered her dead grandparents, a dead aunt, and "the heavenly Father and Jesus." When asked if she wanted to see her mother, the girl said yes and awoke in the hospital.

Reported by pediatrician Melvin Morse in the *American Journal of Diseases of Children*, the incident was the first juvenile near-death experience to appear in medical literature. Morse later interviewed other children who related similar tales after traumatic accidents. One recalled being scolded in heaven; another was carried on a beam of light through a long, dark tunnel.

Although these children were probably raised in religious households, Morse believes their experiences may be more than mere fantasy. The children, he suggests, may have been glimpsing the hereafter or, more likely, recalling the archetypal images that haunt the outback of human consciousness for us all.

Einstein and the Watchmaker

Albert Einstein's theories changed our concept of time, space, energy, matter, and the universe itself, but the physicist remained silent on the subject of religion—except in one instance. Pressed for his thoughts on the existence of God, Einstein replied that he had always been impressed by the mechanics of the universe. Everything from atoms to galaxies functioned as precisely as clockwork, he said, much like a gigantic cosmic watch.

"Someday," he added pensively, "I should like to meet the watchmaker."

Martian Pyramids

For generations, scientists have suspected the existence of life on Mars. Theories about the form of life there have included everything from simple organisms to humanoids who built cities and dug canals. Italian astronomer Giovanni Schiaparelli first described and mapped Martian "canals" in 1877. With the development of more powerful and sophisticated telescopes, observers downgraded the former waterways to natural riverbeds ranging in width from seven to twenty feet. Many believe there may still be water—in the form of ice—on the red planet.

And while satellite photographs have so far failed to reveal any life-forms, some Mars watchers believe there is evidence that Mars may have once supported life. One area—dubbed "Pyramid City" by astronomers—hosts structures that resemble the Egyptian pyramids; the Martian versions, however, are 3,000 feet wide at the base of each side, compared to 612 feet at the base of each side of the Cheops pyramid. Images of an enormous rock or statue depict a partially shaded face, measuring about one mile wide; the visible eye, nose, mouth, and forehead bear a greater resemblance to human features than do those of the Great Sphinx in Egypt. And at the Cofrates depression, possibly a former sea, there is a series of forms that could be the ruins of an ancient port, with square constructions that might have been docks, streets, or buildings.

Further exploration will eventually prove whether these are mere illusions or real artifacts—like the towers and walls of Babylon and Troy—that are unrecognizable until after excavation on and under the surface of Mars.

The Precognition of Nostradamus

●
━━━

Between 1547 and his death in 1566, Nostradamus foretold such future events as plagues, wars, revolutions, earthquakes, massacres, and the development of modern warfare. Anyone who is familiar with history and nature, of course, can make predictions involving wars and natural catastrophes that occur with a certain regularity. Nostradamus, however, was very specific, indentifying individuals by name hundreds of years before they were born.

The sixteenth-century prophet foretold, for example, the rise of Hitler, describing his nationality, rise to power, and successful invasion of France. Uncannily referring to the German leader as "Hister," he added that "the greatest part of the battlefield will be against Hister."

Nostradamus dramatically foretold the fates of numerous historical figures, including Napoleon, England's Edward VIII, Winston Churchill, and Franklin Delano Roosevelt. He often referred to them by nicknames, but occasionally named them exactly, as in the case of Louis Pasteur, who, he said, would be "celebrated as a godlike figure." Writing of Spain's future Franco, as well as Primo de Rivera and his followers, Nostradamus said: "From Castille, Franco will bring out the assembly" and "Rivera's people will be in the crowd."

Recording his prophecies 223 years before the French Revolution, Nostradamus seems to have been most exact in his predictions concerning the fate of France's Louis XVI. The seer referred to the king as the "chosen Capet," the actual royal family name, and as "Lui," capitalizing the French pronoun meaning "him," which sounds like the French name "Louis."

There are also significant similarities between Nostradamus's predictions and actual events during the French Revolution, which took place more than two hundred years *later*. He wrote, for example, that "a conflict would pass over the tile"; in fact, the French word *tuile* refers to the Tuileries Palace, invaded by the revolutionaries. Later, Louis's attempted escape from France, according to Nostradamus, would be thwarted by "two traitors." He named one of these "Narbon," similar in sound to Count Narbonne-Lara, the French minister of war who betrayed Louis. The other, whom Nostradamus named "Saulce," turned out to be the historical Saulce, proctor of Varenne, who stopped the ruler's coach along the escape route and sent the royal family back to Paris.

The deaths of Louis XVI and his queen, Marie Antoinette, Nostradamus also said, would cause "tempest, fire, blood, and slice"—this last referring to the guillotine, not yet invented in Nostradamus's time.

Indians Who Traveled to Europe by Canoe

During the reign of Augustus Caesar two thousand years ago, when the Romans ruled much of Western Europe, a long, narrow, hollow seafaring vessel washed ashore from the North Sea. Speaking a strange language, the copper-colored travelers it carried frequently pointed to the craft and then to the west. Unable to understand the barbarians, Roman soldiers took them hostage and escorted them to the Roman proconsul, Publius Metellus Cellar, who enslaved them.

The travelers would have disappeared into the shadows of history except for a carved likeness of one of them, a bust resembling a Native American. Apparently, the Indians became lost off the North American coast, and the canoe was carried by the upper, easterly Atlantic current—all the way to Europe.

Columbus, who also used the Atlantic current—the lower, westerly stream—during his voyages to the New World, may have been aware of Publius's slaves. A dedicated student of earlier Atlantic crossings, he once described the story of two dead men, dark in color and perhaps Chinese, found floating in a long, narrow boat washed up on the western shore of Ireland, near Galway.

A Portentous Game

Before the arrival of Europeans in the New World, the pre-Columbian people in Central America, Mexico, and some parts of the southwestern United States were *tlachtli* enthusiasts. The object of *tlachtli*, a game similar to soccer or basketball, was knocking a small, hard rubber ball through a hole in a stone above the players' heads. The rules allowed the use of elbows, hips, legs, and the head, but prohibited the hands from touching the ball.

Apparently more than just a sport, *tlachtli* seems to have been a religious ritual as well. Losers not only forfeited their garments and accoutrements, but often their lives. Aztec priests, for example, are known to have ripped out the hearts of players stretched spread-eagle across a sacrificial altar.

The most portentous *tlachtli* match was played between the Aztec emperor Montezuma and Nezahualpilli, ruler of Tezcoco. The purpose was to determine the reliability of Tezcoco's astrologers, who had predicted that strangers would one day rule Mexico. The stakes in the game were three cocks against the Tezcoco kingdom. When Montezuma lost, with a score of 3 to 2, Tezcoco kept his kingdom and won the cocks.

This fateful game of *tlachtli*, in fact, aided the Spanish conquest of Mexico. Montezuma became so depressed by the prophecy of losing his kingdom that he found himself unable to oppose the strangers when they arrived.

Profanity Prohibited by a Royal Saint

Leading the seventh Crusade (1248–1254) to free the Holy Land from the infidels, Louis IX was captured by the Moslems. After his ransom and release, he spent much of his reign imposing his religious views on his subjects.

Louis, the only French king to be canonized after his death, believed it was his responsibility, for example, to eradicate the use of profanity. To cure speakers of the expletives *pardieu* (by God) and *cordieu* (God's Body), he ordered hot irons applied to transgressors' tongues.

It soon became fashionable to utter such expressions as *parbleu* (by blue) and *sacre bleu* (damned or sacred blue), which resembled the forbidden words. (Besides sounding like *dieu*, *Bleu* was also the name of Louis's favorite dog.) The inoffensive oaths eventually survived the Middle Ages and are still part of the French language today.

To Beat the Devil

The day before Halloween 1987, an unusual lawsuit was brought in Little Rock, Arkansas. The suit was filed by Ralph Forbes, formerly a candidate for the U.S. Senate, who sought to bar public schools in the state from celebrating Halloween, classifying the holiday as an "observation of the rites of Satan."

Whether or not the complaint had some redeeming value (outlawing Halloween would probably curb children's tendencies to throw eggs, splash paint, "wrap" houses, tip over farm outhouses, and so forth, every October 31), one of the principal defendants named was obviously a disruptive and eerie character. His name is well known to everyone—"Satan," aka *the devil*. Another defendant, of considerably better reputation, was the Russellville School District. The suit was filed on behalf of Ralph Forbes, Jesus Christ, and minor children.

Ancient Brazilian Semites

When the Portuguese discovered Brazil in 1500, they had no difficulty in naming the place. They had, after all, found what they had sought: the iron ore-rich land called Brazil that, according to ancient legends, lay across the South Atlantic. In several Semitic languages, as well as modern Hebrew, for example, *Brazil* (or B-R-Z-L) means "iron" or "land of iron."

It is a fact that many stone tablets, inscribed in Phoenician and other Semitic languages, have been found along the Amazon. A number of them, some describing the fate of expeditions, were initially considered forgeries. Practical jokers, however, would have been hard-pressed to carve them and then deposit them in the deep Amazonian jungle. If they are, in fact, genuine, then it's also possible that ancient Semites not only traveled to the Brazilian shores long before the Portuguese arrived there and before Columbus's discovery of the Americas, but also named South America's biggest nation almost two thousand years before it was officially discovered.

The Man They Couldn't Hang

Convicted of theft and the murder of a police officer in Sydney, Australia, Joseph Samuels was condemned to die by hanging in September 1803. Still protesting his innocence, he was forced to stand in the execution cart, a noose around his neck. But when the horses were whipped forward, Samuels hung briefly from the rope and then fell out of the cart. In the second attempt to hang him, this time with his hands tied together, the rope suddenly unraveled and Samuels was left strangling slowly, but still alive. On the third try, the rope snapped as the wagon moved out from under him, and Samuels fell to the ground with the noose still around his neck.

After three unsuccessful attempts to hang the convicted man, the crowd, believing that Samuels must be innocent, had become unruly. Rather than try once more, the executioners returned Samuels to his jail cell.

Later, Isaac Simmonds, having made himself conspicuous by jeering at Samuels in the death cart, was found guilty of the crimes and condemned to death by hanging. This time the execution was successful on the first try.

Rats, Cats, and History

Between 1346 and 1350, seventy-five million people died from the Black Death that decimated Europe as it spread across the continent. The great bubonic plague is believed to have originated in Kaffa. According to the theories, ships from the Middle East carried rats infected by plague-carrying lice, and the lice spread the disease to humans.

As the plague progressed, all sorts of remedies, penances, and prayers were used for cures and prevention. Superstition led to an attack on supposed witches and their accomplices, cats. Periodic massacres of the cats, however, only made matters worse since there were fewer rat catchers.

Still, when the plague abated, and the devastated villages and towns recovered, cats returned to their rat-catching duties and regained their places on the hearths.

Film Debut of a UFO

During the 1972 filming of a television commercial on the roof of San Juan's Hotel Sheraton in Puerto Rico, the crew witnessed the sudden approach of a large UFO. Viewing it on the monitors, they could tell that the brightly glowing object was not a plane, a blimp, or a helicopter. It vanished as quickly as it had appeared, but not before it ruined the commercial, which had to be reshot.

That year, there were more reports of UFOs (unidentified flying objects, *not* necessarily extraterrestrial in origin) in Puerto Rico than anywhere else in the world. So the Sheraton incident was no different than a host of other sightings—with one exception. The film footage of the large, glowing UFO was sold to Creative Films, a movie company that needed a shot of a UFO in a film it was making at the time.

Dissecting Relatives

The new medical students seemed nervous as they faced their first set of cadavers in anatomy classes at the University of Alabama. But, according to a letter printed in the *Journal of the American Medical Association*, one of the female med students was horrified when she looked over the corpses. There among the bodies awaiting dissection was her recently deceased great-aunt.

Her relative, it turned out, had been shipped to Alabama by the state anatomical board in Florida, where the woman had passed away. When University of Alabama doctors realized that a med student was faced with watching the body of someone she knew being dissected, they immediately moved the body to another laboratory and instituted a new policy. Now the names of cadavers are checked with incoming students.

"That student [who recognized her great-aunt] quickly recovered from the trauma of the situation," notes psychiatrist Clarence McDanal, a cosigner of the letter.

Ironically, it may have been the med student who was responsible for her dead aunt's body being in an anatomy lab in the first place—before her relative's death, the young woman had talked to her about the merits of body donation.

Dream Headlines

Around 3:00 A.M. on January 29, 1963, Mrs. John Walik of Long Beach, California, suddenly bolted upright in bed—awakened by a terrifying nightmare that seemed unusually vivid.

She had dreamed of an airplane flying low over water. It seemed to level off as it approached a landing strip a hundred feet away. But suddenly it dropped, bounced off the water, and veered into the ground, exploding into flames.

The details of the dream haunted Mrs. Walik. She had clearly "seen" that the plane was a big four-engined Constellation—the same kind of plane her husband flew as a navigator for Slick Airways.

Was the dream a warning that John Walik was in danger? As soon as the Slick Airways office opened that morning, Mrs. Walik called to see if her husband was safe. She was assured that no planes had crashed and that John, who was flying on a plane that was delivering freight to the West Coast, would be home in just a few days.

But Mrs. Walik wasn't reassured. As she told friends, neighbors, and family—anyone who would listen—over the next few days, there was something different about this dream, something frightening. It seemed *real*.

On February 3, 1963, Mrs. Walik decided to check on her husband's safety one more time. Again, the airlines insisted there had been no problems with his plane and John would be landing at the San Francisco International Airport later that morning.

As soon as Mrs. Walik hung up the phone, the details of her dream came rushing back. The plane in her nightmare had crashed near water, she remembered. And to land at San Francisco International Airport, her husband's plane would have to fly over the bay.

Quickly she redialed the Slick Airlines office. But before she could finish explaining her concern, her terrifying dream had come true. Her husband's plane crashed beside a runway and began to burn. Five crew members were killed. Four others—including John Walik—survived.

The next day, the *Long Beach Independent Press* ran a story emblazoned with the headline "Mate's Plane Crash Seen in Wife's Dream." The crash of the ill-fated Constellation was, the newspaper noted, the same disaster Mrs. Walik "had seen in her dreams five days before it happened!"

The Humming House

Back in the 1960s, the family of truck driver Eugene Binkowski of Rotterdam, New York, came down with a host of unexplained ailments. Their heads, teeth, ears, and joints hurt. But why?

The family wondered if a faint humming noise they heard day and night in their house could be related to their aches and pains. The local police and technicians from a nearby General Electric plant were called to the house, but they were baffled by the Binkowski family's claims that they heard a constant hum.

Finally, Eugene wrote to President Kennedy, asking him to get to the bottom of the mystery. A few days after his letter reached the White House, six air force sound experts arrived at the suburban Binkowski home, armed with complex instruments used to detect high frequency sound.

Although they did not identify sounds that could be causing the family's problems, the researchers did make a startling discovery: the entire Binkowski household possessed unusually acute hearing and they were physically able to hear what they claimed to hear. In fact, even six-year-old Terry Binkowski could detect sounds well above the normal hearing range of most humans. The only explanation the air force sound specialists could offer for the constant humming the family experienced was that it might be related in some way to three nearby radio stations.

As word leaked out about the humming house in Rotterdam, hundreds of visitors stopped by to listen for the mysterious noise. Most reportedly heard the hum or said their heads began to feel stuffy. Whatever caused the odd sensations, the Binkowski family finally decided they had to escape the constant drone—so they packed up and moved into a nearby garage.

Ancient Russian Mummies

According to the Russian newspaper *Trud*, in the mid-1980s a group of Soviet cave explorers unexpectedly came across an eerie sight: caves filled with so many ancient mummies that they were soon dubbed the "city of the dead."

But why dozens of men, horses, and wild animals entered the caves in the first place—and how they became mummified—remains a mystery.

Soviet experts speculated in *Trud* that the people could have been fourth-century B.C. nomads trying to hide from the invading troops of Alexander the Great. Emory University historian Thomas Burns agrees that "refugees trying to escape that conquering army could have gotten up to where the mummies were found" in the central USSR. He also theorizes that the people "could have been holing up in a cave because of a family feud."

Brad Shore, professor of anthropology at Emory, says that the doomed nomads could have been turned into mummies by a quirk of nature. "It's unusual, but certainly not unheard of," he notes, "to find people preserved like this after being trapped by a mud-slide or a landslide."

Just how the mummies in the Russian "city of the dead" met their fate may never be known, but the local mountain people have long dubbed the caves where they were found unlucky. According to *Trud*, area residents believe that the black plague originally came from the mite-infested caves. In fact, the Russian speleologists noted that they left the caves with painful body sores—evidence of the biting insects that still share the caves with the mummies.

Sleep Language

When Gene Sutherland of Mesa, Arizona, went to bed, it wasn't unusual for his wife Wilma to find she couldn't get a full night's rest—her husband would often wake her up by talking in his sleep. Usually Wilma would make out a word or two and then drift back off to her own dreams. But one night, Gene's babbling sounded strangely different.

Gene seemed excited and agitated, Wilma recalls, and he was speaking in what seemed to be a thick, foreign accent, using sounds like "ski" and "vich" repeatedly.

Sensing this was not Gene's ordinary sleep talk, Mrs. Sutherland quickly grabbed a tape recorder to document the odd gibberish. When she played the recording back to her husband, he was baffled by his outbursts. But Wilma couldn't get the impression out of her mind that whatever her husband had said in his sleep sounded like Russian. She called the foreign language department at Arizona State and asked Professor Lee Croft to listen to the tape.

Croft not only agreed that Mrs. Sutherland had recorded her husband speaking Russian, but he was able to recognize eight or nine Russian terms, including the words for "a drunk" and "excuse me, it's evident."

Gene Sutherland, however, insisted that he didn't know how to speak Russian. His only exposure to the language had occurred during World War II, when as a United States Army serviceman he met up with Red Army allies at the Elbe River.

Croft theorizes that somehow the experience of hearing Russian left an impression on Sutherland's subconscious, enabling him to speak in Russian as he slept. After word leaked out about Gene's odd talent, however, the Sutherlands soon heard from a host of people with other possible explanations—including reincarnation and demonic possession.

Tasmanian Monster

It's not unusual for dead animals to wash ashore after a fierce storm. But the creature that turned up on a Tasmanian beach in July 1960 after a particularly violent gale was unlike anything that had ever been seen before.

Rancher Ben Fenton and some of his workers were rounding up cattle not far from where Interview River empties into the ocean when two of Fenton's men found the "monster"—a large, circular mass, about twenty feet in diameter and six feet thick at the center, covered with short, coarse hair.

Fenton called local authorities to report the strange find, and soon a government naturalist and other interested scientists were at the remote location to take a look at the mysterious animal.

The thing's inch-thick skin was so incredibly tough that taking tissue samples turned out to be almost impossible. After hacking away with sharp axes for over an hour, however, two scientists were finally able to cut out a segment of the beast's white fibrous interior.

But scrutiny in the lab raised more questions than it answered. Researchers were not able to say what the animal was—only what it *wasn't*. According to scientists who examined the evidence, the creature was not part of any known species on Earth.

Two years passed, but the Tasmanian monster was not forgotten. The Australian Parliament expressed interest in getting to the bottom of the mystery and, once again, a group of government scientists descended on the remote beach where the hairy creature still baked in the sun.

After twenty-four hours of examinations and consultations, the group released an official statement. Their conclusion? The beast remained a baffling enigma, unrecognizable to the world of science.

Angels' Wings

Summoned before the Spanish Inquisition in the sixteenth century, the painter El Greco was interrogated not because of suspected heresy, witchcraft, or a relapse of faith. The Church officials were offended by the way he painted the wings of angels.

According to the inquisitors, El Greco's angels were in opposition to canon law and the Holy Scriptures: They weren't painted so that the wings represented real angel wings at all. However, unlike other victims of the Inquisition, El Greco was able to successfully defend his actions. He presented his theories of form, purity, and grace so convincingly that the judges acquitted him and set him free. Perhaps under their black cowls, the representatives of the Church harbored an appreciation of art—as long as it wasn't too openly paganistic.

Ancient Roman Lead Poisoning

Two Roman cities destroyed and buried during the eruption of Mount Vesuvius in A.D. 55, Pompeii and Herculaneum, are archaeological time capsules, valuable for studying what people were doing at the time of the calamity. The more prosperous

Pompeii is better known because more people escaped. Throughout the Middle Ages, in fact, Italian noblemen had mineshafts dug into the buried city and excavated a number of ancient art masterpieces. Some centuries after the eruption, however, a new city was built on the site of the buried Herculaneum, a situation that still makes research difficult, although not impossible.

Archaeological exploration of Herculaneum during 1988, in fact, unearthed parts of the city and a number of corpses. Study of the preserved human remains has revealed the diseases that plagued the ancient Roman citizens, particularly lead poisoning.

The source of the lead, it's believed, was soldered wine and food containers. Scientists suggest that the ingested lead affected the minds and the reproductive ability of the Romans. Unable to replenish the old Roman stock, the people would have been defenseless against the invading barbarians (who didn't use lead in their utensils). Mental aberrations and instability, not only among the general population but also among such emperors as Caligula and Nero, would encourage the further decline and eventual collapse of the empire.

Frasier's Youthful Old Age

In 1971, southern California's Lion Country Safari attempted to breed twelve young lionesses. Five young male lions were sent in to sire cubs, but the lionesses rejected each of them. One male was even badly mauled.

Later, the safari received an old lion named Frasier from a bankrupt Mexican circus that could no longer afford to feed the animal. Having spent most of his life in a cage, Frasier was scarred, bleary eyed, toothless, and lame. Yet the twelve lionesses found him irresistible, vied for his favor, and even chewed his food for him. With his new harem, Frasier eventually sired thirty-five cubs in sixteen months, after which he died, presumably quite happy and content with his active old age.

Mystery of the Dead Scientists

In August 1986, the body of underwater torpedo guidance systems checker Vimal Sajibhai was found under a bridge near Bristol, England. But that was only the beginning of a mysterious wave of deaths. Nine other scientific researchers working on British defense projects suffered strange and seemingly unconnected deaths. In each case, the death was classified as either a suicide or "unexplained."

Several months after Sajibhai's death, a noose was placed around the neck of Ashhad Sharif as he sat in his car. With the other end of the rope tied to a Bristol park tree, Sharif's neck was broken as the car sped away.

This was followed by the January 1987 death of computer designer Richard Pugh, whose body was found in his East London home. During the same month, the body of Royal Armaments Research and Development Establishment computer expert John Brittem was found in his garage, seated in his car with the motor still running. Metallurgy expert Peter Peapul and computer engineer Trevor Knight were also victims of carbon monoxide poisoning.

The list goes on: Computer expert David Sands, the trunk of his car filled with gasoline, crashed into an empty restaurant and burned to death. Computer specialist Mark Wisner suffocated when a plastic bag was somehow placed over his head. Victor Moore presumably died of a drug overdose. And Russel Smith, of the ultrasecret United Kingdom Atomic Energy Authority, was found dead in his car after it plummeted over a cliff.

The British press has suggested that the deaths may have been a series of planned murders. The purpose: To impede antisubmarine warfare and other defense programs. Members of Britain's House of Commons found the deaths suspicious enough to have called for an official investigation.

Rasputin's Miraculous Cures

The Russian czar Nicholas II and his czarina were greatly influenced by the mysterious Siberian monk Rasputin, whom the czarina referred to as "our Friend." The source of Rasputin's power over the royal family stemmed from his hypnotic ability to stop the internal bleeding attacks of their son Alexis, the hemophiliac heir to the throne. Through his power over the czar and czarina, Rasputin was able to enrich himself with munitions contracts, influence the appointments of his friends to government posts, interfere with military tactics, and live a generally depraved life-style, often involving ladies of the court. Moreover, his increasing influence destroyed public trust in the government and weakened the country's military efforts during World War I.

Although suspected of espionage by some historians, Rasputin has never been proved to be a German spy even though his actions certainly aided the enemy. The Germans reasoned that as long as Rasputin reigned within the palace, the Russian war efforts were doomed anyway. They therefore did everything possible to keep the monk firmly in power.

German agents often bribed Russian soldiers to feign unconsciousness until the arrival of Rasputin, who frequently visited the wounded in Russian army hospitals. When the monk stopped to bless a German plant, the soldier would suddenly sit up, calling out that he had been cured and giving thanks to God, the saints, and Rasputin for the apparent miracle. Such "cures" inflated Rasputin's fame among the Russian people and his influence with the royal family.

Finally, in December 1916, Prince Felix Yusupov contrived to rid Russia of Rasputin. Taking advantage of the monk's interest in attractive noblewomen, the prince invited him to a tryst, got him drunk, fed him poisoned cakes, shot him, and then drowned him in the ice-covered Riva Neva.

It was too late, however. Rasputin's influence and actions had so greatly impugned imperial prestige that the February 1917 revolution, already in the works, would mark the end of the Romanov dynasty and its empire.

Versailles Time Warp

Annie Moberly and Eleanor Jourdain, two British teachers, visited the royal palace at Versailles during a trip to France in 1901. Having explored the main palace, they walked through the world-famous gardens on their way to Petit Trianon, Marie Antoinette's small palace. Since they didn't know the ground plan, they requested the assistance of two men dressed in eighteenth-century garb who they thought were caretakers. The men waved them straight ahead, and as the women moved on, they saw a woman and a young girl also wearing old-fashioned costumes standing in a cottage doorway.

The schoolteachers continued walking until they came to a wooded area. There they encountered a dark man with a malevolent expression sitting in front of a *temple d'amour* (temple of love), a pavilion with a round roof supported by columns. A young man emerged from behind some rocks along a weeded path. He spoke a French dialect unfamiliar to the women, but with the assistance of gestures, directed them toward Petit Trianon, across a wooded bridge over a small gulley. On the other side was the front lawn of the palace.

During their walk, Miss Moberly said later, "everything looked unnatural. . . . Even the trees seemed to have become flat and lifeless. There were no effects of light and shade . . . no wind stirred the trees. . . . It was . . . intensely still."

As they looked ahead at Petit Trianon, Moberly noticed an attractive and obviously aristocratic lady sketching the bordering woods. She was wearing a large hat, a long-waisted green bodice, and a short white skirt. Noticing the teachers, the noblewoman stared at them, as if startled.

Suddenly, the eerie stillness seemed to lift and the surroundings returned to normal. A modern guide appeared and escorted the ladies on a tour of Petit Trianon. The aristocratic artist was no longer anywhere to be seen.

The two teachers did not speak to each other of their experience for several days, and not until 1911 did they jointly but anonymously publish their story in a small but successful book. By that time, they had thoroughly researched what they had seen and concluded that they had walked through a summer day in 1789.

The "gardeners," they declared, were Swiss guards. The dark, menacing man was most likely the Count de Vaudreuil, who was visiting Trianon at the time. The woman and the young girl in the cottage doorway, according to old palace records, could have been peasants living on the palace grounds. The memoirs of Marie Antoinette's dressmaker mentioned making several green bodices and white skirts for what turned out to be the queen's last summer.

There was no mention, however, of a wooden bridge over a gulley in any available records. That missing piece to the puzzle caused the teachers' account to be generally ridiculed—until the royal architect's original plans, which included the gulley and the bridge, were eventually found in the chimney of an old building in a nearby town. The plans had been hidden there long before, perhaps for safekeeping.

Nevertheless, the incident on the grounds of Versailles remains unresolved. Had the Misses Moberly and Jourdain truly seen and talked to ghosts from a summer's day in 1789? Or had the ladies somehow traveled back in time as visible, talking apparitions themselves?

The Widow's Dream

When Ruth Ammer fell asleep on a hot August afternoon in 1962, she was the wife of Syrian-American shoe repairman Joseph Ammer. But by the time she woke up, she had a terrible feeling that she was a widow.

Ruth had experienced a prophetic nightmare. As she later recounted to the police, she dreamed that her husband was in his shop when an assailant attacked him, striking him over and over with a hammer.

When Mr. Ammer failed to come home for lunch as he always did, Ruth began to worry even more about the dream. So she decided to pack Joe's lunch and take it to his shop a few blocks away.

When Ruth arrived, she saw her nightmare come true. She found her husband bound with cobbler's twine, beaten to death. The murder weapon, a hammer, lay nearby.

Although she gave the police a description of the man she had seen in her dream, the officers were not particularly interested—until they learned that a man who answered Mrs. Ammer's description, down to the clothes he was wearing, had been spotted washing his bloody hands in a rest room shortly after Joseph's murder.

Although her dream was not admissible as evidence at the murder trial of William Edmonds, Ruth Ammer did have the satisfaction of knowing that her husband's murderer—the same man she had seen in a nightmare—was found guilty and sentenced to life in prison.

The Socialite Who Dreamed of Murder

Sir Henry Wilson, chief of the British general staff during World War I and a member of Parliament, spent a jovial evening with his old friend, socialite Lady Londonderry, and several other people in June 1922. The group joked and talked at the London socialite's home until close to 2:00 A.M. Then Lady Londonderry went to bed, but it was a fitful sleep. When her husband woke her up, she was screaming and wet with perspiration.

In a terrifying dream, she told her husband, she had watched Sir Henry die. She described how her friend took a taxi through the streets of London, stopping in front of his home. Then Sir Henry paid the driver and walked up to his front door. As he started to unlock it, two assassins approached him, whipped pistols from under their coats and shot him at point-blank range. Then the gunmen raced down the street.

There was one detail of the dream that didn't seem to make sense. Lady Londonderry had "seen" Sir Henry in his full-dress military uniform, but the gentleman's customary attire was civilian clothes.

A little more than a week after the socialite's dream, however, Sir Henry Wilson was asked to unveil a war memorial at Paddington Station. For the occasion, he wore his full-dress uniform. After the dedication, he took a taxi home, where, a few minutes after he paid the driver, two armed murderers shot him to death—a tragedy Lady Londonderry had previewed in her terrible dream.

Impossible Rain

Every school kid knows that clouds and rain go together. But there have been unexplained instances of rain pouring from the sky when there wasn't a cloud in sight.

Mrs. R. Babington arrived home on the clear and sunny afternoon of November 11, 1958, and noticed that water was coming down on her grass and her home's roof. It definitely wasn't raining, so she assumed the neighbor's sprinkler was accidentally aimed toward her house and yard.

But closer inspection revealed no one nearby was watering grass. No pipes had burst and no outside faucets were turned on. The water had to be coming from somewhere. But where?

Soon dozens of people, including the managing editor of the *Alexandria Daily Town Talk*, Adras LaBorde, were watching rain fall on an area about one hundred feet square over Mrs. Babington's house—but no place else in the neighborhood. The downpour kept up for hours and officials at the weather bureau and at England Air Base were unable to come up with an explanation for the phenomenon.

Nearly a century before, a similar event was reported down in Dawson, Georgia. Although there were no clouds in the sky on that

September day in 1886, it rained for more than an hour on an area a mere twenty-five feet in diameter.

A month later that same year, two areas in South Carolina were inundated by cloudless showers. According to the *Charleston News and Courier*, one house and lawn in that seaport town were drenched for hours by a mysterious isolated shower. And as reported by the October 24, 1886 *New York Sun*, for two weeks a small section of Chesterfield County, South Carolina, was saturated by a steady rain that poured from a clear, sunny sky.

The Lifesaving Hunch

Mrs. Hazel Lambert of Pennsbury Heights, Pennsylvania, gave a co-worker a ride home from the Cartex Corporation at about ten o'clock on Christmas Eve morning, 1958. Then she decided to pick up a few things at a nearby food store. But as she drove toward the market, Mrs. Lambert was overcome with the need to step on the gas and race down Franklin Street—a road she had never been on before.

What was behind this strange compulsion? Mrs. Lambert never figured that out. All she knows, she later told reporters, is that she had to follow her strong feelings, which took her to Hillside Street. Suddenly, the woman glanced over at a nearby canal and saw a child's hands, covered in red mittens, holding on to the inside edge of a hole in the ice.

Speeding through the intersection and right over the ice, Mrs. Lambert felt the car slip through the frozen water. The doors jammed as the car settled in four feet of water, so she pressed down on her horn and yelled for help.

The commotion brought George Taylor and his teenage son to the scene to help the trapped driver and the child hanging on to the ice. The younger Taylor quickly used a pole to maneuver himself out on the ice and rescue Carol Scheese—a two-year-old girl who most certainly would have died if Mrs. Lambert had not given in to an odd compulsion.

Bizarre Blackouts

The electricity went out, suddenly and unexpectedly, when the power between two of the main stations serving Denver went down for nearly an hour and a half around midday, February 14, 1963. The outage caused an overload of current, which also zapped relay lines to Cheyenne and Boulder out of commission. To keep the turbines of the Cherokee plant from being damaged, the facility had to be closed down.

What caused the blackout? Engineers sent out to check for line breaks, damaged equipment, and other possible explanations were baffled when everything appeared to be in perfect working order. Then, as mysteriously as the region's electrical power had gone off, it came back on again. "We may never know what happened," a state official was quoted as saying by a local reporter.

There are some, however, who think there may be a link between UFOs and similarly inexplicable power shutdowns. One example was researched by Dr. Olavo Fontes of Brazil and recounted in *The Great Flying Saucer Hoax*, written by Carol Lorenzen, director of the Aerial Phenomena Research Organization.

On an August night in 1959, four automatic keys in the huge electric power station at Uberlândia, Minas Gerais, turned themselves off, shutting down power to all trunk lines. Technicians scurried to find out what was going on. Nothing seemed amiss except that the keys had broken the circuit.

Immediately, a worker from a substation placed a call to the chief engineer at Uberlândia and told him an incredible story: A UFO had soared low over the power station, he said, causing the keys at the substation to kick themselves open.

The chief engineer dismissed the man as a drunk and got back to work. He turned on two of the main keys and found they were still not working. Then he turned the third key and suddenly they all popped open. At that moment, workers at the Uberlândia station began yelling and pointing at the sky. A glowing disc-shaped object was passing overhead on a path right over the power lines. As soon as the "flying saucer" passed out of view, the electric power station began working normally once more.

The Moving Memorial

It's not unusual for a memorial to be moving, in the emotional sense. But there's a memorial in the eastern corner of a Marion, Ohio, cemetery that *literally* moves. And no one knows how or why.

The tapered white granite column, set off by a black granite sphere three feet in diameter, marks the graves of Charles Merchant and six of his relatives. Erected in 1897, it didn't create much of a stir until July 1905. That's when a workman noticed that the heavy black ball topping the monument had been moved several inches, exposing a rough spot on the bottom of the orb where it had once fit.

If pranksters were behind the incident, they must have been incredibly strong—or they must have brought heavy equipment with them. Since the sphere weighs hundreds of pounds, it took a block and tackle to budge it.

Determined that no one would disturb the Merchant memorial again, cemetery officials poured lead cement on top of the granite column to tightly hold the sphere in its original position. But two months later, the black ball had moved again. This time it was ten inches away from where it was supposed to be resting.

Curiosity seekers and scientists, including a geologist, offered possible explanations, but none of them panned out. In fact, the big black ball is said to be restless still—moving from time to time, as if it has a mind of its own.

The Ghost Ships and the Destroyer

The Navy destroyer *Kennison* had two ghostly encounters at sea—events dutifully recorded in the ship's log.

The first took place in 1942 not far from the Golden Gate Bridge while the *Kennison* searched for Japanese submarines. The fog was so thick that the crew had to rely on radar to keep from running aground on the Farallon Islands. But a couple of sailors, a lookout listed as Tripod, and a torpedoman first class named Jack Cornelius, spotted something in the dense mist that the radar never picked up—an ancient-looking, unmanned, two-masted sailing vessel passing within a few yards of the *Kennison*'s stern.

The men yelled over the intercom for the rest of the crew to take a look. The ghostly ship, however, had vanished in seconds. But Tripod and Cornelius gave identical descriptions of the strange craft they had seen plowing across the water.

In the spring of the next year, the *Kennison* was patrolling the coast about 150 miles out from San Diego. The log notes that the sea was smooth and the night sky was clear and starry. Sailors Carlton Herschell and Howard Brisbane were on lookout duty on the flying bridge. As they looked through binoculars, they both saw a freighter heading toward the destroyer. They quickly warned the radarman, who failed to see anything on his scope.

Herschell and Brisbane put down their binoculars. They could now see the freighter with their naked eyes. It was about seven miles away and still coming toward them. Then it simply disappeared.

Time Warps in the Bermuda Triangle

For many years the Bermuda Triangle, an area between Bermuda, the east coast of Florida, and Puerto Rico, has been the scene of hundreds of disappearances of ships from the sea and planes from the sky, or sometimes just the crews suddenly vanish from their ships. Only a few inconclusive last messages have been received. Little wreckage has been recovered. The many theories for the disappearances are varied and speculative:

—Sudden giant seiche waves or eruptions of underwater volcanoes. If wreckage surfaces it may be carried up the coast and farther out in the ocean by the Gulf Stream.

—Human error, compounded by known frequent failure of electromagnetic equipment, including that used for radio communication and motor power.

—Whirlpools and "holes in the ocean" that swallow ships and planes.

—Hijackings by modern pirates or drug traffickers or both.

—Disassociation of matter by sound resonance (a suggestion from the USSR).

—Small, dense, compact fogs on the surface or in the sky, where craft enter but do not exit.

—Selection of human beings and their artifacts by collectors from outer space entering through the Triangle, an area that perhaps allows easy electromagnetic access, functioning as a "hole" in the sky.

—Sudden release of subsurface gas deposits through seismic action causing temporary lack of buoyancy on the sea and whiteouts and loss of horizon by aircraft, which results in their plunging into the ocean.

—Giant sunken pyramids, built by Atlanteans as power sources, that may still function sporadically and interrupt the controls and communication systems of ships and planes.

Besides disappearances, there have been a number of very unusual *appearances*, also without any logical explanation, that may put into question our acceptance of time, space, and matter:

—An oceanic investigative party on the yacht *New Freedom*, in July 1975, passed through an intense but rainless electromagnetic storm. During one tremendous burst of energy, Dr. Jim Thorpe photographed the exploding sky. The photograph when developed showed the burst in the sky, but it showed, too, a square-rigged ship on the sea about one hundred feet away from the *New Freedom*, although a moment before the sea had been empty.

—John Sander, a steward on the *QE-I* saw a small plane silently flying alongside his ship at deck level. He alerted another steward and the officer of the watch while the plane silently splashed into the ocean only seventy-five yards from the ship. The *QE-I* turned around and sent a boat over, but no indication of anything was found.

—Another "phantom plane" silently crashed into the ocean at Daytona Beach on February 17, 1935, in front of hundreds of witnesses, but an immediate search revealed nothing at all in the shallow water by the beach.

—A Cessna 172, piloted by Helen Cascio, took off for Turks Island, Bahamas, with a single passenger. About the time she should have arrived, a Cessna 172 was seen by the tower circling the island but not landing. Voices from the plane could be heard by the tower, but landing instructions from the tower evidently could not be heard by the pilot. A woman's voice was heard saying, "I must have made a wrong turn. That should be Turks, but there's nothing down there. No airport, no houses." In the meantime the tower was frantically giving landing instructions, which were not heard. Finally the woman's voice said, "Is there no way out of this?" and the Cessna, watched by hundreds of people, flew away from Turks into a cloud bank from which it apparently never exited since the plane, the pilot, and the passenger were never found.

The plane had been visible to the people on Turks, but when the pilot looked down, apparently she saw only an undeveloped island. Had she been seeing the island at a point in time before the airport and the houses were built? And where did she finally go?

The Boy Who Lived Before

Indian businessman Parmanand Mohan died in Morada-bad on May 9, 1943. About ten months later, in Bisauli, India, a baby boy was born to college professor Bankey Lal Sharma and his wife. From the age of three, the child, who was named Pramodh, insisted that *he* was Parmanand—he even described how his previous life had ended. "My tummy got wet and I died," he told his father. "Now I have come to Bisauli."

When his son was five, the professor took him to Moradabad, a town the child had never visited before, to see if his tales of life as Parmanand had any basis in fact. The boy quickly led his father and other relatives to a shop where he had been employed in his former lifetime—pointing out in detail how the carbonating machine Parmanand had operated worked. A confrontation with the late Parmanand's wife and sons seemed even more convincing. He identified them by name, talked to them about intimate matters, and even pointed out how their home had been remodeled after "his" death. The visit left both Parmanand's family and Pramodh in tears.

The trip resulted in an explanation for one of the youngster's first assertions concerning his former life. "My tummy got wet and I died" proved to be an accurate, if childlike description, of Parmanand's demise. The man, suffering from an undiagnosed abdominal discomfort, was given a hot bath just before his death.

The Dreams That Saved Josiah Wilbarger

Schoolteacher Josiah Wilbarger of La Grange, Texas, set out one morning in 1838 with four other men to visit his friend Reuben Hornsby, who lived on a farm not far from what is now Austin. But soon after starting the trip, the companions were attacked by a band of Indians. Two of the men immediately fell, mortally wounded. Josiah, shot in the throat, stripped of his clothing, and scalped, was left behind by the two companions who managed to escape with their lives. Josiah must be dead, his friends reasoned—and if it weren't for a woman's dreams, he would have been.

Freezing as he lay naked in the brush, Wilbarger woke up after spending several hours unconscious. Blood streamed from his throat and head. But he was alive and determined to make it to the Hornsby house, about six miles down the trail. Dragging himself a quarter of a mile in that direction, he finally collapsed and drifted in and out of consciousness. Then his sister appeared to him.

"Brother Josiah, you are too weak to go on by yourself," the dreamlike figure said. "Remain here where you are and friends will come to take care of you before the setting of the sun." Then his sister smiled sadly and moved in the direction of the Hornsby's home. Only later was it learned that the woman had died in Missouri twenty-four hours before she appeared to comfort her injured brother.

That evening Mrs. Hornsby, who had been told by Wilbarger's companions that her friend was dead, had a frightening dream. She saw Josiah lying beneath some small cedar trees. He was bloody, naked, and scalped, but still alive.

Mrs. Hornsby woke up from the nightmare and assured herself it was merely a dream. But when she fell asleep again, it returned with the same terrifying vividness. The next morning, due to her insistence, her husband and Wilbarger's companions set out to search for Josiah.

Following the man's bloody trail, they soon found him leaning against a scrub cedar, barely alive. The men cleaned his wounds, wrapped him in warm blankets, and carried him to his friend's farm where he eventually recovered.

The story of Mrs. Hornsby's dreams was not forgotten. The state of Texas eventually erected a monument to the woman whose nightmares helped save a schoolteacher named Josiah.

The Barren Grave

In the early nineteenth century, young Englishman John Davies came to the Welsh town of Montgomery to work for a local widow on her farm. It was the biggest mistake of his short life.

While walking down a road one day, two local men accosted him, demanding money. Davies refused the thugs' request and a fight broke out. Not only was Davies beaten up, but his muggers carried him to Welshpool, where they insisted that *he* had tried to rob *them*.

It wasn't long before the Welsh authorities, never particularly fond of Englishmen, had sentenced Davies to die on September 6, 1821, for highway robbery. Seconds before the noose was put around his neck, he held up his right hand and declared that an innocent man was being sent to his grave: "I die praying to God that He will let no grass grow on my grave and that He will so prove my innocence."

John was buried in the Montgomery parish churchyard alongside rows of other graves—all of which were covered with grass. But Davies's plot remained barren. Local authorities tried topping the grave with green sod, but it immediately turned brown and died. Next, grass seed was tried. None ever sprouted.

Thirty years after Davies's execution, the cemetery was relandscaped. All the graves were covered with two feet of fresh soil and grass seed was planted. Soon the area was covered with a thick, grassy lawn—except for one lonely, brown rectangle that neither seed nor fertilizer could turn green. It was the grave of John Davies. Eventually, a fence was placed around the plot, which remains a barren, mute testimony to one man's innocence.

Who Really Discovered America?

It was back in 1921 that Elwood Hummel found the strange stone. He was fishing along the Susquehanna River near Winfield, Pennsylvania, when he spotted, under the clear water, the small flat object covered with odd markings. On examination, Hummel found it was not a rock after all; instead it was some kind of baked clay tablet. Whatever it was, it didn't seem particularly important to the fisherman, so he just stuck it in the pocket of his fishing coat. It wasn't until thirty-seven years later, when his grandchildren asked about the peculiar object they'd found mixed in with his fishing gear, that Hummel decided to send it to the Field Museum's curator in Chicago.

There scholars pored over the markings and finally translated its message. The clay tablet gave details, they said, about a loan made by an Assyrian merchant in Cappadocia about 1800 B.C. What they couldn't explain was how an ancient Assyrian document got into a river in Pennsylvania.

That mystery has never been solved, but the out-of-place object is just one of many found in the United States which indicate that the New World had a host of visitors long before Columbus—or even native Americans—set foot there.

For example, in Bradley County, Tennessee, J. H. Hooper came across a stone marked with odd symbols. The farmer wondered if there were other strange rocks on his property, and he soon found several more—plus a long stone wall covered with indecipherable signs, numerals, and pictures of animals. A report by the New York Academy of Sciences indicated that the markings on the wall included numerous Oriental characters, which the baffled researchers decided must be "accidental imitations."

The Australian Astronomers and the UFO

When a "flying saucer" is spotted by a couple of teenagers or a tired truck driver, it's easy to brush off the incident as a case of overactive imagination. But when three highly trained astronomers spy a UFO at the same time, that's a different story.

On May 30, 1963, the headlines of the *Melbourne Herald* in Australia declared: "Three Astronomers See Flying Saucer." The article itself noted that the incident was "the best authenticated so far." Professor Bart Bok, a world-renowned authority on the Milky Way; Dr. H. Gollnow, a senior astronomer at the Mount Stromi Observatory; and assistant astronomer Miss M. Mowat, the newspaper reported, had spotted a glowing, reddish orange object around 6:58 P.M. almost directly over the observatory.

The three astronomers tracked the object for one minute as it traveled west to east below the clouds at speeds far too fast to be a balloon. The observers also ruled out a meteor, since the UFO moved slower than those celestial bodies and left no visible trail.

Since the thing was moving under cloud cover, it was far too low to be a satellite, the astronomers reasoned. Besides, a check of satellite charts indicated that none was over the area where the UFO was seen. The Civilian Aviation Control Center also confirmed that there were no planes in the vicinity at the time.

The three scientists concluded that the object, which they noted was self-luminous and did not reflect sunlight, "was definitely man-made!" But just what sort of "man" made this flying craft, which was not a satellite or an airplane, was never explained.

Deadly Warnings

Does death give some people a warning when it is near? In countless cases, the answer seems to be yes.

In February 1958, for instance, twenty-three-year-old Eugene Bouvee found that he couldn't get his seventy-year-old uncle Eugene off his mind. There was no reason to be worried about the old gentleman—he wasn't ill as far as anyone knew. In fact, when young Eugene called one of the elderly Eugene's neighbors the next day, he was told his uncle was feeling healthy and happy. Still, the nephew couldn't shake the feeling that something was terribly wrong.

The young man drove to his uncle's home in Flint, Michigan, but he couldn't get in. The door was locked and smoke was wafting out from around it. He quickly kicked down the door, only to be driven back outside by thick smoke and flames. The fire department arrived shortly afterwards, but it was too late—Uncle Eugene's body was found on the bathroom floor.

In a similar incident, Mr. and Mrs. Richard Ryan of Sheboygan, Wisconsin, received a warning from their son, airman Lawrence Monk, that his death was near. He told his mother he was sure he would die soon and he wanted her to keep his Bible. "I won't be needing this anymore, Mom," he said. "You'll never see me again—but you'll hear about me."

Two days after their son's visit, the Ryans received the tragic news: Their son had been killed, along with sixty-six other passengers, in a United Airlines plane crash in Wyoming.

Not all deadly premonitions turn out to have dire consequences, however. Sometimes they *save* a life. Take the case of thirty-year-old Fred Trusty of Painesville, Ohio, who in 1958 experienced what he called a "strange feeling." It made him drop the tools he was using to build some steps on a hill near his house and compelled him to glance toward a nearby pond. He saw nothing unusual, just some rippling water probably caused by the muskrats who lived in the pond. He picked up his tools again, but the odd feeling returned. Once more he looked over at the pond. This time, he saw a little boy's cap in the water.

Running down the hill, Trusty dove into the pond just in time to save the life of his own two-year-old son, Paul.

The Lost Arms of Venus de Milo

The Venus de Milo was officially found in 1820 on the island of Milos. Now enshrined in the Louvre in Paris, it is one of the most famous and most beautiful of the world's statues. However, seeing that it lacks its arms, art lovers and admiring tourists have long wondered how the arms originally were positioned and what the goddess Venus (or Aphrodite in Greek) was holding in them.

When Venus was first found, she had her arms in place. A Greek peasant living on Milos found her complete, in an opening under a field, perhaps part of an ancient house or temple. He brought the statue to his barn and hid her. He would often go alone, after his day's work, to admire her beauty. He spent so much time this way that his wife suspected he was meeting another woman in the village. She enlisted the aid of a priest. When the priest discovered that the beautiful rival was made of stone, the wife was satisfied, but the secret was out and news of the ancient statue spread far and wide.

Turkish occupation troops who wished to take the find to Constantinople arrived at Milos at the same time as a French frigate sent by King Louis XVIII, who wanted the statue for the prestige of France. A fight started between the French and the Turks. Meanwhile the Greeks were trying to get the statue out to sea, and, as they fled in a small boat followed by the French and the Turks, the statue lost its attached arms, which fell into the sea. The French got to the small boat first, seized the statue, and transported it to Paris, where it now stands in the Louvre as a wonder of the ancient world.

The mystery of the arms' position was not a mystery when the statue was found on Milos. The arms were still in place and a drawing had been made of the statue before the French-Turkish-Greek confrontation. The goddess's right hand was gracefully holding up her robe, already hanging halfway down her body, while the left hand held out an apple, the golden Apple of Discord, connected in legend with Helen, Paris, and the Trojan War.

To find the arms and reunite them with the body of Venus would be an archaeological triumph. Jim Thorne, a deep-sea diver and archaeologist, led an expedition in the 1950s to the area of the coast where the arms were thought to be. On his first dive he found what seemed to be long, lovely white arms reaching up from the bottom. On his second dive he found that they were the graceful and whitened branches of a tree. He never did find the arms.

The lost arms of the world's most famous statue are doubtlessly still lying on the sea bottom not too far from the harbor of the island of Milos.

The Mysterious Demise of Jimmy Sutton

Around 8:30 P.M. on October 12, 1907, Mrs. James Sutton, Sr., told her husband she had just experienced a frightening premonition. "I heard a terrible roaring sound and felt a smashing blow on my head," she exclaimed. "Then I felt stabbing pains in my body and my senses reeled. I don't know why, but I just know that something has happened to Jimmy. Something terrible!"

At 2:30 the next morning, a phone call confirmed Mrs. Sutton's ominous prediction. Her son, U.S. Navy Lieutenant James Sutton, was dead. Navy officials told the family that the young man had committed suicide in Annapolis after getting into a drunken argument with two fellow officers at a Naval Academy dance.

But, according to Mrs. Sutton, as soon as she heard this news an apparition of her son appeared to her and insisted he had not killed himself. "Mama, they beat me almost to death," the grieving mother heard her son say. "I did not know I was shot until my soul went into eternity."

Four days later, the ghostly vision returned, this time to deny published navy reports of how the young man died. Mrs. Sutton claimed that her son gave details of his death that would prove it was not a suicide. For example, Jimmy claimed there was a bruise on his forehead and a lump on his left jaw—facts that directly conflicted with evidence presented at the navy inquest.

Mr. and Mrs. Sutton demanded that their son's body be exhumed and, at a second inquest directed by a nongovernment physician, it was confirmed that Jimmy had indeed died with a large bruise on his jaw and another on his forehead. The doctor also concluded that there was no way the young lieutenant could have killed himself because of the path of the bullet—it had entered from almost the top of the victim's head. In addition, it was learned that the bullet retrieved from Jimmy's body had not been fired by the deceased man's gun, as the navy had claimed.

The second inquest concluded that Jimmy Sutton had not committed suicide. Someone had beaten and then shot him—just as his ghostly apparition had claimed.

Séance for a Murder

Fall was in the air in 1921 when medium Dr. O. A. Ostby and several friends met in Minneapolis to hold a séance. Soon Ostby informed the group that a young girl was in their midst. The spirit, he said, was crying and asking for a favor. She called herself Edna Ellis. It seemed, the medium continued, that Edna wanted someone to write a letter to the St. Louis police department explaining that she had been murdered. She did not want her parents to continue to think that she had run away to lead an immoral life.

The next day, following the ghost's request, Ostby wrote to the chief of police, Martin O'Brien, in St. Louis. O'Brien replied that Edna Ellis had indeed been murdered and that her boyfriend, Albert, was serving a life sentence at the Missouri State Penitentiary for the slaying.

When Ostby and his group met for another séance, the young woman again appeared and thanked the medium. Then she re-

quested that he send O'Brien's letter to her parents in South
Dakota. Ostby was confused by one detail in the apparition's story,
however. The girl spoke of the lover who had killed her as George,
but the police called him Albert Ellis. Edna's spirit explained that
her boyfriend's full name was George Albert, although she had
always referred to him as George.

In November 1922, the Supreme Court of Missouri reviewed
Albert Ellis's case and decided he had been unfairly convicted. The
man was released from prison, but four years later he died in an
accident. Edna Ellis apparently held no bitterness toward her killer.
On July 16, 1928, the spirit of Edna Ellis dropped by another séance
being conducted by Dr. Ostby to inform him that she and George
were happily together at last.

The Two Mr. McDonalds

A person *can* be in two places at the exact same time. At
least that's the decision reached by a New York City jury on July
8, 1896.

The strange verdict came at the end of a burglary trial. William
McDonald was charged with burglarizing a house on Second Avenue. Although the defendant insisted he was innocent, six people
testified that he was definitely the man they had surprised as he
packed up stolen articles inside the home. After a fight, the accused
burglar escaped. McDonald was arrested soon after based on witnesses' accounts.

But at McDonald's trial, another witness gave surprising testimony in the accused burglar's defense. According to Professor
Wein, a medical doctor who performed public hypnotism experiments from time to time, McDonald was hypnotized in front of
several hundred people in a Brooklyn theater at the exact time the
burglary was under way.

Wein testified that he was sure McDonald was the volunteer he
had put in a trance. He remembered him clearly because the man
had been an unusually good hypnotic subject.

"He was . . . very responsive and quick to execute the instructions," the doctor told the courtroom. "I considered him to be in a cataleptic state—that is, deprived for a certain time of all sensations other than those I imposed on his will."

"Was it possible," a lawyer asked, "for this man's spirit to wander while his physical body was in a hypnotic trance and in full view of the audience?"

The professor answered, "Yes. Quite possible."

After hearing this testimony and that of the six eyewitnesses to the burglary, the jury acquitted William McDonald. They decided that everybody was telling the truth—McDonald had been on a theater stage and, at the same time, in a house five miles away.

UFO Landing Strips

If extraterrestrials decide to make their presence known on Earth, they may choose to land at areas built by UFO enthusiasts especially for visitors from outer space.

In 1973, a retired marine officer drew up plans for some fake flying saucers that could be used as decoys to lure alien pilots. His funds ran out, but in the 1980s a group called the New Age Foundation was able to create a similar landing strip designed to attract UFOs. The group christened the fifteen-acre site, near Mount Rainier in Washington State, Spaceport Earth.

Farther south, in Lawson Valley, near San Diego, California, UFO buffs have constructed another saucerport. It's owned by Ruth Norman, head of the Unarius Education Foundation, who believes extraterrestrials will soon be parking their spacecraft in the area.

The Living Dead

Most of us assume that zombies are fictional creatures who dwell only in horror films. But in Haiti, the living dead are taken seriously. In fact, that country's penal code states that turning someone into a zombie is equivalent to murder. And the chief of psychiatry of Haiti, Lamarque Douyon, says he's personally examined three of the creatures. "I am absolutely convinced that zombies exist," he states.

Douyon spent twenty years trying to prove voodoo and related ph. nomena were fakery. Then he had face-to-face encounters with zombies. Douyon learned that they were real people who had been brought to a state of apparent death by drugs—probably a poison derived from flowers of the genus *Datura*. "These people are pronounced dead and publicly buried," Douyon explains. "Then they are exhumed and reanimated by the voodoo sorcerers who administered the drugs in the first place."

The sorcerers enslave most of these zombies for life by giving their victims small amounts of the drug each day. Some of the living dead have managed to escape however. Two are under study at Douyon's Port-au-Prince clinic, where the psychiatrist is working to unravel the secrets of the real-life zombies of Haiti.

Monkeying Around with Evolution

If you go by the fossil evidence, humankind and monkeys haven't been close family members for at least 20 million years. On the other hand, researchers have discovered that only 4.5 million years ago, the DNA in both people and monkeys was pretty much alike. Two British science writers, Jeremy Cherfas and John

Gribbin, have proposed an explanation: Men didn't evolve from monkeys; monkeys *descended* from man.

Gribbin and Cherfas's theory states that a race of walking apes split into two groups about 4.5 million years ago. The group who lived on the plains in time evolved into primitive man. The other walking anthropoids "de-evolved"—they frolicked in trees and eventually became today's apes.

Do Cherfas and Gribbin really think it's time to monkey around with the theory of evolution? Maybe, and maybe not. "We simply want to show how many gray areas there are in fossil evidence," Cherfas comments. "We'd like paleontologists to consult the molecular clock and then reconsider their findings."

Chesapeake Bay Monster Movie

Loch Ness isn't the only body of water in which a dinosaurlike creature has been spotted. One American sea creature, nicknamed Chessie, is said to live in Chesapeake Bay, where it has been videotaped gliding through the water.

It was nearing sunset on the evening of May 31, 1982, when Bob and Karen Frew and their dinner guests first saw a dark object moving in the bay. Bob quickly picked up his video camera and began filming what looked like a thirty-foot-long serpent with humps on its back.

Several Smithsonian Institution scientists agreed to look at the three-minute tape soon afterwards. George Zug, who heads the vertebrate zoology department at the Smithsonian's National Museum of Natural History in Washington, concluded that whatever was in the movie couldn't be dismissed as simply a submerged log or optical illusion. "It was most interesting," the scientist says, although he refuses to speculate on exactly what it was.

Mike Frizelle and Bob Lazzara, members of a Maryland organization called Enigma, which looks into unexplained phenomena, have decided to compare past sightings of Chessie with new reports, including the Frews' videotaped sighting. If they can find out just where the animal is most likely to be seen, Lazzara suggests, then they can go out and look for it.

"We didn't take 'Chessie' so seriously before," Frizelle adds. "But the Frew tape elevated it to a legitimate phenomenon."

Is There Intelligent Life in the Universe?

Even if there are not any intelligent aliens roaming the universe right now, they could exist "within a cosmic eye blink," according to paleobiologist Dale Russell of Ottawa's National Museum of Natural Sciences.

After studying the fossil record of the earth to find out how much brain size and intelligence have increased over the epochs, Russell has concluded that Earth's creatures are quickly developing bigger and better brains. On other planets, the same process could be going on. "Intelligence in the universe may be like a yeast cake," Russell says, "coming up fast."

Russell disagrees with other researchers who think there may be only a few other intelligent creatures in the galaxy. "Their estimates are based on the erroneous assumption that such civilizations will exist for a while, then simply die out. But biology just doesn't work this way."

In fact, Russell points out, even if the humans of Earth become extinct, the planet could still give rise to even more clever species. "It's possible for man to be replaced by an entirely different creature," he explains. "Already the parrot, elephant and dolphin are as large-brained as some of man's ancestors and closest relatives."

He adds that there's no reason to think that earthlings are the only brainy inhabitants of the galaxy. "We haven't yet detected extraterrestrials. But the universe is still evolving and is most likely full of civilizations."

The Constitutional Rights of Extraterrestrials

In an era of odd legal claims and lawsuits of all kinds, an unusual incident took place in 1983. The Pentagon was served with a writ of habeas corpus in the United States District Court of Washington, D.C., by Larry Bryant of Alexandria, Virginia, ordering that there be produced within sixty days the bodies of "one or more occupants of crash-landed UFOs of apparent extraterrestrial origin."

The extraterrestrials in question were allegedly found in three so-called flying saucers that crashed in New Mexico, where a huge radar installation had apparently interfered with the UFO control mechanism. Each flying saucer, as stated in the writ, was manned by three humanoid bodies, dressed in metallic clothing. The writ of habeas corpus was issued under the legal right of citizen's arrest and, according to the complainant, the bodies were kept at Wright-Patterson Air Force Base in Ohio. Bryant further stated that if the extraterrestrials were still alive, keeping them against their wills was depriving them of their constitutional rights.

Nothing since has been released to the public concerning this action, which has been described by Henry Catto, a Pentagon spokesman, as a writ of "habeas corpus extraterrestrial."

The Heavy Fate of Dinosaurs

John Ferguson, an aerospace engineer based in Surrey, England, thinks the earth's gravity has undergone changes as the solar system has passed celestial bodies on its travels through the

Milky Way. Those long overlooked gravitational shifts, he says, probably spelled disaster for the dinosaurs that once ruled the planet.

"During high-g periods everything would weigh more, while during low-g periods everything would weigh less," Ferguson theorizes. Creatures that developed in the sea during a high gravity period, he adds, couldn't live on land until a lower gravity period came along—then they could crawl out of the water.

"Dinosaurs evolved under weak gravity conditions and declined as gravity increased," Ferguson says. Because the massive creatures weighed so much, life became impossible when the pull of gravity was intensified. In addition, the researcher explains, increased gravity must have resulted in the sun generating more energy; otherwise, it would have collapsed under pressure from the earth. With the sun releasing more high-energy, ultraviolet rays and less warm, low-energy infrared light, the climate cooled.

That, says Ferguson, was probably the final death blow to the dinosaurs: Tropical food sources died out and ultraviolet light, raining down on the giant reptiles, caused a cancer epidemic.

Solar-Powered Suicide

When the sun is used as a symbol, it is usually associated with happiness and hope. But one day in the mid-1980s an unemployed Seattle man turned the sun into a vision of death. By rigging up a solar-activated suicide machine, he transformed the warmth of spring sunshine into death rays.

Robert Saylor, who had studied electronics through a correspondence course, called his estranged wife and warned her that he was going to die. He said he'd locked himself in a hotel room; he wanted to see her and their young daughter just one more time. At the meeting, he told the woman that he had created a "foolproof" suicide machine made out of a solar cell, a battery pack, and explosives.

The following day, Saylor called again. This time when he said he was about to kill himself his wife called the police. Just after midnight, the police burst on the scene and tried to talk Robert out of his plan.

According to King County, Washington, police spokesman Dick Larson, the officers thought they had convinced the man to come out of his barricaded room. Instead, as the sun began to rise, a muted explosion was heard. When the police hurried inside, they found Saylor's lifeless body.

He was sitting in a chair with his legs stretched out on a bed. Saylor had put a photosensitive receptor in the hotel room window: It was connected to a battery pack, which was wired to a bomb.

"We'll never know if he really intended to come out," Larson comments, "or if he was just waiting for the sun to rise."

The Satellite from Another World

In July 1960, a *Newsweek* article noted that the number of manmade objects known to be orbiting the earth didn't jibe with the actual number of satellites that had been sent into space. The National Space Surveillance Center said the United States had eleven in orbit and the Soviet Union had two. But according to the *Newsweek* article, several scientists claimed at least one other space-craft was circling the planet. Where did it come from?

"This satellite, the scientists suspect, is a visitor sent by the beings of another star within our own Milky Way—a sort of United Stellar Organization perhaps—interested, for archaeological and anthropological reasons, in how things are going in this part of the galactic neighborhood," *Newsweek* reported.

Could the alien satellite have been the same UFO spotted on December 18, 1957? That evening, around 6:00 P.M., Dr. Luis Corrales of the Communications Ministry in Caracas, Venezuela, snapped a photo of the Soviets' Sputnik II. When Dr. Corrales developed the picture, he was startled to find that he had captured another object on film, too.

Alongside the Russian satellite was a UFO, which showed up as a streak of light because of the short time exposure Dr. Corrales had used. When researchers examined the photo, they concluded that the object wasn't a meteor or star. Instead, they determined that it was an unrecognizable kind of intelligently controlled craft that was able to deviate from the path of the Sputnik II, and then return to its side.

The Woman Who Slept over a Bomb

It's hard to understand how until recently Zinaida Bragantsova ever got a good night's sleep. Since 1941, the woman's bed rested over a bomb that had crashed into her apartment in the Soviet town of Berdyansk and made a hole in her floor. It wasn't that she didn't think about the danger—she simply couldn't find any help for her explosive problem.

Unable to convince anyone that the bomb was real, Bragantsova just moved her bed over the patched hole in the floor where the bomb rested. According to the newspaper *Literary Gazette*, other people in her town made fun of her claims and teasingly called her "the grandmother with her own bomb." Soviet authorities accused her of making up the story just so she could get a new apartment.

In recent years, however, the woman's plight got some attention. When new telephone cables were installed in her neighborhood, demolition experts began searching for buried explosives from World War II. This time when she asked officials to look into her problem they reluctantly complied.

"Where's the bomb, grandma? Under your bed?" an army lieutenant said sarcastically to the seventy-four-year-old lady. "Yes," she answered.

The demolition experts were startled to find that Bragantsova was telling the truth. A five-hundred-pound explosive was discovered and, after two thousand people were evacuated, it was detonated. Bragantsova's home was destroyed by the blast but, the *Literary Gazette* noted, the grandmother finally received a new, bomb-free apartment.

Spacecraft Propulsion Systems

UFO skeptics are quick to point out that there's no way a spaceship could travel the tremendous distances between solar systems without breaking the laws of physics.

Freeman Dyson, a former consultant to NASA who now works at Princeton's Institute for Advanced Study, says that's simply not true: "I think it's quite likely that there are other species zipping around, exploring the far reaches of interstellar space."

Just how extraterrestrials—or humans—could accomplish such a feat is no longer a mystery, according to Dyson. In fact, he says there are several practical spacecraft propulsion systems that could zoom spaceships to the stars. These include systems that would propel a spaceship by shooting either a high-velocity laser beam or solid pellets of light into a kind of "sail" and an orbital electromagnetic "generator" that would launch an interstellar craft by flinging it into space at incredibly high speeds.

By propelling a spaceship at half the speed of light, Dyson predicts, these propulsion systems could probably have a crew of space explorers from our nearest star system neighbor setting down on Earth in less than nine years.

The Mystery Man Who Toasts Poe

Since Edgar Allan Poe wrote about the mysterious and the macabre, it seems appropriate that the anniversary of his death each year is associated with some strange goings-on. Indeed, someone has placed roses and cognac on Poe's grave in the Westminster Churchyard in Baltimore each and every January 19 since 1849.

On a recent birthday of the author, Jeff Jerome, the curator of Poe House, decided to do some detective work to discover the mysterious visitor's identity. After staking out the grave for hours, Jerome and four other Poe fans suddenly heard the cemetery gates rattle at about 1:30 A.M. When they shined a flashlight across the graveyard, the intruder fled—but not before Jerome and his friend Ann Byerly caught a glimpse of him.

Byerly describes the mysterious stranger as a man with blonde or brown hair who was wearing a dramatic-looking frock coat. "He was clutching a walking stick with a golden sphere on its end—like the one Poe carried," Jerome adds. "Before vanishing over the wall, he raised his cane high in the air and shook it at us triumphantly."

Chinese Ape-Men

Chinese citizens have repeatedly reported encounters with seven-foot-tall wild ape-men in the mountainous region of Hubei. The creatures, who are said to swing through trees and eat leaves and insect larvae, are covered all over with brown hair. One witness said he made peaceful contact with a female ape creature who was accompanied by a child. Another man says he ran into a violent ape-man, whom he finally stabbed.

In recent years, Chinese scientists Yuan Zhenxin and Huang Wanpo have proposed that the creatures could be descended from *Gigantopithecus*. Writing in the Chinese journal *Hua Shi*, they note that many fossilized remains of that primate, long believed to be extinct, have been found throughout Hubei.

An ancient myth provides another possible explanation for the origin of Chinese ape-men. According to legend, during the rule of Emperor Ch'in Shih Huang Ti around 200 B.C., a group of people refused to work constructing the Great Wall of China. Fleeing to the mountains, they eventually reverted into primitive beings—"de-evolving," the story goes, into hairy, apelike creatures.

Fossil Dream

As nineteenth-century scientist Louis Agassiz recounted in his book, *Recherches sur les Poissons Fossiles*, a persistent dream directed him to one of his most important discoveries.

The zoologist had tried for weeks to figure out how to transfer a vague outline of a fossilized fish from an ancient hunk of rock. Nothing worked, and Agassiz finally put the stone on a shelf and went on with other work.

But a couple of nights later, he dreamed of what the fossilized fish looked like when it was alive. When he awoke, Agassiz found he couldn't shake the image. So he studied the fossil-bearing slab again. However, he still couldn't see anything other than a vague image.

That night the dream came back. Once more, in the morning, the scientist turned to the stony outline to see if he could make out the prehistoric fish's shape—but he was no more successful than before.

Would the dream return? Suspecting it might, the zoologist put a pencil and paper by his bed. Then he went to sleep and again saw the fish in a dream. Rousing himself to consciousness, Agassiz woke up and in the darkness drew what he had seen.

The next day, the scientist was surprised to find that his drawing contained details that he had never spotted on the fossil. Using the sketch as a guide, Agassiz decided to chip away at the fossilized rock, in hopes that it might reveal additional details of the fish's body.

As he worked slowly and carefully, the scientist found that the fossil had not been completely uncovered. When he removed a paper-thin layer of stone, the image of the fish became clear. This time the prehistoric creature could be seen in sharp relief—it was a previously unknown fish that matched, in every detail, the animal Agassiz had seen in his dream.

A Dream from Prehistory

Anthropologist Joseph Mandemant dreamed it was night and he was standing at an opening of the Bedeilhac cave in France. Inside, a group of Magdalenian hunters, clad only in animal skins, gathered around a campfire. Mandemant could see hunting scenes drawn on the roof of the cave. He also noticed that a young man and woman were sitting apart from the others.

The couple soon got up and went into another of the cave's rooms which contained a ledge. They began to make love in the dark. But the idyll—and the anthropologist's dream—came to an abrupt end when the roof of the cave suddenly crashed down, sealing off the area where the young couple had gone for privacy.

The dream was so detailed and clear that Mandemant wrote it down and set off to visit the actual cave located at Bedeilhac. Everything seemed just as the scientist had dreamed it, except that the main "room" had a wall on the right made of solid limestone.

Could this slab of stone have concealed the room where the lovers retreated for their tryst? Mandemant tapped on the limestone with a mallet and found that it was hollow—another room *was* behind the limestone.

For several days, workmen hacked through the rock. Finally, there was a hole large enough for the anthropologist to climb through. On the other side was the room, just as Mandemant had dreamed it, including the ledge.

There were no signs of the young man's and woman's skeletons, however. Mandemant's detective work showed that when the stone originally fell from the roof of the outer cave, it left an opening just big enough to have provided an escape passage for the young couple.

Despite the fact that much of his dream had been verified by his inspection of the cave, Mandemant still had no tangible proof that while sleeping he had somehow transcended time and space. Then he remembered another detail of his dream—the hunting scenes on the roof of one of the cave's rooms. Following the drawing he had made of the images from his dream, the scientist found the same ancient illustrations he had somehow "seen" when they were new, thousands of years ago.

The Prime Minister Who Dreamed His Own Death

In the spring of 1812, a wealthy Englishman named John Williams had an unusual dream that returned, three times in all, on the evening of May 3. Although he wasn't interested in politics, Williams repeatedly dreamed that he was in the cloakroom of the House of Commons watching a small man in a dark green coat shoot Prime Minister Spencer Perceval in the chest. The dream was so disturbing that Williams thought about warning the prime minister. But when his friends scoffed at the idea, he put the odd nightmare out of his mind.

Prime Minister Perceval, however, learned about the nightmare firsthand—he had the identical dream seven days later. As he told his family on the morning of May 11, he dreamed that while walking through the lobby of the House of Commons, he was shot by a crazed man. The assailant wore a dark green coat set off by brass buttons.

Although Perceval's family urged the prime minister to heed the dream's warning and stay home that morning, he headed off for the day's session of the House of Commons, determined not to let anything so silly as a dream interfere with his official duties. As the prime minister was walking through the lobby, a man whom he had never seen before, wearing a dark green coat with shiny brass buttons, shot Spencer Perceval to death.

Mick to the Rescue

Percy the chihuahua today romps happily around his home in England. But if it had not been for the inexplicably keen senses of another dog, Mick the terrier, he would have been buried alive.

Percy's owner, Christine Harrison, took her pet with her when she visited her parents in Barnsley. The tiny dog refused to stay in the yard and, when he raced into the street, was hit by a car. "We couldn't detect a heartbeat, and his eyes were fixed and staring," Christine recalls.

Sure her beloved Percy was dead, she had her father put him in a heavy paper sack. Then the dog was buried, two feet under, in the garden.

Mick, Christine's parents' dog, refused to budge from Percy's grave. After Christine returned home, she was shocked when her parents reported that Mick had dug up her pet's body and dragged him, still in the burial sack, to her parents' house. Incredibly, the terrier had somehow known that Percy was still alive.

"My dog had come back from the dead," Christine says. Although unconscious, the little canine had a faint heartbeat. He was rushed to a veterinarian, who deduced that the animal had managed to survive because of air trapped in his burial sack. The vet also said that Mick had helped Percy recover by giving him a lick massage that boosted his circulation.

Mick was recognized for his bravery by the Royal Society for the Prevention of Cruelty to Animals. But Christine says she doesn't understand why the terrier saved Percy. "Those two dogs hate each other," she notes. "They always have, and they still do."

Red Army Wonder Woman

In the closing days of World War II, teenage Red Army soldier Nina Kulagina was wounded in the front lines by a German artillery shell fragment. Hurt and sent home, she felt her frustration mounting. While her recovery dragged out, friends and countrymen were dying in the struggle against Hitler and his troops.

"I was walking toward a cupboard," the aggravated Kulagina said later, "when suddenly a jug moved to the edge of the shelf, fell, and smashed to bits."

Lights started turning off and on in her presence. Doors swung open and shut for no apparent reason. Dishes danced on tabletops. Kulagina first suspected a poltergeist, or "noisy ghost," but soon came to recognize the mysterious force as her own. From that realization followed months of concentration and practice, until Kulagina was able to move objects at will.

Edward Naumov became the first Russian scientist to actively investigate Kulagina's psychokinetic abilities. A series of successful experiments conducted by various authorities followed, more than sixty of which were filmed. In the most dramatic of these, an egg was broken and slipped into a saline solution behind glass. Standing several feet away, Kulagina directed her attention toward the egg in the aquariumlike tank. Slowly she separated the egg white from the yolk, moving the two apart with her mind. At the time of the experiment, Kulagina was wired to several instruments, which showed her to be under extreme mental and emotional stress. Her electrostatic field was monitored by Dr. Genady Sergeyev, who reported a four-second pulse cycle as Kulagina separated the egg.

Sergeyev equated the pulsations with magnetic waves. When they occur, he said, "they cause the object she focuses on, even if it is something nonmagnetic, to act as if magnetized. It causes the object to be attracted to her or repelled."

The Wonder Girl from Georgia

A thunderstorm in Cedartown, Georgia, kept fourteen-year-old Lulu Hurst and her cousin, Lora, from falling asleep one summer night in 1883. Then the girls noticed strange rappings and popping sounds that seemed too close to be thunder.

Lulu's parents at first thought the odd commotion was related to the severe electrical storm. But the next evening, it was obvious some other phenomenon was involved—their daughter's bed was thumping so strongly they could feel it, and over a dozen witnesses heard wall-shaking noises in Lulu's room. Observers discovered that the sounds seemed to answer questions. One rap apparently meant "yes"; two knocks were "no."

No one realized, however, that whatever was going on had a connection with Lulu until four days later. That's when a visiting relative was thrown across the room after she touched a chair handed to her by Lulu. Four men who grabbed on to the gyrating piece of furniture found themselves in an exhausting wrestling match with an invisible force that finally broke the chair to bits.

Lulu ran screaming and crying from the scene, terrified by her new powers. But within two weeks she was performing baffling feats in front of live audiences.

The first show by "the wonderful Lulu Hurst," as she was dubbed by the newspapers *Atlanta Constitution* and *Rome Bulletin*, was in a hall in Cedartown packed with curious spectators. Judges, lawyers, bankers, state politicians, and doctors sat on the stage to watch the small, frail teenager's talents up close.

A solidly built man in the audience volunteered to test the girl's powers. He was given a closed umbrella, which he held with both hands across his chest. Told to keep the umbrella still, he braced his feet. But when Lulu simply touched the palm of her right hand against the umbrella, the object jerked violently from side to side. The man began writhing up and down and ended up flung into the laps of the onstage observers.

For the next two years, Lulu demonstrated her powers as she toured the United States. She appeared before the faculty and students of the Medical College at Charleston, South Carolina, an audience that the *Charleston News and Courier* called "notable and critical." After watching the small girl toss people around the stage by simply touching them, the newspaper concluded, "There was not a man in this distinguished and learned array who could explain the mysterious phenomenon."

Nonetheless, twenty scientists from the Smithsonian and Naval Observatory staffs eventually joined Alexander Graham Bell in studying the teenager. They suspected she possessed some kind of electrical force. But their studies failed to solve the puzzle of the amazing Lulu—and when she married and retired a couple of years later, the source of her powers remained as mysterious as ever.

The Strange Trance of Molly Fancher

Molly Fancher of Brooklyn, New York, seemed like a normal and healthy twenty-four-year-old until she suddenly became dizzy and fell unconscious one day in early February 1866. Her mother thought Molly had simply fainted. But when physician Samuel F. Spier came to examine the young woman, he found her in a trancelike coma—the likes of which he had never seen before.

Months passed, and Molly failed to wake up. Dr. Spier examined her clammy body and found that she hardly appeared to breathe at all. Her body temperature was subnormal and her pulse was extremely weak; it sometimes seemed to disappear altogether. Numerous other physicians were called in for their opinions but no one could offer any help.

Dr. Spier was still caring for his comatose patient nine years later when he made two remarkable observations. The records showed that in all the time she had been in a near-death state, Molly had lived with almost no sustenance. Over the years she had only eaten, Spier said, "about the amount a normal person would consume in two days!" In addition, she had developed what the doctor called "supernatural" abilities.

Dr. Spier invited several scientists, including two noted neurologists and the famed astronomer Dr. Richard Parkhurst, to witness Molly's strange talent. "Gentlemen, this girl can fully describe the dress and action of persons hundreds of miles from here, just as they are this instant!" he told the group. "Furthermore, she can read unopened letters and books!"

To test Dr. Spier's implausible claims, the two brain specialists put a message inside three sealed envelopes and had it sent by courier to Dr. Spier's office several miles away. Then Dr. Parkhurst asked Molly what was in the envelope. To his amazement, she answered correctly. "It is a letter," she whispered. "In three sealed envelopes, written on a sheet of paper are the words, 'Lincoln was shot by a crazed actor.' "

To test her powers further, they asked Molly where neurologist Peter Grahman's brother was and what he was doing. Miss Fancher quickly said that Frank Grahman was in New York. He was wearing a coat that was missing a button on the right sleeve and he had left work early because of a headache. A telegram soon confirmed that everything the young woman had said in her trancelike state was true.

Molly outlived her mother and Dr. Spier. For forty-six years she remained in a coma. But in 1912, she woke up as suddenly and mysteriously as she had become unconscious. She lived until March 1915, when she died peacefully in her sleep at the age of seventy-three.

Blind Sight

When European explorers first reached the Samoan Islands, they heard remarkable tales of blind natives who could see through their skin. While this sounds like a fable, it may have been based on fact—there are numerous documented accounts of people who could somehow see without the use of their eyes.

French physician Jules Romain studied this ability in both blind and sighted people for several years after the end of World War I. He found that some people had areas of skin that were photosensitive. So, he theorized, certain nerve endings in the skin could be the pathways by which sight without eyes is possible.

One man who claimed to have this ability was Ved Mehta, an Indian who became totally blind when he was three years old, following an attack of meningitis. In his book, *Face to Face*, published in 1957, Mehta explained that he never needed a cane to get about. In fact, he could maneuver a bicycle through crowded streets with no problem. His secret? Mehta insisted that he possessed "facial vision"—he somehow "saw" through the skin on his face.

Sometimes the sighted claim to have this talent as well. Teenager Margaret Foos of Ellerson, Virginia, was so skilled at "seeing" when her eyes were blindfolded that her father took her to the Veterans Administration Center in January 1960 for special testing. Not only did the fourteen-year-old point out the location and colors of objects while her eyes were taped and bandaged, but she also read newspaper articles aloud.

Syndicated newspaper columnist Drew Pearson, who wrote about the testing of the girl's abilities, said that one psychiatrist noted, "It's conceivable that some new portion of the brain may have just been discovered."

Brains That Baffled Medicine

The brain is so complicated that scientists are constantly working to discover just how it works. It is well known, however, that even seemingly minor injuries and shocks can sometimes cause damage to the brain—and result in anything from a loss of sensation to seizures. On the other hand, medical literature cites cases of severe brain damage that didn't seem to affect patients at all.

In September 1847, twenty-five-year-old Phineas Gage, a foreman on the Rutland and Burlington Railroad, became one of these lucky people. While tapping some gunpowder into a hole, preparing to blast it, the iron rod Gage was using hit a stone. That touched off a powerful explosion that rammed the rod into Gage's skull.

Still conscious, Gage was carried by fellow workers to a doctor's office where the metal was removed—along with pieces of his skull and brain tissue. The two physicians who treated him never ex-pected him to survive, much less endure such a head injury without permanent aftereffects. But, with the exception of losing the sight in his left eye (which was forced almost out of its socket by the accident), Gage soon recovered completely.

A woman working in a mill in 1879 suffered an equally ghastly on-the-job accident. A machine threw a huge bolt that landed four inches deep in the woman's skull. Pieces of her brain were lost during the impact and more brain subst... e was destroyed when physicians took the bolt out of her head. The woman recovered and lived another forty-two years—without even suffering a headache from her ordeal.

According to the 1888 edition of *The Medical Press of Western New York*, about one-fourth of a man's skull was destroyed when he was caught between a bridge timber and the superstructure of the ship he was working on. The sharp corner of the timber clipped off part of the deckhand's head. Doctors who closed the wound found that the man had lost a substantial amount of brain matter, as well as blood. But as soon as the victim regained consciousness, he talked and dressed himself as though he felt perfectly fine. Except for a few dizzy spells, he was healthy despite the loss of part of his brain, until twenty-six years later when a partial paralysis and unsteady gait developed.

For twenty-seven days, a baby born a St. Vincent's Hospital in New York City in 1935 appeared to be a typical infant—it cried, ate, and moved. Only after its death did doctors discover during an autopsy that it had no brain at all.

In a report prepared by Dr. Jan W. Bruell and Dr. George W. Albee which was delivered to the American Psychological Association in 1957, the physicians noted they had been forced to perform drastic surgery on a thirty-nine-year-old man. Although they removed the entire right half of the man's brain, the patient survived. And, the doctors concluded, the operation inexplicably "left his intellectual capacity virtually unimpaired."

An even stranger case was recounted by the German brain expert Hufeland. When he autopsied a paralyzed man who had been fully rational until the moment of his demise, he found no brain at all—just eleven ounces of water.

The Case of the Murder-Solving Mentalist

When Royal Canadian Mounted Police Constable Fred Olsen entered the home of farmer Henry Booher of Mannville, Alberta, in 1928, he was faced with a rare crime—mass murder. Henry and his twenty-one-year-old son, Vernon, had discovered the bodies of Mrs. Booher, her son Fred, and two hired hands. All had been shot to death.

Whoever committed the bloody deed had carefully retrieved all the cartridge cases, except one. Found where it had fallen in a dish of soapy water, it came from a .303 rifle, the kind of gun that had been stolen from a neighbor not long before. There were few other clues to the murderer's identity. But Constable Olsen was suspicious of the glaring looks of hatred and sneering contempt that young Vernon directed in the Mountie's direction when he thought the officer wasn't looking.

Olsen soon learned that Vernon's mother had caused the breakup of his affair with a pretty woman in Mannville and he accused the young man of murdering his mother and the others in a fit of revenge.

"Have you found the rifle?" Vernon calmly asked. When the constable admitted he hadn't, the young Booher added, "You will certainly never get a confession out of me, you know."

Olsen was positive he had discovered the murderer, as was his fellow officer, Inspector Hancock. They even arrested Vernon. But they had no proof that would stand up in court. Desperate for a lead, Hancock finally contacted Maximillian Langsner, who claimed he could solve crimes through his ability to read the minds of criminals. The mentalist, who said he had studied telepathy in the Far East, agreed to tune in to Vernon's thoughts in order to find out where the murder weapon was hidden.

"If he thinks about it, I can pick up the impulses sent out by his brain and interpret them for you," Langsner assured Constable Olsen.

For four hours Langsner sat outside Vernon's cell, staring. Finally, the suspected murderer began to crack. "Get away from here, damn you!" he screamed. "Get away, I say!"

But Langsner didn't budge. He just kept staring. Another hour passed and Booher was clearly exhausted from the mental strain. It was the opportunity the mentalist had been looking for to gain access to the dark recesses of the mass murderer's mind.

"He told me mentally where that gun is hidden," Langsner explained to Constable Olsen. Then he sketched the exact location— under some bushes not far from the Booher farmhouse.

Constable Olsen, Inspector Hancock, and Langsner were soon on their way to the area. The mentalist immediately recognized the spot he had "seen" with his telepathic powers. Running ahead of the others, he fell to his knees by the bushes and began scooping up earth with his bare hands. The murder weapon was soon exposed.

Faced with this evidence, Vernon promptly confessed to the killings and was sentenced to death by hanging.

Although mental telepathy wasn't a usual tool of the Canadian Mounties, Inspector Hancock decided to make Langsner's role in solving the crime public knowledge. He discussed the facts of the case with newspaper reporters and dutifully recorded in the official Royal Canadian Mounted Police files how a mentalist had read the mind of a mass murderer.

Arthur Price Roberts: Psychic Detective

Born in Denbeigh, Wales, in 1866, Arthur Price "Doc" Roberts possessed unusual talents even as a child—he used extrasensory perception to locate lost objects and missing persons. As an adult he became a psychic detective who helped the police as well as private citizens solve mysteries.

For example, Duncan McGregor of Pestigo, Wisconsin, disappeared without a trace in July 1905. Months later, his distraught wife turned to Doc Roberts for help. Unable to come up with an immediate mental impression, Doc went into a trancelike state and soon told Mrs. McGregor not only that her husband had been murdered but exactly where the body was located. Police followed the psychic's directions and found the corpse just where Roberts said it would be—in the Menominee River, trapped under sunken logs by tangled clothing.

Doc also solved the case of wealthy Chicago businessman J. D. Leroy's missing brother. The man had been murdered, Roberts informed Leroy; Doc's psychic impressions told him the body was in a particular area of Devil's Canyon in New Mexico. The victim was found just two hundred feet from a spot described in detail by the psychic detective.

While a guest at the Fond du Lac Hotel, Doc Roberts was approached by local police who asked for help with a two-year-old unsolved murder. Closing his eyes, the psychic "saw" the murder victim and described him accurately. The next day he asked the officers to show him photographs of known criminals. As he flipped through the mug shots, Roberts suddenly stopped and pointed. "There's your killer, gentlemen!" he exclaimed. "You will find him in British Columbia—working for the Mounted Police Service!" Doc's mental detective work proved accurate, as usual.

Roberts was skilled at predicting the future as well as psychically delving into events that had already transpired. According to the *Milwaukee News*, Doc made some astounding prophecies on October 18, 1935. He warned the Milwaukee police to be prepared for bombings. "I see two banks blown up and perhaps the city hall. Going to blow up police stations. Then there's going to be a big blow-up south of the river [Menominee] and then it'll be over!"

Eight days later dynamite exploded in the village hall, killing two children and injuring many others. The next day, bombs went off in two Milwaukee banks and a couple of police stations.

Milwaukee police detective English turned to Roberts for information about the violence. "On Sunday, November fourth, there'll be a big one south of the Menominee. And that'll be all!" Doc predicted.

On November 4, a blast rocked Milwaukee with such power that people eight miles away heard it. As Roberts predicted, it was the final explosion. The police found the scattered remains of the bombers, twenty-one-year-old Hugh Rutkowski, and his nineteen-year-old friend Paul Chovonee, amid the debris. The two had accidentally blown themselves to bits while building more bombs to terrorize the community.

Arthur Price "Doc" Roberts made one of his final predictions at a dinner party in his honor. It was November 1939, and the seventy-three-year-old psychic detective thanked his friends for coming to the get-together. "I am afraid that I won't be present at the next one. As much as I would like to remain, I won't be with you beyond January 2, 1940."

Once again, Doc was right. On January 2, 1940, he died at his home in Milwaukee.

Gladstone's Gift

It was a cold December night in 1932 when off-duty Royal Canadian Mounted Police constable Carey decided to visit a small theater in Beechy, Saskatchewan, for some entertainment. A tall, handsome man who called himself "Professor Gladstone" was on stage performing a mind-reading act.

Constable Carey laughed along with the rest of the audience as hypnotized volunteers performed silly antics under Gladstone's direction. Then the mood changed as the mentalist stood before rancher Bill Taylor and cried, "I have it! You are thinking about your friend Scotty McLauchlin! He was brutally and wantonly murdered!"

Then he pointed at Constable Carey. "That's the man. He is the one who will find the body," Gladstone exclaimed. "And I'll be with him when he does!"

The Mountie knew that Scotty McLauchlin had mysteriously disappeared nearly four years earlier. But the case remained unsolved. Carey approached the mentalist privately and asked how he knew what had happened to McLauchlin. Gladstone explained that he psychically "felt" that Scotty had been murdered.

Detective Corporal Jack Woods of the Criminal Investigation Bureau in Saskatoon decided to question the mentalist further. Gladstone assured him that he didn't know who killed Scotty, but he would know the murderer when he saw him.

The two officers and the mentalist set out to visit people who had known Scotty McLauchlin before he disappeared on January 16, 1929. They stopped by the house of a man named Ed Vogel, questioning him about reported threats made against Scotty in his presence. Exploding in anger, Vogel insisted the Mounties' information was "a bunch of lies."

Suddenly Gladstone pointed at Vogel and began to recite what had happened on the night in question. "You were sick in bed. Schumacher [an acquaintance] pushed through the door and told you he had had a quarrel with McLauchlin and swore that he would kill that damned Scotty," the mentalist said.

Vogel turned white and admitted Gladstone was correct.

Heading to Schumacher's farm, the officers were asked to slow down by Gladstone. He claimed he smelled something foul. The body of Scotty McLauchlin was somewhere in the vicinity, he said.

The officers soon found Schumacher and drove him back to town for questioning. The suspect insisted that he and Scotty had been amiable partners on the farm; when the missing man said he was leaving town, Schumacher had purchased his share of the land.

Gladstone's psychic impressions, however, said the man was lying. "It's the barn!" the mentalist exclaimed. "Now I can tell you how you did it! Scotty left the house. . . . You followed him. You forced him into a quarrel—there was a fight! . . . Scotty fell. . . . But you kept striking and striking until you knew he was dead! Then you buried his body near the barn under some rubbish!"

Schumacher denied the charges. The next day, officers Woods and Carey, accompanied by Gladstone, brought the suspect back to his farm. They were heading toward the barn when the mentalist walked up to a frozen manure pile and announced, "Scotty McLauchlin is buried under there, gentlemen."

The corpse of the long-missing man was soon exhumed, and Schumacher broke down, confessing that the slaying had happened just as "Professor Gladstone" had pictured it in his mind.

The Talking Pencil

Legend holds that King Arthur and Queen Guinevere were buried at Glastonbury Abbey. There are even those who claim that Jesus was a visitor there around A.D. 27. Despite its historical significance, however, the abbey was destroyed by Henry VIII, who plundered the libraries and then blew up the buildings with gunpowder. A thousand years later, the spot dubbed by some the "holiest spot in Britain" was nothing but crumbling ruins.

In 1907, archaeologist-architect Frederick Bligh-Bond began digging at the site, searching for two long-vanished chapels described by early chroniclers of the abbey—one was dedicated to the martyr King Edgar, and another was the Chapel of Our Lady of Loretto. As he noted in his 1933 book *The Gate of Remembrance*, his greatest clues for the excavation project came unexpectedly from a "talking" pencil.

Bligh-Bond first heard about "automatic writing," a method of receiving paranormal written messages from another dimension, from his friend Captain Bartlett. Curious about the phenomenon, Bligh-Bond decided to try it himself. Holding the pencil lightly, he asked, "Can you tell us anything about Glastonbury?"

Following more questioning, the pencil began to move, spelling out, in ancient Latin, details concerning the Chapel of Edgar the Martyr. It described how the structure had been revised and drew a map of the way the abbey once looked, including one of the long-sought chapels.

An entity who identified himself as a monk named Gulielmus noted that Edgar's chapel had extended thirty yards to the east and had windows made of blue glass. Using the directions provided by the "talking" pencil, Bligh-Bond's work crew soon uncovered the ruins of the chapel—including blue glass fragments.

When the archaeologist tried using automatic writing to reveal the location of the Chapel of Our Lady of Loretto, this time he received a message written in early sixteenth-century English. It informed Bligh-Bond that he would find the ruins in the hard bank of earth on the abbey's north side. But only one wall would be uncovered, the writing continued, because looters had removed the rest for private buildings. Digging in the area showed, once again, that the "talking" pencil was correct.

Disembodied entities, one claiming to have been Johannes Bryant, who died in 1533, provided more historical details about Glastonbury. Another spirit, who wrote he was "Awfwold ye Saxon," told Bligh-Bond to dig in a place where evidence of a thousand-year-old wattle-work hut would be found. The archaeologist followed the instructions and once again made the predicted find.

For a decade, Bligh-Bond and his friend Bartlett kept records of the information they received through automatic writing— messages that provided such exact directions on where archaeologists should dig that they were often accurate within a fraction of an inch.

Revolutionary Prophecies

The Duchess de Gramont of France planned a pleasant garden party in the summer of 1788. Among the witty and brilliant guests were the outspoken atheist Jean La Harpe and an eccentric poet named Jacques Cazotte. When Cazotte began uttering strange prophecies, La Harpe wrote them down. Fanatically skeptical of anything supernatural, La Harpe was sure he could use the predictions to ridicule believers. He was destined to use the material— but in a far different way than he dreamed of at the time.

Cazotte's predictions began after Guillaume des Malesherbes, minister of Louis XIV, proclaimed: "A toast to the day when reason will be triumphant in the affairs of men—although I shall never live to see the day!"

Cazotte approached the minister. "You are wrong, sir!" he cried. "You *will* live to see the day—for it shall come within six years!"

Next, Cazotte turned his gaze to the Marquis de Condorcet and told him, "You will cheat the executioner by taking poison!"

The prophet continued moving through the crowd of guests,

stopping by Chamfort, the king's favorite, to tell him he would slash his wrist twenty-two times with a razor. "But it will not kill you," Cazotte said. "You will live a long life thereafter."

The predictions became even more gruesome as he told the famed astronomer Bailly that he would be executed by a mob.

Guillaume des Malesherbes tried to bring back some levity to the evening. He bowed in front of the poet and asked with mock piety, "Can you also end my breathless concern about my own fate?"

"I regret to inform you, sir," Cazotte answered, "that your fate shall be the counterpart of that that awaits your friend Chamfort. You too shall die as a public spectacle."

Skeptic Jean La Harpe had had about enough of this hocus-pocus. "And what of me, sir?" he asked sarcastically. "You do me ill by neglecting my neck. I beg to be permitted to join my friends that we may hiss at the mob together! Surely you can grant me this last favor?"

The atheist and the poet were known to hate each other, so the guests found this exchange hilarious. Cazotte did not smile, however.

"Monsieur La Harpe," he responded, "you will escape the executioner's axe—only to become a devout Christian!"

The crowd roared with laughter. Trying to keep up the renewed good spirits of the evening, the duchess pretended to pout and asked Cazotte why future executioners seemed to spare the ladies.

The poet-turned-prophet held both hands of his hostess. "Alas, my good friend, the executioners have poor regard for the finest of ladies," he said sadly. "It is a day when it will be fatal to be noble. You will die like the king himself, after riding to the scaffold in a woodcutter's cart!"

Five years later, the "impossible" predictions of Jacques Cazotte all came true during the French Revolution. And Jean La Harpe's eyewitness account of the poet's prophecies was willed to the monastery where he had become a devout Christian—just as Cazotte had foreseen.

Dream Translation

Born to poor parents in Cornwall, England, in 1857, E. A. Wallis Budge hardly seemed likely to receive even the most rudimentary education, much less to become the foremost linguistic scholar of his time. But thanks to an extraordinary affinity for Oriental languages—and a mysterious dream—that's exactly what happened.

Prime Minister William Gladstone, who was a master of classical languages, heard of the twenty-one-year-old Budge's natural talent in that field and arranged for the studious young man to attend Christ's College at Cambridge as a charity student.

In order to continue his education, Wallis knew he needed a scholarship for graduate study. So he decided to participate in an upcoming competition that would be conducted by one of the greatest living experts on ancient languages, Professor Sayce. Each student vying for the scholarship would be required to answer four difficult questions at length.

The night before the fateful examination, Budge found he had studied so hard his mind seemed blank. Mentally and physically drained, he quickly fell asleep. Soon he was having a most peculiar dream.

He was taking the examination but he wasn't in a classroom. Instead, he seemed to be in a shed. A tutor entered and handed him the exam. For some odd reason, the questions were written on green paper. Budge easily answered the first part of the test. But when he was asked to translate complicated Assyrian and Akkadian cuneiform characters, he became frightened and woke up.

Drifting off to sleep again, the same dream returned, three times in all. He finally got up and looked at the clock. It was just past 2:00 A.M. Instead of going back to bed, Budge turned to the book *Cuneiform Inscriptions of Western Asia* by Rawlinson. It seemed to him that the difficult passages he had dreamed about were included in the text. For the rest of the early morning hours he pored over the book.

At 9:00 A.M., Budge went to the examination hall but was told the room was full. He was directed to a room he had never seen before. Not only did it look like the shed he saw in his dream, but he also recognized the scarred table and dingy skylights as details he had "seen" while asleep.

The coincidences continued. The tutor who opened the door was the same man Budge had dreamed about. And he presented the young student with questions on *green* paper—the identical questions about cuneiform characters that Budge had studied for hours because of his strange dream.

As Wallis Budge's good friend Sir Henry Haggard recounted in his 1926 book, *The Days of My Life*, Budge won the scholarship and became a renowned scholar, best known perhaps for his translation of the Egyptian Book of the Dead. For a man born to poverty with little hope for such a career, it was a dream come true—in more ways than one.

Somnambulist Theft

In Monroe County, Indiana, in 1881, a local newspaper reporter named D. O. Spencer started dabbling in mind reading. He dubbed himself "Colonel" Spencer and performed his act, which combined some hypnotism with sleight-of-hand magic, around town. Spencer never claimed to have any paranormal powers, but one day he found himself drawn into *real* mind reading—and he solved a mystery in the process. As the *Indianapolis News* wrote, "After that, Mr. Spencer was known as somewhat of a wizard!"

Spencer was performing in a school auditorium. In the audience were Mrs. Harmon and her adult children, three daughters and a son. The family was being torn apart because their savings, about four thousand dollars hidden in five separate places, had disappeared. Since only the family members knew where the money had been stashed, it was clear that one of them was a thief. But which one?

John Harmon rose from his seat and asked if Colonel Spencer

could use his mental powers to find out. Spencer had never been confronted with this kind of request before, and he quickly acknowledged that solving a crime would be an experiment for him. "I'll try if you like," he told the Harmons, adding that "the spirits" would expect 10 percent of anything he found.

The next day, a crowd of about three hundred curious people milled around the Harmons' yard, hoping to catch a glimpse of Colonel Spencer solving the mystery of the missing money. The mind reader found Mrs. Harmon and her daughters sitting nervously in the sitting room. Explaining to the crowd of onlookers that he needed quiet, Spencer began hypnotizing each member of the family and asking them to take him to the money.

Nancy Harmon began to cry, so Spencer turned to her sister Rachel. The young woman was quickly hypnotized, but she was so lethargic that the colonel gave up on getting any information out of her. Next, he tried Rhoda. She was soon in a deep trance.

"You are now going to go straight to the place where the money is hidden," he ordered. "You will walk slowly, following me, straight to the hidden money. If I make a wrong turn you will stop. Now, walk to the money!"

With his hand pressed against the girl's head, Spencer walked backwards as the girl led him toward a corncrib built of logs about a hundred yards from a barn.

"Dig here, men," Spencer told the crowd. "This is the spot!"

Buried in a shallow hole beneath the logs was a roll of yellowed newspaper. Inside was the missing money.

As soon as Rhoda was awakened from her trance, she fainted at the sight of her family's retrieved savings. Colonel Spencer theorized that the woman had stolen the money while sleepwalking and didn't remember her crime.

Spencer changed his mind about "the spirits" taking 10 percent of the recovered money. He also changed his mind about being a professional mentalist and no longer performed his mind-reading act after the Harmon case. There are those who think he may have discovered that there were powers of the mind he didn't understand—and didn't want to tamper with.

Psychic Pill

According to British parapsychologist and researcher Serena Roney-Dougal, people may one day pop psi-pills in order to read minds or peer into the future.

Although that sounds like a scenario out of a science fiction movie, Roney-Dougal says that the drug probably already exists—it's harmaline, derived from the plant genus *Banisteriopsis* in the Amazon. Primitive peoples used the substance for generations to produce mystical changes in consciousness. Because harmaline is chemically similar to a natural substance, melatonin, produced by the pineal gland, Roney-Dougal suspects that harmaline somehow increases psi powers by stimulating the pineal gland and the synthesis of melatonin.

"All these factors seem to point to the pineal gland's being in some way connected with psi, possibly as an organ that stimulates a psi-conducive state of consciousness," Roney-Dougal notes.

The scientist believes that harmaline, considered an experimental drug, should be approved for parapsychological studies. Research subjects would be given the substance and then tested for psychic talents. If the results turn out positive, she thinks other ancient procedures for activating the pineal gland should also be tried in hopes of increasing a person's ESP.

"What is needed," Roney-Dougal says, "is experimental verification of anthropological evidence."

Water Apes

Mankind's apelike ancestors didn't all swing through the trees. About 3.5 to 9 million years ago, some of the anthropoids lived in the sea. That theory, explained by British author Elaine Morgan in her book *The Aquatic Ape*, explains why human bodies have adaptations that aren't found in other land-bound mammals.

Morgan says that when these missing links emerged from the oceans to live on land again after their aquatic evolutionary detour, they were "naked" compared to other apes. This loss of hair has usually been chalked up to the sweltering heat of the open savanna. But Morgan insists if that were the case, then other hunters like the lion and the hyena would also have hairless bodies.

Man lost his hair, she says, for the same reason whales and dolphins lost theirs. "Because if any fairly large aquatic mammal needs to keep warm in water," she notes, "it is better served by a layer of fat on the inside of its skin than by a layer of hair on the outside."

Morgan adds that our aquatic ape ancestors developed long and strong hind legs, perfect for walking upright, after eons of swimming. In addition, they learned to talk out of necessity—speech was essential because being in the water made it difficult to communicate through eye-to-eye contact and facial expressions.

Morgan also points out that while humans are the only weeping primates, seals and other sea mammals cry. "If we view man as a land animal, he is unique and inexplicable," she concludes. "If we view him as an ex-aquatic, he is conforming to the general pattern."

The Boomerang-Shaped UFO

On several nights from March 17 through March 31, 1983, hundreds of Westchester County, New York, residents witnessed a dazzling sight—a boomerang-shaped craft that hovered over them soundlessly, displaying bright rays of light. The multiple reports were unusual, as J. Allen Hynek, director of the Center for UFO Studies in Evanston, Illinois, pointed out, because most UFO sightings are isolated occurrences. "But this UFO was seen in a relatively urban area over a number of days," he stated, "with a broad spectrum of witnesses."

Meteorologist Bill Hele was the first to spot the strange check mark–shaped object with rows of multicolored lights as he drove down the Taconic State Parkway. He saw the lights blink off for a moment; then they came back on—this time flashing a brilliant green. Hele reported that the craft, which hovered one thousand feet in the air for two or three minutes before it drifted out of view to the north, was almost one thousand yards across.

Within a few days, other sightings were pouring in and the Center for UFO Studies launched an investigation headed by Westchester science teacher Phil Imbrogno, coinvestigator George Lesnick, and Hynek himself. The team interviewed a host of witnesses—including doctors, nurses, lawyers, business executives, housewives, and a group of striking Metro-North trainmen—and used an Apple II computer to cross match the information they came up with. The results? All the descriptions of the UFO closely matched Hele's.

But the investigators also came up with some contradictions. Since sightings occurred in towns miles apart at the same time, could multiple UFOs have been in the sky? The evidence pointed to that possibility. However, reports of hundreds of sightings in five Connecticut towns a month after the Westchester incidents seemed to point to a hoax—the witnesses there heard engines and saw maneuvers that could have been performed by small planes flying in formation.

Nonetheless, the investigators declared, this latter event differed substantially from the genuine UFO sightings of a boomerang-shaped craft over New York. Stated Imbrogno, "Single-engine planes cannot hover soundlessly, make ninety-degree turns, or shoot down dazzling beams of light."

How Quick-Frozen Mammoths Taste

The mammoth, the modern-day elephant's hairy ancestor, has been extinct, it is presumed, for thousands of years. Yet everyone from tourists to scientists in Siberia have reportedly sampled flesh from the huge pachyderm: Frozen for eons, it has been fried and roasted and served up for modern man.

Russian scientists are rumored to get together occasionally for "mammoth banquets." And a group of Soviet construction workers got into hot water with paleontologists when they fed mammoth meat to their dogs.

Geologist Robert M. Thorson of the University of Alaska in Fairbanks hasn't tasted mammoth meat yet, although he is currently excavating one of the partially preserved beasts. However, he has snacked on a sample of thirty-thousand-year-old frozen bison. "The piece I ate tasted pretty bad," he notes. His colleagues, who have sampled mammoth meat, say that that wasn't very tasty either—although no one has been known to get sick from eating the ancient fare.

There may be more mammoth to eat in the future, and not just the frozen kind. At a recent symposium on mammoth tissue, held in Helsinki, some scientists suggested that the mammoth may still be alive in remote areas of Siberia. And Soviet zoologist Nikolai Vereshchagin has proposed cloning new mammoth herds from the frozen cells of a long-dead beast.

UFOs and Altered States of Consciousness

Lorraine Davis, a researcher at John F. Kennedy University in Orinda, California, conducted a study under the university's consciousness studies department which she says may show that UFOs have an explanation most people have overlooked. Instead of being spaceships from other galaxies, they could be psychic phenomena related to the bright lights some people see before they die.

Davis came up with the idea after attending a seminar on near-death experiences (NDEs) led by University of Connecticut psychologist Kenneth Ring. Davis noted striking similarities between the altered state of consciousness described by near-death survivors—including seeing an almost blinding light and glimpsing long-dead relatives—and the experiences reported by UFO contactees. Using an NDE questionaire developed by Ring, Davis contacted 261 people who said they had been in contact with UFOs.

When she analyzed the ninety-three replies she received, Davis found that a remarkable pattern stood out. Like people who had been revived from clinical death, those who had seen a UFO consistently said they, too, had undergone three profound changes: Their attitudes toward themselves and other people became less egocentric and their personal religious beliefs moved from atheism or sectarianism to a kind of universal spirituality. They also reported that their psychic abilities had notably increased.

Davis thinks that UFO sightings and NDEs are both examples of altered states of human consciousness. "The UFO participant was thrust into this psychic state by a precipitating event," she says, "just as the NDE subject was transformed by the nearness of death."

This does *not* mean, she emphasizes, that people who see UFOs are just imagining the experiences.

"If the UFO experience does take place in an altered state of consciousness, perhaps a nuts-and-bolts machine *is* materialized for a few minutes," she says. "Who knows? It's certainly possible to perceive and experience in other states of consciousness, sometimes with an even greater sense of reality than that which we experience on a day-to-day basis."

Cigar-Shaped UFO over New Mexico

About an hour before sunset on December 8, 1981, Dan Luscomb watched a huge cigar-shaped object sail across the sky near Reserve, New Mexico. Luscomb, who owns the Whispering Pines Resort seven miles south of Reserve, said the UFO was "as big as four 747s linked together." He also saw a jet pursue the strange object. "But every time the plane got close," Luscomb recalls, "the object slipped away."

The director of the Center for UFO Studies, J. Allen Hynek, learned about Luscomb's sighting from an article in the *El Paso Times*. A few months later, in April, he decided to visit Reserve to investigate the case personally.

Hynek found nine local people who insisted they, too, had seen the same cigar-shaped object at about the same time that Luscomb spotted it. Lance Swapp, an employee at Jake's Grocery Store in nearby Luna, said he saw a bright light while driving home from work. "When I got home, my brother was hollering at me to look up in the sky," he recalled. "There was a large object over our heads, with a jet on its trail."

Housewife Alma Hobbs reported she saw a red ball rising from the ground as she headed toward Luscomb's resort. A few seconds later, it turned sideways and she noted it was tube-shaped.

Hynek stated that whatever these witnesses saw, it wasn't a missile, which would have made deafening noise—the UFO over New Mexico was silent. He also concluded it was probably not a military test vehicle because "no known technology can make a ninety-degree turn in seconds as this object allegedly did. The feat defies Newton's Second Law of Motion.''

Jules Verne's Amazing Prediction

When science fiction writers prophesy future developments, their predictions are often wrong, but occasionally they're incredibly right.

Writing in the 1860s, the French science fiction writer Jules Verne described a moon-bound trajectory leaving a base on the coast of Florida. He named the ship the *Nautilus*. Its travel time to the moon was 73 hours 13 minutes. By an almost unbelievable coincidence, the real moon shot—the Apollo 11—took 73 hours 10 minutes to reach the location in space from which it was to orbit the moon.

In another time jump, Jules Verne predicted the dimensions of an atomic submarine, which he also called the *Nautilus*, 150 years before the atomic submarine was built. The first United States atomic submarine, gracefully christened the *Nautilus* by the United States Navy, was the first submarine to pass through the icy waters under the North Pole, and it gave its name to a whole class of atomic submarines.

The Nostradamus Program

For five centuries, interpreters have labored to decipher the coded prophecies of the astrologer and mystic Nostradamus. Although he was a Christian who claimed to be inspired by God, Nostradamus feared the wrath of the Catholic Inquisition, so he disguised his predictions with all sorts of mysterious literary stratagems, including word-play techniques such as anagrams and aphaeresis (dropping the initial letter or syllable from a word).

About four hundred interpretations of his predictions have been attempted, but none completely broke Nostradamus's complex code until a computer was put to the task. Jean Charles de Fontbrune, a pharmaceuticals manager whose hobby is studying the seer's writings, fed the data he had come up with over the years into a computer network. That allowed him to measure the repetition of letters, words, phrases, and the other linguistic devices Nostradamus employed. Soon it became apparent to de Fontbrune that the mystic had thought in Latin structures and had transposed those structures directly into French—a clue that enabled de Fontbrune to decode six hundred of Nostradamus's eleven hundred verses.

Although he published a book containing his findings in 1980, it didn't create much of a stir. Then someone noticed that de Fontbrune had pointed out that "the year the Rose flourished" would coincide with an uprising of Moslems against the West.

Since the rose was the symbol of the Socialists who took power in France the same year the U.S. embassy in Tehran was seized, people were suddenly interested in what else de Fontbrune's book predicted. Readers discovered that Nostradamus had used his amazing powers to prophesy the death of Henry II in a tournament, the rise of Napoleon Bonaparte, and even the ouster of Iran's shah by "religious zealots."

According to de Fontbrune's interpretation of Nostradamus's verses, Islam will destroy the Roman Catholic Church before the end of the century, when the Arab nations team with the Soviet Union and invade Western Europe. Paris will then swim in blood and the world will be locked in a terrible war. These predictions have created such a stir that some French citizens have reportedly already fled the country.

Future Forms

Physicist Freeman Dyson of the Institute for Advanced Study in Princeton, New Jersey, says that molecular biologists have already begun developing the technology needed to redesign Earth life. One day, he claims, humans will be genetically engineered so that they will be able to thrive in space or alien environments without the need for space suits or artificial life-support systems.

What will these humans of the not-so-distant-future look like? Dyson says they may be noseless ("There's nothing up there in space to smell anyway") and have airtight, crocodile-like skin to protect their greatly reduced internal body pressure from boiling because of a lack of atmospheric pressure. He adds that the new, scientifically altered race of humans could be covered with insulating fur or feathers that would come in handy in the frigid cold of space. The tendency of bones to dissolve during long space flights in zero gravity could also be overcome, he says, by re-adjusting the body's chemical balance.

Ancient Japanese Space Suits

Between 7000 B.C. and 520 B.C., Japanese artisans created small clay statues with pointed heads, slits for eyes, and torsos decorated with intricate patterns of stripes and dots. Known as *dogus*, the objects are usually regarded as representations of ancient Japanese fertility gods. But Vaughn Greene, author of *Astronauts of Ancient Japan*, thinks *dogus* depict just what they look like—humanoids in space suits. In fact, he says, they look surprisingly like they are wearing the extravehicular mobility unit (EMU) suit designed by NASA for space shuttle astronauts to wear outside their ship.

Greene suspects that the top and the bottom of the *dogu* space suit were put on separately, just like the EMU. He also points out that the EMU chest-pack control units are in approximately the same place as the circular knobs found on a *dogu* chest. The stripes around the *dogu* knobs, he theorizes, are not decorations—instead, they are marks used to calibrate the quantity of water or oxygen being released to the creature inside the space suit.

Mystery Cats and Dogs

For the past decade, author Michael Goss has investigated reports of mysterious, flesh-eating creatures in Great Britain that are variously described as either huge cats or dogs.

Goss has documented seventy such sightings throughout the British Isles. Sometimes the animal is described as a tawny, ten-foot-long cat; many of those who have seen carcasses devoured by the creature even say that its eating habits are decidedly feline. However, other eyewitnesses, including a local bus driver and Royal Marine commandos sent to shoot a beast that killed almost one hundred sheep in Stokenchurch, say it resembles a large dog.

One of the mystery beasts was spotted in the summer of 1982, Goss says, east of London in the Fobbing Marshes. A water company foreman working at an isolated storage area one afternoon was startled by the animal. A few days later, a passerby saw what was probably the same creature jump from behind a hedgerow. Neither of the eyewitnesses was sure if he had seen a cat or a dog. On the other hand, in late 1983, three people, one with binoculars, glimpsed an animal just a mile from Fobbing Marshes that they insisted was a large panther.

Some people in Britain, Goss relates, think these reports point to "alien" cats and dogs stalking the country. "If this is a new folklore, we ought to know it," he concludes. "If it is a zoological or paranormal fact, then it is even more essential that we learn what we can."

The Search for Mallory's Camera

On June 8, 1924, while attempting to climb precipitous Mount Everest, George Mallory and Andrew Irvine disappeared without a trace. No one knows how close the two came to being the first conquerors of the highest mountain in the world, but there may be a way to find out. Massachusetts computer engineer Tom Holzel has launched a search for the Kodak Vest Pocket cameras the mountain climbers carried with them.

Holzel learned about the cameras from a small article in the *New Yorker* magazine. He realized if they could be found, they would probably contain undeveloped film that would show how high the explorers got. But finding cameras on the huge mountain, he admits, "is like looking for a needle in a haystack."

However, Holzel thinks it's possible. To help with the search, he had White's Electronics of New England build special, rugged-duty metal detectors specifically designed to tune in to the steel-and-brass bodies of the cameras.

Holzel went looking for Mallory's and Irvine's cameras for three months in 1986. He didn't find what he was looking for, although he did come up with oxygen bottles at what may have been the explorers' campsite.

Why is Holzel, despite enormous odds against his success, determined to continue looking for the cameras and the historic film they contain? He answers in much the same way Sir Edmund Hillary did when questioned about why he was climbing Mount Everest: "Because Mallory's there."

Bigfoot Hunter

Mark Keller resigned from his job at the post office and announced that he was leaving on a five-month hunting trip. He was going after big game, he said—specifically Bigfoot, the legendary ape creature said to roam the deep forests of the Pacific Northwest.

But when word got out that Keller was planning on bagging a Bigfoot, he received more than one hundred threatening phone calls. Some callers said they would find a way to interfere with Keller's plans. Others threatened the hunter's life.

"Some bow hunters up in Washington called and said if I go out and try to kill Bigfoot they will get me," Keller reported.

Arcata, California, police sergeant Jim Dawson notes that Keller also received several threatening letters. However, the police were unable to find out who was responsible.

But all the people who were so concerned that a Bigfoot's death was imminent were soon relieved to hear that Keller's hunting trip had been delayed—indefinitely. He was spotted, not in the wilds of the Pacific Northwest, but in downtown Eureka, California, where county deputy Rich Walton arrested him.

"He had a rifle with a night-vision scope on it," the officer explains. "So I took him in."

Tomb of Ice

Wesley Bateman of Poway, California, was watching a videotape about UFOs one night when he made a curious discovery. He noticed that an ice-covered object allegedly photographed by Apollo 11 astronauts had the rough outline of a TBM Avenger. "The heaviest part of the plane—the nose—is pointed toward the earth," he explains, "and you can easily recognize the bubble turret and the tail."

But what is a 1945 propeller-driven airplane doing in orbit around the earth? Batemen thinks he has the answer. The plane was one of five TBM Avenger torpedo bombers that left the naval air station in Fort Lauderdale, Florida, on December 5, 1945, never to return.

Less than three hours into that routine mission, the planes and their crew of fourteen vanished. A Martin Flying Boat with thirteen men on board sent out to rescue the crew also disappeared. There has been speculation over the past thirty years that aliens were involved in the mysterious incident—especially since some claimed they heard the flight instructor cry, "Don't come after me; they look like they're from outer space," before his voice faded from his radio.

Bateman says the Avenger orbiting the earth could offer solid proof that extraterrestrials were behind the disappearance of the planes. He thinks that when the Avengers dropped depth charges on their training mission, they may have damaged an alien craft under the sea. "When the UFO rose out of the water to avoid further damage," he says, "its rapid departure created a propulsion vortex, sucking up a lot of seawater and the planes along with it."

He adds that anyone who doubts that a 1945 Avenger is circling the earth several thousand miles up should take a look at the photo of the ice-entombed plane. "I can't imagine anyone looking at this and saying it's *not* an Avenger. This is conclusive proof that UFOs exist."

Dreams of the Dead

Some dreams hold clues about life after death. That, at least, is the conclusion reached by Swiss psychologists Marie-Louise von Franz and Emmanuel Xipolitas Kennedy after studying twenty-five hundred dreams.

The researchers say that many dreams about the afterlife simply reveal a psychological dimension of the dreamer. But other dreams have an almost photographic, supernatural quality that sets them apart and convinces the dreamer there is life after death. "These dreams do appear to be encounters with postmortal souls," Kennedy explains. "After having these dreams, people feel it is the dead they have seen."

When the terminally ill are near death, their dreams frequently take on a similar quality, he adds. The dying may appear rejuvenated in their dreams, Kennedy says, or they may encounter someone who has already passed to the "other side."

"Dreams of the dying seem to confirm for the unconscious that impending death is not an end," Kennedy declares. "The ultimate goal appears to be the union of the individual self with the archetypal self we think of as the godhead. These dreams point to the notion that whatever is unresolved in this life must somehow go on, to be continued after death."

Vision of Murder

When Etta Louise Smith, a Lockheed shipping clerk and mother of three youngsters, heard a radio newscast about a missing nurse one afternoon in 1980, she had a strange feeling that the young woman was already dead. The news stated that the police were conducting a house-to-house search for the woman, but Smith kept thinking, "She's not in a house." Then she had a vision "as if there was a photograph in front of me," she recalls. "The woman was dead."

Smith decided to share her psychic insight with the Los Angeles police. After talking to investigators, she visited the remote canyon site she'd "seen" mentally, hours before. Soon she'd discovered the battered and raped body of thirty-one-year-old Melanie Uribe.

Smith was promptly booked on suspicion of murder and spent four days in jail before a local resident confessed that he and two accomplices had committed the crime. The men were later convicted.

Smith filed suit against the city of Los Angeles for false arrest, and Superior Court Judge Joel Rudolf ruled that the police had lacked probable cause and sufficient evidence to arrest Smith for the killing. The jury awarded her $26,184—according to the foreman, the majority of the jurors believed that Smith did have a psychic experience that led her to the murder victim's body.

Smith, however, isn't so sure she should have acted on her extrasensory vision. "Maybe in the future," she says, "I'll call in anonymously."

The Mystery Plane of the Bermuda Triangle

Finally, there appeared to be a break in the mysterious case of the five navy TBM-3 Aztec Avenger planes and the Martin Flying Boat that all disappeared without a trace after leaving Fort Lauderdale on December 5, 1945, and heading into the so-called Bermuda Triangle. Treasure hunter Mel Fisher's crew discovered what seemed to be one of the missing planes partially covered by mud. It was sitting on the ocean bottom about twenty miles west of Key West.

Although UFO enthusiasts have long suspected that aliens captured the missing planes, the wreckage of the Grumman Avenger found by Fisher's men showed no sign of extraterrestrial contact. It simply looked, said K. T. Budde, a member of the salvage crew, "like it had gotten lost and run out of fuel."

So has the mystery of the vanished planes been solved? Far from it. According to David Paul Horan, Fisher's attorney, navy records have revealed that the recently discovered Avenger was *not* one of the famous five planes. "Instead, it was lost from Key West nearly three months prior to those planes' disappearing," he notes. "One survivor who bailed out has been able to identify this plane absolutely."

Horan, who is also a pilot, says he's disappointed that the mystery of the missing Avengers hasn't been solved by Fisher's crew as they comb the ocean bottom seeking buried treasure. "In fact," Horan points out, "nothing that has been found down there looks like it might be related to that whole incident."

Blue People

Curiously colored creatures—like little green men from Mars—are a staple of science fiction stories. But scientists have documented real blue humans living right here on Earth.

When mountaineer-physiologist John West of the University of California at San Diego's School of Medicine visited an area in the Andes near Aucanquilcha, Chile, he made a startling discovery. Researchers had long believed that humans could not live at altitudes higher than 17,500 feet, but West came face-to-face with a handful of men living at nearly 20,000 feet—and they were blue.

Although scientists have long known that certain diseases can give the skin a bluish cast and that genetic abnormalities have caused some people in the Ozark Mountains to be pastel colored, West found that the Andes men were blue for another reason— their coloration seems to have resulted from an adaptation to the air at the extremely high altitude, which has less than half the oxygen found at sea level.

West explains that the miners appear to produce large amounts of hemoglobin, the oxygen-carrying pigment in blood cells. "The hemoglobin is poorly oxygenated," he says, "and it shows through their skin, giving it a bluish color. I suspect these men increase the depth and rate of their breathing and because they were born and bred at five thousand to twelve thousand feet, that may have given them a head start in adapting. But there's a lot we don't yet understand."

University of Pennsylvania physiologist Sukhamay Lahiri has also seen the blue men of the Andes firsthand. He points out that Tibetan priests who spend time at similar altitudes in the Himalayas also have a bluish tint. "But what's startling about the Andes men," he says, "is that they are living and doing heavy labor at these altitudes."

The Cursed Highway

A lot of people might have second thoughts about traveling down New Jersey's new Route 55, a 4.2-mile project in south Jersey's Deptford Township. Part of the road slices through the archaeological remains of an ancient Indian village, including graves of paleo-Indians who inhabited the area eight thousand years ago. Nanticoke Indian Carl Peirce (also known as Wayandaga), the local medicine man, publicly warned that the desecration of his ancestors' resting places would result in disastrous consequences.

"I told them if they proceeded with that road, my ancestors would take revenge," Peirce says. "I warned them that reciprocation from the spirit world could be expected."

Soon after a press conference at which Wayandaga aired his predictions, mishaps and deaths began to plague Route 55. A worker was killed by an asphalt roller and another collapsed on the job from a brain aneurysm. One worker found his feet turning black from a circulatory disorder while another was injured when he fell from a highway bridge. Still another highway laborer suffered three heart attacks. Then a van carrying five crewmen exploded in flames.

"It got to the point that 'What's going to happen next?' was something commonly asked on the job," notes site inspector Karl Kruger.

Wayandaga insists the cursed road will never be safe for travelers: "Until they relocate Highway 55, there will continue to be deaths."

Glimpses of the Future from the Near-Dead

According to psychologist Kenneth Ring of the University of Connecticut, those who have returned from clinical death frequently report they saw more than their past flash before their eyes—they saw the future as well.

Ring, who has studied the experiences of more than a dozen of these people around the country, points out that one man apparently saw himself as a married adult while near death at the age of ten. The vision, which took place during an appendectomy in 1941, included the subject and his two children. He "saw" himself sitting in an armchair and he noticed something "very strange" behind the wall.

In 1968, the man suddenly realized his near-death vision had come true. "When I sat in a chair, reading a book and happened to glance at my children, I realized that *this* was the memory from 1941," he explains. "And the strange object behind the wall was a forced-air heater, something not in my sphere of knowledge as a child."

Other research subjects told Ring similar tales. But there were also numerous reports that, while clinically dead, they had witnessed the fate of Earth. Almost all of these people, Ring says, have foreseen a disastrous era that they insist will start in less than ten years. Earthquakes, volcanoes, famine, nuclear war, and droughts are among the catastrophes predicted. But the near-death survivors also say that peace will eventually prevail. Following a period of disasters, "decades of worldwide brotherhood" will follow.

Ring doesn't think anyone should panic about the predicted worldwide turmoil. "I'm inclined to think the prophecies are metaphors for the fears and hopes of the subconscious," he says.

UFO Movies

A little after 9:00 A.M. on January 11, 1973, near the village of Cuddington, England, building surveyor Peter Day spotted a glowing orange ball in the sky. He reached for the Super-8 movie camera he had in his car and filmed the object as it moved over treetops about a quarter of a mile away.

When the British UFO Research Association (BUFORA) was given the movie to analyze, it announced that the image Day had captured was both "genuine and puzzling." Another examination by UFO-photography specialist Peter Warrington, working with the Kodak-UK laboratories at Hemel Hempstead, concluded, "There has been no trickery." The film was further authenticated by Kodak-UK's technical-information consultant Peter Sutherst, who declared, "Whatever the film shows, it is a real object in the sky."

However, another research team headed by UFO expert Ken Phillips studied the film and concluded that the object in Day's movie was a United States Air Force F-11 jet that had developed a malfunction after taking off from Heyford Air Force Base and then caught fire. The time and date of the crash? It was at 9:46 A.M. on January 11, 1973.

But not everyone agrees. Photography specialist Warrington emphasizes that his team of investigators studied the film under considerable magnification, "and at no point was an aircraft detected."

Day says flatly that he doesn't believe he filmed an aircraft. "A dozen other people, including a schoolteacher and several schoolchildren, also saw the UFO. They were closer to the object than I was, and their descriptions tally with what is on the film."

Brazilian UFO

Most people were napping on the overnight flight between Fortaleza and São Paulo, Brazil, in February 1982, when pilot Gerson Maciel De Britto made an unexpected announcement: "I see a strange object forty or fifty miles to the left and I need eyewitnesses."

The passengers stirred and discovered that they were bathed in a brilliant light. Looking out the plane's windows for the next hour and twenty-two minutes, they observed the sky turn red, orange, white, and blue.

From his vantage point in the cockpit, De Britto made out a "fast-moving, saucer-shaped disk with five spotlights." When the object failed to establish contact after De Britto sent it radio messages in Portuguese and English, he tried communicating through concentration—attempting to send or receive information telepathically.

As the airliner approached within eight miles of Rio de Janeiro for a scheduled stopover, the pilot noted that the UFO was only eight miles from the plane and moving closer. Although radar failed to pick up the object, the Rio tower asked three commercial pilots flying in the area whether they saw the strange light and were told they did. Brazilian military planes were soon soaring after the craft; the official report of the outcome of that chase remains classified.

After major Brazilian newspapers and magazines carried the story, UFO skeptics began pointing out that Venus had risen in the eastern sky at 3:10 A.M. on the morning in question. Could pilot De Britto and his plane's passengers have been fooled into thinking they saw a UFO by the intense and colorful glow of that planet?

De Britto says that's impossible. He insists he saw Venus *and* the strange object. In addition, he says that the light maintained the same orientation to the plane even after he changed course by fifty-one degrees—which suggests an intelligent force was manning the craft. "If what the pilot says is true, then it could not have been Venus," noted J. Allen Hynek, director of the Center for UFO

Studies in Evanston, Illinois. "If it wasn't Venus, then it was a UFO."

Reactions of the Newly Dead

Bodies can and do move after death, as anyone who has seen a chicken's head chopped off can verify.

Reactions of severed human heads and the bodies from which they came were noted from the Reign of Terror during the French Revolution of 1792 when the guillotine was first used. Great numbers of unfortunate people, first the aristocrats and then other dissenters, were decapitated, one after the other. In full view of interested spectators, some macabre results were noted.

Sometimes a victim's mouth would open and close, as if wishing to speak; sometimes eyes would continue to move in their sockets or would alternately open and close. Bodies would also continue to twitch and move, although without heads they were obviously dead.

Equally frightening was the case of the criminal George Foster, executed by hanging in London in 1803. After Foster's execution, a Professor Aldini applied the galvanic process to the corpse in the presence of medical observers to see what would happen. The results were startling and indicated that some motor nerves were still capable of operation. The legs moved, the right hand was lifted and made into a fist, and one eye slowly opened.

In any case, Foster achieved a partial revenge on society. A surgeon named Pass, who had witnessed the postmortem, died on his way back from the experiment. His death was ascribed to heart failure caused by fright.

The Village That Vanished

It isn't unusual to hear about a missing person, but in 1930 a whole village vanished—and it's still missing.

The village was located near Lake Angikuni, about five hundred miles northwest of the Royal Canadian Mounted Police base at Churchill, Canada. Although it was an isolated spot, the Eskimos who lived there were frequently visited by trappers who swapped furs and joined them for meals of caribou. French-Canadian trapper Joe LaBelle, who had traveled through that part of the Canadian wilderness for about forty years, considered the folks who lived on Lake Angikuni old friends.

But in November 1930, when Joe decided to stop by the village for a visit, he immediately knew something was wrong. First of all, the dogs didn't bark. He shouted a greeting but no one answered. Finally, he opened the doors to several of the low sod huts and yelled for his friends. No one replied.

An hour-long search of the village showed that every inhabitant had disappeared. There were no signs of a struggle—pots of food sat over fires that had been cold for weeks. A needle was still in some clothing that a woman had been mending. Kayaks had been left unattended for so long that waves had battered them. Rifles stood gathering dust. The Eskimos' dogs were found dead from starvation, tied to stumps.

The mystery deepened when LaBelle searched his friends' cemetery where bodies were customarily covered with rocks. One grave had been opened and the body exhumed. Stealing a body, LaBelle knew, was taboo for an Eskimo. Whoever had done the deed had stacked the grave stones in two piles—ruling out any possibility that an animal had uncovered the body.

The Royal Canadian Mounted Police investigated LaBelle's report of the village that disappeared. Despite their reputation of "always getting their man," the Mounties were baffled as to how and why thirty Eskimos, in the middle of winter, had disappeared. Months of detective work, including interviews with other tribes in the area, never turned up a clue to explain the village that vanished.

Desert Ship

The *Arakwe* was a wooden ship with huge paddle wheels, like those of the famed Mississippi riverboats, built in the latter days of the War Between the States. Armed with a few small cannons, it was listed as a gunboat in the United States Navy and sent to the Horn of Aconcagua in Chile under orders to show United States support for the Chilean government by displaying the American flag and showing off its guns.

The *Arakwe*'s captain and crew had little reason to believe they would actually see any action, much less that it would occur on dry land. But because of a freak accident of nature, that's just what happened.

Captain Alexander was in his cabin, when, according to his log, he "noticed that the cabin lamp was swinging fore and aft. I hurried on deck and quickly recognized the nature of the disturbance as a submarine earthquake, since the water was rapidly draining seaward from the bay."

Soon the *Arakwe* was caught up for a wild ride on a powerful tidal wave, which carried the wooden ship, and dozens of other boats, far inland. Finally, Captain Alexander and his men found themselves two miles from the sea at the bottom of a cliff. Although the flat-bottomed *Arakwe* was broken up, she was still in good condition compared to the wreckage of other ships scattered all around.

The remains of the destroyed ships' cargoes were strewn for miles, drawing crowds of looters. Some tried to board the *Arakwe*. Captain Alexander and his crew drew their pistols and ordered the looters to back away. But they simply moved just out of pistol range.

The captain knew he needed more forceful weapons—but the crew couldn't reach the shot to load the cannons. The ammunition had been buried somewhere under the boat's damaged deck. There was only one chance, Alexander reasoned, one possible substitution. Quickly, the crew gathered hard, round cheeses from the galley and loaded them, along with the gunpowder, into the cannons.

Holding his fire until the looters moved within a couple of hundred yards of the battleship, the captain finally signaled for the cannons to be fired. The weapons roared as the cheese knocked over enough of the mob to frighten the rest of the looters away.

The *Arakwe* was never seaworthy again, and she is recorded in the navy's official records as lost in action. But she went out with a unique distinction: the only battleship in all the annals of U.S. military history to fight a battle on dry land—with cheese—and win.

The Tennessee Viking Saga

Around 1874, near some Indian graves and earthworks at Castalian Springs in Sumner County, Tennessee, a nineteen-by-fifteen-inch slab of ancient limestone was uncovered. Engraved on its surface was a vivid depiction of a fierce battle—between Native Americans and Vikings.

There are two distinct groups of people portrayed in the scene. Those with almond-shaped eyes appear to have come from over some hills that are represented by four vertical scallops; they have painted faces and wear animal skins, ankle and wrist bands, and elaborate headdresses.

As for the second group, the eyes are outlined with rays. Researchers Ruth Verrill and Clyde Keeler of the Georgia Academy of Sciences concluded that the rays could represent eyelashes, which would have been more obvious on fair persons like the Norse. The leader of the second group holds a square shield. It looks unlike anything used by American Indians—but it's similar to shields used by the ancient Normans. On the ground is a spear shaped like the Viking weapons documented by Johannes Bronsfed in *The Vikings*. The ray-eyed men wear shoes and one wears a Phrygian or Roman-type helmet with a large crescent-shaped crest.

No one may ever know just what the battle was about, but it was clearly bloody. One ray-eyed person is shown decapitated. There are also hints that women may have played a role in the dispute:

An almond-eyed female, wearing a skirt and shoes, holds onto something—perhaps a wampum belt, as an offering of peace. She is being attacked by a male Indian. Another woman, this one a ray-eyed person, kneels inside a structure that Verrill and Keeler have identified as an Indian medicine lodge. She stares upward, as if appealing to her god and smokes a ritual pipe.

The part of the picture that most convincingly identifies the second group as Vikings is the image of a distinctive Viking boat. Verrill and Keeler noted that the boat has the same single mast and yardarm to carry the sail that Vikings used; other features of the boat match those used by North European traders and explorers up to around A.D. 1200. The ship's commander stands at the prow, wearing the famed Viking horns designating his leadership. Five oarsmen are depicted at the rowing level and the paddle ends of their oars are rounded—a feature identical to the Iron Age rock carvings of a Viking boat discovered in Sweden. At the middle of the boat is a landing hook, and, toward the stern, a mooring line extends out into the water. The slab also clearly outlines a type of anchor known to be used in certain instances by Vikings.

If Vikings landed and fought Indians in Tennessee, how did they get there? Verrill and Keeler concluded that a Viking ship could have entered the Gulf of Mexico and sailed up the Mississippi, Ohio, and Cumberland rivers to Rock Creek and then to Castalian Springs—which would have brought them right to where the ancient stone engraving was found.

The Return of John Paul Jones

In 1773, a young Scotsman named John Paul was captain of a British merchant ship. Fighting a mutinous crew, John Paul shot and killed a man, and when the boat reached the port of Tobago, the British authorities arrested him. Knowing he faced almost certain death, he picked the lock on his prison door and fled to the American colonies.

There he met a family who befriended him and he soon changed his name to theirs—becoming John Paul Jones. It was a name that would one day be so beloved by his new countrymen that in the twentieth century the U.S. government would launch a strange mining expedition to recover his body.

Under the leadership of Admiral John Paul Jones, the struggling American fleet outfought the British ships time and again. After the Revolutionary War, he signed on as a mercenary for the Russian navy under Catherine the Great, helping to defeat the Turks.

The proud soldier could not win his battle with failing health, however, and, at the age of forty-five, he died alone in Paris. The U.S. government ordered that his body be embalmed and shipped back to America.

But, perhaps because of bureaucratic bungling, no one ever called for the body and the great Revolutionary War hero was buried in Paris. John Paul Jones was not destined for obscurity, though. One hundred thirteen years later, the American government decided to retrieve his body. There was just one problem: no one was sure where it was.

The cemetery where Jones was buried had been abandoned decades earlier and was covered with factories, businesses, and hospitals. Finally, a researcher discovered old archives that showed where the body should be.

But how could it be reached?

The only solution was to use miners. A shaft was dug near a large building a couple of hundred feet from where John Paul Jones's body was believed to be. Then the miners tunneled around and under buildings until they found the lead casket, emblazoned with the initials J.P.J.

When the coffin lid was cut away, witnesses noted that the body was so well preserved that it still looked remarkably like portraits of the war hero.

The admiral was soon back in the United States, bestowed with honors and laid to rest among the other heroes at Annapolis. Appropriately enough, John Paul Jones was escorted to his final resting place by part of the American battle fleet that he had helped establish more than a century before.

The Psychic Horse

Soon after a Richmond, Virginia, woman named Mrs. Lord purchased a two-week-old colt in 1925, the animal began to behave in odd ways. She came trotting toward her owners before they called her—as soon as they *thought* about calling her. Several years later the horse, named Lady Wonder, could count and spell short words by maneuvering toy blocks around with her nose.

Lady Wonder used her unusual talents to predict the future with startling accuracy. For example, according to the *Chicago Tribune*, the horse predicted that Franklin D. Roosevelt would be the next president of the United States before he had even been nominated. And in fourteen out of seventeen years, the mare correctly predicted the winner of the World Series. In at least two tragic cases involving the deaths of children, Lady Wonder was also able to supply facts that even the police had been unable to uncover.

In the early 1950s, Lady Wonder was asked by authorities in Norfolk County, Massachusetts, if she could help them find four-year-old Danny Matson, who had been missing for months. The horse "told" police to go to a water-filled stone quarry. The site had already been searched without yielding any evidence connected to the case. But the police decided to give it one more try—and they found the body of little Danny.

In October 1955, another boy, three-year-old Ronnie Weitcamp, disappeared after he left three playmates in his front yard and scooted around his family's central Indiana house. Sheriff's deputies and the Indiana state police, accompanied by an estimated fifteen hundred employees of the local navy depot, combed thousands of wooded acres near Ronnie's home looking for the toddler. But there was not a trace of the little boy.

Had Ronnie been kidnapped or murdered? Was he lost? Leads and fruitless clues poured in to the police department, but no solid evidence developed. Ronnie Weitcamp had disappeared. By October 22, the official search was called off.

Remembering the strange tale of Lady Wonder, journalist Frank Edwards, then news director of television station WTTV at Bloom-

ington, contacted a friend who lived within driving distance of
Mrs. Lord and asked him to see if her talking mare could offer any
help in finding Danny.

Although already thirty years of age, extremely old for a horse,
Lady Wonder was still able to "talk," and Edwards's friend asked
several questions.

In answer to "Do you know why we are here?" the horse immediately spelled out "boy," by flipping out large tin letters that
hung from a bar across her stall. When asked the youngster's
name, the mare turned up the letters R-O-N-E, as if trying to spell
Ronnie.

According to Lady Wonder, the boy was dead. He had not been
kidnapped and he would be found in a hole more than a quarter
mile but less than a mile, from his home.

"What is near him?" the horse was asked. "E-L-M," Lady Wonder spelled out. She also indicated the soil around the boy was
sandy, and that he would be found in "D-E-C."

Edwards broadcast the information provided by the "talking"
telepathic horse on October 24, 1955. Predictably, the story received widespread ridicule and criticism. Then two teenagers
found Ronnie's body.

The child was found near an elm tree in a sandy gully, about a
mile from where he was last seen alive. And he was found in
December, just as the remarkable Lady Wonder had predicted
nearly two months earlier.

The Peculiar Death of Meriwether Lewis

Although almost everyone has heard of the famed Lewis
and Clark Expedition, few people know the strange fate that
awaited Meriwether Lewis. The national hero was doomed to die
under such peculiar circumstances that it's unlikely that even
Sherlock Holmes could have figured out exactly what happened.

Just before he was killed in October 1809, Lewis was traveling to
Washington, D.C., with United States Army Major John Neely to

answer accusations that, as governor of the Louisiana Territory, he had mishandled financial affairs—charges that were eventually dismissed. As they made their way along the foothills of eastern Tennessee, several pack mules carrying Lewis's record books bolted during a thunderstorm. Major Neely took off to bring the animals back.

Governor Lewis kept on riding alone. He was a broken man—thin from malaria, worried about the political charges facing him, and lovesick over the rejection he'd suffered at the hands of Vice President Aaron Burr's daughter. When he finally reached the cabin of Mr. and Mrs. John Griner, he quickly asked if he could stay the night and rest.

The tall stranger didn't identify himself. He simply ate his dinner in silence and retired for the evening. Later, the Griners heard someone talking in his room, although they couldn't tell if their guest was muttering to himself or actually carrying on a conversation with someone else. And if he *was* talking to someone else, why hadn't the dogs barked when another stranger entered the house?

Just before dawn, the Griners were awakened by a gunshot. The couple quickly looked around and found that everything seemed to be in place. Then they heard moans coming from the stranger's room.

Entering the bedroom, the Griners saw that the gaunt man was dying. Blood poured from a wound in his left side as he tried to speak. "I am no coward," he said. "But it is hard to die . . . so young . . . so hard to die." Moments later, it was all over.

When the Griners searched through his leather knapsacks for identification, they found a ledger identifying the deceased man as "Meriwether Lewis, Albemarle, Virginia. Capt., U.S. Army."

Had the famous explorer taken his own life? The Griners were both by Lewis's side within seconds of hearing a gunshot. But they insisted there had been no powder smoke in the room—despite the fact that the gunpowder used in those days always left a strong-smelling white fog. Lewis's rifle was found still standing in the corner of the guest room. It had not been fired. No other pistol or gun of any kind was uncovered in the room.

The governor's traveling companion, Major Neely, did not arrive at the Griners' cabin until midmorning the day after Lewis's demise. Why did it take him so long to round up a few mules, and where did he spend the night?

If Meriwether Lewis did not kill himself, is it possible his political enemies arranged his death—and made sure they would have access to his personal records in case they contained evidence that would incriminate them?

No one has ever been able to answer those questions. The peculiar death of Meriwether Lewis remains unsolved.

The Day the Devil Came to Town

When George Fairly, a baker in Topsham, England, went to work early on the morning of February 8, 1855, he noticed curious tracks leading up to the door of his shop. Since a snow blanketed the ground, Fairly could clearly make out the odd nature of the footprints: Somehow, whatever made the curved marks had walked near the base of a wall, jumped on top of it and walked for a while, and then returned to the ground again before heading toward the bay.

This incident would not be particularly interesting except for one thing. George Fairly was only one of *thousands* of residents from around Devonshire, England, who awoke that snowy winter morn to find evidence that a strange visitor had scampered, walked, or slithered over their roofs, fields, and fences—leaving behind clear U-shaped footprints in an unbroken line.

Rumors soon spread that the U-shaped tracks, which sometimes appeared cloven, were devilish in nature, and near panic ensued as people armed themselves against the unknown creature.

In an article published in the February 16, 1855, *Times* of London, the prints were described as ". . . more like that of a biped than a quadruped. . . . The steps were generally eight inches in advance of each other. The impressions of feet closely resembled those of a donkey's shoe, and measured from an inch and a half to . . . two and a half inches."

Whatever made the tracks managed to cover hundreds of miles in a few hours—its trek must have started after the snow stopped falling at around 7:00 P.M. on the night of February 7 and ended before the prints were discovered the next morning. It was also able to cross two large bodies of water, including the Exe River at Exmouth.

No one ever caught a glimpse of the creature who became known as the "devil of Devonshire" and no other U-shaped marks were ever found in the area. But whatever the thing was, it may have also visited barren Kerguelen Island, near the Antarctic. According to the official records of explorer Captain James C. Ross, a landing party found similar, unexplained footprints in the area ". . . described by Dr. Robertson as being three inches in length and two and a half in breadth, having a small and deeper depression on each side and shaped like a horseshoe."

Could whatever made the bizarre footprints have come out of the sea? Two strange finds off the coast of England point to that possibility. In November 1953 a badly decomposed creature, about two and a half feet long, with feet and legs arranged so that it could have walked like a human, washed ashore at Canfey Island. Then, in August 1954, the Reverend Joseph Overs came across another one of the creatures floating dead in a tidal pool. This one weighed about twenty-five pounds, was over four feet long, and had two short legs. The local police who examined the thing reported that it had large eyes, holes where a nose should be, a gaping mouth, and gills. Instead of scales like a fish, it was covered with thick pink skin.

But it is the shape of the creature's tiny feet, documented by the British bobbies, that reminded some people of an incident that happened nearly a century before—the thing had five little toes on each foot, arranged in a U-shape around a concave arch.

ITT versus Sharks

Some of the interference on overseas telephone calls may be caused by sharks biting the new cables that run at considerable depths across the Atlantic Ocean. Sharks have been indicated as the culprits because shark teeth have been found imbedded in the damaged lines. Since oceanic sharks had not presented a problem to undersea cables until now, the attacks on the new cables are surprising, considering that the new cables, which are under an inch in diameter, are somewhat less noticeable than the old ones, which are as thick as one's arm. The cost to repair each of the shark-damaged cables, which cross both the Atlantic and the Pacific oceans, is at least $250,000.

It has been suggested that the taut suspension of the new fiber-optic cables may cause vibrations that the sharks pick up as a food signal. Sharks react to signals produced by an electronic field and would try to snap at and eat anything that generated such signals (a valuable point to remember for swimmers with electronic equipment).

ITT officials are considering countering the shark attacks with cables wrapped in double layers of steel tape on which sharks would crack their teeth.

The Cannibal Tree

Roger Williams came to the American colonies in 1630. Because of his passionate belief in religious freedom, he was soon thrown out of Massachusetts. But he was destined to become the beloved, outspoken leader of the colony of Rhode Island. While history books recount Williams's life, they leave out one of the most fascinating aspects of his death—how some Rhode Islanders accidentally ate him.

It all started in 1683, when he died and was laid to rest, beside his wife, on their farm. A simple headstone marked the graves, and several years afterwards, local townsfolk decided to erect a memorial worthy of Williams's stature.

A commission was duly authorized to disinter the remains of Roger and his wife so they could be given a more proper burial beneath the new monument. But there was a problem: When the two graves were opened, every trace of Williams and his wife had disappeared.

Although it took a while to figure out who had robbed the graves, the thief was finally caught—it was an apple tree, well known for its particularly tasty fruit.

The tree's roots had grown through the coffins that contained the Williamses' remains and penetrated the areas where the couple's chest cavities once lay. Eventually it had completely absorbed both of the bodies. Curiously, the spreading and branching roots, which were preserved and moved to the Rhode Island Historical Society, had taken on a strong resemblance to the circulatory system of the human body.

It soon became obvious that all who had chomped down on the tree's delicious red apples had inadvertently eaten one of America's most famous colonial figures and his wife.

Eyewitnesses to Life after Death

Thanks to the miracles of modern medicine, more and more people are surviving heart attacks and accidents—and living to tell what it's like to die and visit "the other side."

A group of cardiologists from Denver, Colorado, studied twenty-three hundred heart patients who had been revived after facing clinical death. The doctors' 1980 report concluded that 60 percent of these people had remarkably similar stories to tell: They described visits to a place of beautiful light, where they were met by friends and family members who had died.

According to these researchers and others, the tales rarely vary in substance, although not all the details are the same. The clinically dead frequently find themselves at the site of their deaths—an accident scene or hospital room, for example. Aware they are dying, they feel themselves separate from their physical forms, and they begin to move through the power of thought alone. They may watch people work frantically over their unconscious bodies until, finally, they are pulled into a dark tunnel and toward a point of light.

When they reach the light, they find themselves in an exquisitely beautiful outdoor scene and are overwhelmed by feelings of peace. Family and friends who have died before them usually stand behind a barrier like a body of water, either beckoning the clinically dead to come to them or telling them to return.

Finally, the newly "dead" are once again plunged into inky darkness before they are faced with what near-death-experience researcher James Graves calls "a dazzling pillar of light that overwhelms them with joy. They say the being of light does not identify itself, but you see your whole life in front of you and it asks: 'What have you done with the life I've given you?'"

According to Graves, who started collecting reports of these experiences when he was a psychology instructor at Muskegon Community College in Michigan in the 1960s, many people don't want to return to life. They say the light gives them the greatest happiness they've ever known. "It is the last stage," Graves comments. "Any farther, they don't come back."

Not all near-death experiences are so pleasant, however. Researchers have found that some people go through the tunnel of darkness only to find themselves imprisoned in a gray atmosphere full of anger and depression. They go in circles with other people trapped in despair.

The experiences of the clinically dead who have returned to life have been dismissed by some as simply the result of drugs or lack of oxygen to the brain. That doesn't explain, however, numerous examples of near-death experiences that seem to prove the "dead" person was indeed hovering above his lifeless body.

For example, a patient's heart stopped beating during surgery at a Muskegon, Michigan, hospital. When he was revived, the man was able to give the name of the pharmacist who had supplied a frantic nurse with the medicine needed to save his life. While his eyes were closed and he was in cardiac arrest in an operating room, the patient insisted he had been in the corridor with the nurse as she raced into the hospital pharmacy. "I'd always trusted you," the man later told the nurse, "so when I saw you leave the room I followed you."

Monster Turtles

When most people think of sea monsters, they usually envision something akin to a dinosaur or serpent. But there's another type of sea monster that's been sighted repeatedly in the oceans of the world—gigantic turtles.

As he traveled near the southeast tip of Spain in 1484, Christopher Columbus spotted one of the huge creatures. It was, he reported, "a repulsive sea monster big as a medium-sized whale, with a carapace like a turtle's, a horrible head like a barrel, and two wings."

Nearly five hundred years later, in October 1937, a Cuban fisherman caught a monster-sized turtle. Over thirteen feet long and weighing several hundred pounds, the reptile was estimated by zoologists to be at least five hundred years old.

In March 1955, a man stranded on a raft off the Columbian shore without anything to eat or drink for ten days spotted a similar creature that measured about four meters from head to tail. According to a newspaper account written by Nobel prize–winner Gabriel García Márquez, the man "saw a giant yellow turtle with a tigered head and fixed dumb eyes that resembled two giant balls of glass."

A Miami fisherman named Bruce Mournier claims that while swimming underwater off the Bahamas, he met a giant turtle face-to-face. Mournier says the beast weighed about two hundred pounds and "had a monkey's face with its head protruding out in front. And it rotated its neck like a snake."

If monster-sized turtles are real, where do they originate? The creatures have already been sighted in the Caribbean, near Canada, and off the European coast. All three areas have one thing in common: They lie in the route of the Gulf Stream. The Gulf Stream, then, could prove to be the natural habitat and breeding ground of the giant beasts.

The Number of the Beast

Signs carried by protesters are now a normal occurrence in most parts of the world, but a sign seen in Athens in 1986 suggested something more unusual than concern over politics and international issues. The occasion was a public protest over the distribution of new identity cards. Protesters were urging popular rejection not of the cards but of the bar code number keyed to it, which was 666. To anyone familiar with the last book of the Bible—Revelation—666 represents the "Beast" or the "Antichrist" and suggests the work of Satan.

According to Orthodox Archbishop Afxentios of Athens, the number was placed there by "dark forces" inimical to the Christian religion. Several thousand people carried signs saying "No to 666!" showing that public awareness of Satan's war on true believers is still alive in that ancient city.

In any case, the identification in the Bible is specific:

Revelation 13:18—"Here is wisdom. Let him that hath understanding count the number of the beast: for it is the number of a man; and his number is six hundred threescore and six."

The Final Curtain Call

In November 1986, the actress Edith Webster gave her final performance in Baltimore of the play *The Drunkard*. Her role, which she had successfully played over a period of eight years, was that of an elderly grandmother. As part of the script directions, she would sing the song "Please Don't Talk About Me When I'm Gone" and collapse on the stage. But during her final performance, as she was being loudly applauded by the audience, she actually died, and the audience thought it was part of the play, even during the loud cries for a doctor. It took some time before they realized that the death was not feigned but real. Then the applause stopped and most of the audience joined in prayer.

The Eyes Have It

Monsters with multiple eyes may sound like pure fantasy. But strange cases of misplaced eyes have been well documented—and some are even more bizarre than any myth.

In the 1854 edition of the *Boston Medical Journal*, for instance, an English authority related the case of a four-eyed man from Cricklade. The patient sported a double pair of eyes, one pair positioned over the other. "He could shut any eye independently in its orbit or could turn them to look in different directions, which was most distracting to the onlooker," the journal noted, adding that the four-eyed man was strange in other ways as well. For instance, according to the author of the paper, he sang "in a screeching voice to which I could not listen without disgust."

A man named Edward Mordrake, a member of the British aristocracy, also had four eyes, but his extra pair sat on the back of his head. And they were accompanied by an extra nose, lips, and ears. Mordrake's extra face could laugh and cry and its eyes could see, but it never ate or spoke. Instead, it stared and drooled. Mordrake eventually became insane and died a lunatic.

Science has recorded the existence of a real, one-eyed Cyclops as well. The man, who lived for years in the backwoods of rural Mississippi, possessed a normal-sized eye right in the middle of his forehead. He was frequently offered jobs in sideshows and circuses but chose not to exploit his odd deformity—and he gave a menacing one-eyed stare to anyone who tried to convince him to do otherwise.

Pearl Harbor Warning

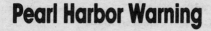

The message scrawled in paint on the sidewalk in front of the public grade school in Owensville, Indiana, was, townsfolk thought, an aggravating bit of vandalism. But what did the cryptic message mean? The huge letters spelled out: "Remember Pearl Harbor!"

The citizens talked about the writing that winter morning in December 1939. What did "Pearl Harbor" mean? They never figured out who painted the words, or why. It seemed just a prank or some mindless vandalism, and the incident was forgotten—until the Japanese bombed Pearl Harbor on the exact day, two years later.

The Face in the Pail

Not all portraits are painted by artists. Sometimes unexplained likenesses of people show up in unusual places without any apparent help from human hands. In 1948, in Northamptonshire, England, a portrait mysteriously appeared in a milk bucket.

Mrs. Margaret Leatherland was milking her cows when she was surprised to see a face smiling up at her from the inside of a shiny pail. The image, which sat just above the milk line, was a portrait of her famous circus entrepreneur brother, Sir Robert Fossett.

Mrs. Leatherland summoned her family to see the strange image, and they too recognized it as a picture of Sir Robert. The subject of the eerie portrait never saw it, however. A few weeks after the face appeared in the pail, he died.

Mrs. Leatherland was determined to scour the picture out of her milk pail, but strong solutions of soda and even acids didn't work.

Sometimes the picture seemed to grow dimmer, but it soon came back just as clear as ever.

The story of the strange face in the pail soon spread. A newspaper published a verified photo of the inside of the milk bucket and the Northampton Society for Psychical Research sent a representative to study the phenomenon. He also saw the picture of Sir Robert inside the pail and went away baffled.

As for Mrs. Leatherland, she eventually became so upset she reportedly disposed of the pail. And with good reason. Every time she filled the bucket, she would look inside to see her dead brother's face drowning in milk.

Frog Survival

According to a report in the February 2, 1958, *Salt Lake City Desert News*, four uranium miners were digging for ore in a Utah mine when they made an incredible find. The workers—Charles North, his son Charles, Jr., Ted McFarland, and Tom North—had hacked through eight feet of sandstone until they reached a fossilized tree stuck in the middle of a bed of uranium. In order to get to the ore, they had to blast the tree out of the way.

The explosion opened up a hole in the stony trunk where a tiny frog sat. The creature was grayish brown and appeared shriveled. It had long, unwebbed toes and suction cups growing out of its tiny fingers. The way the rounded hole was shaped showed that the amphibian had once completely filled the cavity—but, through the eons, it had apparently shrunk to a third of its usual size.

The miners reported that the animal was, incredibly, still alive. It appeared to have somehow survived stuck in the fossilized tree through countless epochs. But twenty-eight hours after being released into the twentieth century, it died.

The Unexplained Portrait

English artist Margaret Moyat woke up on a June morning in 1953 after a strange dream. There was something unusually vivid about the images she had seen in her reverie. An elderly man, whom she didn't recognize, had appeared before her. He smiled, and she assumed he was waiting for her to paint his portrait.

The artist couldn't get the vision out of her mind. In fact, she seemed compelled to paint the old man's picture. The portrait, which showed a striking figure with light blue eyes and a snow-white beard, was completed in just two days.

A few weeks later, two women who had once lived in Eythorne for over thirty years came to visit Miss Moyat. Glancing over at the portrait based on a dream, the two ladies gasped. It was, without a doubt, they told the artist, a portrait of a Mr. Hughes—a minister who had lived in Eythorne and who had been dead for twenty-five years.

Other longtime citizens of the town confirmed that the painting clearly depicted Hughes. But just how Miss Moyat came to paint his portrait remains unexplained—the artist had only lived in Eythorne for two years and had never even heard of the Reverend Hughes until *after* she captured his likeness on canvas.

The Footprints on the Tombstone

Salem, Massachusetts, wasn't the only place that became caught up in witch hunting. Bucksport, Maine, also joined in the frenzy, thanks in large part to the founder of the town, Colonel Jonathan Buck—a cruel man who persecuted one old lady as a witch simply because she had a strong chin and eccentric ways.

The woman insisted she was innocent, but Buck countered that she worked for the Devil and ordered her tortured until she changed her story. The woman, despite hours of pain, still refused to confess. The colonel finally ordered her execution.

As she breathed for the last time, the elderly lady cursed Buck. When the colonel died, she warned, evidence would appear to show he had murdered an innocent woman—her footprint would be found on his tombstone.

Clearly concerned about the woman's prediction, Buck left instructions at the time of his death that his tombstone should be "unblemished and without flaws." Honoring his wishes, his relatives placed a huge, snowy white stone monument over his grave.

But soon both the local sexton and the town's minister noted that an image had appeared on the gravestone. Day by day it became more distinct—a woman's footprint. Buck's family immediately had a stonemason scrape it away. After a few weeks, however, the footprint reappeared.

Buck's grave was drawing throngs of curiosity seekers, so his heirs removed his tombstone and replaced it. But soon the new stone too was emblazoned with the outline of a woman's foot—a legacy that seemed to prove that the murdered old lady had carried out her threat.

The Extra Coffin

Henry and Harry Kalabany of Westport, Connecticut, were digging around their family burial plot in Green Farms Congregational Church Cemetery in September 1956 when one of their shovels hit something unexpected. They had struck a coffin in an area of the burial plot where no member of the family had ever been laid to rest.

Curious about this stranger in their family gravesite, the brothers opened the expensive-looking casket. Inside was the body of a ruddy cheeked gentleman they had never seen before. He appeared to be between forty-five and fifty years old and was dressed in a fine blue suit. The Kalabany brothers had to rebury the coffin; since the man couldn't be identified they couldn't get a permit to move his body. Then they set out to discover who the man was and why he was buried in their family plot.

Finally, the following spring, the local police agreed to help the brothers. Once again, the mysterious out-of-place coffin was dug up. But this time, there was no wealthy-looking, preserved body inside. Instead, all that was found was the skeleton of a man who had been dead at least half a century.

Although the brothers argued that this was not the body they had seen, the police reburied the body where it had been found and closed their investigation of the case.

The Kalabanys never learned the identity of the man they had originally seen. Could he have been a murder victim, later moved and replaced by the disintegrated corpse? Or did the body they found rapidly turn to dust after they opened the coffin? Or could Harry and Henry Kalabany have somehow seen the skeleton as it had appeared in life?

An Ancient Giant

In July 1877, four prospectors moved along the hills of Spring Valley near Eureka, Nevada. They cracked open pieces of rock, looking for outcroppings of precious metal. One of the group spotted something sticking out of a ledge of rock nearby and he climbed up to make out the object's identity. What he found wasn't gold ore, though; instead it was evidence of an ancient giant.

Using their picks, the prospectors soon chipped out human leg and foot bones that had been encased in solid quartzite. The black bones, which had been broken off just above the knee, included the knee joint, kneecap, lower leg bones, and a complete set of foot bones. The man who had once walked on this leg was obviously huge—from knee to heel, the bone was thirty-nine inches long.

The men quickly took their find to Eureka, where it was examined by local physicians. The doctors ruled that the bones were

human, and extremely old. After the Eureka newspaper wrote
articles about the gigantic leg bone, several museums sent archaeologists to look for the rest of the remarkable man's skeleton—but
not another trace of the ancient giant was ever found.

The Pilots Who Walked Off the Face of the Earth

Both temperatures and tempers were blazing in the
summer of 1924 in the Middle Eastern desert. In the area then
known as Mesopotamia, the Arabs were fighting and the British
were trying to keep a handle on the situation. On July 24, Flight
Lieutenant W. T. Day and Pilot Officer D. R. Stewart took off in
their single-engine plane for a routine, four-hour-long reconnais-
sance flight over the area.

When the fliers failed to return, a search party was sent out after
them. The next day their plane was found—in perfect condition.
The craft had not been shot down. Moreover, gasoline was in the
tank and the engine turned over as soon as it was started. But
where were Day and Stewart? And why did they land in an area
of barren desert?

Looking for clues, the search party noted boot marks where the
officers had jumped out of the plane. Their footprints showed that
the men had left the plane and walked along, side by side, for about
120 feet. Then, while still standing next to each other, the men
simply stopped—and vanished.

A half dozen patrols of desert tribesmen, soldiers in armored
trucks, and search planes never turned up a trace of the pilots, who
seemed to have walked off the face of the earth.

Mystery at Sea

It was a clear, quiet night on October 28, 1902, as the steamship *Fort Salisbury* moved through the Gulf of Guinea off the west coast of Africa, heading for the equator. Knowing he had a well-built ship and a trustworthy crew, the ship's captain went to bed and drifted off into a peaceful sleep. The night seemed to be totally ordinary and uneventful. But suddenly, at five minutes past three, the lookout shouted a frantic alarm.

Dead ahead of the *Fort Salisbury*, where nothing was supposed to be, was a huge, round object.

A. H. Raymer, the second officer, rushed on deck and ordered the searchlight to be turned on the thing in their path. It revealed a metallic structure with two small orange-red lights at one end and two blue-green lights near the other. The crew described it as similar to a tremendous airship made out of metal plates. From inside the thing came noises that sounded like machinery working, as well as unintelligible, excited babbling.

As the captain and his men watched the strange object slowly sink beneath the waves, they shouted offers of help. But there was no answer as the giant metal disc slipped out of their sight forever.

A Paranormal Rescue

A religious man, Howard Wheeler was on his knees in prayer in his Charlotte, North Carolina, home about one o'clock Sunday morning on June 10, 1962, when he suddenly stood upright. "I heard an automobile wreck!" he announced to his startled wife, Pat. "I'll be right back!"

Wheeler raced out of his house and jumped into his car. Then he stopped to think for a few seconds. All he had heard was a kind of distant rumble. Where was he going, and why?

Although his neighborhood was crisscrossed with streets, something seemed to guide Howard down Park Road. When he reached Woodlawn, he turned right, down a hill to a shrimp boat. There was no wreck in sight. Then he felt strongly that he should turn around and get back to Montford Drive as fast as he could.

"He went about two hundred yards on Montford, around a curve," the *Charlotte News* reported, "and there was a car smashed against a pole—the engine driven back into the car. He saw no one . . . but a voice said: 'Help me, Humpy, help me!' "

Wheeler soon found an old friend, Joe Funderburke, who had always called him Humpy, trapped in the wreckage. Although Funderburke was badly injured, Wheeler was able to free him from the twisted metal and take him to a hospital. Emergency surgery saved Funderburke's life.

Howard Wheeler could never explain how he heard a car accident happen a half mile from his house, nor how he found it—forty-five minutes before the police or any other passersby discovered the wreck.

Cinque

One of the main participants in the San Francisco kidnapping of Patty Hearst in 1974 had adopted the name Cinque. The original Cinque, who led a slave mutiny on a sailing ship, became famous in the later years of the "Middle Passage," the importation by sea of African slaves.

Cinque, a Mende tribesman captured in 1839 in what is now Sierra Leone, was shipped with others to Cuba, but the slave ship was stopped en route by a British antislavery patrol and sent back to Africa under escort. Once back in Sierra Leone, however, the persistent slavers shipped Cinque and fifty other slaves out again, aboard the bark *Amistad*, its destination Cuba.

When a cook on board, also a Mende tribesman, told the slaves

that they were to be killed and their bodies salted for later eating,
Cinque decided it was time to act. With a nail, he jimmied the locks
of his manacles and those of the other slaves. He found some long
knives, and after killing some of the slavers and keeping the others
as pilots for the voyage back to Africa, he assumed control of the
Amistad.

The Africans knew how to plot directions by following the sun
but could not orient themselves by the stars. Therefore the captive
Spanish pilots steered toward Africa by day but toward Cuba or the
southern United States by night. In effect they veered northeast,
and when they finally landed, they were on the north shore of Long
Island, New York, near Montauk Point. Cinque and others went
ashore to look for provisions and brought back dogs and gin. But
they were followed by the United States Coast Guard, which had
been alerted by duck hunters.

The ship was impounded and the slaves were sent to prison, first
in New London and then in New Haven during the subsequent
trial.

The affair aroused abolitionists, who formed a "Committee for
the Defense of the Africans of the *Amistad*" that included former
President John Quincy Adams, Emerson, and Garrison. The committee was immediately opposed by Southerners, who claimed it
was interfering with due process.

President Martin Van Buren was alternately petitioned and pressured by abolitionists, slave interests, Queen Victoria through the
British ambassador, and the Spanish government. Van Buren decided for neutrality and did not issue an executive order for the
slaves' return. Meanwhile the Africans were aided by students
from the Yale Divinity School and other sympathizers.

The case went to the Supreme Court. Former President Adams
made a plea a hundred thousand words long, including the statement that the slaves "must be considered as free born human
beings" and "be discharged at once."

In 1842 the presiding judge ruled that the captives be returned
to Africa and establish a Christian mission in Sierra Leone, a project
paid for through collections at public appearances and lectures.
(They had been taught English since 1839 by Yale students.)

Cinque returned to Africa with the other slaves, but he did not
stay long at the mission. He went back to the forest from where
there were reports that he had become engaged in the local slave
trade on his own.

The *Lusitania* Nightmare

When lecturer I. B. S. Holbourne left the United States in the spring of 1915 after a highly successful lecture tour, he booked passage home to Great Britain on the huge Cunard ocean liner, the *Lusitania*. There was no way for him to know he would soon witness the vessel's violent destruction. But, somehow, on the other side of the ocean, his wife was able to "see" what lay in store for her husband.

Marion Holbourne woke up on May 7, 1915, in an easy chair in her home's library where she had been taking a nap. While asleep, she had experienced a detailed nightmare. She saw a large liner in terrible trouble. The ship was listing badly and lifeboats were being prepared for launching. Although there was no panic, people were very agitated.

In her dream, Mrs. Holbourne appeared on the upper deck as she watched the ship sink beneath her. A young ship's officer approached her, and she asked if her husband was aboard. The officer answered that the professor had already escaped from the ship in a lifeboat.

On awakening, Mrs. Holbourne told her family about the disturbing dream. They laughed at her and dismissed her vision as "just another nightmare."

Later that day, no one was laughing. The news that the *Lusitania* had been attacked and sunk by a German submarine off the Irish coast soon reached England. Many had lost their lives.

But Professor Holbourne, the family was told, had been saved. After helping other people into lifeboats, he had been ordered to leave the ship himself. When he finally arrived home, he was able to confirm that his wife's dream of the *Lusitania* disaster was accurate—including her description of the young man she talked to. The professor remembered him as being the officer who had ordered him into a lifeboat, saving his life.

Auroras at the Surface of the Earth

During the winter of 1917–1918, according to a 1931 issue of *Nature*, workers at a government radio station in the Arctic "were enveloped in a light mist or foglike substance." Their extended hands seemed to be surrounded by a colored fog, and "a kaleidoscope of colors was visible between the hand and the body." Perhaps most surprising, though, was that there was no apparent dampness in this fog or mist. Stooping down, moreover, they could see under it since it hung just four feet from the ground.

Many explorers have told tales of just such ethereal fog, attributing the phenomenon to auroras—the streamers of light created by electrical charges in the sky. Scientists have refuted this explanation, declaring that auroras never descend lower than fifty kilometers and are usually hundreds of miles above the surface.

Reports of low auroras, nonetheless, persist. Floyd C. Kelley observed such a phenomenon in Hartford, Connecticut, where he was attending Trinity College. "The light effects gave me the impression that the atmosphere was filled with fog and someone was illuminating it by playing a searchlight back and forth," he wrote in a 1934 issue of *Nature*. He also heard "swishing sounds" timed to the flickering of the aurora light.

Lightning Pranks

It's sometimes hard to explain the behavior of lightning. In 1891, for example, the Royal Meteorological Society's quarterly journal reported an incident in which a lightning bolt wrecked a County Mayo, Ireland, kitchen. "All objects of glass or china in the room were upset, but only a few of them were broken; a corner was cut clear off a glass ink bottle, without spilling the ink. The most extraordinary occurrence was what happened to a basket of eggs lying on the floor of the room. The shells were shattered so that they fell off when the eggs were put in boiling water, but the inner membranes were not broken."

An 1886 issue of *Nature* reported lightning's effect on a window in Germany during a particularly violent thunderstorm. Lightning apparently broke a hole—the size of a bullet—in the lower pane. A jet of water shot upward through the opening, striking the ceiling, part of which fell and broke a small table below.

More recently, in Scotland, lightning also drilled a circle in a windowpane at the University of Edinburgh's Meteorological Department. According to a 1973 issue of the journal *Weather*, the missing glass disc was found, intact, inside the room.

The Steamship That Cruised Beside a UFO

There is a curious entry in the logbook of the captain of the *Llandovery Castle*—it tells of how, on the night of July 1, 1947, the steamship cruised briefly through the Straits of Madagascar with a UFO.

It was about 11:00 P.M. when some of the passengers first noted a bright light traveling overhead. As the light passed over the ship, it lost altitude and speed and began to descend within fifty feet of the water. The light was cast downwards at first, creating a search beam that reflected off the water. But then the light went out, and the passengers and crew could see the object beside them.

The witnesses described the craft as gigantic (at least one thousand feet long), cylindrical, and metallic. Some said it was shaped like a mammoth steel cigar with its end clipped. About five times as long as it was wide, the thing had no visible windows or portholes. But because the mysterious craft matched the speed of the *Llandovery Castle* exactly, the crew deduced that something intelligent must be guiding it.

After cruising beside the *Llandovery Castle* for about a minute, the enormous object rose silently. When it was about a thousand feet in the air, it emitted streams of orange flames and shot upwards, disappearing into the night skies.

The Day UFOs Visited Hawaii

Unidentified flying objects have been in the news, off and on, since the late 1940s. At first, researchers could find no patterns to their appearances. Later, "flying saucers" seemed to show up most often in the Northern Hemisphere in the spring and summer months. The rest of the year they were more likely to visit the southern half of the world.

In the early sixties, another pattern emerged—UFOs popped up again and again at satellite launchings and atomic bomb tests. They also seemed to be curious about other aspects of human technology. For example, Captain Joe Walker spotted and photographed strange objects that followed him as he made a test flight in the rocket plane X-15, soaring thousands of miles an hour, high in the sky.

While many of these reported UFOs were only seen by one or two people, an incident on March 11, 1963, involved hundreds—and maybe even thousands—of eyewitnesses. A circular, glowing object followed by a hazy white light soared through the sky for five or six minutes over the island of Hawaii.

Among the people who saw the strange craft were two Hawaiian National Guard pilots who reported spying it from their jets as they flew at a forty-thousand-foot altitude. Lieutenant George Joy noted that the unidentified object had a glowing vapor trail. A Federal Aviation Authority spokesman told newspaper reporters that he and co-workers had also spotted the thing.

Whatever the UFO was, it was clearly not a satellite. And meteors and missiles wouldn't have hovered in the sky for several minutes while hundreds watched. So the case of the UFO that visited Hawaii remains one more unexplained sighting of unknown aerial craft.

Suicide Dream

Mrs. Bertha Stone, a farmer's wife who lived in Jefferson County, Indiana, took a nap each afternoon. On June 10, 1951, she woke up from her customary snooze with a horrible dream on her mind.

She had envisioned herself at one end of a massive bridge, in a city she had never seen before. A middle-aged woman dressed in black, whom she did not recognize, came up to Mrs. Stone and told her: "I came to Abilene to jump in the river."

While Mrs. Stone watched in horror, unable to stop the suicide, the woman climbed over the bridge's railing and jumped off.

The nightmare seemed so real that Mrs. Stone decided to pursue it. Had a woman actually killed herself by leaping from a bridge in Abilene? But which Abilene?

Mrs. Stone wrote letters to the police departments of both Abilene, Kansas, and Abilene, Texas, asking if anyone had committed suicide on the day of her dream.

The Kansas police answered no to her query. But Texas officials wrote that a woman had registered under the name of Ruth Brown at the Wooten Hotel and asked how to get to the nearest river. Then she walked to the nearby bridge and leaped to her death.

The suicide victim was never identified—the name and address she gave at the hotel were fake and her clothing offered no identifying marks. Nor did Bertha Stone ever learn how or why she "saw" in a dream the tragic death as it happened a thousand miles away.

Pint-Sized Aliens

On November 28, 1954, two terrified men burst through the doors of the police station in Caracas, Venezuela. The story they related sounded so farfetched that they were immediately dismissed as drunks. But when medical tests showed they were cold sober—and suffering from shock—it was obvious that something very real and very extraordinary had happened to Gustavo Gonzales and José Ponce.

According to their sworn testimonies, the two men left Caracas in a truck around 2:00 A.M. They were headed for Petare, a town about twenty minutes down the road. Halfway there they found a glowing, curved object blocking the highway.

The craft was floating about five feet above the road and Ponce and Gonzales decided to take a closer look. As they approached the object, a small, dark, hairy, manlike creature clad only in a loincloth came toward them. Gonzales quickly grabbed him and was surprised that the "man" weighed very little, probably about thirty-five pounds. But touching the creature proved to be dangerous.

Immediately, Gonzales was thrown about fifteen feet. Ponce turned and fled toward the police station. As he glanced back, he saw two other small humanoids running toward their luminous ship holding vegetation in their hands.

The tale could not be easily forgotten by the police because it was quickly corroborated by an independent, reliable source. Two days after the men encountered the strange creatures, one of the physicians who had examined them came forward. Although he was hesitant to talk at first because he did not want to be associated with such a strange event, he finally admitted that while driving home from an emergency call he'd witnessed the entire episode. It had happened, he said, just as Gonzales and Ponce had said—UFO, hairy pint-sized alien, and all.

The Nevada UFO Crash

On April 18, 1962, reports came in that a red object had been seen in the skies over Oneida, New York, heading west. Although radar picked up the thing, it could not be identified, so when it went as far as the Midwest, the Air Defense Command scrambled jets from Phoenix to intercept the UFO.

But when the object was about seventy miles northwest of Las Vegas, it disappeared from radar screens. According to the *Las Vegas Sun*, the only newspaper that investigated the tale, the UFO may have exploded over Nevada. At about the same time the object vanished from radar screens, the paper pointed out, an explosion took place somewhere above the Mesquite Range—the blast was so powerful that the streets of Reno became as bright as day. Although many people chalked the brilliant flash up to an atomic bomb test, the Atomic Energy Commission denied that any nuclear tests were underway in the United States at that time.

A few hours later, another strange scenario that may or may not be related was reported by the United Press Service. A huge object had been spotted landing near a Eureka, Utah, electric power station. Once again, *Las Vegas Sun* reporters checked out the story, and, when they questioned a Stead Air Force Base official in Reno, they were told that the landing had occurred. The spokesman, who requested anonymity, also commented that the "impact" of the UFO's landing had knocked the power station out of order.

Curiously, few Americans ever heard about the strange objects that rocked the Southwest that spring evening—only the *Las Vegas Sun* and a couple of regional papers ever printed the news that a "flying saucer" had apparently crashed on Earth.

Biblical Archaeological Hints

Carefully studying literal translations of the Bible isn't just a pastime of the clergy. Archaeologists and geologists contend that activity has helped them find invaluable, hidden loot.

While no one had found evidence that King Solomon had mined copper, Dr. Nelson Glueck, president of Hebrew Union College, suspected that Solomon traded copper with ancient Persian kings. His belief was bolstered by this line in the Book of Deuteronomy: "out of . . . hills thou canst dig copper." But where were the copper mines located?

Glueck used planes to take color photographs of areas around a recently discovered seaport used by King Solomon. Then ground parties searched for long-abandoned water holes. Putting together his evidence, Glueck found the ancient copper mines of King Solomon in the region now known as Wadi el Arabah. He also discovered veins of copper that today, thousands of years later, are back in production.

Another scientist aided by the Bible was Dr. James Pritchard of the University of Pennsylvania Museum, who had long wondered about the pool of Gideon mentioned in the holy Book. After studying the scriptural references, he and fellow researchers located the pool, about eight miles north of Jerusalem. They discovered that when the armies of Nebuchadnezzar had invaded in 587 B.C., the conquerors stopped up the well with tons of debris and its location was soon forgotten. But Pritchard used the Bible's clues to uncover it—and today the pool of Gideon flows again, a blessing for the water-starved Holy Land.

The Restless Coffins in the Buxhoewden Chapel

In the Baltic Sea sits the tiny, rocky island of Oesel. The island's only town, Arensburg, contains many private chapels built by the wealthy few.

When a relative dies, one Arensburg custom is to keep the body in a weighty oak coffin in the chapel for a time. Then it is moved to an adjoining vault. But a mysterious force refused to allow the bodies lying in a chapel owned by the Buxhoewden family to rest in peace. Instead, unseen hands repeatedly tossed the heavy oak caskets around as if they were toys.

The strange happenings began on June 22, 1844, when Mrs. Dalmann visited the grave of her mother. Her horse, which was tied to a post near the Buxhoewden chapel, soon became so excited and heavily lathered that a veterinarian had to be called. Then, a few days later, other people who hitched their horses outside the Buxhoewden chapel returned from church services to find their animals in a similar state. But what could have produced such panic?

Members of the Buxhoewden family decided to inspect their chapel and vault to quash rumors that the place was somehow connected with the horses' attacks of fear. But as soon as the door was opened, it was clear something bizarre *had* gone on there—coffins had been piled in the center of the floor.

The Buxhoewdens put the unopened caskets back in place, locked the chapel door, and then poured lead into the seals to make sure no one could enter and wreak havoc with their relatives' remains again.

Not long afterward, however, eleven horses left in front of the Buxhoewden chapel for a short while became so panic-stricken that three did not survive the incident.

Once again, the chapel was opened. And once again, somehow, the coffins had been thrown in the center of the floor. Some were upside down, and one looked as though it had crashed down from above.

Again the Buxhoewden family put the coffins back where they were supposed to be, locked and sealed the door—and waited. A church court decided to investigate the matter and its representative, Baron De Guldenstubbe, visited the family vault. After the seals were broken and the door unlocked, he entered to find, as before, coffins thrown into the middle of the room.

To make sure the mysterious intruder who was moving the coffins wasn't using a secret tunnel or passageway, the investigators dug up the floor of the vault and made a trench around it. They found nothing.

Then they sprinkled ashes over the chapel's steps and the vault's floor so the intruder would have to leave footprints. Again, the door was locked and sealed and two armed guards were posted outside.

Although the guards never heard or saw any intruders and the ashes were not disturbed, when church representatives once again inspected the crypt they found the coffins moved from the opposite end of the vault where they were supposed to be. Some were standing on end.

Why the coffins were so restless in the family chapel remains unknown. Baffled and tired of the mysterious goings-on, the Buxhoewdens finally removed their ancestors remains and buried them elsewhere.

Dream of a Coming Accident

Winnie Wilkinson of Sheffield, England, could almost never nap in the middle of the day. But one afternoon in the summer of 1962 she found herself drifting off to sleep—and soon experienced a most disturbing dream.

As she later told the police, she dreamed there was a heavy knocking at her front door. When she opened it, she came face-to-face with a woman she had never seen before. The stranger excitedly told Mrs. Wilkinson that her estranged husband had been terribly injured. He had fallen off a scaffold, the dream visitor said, and his wife was to come at once.

Although she was considering divorcing Gordon, Winnie was upset at the thought he might be hurt in any way. So when she woke up she noted the time, 3:12 P.M., and hurriedly called his workplace to make sure he was all right.

Gordon Wilkinson was fine, his employers assured his wife. But the next day, at exactly 3:12 P.M., he was dead—killed when he plunged from a scaffold.

The Sleepy Murderer

While vacationing in Le Havre, French detective Robert Ledru offered to help local police solve the murder of André Monet. A small businessman with few friends but no known enemies, Monet was shot and killed on a nearby beach while apparently out for a midnight swim. There seemed to be no motive and there were only two clues. One was that the bullet had been fired from a Luger, a very common make of gun—even Ledru had one. The other was footprints in the sand, of little value since the perpetrator had taken his shoes off and walked the beach in his stockinged feet.

Examining one of the footprints closely, however, Ledru was suddenly horrified. The murderer lacked a toe on his right foot— just like Ledru himself. He made a print of his own stockinged foot next to the murderer's. He obtained the bullet removed from the victim, went home and shot his own Luger into a pillow, and compared the two bullets. He then reported to his superiors in Paris.

According to the *Encyclopedia of Aberrations, A Psychiatric Handbook,* even the police chief could not deny the evidence. Ledru, who always slept with his socks on, had awakened on the morning after the murder to find his socks inexplicably wet. It was clear that Ledru had murdered Monet while walking in his sleep.

The Calendar Twins

The term *idiot savant* describes an individual who has subnormal intelligence yet possesses an exceptional skill. According to some experts, the idiot savant, rendered important by a particular talent, will often concentrate on it, repeatedly demonstrating his ability and, therefore, improving with practice.

But according to the *American Journal of Psychiatry*, identical twins George and Charles contradicted this idea. The pair had an uncanny acuity for dates. They could recall almost any day and accurately report that date's weather. George, moreover, showed an even more remarkable talent: Although Charles was completely accurate only for twentieth-century dates, George could identify dates in previous centuries. With equal facility, the twins could also identify February 15, 2002, as a Friday or August 28, 1591, as a Wednesday, again George more accurately than Charles. And even though they didn't know the difference between the Julian and the Gregorian calendars, when they identified dates before 1582 (when the change in calendars occurred), they invariably accounted for the ten-day difference. The ability is even more impressive considering the fact that they couldn't add, subtract, multiply, or divide numbers.

Memory, learning, and recall were not abilities available to the twins. They operated, moreover, beyond the usual two hundred-to four hundred-year perpetual calendar, and in fact, could reach beyond the year 7000. While motivational factors may play a part in developing a skill, this alone can't explain the basic skill itself.

A Prince Sees the Flying Dutchman

The legend of the "Flying Dutchman," the ship captain who cursed God and as punishment was condemned to sail a phantom ship eternally over the oceans, has been immortalized in seamen's tales as well as in one of Wagner's operas.

It has often been reported sighted in storms or in fogs. Other sailing ships, drifting and unmanned, have been called "Flying Dutchmen." Encountering the *Flying Dutchman*, in the lore of the sea, has been interpreted as a warning of impending disaster.

An unusual sighting was made aboard the British warship HMS *Inconstant*, sailing the Pacific Ocean on July 11, 1861. In the *Inconstant*'s log of that date, the following entry occurs:

At 4 A.M. "The Flying Dutchman" crossed our bows. She emitted a strange phosphorescent light as of a phantom ship all aglow, in the midst of which light the masts, spars, and sails of a brig 200 yards distant stood out in strong relief as she came up on the port bow where also the officer of the watch from the bridge saw her, as did also the quarter-deck midshipman, who was sent forward at once to the forecastle, but on arriving there no vestige nor any sign whatever of any material ship was to be seen either near or right away to the horizon, the night being clear and the sea calm.

This ghost ship report is different from others because of the identity of the midshipman who wrote it. He was a British prince, doing his tour, as was the custom, in the Royal Navy. He was also later to become George V, the king emperor of the British Empire.

A Time to Keep Silent

During a war it is sometimes difficult and dangerous to admit that an event has helped immeasurably your own side.

Such a dilemma was posed by the disastrous bombing of Coventry, the British cathedral city, by German aircraft in the "blitz" against England in 1940. British Intelligence knew about the projected mass attack beforehand, having broken the German "Enigma" code at the beginning of World War II, but it could not permit even a suggestion that it could "read" secret German radio communication. Therefore, on Churchill's orders, only the usual antiaircraft and fighter plane resistance were able to rise to the defense of Coventry, instead of a mass riposte. The German attack on an unsuspecting target was successful, but the secret of Britain's possession of the key to "Enigma" was safe, to be later used with eminent success in the campaign against Rommel in North Africa and in other operations as well. At the crucial naval battle of Midway, American code translators were able to read Japanese coded communications as fast or even faster than the Japanese.

The top secret "Purple Code," a Japanese version of "Enigma," had been broken by United States cryptoanalysts before America's participation in World War II. During operations in the Pacific, an intercepted Japanese code message indicated when and where Admiral Yamamoto, commander-in-chief of the Japanese fleet, would make an inspection of the Solomon Islands' defenses. Armed with this information, United States Navy planes were able to find and shoot down Admiral Yamamoto's aircraft as well as the escort planes. Despite the propaganda value of this military coup, the operation was kept top secret to protect the United States' knowledge of the code.

Missing Links

To escape the taunts and jeers of the villagers in his Russian home, young Andrian fled into the woods. There he lived in a cave, learning to subsist on his own and eventually fathering his own children. At least two of which—a daughter who died in infancy and a son who survived and traveled with his father—resembled him.

According to a report in *Scientific American*, Andrian was an ape-man. Indeed, when exhibited at a medical seminar in Berlin in his fifties, Andrian had hair all over his body, his face, and his neck.

Andrian, moreover, was not the first human to resemble a missing link between modern man and his cousins on the ancestral family tree. Mexico's Julia Pastrana, for instance, suffered the humiliating fate of having animal-like fur and, according to *Science* magazine, died giving birth to a son who inherited the same trait.

The minds of such freaks, however, are not necessarily impaired or less than human. Discovered in Borneo, six-year-old Kra-o, for example, had thick, coarse hair that ran over her shoulders like a mane and down her back, and her resemblance to a gorilla was even more striking because of a flat nose that diagonally slanted toward her cheeks. She also had baggy cheeks in which she would store food, like apes. But, *Scientific American* said in another report, she learned English quickly and, soon after she was taken to Great Britain, was able to make herself understood.

According to experts, hair such as Kra-o's seems to develop from prenatal *lanugo* common to many mammals, but not modern humans. Among animals, the soft, downy hair gradually develops into fur or feathers. It appears that some genes of our prehistoric ancestors remain in the makeup of human DNA. At rare times, they can still assert themselves.

The Real Sleeping Beauty

On May 21, 1883, Marguerite Boyenval went into a cataleptic sleep induced by fear when the police arrived at her home. Her twenty-two-year-old body was as rigid as a corpse, the arms literally remained outstretched, in the position in which they were originally placed.

Though Boyenval was for the most part unaware of events around her, there were times when she vaguely heard what was said. After about five months, for instance, she suddenly opened her eyes briefly during a physical examination and spoke. "You are pinching me," she exclaimed.

Although she was artificially fed, her health began declining. Developing consumption, her body wasted away and Boyenval finally died in 1903—after a twenty-year-long sleep.

Sunspots and Business

Economist William Stanley Jevons believed that commercial crises were somehow related to the activity of astronomical orbs. To test that notion, his British colleague, economist John Maynard Keynes, decided to trace the history of commercial crises back almost to the beginning of the eighteenth century. Determining that business cycles seemed to occur at intervals of 10 to 11 years, Keynes was able to match economic crises to the cycle of solar spots, which become increasingly intense every 10.45 years.

Keynes, postulating an explanation for the mysterious connection, said, "Meteorological phenomena play a part in harvest fluctuations and harvest fluctuations play a part in the trade cycle. Jevons's ideas are not to be lightly dismissed."

Despite the coincidence of cyclical commercial crises and solar periods, however, the link was never proved.

Huge Slab of Ancient Glass

It wasn't until the mid-twentieth century that engineers and scientists successfully manufactured the largest glass object ever created—the two-hundred-inch reflecting mirror in the Hale Telescope at Mount Palomar. However, someone in Beth She'arim, an ancient center of Jewish learning in southwestern Galilee, managed to create a solid sheet of glass about half as heavy (8.8 tons) *thousands* of years ago.

The slab was discovered in 1956 when an ancient cistern next to some catacombs was being cleared out so that it could be turned into a museum. A bulldozer struck something huge, buried in the ground. It turned out to be a 3.40-meter-long, 1.95-meter-wide slab of solid glass. Since it was too large and heavy to be moved, it was left in the middle of what is now the museum.

The glass is opaque, because of eons of weathering, and filled with tiny crystals. When clean and wet, it appears purple with intermingled streaks of green and purple in one corner.

Researchers concluded that there was no possibility the slab could have been the result of a natural geological occurrence, nor could it be waste from the smelting of ore. Instead, it was documented as man-made—although how and why the giant piece of glass was created remains a mystery.

The Mystery Spheres of Costa Rica

Banana company workers hacked through the dense vegetation of a tropical forest in Costa Rica about fifty years ago, hoping to uncover land suitable for growing bananas. They not only found the rich soil they were looking for, but they also discovered something totally unexpected—a huge round stone about six feet in diameter.

As the workmen searched under nearby vines and brush, they found many more round stones. Some were only a few inches in diameter and weighed just a couple of pounds. But others were eight feet around and weighed more than sixteen tons. They were all so smooth and appeared so perfectly round that it took careful measuring to prove that they were not absolutely perfect spheres.

When the workmen reported their discovery they learned that few people in the area had ever seen the objects. No one—including scientists from all over the world who came to study the mysterious spheres—knew who made them, or why.

The balls were found to be made primarily of granite, although a few were made of limestone. Most were in groups of at least three, but as many as forty-five were found together. Some were inexplicably arranged in triangles and others in circles. Still others were placed in long straight rows pointing north and south, leading to speculation that some long-forgotten ancient people used them to keep track of the position of celestial bodies—in others words, a prehistoric planetarium.

Feline X-Ray Detectors

Biologists at the Veterans Administration Hospital in Long Beach, California, wondered whether cats could sense the presence of X rays. To find out, the researchers exposed the furry felines to five-second intervals of X-radiation. Using a five-millimeter-wide beam directed at specific areas, they found the greatest effect occurred when the radiation was aimed at the olfactory bulb behind the nasal and oral passages. Since directing the ray at the nose itself had little effect, they discarded the notion that the cats actually smelled the ozone created by X rays.

According to the report in *New Scientist*, however, the scientists stopped short of declaring the olfactory bulb responsible for cats' ability to sense the rays. When the olfactory bulb was removed, it turned out, the cats still retained some sensitivity to X rays, particularly when the amount of X rays increased.

There may, the scientists concluded, be more than one sensory receptor capable of detecting X rays. In fact, that possibility is supported by research showing that X-ray sensitivity is probably spread throughout the cat's body.

Mass Strandings of Marine Mammals

On the evening of August 19, 1971, three short-finned pilot whales were found stranded in less than three feet of water along the beach at Sarasota, Florida. Less than a mile away, another six whales were also caught in shallow water near the shoreline. All nine were able to rejoin their herd about 150 yards offshore only after local residents helped push the big creatures into deeper water. Then the herd slowly moved southward along the coast, traveling about 11 miles before more whales became stranded on the shore, again requiring human assistance to move back out to sea. At one point, however, the herd spread out—with some of the whales becoming stranded again—as it followed an aquarium exhibitor towing a young whale to shore. The rescue was repeated, but five days later, the whales were again stranded 160 miles away.

A number of theories, including those involving mass suicide and harassment by sharks, have attempted to explain such behavior among marine mammals. Many studying the phenomenon have pursued the idea that parasites in the sinuses and the middle ear affect echolocation, causing the animals to become disoriented and to float ashore.

Another theory comes from cetacean expert F. G. Wood, who says that marine animals may sometimes revert to the primitive behavior of their terrestrial ancestors, following the instinct to return to land when injured, sick, or attacked. Like other hypotheses, however, Wood's theory lacks hard supporting data.

Those who argue against his theory point out, moreover, that though such a trait may once have been beneficial, it is now self-destructive and should have been eliminated during the evolutionary process.

The cause of whale beachings remains unknown.

Musical Mice

Philip Ryall was often disturbed during the night by what he thought were birds chirping in the chimney. One night, however, he discovered a mouse creeping out of a crevice. It sat up on its hind feet looking around the room, all the while singing in a low warble.

The visits soon became a daily routine—until Ryall caught the fully grown female wood mouse, eventually passing her on to Samuel Lockwood, who reported on the phenomenal mouse in *Popular Science Monthly*. Lockwood kept the mouse, named Hespy, in a cage for everyone's entertainment.

In a similar case reported in *Zoologist* magazine, biologist John Farr suspected that the sound was created by grinding the teeth. But on closer observation, the throat of the mouse appeared to heave, giving the impression of a guttural sound.

If the sound emerged from the throat, however, the mice wouldn't be able to sing while eating as they often do. Nor is the singing a reaction to pleasure, since the mice also sing when chased from their nests.

In an effort to learn the secret of the musical mice, some people have tried to breed singing mice from a variety of mouse species. But this effort has not met with success. That is, no matter how the breeding was done, not all of the offspring would sing. One Maryland man bred hundreds of such mice before he found even a single offspring that could sing.

The Canals of Mars

There is an understandable tendency present among Earth-dwellers to deny the theory that we are alone in the universe or without sentient neighbors in our own planetary system.

When the famous astronomer Giovanni Schiaparelli submitted a theory about the canals of Mars, he was generally believed, because of his international reputation and because the assumption was so logical.

Schiaparelli claimed to have discovered in 1877 a system of lines seemingly connected by terminal points over the bleak Martian terrain. He named these lines "canals" (*canalli*), a name adopted by other theorists who considered them proof that a former Martian civilization had dug them to conserve the dwindling water supply on Mars. Still other astronomers who saw the sometimes straight or sweeping lines thought that they might be "game trails" trodden into patterns by herds of Martian animals over the years or, more probably, by dried up rivers that once flowed into now empty seas.

This last assumption is now more generally held, as there are strong indications that there once were rivers on Mars, and as has been observed, surface ice still exists at its poles.

Dwellers on the Moon

A purely imaginative description of life on the moon was offered as if it were factual to the newspaper-reading public by the *New York Sun* in 1835 through a series entitled "Great Astronomical Discoveries Lately Made by Sir John Herschel at the Cape of Good Hope."

The very name of Herschel, a well-known astronomer, was

enough to inspire the public's confidence, and, without a denial from Herschel, who did not know about the series until after four articles had appeared, the popular articles increased the circulation of the *Sun* by more than 650 percent.

Within a short time a pamphlet edition of the series brought in thousands of additional dollars. For some reason, *The New York Times* editorialized that the series displayed "the most extensive and accurate knowledge of astronomy." The articles were based on statements attributed to Sir John Herschel (but actually prepared by a Richard Locke of the *Sun*) that a new seven-ton telescope, installed at the Cape of Good Hope, South Africa, possessed a 42000x magnification. Focused on the moon, it allegedly made the moon's surface appear to be within five miles of the earth.

The article stated that Sir John had been able to clearly distinguish different kinds of moon animals. Some looked like American buffalos, others more closely resembled bears; there were single-horned blue goats and great cranes and other birds that flew over mountains made of amethyst. There were beaches on great lakes, one 266 miles long. Finally, there were humanoid winged creatures with faces like orangutans that flew but could also walk; these creatures appeared to be about four feet tall (the height frequently reported in modern-day encounters with extraterrestrials).

If the telescope made the moon appear as if it were only five miles away, readers wondered how Sir John was able to see such detail. But it was specified in a follow-up report that the astronomer was able to describe small animals and even the species of trees by adjusting his lens, thus bringing the surface of the moon to within eighty yards of the viewer.

Probably because of the lack of instant news communication in the 1830s, the hoax was not discovered until Locke told the truth to another journalist, who then reported it in the *Journal of Commerce*. When Sir John learned about the matter, he good-naturedly observed that he thought it was a good joke. Nevertheless, many thousands of people believed in the reports of men and animals on the moon and were disappointed when it was revealed to be a hoax.

As the Italian proverb goes, *Se non è vero, è ben trovato*. "If it isn't true, it's still well thought out."

Beyond Coincidence

Sooner or later, coincidences are bound to occur. But they can sometimes mount up to such a degree that there seems to be more than simple coincidence involved—as two car owners at a Sheboygan, Illinois, mall found out firsthand.

Thomas Baker had finished his shopping at the Northgate Shopping Center, and he was ready to go home. He walked up to what he thought was his 1978 maroon American Motors Concord and unlocked the door. But something was wrong. The seat seemed out of whack. He couldn't fit his six-foot-six-inch frame comfortably under the wheel. Glancing around the car, he noticed a caddy holding coffee cups and other unfamiliar items. Baker decided to call the police.

While he was discussing the situation with the officers, an identical Concord drove up. The elderly couple inside explained they were loading groceries into the car when they had found it contained unfamiliar personal objects. A check of the license plate showed that even though the car they were driving looked like theirs, it was someone else's.

According to American Motors Corporation (AMC) spokesman Ben Dunn, the odds of unlocking two AMC cars with the same key are 1,000–1. "But when you consider the matching color and model and the fact that the cars were parked in the same place at the same time," he says, "the odds become more like *ten thousand* to one."

The odds of this particular incident's happening shrank even more when the drivers found out they shared more than the same taste in cars. Thomas Baker and Mr. and Mrs. Richard Baker also had the same last name.

Psychiatrist James Hall of the University of Texas Health Science Center at Dallas says the car mix-up is "a good example of what Carl Jung called *synchronicity*," a term he coined to explain meaningful coincidences for which ordinary chance is not a significant explanation.

Hall adds that these kinds of multiple coincidences may reflect the underlying order of the universe. "There are deeper meanings to these kinds of coincidences," he says, "and they are research-able."

Spirited Novel Ending

Charles Dickens died in 1870, leaving his last book, *The Mystery of Edwin Drood*, unfinished. Did he find a way to complete the novel from beyond the grave? A young Vermont mechanic and psychic named T. P. James insisted that the ghostly spirit of Dickens visited him in 1873 and told him how to complete the novel.

Parapsychologist Jerry Solfvin and fellow researcher Jo Coffey, both of John F. Kennedy University in Orinda, California, are using a computer to analyze the known writing style of Dickens as well as the alleged "spirited" version of his work. The data will then be compared to determine whether the same author wrote all the material.

Solfvin emphasizes the outcome won't absolutely *prove* whether or not the spirit of Dickens actually finished *The Mystery of Edwin Drood*. "That's not our ultimate goal," he says. "What we will demonstrate is that a computer technique can help evaluate psychic information channeled from one person to the next."

The Savant of Lafayette

A native of nineteenth-century Lafayette County, Missouri, Reuben Field was a strong, heavyset man with the intellect of a child. He had never gone to school because he was considered an idiot and could neither read nor write. Nevertheless, he was able to compute and solve the most complicated mathematical problems, although he couldn't decipher written figures.

Told the circumference of the earth, in even figures, was twenty-five thousand miles, for example, and asked how many flax seeds, at 12 to an inch, would be required to circle the planet, Field almost instantly answered 19,008,000,000. If given the date of an event, moreover, he would be able to determine the exact day of the week. According to N. T. Allison in the *Scientific American*, he could also tell the time of day at any given moment without looking at a clock. Once, Allison asked him for the time and Field replied, "Sixteen minutes after three." Engaging him in further conversation, for seventeen minutes, to distract the illiterate man, Allison then asked the time again. Field replied, accurately, "Twenty-seven minutes to four."

Hair-Raising Power

At a meeting of the American Psychological Association in 1940, researcher Donald Lindsley showed the film of a man who had been voluntarily raising the hair on his arms since he was ten years old. He didn't need to scare himself, or even imagine something terrifying. He just raised his hair the same way he worked his muscles, he claimed, but a great deal more was happening than he thought. During the hair-raising experience, Lindsley pointed out, the man's pupils dilated; his heart and respiratory rates increased; even his brain waves changed. Indeed, he gave every physiological indication that he was, in fact, frightened, even though he claimed to feel absolutely no fear.

Strange Beasts of Africa

The natives call it *khodumodumo*, or "gaping-mouthed-bush-monster." In stealthy silence through the dark night, the marauder invades farms, climbing over six-foot-high fences into the pens and seizing sheep, goats, or calves. According to witnesses, the beast's "round, saucerlike footprints, with two-inch toenail marks," are unlike those of any animal known to man.

Some have identified the *khodumodumo* as a mutant hyena. Others disagree, saying the hyena always drags its quarry and is not known to leap tall fences with a calf in its jaw. The hyena, moreover, is not a *quiet* thief—it howls before a kill and shrieks afterwards. For the same reason, many say, the *khodumodumo* is probably not a lion or leopard either.

What's more, the *khodumodumo* is not alone. In the dark continent, tales of mystery beasts abound. Any hunter who has tracked African game, for instance, has heard of the strange, howling, man-eating *ndalawo* of Uganda; the *mbilintu*, a cross between a hippo and an elephant, of the Congo; and the silent, purring *mngwa*, which stalks coconut groves along much of the African coast.

Like the legendary Loch Ness, Africa has its share of water monsters as well. The *lau* and *lukwata*, for instance, are said to be immense serpents that lurk beneath the African lakes and marshes. Reportedly hundreds of feet in length, with the girth of a donkey, they make loud, rumbling noises in the night and attack marine animals and water-traveling humans. Although he never actually saw one, scientist E. G. Wayland, director of Uganda's Geological Survey, was shown an alleged *lukwata* bone and also heard it roaring through the night.

Africans also describe the *agogwe*, a small, furry, ape-man no more than four feet tall. Legend has it that if you leave a bowl of food and a gourd of *ntulu* beer outdoors for the critters, they will take the food and, in return, hoe and weed your yard.

While some of the legendary African beasts may be just myths, *some* may exist. After all, there was a time when scientists doubted the existence of the very real platypus and giant panda as well.

Australia's Enormous Egg

During the 1930s, an Australian farmer found a football-sized egg that has baffled scientists ever since. Researchers confirm that the object is an egg—in fact, a bird's egg. But they say it's thirteen times bigger than an egg laid by the giant emu, the largest egg the scientists of the Australian continent have ever found.

Though the egg remains a mystery to this day, theories abound. The egg could be from a species known as the *Aepyornis*, a bird long extinct in its natural habitat of Madagascar, some four thousand miles west of Australia. The egg could have drifted across the Indian Ocean and floated up to Australia's shore, experts suggest, as does other material caught in the juncture of the Indian and Southern oceans in the area of the find. Or the egg could have been carried by humans and abandoned on the Australian shore.

Then again, some scientists say, the egg might belong to an extinct *Australian* bird, whose fossil footprints and what is possibly its skull were found relatively nearby.

The Mass Death of the Tilefish

It was a cold and stormy Tuesday afternoon, and a strong northwest wind whipped the waves into a frenzy. All around the Norwegian fishing vessel *Sidon*, the shipmaster said, hundreds of dead or dying fish, some three to four feet long, floated on the water's surface. Traveling at a speed of six to eight knots, the *Sidon* ploughed through fifty miles of sea with the fish still slapping against its sides. Soon afterwards, during March and April 1882, the crews of at least twelve other ships related similar encounters.

Hearing the *Sidon* story, United States fish commissioner Spencer Baird began an investigation whose preliminary findings indicated the fish were cod. Still, Baird thought they were more likely tilefish, a Gulf Stream species discovered a few years earlier in 1879. When he actually saw one of the dead fish, he realized he was correct.

According to an article in *Nature Magazine*, Baird and his investigators estimated that about 1.5 million dead fish, with a conservative combined weight of more than 14 million pounds, drifted in an area 170 miles long and 25 miles wide. All manner of explanations were given for the massive kill, from volcanic eruptions and poisonous gases to heat and starvation. The most prominent theory was that the fish, confronted by a current of unusually cold water, became paralyzed and helpless, and eventually died. Be that as it may, the specimens showed no signs of illness or disease.

The species disappeared from human sight for a total of ten years and baffled marine biologists were never able to confirm any reason for the mortality of the fish.

The Mystery of the Inca's Treasure

When Pizarro and his small force penetrated and then conquered the empire of the Incas, an enormous territory covering Peru, Colombia, Ecuador, Bolivia, and parts of Chile and Argentina, he obtained for himself and Spain an enormous treasure in gold.

Much of this treasure came to his hands in a single unit. He had massacred the Indian warriors who tried to protect the Incan king, Atahuallpa, and he had taken the Inca captive. Atahuallpa, in order to secure his release, promised to fill a large room in the palace completely with gold, up to a line indicated on the wall by a standing man's upstretched hand.

Pizarro accepted with alacrity, but, after receiving a large part of the promised treasure, he decided that the Inca should be executed anyway, giving him the choice of being burned or strangled, the preferable strangulation being contingent on the Inca's being baptized. The Inca was then strangled as a Christian.

After the death of the king, the gold of the empire (statues, idols, jars, bars, plates, ceremonial weapons, and chains) continued to be brought in from all parts of the empire. Then suddenly the treasure stopped coming. Pizarro was particularly sorry not to receive the promised forged chain of gold that was said to be so heavy that sixty Indians were needed to carry it. No one ever learned what became of this treasure, often referred to as *el peje grande*—"the big fish."

A curious legend has persisted in Peru: the belief that a lineal descendant of Atahaullpa still has control of an enormous fortune, which he keeps secret, as he does his own identity. The Andean Indians tell of a distinguished and light-skinned Indian, dressed in formal attire like a white man but speaking the ancient Quechua language, who sometimes comes to mountain villages in times of trouble. This may be when certain families or the whole village is desperate for supplies, food, or money. This princely figure arrives in a large, chauffeured black car of a kind seldom seen in the mountain areas. He supplies gold to a village, sometimes for food, or for teachers, or for medicine, and then leaves. His identity is unknown and no one ever seems to remember the license number of his luxurious car, or even if it had license plates.

The Indians, however, are certain of one thing—someone is protecting them in time of need. Perhaps the mysterious benefactor is a descendant of the Great Inca, the "Son of the Sun," who still cares for his people.

The Rain Tree

Ancient journals of travelers in the Western Hemisphere recount stories of a tree that attracted clouds, invariably converting them into rain.

These stories were considered nothing more than tall tales until such a tree, its branches producing a shower of water, was discovered in Brazil during the early nineteenth century. About fifty years later, another was documented in Peru. The leaves of the Peruvian rain tree, *Scientific American* reported, seemed to condense moisture in the atmosphere and, in turn, release the water in the form of showers.

The legend of the rain tree seems to date back to the Fortunate Isles where the only "rain" was the moisture precipitated by trees. Early explorers brought home stories of similar trees in such locales as the East Indies, Guinea, and Brazil.

Today, scientists have posed a possible explanation. Many plants, in a process known as "guttation," they contend, draw moisture up from their roots, usually passing the excess into the atmosphere in the form of gas. If the air is already saturated with moisture and the water reaching the roots is excessive, then the leaves will exude the liquid, sometimes in large quantities. The process occurs mostly at night, when the relative humidity is greatest. In the tropics where atmospheric moisture is high, trees can probably exhibit guttation to such an extent that the name "rain tree" befits them, but the process cannot occur in a dry climate and rain trees cannot, therefore, act as a panacea for drought.

Creatures in the Yard

Marius Dewilde's home was situated among the woods and fields less than a mile from the French village of Quarouble near the Belgian border. Despite the fact that the National Coal Mines' railroad tracks ran along one side of Dewilde's property, the nights were tranquil. During such quiet times, after his wife and son were usually in bed, the French steelworker would sit in the kitchen and read the newspaper before retiring himself. The night of September 10, 1954, however, was different.

Hearing the family's dog barking and howling, Dewilde suspected a prowler. Taking his flashlight, he went to investigate. Outside he spotted something near the railroad tracks, but assumed it was a farmer's truck.

As the dog cringed up to him on its stomach, the steelworker was suddenly startled by a sound to his right. Swinging around, he caught a glimpse of an odd sight: two creatures with very broad shoulders, but no arms, and wearing what appeared to be diving suits and helmets. No more than three feet tall, the entities seemed to shuffle on short legs. They were heading for the dark shape he thought was merely a truck.

Dewilde ran to the garden gate, intending to cut the creatures off. Suddenly a blinding beam of light from the dark shape on the tracks struck and immobilized him; he wasn't even able to shout as he saw the creatures pass within a yard of him and head toward the tracks.

The light was quickly extinguished, however, and Dewilde continued his chase, but it was too late. The creatures apparently reached their destination, and the dark shape rose with a whistling noise as it discharged a cloud of steam beneath. Reaching a height of about thirty yards, the craft then took off toward the east, climbing higher and glowing red as it did so.

Shaken, Dewilde ran to report the incident to the police, who dismissed him as crazy. The commissioner, however, realized that he was neither mad nor joking and initiated a detailed inquiry. Investigators initially suggested that Dewilde may have suffered a hallucination, the result of a head injury.

That may have been discounted had they paid attention to the deeply cut marks in the iron-hard wood of the railroad cars. A railroad engineer estimated that such marks could have been created only by an object weighing at least thirty tons. It would have taken intense heat, moreover, to burn the ballast stones between the cars.

Valencia UFO

The Spanish charter airline flight had been delayed four hours before finally taking off from Salzburg, Austria, en route to Tenerife in the Canary Islands. The passengers' discontent was aggravated further when the plane made an unscheduled landing in Valencia, Spain. It may have been the least of their concerns had they known what precipitated the detour on that Sunday evening in November 1979.

It began after the plane had passed over Ibiza. Shortly before eleven o'clock, flight captain Commandante Lerdo de Tejada saw two bright red lights to the left of the aircraft. The object rapidly bore down on the plane from the left and a little behind. "It was moving upwards and downwards at will, all around us, and performing movements that would be impossible for any conventional machine," Tejada said. He added that it seemed to be as big as a jumbo-jet.

The unidentified object followed the aircraft for about eight minutes. About sixty miles from Valencia, the speed and closeness of the object forced the plane to make a sharp turn to avoid a possible collision. It disappeared after another thirty miles.

The airport's director, traffic controller, and other personnel confirmed seeing something with red lights. News reporter Juan Benitez also learned later that the Spanish air force had picked up the UFO on military radar in the same area as the airliner. Minutes after Tejada had landed at Valencia, two air force planes were dispatched and sighted the object, one pilot reporting close physical encounters with what he described as a UFO.

Cayce's Cosmic Knowledge

Edgar Cayce, America's best-known clairvoyant, once dreamed he was being chased by Indians on the Ohio River and that they were going to kill him. He had told only his immediate family of the dream. So he was rather surprised one day in 1923 when a young boy climbed into his lap and said, "We were hungry together at the river."

Cayce was an active churchgoer throughout his life and was inclined to dismiss reincarnation as unchristian—that is, until he recalled his own former lives. While in a trance state, Cayce was surprised to learn not only that he had been a British soldier in colonial America but also that he had been a high priest in ancient Egypt and an apothecary in the Trojan War.

Although he had been reluctant, at first, to explore reincarnation, Cayce became convinced that past lives were a reality after remembering his own—and having the memory confirmed by a past-life compatriot in the form of a young boy.

Can Animals Reason in Human Terms?

A number of animals, such as horses, donkeys, pigeons, dogs, camels, elephants, and oxen, have been trained to perform work for man. Other animals, bears, monkeys, ponies, goats, lions, tigers, porpoises, seals, and killer whales, have been trained to perform tricks, based on a system of rewards and punishments.

But sometimes it seems that to perform work at higher levels, animals would have to reason beyond instinct, and reason is something commonly believed to distinguish man from the animals.

Can animals reason like man? Certain cases indicate the possibility. German police dogs, for example, were used during World War II in concentration camp mines to count the groups of prisoners entering the slowly moving elevators descending and ascending automatically from the depths of the mines. The dogs were taught to shepherd and count the prisoners as they entered and exited up to the number of twelve and, if there were more or less, to alert the armed guards by barking.

An African baboon was used by an injured railroad worker in Africa in 1877. James Wide had lost his legs in a railroad accident and was given a less active job as signalman. His pet baboon named Jack did the housework that Wide could no longer perform and took care of the garden. Jack pushed Wide as he worked in a railroad car along the rails and worked the levers and signals, and opened and closed siding switches. Wide operated successfully like this for years and never caused an accident or delay.

Herodotus, the famous traveler and commentator of ancient Greece, recounts that the priests of pharaonic Egypt kept baboons in the temples, gave them brooms, and taught them to sweep the temple floors. The baboons learned quickly and kept the temples clean. If the baboons could reason, they may have been flattered by the fact that many temples featured statues of baboon-headed gods.

Meteorite Attack

Bound for Frankfurt, Germany, an Olympic Airlines commercial flight was struck by a foreign object shortly after takeoff from Athens on November 24, 1983. Flying at an altitude of thirty thousand feet over northern Italy, according to Athens newspapers, the plane was struck by "something" that hit the front right window of the cockpit and broke the glass. The crew managed to descend and continued the flight at a lower altitude to maintain internal air pressure. The sixty passengers didn't know that anything out of the ordinary had occurred until the plane reached its destination and headed directly for repairs.

The Fish That Came from Nowhere

In Greek mythology, Hercules once exterminated the *Stymphalides ornithes*, the wild, man-eating birds with iron claws which terrorized the people living in Stymphalis. Today, that locale in the mountains of Corinthia is mostly farmland, except for the nearby Stymphalia Lake, once big and rich in fish.

Fishermen made a fairly prosperous living from the lake until 1976, when drought caused the lake to dry up, its surface eventually reduced to less than half its original surface area of forty-five thousand acres. The fish soon died and completely disappeared from its shallow, muddy water.

Although the drought continued into 1978, the waters began to rise again suddenly in February of that year, and the lake soon returned to its original size. Fish, moreover, mysteriously reappeared. Within a month, the publication *Nea* reported, fishermen were taking their boats out and returning with eighty pounds of fish every day.

Mass Fish Faintings

Fishermen have long cast their nets in the waters around the Greek island of Elaffonisos, near Cape Malea. During the last two weeks of October 1986, however, they found the area ladened with deep-sea fish floating on the surface, alive but unconscious.

Something seemed to paralyze the fish's nervous systems, but curiously, the Greek publication *Ethnos* pointed out, fish that normally live near the surface were unaffected. Icthyological and toxicological studies of the fish were unable to determine the cause of the mass faintings.

It's not the first time, of course, that the phenomenon of mass fish faintings has occurred in Greek waters. From 1984 to 1986 alone, deep-sea fish were found floating in the Bay of Canea near the island of Crete and in the area of Gythium near Elaffonisos Island.

Prehistoric Cretan Flying Reptile

In 1986, according to the Greek newspaper *Ethnos*, Nikolaos Sfakianakis, Nikolaos Chalkiadakis, and Manolis Calaitzis went hunting along a small river in the Asterousia Mountains in western Crete. At about 8:30 one morning during the outing, they heard a strange noise that sounded like the flapping of a bird's wings. At first they paid no attention, but they eventually sighted a huge, dark gray bird gliding not far above.

The winged creature was odd looking, to say the least. Seemingly composed of membranes, its wings reminded the threesome of those of a bat, except they had fingerlike protrusions. Its hind legs, moreover, had large, obviously sharp claws and its beak was similar to a pelican's. The men watched the odd animal until it flew into the mountains and disappeared.

Returning home, the three men searched in several books until they found a similar depiction. The only picture they found that even closely resembled their bird was that of the pterodactyl, a flying reptile that supposedly became extinct millions of years ago.

The Unfriendly Skies of West Virginia.

Delta Airlines flight 1083 departed Pittsburgh on June 15, 1987, bound for Atlanta. En route, the passenger plane was flying over West Virginia when the pilot sighted an object heading toward the craft. The four-foot-long, finned "missile," he told the *St. Louis Post-Dispatch*, was traveling with great speed and narrowly missed the plane as it passed slightly below it and to the side.

The Defense Department denied ownership of the so-called missile, and the National Weather Service claimed it was probably not one of its instruments. At the New York regional headquarters of the Federal Aviation Administration (FAA), spokesperson Kathleen Bergen proposed that it may have been a blimp-shaped helium balloon. The weather service, however, countered that the wind in the jet stream over West Virginia at the time was too weak to make a balloon move as swiftly as the pilot said the object had.

Nevertheless the FAA's official position was that the object was an escaped promotional balloon. "Balloons can travel pretty far," Bergen explained, adding, "We don't acknowledge the existence of UFOs."

Mexican Psychic

Under hypnosis in 1919 to treat her insomnia, Maria Reyes Zierold happened to tell Gustav Pagenstecher, a German physician practicing in Mexico, that his daughter was listening at the door to the office. To satisfy the woman that there was, indeed, no one there, Pagenstecher opened the door, but was surprised to find the child there just as the patient had claimed. The incident intrigued the good doctor and, with Zierold's permission, he began to investigate her possible clairvoyance.

Pagenstecher soon discovered that Zierold was able to give a vivid description of events connected to any object she held in her hands while in a hypnotized state. While holding a piece of string, for example, she envisioned a battlefield on a cold, foggy day. There were groups of men and continuous gunfire. "I see a big ball coming through the air with great speed," she suddenly exclaimed. "It's dropping in the middle of fifteen men, tearing them to pieces." The string, it turned out, had originally been attached to a German soldier's dog tag. The scene Zierold reported was, the soldier said, "the first great impression I received of the war."

Hearing of Pagenstecher's studies of Zierold, the American Society for Psychical Research's Walter Prince soon arrived to determine whether Zierold was telepathic or genuinely clairvoyant. One experiment he used involved two identical pieces of silk enclosed in identical boxes. He mixed them up so that even he didn't know which was which. Holding one box, Zierold described a Mexican church and dancing Indians; the other, she said, gave her the impression of a French ribbon factory. In fact, the first was from a church altar while the second had come directly from the manufacturer.

Bridey Murphy

A good dancer of Irish jigs, Bridget (Bridey) Murphy, the daughter of Duncan and Kathleen Murphy, Irish Protestant residents of Cork, also read Irish mythology and sang Irish songs. In 1818, Bridey married a Catholic named Brian MacCarthy and they traveled by carriage to Belfast. Bridey, however, wasn't an outstanding person in Irish history and we would probably know nothing about her had it not been for Virginia Tighe, a resident of Madison, Wisconsin, who grew up in Chicago.

During a number of hypnotic regressions from November 1952 to October 1953, Tighe revealed her previous life as Bridey Murphy in early nineteenth-century Ireland. Speaking as Bridey, Tighe had an Irish accent, often accurately using words with meanings that had changed since the nineteenth century: Referring to a child's pinafore, for example, she used the word *slip* and not the more common modern word *petticoat*.

Tighe had never visited Ireland and strongly denied allegations that she had ever associated with Irish people. Yet while still under her trance, she once danced "The Morning Jig," ending her performance with a stylized yawn. Her description of another dance was confirmed by a woman whose parents had danced it. Tighe also correctly described the procedure used during Bridey's lifetime for kissing the Blarney Stone.

According to Bridey (through Tighe), among other family details, her brother Duncan was born in 1796 and married Aimee, the daughter of the headmistress at a school Bridey attended when she was fifteen years old. After her own marriage, she and her husband traveled by carriage to Belfast through towns that she named. They worshiped at Father John Gorman's St. Theresa's Church and shopped in stores, which she named; she also correctly described the coins used during that period. And uillean pipes, she said, were played at her funeral.

Commissioned by the American magazine *Empire*, William Barker spent three weeks in Ireland investigating Bridey's story. He was able to confirm some of the facts, particularly the insignificant details; he proved some to be wrong, however, and was unable to confirm others.

Barker couldn't verify dates of births, marriages, or deaths because Cork officials didn't keep such records until 1864; and if the Murphys noted the occasions in the family Bible, as was the custom, its whereabouts was unknown. Nor was any information found concerning Father Gorman or St. Theresa's Church. But after painstaking research, Barker did discover that Carrigan and Farr, two shops mentioned by Bridey, had both existed. The uillean pipes, moreover, had been once customarily played at funerals because of their soft tones.

Argentine UFO

Two miles outside the small town of Trancas in northwestern Argentina, the Moreno family's Santa Teresa Ranch has its own electric power plant. When it broke down on the evening of October 21, 1963, the household retired early, while twenty-one-year-old Yolie de Valle Moreno stayed awake to feed her infant son.

The house was still and quiet when the maid, Dora, suddenly knocked on Yolie's door, crying that there were strange lights outside. The whole farmyard seemed to be illuminated. Both Yolie and her sister Yolanda went out to investigate. In the distance to the east, near the railroad tracks, they saw two bright, disc-shaped objects connected by a shining tube. It looked, Yolie said, "like a small train, intensely illuminated." They could also make out a number of shadows moving within the tube. They suspected, at first, that there may have been a derailment.

As they walked around to the front of the house, they saw two pale greenish lights near the gate of the farm. As Yolie directed the flashlight toward it, she realized it was a disc-shaped, domed object, about thirty feet wide. It hung in midair while emitting a slight hum. Through its six windows the women could see a band of multicolored light begin rotating as a white mist enveloped the object. Without warning, flames shot out, knocking the women to the ground.

Next, a tube of light, about ten feet wide, emerged from the top of the object and probed the features of the house. Three more objects appeared on the railroad tracks and directed ten-foot-wide beams of light toward the henhouse, the tractor shed, and a neighbor's house. Yolie ran inside where the temperature had risen from 60°F to a stifling 104°F, and the air smelled of sulfur.

After about a total of forty minutes, the object at the farm's gate retracted its light and joined the others on the tracks. Finally all six objects rose and flew off toward Sierra de Medina, a mountain range to the east.

The cloud that had enveloped the object nearest the house didn't dissipate until four hours later. A journalist who visited the family the next day said the heat and the smell of sulfur still lingered. What's more, a pile of small white balls, forming a perfect three-foot cone, lay beneath the spot where the object had hovered outside the gate; similar balls were found on the tracks. Later analysis at the University of Tucuman's Institute of Chemical Engineering determined they were composed mostly of calcium carbonate, with a small percentage of potassium carbonate.

In a later inquiry, half a dozen other members of the community told local police that they had seen the illuminated objects on the railroad tracks as well. One man said he saw six disc-shaped objects flying across the sky at 10:15 P.M., about the time the Moreno's ordeal ended.

Lake Guns

Each autumn, Albert Ingalls returns to Seneca Lake, where he spent months swimming, camping, boating, and fishing in his youth. Almost every day during the season, he hears distant, muffled explosions reverberating over the area. Indeed, even before the first settlers arrived, Native Americans in the region experienced the sounds, resembling the explosion of guns.

Booming lake guns, of course, have been reported in a number of countries, including Italy, Haiti, Belgium, and throughout Africa. In Northern Ireland, for example, cannonlike sounds are heard throughout the year at Lough Neagh, a lake covering 150 square miles which was created by volcanic eruptions. Although fishermen are often on the lake, no one has ever noticed any movement in the water and the booming seems always to be heard in the distance. Near the North Sea, the lake was frozen over during the winter of 1896. In that year, the Reverend W. S. Smith reported that he and other skaters on the lake heard the explosions and estimated they occurred about a half mile away. The ice, they noticed, was not disturbed.

No one knows the origin of the lake guns for sure, though theories have been kicked around. In one hypothesis, for instance, scientists have suggested that the gun sounds are created as natural gas escapes from sandstone stratum hundreds or even thousands of feet below the surface of the lakes. The gas shoots upward through the water, exploding at the surface. No large bubbles or volumes of gas have ever been seen in the lakes, the theory goes, because the gas breaks up into small bubbles before it reaches the surface.

One investigator, Rochester Gas and Electric Corporation geologist A. M. Beebee, has suggested that the guns heard in Seneca Lake may eventually die out. The reason: Rochester Gas and Electric's drilling in nearby gas wells will diminish gas pressure below the lake. The natural gas will then no longer escape through the lake.

Acoustic Mirages

Ann H. Bourhill of Transvaal, South Africa, was awakened by the apparent sound of cannons on June 14, 1903. The noise was followed by a long "whizzing," with a second explosion a few seconds later. Not long afterward, another acoustic episode occurred, giving the impression that a large structure may have been bombed. What's more, similar sounds were heard by others as far as ten or twelve miles away.

This incident, moreover, is not unique. Unexplained detonations have been reported for decades around the world. Though the cause remains a mystery, some modern experts now suggest that the sounds result from electrical disturbances in the atmosphere at the time.

One observer in Texas, for instance, claimed to have heard a whizzing sound before he actually saw a meteor entering the atmosphere. Studying the phenomenon, American meteor expert H. H. Nininger hypothesized that the sound resulted when the human ear converted the electrical activity surrounding the meteor to sound. Though no one has proposed the mechanism by which this might occur, researchers have suggested that acoustic mirages might result from electrical activity generated by supersonic jets and earthquakes as well.

Whispering Lake

S. A. Forbes was boating on Shoshone Lake in Yellowstone National Park when he heard a mysterious sound. Like others who have experienced the phenomenon there and at Yellowstone Lake, he thought of a vibrating harp or the sound of telegraph wires "swinging regularly and rapidly in the wind," or even voices heard faintly overhead.

The noise began softly, seemingly in the distance, he reported in the *Bulletin of the United States Fish Commission.* Then it grew increasingly louder as it approached, and it finally died out as it moved onward in the opposite distance. Occurring repeatedly, the traveling sound lasted from a few seconds to more than half a minute.

The sound at Shoshone Lake, as well as at Yellowstone Lake, where it occurs even more frequently, is usually noticed on bright, still mornings shortly after sunrise, but it has also been heard later in the day when the wind is blowing. Numerous theories have emerged to explain the phenomenon—electricity, whistling of ducks' wings, insects, waterfalls and geysers, or simply the wind.

Erratic Meteors

Spotted on August 10, 1972, over the western United States and Canada, the bluish white meteor was a blazing ball of fire. Traveling slowly across the sky, it left a trail of smoke that remained for at least an hour after the fiery sphere disappeared.

Once entering Earth's atmosphere, a meteor almost always strikes the earth. But this one, according to *Nature* magazine, "bounced off the atmosphere and flew back into space."

On other occasions, slow-moving meteors have been observed to bounce or dip during their trajectory en route to Earth's surface. On November 14, 1960, for example, an officer on the S. S. *Hector*, sailing from Adelaide, Australia, to Aden in South Yemen, observed such a meteor. Unusually brilliant and visible for just two seconds, it appeared to suddenly dip and then climb again. Yet other erratic meteors have never penetrated to the surface, instead skipping across the upper atmosphere like stones upon water.

Gas and other volatile materials in a meteor's composition are heated by atmospheric friction and expand, sometimes throwing the celestial object off course. Meteors, after all, are not perfectly formed spheres and, therefore, do not always appear to behave in rational ways.

The Fata Morgana

When the sun reaches a certain point in the sky and the sea is calm, you can look out across the straits of Messina and see images of arches, towers, and palaces with their balconies and windows. Also visible are rows of trees, as well as figures on horseback and on foot.

If a fog hangs over the water, moreover, the reflections of the objects appear in the air as well. Named after King Arthur's sister Morgan le Fay, who conjured up towns and harbors to lure seamen to their deaths, the fata morgana is a mirage of fantastic cities and countrysides and occurs in a number of places around the world, but most often in colder climates—in the Firth of Forth, Scotland, for example.

No one has ever adequately explained these spectral visions, though some pundits have claimed that if you fixate on rocks and a beach coast long enough, you may see things that are not really there.

Mirage at Sea

On April 15, 1949, the second officer of the *Stirling Castle* spotted a vessel off its port bow and five miles away in the English Channel. Through his binoculars, the crewman reported in the *Marine Observer*, he saw the boat's lights move for brief periods. The lights seemed to generate a double image, and as the higher image merged with the lower one, the crewman actually saw vertical strips of light.

Such mirages are usually responsible for the double images of low-altitude stars and planets, terrestrial ghost lights, and probably a number of UFO sightings. They aren't classic fata morganas, but the elongation of the images is part of the same optical process that distorts distant shores.

Apparitions of the Virgin Mary

It's not unusual for a lone witness to claim he or she has seen a ghostly apparition. But in Zeitoun, Egypt, *thousands* of people insist they've seen an eerie shining figure, believed by many to be the Virgin Mary, atop St. Mary's Coptic church.

The strange sightings began in April 1968 and continued until 1971. Then they started up again in the mid-1980s, this time over another Coptic church outside of Cairo, St. Demiana's. The figure, accompanied by a bright light, at first appeared only in the early morning. Later on, she was seen briefly several times each night.

Huge crowds gathered in the streets below, and several witnesses said the dome of the church inexplicably glowed during these visitations. Others reported that the smell of incense sometimes pervaded the entire area.

On one occasion the mysterious lady "stayed for twenty minutes," according to journalist Mousaad Sadik, who wrote about the apparition in the Cairo-based paper *Watani*. "Spellbound," he reported the next day, "the people started to plead and pray."

Pacific Coast Vikings

●────────────────────────────────────

With the discovery of the ancient remains of Norse villages in Newfoundland and northern Labrador, few people now doubt that seafaring Vikings visited the New World long before Columbus. But there are also scattered clues that the seafarers didn't stay put on America's eastern shore. In fact, they appear to have made it all the way around the top of North America to the Pacific Coast.

As D. and M. R. Cooledge pointed out in their book *Last of the Seris*, during the tenth and eleventh centuries, when the great Viking explorers Eric the Red and Leif Ericson were roving the oceans, the Northern Hemisphere was the warmest it had been since the Ice Age. With ice floes melted or greatly diminished, Viking ships would have had little trouble navigating through the islands dotting the Northwest Passage above Canada.

The tribal legends of the Seris suggest that Norse explorers visited the Indians' homeland on Tiburón Island in the Gulf of California. According to a paper presented at the 1953 Toronto Meteorological Conference by Ronald L. Ives of the Cornell Aeronautical Laboratory, the Seri tribe told of the "Come-from-Afar-Men" who landed on Tiburón from a "long boat with a head like a snake . . . a long time ago when God was a little boy." The Seri tradition holds that these men had white hair and beards; their women were redheads.

According to the Indian tale, the strangers hunted whales in the gulf and cooked them on shore. They sailed away to the south but their ship was soon torn apart by the pounding breakers. The survivors of the shipwreck swam to shore where they were helped by the Mayo tribe. The strangers eventually intermarried with the Indians.

Is this historical fact or fantasy? To this day, some Mayo Indians are born with blonde hair, blue eyes, or both, which they say are passed down from the "Come-from-Afar-Men." In fact, until the 1920s, anyone who married outside of the tribe was expelled because the Mayos were adamant about retaining this ancient heritage.

Authors Brad Williams and Choral Pepper point out in *The Mysterious West* that actual Viking ships have been found in the American West. An elderly widow in Baja, California, found the hull of an ancient ship, with shields like those used by the Norse on its gunwales, on a canyon floor near the United States and Mexico border. And noted antiquarian researchers Louis and Myrtle Botts of Julian, California, found the dragon prow of what appeared to be a Viking ship in March 1933. It was sticking out of a canyon wall near Agua Caliente Springs, on the United States side of the Mexican border. Before they could excavate it, however, an earthquake triggered a rockslide that sealed off the canyon.

Ancient Roman Artifacts in Arizona

On September 13, 1924, Charles Manier found something on Silverbell Road northwest of Tucson, Arizona, that, according to the accepted record of world history, shouldn't have been there. The find included an array of ancient Roman relics made of lead. The anachronistic trove included more than thirty relics, including a sixty-two-pound cross, daggers, batons, spears, and swordlike weapons.

Archaeologists and mine engineers present during the digs noticed that the objects were found encrusted in caliche—a sheet of hard, crusty material that "grows" because of a reaction of chemicals and water in desert soils over many years. That such heavy deposits of caliche had developed around metal objects at such depths, they concluded, meant the Roman artifacts had to have been very old.

As the caliche was removed from the objects, Latin words, letters, and graphic symbols became visible on many of the items. Researchers, who used this information to date the artifacts to between A.D. 560 and 800, suggested that, just maybe, a band of Roman adventurers had once explored what is now Arizona.

The Arctic Metropolis

When archaeologists Magnus Marks and Froelich Rainey were in the Arctic for a second season of digging at Ipiutak in June 1940, they made an astonishing discovery. They had arrived just at the time when grass and moss in that location were becoming green—but not everywhere. Some areas of grass were higher and literally yellow, and the researchers noticed that the discoloration created a clear pattern of yellow squares. Further investigation showed that the yellow grass was growing over the ancient ruins of what Rainey called an "Arctic metropolis."

Long avenues of yellow squares marked over six hundred houses, extending east and west along the north shore. Later digs showed that more than two hundred additional houses were also buried far beneath the sand. The town was almost a mile long and about a quarter of a mile wide. Rainey estimated that around four thousand people lived in the town—an incredible number of inhabitants for a hunting village in the Arctic.

Rainey and Marks discovered elaborate and sophisticated carvings at the Ipiutak site which show that the people were most likely not related to primitive Eskimo cultures. Instead, Rainey theorized "the people of this Arctic metropolis brought their arts from some center of cultural advance."

Castles in the Sky

Every year from June 21 to July 10, "The Silent City of Alaska" appears on the Mount Fairweather glacier. Visible for about two hours between 7:00 and 9:00 P.M., the mirage is believed to be a mirror representation of Bristol, England, some twenty-five hundred miles away, further than any other mirage has been seen. (The greatest distance of any other projected mirage has been just six hundred miles.) Indeed, according to investigators, the vision includes a tower that seems to be an exact replica of one at St. Mary Redcliff.

The explanation for this mysterious mirage is not known for sure, but many experts suggest it may be the result of lenslike layers of air that magnify distant scenes.

Magnificent Memory

There have been many tales of individuals, from Mozart to King George III, who possessed the gift of remarkable memory in particular areas of knowledge. Some calendar experts have been able to report the day of the week for any date given in the span of a hundred years.

But Englishman Daniel McCartney had the distinction of remembering everything that had ever passed through his mind during most of his life. Once, at a public meeting to demonstrate and prove his ability, with someone prepared to verify McCartney's accuracy, a man in the audience asked McCartney to identify the day of the week for a particular date fifteen years earlier. McCartney replied, "Friday," and the questioner told him he was wrong. It had been the man's wedding day, he said, and it had been a Thursday. To settle the argument, the verifier checked an old calendar and determined that, indeed, McCartney was correct. McCartney's ability, however, went beyond just dates and weather reports—he could even remember what he had had for breakfast, lunch, and dinner for the last forty years. He retained his remarkable memory until the day he died in 1887 at the age of seventy.

The Incredible Building Rocks
of the Incas

Many of the monumental stone ruins of Peru and Bolivia pose architectural and archaeological mysteries. The enormous stones of the walls of Sacsahuaman and Ollantay in Peru and Tiahuanaco in Bolivia were built by pre-Incan cultures. Somehow these early peoples transported great building stones, many weighing 150 tons each, across mountains, rivers, and deep valleys and then set them up on other mountains. They remain in place today despite earthquakes that have leveled later cities built on their sites. The intervening earthquakes have not tumbled these rocks, which were linked together by angles, curves, and interstices indicating that the stones were cut and fitted together exactly more or less like a three-dimensional jigsaw puzzle.

There is no indication of how the builders could have succeeded in getting these enormous rocks to fit so closely together. Not even a thin blade can be pushed between them, and there is no sign of the use of mortar. It seems impossible that such stones could have been shaped with stone hammers or other primitive means and then lifted in and out of position until the builders obtained a perfect fit.

Colonel Percy Fawcett, the British writer-adventurer who explored the mountain and jungle regions of central South America for many years, has suggested that the unusual and cohesive joining together of the huge stones may have been made possible through the use of a liquid or paste employed by the ancient builders.

Drawing on his own experience, he tells of some wet leaves carried by jungle birds in their beaks to soften stone in walls of canyons over rivers, thus enabling them to peck out rookeries for themselves in the canyon walls. A further report tells of a man who, after crossing a field covered with low plants with red leaves, found that his long spurs had softened and melted at the ends. Indians later asked him whether he had walked through a field of such plants and told him that the plants were once used by the Incas to "melt" rocks.

A like experience of melting occurred, according to Fawcett, when some American engineers dug up a sealed container from an ancient tomb. It still had in it some liquid that they presumed was *chicha*, a strong Andean drink. When they offered it to one of their workmen, the man refused. When they tried to force him to drink it, there was a struggle and the jar fell and broke on a rock. As they watched, the rock under the puddle of liquid began to soften and then, as others came from the camp to look, it reverted to its original hardness.

Colonel Fawcett could not explain the mystery. Several years after the incident, in 1924, he made his personal contribution to South American mysteries by disappearing near the Xingu, one of the tributaries of the Amazon.

Musical Sands

Jebel Nagus, a high sand slope along the west coast of the Sinai peninsula, creates loud musical sounds when the sands are disturbed. According to native legend, the music comes from the *nagus*, or wooden gong, of a monastery buried in the area. The sound is difficult to describe, according to visitors who have heard it. In fact, it doesn't really resemble the sound of a gong or bell at all. Some have said it sounds like a harp or the noise produced by drawing a finger around the wet rim of a glass. Others have compared it to the air rushing into the mouth of an empty metal flask, the deeper tones of a cello, or the hum of a spinning top.

Similar singing sands have been heard around the world—at Reg-Ravan, north of Kabul, Afghanistan, and on the Arequipa plains of Peru, for example. Most, however, sound more like roars, booming noises, or simply squeaks. In the eastern part of Churchill County, Nevada, a four-square-mile hill of moving sand produces a deafening sound that reminds some residents of telephone wires vibrating in the wind.

The Surviving Sister

Retired teachers Margaret and Wilhelmina Dewar had been respectable citizens of Whitley Bay in Northumberland, England. Margaret's character was soon impugned, however, after Wilhelmina's sudden death. In the early morning hours of March 23, 1908, a shocked Margaret summoned neighbors and ushered them up to Wilhelmina's bedroom. There they discovered Wilhelmina's charred body lying in the bed. The linens were mysteriously untouched and there was no sign of a fire anywhere else in the house. This, Margaret said, was how she had found her sister.

At the inquest, the local coroner found Margaret's story difficult to believe. The police, moreover, claimed Margaret was so drunk at the time she couldn't have known what she was saying. The coroner decided to adjourn the investigation to give Margaret time to think about her story.

When the court reconvened, Margaret did, in fact, change her story: She had found Wilhelmina on fire, but alive, elsewhere in the house, she said. She then helped her sister upstairs, where she died. The court accepted this more plausible story, and no one even questioned how Wilhelmina had been incinerated in a bed that she apparently left unscathed.

The Largest Mammal Population

As other animal species have disappeared, or nearly disappeared, two animal groups have continued to grow, rivaling each other in numbers—human beings and brown rats.

Now, in the latter part of the twentieth century, the human

population of Earth has passed the rat population in number for the first time, and the rate of increase of the human population has been estimated to be doubling every thirty-five years. Up to now certain controls, such as wars, famines, plagues (usually spread by rats), and other disasters have served to keep the human population in check, but now, with new medical developments, the surge in the number of humans is greater than ever before. This remarkable increase may soon lead to a world food shortage as well as a lack of living space. This may already be observed in a number of countries throughout the world.

There exists an interesting human-rat symbiosis, especially beneficial to the rats, in that rats congregate in and under human cities and farmlands—in fact, anywhere people live and provide such sustenance as stored food supplies or garbage. Rats have been carried by human-engineered transportation, notably ships, to all parts of the Earth. Attempts to cut down the rats' rate of increase (female rats can have litters of five or six every six weeks!) by poison, chemicals, the use of ferrets, dogs, and cats have shown results in some areas, but rats, by some believed to be the most intelligent of mammals, seem to successfully resist all attempts to destroy or significantly limit their species.

As space probes sent to the planets and beyond become more commonplace and the search for new habitats for the world's surplus human population is intensified, it is hoped that experimental rats will not be included on space vehicles, lest they find a way on new planets to dispute man's dominion— as they have so long done on Earth.

Human Incinerators and M.D.s

While driving through Ayer, Massachusetts, on May 12, 1890, Doctor B. H. Hartwell was stopped and called into a nearby woods. There he and other witnesses saw a woman crouching as flames engulfed her body. Neither Dr. Hartwell nor other witnesses were able to determine the cause of the fire.

Although there have been relatively few open admissions, Dr. Hartwell has not been the only physician to encounter incidents of spontaneous human combustion. At a Massachusetts Medico-Legal Society lecture, held in the autumn of 1959, many doctors said they'd had experience with spontaneous human combustion as well. British physician D. J. Gee of the University of Leeds gave the keynote lecture. He was met with a round of applause and, much to his surprise, found that several doctors in attendance claimed similar experiences as well. The phenomenon was not as uncommon as it might appear based on written reports, the group declared. One doctor even said he came across cases of spontaneous human combustion once every four years.

Talking Chopper

"You needn't bother going. It won't do the slightest good," a voice said, interrupting West German dentist Kurt Bachseitz as he spoke on the phone with a patient.

Over the next couple months, Bachseitz repeatedly heard the voice. Often it was wisecracking and insolent. Calling itself "Chopper," the voice even developed an interest in the doctor's receptionist, Claudia. It was soon projecting from everywhere, including the sink and the toilet.

Suspecting electronic interference from a ham radio operator, the local telephone company investigated. It decided to install a new line in the doctor's office and re-lay the telephone cable throughout the building. Not only did the voice continue its pronouncements, but eventually it was heard over a Munich radio station. "You've taken away my switchboard," Chopper said. "But I can hear you just as well. So don't think I'm not listening in!"

Chopper's story hit all the newspapers and it seemed everyone had an explanation for the voice; psychics suggested it was a paranormal phenomenon. A philosopher said it might be a manifestation of the subconscious. Some doctors proposed that it was the mental projection of a cancer patient whose vocal chords had been surgically removed.

The truth, however, was revealed in March 1982. It had been a practical joke instigated by the dentist himself, who was also an accomplished ventriloquist. Thereafter, Bachseitz closed his office and was admitted to a sanitorium.

A Movable Light

A torpedo-shaped cloud of light appeared on the horizon of northern Europe on November 17, 1882. For months afterward, scientists debated its nature, finally terming it an "auroral meteor" because it swept purposefully across the sky like a large meteor.

A stranger event occurred over Cincinnati in 1849: A bright streak of light suddenly appeared and, after rising to a certain point above the horizon, seemed to explode, spreading over the entire sky. It was then followed by five consecutive bursts of light, all originating from the same point.

Unlike actual meteors composed of rock and metals, auroral meteors are probably disturbances moving through the upper atmosphere. No one knows exactly what causes them, but two possible suspects are gravity waves and gusts of solar wind.

The Man Who Took Photos with His Mind

When Ted Serios of Chicago recovered from a serious illness, he found he'd developed a most unusual talent. He could take Polaroid photographs of scenes miles away by just turning the camera toward his head and snapping a picture.

In 1963 a publisher in Evanston, Illinois, decided to test Serios's unexplained powers. He presented Serios with a Polaroid camera loaded with fresh film and watched as the psychic photographer held the camera at arm's length so that the lens faced him. Then Serios pushed down the shutter release.

The photograph was pulled from the camera and the publisher observed it being developed. The words "air division" showed up clearly on some kind of airplane hangar. Other fragments of words that appeared seemed to refer to the Canadian Mounted Police.

The snapshot was sent to the Mounties' headquarters and was soon identified as the Canadian Mounted Police hangar in Rockcliffe, Ontario. Somehow, Ted Serios had managed to take a photograph of an airport hundreds of miles from where he sat—just by pointing a camera at his mysterious brain.

The Native American Messiah

Sometime in the late 1880s, a Cheyenne set out from his tribe to grieve for the loss of a relative, as was the custom. During the process, he fell into a trance and dreamed that he wandered the country. He saw wildlife that had long disappeared from his people's hunting grounds, and he eventually came upon an encampment of dead family members enjoying an abundant life. As he gazed upon the settlement, he noticed a great, brilliant light that grew and extended from the village to the horizon. Along the path's light, a robe-clad figure, with skin lighter than that of the Cheyenne's own people, approached and proclaimed himself to be the Son of God. He had come, he said, to help the Indians. He could restore their game, eliminate hunger, and reunite the living and the dead. The wicked white race, he added, would perish if only the Indians worshiped and followed him.

When the Cheyenne returned home, he told no one of his dream. Shortly afterward, however, various people among the Cheyenne and other tribes began having similar visions and some heard songs and voices as well. They gathered to sing the songs, dancing to the rhythms. As in ancient traditional Indian cults, the people would fall into trances as they practiced their ritual. Soon, people were repeating tales of having seen the Messiah in the mountains near Mexico.

Although the belief in a messiah is a fundamental myth, no one could ever explain why the visions of the Cheyenne incorporated the image of Christ.

Phantom Rock Throwers

On one suburban street in Birmingham, England, the residents live a comfortable middle-class life in every way but one: Night after night, for years, stones have been hurled at the backs of their homes. Windows were broken, doors marred, and roofs damaged. And finally, unable to locate the culprits, the beleaguered residents of Thornton Road went to the police.

A routine investigation failed to reveal anything, and the matter was finally turned over to Chief Inspector Len Turley. To get to the bottom of the mystery, Turley and his men tried everything: They conducted all-night stakeouts, used automatic cameras, and even monitored the houses through periods of bitter cold. Studying the rocks themselves, investigators found they were of the type found in almost every garden, though devoid of any markings, prints, or even soil, as though they had been washed.

Resigned to this fate, the residents have boarded up their back windows and erected chicken wire screen to protect their homes. They go to the backyard at dusk only if necessary, and, they say, it is an ordeal.

Transcending Death

Does the spark of human consciousness survive death? Maybe so, according to Polish physicist Janusz Slawinski.

To prove this notion, Slawinski points to a well-known phenomenon in which a collection of cells in a laboratory dish emit a burst of radiation as they die. According to Slawinski's calculations, this burst is powerful enough to encode reams of complex information, including human memory and consciousness itself.

Slawinski believes we may sometimes emit what he terms the "death flash" while we are still alive, accounting for the out-of-body experience. This burst may also be the raison d'être for the near-death experience, in which consciousness literally leaves the body as it dies.

Says Slawinski, "electromagnetic radiation released by living systems provides a realistic basis for the possibility of life after death."

Therese Neumann

The stigmata—bodily marks resembling the wounds of the crucified Christ—usually manifest themselves in female subjects. One of the more renowned women to suffer the experience was Therese Neumann, a poor peasant girl born in Konnersreuth, Bavaria, in 1898.

Neumann's childhood seemed normal, even mundane. She worked as a domestic on neighboring farms, until a series of inexplicable illnesses rendered labor impossible. Then during the Lenten season of 1926, she "saw" Jesus and her current illness was cured. In its stead, however, her body was wracked with the

Passion—the five traditional wounds associated with Christ's crucifixion, as well as whip lashes across the back and thorn pricks on the head.

Neumann's wounds would open every Good Friday and during Lent for the next thirty-two years, sometimes gushing as much as a pint of blood and causing her to lose as much as eight pounds during the course of a single affliction.

Neumann spent a largely reclusive life, passing much of her time in bed shrouded in white linens. She was examined extensively by the medical profession of the day, but no hint of a hoax or trickery was ever remotely entertained.

Almost as startling as Neumann's stigmata was her ability to go without food or water for extended periods of time. She survived on wine and Communion wafers for the last three and a half decades of her life. Given her circumstances, Neumann remained reasonably healthy. She continued to have visions and ecstatic trances until her death in 1962.

First UFO Report

Washington State businessman Kenneth Arnold was about to fly from Chehalis to Yakima in his private jet when his flight was delayed. A Marine Corps transport plane was missing in the region, it seemed, and the air space was reserved for a search. At about 2:00 P.M., however, Arnold got the okay to take off, and he headed toward majestic Mount Ranier. He swung west to give the terrain a quick glance of his own but, finding nothing out of the ordinary, headed on.

He reported the sky clear and the air smooth, and noted that a DC-4 was behind him flying at about fourteen thousand feet. Then, suddenly, he saw a flash of light, as if the sun were being reflected off bright aluminum. Finally he saw nine vehicles in formation, heading from the north toward Mount Ranier. The craft were traveling so fast that Arnold guessed they were new fighter jets on a test flight. The size of each, he determined, was somewhat smaller than the DC-4 still overhead. Later calculations showed the diagonal line of objects, which swerved through the mountain peaks without breaking formation once, to be about five miles long. Arnold clocked the objects as moving at a speed of 1,656.71 miles per hour.

Occasionally, Arnold reported, one of the objects would dip or turn sideways, and he was surprised that he could find no tail. As he scrutinized the strange craft further, however, he was shocked to see a series of saucerlike objects with bubble tops.

Word of Arnold's sighting quickly reached the news media, and the term "flying saucer" was coined. Arnold was flooded with calls from interested citizens around the country. But no government official ever tried to follow up on his case.

In fact, the air force not only denied any unusual sightings that afternoon, it also declared that Arnold had seen a mirage.

Still, wondered Arnold and his supporters, what had happened to the pilot of the DC-4? And what became of the lost transport, which was never accounted for and, they suggest, may never have existed at all?

Croesus and the Oracles

More than two thousand years ago, Croesus, the king of Lydia, became increasingly concerned about the powerful Persians. Before taking any action against his enemies, however, the great leader decided to consult an oracle. But which one? To make his choice, Croesus decided to test seven candidates, six Greek and one from Egypt.

To conduct the test, Croesus dispatched seven messengers. Each visited a different oracle, instructing him or her to describe the king's activities at a specified time and day. Anyone, of course, could have correctly guessed the answer if the monarch had performed a routine task. So old Croesus came up with an elaborate ritual, something only a truly talented oracle would possibly know: He cut a lamb and a tortoise into pieces and boiled the flesh in a brass cauldron covered with a brass lid.

The messengers returned from their mission and the king read the descriptions. Only the oracle at Delphi had known what the king had been doing. In fact, the historian Herodotus tells us that the Pythoness, as the oracle was called, answered even before hearing the question. Croesus was so impressed he showered the oracle with gifts worth more than $100 million by the standards of today.

The Ipswich UFO Incident

At 10:55 on the night of August 13, 1956, a radar operator at the American-leased Royal Air Force (RAF) Bentwaters base near Ipswich, England, picked up a fast-moving target. It appeared when it was just thirty miles to the east, traveling at two thousand to four thousand miles per hour as it headed in from the sea.

A tower operator described the object as "blurred out by its high speed" as it passed directly over the base. Alerted by ground control, an American pilot saw a fuzzy light flash between his aircraft and the ground.

Bentwaters' controller notified the Americans at the RAF's Lakenheath base, where the UFO seemed headed. Shortly afterwards, Lakenheath radar recorded objects traveling at incredible speeds, stopping suddenly, and instantaneously changing course. Ground observers sighted two white lights that came together and disappeared. Officials hesitantly notified the RAF.

The RAF's chief controller dispatched a fighter plane toward the UFO. As the aircraft closed in , however, the UFO suddenly and mysteriously appeared behind the plane. Witnesses said the UFO seemed to flip over as it moved behind the RAF fighter, which then attempted to get behind the UFO.

According to Arizona University atmospheric physicist James McDonald, "The apparently rational, intelligent behavior of the UFO suggests a mechanical device of unknown origin as the most probable explanation."

The United States Air Force Condon Report on UFOs described

the sighting as one of "the most puzzling and unusual cases" ever to emerge.

UFO Photographs

Paul Trent's wife was in the yard feeding the rabbits at 7:45 P.M. on May 11, 1950, when she saw a disc-shaped object moving westward in the northeastern Oregon sky. Responding to her cries, Trent soon realized the unusual nature of the object and ran for his camera, already loaded with a partially used roll of film.

The silent, silvery UFO was slightly tilted, Trent recalls, and appeared to be gliding as it approached. Just before the craft passed overhead, the McMinnville couple felt a breeze. After taking one shot, Trent advanced the film and snapped a second photo, moving to the right to keep the object in view.

Hoping to avoid publicity, Trent had the film developed at a local shop and told few people about the unusual event. Nonetheless, a reporter from the *McMinnville Telephone Register* got wind of the sighting and decided to follow up. The story appeared in the local papers on June 8 and papers in Portland, Oregon, and in Los Angeles picked up the story on June 9 and 10. A week later, *Life* magazine ran the photos.

When the United States Air Force investigated the incident seventeen years later as part of what would become the Condon Report, investigators submitted the photographs to rigorous scientific examination. Afterwards, they had to admit that the photos were genuine.

According to the Condon Report, "This is one of the few UFO reports in which all factors, both psychological and physical, appear to be consistent." To be sure, Trent's photos are not the only UFO pictures that exist. But according to experts, they represent one of the few sets of UFO photos that seem to be legitimate and not the result of accidentally damaged film or a hoax.

UFOs in France

As bizarre as it sounds, grotesque dwarflike aliens in diving suits were reported in Quaroble, France, on September 10, 1954. A week later, a French farmer was bicycling near the town of Cenon when he suddenly started to itch all over. When he stopped alongside the road and dismounted, he became immobilized at the sight of a "machine" ahead of him. A small diving suit–clad creature approached, uttered strange sounds, and touched the farmer's shoulder. It then returned to the object and disappeared inside. The UFO glowed green as it rose into the air and sped away.

Some ten days later, four French children were playing in their father's barn. Hearing the dog bark, the eldest boy went out to investigate and confronted a rectangular creature that, he said, resembled a "sugar cube." Throwing pebbles and shooting a toy arrow at the ET, the boy was pushed to the ground by an invisible force. As he scrambled away, he saw the creature waddle off toward the meadow. Running back to the house, the children saw a glowing red object hovering over the meadow. The next day, investigators discovered a circle of burned grass.

A couple of weeks after that, yet another Frenchman reported an encounter with a four-foot-tall creature in what, again, resembled a diving suit. The creature shuffled along the road before disappearing into the adjacent trees. And the next day, three children saw another four-foot-tall being emerge from a "shiny machine." Later describing the creature as a "ghost" with a hairy face and big eyes, dressed in something akin to a priest's cassock, the children said the being spoke words they didn't understand.

The following day, three men from Bordeaux were driving near Royan on the Atlantic coast of France when they observed a craft hovering about thirty-five feet above the ground. Getting out of their car to investigate, they came upon four three-foot-tall creatures seemingly making repairs under a craft.

According to the experts, UFO reports seem to occur in waves. There was a rash of sightings throughout the Western Hemisphere as well as in Australia and Asia from 1957 to 1958; in South America from 1962 to 1963; and in the United States in 1964. Britain and Italy experienced a wave of sightings from 1977 to 1978. But out of all the UFO waves, the 1954 French wave was the most intense.

Prince Bernhard's Narrow Escape

The long road passed through a meadow and led to the crossing gate at the railroad tracks. Speeding down the road, a car suddenly blew a tire and ran into the gate. A lorry stopped behind it. To complete her dream, she saw the driver, lying dead on the ground. It was Prince Bernhard of the Netherlands.

When she awoke, the dreamer immediately wrote to W. H. C. Tenhaeff, who, describing the case later in the *Journal of the Society for Psychical Research*, identified his subject only as "Mrs. O of Amsterdam."

Mrs. O had described her psychic abilities and precognitive dreams to Tenhaeff before. This dream, however, disturbed her more than most. She mailed the letter almost immediately and it arrived at Tenhaeff's postmarked Saturday, November 27, 1937.

While listening to the radio the following Monday evening, Tenhaeff heard a news report about Prince Bernhard having been in a car accident that day. With the newspaper stories that later appeared, Tenhaeff was able to compare the actual accident with Mrs. O's dream:

Railroad employees, news reports indicated, were working at the viaduct of the Hilversum-Amsterdam Railway, digging sand and loading it onto lorries. As the prince's speeding car approached, one full lorry was being maneuvered onto the road that passed through meadows on its way from Diemen to Amsterdam. The right front of the car collided with the rear of the lorry on the left side. Several people who lived nearby rushed out of their houses with blankets and helped place the two drivers on them until the doctor arrived. Reports mentioned nothing about a flat tire or a collision with the gate visible in newspaper photos. Prince Bernhard, moreover, did not die.

The Year Summer Never Came

"I well remember the seventh of June," Chauncey Jerome of Plymouth, Connecticut, wrote of the year 1816. "I was dressed in thick woolen clothes and had an overcoat on. My hands got so cold that I was obliged to lay down my tools and put on a pair of mittens."

Throughout the entire northeastern United States, the weather that summer was more than unseasonable. From June 6 to 9, severe frosts killed crops. Snow fell on two occasions, though it was heaviest in northern New England, where some areas reported eighteen to twenty inches.

Summer seemed to return toward the end of the month, but in July another frost killed the replanted crops. And on August 20, temperatures dropped again, with frost as far south as northern Connecticut.

No one has ever explained the bizarre summer of 1816. But some modern meteorologists have suggested a possible culprit: volcanic dust from three major eruptions occurring between 1812 and 1817. The volcanic eruptions certainly dispensed great quantities of dust into the atmosphere, the researchers say. This might have blocked the sunlight and caused the extreme cold. Critics of this theory, however, note that when Krakatoa erupted in 1883, it created a spectacular sunset seen around the world—but no change in climate at all.

The Giant Bird of Egypt

In 1821, James Burton discovered three huge conical birds' nests along Egypt's Red Sea coast. Approximately two and a half to three feet wide at their apex and fifteen feet wide at their bases, the nests were each about fifteen feet tall. They were eclectically composed of materials that included sticks, weeds, fish bones, and pieces of woolen clothing. Fashioned into the structure of one nest was an old shoe and a silver watch designed by a watchmaker in the eighteenth century; another included a human thorax. Based on what he learned from neighboring Arabs, Burton determined that these were the nests of a giant bird that had only recently deserted the area.

Reporting on his discovery in the *American Journal of Science*, Burton said that area residents compared the species to the giant bird depicted in the tomb of the pharaoh Khufu, whose pyramid was built around 2100 B.C. The storklike avian of the pharaoh's day had white feathers, a straight, long beak, and long tail feathers. The male of the species had tufts at the back of the head and on the breast. The bird was apparently often caught by people living along the Nile Delta and offered as a gift to the pharaoh.

Because later Egyptian pyramids have no engraving or paintings depicting the birds, it had been assumed, up until Burton's modern discovery, that the creatures had probably become extinct.

Alligators in the Sewers

Claims of alligators in New York sewers might qualify for the most persistent of the urban myths. New Yorkers vacationing in Miami, the story goes, are said to have returned home with baby alligators as pets for their children. The more the alligators grew, however, the less desirable they seemed as playmates. Rather than have them skinned for their hides, parents flushed them down the toilet. Some apparently survived, living in New York City's sewers on a diet of rats and reaching a formidable size.

Is there any truth to this tall tale? Investigating the sewer alligator, cryptozoologist Loren Coleman went searching for the *real* story behind the sewer 'gators—and the origin of the myth. Reporting in the *Journal of American Folklore*, he said that he ended up with many "alligator in the sewer" reports between 1843 and 1973, but few appeared to be real.

One case, however, stood out from the rest. Recorded as fact in the *New York Times* on February 10, 1935, the story's headline read, "Alligator Found in Uptown Sewer."

Boys seemed to be having a great time as they shoveled the last of the winter's snow into a manhole on East 123rd Street near the Harlem River. Noticing that snow seemed to be backing up, however, sixteen-year-old Salvatore Condulucci investigated more closely and he saw something move. After a closer look, he called his friends, insisting there was an alligator below. One by one, they peered down into the manhole and confirmed the story. Yes, there was indeed an alligator, apparently trapped, slashing around in the ice and snow.

Using clothesline they quickly acquired from a nearby store, the boys fashioned a slipknot and lowered the rope into the hole. They maneuvered it until they worked it around the alligator and then, with great difficulty, slowly pulled it up to safety and the street.

Once the critter had been rescued, one of the boys moved to loosen the rope. Opening its jaws and snapping at him, the half-dead alligator certainly didn't seem to be very grateful for its rescue. The boys' curiosity and sympathy quickly turned to fear and animosity. Using their snow shovels, they finished the job begun by the cold water and the melting snow. They then dragged the animal to the store where they'd gotten the rope.

Measuring seven and a half to eight feet long and weighing about 125 pounds, the alligator, authorities theorized, had apparently fallen off a steamboat traveling from the Everglades which had passed 123rd Street. Attempting to escape the cold Harlem River, it swam toward shore and apparently found the opening to the conduit. Struggling through the torrent of melting snow, and already half dead, it finally arrived beneath the manhole.

In Search of Atlantis

According to the theory of continental drift, all of the earth's land masses were once joined together in a single piece. Gradually that piece broke up and moved apart to form the continents as we know them today.

The theory explains the fact that the shapes fit together like pieces of a jigsaw puzzle—all except for the bit between Europe and the United States. That missing piece seems to be the same size and shape as that of the Atlantic's underwater plateau. Could that submarine land mass once have been the lost continent of Atlantis, relegated by most to the status of myth?

Indeed, though many scientists consider Atlantis nothing more than legend, tales of the lost city can be found in every culture on earth. All races, for example, share the story of a great flood that destroyed an entire civilization. And even the name Atlantis appears in various forms around the world. In the Canary Islands there is the term *Atalaya*, whose original inhabitants were supposedly the only survivors of a continent whose mountain peaks became islands as the world was flooded. The Basques of Northern Spain, whose traditions go back to the Stone Age recall a great island in the ocean called *Atlaintica*. The Vikings described the wondrous western land known as *Atli*. In North Africa, there is *Attala*, described by the Berbers as a warlike kingdom once rich in gold and silver. The Aztecs' lore had its form of Atlantis—the legendary land of origin, Aztlán. And North American Indians living near Lake Michigan frequently referred to *Azatlán*, after their ancestors' island in the sea.

Whatever happened to Atlantis? Some six thousand years ago, legends say, the land was struck by some sort of sudden catastrophe. That catastrophe, today's researchers speculate, might have been the melting of glaciers, volcanic eruptions, violent earthquakes, tidal waves, or meteors colliding with Earth.

According to modern-day investigators, moreover, there is now solid physical evidence for the existence of Atlantis. Using sonar equipment and other high-tech tools, scientists have located un-

derwater islands with fresh water springs in the middle of the
ocean, and land vegetation has been retrieved by scientific probes.

ESP in Prague

A simple, genial Czechoslovakian, Pavel Stenpanek
never claimed he was psychic. He merely volunteered to take part
in an experiment designed by Czech scientist Milan Ryzl, who
thought it might be possible, under hypnosis, to train someone in
psi.

The project seemed straightforward enough to Stenpanek. And
before long, he was showing proficiency in ESP. Ryzl's basic procedure involved placing a set of target cards, green on one side and
white on the other, in a cardboard cover. They were first shuffled,
then coded, and finally placed in covers to prevent any visual clues.
At last they were presented to the subject, whose job it was to guess
whether the green side or the white side was uppermost in the
pack.

Stenpanek's performance went through various stages. At first
it was merely slightly better than average. By 1964, however, his
scores had declined so that he demonstrated ESP *less* than would
be expected if he had randomly picked a color. Ryzl feared Stenpanek's ability was fading—until parapsychology researcher J. G.
Pratt engineered a cure.

Instead of asking Stepanek to focus on the pack, the investigators
now asked him to report the color of one card at a time. In that new
experimental format, Stepanek's ability proved extraordinary. He
was able to guess the color of the cards much more frequently than
if he had chosen the color at random.

Mystery of the Healing Needle

After unsuccessful drug therapy for myelitis, a crippling inflammation of the spinal cord, a young girl is able to walk again. A man recovers from appendicitis without surgery. Another's dysentery is cured not by destroying the disease's bacteria, but by increasing the body's resistance. The miracle worker is not a religious healer, but rather the ancient technique of acupuncture—a medical art form that can cure a wide range of afflictions as long as no irreversible organic deterioration has occurred.

Acupuncture as a medical art evolved, one legend says, from observations of Chinese soldiers who, when wounded by arrows sometimes recovered from ailments they had endured for years. The earliest written reference to the art appears in the *Nei Ching*, or *The Yellow Emperor's Classic Book of Internal Medicine* dating back from 3,000 to 4,500 years ago.

The basis of acupuncture involves something the Chinese call *qi* (*chi*), which, loosely translated, means "life force" or "vital energy." If *qi* stops flowing harmoniously through the body, the result is illness. *Qi*, the Chinese say, circulates through the body by means of a series of meridians, invisible channels flowing under the skin. There are two central meridians—the governor vessel, which runs up the spine, and the conception vessel, which runs up the front of the body. A dozen other meridian pairs on each side of the body are linked to the heart, lungs, kidneys, and other specific organs, including two not even recognized by Western medicine—the heart constrictor, which controls circulation, and the triple heater, which keeps the body warm.

On each of these meridians lie the "acupuncture points," two thousand in all. Stimulating the points with needles or massage affects the meridians and their corresponding body parts by easing the flow of *qi*.

The results of acupuncture vary: There may be instant relief or slow improvement over weeks or even months. Experiences range from a feeling of tranquility to an abundance of energy. Some patients have a feeling of being pleasantly exhilarated; others actually feel worse for a time. Some notice no effect at all.

Claims that acupuncture results are due to faith or suggestion are countered with proof that it's consistently successful and equally effective on animals. Why sticking a needle in someone is able to restore the body's energies, however, still remains totally unknown.

The Ghost of Redmond Manor

Sounding like a rat gnawing at timber, the tapping was heard close to the foot of the bed for about five minutes. At first slow, the sound gradually became faster and louder. Then the bedclothes began sliding off the bed as if someone were pulling them, or as if a strong breeze were blowing through the room.

N. J. Murphy had heard the rumors about the Court Street house owned by one Nicholas Redmond, who admitted that it was haunted; indeed, Redmond's wife and two boarders, John Randall and George Sinnott, agreed.

Not accepting anything on hearsay, however, Murphy and Owen Devereux decided to spend the night in the house, sitting in the boarders' room, where the activity usually occurred.

The tapping and the movement of the sheets began around 11:30 P.M., about ten minutes after the investigators put out the lights. They checked under the bed for strings or wires, but found nothing suspicious at all. After another ten minutes, the noise recommenced, gradually increasing as it had before, and the sheets began to slide off the bed. This time, when the tapping stopped, Randall began screaming. He was being pulled off the bed and onto the floor. Terrified, he was soaked in perspiration. Helping him from the floor, Murphy and Devereux persuaded him to get back into bed.

Around 1:45, the tapping began once more, but this time it came from the middle of the room. It continued for fifteen minutes and then stopped. Murphy and Devereux were unable to offer any explanation for the phenomenon. And to this day, the ghost of Redmond Manor is unexplained.

Fish from the Skies

━━━━━━━━━━━━━━━━━━━━━━━━━━━━

A. D. Bajkov, a scientist with the United States Department of Wild Life and Fisheries, was in a Marksville, Louisiana, restaurant having breakfast on October 23, 1947, when a commotion arose outside. Not believing the waitress who told him fish were falling from the sky, he went out to investigate for himself. Sure enough, within an area of approximately one thousand by seventy-five or eighty feet, fresh, cold, but not frozen, fish littered the streets and yards—large-mouth black bass, sunfish, and minnows, but predominantly hickory shad. There were some spots averaging one fish per square foot. A Marksville Bank officer and two merchants had been struck by the falling fish as they walked to work.

Once when Bergen Evans, a noted debunker of scientific anomalies, asserted that all fish falls were merely myths, E. W. Gudger, a scientist at the American Museum of Natural History, responded with an array of evidence he'd been accumulating for years. In September 1936, for example, a fall on the Pacific island of Guam comprised the tench fish, common to the fresh water of Europe and western Asia.

Most often accompanying violent thunderstorms and heavy rains, fish rains usually involve a single species of fresh fish falling within an elliptical area a few hundred feet long. The explanations that a waterspout or whirlwind deposits them is acceptable when the fish comprise those that school in shallow waters. But the falls often include deep-water fish, some dead, dry, and even headless. No one has explained this last type of fish rain at all.

Driesch's Theory of Evolution

Expecting that half an egg would produce half an embryo, nineteenth-century biologist Hans Driesch used a hot needle to kill half of a sea urchin's fertilized egg. To his amazement, he discovered that each half developed into a complete, but smaller embryo of a whole sea urchin. Each half of the egg, it turned out, had a blueprint of the whole. Two whole eggs forced together, moreover, would fuse and develop into one embryo that was larger than normal. Driesch argued, therefore, that life itself is a dynamic force that "aims" for wholeness, independent of its chemistry.

According to the tenets of orthodox science, life on Earth happened by pure accident and can be explained by the laws of physics and biology. There is a reason for everything, most scientists will insist, and there is no such thing as free will in nature. Driesch and others, however, have dared to suggest that life may have its own program and its own laws.

Intrigued by Driesch's ideas, Harold Saxton Burr studied the electrical forces that initiated the construction of an organism's blueprint in the egg. He attached a voltmeter to trees and other organisms, keeping an ongoing record of their voltage. The trees' voltage, it seems, varied according to the seasons, sunspot activity, and the phases of the moon. In rabbits' ovaries, the voltmeter registered a sudden jump whenever follicles ruptured and released an egg. Attached to psychiatric patients, its reading coincided with the degree of mental illness. It could also record the highs and lows in physical illness, according to Burr, for instance detecting cancer at an early stage.

The experiments, Burr concluded, showed that all living things were influenced by their electric fields, their "life fields," as he dubbed them. A frog's egg, for example, had various lines of electrical force; when it developed into a tadpole, these lines became the nervous system. It was as if living matter were poured into the life field's mold.

Others in the twentieth century have contributed studies that support Burr's conclusions. In the 1930s, for example, Semyon

Kirlian seemed to have actually photographed the life field of a flower. Made by using high-voltage film plates, the photograph showed a glowing corona that surrounded the plant. A photograph of a torn leaf, moreover, appeared to show a dim outline of the leaf's missing portion.

In experiments at the University of Wisconsin in the 1970s, Daniel Perlman and Robert Stickgold grew bacteria in a solution containing an antibiotic that would normally destroy the bacteria. This particular bacteria, however, contained a gene that destroys the antibiotic, ensuring its own survival. According to accepted scientific views, this occurs by simply activating the defense system, which then shuts down when the danger has passed. Instead, the bacteria actually reacted by replicating the protective gene, as if it chose a more effective defense.

If life exists independently of matter, then life is the master of matter, and not the other way around, as most scientists now believe. And if it is the master, it can overrule the laws of nature. Having studied DNA programming, cyberneticist David Foster contends that Darwinian biology is most likely all wrong. He contends that complex genetic programming indicates the probability of higher intelligence than anything found on Earth. He believes the universe is, therefore, akin to a magical being and cannot be described in purely physical terms.

Dreaming of Comets

Charles Tweedle awoke around four o'clock one morning in 1886. Having just dreamed of a comet crossing the eastern sky and appearing before the rising sun, he immediately dressed and went outside. He gazed through a telescope on his observation platform, he wrote in a 1905 issue of *English Mechanic*, and saw thousands of stars shining brightly in the clear sky. Then he saw the comet sail into view. It was extremely bright and pearly white, its dense center swirling outward.

Observing the comet for the rest of the night, Tweedle was

thrilled. It was his first comet discovery, and, as soon as the post office opened, he sent off a telegram announcing his find. Almost immediately afterward, when the morning mail arrived, he read of the comet's discovery, individually viewed by astronomers Barnard and Hartwig. It came to be known as the comet Barnard-Hartwig.

Tweedle never discovered another comet, and he was never able to bestow his name on a heavenly body.

The White Blackbird

When an old woman of Somersetshire, England, had become particularly obnoxious toward her neighbors, they retaliated by following an old Shrove Tuesday custom called "crocking." Bombarding her door with all the pots, pans, and other crockery they'd collected and saved during the previous year, the townspeople created as much racket as possible to annoy her. The event, however, had an unintended victim.

Known around town for its sleek coat and sonorous voice, one neighbor's tame blackbird seemed panic-stricken by the discordant noise. For two days, it jumped around its cage and refused to eat. Although the bird eventually calmed down, the stress experienced during the Shrove Tuesday antics had a long-term effect. The bird began moulting, Alfred Charles Smith reported in *Zoologist*, and many of the shiny, black feathers were replaced by white ones. Fear had turned the poor bird gray.

Asthma Cured by Lightning

Martin Rockwell was looking out the window watching the sky grow dark and menacing. He stood with his weight on his left leg, his right hand resting on a wet board connected to the sink. Suddenly he felt his right arm and left leg go numb. In the very next instant, lightning struck the building within ten feet of him and knocked him unconscious. He came to a few minutes later, but it was days before he regained full use of his limbs.

There was a positive side to the lightning attack, however. Since childhood, and most often in the autumn, Rockwell had suffered from asthma and was often forced to rest in bed for weeks on end. But after the lightning incident, according to the *American Journal of Science*, he never had another attack.

Barisal Guns

All day long the noises aboard the steamer prevented G. B. Scott from hearing any other sounds. But at night, with his boat moored near the delta of India's Ganges River, he detected the dull, muffled booms of distant cannon—sometimes a single report, at others a succession of two, three, or more. These were the mysterious sounds of the Barisal guns.

The Barisal guns, heard no where outside the Ganges delta and emanating from the south or southeast, occur most frequently from February to October and always in connection with heavy rainfall. Many residents claim they can't tell the difference between the Barisal guns and the festive bombs fired during weddings and festivals. The wedding season, however, is very short. The guns, moreover, are heard even during the annual fast when there are no festivals of any kind.

Some researchers have attributed these detonations to underwater earthquakes or volcanic eruptions. But to this day, most experts agree that no satisfactory explanation has been found.

The Case of the Last-Minute Errand

On Saturday, January 3, 1891, at precisely 8:00 A.M., a man walked into a photo store and asked for overdue photographs in the name of Thompson. He was told they would not be ready until later that day. Explaining that he had traveled all night and could not return, the man abruptly left.

The store owner, a man named Dickenson, decided to mail the prints. First he looked up the negatives and realized that the man in the photos was the one who had stopped at the store. Two days later, he set out to make the prints. While working, however, he smashed the glass plate negative by mistake.

Dickenson then wrote the Thompsons to make arrangements for a new sitting. He learned from Thompson's father, however, that it was too late. Thompson had died on the same Saturday Dickenson saw him at the store. At that exact moment, 8:00 A.M., in fact, Thompson was actually unconscious and lying in his deathbed. The man's father added that his son had been delirious the day before and insistently asked for the undelivered photos.

Mind over Fungus

Parapsychologists have been fascinated by the subject of psychic healing for years. But studying the results of such practices is difficult since people tend to recover from sickness and biological damage for many reasons. This has led some parapsychologists to simply explore whether some individuals can use psychokinesis to disrupt small biological systems or cultures.

The researcher who pioneered this type of experiment was Dr. Jean Barry, a French physician who worked in collaboration with the Institute of Agronomy in Paris. Dr. Barry wanted to see if his subjects could use mind over matter to inhibit the growth of fungus cultures, since fungi can cause disease. Petri dishes were prepared by the institute the day before the experiments and were subsequently placed in an incubator, where the cultures could thrive. The following day, Dr. Barry's subjects would each be given ten dishes filled with the cultures. They would be asked to concentrate for fifteen minutes on five of the dishes, trying to mentally inhibit the growth of the cultures. The other dishes served as the controls.

By the time the experiment was completed, eleven subjects had been employed for a total of thirty-nine sessions. The result: The control cultures were significantly larger than the experimental ones, indicating that the subjects had successfully used psychic skills to inhibit fungus growth.

The Magus of Strovolos

Each year, Dr. Kyriacos C. Markides journeys to Cypress to talk with Spyros Sathi, a psychic healer and teacher known as *Daskalos*, or "The Magus of Strovolos." While visiting the psychic, Dr. Markides, a sociologist from the University of Maine, personally documented his powers of clairvoyance.

The incident took place when Markides brought a colleague to meet Daskalos. The gentleman had recently been bitten by a dog and was limping, so the healer asked to examine the leg. After the man had untied the bandage, Daskalos moved his hand over the wound to heal it—claiming that he was dissolving a blood clot he psychically saw forming.

"The blood clot is dissolved," he told his visitor, "but I have to warn you, you have an infection of the liver. You must avoid alcohol."

Dr. Markides's colleague didn't believe the diagnosis since he felt perfectly fine, so he ignored the remark. It wasn't until three months later that he wrote to Dr. Markides from Connecticut that he was suffering from a case of hepatitis, which inflames the liver. When the illness first struck, he suddenly recalled Daskalos's diagnosis and was attempting to find out if Dr. Markides recalled it, too. Luckily, Dr. Markides had taped their conversation with the healer, and the prediction was easily documented.

But just how did Daskalos know of the disease, which hadn't yet produced any symptoms? The healer claimed that he "saw" right into the professor's body. "Now when I was examining the professor's leg," he later told Dr. Markides, "and I concentrated within his body, I noticed inside the liver a little brown spot touching the bile. From experience I knew that there was trouble coming."

This possibility is consistent with our medical knowledge, since with hepatitis, symptoms can develop three months after the initial infection sets in.

Misguided Psi

Dean Kraft is one of this country's best-known psychic healers. In 1976, he and several other psychics cooperated in a lengthy research project conducted by parapsychologists at the Washington Research Center in San Francisco. The experimental team was headed by Roger MacDonald, who wanted to determine whether the healers could disrupt electrical and magnetic fields, cause perturbations within a sealed cloud chamber, rebond water molecules, and so forth.

Kraft's success at these tasks was fairly marginal. But something unexplained—and morbidly amusing—happened during the tests when he tried to "heal" a rat especially bred to be hypertensive. The rat was brought to the lab on the day of the experiment and placed in a restraint cage, where its blood pressure was recorded by a probe hooked to its tail. Kraft was admitted to the room only after the experimental preparations had been made. He took a dislike to the rodent as soon as he saw it.

"I tried to explain that my only previous experience with rats had been in the music store where I once worked," says Kraft. "There, fat long rats that lurked in the basement sometimes ventured upstairs and scared the hell out of everyone. I felt only hate and fear for rats, and was worried, for it had always seemed to me that I needed to have positive thoughts—loving thoughts—toward the subjects I tried to heal."

Kraft tried to lower the rat's blood pressure, despite his trepidations, by sending it healing energy. Everybody left the room when the test was complete. The shock came moments later, when a technician went back to check the rat's blood pressure for a final time. The rat had dropped dead!

No explanation for the death was ever found.

Invasion from Mars

In the years before television the performance of one particular science fiction radio show, broadcast at a critical moment in world history, had an almost incredible effect on the listening audience. It happened in 1938, when the listening public was already psychologically prepared for the possibility of a world war, just after the Munich debacle and the threatened invasion of neighboring countries by the governments of Germany and Italy.

The radio show was a dramatization of an imaginary invasion of Earth by forces from Mars, based on a science fiction fantasy, *The War of the Worlds* by H. G. Wells. The actor Orson Welles was the narrator. Although the program was pre-announced as a radio dramatization only, Welles's masterful and exciting report of the invasion of Earth, specifically of northern New Jersey, by gigantic extraterrestrial-controlled robot towers that spread destruction through "death rays" aimed at civilians and troops, as well as the on-the-spot interviews with "refugees" spread panic among the listeners who had tuned in after the program had started and, therefore, thought it was the latest news. As the listeners telephoned their friends and compared notes, they convinced each other that the invasion was actually taking place. The telephone lines were jammed with calls and the excitement mounted. There was no further declaration on the air that the program was fictional. The panic spread, and the roads in New Jersey, parts of New York, and Long Island became blocked with cars filled with refugees, police cars, fire trucks, and motorcycles. The number of cars and accidents soon brought traffic to a standstill, and it took hours for state and local police to disentangle the traffic and restore order.

Even then, many of the fleeing thousands still believed that the space invasion was taking place and was being kept secret to avoid nationwide panic.

Some time after the "Mars invasion" had calmed down, the program was rebroadcast in Spanish at at theater in Lima, Peru. Here public excitement reached such a point that rioting broke out during the show, causing fifteen deaths and many more injuries.

And two years later, in September of 1939, similar public panics occurred in Western Europe—but this time the invaders were not from Mars.

Has Noah's Ark Been Found?

Among the earliest legends known to man is one that tells of a great flood and a great ark that survived it, carrying people and animals to renew life in a drowned world.

This legend is part of the lore of ancient nations and tribes of all continents. In the Hebrew, Christian, and Moslem traditions, the landing place of the ark was Mount Ararat, now in northeastern Turkey.

The word *Ararat* comes from *Urartu*, an ancient Assyrian word for Armenia. The Bible specifies Ararat and also "the mountains of Armenia" as the landing place of the ark. But it does not specify on which mountain it landed, although Mount Ararat has become sanctified through tradition and legend as the resting place of the Great Ship.

For many centuries travelers claim to have seen it frozen in the ice, mountaineers have taken purported pieces of it as religious keepsakes, military pilots have reported flying over it in both world wars, and an ERTS satellite report of 1974, taken at fourteen-thousand feet, shows something in a great crevasse "clearly foreign to anything else on the mountain." In the opinion of Senator Frank Morse, chairman of the Senate Aeronautical and Space Sciences Committee, it was "about the right size and shape to be the Ark."

Since Ararat through the centuries has been shaken by a number of earthquakes and volcanic explosions, the ark, although protected in "deep freeze" may have been damaged or broken apart. This could explain the finding of what seems to be the lower portion of the great ship at the seven-thousand-foot level. This part of the ark may have slid down the mountain and been buried in a mud bank about twelve miles from its original site (great drag anchors and part of its port side have been found along the path of its presumed downward slide). If this hull is part of the ark, the remaining upper portion must still be at the fourteen-thousand-foot level, under the ice.

This "hull" surfaced from a frozen mud slide in 1948 and has been examined by a number of researchers who, until the 1980s, were puzzled, considering that the artifact, although in the shape of a great ship, was made of stone. The measurements of the hull are almost exactly those given in cubits in Genesis, the first instance in the Bible of exact statistics. The artifact has slowly risen out of the frozen mud since 1948 and, as it does so, its lines appear consistently more shiplike.

Subsurface interface radar, brought to the site, shows metal and attached beams supporting the hull, bow to stern and port to port, as well as divisions of several decks into numerous sections. As for the stone ship, it now appears that a reed and wood framework was coated with cement (K-F-R)—mistakenly translated from the original Aramaic as "gopher" wood.

The hull is filled with solidified earth and mud and is now under the protection of the Turkish government for projected investigation by archaeologists. A newly made sign pointing the way to this unusual artifact states simply: *Nuh'un Gemesi*—Noah's Ark.

Whether or not this is really Noah's Ark, it is obviously the preserved remains of a great ship, larger than any other that we know to have existed in remote antiquity.

CHARLES BERLITZ'S

World of

STRANGE PHENOMENA

━━━ **VOLUME 3:** ━━━

The Odd and the Awesome

Foreword

The realm of the odd and the awesome – where human eyes cannot see and our intelligence becomes insignificant – is all around us. It abounds with mysteries. Mysteries of unusual appearances, mysteries of phenomenal strength or odd creatures constantly remind us that we do not truly know all that we suppose. What, for example, happened to Judge Crater, Amelia Earhart or Jimmy Hoffa? Did Napoleon actually end his life on St Helena or, as some surmise, did he live out his life in New Orleans? But these examples are personal mysteries that can be (and perhaps already have been) solved.

Greater mysteries include the disappearances of cities, cultures, great islands and entire civilizations, like those of the Maya, the Toltecs, the Indus Valley, the islands of the Pacific and the peoples who preceded the Incas in South America. Many of these early civilizations achieved remarkably accurate concepts of the world and the universe, well in advance and in different parts of the world from civilizations that followed them, often attaining scientific expertise not to be equalled again for thousands of years. Some impossibly advanced civilizations have burst into flower and then disappeared or regressed, for reasons unknown, either into more primitive jungle and desert tribes, or have been absorbed by other less advanced populations.

Despite our own advanced state of technology, we are frequently visited by mysterious 'ghosts' – and not just the kind that haunt our houses but more modern ghosts such as those of radio and television shows of years past suddenly appearing and disappearing on channels showing regularly scheduled programmes. Do such unexplainable events point to the possibility that there exists a curvature in space or time? More and more reliable witnesses are reporting such events which are said to occur by day as well as night. And so many reports can't be ignored. They have become the object of study by scientists as have numerous cases of possession or poltergeist activities, the latter being violent out-of-body projections of one's own personality or 'soul'. It has even been suggested that the increasing number of sightings of UFOs, now firmly believed in by more than 50 per cent of the world's population, may be the modern equivalent of ghosts at a time when haunted houses are being replaced by haunted skies.

The greatest mysteries of the world do not consist of incidents, however fascinating, but of the potential solution to elusive questions pertaining to the nature of time and space. Space, with its suns, planets and denizens (if any) has long been the object of intensive study, and it is likely that, within a very few years, the surface of Mars will be explored in detail by expeditions from Earth to learn, among other things, whether what appears to be gigantic pyramids and an enormous stone human face in a section of Mars now called Cydonia are really what they seem to be, and whether they have been constructed not by nature but by living entities. Also scheduled to be examined on Mars are the apparent ruins of a seaport city on the shores of a now dry ocean bed. These and other ruins have been photographed by American and Russian astronauts and, if verified as true constructions, their existence – regardless of being hundreds of thousands of years old – should provide a comforting thought to the inhabitants of the Earth – that we are not alone in the universe. (Unless, of course, the constructions were built by our own ancestors before they came to Earth!)

As we penetrate further into the exploration of space and time we will be opening up new worlds of wonder, changing our own consciousness and destiny. This, again, is the kingdom where our imagination will be as important as our intelligence.

Consider what the famous French scientist, Marcellin Berhelot, wrote in 1887 regarding the progress of science and the exploration of space:

From now on there is no mystery about the universe. . .

If he had had the capability of listening, he and others might have heard in response to their insular surety, echoes of cosmic laughter from somewhere beyond space and time.

Double Coincidence Times Three

One of the oddest coincidences ever recorded spans a period of nearly 200 years and involved three ships that sank in the Menai Strait off the coast of Wales. The first vessel went down on December 5, 1664, and of its 81 passengers only one, Hugh Williams, survived. On December 5, 1785, 121 years later, another ship sank in the Menai Strait and, again, all of the passengers perished except one – named Hugh Williams.

Two ships sinking in the same area on the same day of the month certainly isn't earth-shattering. When each of them has only one survivor and both are named Hugh Williams, it's a little eerie. But the story doesn't end at that.

On December 5, 1860, yet another ship, a small 25-passenger vessel, sank in the Menai Strait. And once again there was only one survivor – and once again his name was Hugh Williams.

Coptic Vision

In the suburbs of Cairo, Egypt, a glowing apparition has been seen over the roofs of two Coptic churches, mystifying believers and sceptics alike since April 1968. Appearing in the early morning hours and described by some as resembling the Virgin Mary, the vision first appeared over St Mary's Coptic Church in Zeitoun. For three years, thousands of people flocked to the church to witness the nightly phenomenon.

After its last occurrence in 1971, the apparition didn't appear again until 1986, when the figure rematerialized above St Demiana's, another Coptic church outside Cairo. According to eye-witnesses, the vision was often accompanied by the scent of incense and the entire dome of the church would glow while the image hovered over it.

The crowds grew so large outside St Demiana's that the Cairo police were called in to keep order. Mousad Sadik, a journalist who regularly covered the story for a Cairo-based newspaper, reported one occasion when the spirit was visible for a full 20 minutes. While scientists have attempted to credit fraud, mass hallucination, a natural optical phenomenon, or electrical discharges from the roof of the church, no one has definitively explained the phenomenon.

Orchard Family Justice

Joe Orchard, a former petty officer in the Royal Navy, and his family began experiencing strange phenomena in their home in Adisham, Kent, in the mid-1970s. Doors and water taps would inexplicably detach themselves and fly around. A ceiling collapsed for no apparent reason, furniture would mysteriously become soaking wet and electrical appliances regularly malfunctioned. Circumstances finally convinced the Orchards to flee their home.

After some consideration, Orchard concluded that 'electro-osmosis' was causing the disturbances in his home. A power cable near the cottage, he presumed, was leaking electricity which was subsequently affecting the mechanics of the house. The Orchards moved back in only after burying electrodes in the lawn to deflect the leaking power.

They then took legal action against the South Eastern Electricity Board, seeking restitution for the damage done to their home. The Electricity Board denied responsibility, however, and enlisted a sympathetic judge to discount the Orchard's claims. After a 12-day trial, the judge declared that Joe, his wife June, and their 23-year-old son had staged the whole ordeal to cheat the electric company. 'We told the truth in court, but we were branded liars,' June stated afterwards.

Transposing Senses

It's generally believed that when people lose the ability to see or hear, their other senses somehow compensate for the deficiency and become noticeably more acute. But in several documented cases, the lost sense has actually been shown to relocate.

The most celebrated case of transposed senses was reported by Dr. C. Lombroso, a highly regarded neurologist and psychiatrist. Three months after a 14-year-old girl had suddenly become quite ill, she completely lost her sight. Even though her eyes were non-functional, however, the girl claimed she could see. Her mystified parents took her to Lombroso who conducted a series of tests to determine if she was telling the truth.

The neurologist placed blindfolds over the girl's eyes and then placed objects in front of her. Amazingly, she could in fact see them, identifying colours and even reading a letter. A bright light shone against her ear lobe, however, caused her to wince in pain. And when the doctor poked his finger at the tip of the girl's nose, she angrily exclaimed, 'Are you trying to blind me?'

Evidently, the girl's sense of vision had relocated to the tip of her nose as well as her ear lobe. But more than her sight had been transposed: apparently she could also smell through her chin.

Return from Suicide

On November 8, 1952, Theresa Butler took an overdose of sleeping pills and was found hours later in her bath. She was taken to the morgue after she was pronounced dead by the local coroner who found no pulse, no blood pressure and no perceptible reflexes.

The morgue attendant on duty was accustomed to seeing an occasional bout of rigor mortis, a condition that can cause a dead body suddenly to move reflexively. He wasn't prepared, however, to see Butler's corpse working its jaw and gasping. Stunned, and not a little frightened, he called his boss who determined that Butler wasn't dead after all and immediately rushed the now comatose woman to the hospital.

It's not often that someone recovers from having been declared legally dead. But that's exactly what Butler did, and five days later she was discharged from the hospital. Fortunately, her condition had been discovered before she could be buried alive.

Psychic Sea Search

In 1977, the Mobius Society, a parapsychology research group based in Los Angeles, USA, set out to test the ability of psychics to predict the locations of sunken ships. Director Stephen Schwartz sent sets of four Pacific Ocean navigation charts to five volunteers, all of whom claimed to have some psychic ability but did not practise professionally. They were asked to locate and describe the shipwreck site through nothing more than remote viewing, using a mental image to sense an actual ship.

In what was already a great coincidence, four of the five participants selected a single site: 10 square miles near Santa Catalina Island. According to the four psychics, a wooden sailing ship with a steam engine had exploded some time between 82 and 93 years earlier. They also described such objects as the ship's wheel and a stone slab that would be found at the site, located some 277 feet below the surface.

That June, Schwartz and two of the psychics set out to determine the accuracy of the prediction. Also aboard the ship was Al Witcombe, who would pilot the *Taurus I*, a 32-foot submarine. After three hours of fruitless searching, Witcombe dropped a radio-homing device into the target zone. *Taurus's* manipulator arm dug into the sand on the ocean floor and pulled out the first of many relics from the sunken ship located by the homing device.

Three days of diving proved incredibly successful. Every object the psychics had envisioned in the remote viewing experiment was found, including the wheel and the stone slab. The distribution and type of wreckage, moreover, supported the psychics' claim that the sunken ship was made of wood and had, indeed, exploded. And the marine growth on the wreckage indicated that the ship had been underwater for decades, at least.

The Many Lives of the Dalai Lama

To practitioners of the centuries-old religion of Tibetan Buddhism, the epitome of spiritual leadership and perfection is the man-god known as the Dalai Lama. His significance stems from the Buddhist tenets regarding reincarnation.

To Buddhists, the ultimate goal of reincarnation is *Nirvana*, the point at which all the karmic requirements of human life have been satisfied and the soul may rest in its enlightened state. More advanced souls, however, may choose to remain in the cycle of reincarnation in order to help others on their own paths towards *Nirvana*. Among such beings, called *bodhisattvas*, the most sacred is *Avalokitesvara*, the *Bodhisattva* of Compassion. Each Dalai Lama, throughout the history of Buddhism, has been believed to be the reincarnation of *Avalokitesvara*.

Upon the death of each Dalai Lama, the monks consult oracles to determine within which child the spirit of the *Avalokitesvara* has been reincarnated. Once found, the child is tested to verify the spirit's presence and to determine if the child will be the new Dalai Lama. The ritual requires the child to select correctly his predecessor's possessions among a miscellaneous collection of objects. This is possible because, unlike mere mortals, *bodhisattvas* retain their memories of past lives.

Many other stories surround the Dalai Lama. For example, when the Chinese Red Armies had consolidated their control over China in 1950, the Communists re-established Chinese sovereignty over Tibet, signing a treaty with the Dalai Lama in 1950. The Tibetans, however, continued to resist but were finally overcome in 1959. One of the prizes of the Chinese victory would have been the capture of the Dalai Lama, the spiritual head of millions of Tibetans and Chinese. But the Chinese never captured him, although he was accompanied by numerous escorts which the special Chinese troops using advanced aircraft should have found easily.

As the Dalai Lama approached a mountain pass leading to freedom in India, a heavy and unexpected fog suddenly covered the border area making it impossible for planes to locate him, and a convenient blizzard obscured the traces of his passage from the pursuing troops.

He established himself in India, where he still is today, fortified by his claim to the stewardship of Tibet, and evidently protected by the Tibetan gods of snow and fog.

The Lost Fleet of Alexander the Great

In 234 BC, Alexander the Great, after extending his conquests as far as western India, ordered Admiral Nearchus to return to the Persian Gulf and transport the exhausted and depleted Greek troops back to Greece. Some of the fleet, however, never reached their homeland. Some historians speculate that their ships continued past India into the Pacific Ocean, eventually reaching Tahiti and Hawaii. There has been some evidence to support the idea that the Greeks even made it all the way to the western coast of the Americas.

On the east coast of North America, the first white men to reach the shores of Maryland and Virginia discovered a river the natives had named Potomac. The Greek word for river is, oddly enough, *potamós*.

When sixteenth-century Spanish conquistadors invaded the Aztec empire, for example, they learned that the word for the Aztec pyramid temples was *teocalli*, meaning 'dwelling of the god'. Later study by historians revealed that *teocalli* is remarkably similar to two Greek words – *theós* and *kalías* – which, when used together, also mean the same thing as *teocalli*.

And in Hawaii, a number of words such as *aeto* (eagle), *mele* (song) and *noo-noo* (intelligence) for example, are strikingly close to Greek words with the same meaning *aétós*, *melodía*, and *nous*. Hawaiian war helmets, moreover, although designed in wood and feathers instead of metal and horse-hair, were nearly identical to their Greek counterparts.

The simple, but intriguing, explanation for the appearance of Greek words and artefacts in far-flung cultures centres around Alexander, conqueror of most of the ancient world. After overpowering the mighty Persian Empire, Alexander's land troops pushed eastward into India and northward into what is now the Soviet Union. Meanwhile, his 800-vessel fleet, led by Admiral Nearchus, explored the Indian coast.

If the Greeks did find their way to lands in the South Pacific and the Americas, they would probably have seemed at least like demi-gods to the indigenous peoples and their language and art worthy of adoption into the native cultures.

Talking Porpoises

Some years ago, a shipment of recently captured porpoises was placed in a holding pool at the Seaquarium in Miami, USA. The pool was located near another one containing tamed porpoises, but it was out of sight. The intention was to train the new porpoises so that they, too, could entertain the Seaquariam audiences.

The lessons, however, would not begin until the following day.

During the night, J. Manson Valentine, curator honoris of the Museum of Science of Miami, heard a barrage of sounds emanating from both porpoise tanks. In the morning, when it was time to start teaching the new additions, Valentine and his training team discovered that the lessons weren't necessary: the new porpoises were able to perform most of the tasks on the first attempt.

Valentine surmised that through some form of inter-porpoise communication, the veteran porpoises had informed the new ones what would be expected of them.

Haunting at Haw Branch

Haw Branch Plantation had once been a magnificent estate, with its gardens, rolling lawns, dry moat and stately chimneys gracing the classic antebellum manor house. But in 1964, after 50 years of neglect, the property had fallen into grave disrepair. When Gibson McConnaughey inherited Haw Branch, she and her husband Carey immediately set about restoring the estate to its former grandeur. But there was at least one ancestor who would also return to Haw Branch.

Soon the McConnaugheys began hearing strange noises throughout the house. Sometimes the scent of oranges or roses would waft through the air, when neither fruit nor flower were present. On one occasion, moreover, the McConnaugheys saw someone carrying a lantern as he came out of the barn and approached the house, but as he drew near they could only see the kerosene lamp bobbing in the air.

Three months after they had moved into Haw Branch,

the couple and their children were awakened in the middle of the night by a woman screaming in the attic. Petrified, they waited until morning to investigate, but found nothing to account for the noise. The screams recurred at six-monthly intervals, but it wasn't until the summer of 1967 that Gibson witnessed an image connected to the voice.

'She was not transparent, just a white silhouette,' Gibson later recalled. Although she was unable to discern any facial features, Gibson noticed that the apparition wore a floor-length dress from some earlier era. Standing only briefly in front of Gibson, the women stared silently into the distance as she repeatedly disappeared and reappeared.

By 1969, the family had grown accustomed to the woman and their other ghostly housemates. The bi-annual visit of the woman's voice, however, began to occur more frequently after the arrival of a family heir-loom. Gibson's elderly cousin sent the McConnaugheys the portrait of a long-dead relative named Florence Wright. From the description they received, the family expected a portrait in vivid pastel colours depicting the young Florence, shortly before her sudden death. When it arrived, however, the McConnaugheys were surprised that the painting was awash in dark greys, browns and dirty whites. Even so, they hung it over the library fireplace.

Then, in February 1970, the portrait began to trans-form. The charcoal-black hair seemed to be a lighter shade. A rose at the base of the painting was turning from dusky grey to pink. And Florence's skin was taking on a life-like hue. In fact, every detail was inexplicably brighter and more colourful. As the process continued, the image of Florence Wright soon depicted a blue-eyed, red-haired beauty sitting in a bright green chair.

According to a psychic who subsequently examined the portrait, Florence's spirit had been locked in the painting at the time of the woman's death. She, therefore, had the power to drain the painting of all colour until she was happy with its location. The voices heard at Haw

Branch were fellow spirits who had been enlisted to aid the woman to regain her lost colour. Evidently, the psychic believed, Haw Branch, with its vibrant spiritual atmosphere, was a satisfactory home for Florence Wright.

UFOs over Japan

Some 700 years before the term 'flying saucer' appeared in Western descriptions of UFO sightings, the Japanese were recording incidents of their own. Ancient documents, for example, describe an unusual object heading north from a mountain in Kii province on October 27, 1180. The craft then simply disappeared over the horizon, leaving a luminous trail in its wake. In another instance, a poet's execution was stayed in 1271 when an object suddenly appeared in the sky on the day of the scheduled beheading.

It was also a Japanese military officer who ordered the first known UFO investigation in 1235. On the night of September 24, General Yoritsume and his army witnessed mysterious lights that remained visible in the sky for many hours, swooping, circling and performing other then-unimaginable aerobatics. The general's experts, however, finally reported that the phenomena was the result of 'the wind making the stars sway'.

Indian Observatory

In Arizona, USA, Saskatchewan, Canada, and some 50 other sites throughout North America, there are distinct wheel designs laid out on the ground which are discernible only from above. The wheels are simply constructed out of thin ridges of stones making up a rim, hub and often a number of spokes. Some wheels also feature piles of stones called cairns strategically placed within the wheel's outline. The Bighorn Medicine Wheel is the best preserved and best known of the North American wheels. So-named by the Plains Indians because of its supposed spiritual properties, the Bighorn Medicine Wheel is located high on a plateau in Wyoming's Bighorn Mountains.

Historians suspect that the wheels, like their European counterparts, the megaliths, were astronomical observatories used by local tribes as early as the 1100s. A particular cairn of the Bighorn faces the wheel's hub and directly toward the rising sun of the summer solstice. Other rock piles point toward the rising and setting of three brilliant stars during seasonal changes. All the wheels, moreover, were evidently designed to afford a clear view of the horizon.

But while historians are reasonably sure of the wheels' mechanics, they are still puzzled by their purpose. Some researchers speculate that the medicine wheels would be especially helpful to agricultural tribes to keep track of the planting seasons. Nomadic hunting tribes could also use them to observe the roaming bisons' migratory patterns, or perhaps their own migration to warmer climates during the winter.

Death of the Oceans

Oceanographer and conservationist Jacques Cousteau proposes a horrifying vision of the consequences of mankind's present exploitation and pollution of the world's oceans.

If all the oceans' aquatic life were to die suddenly, the decaying organic matter would create an unbearably foul stench. The wafting odour would drive people from the fertile coastlines and into the mountains and highlands that could hardly support the overwhelming influx of new inhabitants.

Far worse, however, would be the release of carbon dioxide into the atmosphere. Without the action of aquatic life which helps to balance the Earth's salts and gases, the carbon dioxide would steadily increase, aggravating the Greenhouse Effect. Rather than the Earth's heat radiating into space, it would be trapped beneath the stratosphere, raising sea-level temperatures to an intolerable point. Polar ice caps would melt, causing flooding of unimaginable proportions.

As nightmarish as such prospects may seem they aren't the only likely possibilities. As the thick film of dead organic matter coated land and sea, the slime would interfere with evaporation and subsequent rainfall. The result would be global drought and famine.

The ultimate consequence, 30 to 50 years after the oceans officially die, would be the extinction of the human race and most other species of animal. Confined to overcrowded areas between dead seas and sterile mountains, and suffering from starvation, disease epidemics and severe weather conditions, humans will finally succumb to anoxia, or lack of oxygen. And then life on Earth will be reduced to bacteria and a few remaining species of insects.

Nazca Patterns

Pilots flying over southern Peru's Nazca desert in 1939 unexpectedly observed strange patterns on the ground. They reported depictions of animals and birds as well as spirals and straight lines which, the pilots claimed, resembled the runways of modern airports. Even more amazing, the designs' measurements were incredibly accurate.

Some 50 years later, scientists are still unable to explain the origins of the massive drawings. Because the designs are discernible only from the air, however, many researchers speculate that their ancient creators must have also been able to fly – or were directed by someone else who could.

To space buffs like Swiss author Erich von Daniken, the designs' explanation is simple. The Nazca drawings, he believes, are signal markers for aircraft guidance and were placed in the Peruvian desert by extraterrestrial visitors. In his 1967 book *Chariots of the Gods*, von Daniken proposed that the alien beings arrived on Earth about 10,000 years ago and proceeded to manipulate monkey genes to develop a species of humans. Their creations would then perceive the aliens as gods.

The Book of Genesis and other creation stories, von Daniken suggests, stem from those early extraterrestrial visits. Archaeological findings like Nazca are the relics of ancient astronauts.

The Mysterious Mayan Calendar

Devised more than 5,000 years ago, the ancient Mayan calendar is amazingly accurate. Its computer-like complexity still baffles archaeologists and astronomers. Among their other feats, the Mayans correctly determined that the Sun, Moon and the planet Venus appear in the same alignment only once every 104 years.

How were the ancient Mayans able to make such precise astronomical observations long before the invention of the telescope? According to the civilization's own legends, the calendar was a gift of 'strangers from the star world'.

Of all ancient races the Maya came the nearest to recording the exact length of the solar year. One present reckoning is 365.2422 days while the Maya using their own calculations and instruments from their high pyramids came to 365.2420 – two ten-thousandths of a day's difference – thousands of years before anyone else came near it.

Group Reincarnation

In 1962, English psychiatrist Arthur Guirdham began treating a young woman who experienced terrifying nightmares. During the next four years, 'Mrs Smith' (as Guirdham called her in three books about the curious case) recounted the torments she endured as a member of the Cathars, a medieval French religious sect whose followers believed staunchly in reincarnation.

The historical details and portrayals of thirteenth-century life of Smith's accounts were amazingly accurate, Guirdham found. Smith claimed, for example, that the Cathars' robes were dark blue, contradicting most historians who had always asserted the garments were black. Digging into reams of research and data, Guirdham was finally able to determine that Smith was right.

Smith was only the first of several reincarnated Cathars Guirdham began to attract. Eventually six others joined her, forming a closely knit group. And having sensed something familiar about Smith's tales from the very beginning of their association, Guirdham also began believing he was the reincarnated Roger Isarn de Fanjeaux, Smith's lover during her thirteenth-century incarnation. It would certainly explain why Smith originally sought his help.

Psychic Witness

When a seven-year-old boy disappeared from his Los Angeles home in 1978, police were stymied in their efforts to find substantial leads in the case. In frustration, they turned to a local psychic known simply as Joan.

Joan soon told the detectives that the boy had been murdered by a man she described to a police artist. She later disputed the accuracy of the subsequent sketch, arguing that the face should be longer and the nose smaller. The missing boy's father, however, was still able to identify the depicted suspect as a family acquaintance, who was arrested.

At the beginning of the trial, the defence lawyer argued for the dismissal of charges against the accused acquaintance. Based solely on psychic predictions, the suspects's arrest had been illegal, the lawyer stated. Even so, the judge overruled the courtroom objection and the acquaintance was eventually convicted of murder.

The Casket Lid of Pacal

A carving found in Palenque, Mexico, on the cover of a Mayan nobleman's casket proved to be a surviving treasure of Mayan pictorial art. It was excavated in a crypt beneath a pyramid temple and is assumed to be the casket and portrait of someone named Pacal. Archaeologists have offered the theory that Pacal was a former Mayan ruler, although it is difficult to ascertain much about him since the Mayan system of writing – a series of hundreds of complicated glyphs – has not yet been satisfactorily deciphered. Regardless of his name, however, Pacal must have been a person of supreme importance to have been so entombed.

It is not certain what the coffin lid represents. When the rectangular lid is viewed on its long side, it looks like a feathered and jewelled Mayan figure riding or straddling some sort of stylized form, thought by some archaeologists to be the Tree of Life. In addition, there seems to be some sort of monster depicted in the lower part of the lid.

Another theory, held by certain Russian space engineers, scientists and writers such as Aleksandr Kazentsev and others, suggests that the picture is a stylized rendition of an astronaut or cosmonaut. Kazentsev has pointed out that many of the unique details in the carving evoke the peculiar control panel of a capsule designed for space travel. When the carving is placed horizontally, the seated position of the figure appears correct for an astronaut in a space probe. Kazentsev has pointed out details such as a recognizable antenna, space directional system, control panel, turbo compressor and, behind the picture of Pacal, items that resemble fuel tanks and a turbine and combustion chamber.

While it is evident that in this instance, as with many other mysterious archaeological finds, what you see in the carving depends on the way you look at it, it can't be denied that the coffin lid of Pacal represents at the very least an extraordinary coincidence.

Out-of-Body Experiences

Intentional and random out-of-body experiences (OBEs) have been reported throughout history by people of every age, race, creed and culture. OBEs are as common among Russians and Americans, say, as they are in the tribes of Africa and Australia.

Writers and artists especially claim that OBEs serve as creative inspiration and they have been able to describe them in vivid detail. Famous out-of-body travellers include D.H. Lawrence, Aldous Huxley, Emily Brontë, Jack London and the German poet Goethe.

For example, during World War I, American author Ernest Hemingway served in the United States ambulance corps. One hot July night in 1918, he was crouched in a cramped trench on the Italian front near the village of Fossalta when he suddenly heard a mortar shell hurtling through the air. The bomb exploded and shrapnel seared his legs. Afterwards, he told friends that the pain was excruciating and he had believed that he had been near death when he actually felt his spirit leave his body.

Hemingway immortalized his experience in the 1929 novel *A Farewell to Arms*: 'I tried to breathe, but my breath would not come,' says the protagonist Frederic Henry. 'I felt myself rush bodily out of myself and out and out and out and all the time bodily in the wind. I went out swiftly, all of myself, and I knew I was dead and that it had been a mistake to think you just died. Then I floated, and instead of going on I felt myself slide back. I breathed and I was back.'

A Glimpse of Heaven

Father Filippo Neri was considered an extraordinary holy man in sixteenth-century Rome. Parishioners had observed him levitate during Mass, perform exorcisms, and even raise the dead.

At dawn on March 16, 1589, Neri was summoned to the palace of Italy's Prince Fabrizio Massimo. The priest was told that the prince's 14-year-old son, Paolo, was gravely ill and not expected to live much longer. Even though the boy had died half an hour before Neri arrived at his bedside, the priest knelt to pray for the departed soul, blessing the body with holy water.

As the grieving family looked on, the holy man blew into Paolo's face, placed a hand on the youth's forehead and called out his name. In a moment, Paolo's eyelids miraculously flickered and opened.

Paolo told the people gathered around his bed that he had gone to heaven and had seen his mother who had passed away eight years earlier. Heaven was a beautiful place, the exalted child said, and he desperately wanted to return. 'Well, then,' the priest told him, 'go in peace and be blessed.' With that, Paolo closed his eyes and died – again.

The Sharks in the Forest

Scuba divers who encounter sharks in clear water generally believe that sharks, unless aroused to a feeding frenzy by another source, will not attack them on sight. The divers, with their bulky tanks, safety equipment and clouds of bubbles seem to give sharks the instinctive feeling that they represent an opponent who requires further reconnoitering prior to attack. In other words, people are in greater danger swimming on the surface, kicking their legs like a wounded or dying fish – an easy prey to a shark – than a diver cruising slowly through deep water like a fellow predator.

Unusual exceptions to this rule, however, have been reported in the Pacific area south of San Francisco, where sharks have taken to attacking and killing divers for food in the underwater kelp forests off the coast. The kelp rises from the ocean floor like trees with branches and leaves. This not only makes it harder for divers to distinguish hungry sharks but also seems to convince the sharks that the divers, who they might not ordinarily attack, are really seals, a local shark delicacy. Divers may resemble seals to them because of their glistening diving suits, fins, and even their method of propulsion as they swim.

Lifelines of the Not-Quite-Dead

Among the medical community of nineteenth-century Europe and America, the determination of death was often a difficult task. Bodies were often interred as quickly as possible to avoid contagion, particularly during cholera and typhoid epidemics. And in the absence of modern embalming techniques, it was not uncommon for people to be buried when, in fact, they weren't really dead. In Germany alone, it was estimated that thousands of premature funerals occurred every year.

Children's fairy-tale writer, Hans Christian Andersen and others wrote about the possibility of waking to find themselves buried alive. Andersen, moreover, never went to bed without leaving a note on his nightstand. It read: 'Am merely in suspended animation'. And a few days before he died, Anderson instructed a friend to cut open the writer's veins once he died to guarantee absolutely that he was no longer living when buried.

This common fear of being buried alive created a burgeoning market for various safeguards. One of the most basis was a set-up that included a bell placed at ground level attached to wires running into the coffin. In this way, a person who revived after burial could ring the bell to alert the living. More advanced versions featured a pneumatically operated signalling device triggered by the slightest movement inside the çasket.

Perhaps the most elaborate deathguard, however, was a Viennese mechanized morgue, planned in 1874. Corpses would be monitored by metal plates that could detect body movement and then send an electrical impulse to trigger an alarm in the central control room. An identification number on each bell would enable watchmen to determine which body had moved so they could rescue the person.

The morgue plans, however, were abandoned when a

new cemetery, complete with the popular above-ground bell system, was laid out nearby. There are no indications in the cemetery records that any of the presumed dead ever rang the bells.

Keeper of the Psychic Wolves

When Jack Lynch took over the wildlife reintroduction project to save the American buffalo wolf from extinction, he didn't expect his wards to display an uncanny psychic ability. The animals, however, seemed to have developed intense ties to their saviour, E.H. McCleery, who had established the sanctuary. Lynch, familiar with wolf behaviour, took over the job as caretaker when McCleery, suffering with colon cancer, became too ill to continue tending his beloved wolves.

On the night of May 23, 1962, Lynch was surprised by the animals howling in unison. 'If they are disturbed by something, they might howl for about 20 seconds,' Lynch explained. 'But this time, they kept it up for 10 minutes.'

The next day, Lynch learned that McCleery had died at the exact time the wolves had begun howling. 'I have no explanation for it,' Lynch said, 'especially since [McCleery] was in a hospital 36 miles away. I just know what I saw and heard.'

Dream of the Cave Dwellers

Anthropologist Joseph Mandemant once reported a prophetic dream in which he found himself in the famous Bedeilhac Cave. In the French cavern, prehistoric hunters gathered around a fire. On the ceiling Mandemant could clearly see hunting scenes obviously painted by the cave's occupants.

Mandemant was struck by the presence of a man and a woman, who he presumed were lovers. They left the main area and disappeared through a short cleft which led into a smaller, more private space and onto an outcropped ledge. As the anthropologist watched the two humans huddle in the darkness, a sudden loud roar erupted as the ceiling of the cave collapsed, sealing the room where the couple had been.

When he awoke, Mandemant recorded every detail of the dream and then set out for Bedeilhac Cave. At first, he seriously thought the trip was a wild goose chase. Inside the cave, however, he located a huge slab of limestone at the spot, in his dream, that seemed to be where the cleft leading to the lovers' private space had been. He tapped on it in various spots and heard an encouraging hollow sound. He hired workmen to break through the stone and, sure enough, on the other side found the lovers' space and the ledge.

While there was no trace of the prehistoric lovers, Mandemant did find the crude but elaborate hunting scenes he had first seen in his dream.

The Human Blowtorch

At first, it might have seemed like an entertaining gift but A.W. Underwood grew tired of his ability to set objects aflame by simply breathing on them. It was, after all, a talent he had to guard carefully. And despite months of tests, and the eventual celebrity status he achieved, not a single expert could explain what caused this bizarre phenomenon.

According to L.C. Woodman, the first physician to examine the fire-starter, when Underwood held items such as a cotton handkerchief or dry leaves against his mouth, they would burst into flames in a matter of seconds. The doctor rinsed out the 24-year-old man's mouth with various solutions. He made him wear rubber gloves. No matter how rigorous the examination, neither Woodman nor his colleagues could find any trace of trickery. Nor could they determine any medical condition that would have such symptoms.

Roger Williams' Apples

Roger Williams was one of the most honoured and beloved of the New World's early settlers. Having first arrived in Massachusetts from Cambridge, England, in 1631, he was later banished to Rhode Island for his outspoken religious views. In his new home, however, Williams became the leader of the tiny colony, famed for its unprecedented religious freedom.

When Williams died in 1683, he was buried in a grave

marked by a modest headstone. Some years later, however, Rhode Island officials decided to erect a more appropriate memorial. But when the grave was opened, to everyone's amazement, it was empty.

At first, the Roger Williams' Memorial Commission members suspected grave robbers had stolen the leader's remains. But, in fact, it was nothing so sinister. It seems that as the roots of a nearby apple tree had grown, they pushed their way into the coffin where they overtook and eventually absorbed the remains of Roger Williams. The evidence was the tangle of roots the shape of which bore a remarkable resemblance to a human body.

The Commission decided to remove and preserve **the** roots which are now in the possession of the Rhode Island Historical Society.

The Former Life of Shanti Devi

Born in 1926 in Delhi, India, Shanti Devi was only three years old when she began talking about people she referred to as her husband and children. Questioned by her mystified parents, Shanti said her spouse's name was Kedarnath. Both he and a son, moreover, lived in Muttra.

Thinking the girl was suffering from some sort of delusion, her parents took her to the doctor. While there, Shanti recounted even more details of her previous life, including her pregnancy. She had died during childbirth in 1925, she told the physician.

By the time she was eight years old, Shanti had been examined by half a dozen doctors, but no one had gone beyond questioning the girl. Her great-uncle, however, finally decided to investigate her story and tracked down the man Shanti said was her husband. Kedarnath did, indeed, still live in Muttra with his two children, the youngest being the child his wife had died delivering in 1925. But believing he was being tricked, Kedarnath declined to meet the girl himself and sent a cousin to Delhi in his place.

When the cousin arrived at the Devi home on the pretext of conducting business with Shanti's father, the girl immediately recognized him,. After discussing and agreeing on many details of the deceased woman's life, the cousin was convinced of Shanti's recollections and he sent for Kedarnath.

Some time later, Shanti finally went to Muttra to meet her former family, but they wanted nothing to do with her and Shanti had to learn to live in the present. By this time, however, the case had attracted the attention of the press as well as past-life researchers. Many of them investigated her claims thoroughly before Shanti could begin the process of adapting to her new life. The case remains one of the best documentations of past-life recall in history.

The Garrulous Glastonbury Monks

During his research of Glastonbury Abbey in 1907, prior to its eventual excavation, Frederick Bligh-Bond was frustrated in his attempts to locate the sites of two particular chapels mentioned in many early descriptions. Since all other alternatives had failed, the British architect and archaelogist considered the use of automatic writing to enlist the aid of the spiritual world.

As one of the most famous historical sites in England, Glastonbury Abbey is said to have existed during the lifetime of Jesus Christ. In fact, according to legend, Christ himself had visited the religious enclave. Kings – including, many believe, Arthur – had been buried in its chapel. By 1086, it had become a shrine and the object of pilgrimages. During the reign of Henry VIII, however, the abbey was destroyed, a consequence of the King's battles with the Catholic church. Eventually, the remains of the massive structure crumbled until finally nothing remained of the former magnificence.

Although Bligh-Bond initially planned nothing more than an experiment in automatic writing to locate the chapels, he called upon a friend, a certain Captain Bartlett who was proficient in producing written messages from otherworldly entities. Amazingly, the 'spirits' were sympathetic to Bligh-Bond's plight. Soon they began spouting incredibly detailed information about the location and measurements of the abbey's chapels. The communicators, moreover, identified themselves as former Glastonbury occupants, principally monks. At least one, for instance, had lived there about 1,000 years before construction of the actual abbey and described the support for the roof of a hut he had designed and that was later uncovered by Bligh-Bond's workmen. Each communicator would respond to particular questions relating to his own tenure at the abbey.

Using the information furnished by the spirits, Bligh-Bond surveyed the area around the site of the abbey. Subsequent excavations prove all the details to be correct, often accurate to within a fraction of an inch. Authorities had no doubt that the Glastonbury discoveries were legitimate. When Bligh-Bond revealed how he located them, however, he lost a great deal of credibility. Although the excavation continued, Bligh-Bond was soon driven off the project in 1922. Ten years later, in his book *The Gate of Remembrance*, he not only wrote about the messages he had received and verified by the excavation, but also revealed other descriptions of the abbey which were also later confirmed.

Velikovsky, the Bible and the Planets

Immanuel Velikovsky, a Russian-born author who emigrated to America in 1939, provoked a scientific and astrological storm 11 years later with his book, *Worlds in Collision*, the echoes of which are still reverberating in the world of science. Based on his studies of ancient history, Velikovsky attempted to show that the stories from the first books of the Bible, so often considered purely legend, were basically historical and could be corroborated by the legends of other ancient races existing at the same time.

Velikovsky claimed that the Earth had indeed experienced planet-shaking catastrophes as 'recently' as 2,000 years ago when, as recorded in the Bible, the sun had stood still in the heavens, the Red Sea had parted and joined again, manna had fallen from the skies and sustained the Israelites, great plagues had beset Egypt – in short, that the miracles of the age of Moses were in fact true. He maintained his theories by even more surprising suppositions: that part of the planet Jupiter had torn off and formed a comet; that the comet had swerved near Mars, knocking Mars off its orbit to a near collision with Earth, and that the comet had continued its path within our own solar system periodically causing tidal waves and enormous earthquakes on Earth until the comet became the planet Venus.

According to Velikovsky human mass destruction has been detailed in almost all ancient records, and mass animal extinctions are evidenced by remains in caves and rock strata throughout the world. Despite Velikovsky's assiduously compiled corroboratory evidence from ancient writings and legends, his theories were generally ridiculed by the scientific establishment. A distinguished

British astronomer stated that his book was 'all lies', adding that he 'had not read and would never read (it)'. Another astronomer said it was 'the worst book since the invention of movable characters'. The public, as might be assumed, read it with enthusiasm.

This author asked Velikovsky shortly before his death how he had been able to predict, long before it was 'officially' known, that the surface of Mars was covered with craters, that Venus spins in the opposite direction to other planets in our system, and that the planets and the sun have positive and negative electrical charges. He also was asked how he knew in advance that the temperature of Venus would be 800°F when Einstein himself had predicted that it would be −25°F?

Velikovsky answered in a somewhat indirect manner. He said: 'You know the British Museum has thousands and thousands of Babylonian baked clay tablets which have not yet been translated or published. They offer interesting and pertinent information about the solar system to anyone who takes the trouble to read them'. It should be added that Dr Velikovsky had great expertise in the languages of the ancient Middle East and was able to read the inscribed cuneiform texts of Assyria and Babylonia.

The Ancients Knew About Antarctica

In 1513, Piri Ibn Haji Mehmed, an officer in the Turkish navy who was known as Piri Re'is, commissioned cartographers to prepare a map of the Atlantic Ocean and its bordering lands. After completion, the map was forgotten until 1929 when it was found in the Turkish

Imperial Archives in Constantinople. Drawn just 21 years after Columbus discovered America, it was one of the most accurate early maps of the New World. An inscription on the map indicated that Piri Re'is based the western portion on maps that Columbus himself had used during his first voyage. It was the first evidence that there had been earlier maps, and supported the idea held by many researchers that Columbus had known about and used them. Another inscription, moreover, stated that the Turkish officer had also consulted even older maps, some dating to the time of Alexander the Great.

The map also presented proof that the unexplored Antarctic continent had been mapped by someone thousands of years before it was rediscovered in 1820. It shows, in correct proportion, parts of Africa and eastern South America. Beneath the southern tip of South America, there are contours of another coastline. Cartographer and historian Charles Hapgood has identified these as the coastline and mountains of Antarctica as they actually exist under the covering ice sheet. What is more unbelievable for an ancient map is that it was drawn using spherical trigonometry and adapted to the curvature of the Earth, thousands of years before it was possible to calculate longitude.

As it is known that Antarctica was largely ice-free about 8,000 to 10,000 years BC, a number of explanations for the advanced mapping have been offered, including the theory that this was an air map made by extraterrestrials from a UFO.

Charles Hapgood disputes the UFO theory as follows:

It is . . . reasonable to suppose that the land was occupied and that the occupants could make maps. I feel that only commercial motivation could have led to the mapping: somebody wanted the natural resources and the trade of the continent.

It is unrealistic to jump to the conclusion that . . . extraterrestrials made the maps. The maps in their present state do not suggest the accuracy we should attribute to people capable of crossing billions of miles of interstellar space.

With the mention of commercial motivations, Hapgood may have explained the survival of the Greek or proto-Greek maps of an earlier world. They were preserved by constant copying by shipmasters who wished to keep secret the trade routes to distant places. The Oronteus Finaeus map, last copied in 1532 from an ancient original, shows rivers flowing through Antarctica which follow the path of present glaciers. Still another, the Bouache world map, dated 1754, shows Antarctica at the bottom of the world and explains that the undiscovered continent must exist to balance the world's land areas. But the then unknown continent was drawn correctly – with one seemingly notable exception: it was shown as two enormous islands, separated by a sea. This is, in fact, the actual shape of Antarctica without the ice.

The existence of Antarctica was finally accepted as a reality in 1820. But it was not until the Geophysical Year of 1955 that an international scientific expedition verified that the true coast of Antarctica is obscured by the ice; that there are mountains and riverbeds under the two-mile high ice cover, and that the continent itself consists of two enormous islands.

One mystery remains. What was the advanced civilization whose representatives charted the land around the southern pole when humanity was young and Antarctica had not yet been frozen over?

UFOs over Africa

Zimbabwe Air Force officials are still baffled by a round, shiny, unidentified object with a cone-shaped top that swooped over the southern part of their African nation in 1985. According to Zimbabwe's Air Commodore David Thorne, air traffic controllers watched the craft hover overhead and even tracked it on radar. Pursuing the UFO, air force pilots got a good look at it as the craft streaked across the sky. They described it as being so shiny that at first it seemed to reflect the colours of the sunset, but as the sky grew darker, they realized that the UFO was creating its own light. The pilots also estimated that the UFO was travelling at twice the speed of sound. 'Our pilots are completely reliable,' Thorne insisted. 'This cannot be dismissed as a 'plane, weather balloon, or natural phenomenon.'

Celestial Swastika

The swastika, in modern times, has become a symbol of evil, but according to two University of Texas scientists, the Nazi emblem may have mystical connotations.

When physicists C.J. Ransom and Hans Schluter exposed hydrogen gas to electricity and magnetism, the hydrogen glowed. Then the gas suddenly dispersed to form the silhouette of a swastika. The experiment led the scientists to speculate that a comet, passing through the Earth's magnetic field, might create a similar effect. If so, then the swastika would have first appeared to humans as a naturally occurring phenomenon, but awestruck observers would have taken it as a supernatural sign. That, they concluded, would explain why the modern symbol of evil was once revered by the Hindu and other religions. Swastikas are carved, for example, on ancient tombs near the city of Troy. And even Christians portrayed it as a holy symbol during the Middle Ages.

Roman UFOs

In his manuscript, *Predigerium liber*, fourth-century Roman historian Julius Obsequins recorded numerous accounts of UFO sightings. In one particular incident, for example, a round, ship-like shield with flaming torches gyrated and fell to the ground near Spoletium, north of Rome. 'It then seemed to increase, rose from the earth, and ascended into the sky, where it obscured the disk of the sun with its brilliance,' he wrote.

Obsequins' reports, however, were not the only ones to be recorded and to survive into the twentieth century. In *Prodigerium ac Ostentorium Chronicon*, a professor of grammar and dialectics compiled other Roman sightings whose descriptions are remarkably similar to modern accounts of UFOs seen flying in formation. During the reign of Emperor Theodosius, for example, in the last years of the fourth century, a glowing orb suddenly appeared in the sky, shining almost as brightly as Venus. As witnesses gazed in awe, a great number of other similar objects amassed, like a swarm of bees flying around a bee-keeper. They seemed, moreover, to be dashing violently against each other, and eventually joined to form a shape resembling a two-edged sword.

The Image in the Challenger Smoke

When the space shuttle Challenger exploded on January 28, 1986, a nation watched in horror as the lives of seven American astronauts, including one teacher, ended tragically. That night, one witness repeatedly watched a videotape of the disaster hoping, perhaps, to grasp its reality. Viewing the tape closely, however, she noticed an image that greatly affected many devastated employees at the Kennedy Space Centre.

Now a Kennedy Space Centre medic, Debi Hall had witnessed the disaster first-hand, seated alongside reporters and the astronauts' families. At home, exhausted and emotionally drained by the day's events, Hall initially thought she was imagining things when she sat in front of the television. She kept rewinding the tape and playing the scene back until she convinced herself that, yes, there was an image of Christ in the clouds of smoke enveloping the Challenger.

The following day, she and her husband viewed the tape together and he agreed that there was clearly an image of a large, bearded face. And when Hall took the videotape to the space centre, others also saw the face, without it being pointed out to them. Hall's explanation? 'I think it shows divine intervention,' she says.

Captive Extraterrestrials

During the summer of 1983, Larry Bryant of Alexandria, Virginia, USA, served a writ of habeas corpus on the United States Departments of Defense and State, the Air Force, the Army, the National Security Agency and the Federal Bureau of Investigation (FBI). His charge? All the defendants had conspired to cover up the crash of an extraterrestrial vehicle in the New Mexico desert in 1950. What's more, the Air Force actually possessed one or more bodies of the UFO's occupants.

An FBI document appended to the court order quoted an Air Force investigator as saying three flying saucers had been recovered near the Pentagon's huge radar apparatus in New Mexico. Evidently the radar had interfered with the crafts' controlling mechanisms. According to the memo, each circular craft had a diameter of approximately 50 feet and contained a raised section in the centre. Their occupants were humanoid, it continued, three feet tall and wearing metallic bodysuits.

Bryant believed the extraterrestrial visitors were still alive and being held against their constitutional rights. They could not be held without being charged with a crime, he argued, and by serving the writ, Bryant hoped to have the aliens released by the government or, at least, recover their bodies. Perhaps he wished mostly to make the affair public but it was unlikely that the government, after years of denying the existence of UFOs was now going to acknowledge them, let alone admit to the custody of the aliens themselves, just because they had been served a writ of habeas corpus.

The Bermuda Triangle Revisited

An area bounded by an imaginary line stretching from Florida to Bermuda to Puerto Rico and then back to Florida, the Bermuda Triangle has been the site of many mysterious disappearances of boats, planes and people. One of the oddest incidents occurred during a short flight to Turk Island in the Bahamas.

As Helen Cascio piloted her Cessna 172 on the approach to the island, the control tower imparted her landing instructions. But Cascio didn't respond, although her radio channel was open. The tower operators then heard the pilot telling her lone passenger, 'I must have made a wrong turn. That should be Turk, but there's nothing down there. No airport. No houses. Nothing.'

The controllers continued frantically to contact the pilot, but Cascio obviously could not hear them. Then they received what would be the final query they would hear: 'Is there no way out of this?' No trace of the plane, pilot or passenger was ever found.

Many investigators' explanations for the bizarre disappearances in the Triangle range from hijackers by modern pirates to simple human error. There is also some speculation that in the area there is a whirlpool or a hole in the ocean that swallows vessels and aircraft unfortunate enough to pass directly overhead.

Another possibility, however, is that the parts of Atlantis lie beneath the Bermuda Triangle. Fabled Atlantean pyramids, constructed as power sources, may still function sporadically and disrupt vessels' and aircrafts' communication and control systems.

Then, of course, those who believe we are being invaded by malevolent or devious extraterrestrials speculate that these aliens can somehow lock into the Bermuda Triangle's magnetic field and extricate human specimens and artefacts for their own research purposes.

While many disappearances in the Bermuda Triangle have been widely reported, however, less has been heard about craft appearing in the area. In July 1975, for example, Jim Thorne, a member of an oceanic research group aboard the yacht *New Freedom*, photographed a dazzling electrical storm above the Triangle. Examining the developed film, he was shocked to see a clear image of a square-rigged boat an estimated 100 yards from the *New Freedom*. Yet on the night of the storm, he knew there had been no other vessels in the vicinity.

The Mysterious Martian Canals

When Italian astronomer Giovanni Schiaparelli discovered a grid of lines on the surface of Mars in 1877, he theorized that the canals, as he called them, had been created by inhabitants of the red planet as some kind of irrigation system to conserve their dwindling water. Later, some observers thought the lines might, instead, be trails followed by herds of migratory Martian animals.

Many others, particularly today, suggest the so-called canals were actually dried-up river beds. There are, in fact, strong indications that there is still surface ice at the planet's poles. But until spacefarers are able to explore the planet, the explanation for the Martian canals will remain a mystery.

The Unknown Planet

Every school child is taught that there are nine planets in our solar system. But for more than 100 years some astronomers have postulated that there may, in fact, be a tenth.

The scientific speculation began in March 1859 when a French country doctor and amateur skywatcher named Levearbault observed an object orbiting the sun. It seemed to be even closer to the sun than Mercury, considered by most astronomers to to be the closest planet orbiting the sun. Levearbault meticulously tracked and timed the assumed planet's path, recording his observations on a pine board.

When France's most illustrious astronomer, Urbain Jean Le Verrier studied Levearbault's records, he agreed that there was, indeed, another planet, which he subsequently dubbed Vulcan. According to Le Verrier, Vulcan's presence would explain why Mercury moves 43 inches closer to the sun every year. Vulcan's gravity, he proposed, was actually pulling Mercury towards it.

Even so, no one since has observed Vulcan – perhaps because many don't believe the planet exists and are, therefore, not looking for it. Yet some of these same sceptical astronomers have speculated that a tenth planet, which they have likewise never seen, does exist, but in the other direction, beyond Pluto.

The City That Vanished Twice

There are a number of legendary lost cities on the bottom of the Atlantic Ocean and the Mediterranean, Aegean and Caribbean seas. There are also a number that are certainly drowned but not lost as their locations are known. The ancient Roman seaside resort of Baiai, for example, is not far from Naples and has been explored and extensively photographed by divers working at a depth of 50 to 60 feet. Sybaris, whose name has become synonymous with luxurious or 'sybaritic' living, lies on the sea floor of the Gulf of Taranto. Parts of Carthage, Leptus Magna, Tyre, Caesarea, Alexandria, and other large cities still lie under the waters of the Mediterranean.

Such cities have usually subsided into the sea as a result of seismic action, and are easily located because the ancient chroniclers told us where they were. Something unusual, however, happened to Helike, a large city of classical Greece which, in 373 BC, disappeared from the surface during an earthquake and tidal wave with all of its buildings, streets, ships and thousands of inhabitants. No one escaped the final towering wave which swept away not only the ships of Helike but also ten visiting warships from the Spartan fleet anchored in the harbour. Where Helike used to be there were only the waters of the Gulf of Corinth.

When the waters cleared it was possible to see the ruins of the city on the sea floor. For hundreds of years Helike stayed in its undersea location, perfectly visible through the clear water. Roman tourists of a later epoch would contract Greek boatmen to row them over the well-preserved ruins. The tourists would often employ divers to bring up coins and other finds from the undersea city. The divers plunged up to 60 feet through crystal clear water. From the surface, a statue of Zeus (Jupiter to the Romans) could be seen still standing amid the ruins of his temple.

Towards the end of the Roman occupation of Greece, however, another earthquake opened the sea floor under the underwater city and then closed over it. Helike, now lost, may have contained treasures of considerably greater value than the silver and gold coins the divers were seeking.

Unless a new shock brings the city to the surface again, Helike may lie where it is forever, both lost and not lost several miles east of the present town of Aiyion on the northern shore and an unknown distance beneath the sea floor of the Gulf of Corinth.

The Pharaoh and the Aliens

An ancient Egyptian papyrus may contain one of the first known written accounts of a UFO sighting. According to the record, dating from the time of the Pharaoh Thutmose III, who reigned from 1504 to 1450 BC, scribes in the House of Life sighted a 'circle of fire' travelling silently through the sky. 'It had no head,' the papyrus states, 'and the breath of its mouth had a foul odour.' The awestruck observers fell to the ground, not knowing whether to fear or worship the strange celestial flame. During next few days, more and more similar fireballs, as bright as the sun, appeared over Egypt.

In an effort to ward off the objects' power, the Pharaoh directed the priests to burn incense to encourage the peaceful intercession of the gods. And when the unidentified objects finally departed, Thutmose ordered the written record so that the incident would be always remembered.

Lizard Man

There have been numerous Bigfoot or Yeti sightings around the world. The human-like creatures are usually said to be large and hairy with glowing red eyes. During the summer of 1988, however, residents of Bishopville, South Carolina, USA, reported accounts of a rare breed of Bigfoot: a seven-foot-tall lizard man with scaly green skin. According to witnesses, unlike other Bigfoot creatures, Lizard Man has only three toes on each foot, as well as long ape-like arms that end in three finger tipped with four-inch claws. Only the second Bigfoot to have only three fingers on each hand, and the first to have three toes on each foot, Lizard Man is the most unusual Bigfoot ever reported.

Seventeen-year-old Chris Davis first encountered Lizard Man around two o'clock on the morning of June 29. On his way home, he stopped near the brackish waters of Scape Ore Swamp outside Bishopville to change a flat tyre. While replacing the jack in the car's boot, he glimpsed something running across the field toward him. Jumping into his car, he was quickly engaged in a tug-of-war with the reptilian creature as he tried to pull the door closed. Then Lizard Man jumped onto the car's roof, where he left scratches in the paint as evidence of his attack.

Hysterical, Davis returned home and told only his parents and a few close friends about the experience. Law enforcement officers, however, interrogated him after neighbours said the boy might know something about the strange bite marks and scratches found on another car.

Davis, of course, wasn't the only person to encounter Lizard Man. Soon other reports were flooding the sheriff's office. Teenagers Rodney Nolfe and Shane Stokes, for example, were driving near the swamp with their girlfriends when Lizard Man darted across the road in front of their car. Construction worker George Holloman also claimed Lizard Man jumped at him as he was collecting water from an artesian well.

Investigating the area around the swamp, state trooper Mike Hodge and Lee County deputy sheriff Wayne Atkinson found three crumpled, 40-gallon cardboard drums. The tops of saplings were ripped off eight fee above the ground. And there were, according to Hodge, 'humongous footprints', fourteen-by-seven-inch impressions in hard red clay. Following the tracks for 400 yards, the officers backtracked and found new prints impressed in their car's tyre tracks. According to state wildlife biologists, the footprints matched no known animal species.

Cities without Names

The jungles and deserts of the Earth contain a number of 'lost' cities, lost because their impressive ruins leave few clues as to which civilization built them, and why they were abandoned. Their locations, often in deserts, deep forests, or under the sea, bear witness to past cataclysms, man-made as well as natural. Time has covered them under a jungle canopy or buried them under great mounds of earth.

Most of the lost cities of Europe, the Middle East, and Southern Asia can be linked to an identifiable culture. The ruins of Angkor Wat in Cambodia, the mound-covered cities of Babylonia, the sunken cities of the Mediterranean, and even the island ruins of the Pacific can be identified because of their similarities to other cultures. But what once were huge cities, like Mohenjo-daro and Harappa in Pakistan are not referred to in ancient records. These larger metropolises, which flourished thousands of years ago, once contained populations of over a million inhabitants. But no one knows their true names or what race built them. All available records are written in a hieroglyphic language which no one yet has been able to decipher. The only other place this language has appeared is on Easter Island, the Pacific island of colossal statues, almost exactly on the other side of the Earth from Mohenjo-daro and Harappa.

Some of the prehistoric cities of South America are especially puzzling because their location on the top of high mountains makes one wonder how enormous stones, weighing hundreds of tons, could possibly have been transported and set exactly in place. We do not know what these cities were originally called because they were already deserted when the Spanish conquistadors arrived. The American peoples who greeted and later fought the Spanish had given the ruins different names and, when questioned, said that the cities had been built by the gods.

There is an intriguing legend of a lost city which is said still to exist in the Amazon jungles. The city is reputed to contain great treasure, not buried but, in some versions, still in use by the inhabitants. These survivors are said to preserve their isolation by being surrounded by bellicose Indian tribes, notably unfriendly to explorers. The inhabitants of this lost city are said to be of a white race, and it is reported that they still possess an advanced culture and many accoutrements of civilization, including a means of illumination, not electric but a constant glowing light which is not fire.

Portuguese and other explorers have been trying to locate this mysterious city since the seventeenth century. One early expedition, led by a Francisco Raposo, ascended a precipice over the jungle and reached a plateau. They saw a large city about four miles away. When they approached the city they found it was apparently abandoned but only partially in ruins and a number of large stone buildings were still standing. There were streets, plazas, walls, arches and obelisks decorated with what appeared to be writing. Statues, carvings and the style of architecture were superior to those of other pre-conquest South American cities. Mine shafts outside the city indicated a high content of silver ore. While exploring, Raposo and his men saw some 'white Indians' in a canoe dressed in strange garments. The expedition, fearing an unequal combat, left the area. Other expeditions have tried unsuccessfully to retrace the route and one of them, comprising hundreds of men, disappeared in the jungle.

Colonel Percy Fawcett, a retired British Army officer, was undoubtedly the most dedicated among the explorers who continued the search. At different times from 1906 to 1925 he searched for and compiled information about this lost city which he considered to be in the vicinity of the Xingu River, a tributary of the Amazon, in Brazil. He thought it was part of a whole civilization, and that there were other cities also buried in the jungle. He believed too that the lost city was a remnant of an ancient advanced civilization, its people now degenerate, but who still preserved the remnants of a forgotten past.

His dedication to his research ended in 1925 when he disappeared himself on an expedition. The last entry in his diary, found later, indicated that he thought he was within a two-week trek of the city that he had so long tried to find.

Did he find it? Or was he killed by the Indians he once said might be guarding it? The disappearance of Colonel Fawcett is one of the major mysteries of exploration. His own words would be a fitting epitaph: 'What can be more enthralling than penetration into the secrets of the past and throwing light onto the history of civilization itself?'

The Prophecies at Fatima

More than 70 years ago, three shepherd children claimed they saw the apparition of 'a beautiful lady from heaven' who eventually entrusted them with three secrets. Although two were eventually disclosed, the third remains locked in a vault in the Vatican.

Lucia, Francisco and Jacinta claimed to have seen the apparition in a cloud hovering over a tree near the village of Fatima in Portugal. The mysterious woman told them to return to the same spot on the thirteenth of each month. On the appointed day, one month later, the children trekked back to the oak tree, followed by some 50 other villagers who had heard the children's tale spread throughout Fatima.

While some witnesses later claimed that there was, indeed, a low-hanging cloud over the tree, no one except the children saw the woman. The results were no different the following month, and soon sceptics were berating the children as well as the adults who had been taken in by the game. The children, however, insisted they were telling the truth.

Despite the seething of church officials, the children continued to return to the tree on the thirteenth of every month. On a rainy October 13, 1917, which would prove to be the last sighting of the apparition, the place was mobbed by faithful Catholics desperately hoping to experience a miracle. Although the children were still the only ones to see her, the woman identified herself as 'Our Lady of the Rosary' and divulged the three secrets. Then the vision vanished. Suddenly, villagers later reported, the rain stopped and the clouds dissipated, revealing a sun that seemed to begin spinning and then plummet to the ground. The terrified crowd was certain that the world was coming to an end, before the sun returned to its normal position. The bizarre behaviour was said to occur twice more.

But what about the secrets kept by the children? They were never divulged by Francisco or Jacinta, who died during the influenza epidemic of 1918. Lucia, however, later wrote an account of the experience in which she described the predictions, at the request of the Holy See. One was a vision of hell, she wrote, and another concerned the outbreak of World War II, even describing a 'great, unknown light' that accompanied Hitler's annexation of Austria in 1938.

At the Lady's request, Lucia said, the third secret must never be divulged and, indeed, remained in a sealed envelope until Pope John XXIII opened it in 1960. The revelation so terrified His Holiness that he reportedly ordered it resealed and never made public.

A Curious Meeting of Compatriots

The now-legendary sinking of the passenger ship *Andrea Doria* was a world-wide news event. But one of the lesser known tales associated with the disaster involved a bizarre meeting of compatriots.

The *Andrea Doria* was destroyed when a Swedish ocean liner ploughed into its side, penetrating the passenger cabins. In one of the cabins a young Norwegian girl, alone and panic-stricken began screaming in her native language.

It just so happened that one of the Swedish liner's crew, a Norwegian sailor, heard the girl's cries for help. They seemed to be right outside his own cabin. Pushing through the splintered wall of the ship, he was able to reach directly into the girl's cabin aboard the *Andrea Doria* and pull her into his cabin.

The ships had collided at the exact point where the two Norwegians had their cabins.

The Meteor at Forest Hill

The morning of December 8, 1847, was clear and sunny in Forest Hill, Arkansas, USA. By the end of the day, people would be debating the cause of events that had transpired.

By mid-afternoon of that early winter's day, churning grey clouds had mysteriously accumulated, blotting out the sun and darkening the sky. The clouds seemed to be illuminated by 'a red glare as of many torches', according to one eye-witness account. Suddenly, there was an ear-splitting explosion. Buildings shook and the church steeple's bell began ringing. Then, a barrel-sized object with a trail of flames hurtled from the sky.

The fiery ball struck the ground just outside Forest Hill, creating an indentation that measured more than two feet in diameter and eight feet deep. At the bottom of the hole, a huge rock steamed. It was, in fact, so hot that water instantly condensed into steam when poured into the hole. The air, investigators also noticed, was pungent with the aroma of sulphur.

Some experts, of course, believe the hurtling ball from the sky was a meteor, even though meteors are not known to be accompanied by sudden cloud formation. According to others, a flash storm produced lightning that struck the ground, fusing the soil into a type of rock called fulgurite. But this explanation doesn't account for the projectile that witnesses saw fall from the sky.

Starvation in the Palace

Robert Nixon, a ploughboy in fifteenth-century Cheshire, was a quiet, mentally retarded young man. Few people paid attention to his occasional outbursts of babbling verbiage. And it wasn't until he was called into the service of the King that anyone realized his talent.

One afternoon while working in the fields, Nixon suddenly inexplicably exclaimed, 'Now, Dick! Now, Harry! Oh, ill done, Dick! Oh well done, Harry! Harry has gained his day!' It meant nothing to his co-workers, and they would have normally forgotten all about the incident. But the next day, a passing courier from London reported that King Richard III had died in combat against forces commanded by the King's rival, Henry Tudor. The battle, the Cheshire folk learned, had occurred the previous day and, it seemed, at approximately the same time of Nixon's puzzling declaration.

When Henry Tudor, now Henry VII of England, heard about the incident, he sent for the retarded visionary. But Nixon became hysterical when the command was delivered. He was petrified of going to London and begged not to go. If he did, he said, he would surely starve to death. But despite his protestations, he was soon escorted to the palace where Henry intended initially to test Nixon's abilities.

As he had planned, Henry hid a valuable diamond, claimed that he had lost it, and asked Nixon to find it. Nixon, however, was more talented than the King presumed. He calmly and coherently said, quoting an old proverb, that anyone who hides an object should certainly be able to find it afterwards. So there was no need, he told the King, to tell his Majesty, where the diamond was.

Henry was so impressed, it's said, that he installed Nixon in the palace so that he could record the new

palace prophet's predictions. During his royal employment, Nixon foresaw the English civil war and the war
with France, as well as the deaths and abdications of
kings. Only one of his prophesies – that the town of
Nantwich will be destroyed during a great flood – has
yet to come true.

Despite his successful tenure in the King's service,
however, Nixon was continually plagued by the fear of
his own starvation. To ease his prophet's mind, Henry
ordered that Nixon be fed whenever and whatever he
wanted, which did not endear Nixon to the kitchen staff.
And when he was away from the castle, Henry also
assigned an officer to watch over Nixon's welfare.

The officer, it seems, took his orders quite seriously,
locking Nixon in a closet to protect him from any violence. Once, however, when he was suddenly called away
from the palace during the King's absence, he forgot that
Nixon was in the closet, and by the time anyone found
him, Nixon had starved to death.

Pure Chance

Frederick Chance was speeding down a lonely
road in Stourbridge, Worcestershire, when he saw the
headlights of an oncoming car. As vehicles were travelling at high speed, they were unable to swerve in time
to avoid a collision. Emerging from the wreckage with
only minor injuries, Chance checked in the other car
and satisfied himself that its driver was also relatively
unharmed. Thankful that the accident had not been
worse, Chance introduced himself to the other driver.
The motorist was incredulous, for he, too, was named
Frederick Chance.

Early Flesh Eaters

Modern anthropologists hold that tales of cannibalism among primitive tribes are largely myth. But evidence unearthed by archaeologist Jean Courtin indicates that as far back as the Stone Age at least one group of Stone Age dwellers did, in fact, eat human flesh.

Investigating a cave near Fontgregoua in south-eastern France, Courtin and his colleagues found the remains of six humans who had been dead for some 6,000 years. When closely examined, the bones revealed tiny cuts and chop marks. The flesh of the deceased had apparently been systematically stripped from their bones.

While it doesn't prove that whoever removed the flesh actually ate it, Courtin's find at least indicates that same-species butchering with some sort of tool had taken place. Anthropologist Paola Villa who examined the bones, believes that the six skeletons may have been prisoners of war who were killed and eaten by their captors.

Phantom Fountains

While watching television one mild, dry October night in 1963, Francis Martin and his family noticed an expanding wet spot on the wall of their Metheun, Massachusetts, USA, home. Then, they heard a distinct popping sound, and watched a fountain of water spurt from the site. The water flowed for about 20 minutes, stopped, and resumed 15 minutes later. During the succeeding days, the phenomenon spread to other sites around the house.

Soon the Martin's home was too water-logged to inhabit and the family was forced to move in with Mrs Martin's mother in nearby Lawrence. The phantom fountains, however, soon began occurring in the Lawrence house as well. The deputy fire chief, called in to examine the pipes thoroughly, was unable to find any leaks that might have caused the water flows which he also witnessed.

Deciding to return to Metheun, Martin turned off the water main and drained all the pipes in their own house. Although the pipes were all in perfect repair, the flooding persisted. When the family relocated once more to Lawrence, the fountains followed again, too.

Eventually, the water assaults ceased as mysteriously and suddenly as they had begun.

The Vision of Cyrano de Bergerac

Cyrano de Bergerac's legendary nose has been immortalized in many modern tales, but the French author's own tales deserve even greater attention. Few people are aware that the man may have been a prophet in his own right.

In his posthumously published tales of trips to the Sun and Moon, he described the orbits of the planets around the Sun, which at that time was not a popularly accepted idea, and he described a form of rocket propulsion. Cyrano also expressed the idea that traditional myths and religions were bequeathed to human beings by extra-terrestrial visitors to Earth.

The celestial travels in Cyrano's writings involved the

use of an amazing array of apparatus unheard of in the seventeenth century. To his contemporaries, de Bergerac's ideas – which included moveable dwellings, devices to record and replay speech, tubes that illuminate the dark – would certainly have seemed bizarre. Today, they seem remarkably similar to mobile homes, tape recorders and light bulbs.

The Doom of Seaforth

Bored with the tedious life at Brahan Castle, the Earl of Seaforth packed his bags in 1660 and left for Paris where he would remain indefinitely. But he didn't expect such an action to affect the entire Seaforth family line.

As each day passed and the Earl had still not returned to Seaforth, his suspicious wife Isabella grew angrier. One evening, during a gathering of guests at the castle, she summoned Kenneth MacKenzie, a local seer known as the Warlock of the Glen, whose abilities were known throughout the Scottish countryside. Gazing into the hole of a small white stone, he could foresee future events and predicted, amongst other things, the bloody battle of Culloden and other historic events.

Isabella, however, was not concerned about war and politics. She wanted to know what her husband was doing and where he was doing it. To answer her query, MacKenzie began to peer into his stone, only to begin laughing. With Isabella demanding to know what amused him, MacKenzie reluctantly replied that he had, indeed, perceived an image of the Earl. Yes, he was still in Paris, he told her, and he was enjoying himself in the company of two beautiful young women, onє sitting on his knee, the other stroking his hair. Humiliated in front of her guests, Isabella was furious and ordered the seer to be executed. But before he was put to death, MacKenzie placed a curse on Isabella and her family.

According to what became known as the Seaforth Doom, the Seaforth family line would eventually become extinct, MacKenzie declared, detailing the fate that would befall the cursed descendants. The last living descendant would be deaf and mute, and he would outlive his four sons. Brahan Castle would end up in the hands of a woman, who would eventually be responsible for her sister's death. The Seaforth Estate, moreover, would cease to exist.

In time, as the family continued to prosper, despite some minor setbacks during changing political climates, the curse was forgotten. Then in 1783, the only living Seaforth heir, Francis Humberston MacKenzie inherited the castle and the estate. During childhood, the new master of Brahan Castle had contracted scarlet fever. As a result, he was deaf and mute, although he regained limited speech later in life, married and fathered 10 children, including four sons.

When Francis died in 1815, having outlived all of his four sons, there were no male heirs to the Seaforth title. The estate, then, went to the Earl's daughter, Mary Elizabeth Frederica. Soon afterwards, Mary took her younger sister Catherine out for a fateful carriage ride. During the excursion, one of the horses bolted and caused the entire team to run out of control, dragging the carriage along with them. The carriage hit a rock along the road, overturned and rolled down a bank, killing Catherine almost instantly.

Eventually, devastated by financial mismanagement, extravagance and government fines, Mary was forced to sell the Seaforth estate, piece by piece, until there was nothing left. With the land, the castle, and even the family name gone forever, the Seaforths were no more – just as the Warlock of the Glen had predicted.

Revenge of the Fish

One of the favourite dishes among natives of Papua New Guinea is needle fish, a thin, silvery, foot-long marine creature with a three-inch-long bony snout. At one time, however, the fish began attacking its potential predators – as many as 20 victims a month – in deadly fashion. And natives began calling on the spirit world for protection, chanting incantations as they sat in their boats waiting for a bite.

Physician Peter Barss first encountered the results of needlefish attacks a week after he began working at the Milne Bay Hospital. Villagers presented him with the body of a fisherman who had died when a sharp piece of bone had pierced his chest. The cause of the fatal wound became evident a week later when the natives arrived with another dead fisherman. This time, the bone was still attached to its owner: a lice needlefish imbedded in the man's stomach.

During the ensuing weeks, Barss saw numerous other cases of needlefish attacks, most of them occurring at night. Initially, the doctor speculated that the fish were attracted by the light of the lanterns, somewhat like moths, and they had accidentally 'stabbed' the unsuspecting fishermen. But there were other people who had been assaulted in broad daylight, including a three-year-old girl who was paralyzed as a result of a needlefish attack. So Barss concluded that the fish were purposely hurling themselves at the occupants of fishing boats in a sort of kamikaze mission to exact revenge.

The Philadelphia Experiment

In 1943, a top-secret experiment at the US naval yard in Philadelphia was designed to test the ultimate weapon – an invisible battleship. As a result, however, numerous people involved in the experiment suffered bizarre after-effects, most notably spontaneous human combustion, and the government eventually cancelled – and covered up – the project.

The navy was using a powerful electromagnetic field (EMF) in its attempts to render the destroyer escort *USS Eldridge* invisible to radar and magnetic mines. During World War II, scientists didn't understand the harmful effects that EMFs could have on the central nervous system. Consequently, while working to build the ship, some crewmen may have inadvertently been too close to the source of electromagnetic energy.

The navy continues to deny that there was ever such an experiment, claiming it was concocted in a 1955 book about UFOs. But the case files are still open and from time to time new evidence emerges.

Blind Vision

People often recall previous lives in such detail that it's almost impossible not to accept reincarnation as fact. Science, however, demands evidence. Philosophy professor James Parejko postulated if a person born blind had visual memories of a previous lifetime, it would go a long way towards proof of reincarnation. To that end, he set up an experiment at Chicago State University to test his hypothesis.

Parejko began by hypnotizing three blind subjects and regressing them into past lives. Just as he had hoped, all three reported *seeing* things. They spoke, for example, of flickering candles, yellow teeth and people with blotches on their faces. And their accounts indicated the reactions of a sighted person: in one case, a subject spoke about having to look away when the sun shone on the jewellery of someone else. Would a sightless person have any idea that such an action was necessary?

Parejko doesn't agree with sceptics who suggest that the three blind people could easily have taken their descriptions from books. He cites the case of a man who, once his sight was restored, was baffled by the difference between the way he had imagined things and what he actually saw. The blind, moreover, report that their past lives are much more vivid than their dreams.

The Quest for Jason

One of the greatest explorers in Greek mythology, Jason and his crew of Argonauts successfully battled such legendary foes as the Amazons and the half-bird, half-woman creatures known as Harpies in their quest for the Golden Fleece. Oxford University scholar Tim Severin believes Jason was much more than a fictional hero.

According to Severin, Jason lived during the Bronze Age, some 3,000 years ago. Because there is no written history of the period, Severin decided to embark on an expedition to trace the Argonauts' ancient route and to gather archaeological evidence of Jason's existence.

Severin and a group of 20 colleagues set sail in March,

1984, from Volos, Greece, in a ship that the Oxford scholar christened *Argo* after Jason's famous vessel. Volos, of course, is said to be the site of Jason's home, the ancient city of Pegasae. From there, Severin hoped to proceed through the Black Sea to find the kingdom of Colchis, the home of Jason's wife, the sorceress Medea, which is believed to have been located somewhere near the modern Soviet Republic of Georgia.

The evidence still hasn't been found, but Severin is confident that Soviet archaeologists will be able to provide concrete proof that in ancient times Jason had, indeed, roamed what is now Georgia. After all, Severin points out, it's rare, if not unheard of, to have an epic story that is entirely imaginary.

Great Balls of Fire

Except for thunderclouds some 60 miles away, the sky was clear as the Russian passenger plane departed the town of Sochi in 1984, all signs pointing to a routine flight. Soon after they left the local airport, however, the pilots saw a glowing fireball, with a diameter of about four inches, outside the cockpit window. With a deafening noise, the fireball suddenly shot through the metal wall of the fuselage and appeared in the main section of the plane. The shocked passengers watched as it swooped over their heads and zipped toward the rear where it split into two crescent-shaped halves. In another moment, it had reformed and exited through the rear, vanishing without a trace.

The pilots turned the plane around and headed directly back to Sochi, where investigators discovered that the plane's radar equipment had been severely damaged.

There was a hole, moreover, in both the fuselage and the tail.

The fireball, Soviet scientists decided, was a rare and little-understood phenomenon known as ball lightning, which years earlier was also experienced by a United States military plane. In a fashion similar to the Soviet experience, the fireball entered the cockpit, passed between the two astonished American pilots, drifted through the plane, and then shot out of the back.

The Human Lightning Rod

Most of us fear being struck by lightning during electrical storms, but the chances of that happening are, in fact, rather slim. Being struck more than once is even more improbable. For Betty Jo Hudson of Winburn Chapel, Mississippi, USA, however, the odds are much higher. She has come to the conclusion that she's a human lightning conductor.

Hudson first noticed her electrical affinity when she was a child and lightning struck her in the face. Not long afterwards, her parents' home received a powerful electrical jolt and, in 1957, the house was completely destroyed by yet another lightning blast. When the woman married Ernest Hudson, however, the lightning seemed to change course. Her new home became the focus and was struck three times. Even the neighbours were being hit during electrical storms. And lightning has struck trees as well as a water pump in the yard. One bolt even killed the Hudsons' dog.

One of the more recent episodes occurred when the Hudsons were shelling butter beans on their front porch one summer afternoon. A flash storm passed through, sending the couple scurrying inside. As they huddled together, they heard a horrifying crash: the lightning had devastated the bedroom.

Dying for Publicity

Some common motives for suicide are escape from sorrow or unbearable difficulties, protest, honour – fairly common in Japan and other parts of Asia – escape from incurable illness, and unrequited love, perhaps not now so common as it was in past, more romantic eras. But a recent offer by Portuguese poet Joaquim Castro Caldes to commit suicide for the sake of personal publicity is an interesting exception. He made the offer in good faith to the Gulbenkian Foundation, a world organization dedicated to the arts.

Castro offered to commit suicide for US$7,000 (it sounds better in Portuguese currency – 1,320,000 escudos). He even submitted a breakdown of how the money was to be spent: esc 70,000 for revolver and bullets; esc 500,000 for cremation and scattering of his ashes on the Tagur river flowing through Lisbon; esc 500,000 for a good orchestra to play Mahler's *Kindertotenlieder*; and esc 250,000 for an orchestrated performance by 200 clowns.

Not surprisingly, the Foundation refused the detailed and imaginative offer which nevertheless, became known to the press, possibly through information furnished by the prospective 'victim'. In any case, the poet got the publicity he wanted, without having to kill himself for it.

Canine Hero

When Christine Harrison visited her parents in Barnsley, Yorkshire, she took along her chihuahua, Percy. The dog ran into the street and was hit by a car. As far as anyone could tell, Percy was dead. The family wrapped the beloved pet in a heavy paper bag and buried him in a two-foot-deep grave in the garden.

Christine's parents' dog, Mick, however, wouldn't leave the grave alone. The terrier frantically sniffed and scratched at the soil. Finally unearthing the burial sack, Mick carried it into the house, where he began licking the chihuahua. Percy, it seems, was unconscious but with a faint heartbeat.

The family rushed the chihuahua to the veterinarian who revived him and concluded that Percy had been in shock and survived underground because of the air trapped in the paper bag. Mick's lick massage, moreover, had stimulated the smaller dog's circulation.

Percy fully recovered, and the Royal Society for the Prevention of Cruelty to Animals nominated Mick for an animal lifesaving award. What impressed Christine the most about the remarkable canine heroism, however, was the fact that the two dogs had always hated each other.

Storm Drain Crocodiles

Tales of alligators in New York City sewers have flourished for years, despite the lack of evidence. But in Cairns, Australia, three- to four-foot-long crocodiles often roam through sewers. Although the crocs rarely bother residents, at least one developed a taste for people.

One afternoon, 21-year-old Leon Phillips was walking down the main street in Cairns, Australia, when a hefty crocodile stuck its head out of a sewer and grabbed the young man by the leg. Fortunately, Philips was able to kick the crocodile away with his heavy cowboy boots and the help of a passing cab driver.

No one is quite sure how the crocodiles found their way into the sewer system, but some suggest that somebody may have had a small croc or two that grew too large and released them into the storm drains.

The Eye of the God

The medical symbol that looks like an 'R' with a cross at the bottom and appears on doctors' prescriptions is not a letter at all. It is a shortened form of the hieroglyphic for 'eye' – specifically the eye of Horus, the Egyptian god of medicine and cures. Adopted by doctors of ancient times as a symbol of their craft, its use has survived the civilization of pharaonic Egypt by thousands of years. So today, when doctors write prescriptions, they may not realize it, but they're paying homage to the god of medicine and cures.

The Zombie in the Fields

Zombies, legendary or not, are an accepted fact of life in Haiti. A possible explanation for so many cases of the seemingly dead and buried being brought back to life to do manual labour is that the so-called death is not really death but a deep coma deliberately induced by drugs. The victims, seemingly dead, are buried and then dug up, resuscitated by different drugs and sold as field workers by the voodoo practitioners.

Mrs Gloria Andrulonis, a woman who lived on an estate in rural Haiti some years ago, had an unusual experience related to zombies when her cook's daughter died. The girl was duly buried but, a few days after the funeral, servants from the next estate told the cook that they had seen her daughter working in the fields of a neighbouring plantation with a group of zombies.

When Mrs Andrulonis asked her cook what she would do about this, the woman replied, 'Nothing. What can one do? She is dead. She has been buried and her soul has gone.'

It is believed that zombies are supposed to be fed only unsweetened and unsalted food. A number of cases have been reported in Haiti about so-called zombies, who ate sweets, remembered their death and tried to go back to their graves.

The Mysterious Soviet Mummies

Soviet speleologists exploring caves in central Russia discovered a virtual city of the dead, composed of dozens of ancient, mummified men, horses and wild animals. Soviet scientists speculate that the men had been fleeing the armies of Alexander the Great, who reached modern day Afghanistan in the fourth century BC. On the other hand, they could have been driven into the caves by a family feud and ended up meeting a mysterious collective death. Others, like Emory University anthropologist Brad Shore, believe that the men may have been the victims of a natural disaster: a mudslide or landslide could have trapped the victims, burying them alive and then preserving their bodies.

The mummies, however, also disclosed evidence of mite infestation that had left the men with painful body sores, which didn't surprise the mountain people who live in the area today. They have always believed that the black plague originated in mites from the nearby caves.

The Bedside Bomb

The Nazis were approaching the Soviet town of Berdyansk in 1941, heralding their arrival with gunfire and bombs. Zinaida Bragantsova sat by the window, sewing and trying to remain calm. Suddenly, a harsh blast of hot wind knocked the woman unconscious, and when she came to she discovered a huge hole in the floor. Inside lay a German bomb. During the continued shelling, Bragantsova was unable to seek the help of authorities, so she simply patched up the floor and waited for the end of the war.

For years afterwards, Bragantsova pleaded with anyone who would listen, but no one would believe her story about a bomb under her bed. Her neighbours thought she was crazy. Soviet officials even accused the woman of fabricating the whole incident in order to get a new apartment.

In 1984, however, a telephone cable was being installed in Bragantsova's neighbourhood and demolition experts were in Berdyansk to check for unexploded World War II bombs that might still be lying around. Bragantsova again pleaded for someone to remove her bomb. And this time an army lieutenant was sent to investigate. Sure enough, a 500-pound German bomb was found in the hole, now under the old woman's bed which she had placed over the spot to hide the ugly patchwork.

After the Berdyansk neighbourhood was hastily evacuated, the bomb was detonated, destroying Bragantsova's home in the process. But the grandmother was finally rid of the bomb and would receive a new apartment.

The problem with decades-old bombs is that, for no known reason, they can suddenly go off. Fortunately for Zinaida Bragantsova, the bomb under her bed waited 43 years to be found before exploding.

The Demon Sea of Japan

The Bermuda Triangle may have an equally mysterious counterpart in the Pacific Ocean, off the coast of central Japan. Known as the Demon Sea, or the Devil Sea, the fateful area had claimed nine ships when the government decided to send a search party to investigate in 1955. The expedition ship not only found no traces of the first nine ships, but it also disappeared within days.

During the next 15 years, the Demon Sea swallowed at least a dozen more ships. And more recently the Japanese Transport Ministry launched another expedition, this time using robots instead of humans to do the job. A robot-buoy will perform the possibly dangerous task of analysing the wind, weather and wave conditions in the Demon Sea.

Some scientists speculate that severe winter weather conditions and extremely large waves may be responsible for the accidents. One trait, however, is already known about the Demon Sea: magnetic and true north are aligned at the site, making them indistinguishable.

The Pyramid at the Bottom of the Sea

East of the Florida Keys, about 27 miles north of Cuba and at a depth of 1,000 feet, a pyramidal formation rises from the bottom of the sea. It is so regularly shaped that it appears to be a man-made construction. Its height, as indicated on the radar screen, appears to be about 400 feet, making it of comparable size to the pyramids of Egypt. If this is, in fact, a pyramid it would be one more proof of the existence of a now-submerged ancient culture whose ruined buildings, roads, stone walls, stairways and shaped monoliths are scattered along the sea floor of the Caribbean and the western Atlantic. These would be the remnants of settlements covered by water when the ocean levels rose and the land sank during the changes that occurred at the end of the third glaciation more than 10,000 years ago.

The huge stone formation or man-made pyramid was outlined in the 1970s by a fishing captain, John Henry, using sonar to track schools of fish. It is located not on the Bahama Banks but on the ocean floor, after dropping off in the vicinity of Cay Sal.

According to the sonar image, its top is several hundred feet below the surface, making it impossible for scuba divers to examine it in sufficient detail. Its profile, although regular, does not resemble an Egyptian pyramid but rather an Aztec or Mayan one with a small construction at its flattened summit.

It has been researched and photographed by several expeditions. Photographs and films from lowered cameras have been taken by researchers Jacques Mayol and Ari Marshall. These photographs indicate the curious presence of flashing globules of light in the lower section of the pyramidal mass.

About 10 years ago, according to the account of several crew members, a United States nuclear-powered submarine struck something solid as it was cruising near the bottom of what they referred to as the 'Bermuda Triangle'. The submarine personnel were not hurt and the submarine, which had ice-breaking equipment, was not damaged. Depth maps showed no underwater cliffs or mountains in the area but sonar mapping might easily miss a pyramidal formation even if crossing it at a lower level.

Since no further information was released by official sources we are left only with an intriguing concept. Perhaps man's most modern and perfected underwater combat vehicle collided with a pyramid so old that the land it was built on has since sunk beneath the sea.

Near-Death Experiences of Hell

Near-death experiences, in which individuals report leaving their bodies and heading toward a bright light, are an increasingly recognized phenomenon. But according to Maurice Rawlings, Clinical Professor of Medicine at the University of Tennessee College of Medicine in Chattanooga, USA, some of the trips to the outskirts of heaven may possibly be glimpses into hell.

Rawlings interviewed nearly 300 patients immediately after their resuscitations. And the stories he heard from at least half of them convinced him that they'd seen lakes of fires and demonic figures, not the benevolent images reported in better known near-death stories. Rawlings believes that many people substantially alter their accounts simply because they're ashamed to admit they might not be going to heaven.

Alien Jump Start

On a Sunday night in November 1976, Joyce Bowles and her neighbour Ted Pratt were driving to the village of Chilcomb to pick up Bowles' son. On the way, the car began to shake violently and careened on to the grassy shoulder alongside the road. The engine inexplicably stopped running and the headlights blacked out.

Then Bowles and Pratt saw a glowing, cigar-shaped orange craft howevering over the road near them. Through a window in the side of the vehicle, Bowles and

Pratt saw three heads lined up as if they were passengers on a bus.

One of the occupants of the mysterious ship emerged and approached the humans. Wearing a silver jumpsuit, the creature had intense pink eyes without pupils or irises, Bowles later reported. 'He peered through the window at the dashboard controls,' Bowles recalled. When he did so, the engine fired and the headlights flashed back on. 'Then, he and the cigar simply vanished.'

Some experts believe that the point of encounter was especially attractive to extraterrestrials. It lies at an intersection of a grid of lines drawn between local ancient burial grounds.

Dowsing Technology

In 1951, when the General Motors (GM) Corporation opened a huge plant in semi-arid Port Elizabeth, South Africa, the area was suffering a major drought. The GM plant, like other large factories, required a dependable water supply. Even when the surface is bone dry, water usually runs deep under the ground but there were no reliable wells at this plant. Scientific searches for the sub-level water, moreover, had been unsuccessful.

With everything to lose, the desperate GM officials resorted to the use of a dowser to find water by simply sensing its location beneath the surface. The plant's superintendent called in C.J. Bekker, a local dowser who also happened to be a GM employee and who agreed to help.

With his arms folded across his chest, Bekker wandered around the grounds of the GM plant for half an hour. Then, he suddenly stopped and began to shake uncontrollably. GM officials would find fresh water, Bekker said, if they dug exactly where he was standing. The dowser then went on to find two more places.

Although they marked the sites for future reference, the officials were sceptical. To convince themselves to trust Bekker, they blindfolded him and asked him to go through the process again. Without being able to see where he was walking, Bekker returned to the same areas he had previously indicated.

The company only had to drill in one of Bekker's locations to find enough water so that no further wells were needed.

The Resilient Brain

While the brain is considered our most delicate organ, there have been numerous recorded cases of injury to the brain that mysteriously have had no adverse effects on the patient. One such incident involved a young millworker who, in 1879, was struck above her right eye by a machine bolt. The impact of the bolt drove fragments of bone four inches into the woman's brain, destroying parts of it in the process. Subsequent surgery, moreover, resulted in even more physical damage to the organ. Yet the woman recovered fully, not even suffering a headache during the next 42 years of her life.

The brain of Phineas Gage, however, was perhaps one of the most remarkably resilient of all time. A 25-year-old railway foreman, Gage was ramming explosive material into a hole on September 13, 1847, using a long metal rod with a sharp point at one end. When the bar struck a rock, it created a spark and, and in the subsequent explosion, the rod shot through Gage's cheekbone with bullet-like speed. Nearly forcing his eye out of its socket, the rod went straight through the man's skull, with about 18 inches protruding from the top of his head.

Amazingly, Gage did not lose consciousness. He was rushed to a hotel where his colleagues could summon a doctor. On arrival, Gage got up and walked into the building. The doctor called in a surgeon who removed the bar, extracting bit of bone and brain with it. Although neither physician expected Gage to live, he astounded all the medical authorities who examined him. Miraculously he recovered and only lost the sight in his left eye.

Dreams that Come True

While there are those who doubt the veracity of prophetic dreams, many people have foreseen the future during their sleep. Author Rudyard Kipling, for example, reported a dream in which he was at a formal event. His view of an unidentifiable ceremony was obstructed by the belly of a fat man in front of him. And at the end of the dream, a stranger approached and asked to have a word with Kipling. Six weeks later, Kipling was at an affair that he soon recognized as the one he'd attended in his dream. The entire event, in fact, was exactly the same as he had seen it, including the details of the fat man and the stranger.

There have been countless ordinary people who have also shared a vision of the future in their dreams. Four-year-old Robert Beresford of Buckinghamshire wasn't exactly concerned about World War I in October 1918. But on the eighteenth of the month, while taking his afternoon nap, he began muttering in his sleep. 'Poor Mrs Timms,' Robert's parents heard him saying. 'Won't someone please tell her?' The parents were baffled. They knew no one named Timms or Edwin. While the boy still lay sleeping, they asked him what they should tell Mrs Timms. 'It's about Edwin,' he replied after several minutes. 'He's dead, dead in the mud.' When he awoke, Robert remembered nothing about the dream.

Having mentioned the episode to the family doctor, he recalled a woman named Mrs Timms who lived about 20 miles away. When he enquired, he learned that she also had a son named Edwin stationed in France. On the day of the dream, Edwin had been killed in battle. Robert Beresford had obviously reported Edwin's death even before his mother had received official notification.

Helen Watson of Ellerbuck also experienced a prophetic wartime dream involving her son, Teddy, who had been among the missing since the 1940 battle at Dunkirk. Many vital records had been destroyed during the evacuation of Dunkirk and there had never been official documentation of where Teddy had been buried. One night in 1956, however, Helen dreamed she was in a military cemetery at Dunkirk amid rows and rows of unmarked white crosses. As she approached one particular gravesite, her son appeared, smiled at her, and then disappeared.

Afterwards, when she travelled to the Dunkirk cemetery, Helen Watson found the gravesite her son had indicated in the dream. She contacted officials who agreed to exhume the coffin. Inside, they found the rosary, locket, and monogrammed cigarette holder belonging to Corporal Teddy Watson.

Optical Anomalies

A legendary one-eyed giant, the figure of the Cyclops appears in myths throughout the world. But a man living in a Mississippi backwoods community may have been the first truly one-eyed human being. His single orb, completely normal in every way, was located in the centre of his forehead, according to the *Boston Medical Journal*. For years, sideshow and circus promoters pursued the man, but he adamantly refused to become a public spectacle.

The Mississippi man, of course, isn't the only person in the world to have ever endured an anomalous collection of eyes. There was an English four-eyed man, for example, who could open and close each eye independently and look in four different directions at once.

The Retirement of a Monster Lobster

When physician George Macris of Palmer, Alaska, USA, was out shopping for lobster, a favourite local dish, to serve at a forthcoming dinner party, he came upon a monstrous beauty in his grocery store's tank. Macris, a long-time lobster diver, had never seen one like it before: it was more than three feet long and had claws 'the size of catchers' mitts'. And Macris, whose hobby was marine biology, knew it was a perfect genetic specimen of a nearly 90-year-old arthropod. He knew the fate of a lobster that size would have to be secured. So he bought the old lobster to save it from being boiled to death.

Macris subsequently purchased a one-way plane ticket to Maine, on the east coast of the United States, where state law prohibits the capture of lobsters that are larger than usually found. He then packed his huge charge, dubbed Monster Mike, in ice and saline-soaked rags, and put him on the Maine-bound plane. Although Monster Mike later missed the connecting flight in Chicago, he arrived in Portland, Maine, 24 hours after leaving Alaska and was met by marine patrol lieutenant Joseph Fessenden. The following day, Fessenden dropped the lobster off at the mouth of Portland Harbor, where he has been ever since, enjoying a protected old age.

The Rescue of a Shipwrecked Woman by a Giant Sea Turtle

Candlearia Villanueva was sailing on the *Aloha* when it caught fire and sank 600 miles south of Manila in the Philippines. With a life jacket strapped around her body, the woman floated in the sea for more than 12 hours before a giant sea turtle appeared beneath her. Some 36 hours later, the crew of a Philippine navy vessel rescued her, thinking the woman was clinging to an oildrum. They didn't realize that the turtle was holding her afloat until after they pulled the woman aboard. Villanueva later reported that there was also another smaller turtle that had crawled up on her back and seemed to bite her every time she was about to fall asleep. She thought that, perhaps, it wanted to prevent her from dipping her head into the water and drowning.

The Cement Pillars of New Caledonia

As far as any knows, the first human visitors to New Caledonia, about 750 miles east of Australia, arrived from Indonesia around 2,000 BC, which is why archaeologists have a hard time explaining the odd presence of cement pillars. Perhaps tens of thousands of years old, the pillars lie on the New Caledonian Isle of Pines, some 40 miles off the southern coast.

Scientists have long known about the Isle of Pines' 400-odd tumuli. These anthill-shaped land formations are eight to nine feet high, 300 feet in diameter and virtually bare of vegetation. It was during the excavation of the geological curiosities during the 1960s by L. Chevalier of the Museum of New Caledonia at Noumea (the island's capital) that one cement pillar was found unexpectedly in each of three tumuli, and two pillars lying side by side in a fourth. Their heights ranged from 40 to 100 inches, and their diameters from 40 to 75 inches. They were made, strangely enough, with a lime and mortar mixture – technology unheard of before a few hundred years BC. Even so, based on radiocarbon-dating, the pillars were created between 5,120 and 10,950 BC.

What Chevalier found most baffling about the find, however, was that there were no human remains found anywhere around the site. Given the apparent age of the cylinders, the absence of human or other life in the proximity, and the sophistication of their construction, the origin of the pillars remains a complete mystery.

The House on Haunted Hill

During the excavation of their garden for a swimming pool, Sam and Judy Haney unearthed two human bodies. But that was only the beginning of their problems. It wasn't long before the television was glowing even when it was turned off; sparks flew from unplugged clocks; and shoes disappeared, being found later on top of one of the graves in the backyard.

The Haneys' home and others like it in the suburban development, it turned out, were built over a nineteenth-century cemetery. Disturbances have also affected some of the other homeowners: cups have broken while sitting on shelves; appliances stop working with no apparent cause, and lights and water taps have been mysteriously turned on. An apparition, known as Betty, has also appeared and frightened some residents away.

Claiming mental anguish and stress-induced diabetes, the Haneys sued the developer for US$2 million. The jury recommended a settlement of US$142,000, but the judge overturned the jury's decision and awarded the Haneys nothing. The developer had not been negligent, the judge decreed, and had not intentionally misled them about the presence of the graves.

The Haneys subsequently moved and there's been no mention of an appeal.

Spontaneous Human Combustion Inside Parked Cars

Two of the most unusual cases of spontaneous human combustion occurred while the victims sat inside their cars. The first occurred in December 1959, and was initially dismissed as a suicide. Billy Peterson, a despondent auto worker in Pontiac, Michigan, USA, had, indeed bent his car's exhaust pipe into the passenger compartment and the official cause of death was listed as carbon monoxide poisoning. But doctors were unable to explain the third-degree burns on the body's back, legs and arms, especially as his clothing – even his underwear – had not been burned. They were even more baffled by the fact that hairs on the charred parts of the body were not even singed.

In October 1964, 75-year-old Olga Worth Stephens of Dallas, Texas, was sitting in her parked car when, according to eye-witnesses, she suddenly burst into flames. By the time rescuers arrived on the scene, Stephens had been burned beyond recognition, yet nothing else in the car had been affected. The subsequent investigation was unable to explain the fatal fire.

Dwellers on the Moon

In 1835, the *New York Sun* published a purely imaginative series of articles that gave readers their first glimpse of life on the moon. Entitled 'Great Astronomical

Discoveries Largely Made by Sir John Herschel at the Cape of Good Hope', the articles were based on statements attributed to the world-famous astronomer, which gave credence to the speculations.

Herschel, the reporter Richard Locke claimed, had used a new seven-ton telescope located at the Cape of Good Hope in South Africa to view the surface of the moon in greater detail than had ever before been possible. Magnifying the moon by 42,000 times, and bringing it into sight within the equivalent of five miles, Herschel was able to see clearly mountains of amethyst and beaches along great lakes, the largest being 266 miles long. By adjusting the telescope's lens, Herschel could focus on the surface within 80 yards and observe an array of creatures, including blue, single-horned goats, huge cranes and other birds, as well as beasts that resembled American buffalos and bears. He could even identify species of trees. Most surprising of all, he had witnessed four-foot-tall humanoid creatures with wings and monkey-like faces roaming the lunar surface.

In an editorial in *The New York Times* it was suggested that the 'Great Astronomical Discoveries' series displayed 'the most extensive and accurate knowledge of astronomy'. And the reports, later compiled and published in a separate pamphlet and sold on news-stands, resulted in the newspaper's circulation increasing by 650 per cent.

The truth wasn't revealed, however, until Locke admitted to another newspaperman that he had, in fact, fabricated the entire series. When this news appeared in the *Journal of Commerce*, thousands of credulous people were disappointed. Herschel, however, thought it was a great joke.

The Winning Entry of two Walter Kellners

When the German magazine *Das Beste* ran a reader competition in 1979, the editors had no idea that the winning entry would reveal a bizarre coincidence. Responding to the contest for the most interesting personal experience, a pilot named Walter Kellner of Munich, West Germany, submitted his story of survival. He had been flying a Cessna 421 over the Tyrrhenian Sea between Sardinia and Sicily, he wrote, when the plane experienced engine trouble. Plunging into the sea, he survived by floating in a rubber dinghy until he was rescued.

Impressed by the tale, the *Das Beste* editors placed Kellner's account among the competition's finalists. They then set out to verify the incident with German and Italian officials. Kellner's personal story was true in every detail and he was named the winner in the magazine's contest.

The competition results were announced and Kellner was to be awarded his prize on December 6. That day, however, *Das Beste* editor-in-chief Wulf Schwarzwaller received a strange letter from a Walter Kellner of Kritzendorf, Austria, who claimed the German Kellner's story as his own, although it had a different ending. According to the Austrian Kellner, he had been flying his Cessna 421 over the Tyrrhenian Sea when engine trouble forced him to land at Cagliari airstrip in Sardinia. The second Kellner accused the first pilot of being an impostor and that his personal story was a hoax.

The first Walter Kellner admitted that he was aware, from the plane's records, that another pilot named Kellner had flown the same Cessna but, he said, he hadn't known they shared the same first name and had experienced similar mechanical failures while flying over the same location.

With further checking, the editors learned that *both* stories were indeed true.

The Ghosts of the Tower of London

In 1605, Henry Percy, ninth Earl of Cumberland, was sentenced to London's Martin Tower for his involvement in the Gunpowder Plot to blow up Parliament and, with it, King James I. The Earl remained there for 16 years before buying his freedom for £30,000. Even though he was released and never executed, however, his ghost has haunted the Tower ever since his death, and has been seen walking the battlements where Percy often took the air during his imprisonment.

Lady Jane Grey, of course, was an even more illustrious resident of the Tower, sentenced for her role in an abortive attempt to make her Queen of England. On February 12, 1554, she was beheaded in the grounds outside the Tower and her ghost has haunted the edifice ever since. As recently as 1957, on the anniversary of her death, a Tower guard saw a white mass form into the image of Lady Jane. He immediately called another guard who also saw the apparition.

While Martin Tower is rich in spectral lore, not all of it involves the ghosts of former prisoners. One of the strangest sightings apparently happened only once and has defied all efforts to explain it. In October 1817, Edmund Lenthal Swifte, Keeper of the Crown Jewels, was dining with his family in Martin Tower where the jewels were then stored. They looked up suddenly from their meal and saw a glass cylinder filled with a swirling blue and white liquid hovering just above the table. It slowly moved behind Swifte's wife who began screaming. And when Swifte threw a chair at the spectral container it disappeared and was never seen again.

Beginning in the reign of Henry I, moreover, the Tower was often used to house a collection of animals for royal entertainment. These ranged from lions, tigers and bears to monkeys, zebras, hyenas, and even elephants. The practice ceased in 1835 when a Tower guard was mauled by a lion. Before that in 1815, however, a Tower sentry was patrolling the entrance when, on the stroke of midnight, he saw a huge bear rising on its hind legs in front of him. Terrified, the guard lunged his bayonet, only to watch in amazement as it passed through nothingness and lodged in the oak door where the bear had been. The sentry reported the incident the following morning, but died the day after that, some say from shock.

Accidental Coincidence

On a June night in the 1930s, highway patrolman Allan Falby from El Paso, Texas, USA, was pursuing a speeding truck. When the vehicle slowed down as it went around a corner, Falby's car ploughed into it at full speed. His leg spurting blood from a ruptured artery, Falby would have surely died had it not been for Alfred Smith, a mere passer-by who stopped to assist him. Smith applied a tourniquet to the patrolman's leg to curb the flow of blood until the ambulance arrived.

Five years after his near-fatal accident, Falby responded to a radio call for assistance at the scene of a one-car collision. The car had crashed head-on into a tree and the unconscious driver had severed an artery in his leg.

Recalling his first aid training, Falby quickly applied a tourniquet, thus saving the man's life. Then on closer inspection, he realized that the injured driver was none other than Alfred Smith, the same man who had saved his life five years before.

Revitalizing Decapitated Heads

The guillotine was the preferred instrument of execution in nineteenth-century France. In 1887 these decapitations provided a bounty of severed heads for one enterprising scientist attempting to attach the heads to the bodies of dogs. Although the gruesome series of experiments failed, modern researchers believe it may soon be possible to revive a detached head and perhaps someday even organically grow an entirely new body for it.

In his book entitled *If We Can Keep A Severed Head Alive. . .*, attorney and engineer Chet Fleming cites one Cleveland experiment in 1971 in which severed monkey heads regained consciousness for 36 hours. Fleming has even patented a blood-processing system used for perfusing animal heads to keep them alive. He is quick to point out that no one can use his procedure without his permission. He wants to make sure that scientists work on live, severed heads with full regard for the ethical, legal and social issues involved.

Some scientists are actually looking at the possibility of preserving heads for future use. Since cloning technology may be possible around the same time in the future as viable cryonics (the freezing of animals as well as human beings for later resuscitation) they are hoping to be able to clone a new body for the frozen head.

The Explorer and the Friendly Cannibals

The word 'cannibal' comes from *caribal* which refers to the eating habits of certain of the Caribbean Indians as observed by Columbus when he first arrived in the Americas.

There have been many reasons cited for cannibalism. One group of cannibals on the islands of the South Pacific used to eat the heart and other body parts of their enemies to absorb their bravery and force. In other areas, as far apart as Ireland and China, cannibalism has occurred sporadically during the great famines of the 1840s (Ireland) and the 1930s (China). A number of incidents of cannibalism have occurred at sea among survivors of shipwrecks and other disasters who were stranded with no food.

The Aztecs, as noted by the Spanish conquistadors when they first arrived in Mexico, limited their cannibalism to eating the arms and legs (usually cooked in spicy chocolate sauce) of the captives sacrificed on the altars at the top of their lofty pyramidal temple. They gave the torso of the victim to the animals in the imperial zoo but kept the heads for decorating a special building in front of the main temple in what is now Mexico City.

Cannibalism continued to be practised deep in the jungles of South America, New Guinea and parts of Central Africa until well into the twentieth century. An American author and explorer, William Seabrook, in describing an encounter with ritual cannibalism in Africa, wrote that he was offered some of the meat by a tribal chief. He deemed it was politic to accept and, like a true researcher, tried portions of it fried, stewed and roasted. He found the roasted samples to be best, and wrote that it tasted like pork. In this he agreed with the former cannibals of the South Seas, who referred to human meat as 'long pig'.

Reincarnated Prodigies

There has been intense debate over the years about the source of child prodigies' incredible talents. Most psychologists contend that children like Wolfgang Amadeus Mozart, who was composing complex music at the age of five, are simply born with extraordinary memory and organizational skills. Others, however, believe that because their apparently learned abilities appear so early in their lives, these amazing children are the products of reincarnation.

As evidence that their abilities are talents displayed in previous existences, proponents point to the cases of an eighteenth-century French boy, Jean Cardiac – who could recite the alphabet at the age of three months and spoke half a dozen languages by the time he was six years old – and of a nineteenth-century blind four-year-old slave in Georgia, USA, called Blind Tom. According to one teacher, Tom played the piano expertly the first time he tinkered the keys and 'knew more of music than we know or can learn.'

The Dream Stories of Robert Louis Stevenson

Robert Louis Stevenson always admitted that the plots of his popular stories were derived from dreams. He even claimed to dream plots at will. Early in his career, he wrote a story about dual personality – one good, the other evil – entitled 'The Travelling Companion'. The story was summarily rejected by an editor who said that the idea was ingenious, but the plot was weak. Frustrated by his inability to improve the story, Stevenson decided to try dreaming up a solution. Blessed with extraordinary recall, he was able to remember every detail of his newly dreamed plot. And as he wrote what he had dreamed, 'The Travelling Companion' was transformed into the classic *Dr Jekyll and Mr Hyde*.

The Grim Pun of Qin Shi-Huang-di

The Great Wall of China, built 2,000 years ago, is the largest single artefact on Earth and is also the only man-made construction visible from space, as noted by the first astronauts.

Over 2,500 miles long, the wall represented an enormous cost in human life. But spending lives did not greatly concern the Emperor, Qin Shi-Huang-di, whose priority was to defend the northern borders of China. On the Emperor's orders, slaves, prisoners, farmers, soldiers and, as a gesture of the Emperor's contempt for any learning that pre-dated him, a number of scholars and historians toiled and died building the Wall. As the death toll mounted, a frightening prophecy was passed along the wall – 10,000 people would be buried in the Wall before it was finished.

When the Emperor learned of the prophecy, he said, 'We will fulfil the prophecy,' adding that everyone would then cease to worry and be able to work even harder. For he found a man named Wan whose name meant 'ten thousand' and had him buried within the 'Ten Thousand Mile Wall', or as it is called in Chinese, *Wan-li Chang-Ching*. Thus the name of the Wall still contains the name of Wan, as well as Wan's skeleton along with an estimated 10 times 10,000 bodies of others.

Chesapeake UFO

Captain William Nash and his co-pilot William Fortenberry were making a routine New York to Miami run in a Pan American DC-4 around eight o'clock in the evening of July 14, 1952. The sky was clear and visibility was unlimited, a perfect night for flying at an altitude of 8,000 feet.

Then, near Norfolk, Virginia, Nash and Fortenberry noticed an eerie glow not far off. It became apparent that the light was emanating from six fiery red objects, each about 100 feet in diameter, and flying in formation. 'Their shape was clearly outlined and evidently circular,' Nash reported. 'The edges were well defined, not phosphorescent or fuzzy in the least.'

Flying about 2,000 feet above the Chesapeake Bay, the six discs were then joined by two others. And when they were nearly aligned below the DC-4, the lights dimmed slightly and the craft flipped on their sides.

The DC-4 flight team communicated a radio report to be forwarded to the Air Force, and the next morning, were told that there were at least seven other reports of the same glowing discs in the area. But after checking the positions of all known military and civilian craft in the vicinity at that time, the Air Force was unable to account for what the UFOs might have been. The case remains in the Air Force files, classified as officially 'unexplained'.

Heavenly Music

The spirit of Franz Liszt is said to have appeared to Rosemary Brown in 1964, keeping a promise he made to her many years before when she was only seven years old. He returned to give her his music. But he also brought the spirits of Chopin, Schubert, Schumann, Beethoven, Bach, Mozart, Brahms and many others. Each of them asked her to transcribe their music composed after death. Her cupboards and drawers were soon overflowing with more than 500 pieces of music.

'The music is absolutely in the style of these composers,' insists concert pianist Hepzibah Menuhin, Yehudi's sister, who agreed with many critics. And according to composer Richard Rodney Bennett, 'A lot of people can improvise, but you couldn't fake music like this without years of training.' In fact, Brown had had extremely little training, and as a child she had attended the opera against her will.

Brown, however, does profess a strong background in psychic phenomena. Both her parents and her grandparents were psychic, and Brown became aware of her own ability when she was very young. In fact, by the time she was seven and Liszt first appeared to her, she was already accustomed to being visited by spirits.

As for her channelling the music of many of the world's greatest composers, musicians and psychologists have investigated Brown and all have agreed there was no way that she could be cheating.

Crimes of Psychic Vision

When Lockheed shipping clerk Etta Louise Smith heard a radio broadcast about a house-to-house search for a missing nurse, she immediately thought: she's not in the house. The she received a visual picture, as if there were a photograph in front of her, and Smith knew that the nurse was dead.

Then the 39-year-old mother of three went to the police station to speak with the investigators. From there she went out to a remote canyon site she'd visualized. There she found the body of 31-year-old Melanie Uribe.

But 12 hours later, Smith was arrested on suspicion of murder. During her four-hour stint in jail, however, one of the killers was arrested. He confessed and implicated two accomplices, who were also arrested and later convicted. Subsequently Smith sued the city of Los Angeles for false arrest.

The judge ruled that the police had lacked probable cause as well as sufficient evidence to implicate Smith in the murder, and the jury awarded her more than US$26,000. Still the police as well as the attorney representing the city continued to doubt that Smith had had a psychic experience and insisted that somehow she had heard about it, perhaps through talk in the neighbourhood.

Smith thinks that she may phone the police anonymously with any future visions.

The Reincarnation of a Minister's Wife

Married to a minister and the mother of four children, Dolores Jay doesn't believe in reincarnation, neither speaks nor understands German and has never been to Germany. But when the American housewife is hypnotized she regresses in time, beyond her childhood and her infancy, until she suddenly becomes an adolescent girl in nineteenth-century Germany who remembers her dolls, her home and her own death.

As 16-year-old Gretchen Gottlieb, she is terrified and hiding from anti-Catholics who have already killed her mother. Her head aches. She mumbles German, mentions a gleaming knife, but desperately evades questions. She finally wails. And there it ends. Jay doesn't recall anything else until her own birth in 1923.

Gretchen Gottlieb's home was in Eberswalde, a small town in what is now eastern Germany, close to the Polish border. During World War II, it was the site of the Germans' last stand against the Russians who almost completely razed it. Any records that may have proven the existence of Gretchen have been destroyed.

Mutilated Farm Animals

Throughout 1988, something vicious and deadly was mutilating farm animals in Geneva in southwest Alabama, USA. Despite the fact that more than 40 animals have been killed – including a horse whose genitals were ripped off and pigs whose entrails were torn out of their bodies – no one has been able to spot the creature responsible.

Among the casualties were several 60-pound pigs and a 250-pound boar owned by the Stinson family. 'Whatever it is, it seems more interested in tearing its prey apart than eating it,' says Lance Stinson, whose parents and sister think they may have heard the killer one night. 'They heard a high-pitched scream – it seemed to come from different directions at the same time.'

According to Dot Kirkland, spokeswoman for the Geneva County Sheriff's Department, an official investigation of the mysterious animal deaths was hampered by droves of sightseers bent on catching a glimpse of the unknown killer. 'We couldn't tell if there were any tracks because so many people were walking around out there,' she says. 'No new evidence has turned up and the killings seem to have stopped. We now think the animals were probably attacked by wild dogs.'

Lance Stinson isn't so sure. 'Some old-timers think it could be an injured, crazed bear. Others think it's a panther or even wolves,' he says. 'One thing is apparent, though. By the marks on our dead animals, whatever killed them had four claws on one foot and only three on the other. The Sheriff's department may believe dogs did this. But a lot of other people aren't convinced.'

Intra-Dimensional Travelling Maya

Mayan culture has always been an enigma for researchers who can't understand why a Stone Age society would have such an astute knowledge and understanding of mathematics, astronomy and recorded time. One theory, explains Colorado art historian Jose Argüelles, is that the Maya were intra-dimensional travellers who settled in Mexico around 600 BC. Their mission: to place Earth and its solar system in alignment with the Universe.

Arguelles was first confronted with the idea of the Mayan travellers when he met a Mayan holy man who told him that our solar system is the seventh one navigated by the Maya. The leaders departed in the ninth century AD, leaving behind their sacred calendar as a system of prophecy. And when the Mayan calendar ends in 2012, moreover, mankind will shift to a decentralized, nonindustrial culture in which contact with alien beings is commonplace.

The Mother of Us All

According to the Bible, the first woman was Eve – Adam's mate – the mother of Cain and Abel and the matriarch of mankind. Some scholars, however, have considered Eve, as well as Adam, of course, to be merely representational of the beginnings of the human race.

But a recent study actually traces modern humans to a single ancestor, a woman who lived in Africa some 200,000 years ago.

The single ancestor theory is based on the study of DNA (deoxyribonucleic acid) from the mitochrondria (the part of the cell that converts food into energy) in 147 people. Biochemist Mark Stoneking at the University of California at Berkley mapped the DNA, which is passed on only by the female of a species, and traced it backwards in time. Estimating the mutation rate, he then determined that not only would the common ancestor be a female, but that she would have lived between 140,000 and 280,000 years ago.

Christmas Combustion

In 1885, Patrick Rooney and his wife invited their son John and their hired hand, John Larson, to join them for a Christmas Eve drink. The four sat around the kitchen table, enjoying the whisky bought by Patrick in town. After a few drinks, young Rooney headed back to his own farm a mile away, and Larson retired to his room, leaving the hosts to finish off the bottle.

Larson rose before dawn, even though it was Christmas morning, to perform his routine chores. But when he walked into the kitchen, he found Patrick Rooney slumped in the chair where he'd been sitting the night before. He was dead. And Mrs Rooney was nowhere to be found. In a daze, Larson raced to John's farm. When the two men returned to the death scene, they discovered a three-by-four-foot hole in the floor. At the bottom lay the remains of the 200-pound Mrs Rooney: a burned piece of skull, two charred vertebrae, and a foot in a pile of ashes. She had evidently burned to death, the two men concluded. But why had nothing else in the kitchen been burned? And what had killed Patrick Rooney?

When the police and the coroner arrived, suspicion quickly fell on Larson, but no case could be made against him. The rising soot, they found, had left an outline of Larson's head on the pillow while he obviously slept through the ordeal. The coroner concluded that Mrs Rooney had been the victim of spontaneous combustion. Her husband, he suspected (and the jury agreed) had been asphyxiated by the fumes rising from his wife's burning body.

The Woman Who Was Resurrected by the Man She Loved

Young, beautiful and born into the French nobility, Victorine Lefourcade was in love with a poor journalist named Julius Bossuet whom her parents refused to allow her to marry. Instead, they forced her to wed a man of their choosing, someone of appropriate class and status. It was a loveless marriage in which Victorine was like a grieving widow, and in 1810, after several years of misery, she became ill and died.

When Bossuet heard about her death, he travelled to the village graveyard where his beloved was buried. Desperately wanting a remembrance, some token that could be dear to him for the rest of his life, he began digging up the woman's coffin to snip a lock of her hair. As he began to cut the hair, however, Victorine opened her eyes.

As far as everyone else was concerned, Victorine was dead. So the two lovers remained hidden until Victorine regained her health, and then they sailed for the United

States. Some 20 years later, confident no one would recognize the woman, the couple returned to France.

Someone did recognize her, however, and word soon reached her husband in her former life. Although he had Victorine arrested, the court refused to honour his claim against her and Victorine and Julius Bossuet were free to remain together and live in France.

Stock Market Psychics

Organized by clinical psychologist Judith Kuriansky and William Flanagan, the editor of *Forbes* magazine, the three-hour cruise bringing together 120 stock market experts with five professional psychics was initially intended as a lark. According to Flanagan, he thought it might be an amusing way to 'pick up on the vibrations and energy levels coming from Wall Street.' But the East River cruise turned spooky when every one of the psychics reported negative energies pouring from downtown New York City. One psychic, a woman named Wendy, was convinced that at least two years of economic turmoil were forthcoming, with the Dow Jones average dropping as low as 1,100 by the end of 1989. Her prediction, however, was in direct contrast to the then current market analysis which was overwhelmingly bullish. Even so, a week after the cruise, in October 1987, the financial world was devastated by Black Monday, when the market plummeted by 500 points.

Amelia Earhart: Lost Heroine

One of the most celebrated disappearances in recent history involved pilot and American heroine Amelia Earhart. Earhart and her co-pilot, Fred Noonan, took off from California, USA, on May 20, 1937, commencing what was to be an eastward circumnavigation of the globe. The flight was carefully tracked as the flight team passed over Florida, Brazil, Africa, India and Australia in the specially equipped twin-engine plane.

On July 2, Earhart and Noonan refuelled in Lae, New Guinea, and resumed their flight, intending a rendezvous with the Coast Guard ship *Itasca* in the central Pacific. The last transmission received from the pair, however, was confusing and fragmentary. No further messages went out over the radio and the plane was never seen again.

Frantic searches were conducted, even employing George Plutnam, a friend of Earhart, and her husband. According to psychic Jacqueline Cochran, soon after losing contact, Earhart was alive on an unidentified Pacific island. There was some speculation that the plane had gone down on a volcanic island that was subsequently submerged (or sank). Other possibilities included their capture by the Japanese who summarily executed her as a spy. In any case, no trace of the pilots or the aircraft was ever found.

Brains That Baffled Medicine

The brain is so complicated that scientists are constantly working to discover just how it works. It is well known, however, that even seemingly minor injuries and shocks can sometimes cause damage to the brain – and result in everything from a loss of sensation to seizures. On the other hand, medical literature cites cases of severe brain damage that didn't seem to faze patients at all.

According to the 1888 edition of *The Medical Press of Western New York*, about a quarter of a man's skull was destroyed when he was caught between a bridge timber and the superstructure of the ship he was working on. The sharp corner of the timber clipped off part of the deck hand's head. Doctors who closed the wound found that the man had lost a substantial amount of brain matter, as well as blood. But as soon as the victim regained consciousness, he talked and dressed himself as though he felt perfectly fine. Except for a few dizzy spells, he was healthy despite the loss of part of his brain until 26 years later when a partial paralysis and unsteady gait developed.

For 27 days, a baby born at St Vincent's Hospital in New York City in 1935 appeared to be a typical infant – it cried, ate and moved normally. Only after it died did doctors discover during an autopsy that it had no brain at all.

In a report prepared by Dr Jan W. Bruell and Dr George W. Albee that was delivered to the American Psychological Association in 1957, it was noted that the physicians had been forced to perform drastic surgery on a 39-year-old man. Although they removed the entire right half of the man's brain, the patient survived. And, the doctors concluded, the operation inexplicably 'left his intellectual capacity virtually unimpaired.'

Dr Augustin Iturricha and Dr Nicholas Ortiz of Brazil have documented another baffling brain story. In an address presented before the Anthropological Society at Sucre in 1940, Iturricha told of a 14-year-old patient with an excruciating headache who was believed to have an abscess of the brain. The boy died, and on autopsy, it was found that his brain mass was virtually detached from the bulb – a condition with medical consequences similar to decapitation. Yet the youngster possessed all his faculties up to the time of his death.

An even stranger case was recounted by the German brain expert Hufeland. When he autopsied a paralysed man who had been fully rational until the moment of his demise, he found no brain at all – just 11 ounces of water.

Florida UFO

Some of the most spectacular UFO photos ever to emerge were published in Florida's *Gulf Breeze Sentinel* in 1987. The pictures, taken by a local businessman, portrayed a squat, portholed, teapot-shaped UFO. According to the photographer, who asked that his name not be published, a blue beam of light coming from the craft lifted him three feet into the air as he took the photos.

Though the story seemed incredible, it soon turned out that the first photographer was not alone. About a month after the publication of the pictures, another group of similar photos turned up in the *Sentinel's* night drop. They were taken by an anonymous reader corroborating the account. What's more, over the days and weeks that followed, more than 100 *Sentinel* readers wrote in to say that they had seen the strange UFO as well.

Walt Andrus, director of the Mutual UFO Network in Seguin, Texas, eventually heard of the case. Deciding to evaluate it, he went to the *Gulf Breeze* himself. 'I had been expecting some kind of hoax, but I don't know what to think now,' Andrus says. 'These pictures are the best I've seen in more than 30 years of investigation.'

Laser physicist Bruce Maccabee of Silver Spring, Maryland, agrees. 'If it's a hoax,' he says, 'it's just about the most sophisticated one I've ever seen.'

The Priest of Bel

In March of 1892, Herman Hilprecht, Professor of Assyriology at the University of Pennsylvania, was putting the finishing touches to his master work, a survey of ancient Babylonian inscriptions. But two items – fragments of agate that Hilprecht believed were rings from the Temple of Bel at Nippur – defied identification. Tired and frustrated, the Assyriologist assigned the two pieces to his 'unclassified' category and reluctantly finished his book.

That night, Hilprecht dreamed that a tall figure dressed in priestly Babylonian garb took the scholar to the treasure chamber of what Hilprecht immediately recognized as the Temple of Bel. The figure then proceeded to explain that Hilprecht's two puzzling pieces of agate were, in fact, two portions of the same ring and, due to a shortage of agate, it had been divided to form earrings for a statue of the god Ninib. If the two pieces were put together, the dream's priest said, they would reveal the entire inscription Hilprecht had laboured to decipher.

The next morning, excited by his dream, Hilprecht immediately examined the agate fragments. Sure enough, the two pieces placed side by side read: 'To the god Ninib, son of Bel, his lord, has Kurigalzu, High Priest of Bel, presented this.'

The Earliest Human Beings?

Mankind has been roaming the Earth for only one or two million years, according to accepted palaeontological theory. But if some of the fossils discovered in North America are any indication, human beings – or something very like humans – have been around for hundreds of millions of years.

One amazing discovery was made in the Cumberland Mountains in Jackson County, Kentucky, in the 1880s. As it crossed Big Hill, a wagon train proceeded to break up the sandstone on the peak's summit. When the debris was cleared away, a layer of rock was uncovered and later determined to be more than 300 million years old. Embedded in the ancient rock, excavators found various animal tracks as well as two human footprints, described as being 'good sized, toes well spread, and very distinctly marked'.

Even earlier, another strange set of footprints was unearthed on the west bank of the Mississippi River at St Louis in 1816. The prints were 10½ inches long and 4 inches wide at the toes. According to Henry Schoolcraft who examined them, the footprints seemed to have been made by someone used to walking great distances without the benefit of footwear. Schoolcraft described them as being 'strikingly natural, exhibiting every muscular impression and swell of the heel and toes, with a precision and faithfulness to nature, which I have not been able to copy'. However confident he was that the footprints were genuine, Schoolcraft was nonetheless unable to explain how they managed to appear in a layer of limestone that had hardened 270 million years earlier.

Cure by Lightning

Samuel Leffers woke one morning in the summer of 1806 with an unusual numbness on his left side. At first, he wasn't alarmed, assuming that he had lain too long on the one side. He soon realized, though, that he also had difficulty speaking and he was unable to close his left eye. Although the condition abated somewhat, it seemed to centre thereafter in his eye, which remained permanently opened.

Later that summer, according to an account in the *American Journal of Science*, Leffers experienced another misfortune, or so he thought, when he was struck by lightning and knocked unconscious. When he regained consciousness, however, he had also regained use of his limbs. The following day, he noticed that his eyesight improved and could soon move the lid. There was only one set-back: the electrical shock had impaired his hearing.

Napoleon's Double

While still the powerful Emperor of France, Napoleon Bonaparte sent his representatives all over Europe looking for men who could pass for his double. Four stand-ins were found. One was murdered shortly before Waterloo and another suffered an injury that left him useless as a Napoleon look-alike. but two other men, who looked virtually like the Emperor's twin brothers, remained attached to Napoleon's staff for the rest of his reign. One of these doubles, François Eugène Robeaud, may have played the role of Napoleon until his death.

After his defeat at Waterloo, Napoleon was at the mercy of his conquerors. The British decided he must be imprisoned where he could never escape, on the isle of St Helena. Meanwhile François Robeaud returned home to Baleycourt to be a farmer.

According to historical accounts, Napoleon lived in exile off the coast of Africa until his death. But a series of coincidences suggest that he may have escaped and substituted a double in his place.

In 1818, something unusual happened in Baleycourt. A fine coach pulled up at the home of Napoleon's double, Robeaud. Could the visit have had anything to do with the return to France of General Gourgard, who had just been replaced at the command post at St Helena? Gourgard's friends were known to include wealthy supporters of Napoleon.

Robeaud told his neighbours that the man in the coach was only a man who wanted to buy some rabbits. But soon afterwards Robeaud and his sister disappeared.

Authorities trying to track down the Napoleon double finally located his sister, several years later, living in unexplained luxury in Tours. But where was her brother? She told the inspector assigned to the case 'He went away on a long voyage.'

Coincidentally, a stranger named Revard settled in Verona, Italy, in 1818, just after Robeaud disappeared. Along with a business partner named Petrucci, 'Revard' opened a small shop. The proprietor looked so much like Napoleon that he was quickly nicknamed 'The Emperor'.

Meanwhile on St Helena, the prisoner known as the real Napoleon was becoming forgetful. His handwriting changed. He was uncouth. French authorities attributed all this to changes 'brought on, no doubt, by his imprisonment.'

On May 5, 1821, Napoleon died in exile. Or did he?

Two years later, the Italian shopkeeper who bore such a striking resemblance to Napoleon abruptly deserted his business and never returned to Verona. Then, 12 nights after 'Revard' disappeared, on September 4, 1823, an intruder was killed as he ran towards an Austrian castle in Schönbrunn, where Napoleon Bonaparte's son lay near to death from scarlet fever.

When the authorities saw the dead body, they placed the building under guard. Napoleon's wife insisted the body be buried at the castle. The mysterious, unnamed 'intruder' was buried in a grave in direct line with the plots where Napoleon's wife and son were eventually laid to rest.

Some 30 years later, Petrucci confessed that he had been paid 100,000 gold crowns for his silence about the true identity of his fellow shopkeeper. The man who had been in business in Verona with the mysterious Napoleon look-alike was positive that 'Revard' was none other than Napoleon Bonaparte himself.

The Gazelle Boy of the Spanish Sahara

In 1970, French anthropologist Jean-Claude Armen discovered a wild child living among a herd of gazelles in the Spanish Sahara. The dark-haired, approximately 10-year-old boy galloped in gigantic bounds with the best of the species, and he seemed perfectly adapted to his environment, living among the gazelles as if he were one of them. Although the boy was never captured, Armen was convinced that he couldn't have been retarded, believing that a retarded child could not be nearly as successful in the wild as the Gazelle Boy clearly was.

Bloodscope Readings

According to psychologist Takeji Furukawa, in his book *Blood Groups and Temperature*, a person's blood type can reveal a great deal of information. People with type O blood, for example, are the best employees; type Bs are freedom-loving people; type As are more successful when they're in structured environments. Although published during the 1930s and dismissed by medical authorities, the book became the impetus for a national Japanese craze 50 years later.

During the 1980s, the Japanese Red Cross began reporting an unprecedented response among 16- to 19-year-old students to their blood-donation appeals. The teenagers responded not only because they felt it was their civic duty, but also because they wanted to learn their blood types. Then, consulting Furukawa's book, they could determine their traits accordingly. Blood-based horoscopes even made their way into Japanese women's magazines and a matchmaking service began requesting blood type on prospective clients' applications. Even a Japanese polling institute indicated blood types among its demographic data. Medical authorities resumed the debunking of *Blood Groups and Temperature* but this had little effect on the popularity of bloodscopes.

The Riddle of the Sphinx

The Pharaoh Chephren is said to have built the legendary half-man, half-lion monument known as the Sphinx at Giza around 2,700 BC. But if the theory of Egyptologist Anthony West, author of *The Travellers' Key to Ancient Egypt*, is correct, the Sphinx was actually constructed much earlier. And if so, then it follows that the Egyptian civilization is also much older than previously believed.

West points out that the erosion suffered by the stone sphinx is much worse than its supposed contemporaries, the Pyramids. And the two-foot-deep channels splicing its walls he says, were cut by water from the Great Floods of Egypt that ravaged the region from 15,000 to 10,000 BC. If the Sphinx at Giza was, in fact, built before the floods, it would explain why Egyptian culture blossomed so rapidly afterwards: its foundation had already been laid and somehow survived the devastating waters.

Climbing Fish

In perhaps some kind of arrested evolution, the *Periophthalmus Schlosseri*, a fish native to Malaysia, often leaves its aquatic environment to climb trees. When the tide is out the fish squirm around in the mud and wriggle up nearby trees in search of insects. With uncanny agility, they propel themselves by means of two leg-like fins.

The World's Largest Time Capsule

It has been the custom to bury time capsules containing articles of contemporary life and past epochs in certain World's Fair cities, such as New York, Chicago and others. But the greatest time capsule of all is not buried; it is over 45 storeys high. The Great Pyramids of Egypt, reputedly the tombs of the Pharaohs Khufu and Khafra of the fourth dynasty have been finally recognized as compendiums of ancient knowledge, geography, astronomy and science.

Egyptian legends have implied that the purpose of the two greatest pyramids were not so much to function as tombs but to store knowledge (the pyramid of Khufu) and hidden treasure (that of Khafra). During the Middle Ages, the Arab rulers of Egypt had tried mining both pyramids. They were unsuccessful except for removing the smooth limestone facing blocks covered with hieroglyphics from the Great Pyramid and using them, face reversed (and therefore unreadable), for building the Mosque of Ibn Tulum in Cairo.

When Napoleon invaded Egypt in 1798 and defeated the Egyptian armies he ordered his surveyors to use the Great Pyramid as a basis for triangulation for military mapping. To the surprise of the French surveyors they found that a continuation of the diagonal lines crossing the base would neatly enclose the Nile Delta and that the longitudinal meridian would pass through the apex of the pyramid and cut the delta into two equal parts.

French scientists who followed the surveyors discovered a series of remarkable coincidences. For example, they calculated that the total distance around the base divided by twice its height (taking into account the original height, before some of the great apex stones were removed) was 3.1416 – the exact number of pi – not the later Greek approximation of 3.1428.

Scientists have since calculated that a straight line drawn due north from the intersection of traverse lines at the base would miss the North Pole by a little over four minutes, a fraction of a degree, but since the time when the pyramid was built, the North Pole itself had shifted the same amount of time distance. They found that a shaft from the King's Chamber of the pyramid pointed directly to the Pole Star, then in the Dragon constellation but now in the Big Dipper.

Each side of the pyramid gives, in Egyptian cubits, the number of days in the year as 365, subject to recalculation every 1,460 years. The original height of the pyramid times one billion gives the approximate median distance of the Earth to the Sun.

When the French, before going to Egypt, had adopted the metre measurement as one ten-thousandth part of the meridian they did not know that the metre was similar to, but not exactly, the length of a pyramidal cubit, which equals one ten-millionth of the polar axis, making the ancient Egyptian measure basically more accurate because the meridians vary according to the Earth's surface.

Perhaps the most striking figure of all, demonstrating a culture reaching into the very distant past, is suggested by adding together the diagonal lines at the base of the pyramid which, in pyramid inches, gives a figure of 25,826.6. This figure, coincidentally, represents almost exactly the number of times that the Earth's polar axis takes to return to its original position in relation to the sun as it travels through space – 25,827 years.

These are only some of the coincidences that suggest that the Pyramid of Khufu is not a tomb but rather a time capsule, made of stone, re-telling ancient knowledge lost for thousands of years but ever more readable as scientific knowledge catches up with what was once known in the distant past.

The Gloucester Monster

One of the most well-documented sightings of a sea monster occurred in Gloucester Harbour, Massachusetts, USA, in August 1817. So many people witnessed the giant marine creature that a special committee of the Linnaean Society of New England was established to gather sworn affidavits.

A ship's carpenter, Matthew Gaffney, for example, reported that he was aboard a boat in the harbour around half past four on August 14 when the sea serpent rose from the water not 30 feet away from the vessel. Its head, he said, was as large as a four-gallon keg, his body the width of a barrel, and its length he judged to be about 40 feet. The creature seemed to approach the boat as if it were going to attack, but then suddenly dived beneath the water. It reappeared 100 feet away soon after, moving at an estimated rate of one mile every two or three minutes.

The Psycho-Kinetic Adolescent

Bizarre occurrences began to happen in the Resch household on March 3, 1984. Lights switched on and off, without apparent cause. Electrical appliances turned themselves on. The television made mysterious noises even though it was turned off and the screen blank. The shower began running while no one was in the bathroom. Through it all, there was one common thread: 14-year-old Tina Resch, who always seemed to be near the action although not physically responsible for it.

During the next few weeks, Tina made candlesticks dance and hanging lamps swing with frightening regularity. Soon, the entire neighbourhood was aware of the phenomenon and family friends and relatives also witnessed objects flying around the house. It wasn't long before researchers and reporters descended in waves upon the frazzled Reschs. Two religious groups even attempted an exorcism.

A television videotape, however, stirred up even more controversy. When the tape, clearly showing Tina levitating a lamp, was played in slow motion, some observers said they saw Tina holding the lamp's cord in her hand. Cries of fraud rose throughout the psychic research community. But others, like *Columbus Dispatch* photographer Fred Shannon, insisted that what was happening was no hoax. Shannon, who expressed his concern for Tina's safety, recounted an incident in which the living room couch moved 18 inches from the wall and 'attacked' Tina, who was sitting in a nearby chair. He also observed the phone move through the air on at least seven occasions, several times hitting Tina so hard she screamed.

To try to resolve the situation and the controversy, Tina's parents agreed to have Tina tested at a laboratory near Chapel Hill, North Carolina. During a remarkable series of experiments, Tina was asked to alter the nerve cell firing patterns of giant sea slugs, using nothing more than her mind to accomplish the feat. According to biomedical engineer and neuroscientist Steve Baumann, the tests were successful.

Although the sea slug's nerve cells emit a signal every second or two, the scientists didn't pick up a single signal for an interval of 23 seconds, during the time when Tina's mind was controlling the slugs.

Of course, sceptics are still unsatisfied, insisting there will be no proof of Tina's psycho-kinetic powers until the test results are replicated.

Premonition Insurance

When Jaime Castell, a Spanish hotel executive, woke from an eerie dream, he thought better than to wake his six-month pregnant wife to tell her about it. There was no need to concern her with the knowledge imparted to him. The voice in the dream, after all, had specifically mentioned the child she was carrying, saying that Castell would not live to see it. Concerned by the portentous dream, Castell followed up the next morning by taking out a life insurance policy for the value of more than £50,000 payable to his wife immediately upon his death.

A few weeks later, Castell was routinely driving home from work when he saw a car travelling from the opposite direction and at more than 100 miles per hour. As Castell watched in horror, the speeding vehicle careened off the road, across the metal safety bar dividing the roads' lanes and flipped end over end into the air. It was the last thing Castell saw before the car landed on top of his own car. Both drivers were killed instantly.

Often an insurance company will rule an insurance policy invalid if it appears it was purchased with the knowledge that the holder knew he was about to die. Due to the freakish nature of Castell's accident, however, the company couldn't dispute the claim filed later and immediately paid Castell's wife as beneficiary.

The New Jersey Bigfoot

In May, 1977, in Wantage, New Jersey, USA, several of the Sites family's pet rabbits were squeezed to death by something that had clawed at boards and ripped open the wooden barn door to get at the animals during the night. The culprit showed up again the following night, appearing in the now brightly lit garden. Big and hairy, it looked like a human with a beard and moustache, but it had large, glowing red eyes. It swatted at a dog that leaped at it, flinging it 20 feet away.

On the third night, Mr Sites and three others sat in wait with loaded shotguns. When it showed up they fired at it several times. It growled and ran off into the woods. They were sure they'd hit their target, but they could find no traces of blood afterwards.

Investigators for the Society for the Investigation of the Unexplained searched the area but they never saw the creature, although they heard what they were told was its screaming. Following their examination, the creature was seen several more times, once by the Sites' children who saw it crawling through the grass. Its arm was outstretched as though it were injured and seeking help.

Musical Aspirin

A woman heard music, songs from the 1930s and 40s playing all day long in her head. In frustration, she sought the help of James Allen of the Minneapolis Clinic of Neurology.

Allen investigated every conceivable possibility: were the woman's neighbours, perhaps, playing their music too loudly? Was her hearing aid malfunctioning and somehow picking up a local radio station? No. Even when the woman was placed in a sound-proof room, she still heard the songs.

Allen then undertook a thorough physical examination: the woman was mentally sound, with normal brain wave patterns. With the exception of limited hearing and her rheumatoid arthritis, she was otherwise healthy.

Allen finally realized that the melodies were caused, in fact, by the 12 aspirin per day she took for her arthritis, as the drug sometimes causes ringing in the ears. Because the memory for music is stored in the auditory centre of the brain's temporal lobe, the combination of the woman's hearing loss and her heavy use of aspirin stirred her musical memories and brought them into her consciousness. When her aspirin intake was reduced by 50 per cent, the sounds gradually subsided, Allen reported in the *New England Journal of Medicine*.

Dream Murders

Baffled police in Oak Park, Illinois, urged residents in the area to come forward with information regarding the murder of a 24-year-old nursing student on October 4, 1980. One young man, Steven Linscott, felt compelled to tell investigators about the bizarre dreams he had between one and three o'clock that morning while sleeping next to his wife.

In the dreams, according to the 27-year-old Bible student and counsellor at the Good News Mission, he had seen a man and a woman engaged in what seemed to be a friendly conversation in her home. Suddenly, the man's mood changed and, with a malicious grin, he grabbed a long, heavy, metal object and bludgeoned the woman to death. What particularly shocked Linscott, however, was that the woman had not protested at all during the entire dream beating.

Police were stunned by the amazing similarity between Linscott's dream revelation and the details of the actual homicide. The victim had been bludgeoned by a heavy metal object and had been struck numerous times. A student of yoga, moreover, she had been found with her fingers in a Kriya Yoga gesture signifying the acceptance of death. Added to the coincidence, Linscott had, on one occasion at the police station, worn a shirt resembling the one worn by the man in his dream. Concluding that these details could only have been known by the murderer, the police arrested Linscott. Two years later, Linscott was convicted and sentenced to 40 years in jail.

In 1984, however, Linscott's conviction was overturned by two of three judges who heard Linscott's appeal, ruling that the dream could not be considered a confession. The evidence merely raised the possibility of guilt. Enough inconsistencies, moreover, existed between the dream and the actual murder, including the race of the victim. Although the third judge believed that Linscott was guilty, the majority held that the evidence 'was plainly not sufficient to exclude every reasonable theory of innocence'.

The Loch Morar Monster

Loch Ness isn't the only Scottish lake that boasts the habitation of a mysterious marine monster. Sightings at Loch Morar, in fact, go back to 1887, although it wasn't until 1969, that the Lake Morar monster was dubbed Morag.

Duncan MacDonnell and William Simpson were on the lake in their cruiser on the afternoon of August 19, 1969. After a day of fishing, they were heading home when they heard a splash. When they looked out, they saw the Morar monster coming directly at them. When it grazed the side of the boat, it seemed to slow down almost to a full stop, as if running into a vessel had been unintentional.

Morag, they reported, was huge, about 25 to 30 feet long, with a snake-like head about a foot wide. It had a rough-textured, brown skin and on its back three bumps raised about 18 inches above the water-line.

For several minutes, the two men tried to prevent the creature from capsizing the boat. One of the men grabbed a gun and shot at the beast which then slowly sank and allowed the men to escape.

Solar Suicide

Despondent over his pending divorce, Robert Saylor decided that if his wife wouldn't have him, then life wasn't worth living. As a graduate of a correspondence course in electronics, he built a 'foolproof' suicide machine out of a solar cell, a battery pack and a .22-calibre cartridge. The unemployed Seattle man took the machine to a local hotel, barricaded himself in the room, and then called his estranged wife. Telling her of his suicide plan, he asked to see her and their young daughter one last time before he died.

Saylor called his wife again the next day and said he was going through with his plan. His wife immediately alerted the police who arrived at the hotel shortly after midnight. For more than five hours, they tried to talk him out of killing himself and, in the end, were sure they had succeeded. But as dawn broke, they heard a muffled explosion inside the hotel room.

When the police broke into Saylor's room, they found the man sitting in a chair, his legs propped up on a bed. He was dead. Investigating the scene, police found a photo-sensitive receptor in the window which was connected to the battery pack. The first rays of the sun caused the solar cell to trigger the battery which was connected to the .22-calibre cartridge taped over Saylor's heart. The explosion killed him instantly.

The Lake Monster of British Columbia

Since the year 1700, there have been about 200 reports of a huge aquatic animal sighted in the Okanagan Lake in British Columbia, Canada. Popularly known as Ogopogo, the creature was observed in 1949, for example, at close range by several people. Leslie Kerry was out in his boat with a holidaying Montreal family when they spotted a large, snake-like form, undulating vertically just at the surface of the lake. It appeared to be about 30 feet long and a foot thick and had a forked tail. Meanwhile, on shore, Kerry's wife noticed the creature as well, and called her neighbours to take a look. Watching it through binoculars, they described it as smooth and black, and had 'undulations or coils'. They also thought there might have been two creatures, based on the distance between some of the coils.

The Travelling Prophet and the Glasgow Earthquake

Edward Pearson, a self-proclaimed 'unemployed prophet' from Wales, awoke one morning in late November 1974 with a horrible premonition. Earthquakes in the British Isles, he knew, were as common as snow in July. Even so, Pearson had the impression that the city of Glasgow would soon be wrecked by a substantial tremor.

Seeing no alternative, he felt he must warn Glasgow's citizens of the imminent quake. Although he lacked the necessary funds to travel to the city, the Welshman boarded a train without a ticket at Inverness on December 4, certain that the importance of his visit would convince the train's guard to make an exception in the prophet's case.

Unfortunately for Pearson, the train authorities weren't as understanding as he had expected and his passage was denied. His story was reported, somewhat tongue-in-cheek, the following day in the Dundee *Courier and Advertiser*. Three weeks later, however, when an earthquake rattled Glasgow, destroying numerous buildings in the city and surrounding area, the newspapermen realized they had scoffed at a most accurate prediction.

Auto Coincidence

When Thomas Baker came out of the Northgate Shopping Centre in Sheboygan, Illinois, USA, his first thought was that his car had been stolen. But after a few minutes of searching, he saw the maroon car not far from where he had originally parked it. He unlocked the door and slid inside, but was baffled when his six-foot, six-inch body didn't fit comfortably between the seat and the steering wheel. And when he looked around him, he noticed many unfamiliar objects in place of what should have been there. Confused, and unsure of what else to do, Baker called the police.

Later, while Baker was explaining the puzzling situation to the patrolman who responded to his call, an elderly couple pulled up in an identical maroon car. They, too, had been mystified when they realized there were unfamiliar items in the car they had thought was their own. A subsequent check of licence plates proved that Baker and the elderly couple had, indeed, confused their cars.

According to the manufacturers, the real coincidence lay in the fact that each owner's key opened the other's car door, something that had a one in 1,000 chance of occurring. But when you consider the matching colour and model, as well as the fact that the cars were parked in the same place at the same time, the odds become more like 10,000 to one.

In an even more bizarre twist, however, Baker and the elderly couple had the same surname.

The Cursed Kimono

In the annals of legendary cursed clothing, perhaps none created nearly as much furore and destruction as that attributed to a mid-seventeenth-century Japanese kimono.

Three young women each successively owned the garment and all three died before they ever had a chance to wear it. Believing the kimono was evil and the cause of the girls' deaths, a Japanese priest declared that it should be cremated in February 1657. But as the kimono was set ablaze, a sudden and violent wind blew up and fanned the flames until they were out of control. The ensuing fire destroyed three-quarters of Tokyo and killed 100,000 people.

Bismarck, Jefferson and the Lucky (or Unlucky) Number 3

They may have lived during different periods and in different countries, but Thomas Jefferson and Prince Bismarck had at least one thing in common: the number 3 figured greatly in their lives. Among other tertiary facts, the third President of the United States, Thomas Jefferson was his parents' third son and the family's third Thomas. He wrote the Declaration of Independence at the age of 33, for three years served as the third ambassador of France, was appointed the third president of the American Philosophical Society, and lost the presidential election in 1796 by three votes.

A passionate lover of the three arts, architecture, painting and music, Jefferson hated three things: royalty, nobility and fanaticism. Jefferson would probably, then, have been displeased by Bismarck's three titles: Count, Duke and Prince. Like Jefferson, however, Bismarck studied in three schools, although the Prince then went on to serve three kings, fight in three wars, had three horses killed under him, signed three peace treaties, served as ambassador to three countries and established the Triple Alliance. And unlike Jefferson, Bismarck, the father of three children, escaped three attempts on his life. His coat of arms, moreover, bore a three-leaf intertwining three oak leaves.

The Shod Foot That Killed Trilobites 280 Million Years Ago

William Meister, along with his wife and two daughters, was on a rock and fossil hunting expedition in Antelope Spring, near Delta, Utah, USA. Amateur fossil buffs, the Meisters had already unearthed the remains of several trilobites – small marine invertebrates that had become extinct 280 million years ago, but had been the forerunners of crabs and shrimp. From the same rock strata, Meister pulled out a two-inch thick slab. Splitting it, he was surprised to find what seemed to be a fossilized footprint. If that wasn't unusual enough, the foot had apparently been wearing a sandal and had crushed a trilobite beneath it.

If Meister's fossil evidence meant what it seemed to indicate, Meister reasoned that palaeontologists must be wrong on at least one of two arguments. Either trilobites, known to have thrived for more than 320 million years, had not become extinct 280 million years ago; or contrary to theory, humanoids have been around much longer than the two million years that palaeontologists have estimated. The footwear, moreover, is another puzzle as historians have projected that sandals, shoes and other footwear have only been worn for several thousand years.

Meister attempted to have his find examined by local university geologists, but they weren't interested. Meister was simply wrong in the assumptions he had made about the find. So he finally went to the press with his discovery. Still the academic community was uninterested. James Madsen, curator of the Museum of Earth Science at the University of Utah, for one, flatly refuted Meister's claim that he had evidence of humanoids existing at the time of the trilobites. 'There were no men 600 million years ago,' he stated. 'Neither were there monkeys or bears or ground sloths to make pseudo-human tracks. What man-thing could possibly have been walking around on this planet before vertebrates even evolved?'

What indeed? Some people familiar with this case speculate that, perhaps long before the appearance of *homo sapiens*, some shoe-wearing biped from another world may have walked upon the Earth.

Code Words in Wartime

The absolute secrecy surrounding the Allies' plan to invade Europe during World War II made it necessary to devise an elaborate system of code words to alert agents to intended actions. Called Operation Overlord, the invasion plan included distinct phrases, each with its own code name. The naval initiative, for example, was known as Neptune. The French destination and rendezvous points were known as Omaha and Utah, and Mulberry was an artificial harbour, where the arsenal and supplies were to be stationed. But 33 days before the scheduled invasion date, many of the code words curiously appeared in the crossword puzzle of London's *Daily Telegraph*. Then, only four days before the plan was put into operation, the word 'overlord' showed up in the crossword puzzle.

Concerned that a Nazi spy had somehow obtained the code and was publicizing Operation Overlord through the crossword puzzle, security agents stormed the *Daily Telegraph* offices. To their surprise, they found only a bewildered schoolteacher named Leonard Dawes who had been composing the *Daily Telegraph* puzzle for 20 years. Dawes finally managed to convince the agents that the appearance of the key code word in the crossword puzzle was just a coincidence.

The Star of Nine Moons

Living among the Efe pygmies of the isolated Ituri forest of Central Africa in 1957 and 1958, French anthropologist Jean Pierre Hallet learned that the Efe referred to the planet Saturn as 'the star of nine moons'. The fact about Saturn's moons, of course, wasn't a surprise. Astronomers, in fact, had known about the moons since 1899, when the ninth was discovered. A tenth moon, moreover, was observed by the Voyager space probe when it orbited the planet in 1980. Even so, no one has any idea how the Efes knew about even nine moons, since none of the moons can be seen with the naked eye, and the pygmies' lack of technical development certainly precluded even an awareness of the telescope.

The Teleportation of Mrs Guppy

London mediums Frank Herne and Charles Williams were holding a joint séance with a circle of visitors when they heard the voices of the spirits of John King and his daughter Katie. Katie agreed to bring something to the sitters and someone asked her to produce well-known medium Mrs Guppy. Katie laughed and, despite her father's protests, insisted that she would comply.

The sitters were all laughing when they heard a loud thump on the table, and several of them screamed. One of them lit a lamp, and there in the middle of the table sat Mrs Guppy. She seemed to be in a trance and held a pen and an account book in her hand.

When the medium was gently roused from her trance, she was a little perturbed. The last thing she remembered was sitting at home three miles away. The sitter escorted her home, where an anxious friend awaited. Apparently, the two had been in Mrs Guppy's room together when Mrs Guppy suddenly disappeared, 'leaving only a slight haze near the ceiling'.

The Preserved Body of St Bernadette

In 1858, Bernadette Soubirois, then a 14-year-old French girl, saw visions of the Virgin Mary at a spring in Lourdes, France, now one of the most famous Catholic shrines. Bernadette later became a nun in the order o the Sisters of Nôtre Dame and died at the age of 35. Fof 45 years following her death, however, Bernadette's body was exhumed three times to determine the condition of her corpse, its possible incorruptibility being a sign of sainthood, according to Catholic church tradition. Although there had been some decomposition as a result of the examinations, investigators found that Bernadette's body remained remarkably well preserved. Today, it's on permanent display in the chapel of the Convent of St Gildard in France.

Ocean Oasis

Captain Neal Curry, his wife and two children and a crew of 32 set sail in Curry's ship *Lara* from Liverpool, England in 1881. On their way to San Francisco, a violent fire broke out on board and they were forced to abandon the vessel off the western coast of Mexico. The three lifeboats drifted aimlessly through the Pacific Ocean, with no land or other ships in sight. Soon, debilitating thirst and hunger overwhelmed the passengers and before long seven people had lapsed into unconsciousness.

While asleep one night, Curry dreamed that the water changed colour from blue to green. He tasted it and found that it was fresh and drinkable. When he groggily struggled awake, weaker than he ever thought possible, Curry was astonished to see the water surrounding the cluster of lifeboats was indeed green. And just as he'd foreseen in his dream, he mustered enough strength to lower a container into the ocean. Lifting it, he raised the water to his lips. Sure enough, the water was fresh – and drinkable.

Having been in the lifeboats for 23 days after abandoning their burning ship, Captain Curry, his family and crew landed on the Mexican coast. Because of the mysterious fresh water oasis they'd accidentally discovered in the middle of the ocean, all 36 lives were saved.

The Healing Powers of Padre Pio

The spontaneous appearance of stigmata, the replication of the wounds Jesus Christ suffered on the cross, on a seemingly normal person is considered a holy occurrence in the Catholic church. A most remarkable case of such stigmata, for example, was reported in the Italian town of Loggia in the early part of this century. A Capuchin monk known as Padre Pio was not only marked by the nail wounds in his hand and feet and that of the sword that pierced his side, but he was also able to heal the sick and injured by simply laying his hands on their bodies. On one such occasion, a nine-year-old boy, so hunchbacked that he could only crawl through the streets, was suddenly able to stand up straight after one touch of the monk's bleeding hand.

Padre Pio, born in 1887, first felt pain in his feet, hands and side when he was 28 years old, but doctors were unable to determine the cause. Three years later, he was praying at the altar when he collapsed in pain. Fellow monks found him unconscious some time later, bleeding from his hands, feet and side with no apparent cause. The monks immediately realized that he displayed the stigmata of Christ.

While Padre Pio was revered and respected throughout Italy and later the world, he still encountered sceptics and critics. One of them, a Doctor Ricciardi, who lived in the town of San Giovanni Rotondo not far from the Capuchin monastery, was stricken with a brain tumour in 1929. Wanting to die in peace, he refused to admit Padre Pio into his bedroom. But death did not come easily to Dr Ricciardi and when Padre Pio unexpectedly appeared at the physician's bedside, he was willing to accept the administration of the monk's healing power. By the end of that year, Dr. Ricciardi had fully recovered.

Blue-Skinned People

Blue-skinned people are an oddity of nature, but in most cases they can be biologically explained. Some natives of the Ozarks, for example, have a pastel blue hue due to genetic abnormalities caused by decades of in-breeding. Several known diseases can also cause a bluish discolouration of the skin. But high in the Chilean Andes, a group of true blue-skinned people were discovered at an altitude 2,500 feet higher than human beings were thought capable of surviving over prolonged periods. Mountaineer and physiologist John West of the

University of California at San Diego's School of Medicine discovered the small group of miners whose skin evidently turned blue to adapt to the lack of oxygen at nearly 20,000 feet above sea level.

The miners apparently produce large amounts of haemoglobin, the oxygen-carrying pigment in human blood cells. The excess haemoglobin can be seen through the skin, giving it the bluish tint. The men have probably also increased the depth and rate of their breathing. And because they were born and raised at high altitudes, they already have a headstart in their adaption.

Tibetan priests also spend a great deal of time at equally high altitudes, but the miners in the Andes are also having to work strenuously so their bodies need more oxygen.

The Lawyer Who Presented His Case Too Well

Thomas McGean was a local trouble-maker who, in 1871, was accused of shooting and killing a man, Myers, in a bar-room brawl. His defence lawyer, Clement Vallandigham, contended that Myers had shot himself as he attempted to draw his gun from his pocket while trying to rise from a kneeling position. One evening, Vallandigham met up with fellow defence lawyers and demonstrated how the scenario occurred.

Earlier, the lawyer had placed two pistols on the bureau, one empty and one loaded. Grabbing the loaded one by mistake, Vallandigham put it in his trouser pocket and cocked it. He re-enacted the scene as he imagined it occurred. But when he pulled the trigger, he shot himself, exactly as he'd argued the dead man had. Vallandigham died 12 hours later – and McGean was subsequently acquitted.

The Man Who Would Not Hang

Young Will Purvis was tried for the murder of a farmer in Columbia, Mississippi, and although he insisted he was innocent throughout the trial, the 12 jurors found him guilty. He was sentenced to hang and as he was leaving the courtroom, Purvis shouted at the jurors, 'I'll live to see the last one of you die!'

On February 7, 1894, Purvis stood on the gallows, a heavy noose tied securely around his neck. But instead of dangling and his neck breaking when the trap door opened, Purvis fell right through. The knot on the noose had mysteriously become untied and the noose, therefore, had slipped over the convicted man's head. Officials re-tied the noose and prepared for a second attempt. But the crowd gathered to watch the execution was of a different mind. To them, Purvis's salvation was a miracle and he was obviously not meant to hang. Screaming, singing and shouting their praises to God, the onlookers had enough influence to postpone the execution. Several appeals filed by Purvis's lawyer were denied and the hanging was re-scheduled for December 12, 1895, despite the fact that Purvis was now a popular figure.

A few nights before the second scheduled execution, a small group of admirers broke Purvis out of prison and he went into hiding to await the inauguration of a new governor sympathetic to his plight. In 1896, however, he surrendered and his sentence was commuted to life imprisonment.

By 1898, the outpouring of letters and favourable public opinion finally had an effect: Purvis was pardoned and released from prison. It wasn't until 1917, however, that he was vindicated. On his deathbed, a man named Joseph Beard confessed to the murder for which Purvis would have been executed.

In a postscript to this curious tale, Purvis died on October 13, 1938, three days after the death of the last surviving juror at his trial. Just as he had promised, Purvis had outlived them all.

Bigger Than 'Jaws'

Life in the oceans still remains a mystery to even the most ardent researchers. In fact, many marine biologists believe that there are probably countless sea creatures still to be identified. Two sharks captured off the coasts of Hawaii and California, for instance, may be examples of a shark species thought to have been extinct for millions of years. The two 15-foot-long specimens, dubbed 'megamouths' because of their scoop-like jaws, are tantalizing evidence that there are probably many more unknown animals where these two came from.

Richard Greenwell of the International Society of Cryptozoology, cites eye-witness accounts from around the world attesting to the existence of abnormally large sharks. Author Zane Grey, for example, reported seeing a 40-foot long, yellow and green shark in the South Pacific during the 1920s. And in 1977, some fishermen pulled their boat alongside a giant white shark that they estimated to be more than 30 feet long. Beside such unusually long sharks, Greenwell says there's no reason to think that prehistoric sharks, such as the previously presumed extinct *Carcharodon megalodon*, couldn't still be alive and well hidden deep below the ocean's surface.

Blazing Beach

Just after dinner on September 1, 1905, the guests at Kittery Point's Hotel Parkfield on the coast of Maine, USA, were enjoying the late summer air when they were startled by an amazing sight: the beach had burst into flames. Both the sand and the surface of the water were spouting fire and thick, sulphurous smoke. A loud crackling sound could be heard up to 100 yards away, and the flames, rising to a height of one foot, continued to burn for more than 45 minutes.

One curious guest grabbed a handful of sand, but quickly dropped it when the intense heat scalded his skin. Other guests scooped up some sand in a pot and took it into the hotel where they added water to it. To their surprise, gas bubbles escaped from the sand and, as they broke at the surface of the water, they ignited.

According to one explanation for the bizarre event, a layer of seaweed buried beneath the sand – both on the beach and below the water near the shore – had fermented, creating pockets of a flammable gas that, when it reacted with the air, caused the fire. That was only one possibility, however, and was never actually proven to be the cause.

Burn Immunity

Despite its mystical quality, the phenomenon of fire-walking – the ability to cross a bed of hot coals barefooted – can be explained as a simple case of the mind being trained to control the sensation of pain for a limited period of time. But the amazing abilities of a nineteenth-century Denton, Maryland, USA, blacksmith suggests an actual immunity to intense heat.

Nathan Coker was born in 1814, a slave belonging to a Hillsborough, Maryland, lawyer named Purnell. His owner's mistreatment of the boy included starving him, and it was his constant hunger that prompted the discovery of his unusual gift. One afternoon, when the cook was out of the kitchen, Nathan reached into a vat of boiling water, pulled out a cooking dumpling and popped it into his mouth. He then realized that he felt no pain, not on his hand or in his mouth. He soon found that he could touch and eat any food, no matter how hot. He'd drink the fat off the top of boiling water and would even down scalding coffee. He claimed, in fact, that it was *cold* liquids and food that gave him the greatest discomfort. After he was freed, Nathan went to work as a blacksmith where his unique ability came in quite handy. As Nathan told it, 'I often take my iron out of the forge with my hand when red hot, but it don't burn'.

As word of Nathan's gift spread, he was invited to give a demonstration before prominent Easton, Maryland citizens including two newspaper editors and two physicians. The feat was even reported in the pages of the *New York Herald* in 1871. According to eye-witnesses, Coker placed an iron shovel, heated until it was white hot, on the soles of his bare feet. After the shovel was re-heated, he ran his tongue over it. Lead pellets were also melted into liquid and poured into Coker's hand and the blacksmith then poured the substance into his mouth. As the astonished audience watched, Nathan rolled the molten lead around his teeth and gums until it had solidified.

After each feat, the physicians examined Nathan, but found no indication that his flesh had been affected.

Nineteenth-Century Flying Saucers

A story that appeared in the January 25, 1878, issue of the Denison, Texas, *Daily Herald* may have contained the first known use of the word 'saucer' to describe a UFO. The article recounted the experience of John Martin, a farmer living just south of Denison.

On the afternoon of January 24, Martin was working in his fields when he looked up and suddenly saw a dark, disc-shaped object in the clear sky. The object travelled 'at a wonderful speed', he told the *Daily Herald* reporter, and it resembled a saucer skimming across the heavens.

The Mystery of Dowsing

Dowsing is traditionally the ability of locating underground water, but many practitioners nowadays also seek buried objects. Their instrument is nothing more than a forked stick. Regardless of what dowsers seek, however, the art has probably been around since prehistoric times, if Algerian rock paintings are any indication. Ancient Egyptians as well as the early Chinese also seemed to have dabbled in the art. Written accounts, however, date back only to the Middle Ages.

Although little is known about how it works, speculation falls into two categories: physical and psychic. According to those who practise dowsing, some force emanates from subterranean water or buried objects and is transmitted to the dowsing stick. The force, they believe, may be an energy field, electromagnetism, or even radiation. But this doesn't explain how a pendulum swinging over a map can pinpoint an object's actual buried location.

Map dowsing falls more in line with the psychic explanation. The theory is that the dowser attunes his or her mind to a universal consciousness which then provides information that causes the dowser's muscles to react involuntarily. Such a reaction then stirs the pendulum to vibrate, indicating the site where the object will be found. Some dowsers, in fact, claim not even to need an instrument; they simply 'know' where the object is.

Abraham Lincoln and the Dancing Piano

During the 1860s, even American President Abraham Lincoln was attracted to spiritualism which was at the height of it popularity. At a seance in the home of a Mrs Laurie and her daughter Mrs Miller, Lincoln watched Miller make a piano beat time with heavy thuds on the floor as she played during a trance.

As she began to play, the piano's front legs repeatedly rose then dropped back to the floor. One guest asked to sit on the piano to verify that it moved and the medium replied that anyone who wished could sit on it. Four people did: a congressional lobbyist, a judge and two soldiers who were accompanying Lincoln. When Mrs Miller resumed her playing, the piano again began rising, as much as four inches off the floor, and then falling.

An Orphan's Visit from Mother

One night in 1878, the Reverend Charles Jupp, warden of the Orphanage and Convalescent Home at Aberlour, Scotland, gave up his bed to unexpected overnight guests at the orphanage. So he slept with the children in the dormitory, on a cot near three children who had just arrived following their mother's death.

In the middle of the night, jolted out of his sleep for no apparent reason, he surveyed the dark room. Then he noticed a strange and wonderful sight: a small, glowing cloud, in his own words 'as bright as the moon on an ordinary moonlit night', hovering over the youngest of the three recently orphaned children.

Certain that he wasn't dreaming, the Reverend felt he just had to touch the otherworldly apparition. But as he went to rise from the bed, some invisible but benevolent force seemed to keep him from getting up. He heard nothing, but felt and perfectly understood the directive, 'Lie down. It won't hurt you'. Calmed by the spectral force, he fell back to sleep.

The next morning, he rose at his customary time and, at six o'clock, began dressing the children. When he went to the child who had lain sleeping beneath the spectral cloud, he found the boy unusually silent. He looked up at the Reverend with an extraordinary expression on his face and said, 'Mr Jupp, my mother came to me last night. Did you see her?'

The Reverend didn't answer, but simply smiled and told the boy to get ready for breakfast.

The Mystery of Cawdr Castle

According to legend, Scotland's Cawdr Castle was the scene of King Duncan's murder by Macbeth in 1040, a tale immortalized by William Shakespeare. But the castle is interesting for another more unusual reason; on its chimney is a carving representing a fox smoking a tobacco pipe and holding it exactly as a human smoker would. The date engraved on the stone is 1510. But tobacco was introduced into England by Sir Walter Raleigh in 1585, 75 years *after* the smoking fox was carved.

Five Fiery Days in January

Mysterious and spontaneous flames plagued the Williamson family for five days in January 1932. During those cold winter days in Bladenboro, North Carolina, their clothing as well as household items suddenly ignited for no apparent reason. Neither the police, utility company officials, nor arson experts were ever able to determine the cause or offer any logical explanation for the phenomenon.

On the first occasion, Mrs Williamson's dress flared up. Soon after, the family discovered Mr Williamson's trousers ablaze as they hung in the wardrobe. Then a bed, curtains and other articles went up in flames. On each occasion, there were bluish, jet-like flames unaccompanied by any smoke or odour. Even more bizarre, nothing else nearby was ever affected.

The Nightmare of Being Buried Alive

The night after Max Hoffman was buried, his mother had a nightmare, dreaming that her son was trapped inside his dark grave. His hands clenched below his right cheek, the five-year-old boy was tossing and turning as he struggled to escape his prison of death.

Waking from the horrible dream, the mother pleaded with her husband to have the coffin disinterred, but he refused, believing that she was refusing to accept the fact that their son was dead. The next night, however, Mrs Hoffman had the same dream. Her husband finally agreed to appease the distraught woman.

With a neighbour's assistance, Mr Hoffman went to the cemetery at one o'clock in the morning, and exhumed his son's body. It lay exactly as Mrs Hoffman had dreamt, but showed no sign of life. Even so, they took the boy's body to the doctor who had pronounced him dead. Reluctantly, the doctor attempted to revive him. An hour later, they were shocked to see an eyelid twitch.

Within a week, Max had fully recovered and went on to live to be nearly 90 years old.

Matthew Manning's Personal Poltergeist

The house in Cambridge, England, was neither strange nor spooky, and it wasn't old enough to have a history of hauntings. But in February, 1967, Derek

Manning began to notice that objects were mysteriously moving around.

It started with a silver beer tankard that Manning kept on a wooden shelf. One morning, and for several mornings afterwards, the tankard was found on the floor, and Manning's three children denied any responsibility. Sprinkling talcum powder on the shelf around the tankard to try to catch the culprit, Manning was astonished to find the powder undisturbed in the morning, even though the tankard was once again on the floor.

Manning finally called the police who referred him to the Cambridge Psychical Research Society. Professor A.R.G. Owen of the Society suggested that a poltergeist – a mischievous ghost – was the probable cause of the moving objects and that the activity centred around the children, particularly 11-year-old Matthew. And in fact, the disturbances ceased when the children were sent to visit relatives for a while. As soon as they returned, however, so did the poltergeist, and this time, even heavy furniture was displaced. The activity continued until Matthew went off to boarding school.

The phenomenon reached a peak when Matthew was home during the Christmas holidays in 1970. Matthew himself often heard a scratching noise behind his bedroom wall and footsteps outside his window. On one particularly frightening night, the scratching seemed to come from the direction of a cupboard in his room and, when Matthew flicked the light on, he noticed the cupboard had been moved at least 18 inches away from the wall and towards him. He quickly turned the light out and almost simultaneously, the bed began to shake violently. Too terrified to move, the boy simply waited to see what would happen next. When he felt the lower end of the bed rise, however, Matthew raced from the room and spent the rest of the night in his parents' room. The remainder of the night passed without incident, but in the morning, the family found the house in a shambles.

As if the overturned furniture were not enough, bric-a-brac began flying around. It got to the point that family members would ask for something to be moved and the poltergeist complied. Puddles also appeared on the floors throughout the house and ghostly messages were scrawled in childish handwriting on the walls. One eerie inscription read, 'Matthew, beware'. With that, Matthew quickly returned to boarding school, but the poltergeist evidently followed him, wreaking the same kind of havoc there as it had in the Manning household.

Finally, Matthew attempted to re-channel the spirit's energies through automatic writing and spontaneous drawings and figured that, perhaps, five per cent of the results actually came from external entities and not from his own mind. In any event, the disturbances eventually ceased, and Matthew went on to continue his paranormal experiments and developed considerable psychic talents of his own.

The Man-Beast of Washington State

In Grays Harbour, Washington, USA, Deputy Sheriff Verlin Herrington was driving home late one night when he encountered what he first thought was a bear. Proceeding along Deekay Road at approximately half past two in the morning of July 26, 1969, he slammed on his brakes and screeched to a halt. Turning his spotlight on the beast, he realized it wasn't a bear. And although it walked upright, it wasn't human either. It was covered with thick brownish-black hair, except on its human-like face that had a dark leathery appearance. Instead of paws it had feet, its toes as well as its fingers quite distinct. And it appeared to be about seven-and-a-half feet tall and must have weighed at least 300 pounds.

Fearful, Herrington drew his gun, but before he could have taken a shot at it, the creature strode quickly into the woods and out of sight. The next day, the deputy returned to the site where he found and photographed a footprint that measured 18½ inches long.

Prehistoric Saunas

Archaelogists have long thought that the European features known as burnt mounds were nothing more than cooking areas. But that was an assumption based mostly on historical references to the use of hot stones to boil water. That may be true, but the purpose may not have been for cooking as much as for steaming. Recent excavations, in fact, have unearthed evidence to suggest that the burnt mounds may actually have been early versions of our modern saunas. According to University of Birmingham Professor of European Prehistory, Lawrence Barfield, the mounds may have been sweathouses or sauna baths. To support his idea, Barfield cites the absence of animal remains which would have been proof that the mounds had been used for cooking, but there are troughs that could have held water for steam.

The evidence, coupled with historical accounts that indicate a prevalence of marijuana use, leads Barfield to speculate that as early as the first millenium BC, our ancestors may have been purposefully engaging in recreational drugs while sitting in the prehistoric equivalent of a hot tub.

The Rainmakers

In the final days of the nineteenth century, an Australian named Frank Melbourne arrived in America advertising himself as a professional rainmaker. He'd set up a canvas wall around a 30-sqaure-foot area where he would mix his secret formula. Soon the fumes from the formula would rise through a 30-foot-high smoke-stack and then escape into the atmosphere.

Melbourne's wasn't a new idea, of course. Knowing that rains always followed forest fires, shamans would create great fires in time of drought. Even American Civil War soldiers accepted rain as a natural consequence of battle and referred to them as 'battle storms'. The clouds of cannon smoke that rose into the sky, they knew from experience, were soon followed by rain clouds. Perhaps it was just coincidence, maybe not.

In 1891, in Goodland, Kansas, farmers collectively hired Frank Melbourne to break the drought they were suffering. When he began his routine, there hadn't been a cloud in sight for days. But then Melbourne's chemically-created smoke filled the air and by mid-afternoon the clouds rolled in thick and dark. That night, the farmers stood in the downpour, rejoicing.

The following year, Melbourne's miracle working was not needed. The rains came in abundance. So the last anyone heard of the Australian rainmaker, he was off to Africa. In his stead, however, there were other rain-makers. C.B. Jewell's spectacular method of producing rain employed a bundle of dynamite attached to a small balloon sent 500 to 1,000 feet in the air, where the explosives were detonated via a telephone wire. He entertained the public with fireworks and satisfied the farmers who hired him with great downpours.

Perhaps the best known rainmaker, however, was Charles Mallory Hatfield. He had practically a lifelong interest in rainmaking, conducting his own experiments after reading Edward Powers' 1871 book on the 'science of pluviculture', which attracted so much attention that even the United States Congress appropriated money in 1891 to investigate Powers' theory that rain could be coaxed out of the sky through scientific methods.

By 1902, Hatfield was a full-time rainmaker. He built huge wooden tanks standing on stout legs that held the tanks 12 feet above the ground. He, too, used chemicals, dumping them into the tanks, stirring and mixing them, adding water and a few gallons of acid, then tightly covering the tank with a wooden lid. After about 20 minutes, he'd lift the lid and the malodorous vapour would escape into the atmosphere.

In 25 years, he contracted 500 rainmaking jobs in the Los Angeles area, ranging in cost from US$50 to US$10,000. In one experiment, he agreed to fill the Lake Helmet reservoir, producing 11 inches of rain and raising the reservoir's water level by 22 feet. Hatfield's greatest and unequalled success, however, occurred in the Mojave Desert where he produced 40 inches of rain in three hours.

The Bardin Booger Man

Deep in the pine forests of Bardin, Florida, a big, hairy, man-like beast with a pug nose lurks, waiting to leap out and shake passing cars. Local residents call him the Bardin Booger, and he's become something of a celebrity in the town. Bud Key, owner of Bud's Grocery in the heart of Bardin, sells T-shirts emblazoned with pictures of the monster. And a local country music performer even wrote a song about the Booger Man.

Size 13 footprints have been found in the areas where

the Booger has been spotted. Eye-witnesses include Doug Crew, a long-time Bardin resident who was sitting with two young women in his truck one evening when the van began to vibrate violently. 'The best way I've come to describe it.' Crew said afterwards, 'is that it's like a dog when it shakes water off its back.'

While the phenomenon has included some pranksters to fake Booger prints and rig up sound systems to produce weird sounds, a number of folk have actually seen the Booger. And as Key says, 'As far as I'm concerned he's still around.'

Out-of-Body Rescue

At sea for weeks, a British ship out of Liverpool, England, was moving through the icy North Atlantic waters and headed towards Nova Scotia in 1828, when the first mate, Robert Bruce, encountered a stranger in the captain's cabin. The man, who Bruce knew wasn't a crew member, was writing on the blackboard. Suspecting the scribbler was a stowaway, Bruce ran to get the captain. When the two men returned to the cabin, the stranger was gone, but he had left a message on the blackboard, reading: 'Steer to the Nor'west'.

Calling all hands on deck, the captain had each one write the message, but no one's handwriting matched that of the stranger. Even so, the captain felt it might be wise to follow the mysterious suggestion and ordered the ship's course to be altered.

Not long after the captain ordered the crew to steer to the north-west, the ship's look-out spotted another ship that appeared to be wedged in the ice of the freezing ocean. When all its passengers were brought safely aboard the British ship, Bruce spotted a man resembling the stranger in the captain's cabin. His handwriting was tested and, sure enough, matched that on the blackboard.

According to the ice-bound ship's passenger, he had fallen asleep just after the vessel had become stuck in the ice. When he awoke, he had a strong feeling that they would be rescued. Evidently, the man had had an out-of-body experience, projecting himself onto the British ship to deliver an SOS call.

Geomagnetism and ESP

Based on the often unsuccessful demonstration of ESP abilities in controlled test situations, sceptics have long argued that so-called ESP is nothing more than chance or luck. After all, if the phenomenon were real, there is no reason why a subject should perform well one day and poorly the next. But two separate research groups have shown that changes in the Earth's magnetic field might actually be responsible for the inconsistency of the psychic ability. Since it's known that fluctuating geomagnetism affects biological activities, it is reasonable to assume it also influences PSI.

In a survey of remote-viewing experiments conducted during a five-year period, Marcia Adams, president of the Time Research Institute of Woodside, California, found a clear correlation between successful tests and geomagnetic fluctuations. In the 24- to 48-hour period before successful tests, the geomagnetic field measurements were generally low; the exact opposite was true before unsuccessful tests.

Professor Michael Persinger, researcher of psychology and neuroscience at Canada's Laurentian University, moreover, supports Adam's findings. Persinger chose to look at 'crisis apparitions' – those situations in which an individual is able to sense a disturbing occurrence before it actually happens. Going through collected accounts taken from as far back as 1868, he was able to determine a significant connection between such premonitions and periods of low geomagnetic activity.

Lepenski Vir

The west bank of the River Danube in Yugoslavia was not thought to be significant in terms of prehistoric civilization. It had been assumed that Neolithic Europe had not been the birthplace of any independent civilization, but that its cultural development had been, in large part, determined by Near Eastern influences. But in 1965, archaeologists made an amazing discovery at a horseshoe-shaped bend in the Danube where they found a small, but highly organized settlement that dated to 5,800 BC.

Remarkable as a model of social, economic, religious and artistic organization, the prehistoric European settlement, which the archaeologists dubbed Lepenski Vir, seems to have developed independently of any outside influence; unless the builders were traders or refugees from a distant area. In addition to a sanctuary containing stone sculptures of extraordinary sophistication, a central plaza fanned out into streets lined with trapezoidal and other geometrically shaped buildings. The floors of the dwellings, moreover, had been paved with an ingenious mortar of limestone, water, gravel and sand.

The Missing Lake

A small lake had nestled in the Italian Dolomites for hundreds of years. In July 1980, however, the calm, peaceful body of water vanished into thin air, leaving nothing but mud and a few fish behind. One minute people had been fishing and swimming in the lake. The next, a great spiral of water roared out of the centre of the lake and continued to rise until the lake was completely gone. Hydraulic engineers and geologists have never been able to explain the phenomenon.

Paranormal Phenomena and Exorcisms

Adolf Rodewyk, the Jesuit priest who wrote *Possessed by Satan*, the 1963 definitive handbook on exorcism, urged priests to rule out all medical explanations for an apparent demonic possession before undertaking the dangerous ritual. He may or may not have followed his own warning before submitting a German student to an unsuccessful exorcism that ended tragically in 1976.

A student at the University of Würzburg in Germany, Annaliese Michel had been under medical care for epilepsy for four years before she began displaying unprovoked rage, violence and other abnormal behaviour. At the request of the young woman's parents, the local parish priest counselled the girl and, after consulting Rodewyk, then 81 years old, recommended exorcism.

The ritual soon began under the guiding hands of the Reverends Arnold Renz and Ernst Alt.

After several months of harrowing yet fruitless exorcism, however, the 23-year-old woman, now weighing only 70 pounds, died of malnutrition and dehydration on July 1, 1976. Less than two years later, Renz, Alt and Annaliese's parents were charged with negligent homicide. The priests were eventually convicted, but their six-month prison sentences were suspended. The tragic case led the German Bishops' Conference to rule that no exorcism could take place without the presence of a doctor.

But was Annaliese's demon the successful party in the exorcism? Or did the young woman die because she wasn't possessed? Some familiar with the case believe that it may actually have been one of a multiple personality, a syndrome that manifests two or more different personalities each opposed to the others or ignorant of them, in the same body. If one of them appears to be diabolical, the church authorities' only means of determining whether it is a case of possession are the same ones used to distinguish hysteria from possession.

The church considers paranormal phenomena an indication of possession, while on the other hand, many physicians and psychiatrists reject them as misperceptions or hallucinations. Even those less sceptical, however, may not consider paranormal phenomena as the work of demons. But the church's test is based on whether such phenomena occur in the context of a hateful aversion to religion.

The Booby-Trapped Tomb

China's first Emperor, Qin Shihuangdi was entombed in a massive, intricate burial complex built especially for him. As described by historian Sima Qian in the second century BC, the complex was surrounded by a river of mercury that was circulated manually.

Even though Sima Qian was the most famous of all Chinese historians and a highly regarded scholar, his descriptions of rivers of mercury and other details of the Emperor's tomb were considered myths. Recent excavations in China, however, have tended to bear out much of what Qian said. As reported in the *Guangming Daily*, the official Chinese newspaper, an analysis of the soil around the burial complex revealed unusually high levels of mercury.

In fact, Sima Qian's description of the tomb has become so believable that archaeologists excavating the tomb are now being very cautious. Qian, after all, also warned that the burial ground was booby-trapped with 'mechanically triggered crossbows set to shoot any intruder'.

The Dream of Assassination

On May 3, 1812, British aristocrat John Williams dreamed he was in the cloakroom of the House of Commons when he observed a crazed man in a green coat shoot and kill another man. When he asked the identification of the slain man, he was told it was the Prime Minister, Spencer Perceval. Awakening, the shaken

Williams recounted the dream to his wife and then fell back to sleep. The nightmare recurred twice more before dawn, awakening him each time.

Not a particularly political man, Williams wondered about the meaning of the persistent dream, even debating whether he should warn the Prime Minister. Little did he know that Perceval had dreamed a similar scenario. In his recurring nightmare, the Prime Minister told his family in the morning, he was walking through the House of Commons lobby when he was accosted by a lunatic wearing a dark green jacket with shiny brass buttons. The man aimed and fired his pistol. Then, Perceval reported, everything went black.

Although his family tried to convince him to remain at home, Perceval arrived at the House of Commons and, as he entered the lobby, was shot by a madman wearing a green coat with brass buttons.

Revenge from Beyond the Grave

In County Durham, England, in 1681, a miller named Jason Graeme was visited not once but three times by a female ghost bent on revenge. The apparition, who told Graeme her name was Anne Walker, presented a hideous appearance: covered in blood, she had five gaping wounds in her head. She had been murdered, she said, by Mark Sharp, a man hired by a relative by whom Walker had been pregnant. The ghost now wanted Graeme to go to the authorities and tell them her story.

Refusing to believe that Anne was anything more than a disturbing figment of his imagination, Graeme did not comply with the request. Anne Walker appeared twice more to plead her case before the miller went to the local magistrate, telling him the location where Sharp had buried his victim. When the pit was searched a body was found, bearing the wounds as described by Graeme. As a result of the grisly discovery, the relative and Mark Sharp were arrested, tried, and hanged. Anne Walker had exacted her revenge.

The Mysterious Greek Plague

Do diseases die out and become extinct? Or do they merely lie dormant, awaiting the conditions that will trigger their resurrection? A mysterious plague, for example, ravaged Athens between 430 and 427 BC, leaving death and suffering in its wake and so weakening the army that Athens was defeated in the war with Sparta. According to the Greek historian Thucydides, the symptoms included cough, vomiting, diaorrhea and thirst, as well as blisters, gangrene and amnesia. Originating in Ethiopia, the disease, he wrote, spread through Egypt, Libya, Persia and then struck the port of Athens. For centuries, scholars have attempted to determine what the disease was.

Retired epidemiologist Alexander Langmuir, who formerly headed the epidemiology department of Atlanta's Centers for Disease Control, reports that many of the symptoms cited by Thucydides resemble those of pandemic influenza, similar to the 1918 outbreak. But other symptoms, like convulsive retching and gangrene of the hands and toes, appear compatible with a staphylcoccus infection very much like today's toxic shock syndrome, considered a new disease. It raises the idea that the plague of Athens is not an extinct disease and could, in fact, erupt again in the future.

Star Maps of the Sumerians

The Babylonians have long been acknowledged for their vast celestial knowledge, developed thousands of years before the European astronomical revolution led by Copernicus. But newly translated Babylonian texts indicate that the civilization's wealth of information was actually inherited from the Sumerians who preceded them. The Babylonians, it seems, knew only how to use the Sumerian charts and actually understood very little if anything about the basis for the calculations.

The basis for our modern calendar, then, was developed some 5,000 years ago by the Sumerians who recognized that the planets were spherical and revolved around the sun. And they understood that the Earth wobbles on its axis, affecting the position of the North Pole. And they calculated that it takes nearly 26,000 years for the North Pole to return to the same position. Even more interestingly, they measured precisely the distances between stars, valuable information for space travel. But why were the Sumerians, with no conceivable mode of interstellar transportation, so interested in establishing the *distance* from one star to another?

Friendly Ghosts

According to Carol Mitchell at Colorado State University, most ghosts today are friendlier than in days gone by. In a survey of 400 people who had encountered ghosts, Mitchell found that the otherworldly entities have become less outlandish and wild and more prosaic. Survey respondents described ghosts as blue or white lights, fireballs or vague human figures that appeared briefly in a variety of settings, including cars, homes and gardens, but particularly bedrooms. They would talk with family members, give advice and even ask to hold children. The survey results, moreover, refute the idea that ghostly encounters have decreased in recent years.

The Scent of Violets

After his disastrous performance in the Franco-Prussian War in 1870, Emperor Napoleon III and his family fled France for Great Britain, where they were given refuge by Queen Victoria. The Emperor's son Louis became so attached to his adopted country that he volunteered for military service in South Africa. And in 1879, he gave up his life for England in the battle of Isandlahvana against the Zulus. He was buried in the jungle not far from the place where he died, although no one was quite sure where.

Believing that her son should be interred in England in the family tomb, Empress Eugénie accompanied an 1880 expedition to find Louis' body. Day after day, the search party scoured the African jungle, unable to locate the burial site. Then, with her health affected by the tropical climate and her spirits sagging, the Empress suddenly detected the scent of violets, her son's favourite flower. She followed the scent until it faded, at which point she stood directly over Louis' grave, overgrown and hidden in the underbrush.

Leech Prescriptions

Before the dawn of twentieth-century medicine, physicians often used leeches to treat illness. Only now are modern doctors realizing that the bloodsuckers may be medically valuable. In fact, zoologist Roy Sawyer says the secretions from leeches will be to heart-related diseases what penicillin was to infectious disease. They are already used by plastic surgeons to restore healthy circulation in patients with skin grafts and re-attached limbs. It has been found that two powerful enzymes in leech saliva can actually break down blood clots, another could possibly cure glaucoma by attacking and destroying the build-up of jelly behind the eye that causes the disease. And leeches are also helping researchers to learn more about Parkinson's disease. Nineteenth-century physicians and other medical practitioners may have actually been on to something, even if they didn't know how leeches affected human bodies.

The Bishop and the Assassination of the Archduke

Bishop Joseph Lanyi awoke from a frightening dream involving a letter from his former student, the Archduke Franz Ferdinand of Austria. In the top margin of the note paper there was a small drawing of the Archduke's car. A general sat opposite the Archduke and his wife, and an officer was positioned next to the chauffeur.

A crowd thronged the streets as two young men bearing guns approached the vehicle. Beneath the disturbingly detailed illustration, the text of the letter offered an eerier portent: 'Dear Dr Lanyi,' it began, 'I wish to inform you that my wife and I were the victims of a political assassination.' It was signed 'Your Archduke Franz' and dated June 28, at 3.15 AM.

According to the clock when the bishop awoke, it was a quarter past three in the morning and the date happened to be June 28, 1914. Writing down the details of the dream, Lanyi later recounted it to his mother and others.

Around half past three that afternoon, Bishop Lanyi received a telegram with the news of Archduke Franz Ferdinand's assassination in Sarajevo, Yugoslavia, an event that triggered the outbreak of World War I. There had been only one murderer and the officer was standing on the car's running board, not next to the chauffeur, but otherwise, the details of the bishop's dream had been accurate.

Chinese Yeti

Surrounded by the Chinese provinces of Hubei, Shaanxi and Sichuan, the mountainous region of Shennongjia is apparently the home of a large, man-like beast, the Chinese Yeti. In May, 1976, six Communist party officials travelling by jeep through the southern part of Hubei came across the strange creature in the road ahead of them. It had fine, light-brown body hair, with a dark red streak down the back, a human-like face with a wide forehead and narrow chin, and a broad, gaping mouth. Motionless, it crouched in front of the vehicle and stared directly at the passengers. They got out and surrounded it, throwing an occasional rock to prod it along, and the creature finally rose on its long, muscular legs and silently lumbered off into the woods.

Another sighting occurred a month later. Gong Yulan and her four-year-old son were gathering fodder for pigs when they saw a large animal with reddish-coloured hair rubbing its back against a tree less than 20 feet away. Yulan grabbed her child and ran, but, to her horror, the beast followed, screaming something that sounded like 'Ya, ya'.

Numerous other reports of mysterious man-like creatures in the Shennongjian region beginning in 1976, prompted the Chinese Academy of Sciences to organize an investigation. Searching and gathering evidence for eight months, 100 biologists, zoologists, photographers and soldiers were never able to catch a specimen of the creature, but they did observe it. According to the leader of the research team, Ghou Guoting, the beast was neither human nor bear, but something in between, perhaps an as-yet-unidentified primate species. Archless footprints, measuring 12 to 16 inches long, indicate that it has three distinct toes, one of which appears to be three digits which have grown together. And it is evidently not carnivorous, preferring to dine on nuts, leaves, roots and insects.

Dreamy Encounters with Postmortal Souls

Two Swiss researchers who have conducted a study of more than 2,500 dreams believe that some nocturnal imaginings may actually be glimpses into the afterlife.

Psychologists Marie-Louise von Franz and Emmanual Xipolitas Kennedy have found that while not all dreams about life after death are significant, many have a special, supernatural quality that sets them apart. According to Kennedy, they appear to be encounters with postmortal souls much like those that typically occur among the terminally ill. The dreamers sometimes describe themselves as rejuvenated in their dreams, or they may meet up with close friends or relatives who have already passed away.

Kennedy believes that even if they are not actually proof of life after death, these dreams have considerable value in confirming for the unconscious mind that impending death is not an end, which then eases the patient's passage from life into death. They point to the notion that whatever is unresolved during life must somehow, Kennedy asserts, be continued after death. The purpose is somehow to unite the individual with the archetypal being we think of as God.

Death by Overdose of Water

Tina Christopherson, a 29-year-old Florida woman with an IQ of 189, was obsessed with the idea that she had stomach cancer, the same disease that had killed her mother. To cleanse her body, she often went on water fasts, eating no food, but drinking as much as four gallons of water a day. She eventually drank so much water that her kidneys were overwhelmed and the fluid began draining into her lungs. She died of internal drowning, or 'water intoxication'.

The Spectral Soldiers of Looe Bar

In 1974, Stephen Jenkins returned to Looe Bar on the Cornish coast near where King Arthur is said to have died. Jenkins arrived with a map in his hand and his wife by his side. His first visit to the area had been in August 1936, as a teenager. At that time, he had been gazing around the landscape when he saw a battalion of medieval warriors, mounted on horseback and wearing cloaks of red, black and white. One soldier stood in the centre of the group, his hand on his sword and stared directly at Jenkins. But when Jenkins moved forward to get a better look, the entire army vanished.

Now, the vision reappeared exactly as it had nearly four decades earlier, but this time, Jenkins' wife was also a witness. And with the map, he was able to pinpoint the exact rendezvous site of the spectral army. Plotting a grid between ancient burial grounds in the area, Jenkins concluded that the soldiers became visible only at the specific spot because of the psychic energy emanating from the surrounding burial grounds.

The Disappearing and Reappearing Spanish Mission

No one is exactly sure where the Mission of the Four Evangelists lies, but it's believed to be within a 40-mile radius of Yuma, Arizona, perhaps in the south-

western state itself. Many believe, however, that the
Spanish mission probably rests alongside Laguna Prieta,
a lake south of the border in Mexico, although no one
can find the lake either. Hiding under the desert sands
for years, the Spanish mission magically reappears only
to disappear again. It may be covered by a natural
phenomenon called 'walking dunes', mounds of sand
that form around objects and constantly change shape,
occasionally reaching heights of 300 feet or more.

Ancient Japanese Mexicans

In more than 50 years of examining pre-Columbian art, Alejandro von Wuthenau has found dozens of
statues with Asian features, some dating from 2,000 BC.
One, for example, is a terracotta reproduction of an Asian
wrestler dating between 1,000 and 800 BC which was
found in the Mexican mountains of Guerrero. The artefacts, von Wuthenau insists, indicate that the Japanese
visited the Americas long before Europeans did. The only
question is, how did they get there?

In 1986, von Wuthenau discovered what he believes
may be a replica of a seafaring vessel used by early Asian
explorers. The foot-long tarracotta boat contains 10 figur-
ines of oarsmen, all with distinctly Japanese faces.

The Missing Mariner

When *The Times* of London sponsored a round-the-world boat race, scheduled to begin on October 31, 1968, Donald Crowhurst thought the publicity, not to mention the prize money, would be ideal to give his failing business a shot in the arm. So the marine electronics entrepreneur entered the race with his newly built *Teignmouth Electron*. Two weeks into the journey, however, he decided to loiter in the South Atlantic and fake his logbooks. Then, when it was apparent that only the *Teignmouth Electron* and one other ship remained in the race, Crowhurst decided that his only alternative was to let the other ship win. But on May 21, 1969, his sole rival went down near the Azores.

Distraught that the publicity surrounding his victory would reveal his fraud, Crowhurst seemed to lose his mind, as evidenced by the increasingly incoherent and rambling logbook entries and radio messages, which ceased on June 30. When the *Teignmouth Electron* was found adrift in the mid-Atlantic on July 11, Crowhurst was not on board. It's assumed that he jumped overboard rather than face up to his 'sin of concealment', as he called it in his logbook.

A Test of Telepathy

Before his flight to the Arctic by way of Alaska in October 1937, Sir Hubert Wilkins and Harold Sheran agreed to try communicating telepathically, setting up a

strict experiment. For three 30-minute periods, from half
past eleven to midnight, Eastern Standard Time, on
Monday, Tuesday and Thursday evenings, Sherman
would sit quietly and await Wilkins' messages. For his
part, Wilkins would attempt to project information about
what was happening to him during those particular periods. There would be two controls to ensure the test's
legitimacy: each night Sherman would write down the
impressions he received and mail them to Gardner
Murphy, the head of Columbia University's department
of parapsychology. And Reginald Iverson, chief operator
of *The New York Times* short-wave station would report
to Wilkins on the experiment's progress. A.E. Strath-
Gordon and Henry Hardwicke observed Sherman on Wilkins' behalf.

The results: an amazing number of impressions recorded by Sherman of events during Wilkins' expedition
as well as the flyer's personal thoughts and reactions
were approximately correct and impossible to have been
guesswork.

On March 14, for example, Sherman wrote: 'Believe
you discovered crack of framework in tail of fuselage
which needed repair. Seem to see you manipulating hand
pump of some sort in flight. One engine is emitting
spouts of black smoke – uneven, choked sound – as
though carburettor trouble.'

According to his own daily records, Wilkins had, in
fact, discovered the crack in the framework. His trouble
with the engine, caused by changing from one fuel tank
to another, had occupied his mind all day.

Wilkins himself was surprised by some details in Sherman's reports, including the mental image Sherman
received about Wilkins' evening attire at a ball in Saskatchewan. Of course there were times when Sherman
received no telepathic messages and his impressions were
wrong. But that he received anything at all was remarkable.

Native American Freemasons

In the mid-1970s, photographer and former newspaper publisher John Loughran was photographing Anasazi archaeological sites in the American south-west when he noticed remarkable similarities between the Indians' men's temples and his own masonic lodge. Well versed in the traditions and symbolism of freemasonry, he realized the Anasazi temple furniture was placed the same way, and the area where the main rituals occurred seemed 80 per cent identical to those in today's American masonic lodges. The only difference was that the Indian temple was round. After further research, however, Loughran discovered the masonic temples in northern Africa were initially round too.

Loughran speculates that if native Americans practised freemasonry, then they would have possessed a written language, despite beliefs to the contrary, because masonry is based on learning.

By using his knowledge of masonry to decipher symbols left by the Anasazi, Loughran was able to follow clues to a hidden, ancient Indian library containing rock and clay tablets, ranging in size up to two feet by one foot and dated between 1,000 and 1,200 AD. The most surprising find, however, is that they appear to have been written in a script resembling Arabic.

The Strange Lights of the Moon

Since the eighteenth century, astronomers have observed mysterious lights emanating from the surface of the moon, the earliest record dating back to 1787. On the nights of April 19 and 20 of that year, British astronomer Sir William Herschel had focused his telescope on the moon and was surprised to detect three brightly shining lights, which he concluded came from lunar volcanoes. And in 1790, Herschel observed more than 150 of the same kind of lights that he described as 'red, luminous points . . . small and round'.

Even though Herschel was a respected scientist, his volcano theory was, for the most part, discounted. According to a report published in *The American Journal of Science and Arts* in 1822, lunar volcanoes were unlikely because any molten rock at the moon's core would cool rapidly due to the moon's size. Instead, it was postulated that the lights observed by Herschel and others near the crater Aristarchus were just reflections of light from Earth.

By 1965, astronomer Zdenek Kopal had recorded 16 separate cases of lights at the Aristarchus crater and other regions, but the source was still disputed. Kopal was able to obtain pictures of the moon that showed a distant brightening in dark areas of the surface. These he attributed to particles emitted by solar flares that had occurred shortly before. But Kopal could not apply the same explanation to the spots of light discerned in sunlit areas of the moon, leading him to the idea that 'the effects of solar activity may depend on processes that are not yet understood.'

A few years later, in the magazine *Nature*, A.A. Mills proposed another theory for the lunar lights: 'fluidized beds' of fine dust were being churned up by gases beneath the moon's surface. These beds would, in turn, give off a hazy 'glow discharge' of static electricity that, from Earth, appeared to be points of light.

None of these hypotheses has yet been proven or disproven. Another observation of the lights defies all of them, however. In 1788, German astronomer Johann Hieronymus Schroter saw what he described as 'a bright point, as brilliant as a fifth-magnitude star' to the east of the lunar Alps. After 15 minutes, the light simply disappeared. Schroter continued to observe the moon until the same area reappeared, this time in full sunlight. He was astonished to see a round black and grey shadow exactly where the light had been on the moon's previous revolution.

Ancient Butter Ball

From as early as the Middle Ages and until at least the nineteenth century, homemakers would store dairy products in Ireland's peat bogs. But no one has ever found anything quite like a ball of butter unearthed recently. Rancid but edible, the huge ball of butter weighs nearly 100 pounds and lay buried at a depth of five feet, indicating that it is approximately 1,000 years old. Stored in what is believed to be the stomach of a cow, the butter was well preserved by the moist conditions of the bog. Like the discovery of the world's oldest preserved human brain matter in a watery burial ground in Florida, the find is another example of the incredible preservation qualities of saturated soils.

Pets that Sense Earthquakes

The Chinese have long noted that animals can somehow sense an imminent earthquake. They sense the drastic changes in the Earth's magnetic field, the precursor to earthquakes, and become nervous and frightened, often going into hiding. For instance, in Japan, before an earthquake, goldfish have tried to jump out of their bowls and in China pet birds have attempted to escape from their cages.

Jim Berkland became convinced of the Chinese earthquake-warning wisdom, in part based on his observations of animal behaviour, and after his own cat ran away right before a large earthquake. It returned a few months later – just before another quake.

Berkland, chief geologist for California's Santa Clara County, now goes through the lost-and-found classified sections of three major California newspapers, counting the number of missing cats and dogs. When the number of lost pets increases, it means the state may be hit by a quake.

He combines the number of animals advertised as missing, data on geyser and tidal activity and the position of the sun and moon, to ascertain when conditions are most favourable for earthquakes to occur. Then he compares it all to make his earthquake predictions, boasting an 82 per cent success rate.

Montreal's Day without Sunshine

The morning of November 10, 1819, dawned dark and ominous over the city of Montreal, Canada. When residents saw the heavy clouds that quickly changed from a murky green to pitch black, they expected the same thick, soapy rain that had left behind a sooty residue two days before. They were unprepared, however, for the mysterious and terrifying bout of violent weather that ensued, the likes of which had never been seen before or since.

By noon of that Tuesday, the city lights were ablaze as if it were night. The sun, when it could be seen through the thick clouds, ranged from a dark-brown colour to a sickly yellow, to orange and finally to blood-red. At about two o'clock in the afternoon, a wave of clouds rushed over the city, followed by a glaring flash of lightning that illuminated the sky like the sun. Then thunder rattled windows and shook the buildings to their foundations.

Another rush of clouds came, and then a light rain, similar to the shower that fell two days earlier, began to fall. Terrified residents watched as the next blaze of lightning struck the spire of the French parish church. Electricity danced around the iron cross atop the ball at the steeple's summit. The cross plummeted to the ground and shattered.

When Montrealers awoke the next morning, however, the sky was clear and blue. The only trace of the storm was the broken cross lying on the ground.

The Man in the Black Velvet Mask

In 1848, Alexander Dumas wrote the classic novel, *The Man in the Iron Mask*, based on a true but mysterious incident that took place during the reign of Louis XIV of France in the seventeenth century. In Dumas' tales, a man was secretly held prisoner for 34 years in a variety of prison suites, and wore an iron mask to conceal his identity. The prisoner, according to Dumas, was the King's twin brother, whose face would have been recognizable to anyone who saw it. In reality, however, the historical identity of the prisoner has never been determined.

What is known? In July 1669, a man was captured near Dunkirk. Apparently too dangerous to set free and, for some reason, too valuable to kill, he was imprisoned in the Bastille, where he lived in solitary confinement until he died in 1703, probably of natural causes. And unlike the character in Dumas' story, the historic prisoner wore a black velvet mask, not an iron one.

Some people believed the man in the black velvet mask was the king's older brother, imprisoned to avoid a dispute over who was the rightful heir to the throne. Still others surmise that he was Louis himself, his throne usurped by an impostor, an illegitimate half-brother. But perhaps the most feasible explanation is that he was Louis' real father.

Louis' parents had been estranged for many years when the future king was born in 1638. And Louis XIII, moreover, was old, ailing, and probably impotent. With the need for an heir to succeed the King, royal advisors might have provided the Queen with a surrogate father. If, then, the prisoner was Louis' biological father, and if the son had him executed, it would have been akin to patricide. And Louis probably did not have anything against him. But imprisoned, ordered by royal decree to speak to no one (and others ordered not to listen) under pain of death, the man could not reveal Louis XIV's true heritage.

The Curse of the *Charles Haskell*

Fisherman are a superstitious lot, and those who ply their trade in the particularly treacherous waters of Grand Banks off the coast of Newfoundland may be a bit more warier than most. So when in 1869 a workman inspecting the schooner *Charles Haskell* slipped off a companionway and broke his neck, many decided that the ship was cursed. But despite its reputation, Captain Curtis of Gloucester, Massachusetts, assumed command, and eventually managed to assemble a crew willing to sail the *Haskell*.

In 1870, the *Charles Haskell* was among the hundred or so vessels in the waters of the Grand Banks when they were hit by a hurricane. While the sea churned and the fishing ships pitched, the *Haskell* rammed the *Andrew Johnson*, destroying it and killing everyone on board. Although badly damaged, the *Haskell* managed to limp back to port.

Repairs made, the *Haskell* ventured back out into the Grand Banks again the following spring. Six days after setting sail, two men on midnight watch duty experienced a horrifying vision: 26 phantoms in rain slickers boarded the vessel. Their eyes were just hollow sockets, but they proceeded to take up their positions as if to commence fishing. Some time later, their mission evidently completed, the ghostly fishermen returned, single file, to the murky waters.

The watchmen reported what they had seen to the captain who, sufficiently alarmed by the guards' terrified faces, turned the boat around. But on their way home, the fishing apparitions appeared once again. This time, as the *Haskell* approached shore, the 26 marine ghosts walked over the water toward the port of Salem.

That was all it took to convince the fishermen, including Captain Curtis, and the *Charles Haskell* never sailed again.

Waldo's Mountain

In the early 1960s, an eccentric land developer named Waldo Sexton decided that his hometown of Vero Beach, Florida, was far too flat. What it needed was a mountain. So he built one. On the sides of the 50-foot high hill, Sexton carved steps that led to two solitary lawn chairs perched on the summit. Sexton later donated his mountain to the city for the enjoyment – and the amusement – of everyone.

When the mountain was levelled in 1972, just five years after Sexton's death, a restaurant was built in its place. But ever since it opened, the restaurant has been plagued by strange happenings. Glasses break and objects fall off the walls for no apparent reason. One night, after the proprietor Loli Heuser had closed the restaurant she saw a vision of a bronze statue of Waldo Sexton himself and realized what was affecting the restaurant. Waldo, disturbed by the razing and replacement of his mountain, had been exacting his annoying revenge.

Heuser's solution to the problem? Hoping to appease the deceased land developer, she plans to erect a statue of Waldo Sexton and a miniature replica of his mountain in the restaurant's grounds.

Instilling the Fear of Death

A most bizarre method of execution was perfected by Australian aborigines. The ritual, called 'bone-pointing', was brought to national attention in 1953 when Kinjika, a tribal member of the Mailli in Arnhem Land, was hospitalized in Darwin. Although he had no symptoms of poisoning, disease or assault, the aborigine died after four days of intense suffering.

Kinjika had fled his homeland after being condemned to death by the Mailli tribal council for breaking the taboo of incest. In an elaborate ritual, the executioner began preparing the *kundela*, or killing bone, derived from a human, kangaroo or emu bone. Sometimes even made out of wood, the *kundela* is six to nine inches long and usually includes a tail of human hair. When fashioned, it is then charged with powerful psychic energy.

Since Kinjika had left the confines of the village, the ritual executioners, or *kurdaitcha*, were enlisted to find and kill the convicted man. Traditional *kurdaitcha*, covered in human blood and kangaroo hair, travel in pairs or threes, wearing masks made of emu feathers and slippers that allow them to tread silently. When they find their victim, they pose as if ready to shoot but, instead, merely point the *kundela*, utter a chant, and then depart.

Whether, in fact, the result of the bone's psychic energy or his mental state, the victim is left a pitiful sight, imagining the lethal weapon's venom pouring into him.

His eyes glaze over, his face becomes horribly distorted, his muscles twitch uncontrollably. He may froth at the mouth while attempting to scream, the sounds caught in his throat. He becomes increasingly sick and lethargic, refusing to eat, and inevitably dies within days.

Only one thing can alter the effects of bone-pointing and that is a counter-charm administered by the tribe's medicine man.

Galactic Close Encounter: When Galaxies Collide

Of all the scenarios for an apocalyptic end to the world, the grandest is probably a catastrophic collision between our galaxy, the Milky Way, and another. Astronomer Marshall McCall has, in fact, estimated the likelihood of such an event actually occurring and, he's determined that it will, although not in our lifetimes.

The Milky Way is linked by gravity to a neighbouring galaxy known to astronomers simply as M31. With their common centre of gravity, their present course will bring them together, McCall speculates, in about four million years. All the planets in our solar system, however, will remain clinging to the sun because their gravitational bonds are stronger than the intergalactic forces.

At worse, perhaps our solar system could be ripped out of the Milky Way and sent on an independent course through space.

The Curse of Dunnellen Hall

After her husband died of a heart attack while being driven home by their chauffeur, Lynda Dick put the 28-room Dunnellen Hall up for sale. She compared the mansion in Greenwich, Connecticutt, to the Hope Diamond, and told the real estate agent that it brought bad luck to everyone who owned it. Indeed, since it had passed out of the hands of the original family owners, most of the occupants had suffered financial difficulties, with some being indicted.

Dunnellen Hall, a Jacobean mansion on 26 acres of land with a view of Long Island Sound, was built in 1918, commissioned by Daniel Grey Reid as a wedding present for his daughter Rhea and her husband Henry Ropping. In 1950, their sons sold the estate to Loring Washburn, president of a steel-manufacturing company.

In 1963, after Washburn suffered financial difficulties, Dunnellen was taken over by a finance company and remained vacant until bought by Gregg Sherwood Dodge Moran. A show-girl and former wife of an heir to the Dodge automobile fortune, she married Daniel Moran, a New York City police officer who later shot himself.

Financier Jack Dick paid US$1 million for Dunnellen Hall in 1968. Soon after, in 1971, he was indicted and charged with stealing US$840,000 through the use of false documents to obtain a loan. He died in 1974, before the case went to trial.

Despite Lynda Dick's conclusion about the estate being cursed, the price for Dunnellen Hall increased to US$3 million when Indian-born oil supertanker owner Ravi Tikkoo bought it in 1974. A slump in the oil market during the oil embargo of the mid-1970s forced Tikkoo to sell the property to its most recent owners, real estate and hotel tycoon Harry Helmsley and his wife Leona. In

1988, the Helmsleys were indicted on federal charges of evading more than US$4 million in income taxes.

South American Super Snakes

Some of the longest snakes ever reported made their homes in the Amazon River basin of Brazil. In the early twentieth century, for example, two reputable observers spotted monster specimens and took their stories back to civilization. But sometimes, no matter how reliable the witness, people refuse to believe.

In 1907, for example, Colonel Henry Fawcett was surveying the Amazon basin for the Royal Geographical Society. He and his Indian crew were making their way down the Rio Abuna when the triangular head of an anaconda appeared below their boat's bow. Fawcett grabbed his rifle and fired a bullet into the reptile's spine. There was a sudden flurry of foam and a thumping against the boat's keel before the snake died, its body continuing to writhe horribly. Fawcett estimated the snake's length to be 62 feet – 17 feet in the water, with another 45 feet still on shore.

An even larger water snake was sighted by Victor Heinz, a Brazilian missionary, on May 22, 1922, at three o'clock in the afternoon. Heinz was travelling up the flood-swollen Amazon when he was startled by a huge shape 30 yards ahead. It was a giant water snake, wrapped into two coils and drifting placidly downstream. As thick as an oil drum, its visible length was roughly 80 feet.

The priest and his crew passed the snake, keeping silent and trying not to rock the boat too much with their collective trembling. When the vessel was clear of the monstrous reptile, one of the guides explained that the reason the snake was so calm was because it had just feasted on several enormous rodents known as capybaras.

King Solomon's Mines

According to the Bible, King Solomon was phenomenally rich, and imported most of his precious metals and stones, as well as other exotica and luxuries, from far-distant lands. Much of it is now thought to have been copper or brass.

Mystery shrouds the location of the fabled mines, but the Bible's clues focus on two places: Ophir, where the gold came from, and Tarshish, connected with the navy that collected it. Unfortunately, there's no indication of the cities' locations. There are a number of possibilities, at least for Tarshish. First, there may have been more than one Tarshish (which can be translated as smeltery) where Solomon obtained his metals. Or, according to Jewish historian Josephus, who translated the Old Testament in the first century AD, Tarshish actually meant Tarsus, an ancient Roman port. But since Solomon was linked with the sea-trading Phoenicians, who colonized what is now Spain, Tarshish might be Tartessos, a kingdom near Cadiz and described by the Greeks as being rich in silver.

Tartessos may have been the starting point for even greater sea adventures around Africa and, maybe, America. Voyages to the western hemisphere are a possibility, made more tantalizing by the discovery, on the Mediterranean coast of Israel, of a text that mentions the 'gold of Ophir' and suggests that Ophir could be reached via Gibraltar. The Phoenicians, then, may have visited Brazil, which means 'iron' in Aramic and Hebrew, a striking example of an ancient name being applied to a land and its chief product before the country was 'officially discovered' by later explorers.

The Walking Dead

In Haiti, the blending of African religions and European Catholicism resulted in a curious spiritual amalgam known as voodoo. The *loas*, or gods, imbue the priests, in particular, with special powers that enable them to reanimate supposed corpses into mindless automatons or zombies.

Some of the most striking zombie manifestations are the result of love of revenge, which play major roles in the practice of voodoo. In one recorded case, a voodoo priest, or *houngan*, attempted to possess a young woman who was engaged to marry another man. She rebuffed the *houngan's* advances, and the angry priest was heard muttering threats and curses as he departed the woman's company. Within a few days, the woman fell ill mysteriously and died. When the body was being prepared for burial, her head had to be tilted slightly so that she would fit inside the coffin. And someone also inadvertently burned her foot with a cigarette.

Not long after the funeral, it was rumoured that the woman had been seen with the very same *houngan* she had previously rejected. There was no concrete evidence, however, and the possibility of her being alive wasn't pursued. Then, years later, the dead woman returned to her home, telling the family she'd been turned into a zombie by the voodoo priest, but was released when the *houngan* repented. She was positively identified by the scar from the cigarette burn on her foot and by her neck which was permanently bent from her placement in the coffin.

The Legend of Count Saint-Germain

He was an advisor to kings, a social celebrity, an alchemist and a wise man of great repute. But everything about the man known as Count Saint-Germain is shrouded in mystery. It is not known, for example, where or when he was born, or when he died. There are some, in fact, who believe Count Saint-Germain is still alive.

A vibrant conversationalist, a talented violinist, a skilled painter, and incredibly knowledgeable in every conceivable subject, Count Saint-Germain first became a celebrity during the mid-eighteenth century through his close association with Louis XV of France. Some called the count a genius: others believed him to be a charlatan of considerable proportions. He was especially mistrusted by members of the king's court who envied the count's position as royal confidant. Saint-Germain even involved himself in foreign policy decisions, to the chagrin of the rest of the government. Under the threat of arrest, Count Saint-Germain fled to England.

It was commonly believed that Saint-Germain was also a member of a secret society, perhaps the Freemasons or Rosicrucians and was familiar with their ancient rites. Some 15 years before the French Revolution, he warned the king of the coming bloodbath. And in addition to predicting the future, the Count was also a historian who recounted events as if he had been there.

Saint-Germain's death, moreover, is as mysterious as his life had been. According to court records, the Count died on February 27, 1784. At the time, he was practising alchemy with Prince Charles of Hesse-Kassel in Germany, and later whenever he was asked about his friend's death, the prince would always change the subject, as if trying to cover something up. In fact, Saint-Germain was registered at a convention of Freemasons in 1795, and was sighted by reputable sources in Vienna and the Far East as late as the 1800s.

Cattle Mutilations

Satanic cultists or UFOs? It's a question cattle ranchers in the American midwest have often pondered following numerous incidents of bizarre mutilations among their herds. Whatever the answer, something destroyed their cattle in a grisly and puzzling manner.

In the late summer of 1975, a Colorado rancher found a blue plastic valise containing a cow's ear and tongue as well as a scalpel. This was viewed by investigators as the first concrete clue linking the killings to some kind of cult. Then in August of that year, a motorist in Blaine County, Idaho, reported seeing a group of hooded figures near a ranch where two cows were found mutilated the following day. Subsequent searches failed to turn up any further signs of cultists. Even so, investigators were convinced that the culprits were human, even if their activities were inhumane.

Other incidents, however, were not so easily explained. In Washington County, Colorado, for example, mutilated cattle seemed to have been dropped from the sky, leading ranchers to the conclusion that aircraft were involved. And in Copperas Cove, Texas, a farmer saw an orange light hovering over his farm on the night his calves were butchered. The following day, inspection of the area revealed that the grass was flattened in concentric circles, as if pressed down by a blast of air from above.

One of the most puzzling cattle mutilations took place in Whiteface, Texas, in March, 1975. Not only was the heifer found in the centre of a scorched circle of wheat, but the mutilation was particularly horrible and inexplicable. The animal's tongue and external organs had been removed; its neck was grotesquely twisted; and its navel appeared to have been bored out. Yet amazingly, there were no signs of blood anywhere on the ground around the animal.

The Hermit Czar

Almost immediately after it was announced that the Russian Czar Alexander I had died at the age of 47, people began wondering if he was, indeed, dead. Rumours spread that he had actually abdicated in order to live the life of a hermit. Residents of Tomsk, in fact, claimed that a hermit named Fedor Kuzmich had suddenly appeared in their eastern Russia town and was really the former czar. When Kuzmich died in 1864, moreover, his last words were 'God knows my real name'.

Having become czar following the death of his father, Nicholas I, Alexander II attempted to put an end to the stories about his uncle. In 1865, he ordered the casket to be opened, but found it empty. A subsequent examination in 1926 confirmed that the body was, indeed, not inside the casket.

The Man Who Witnessed His Own Funeral

An anonymous English victim of typhoid fever was exhumed four days after his burial in 1831 and taken to a group of medical students for dissection. When the professor began cutting into the chest, however, the corpse cried out and grabbed the professor's arm. The events leading up to his assumed death make his story even more bizarre.

Although his physical strength declined as a result of the typhoid fever, the Englishman explained that he had never lost his mental awareness. Unable to speak or otherwise communicate, he heard the doctor pronounce him dead and felt his face being covered. He lay alert as family and friends mourned for three days. Following what he called brutal treatment by the undertaker, he 'heard the crashing of the wood as they drove in the nails fastening the lid. Crammed into the narrow box, I experienced a sensation as if my head and limbs were being torn asunder.' Then he heard a friend reading the graveside sermon.

He remained alert during the next four days. But when the professor's knife began to cut him, though, 'I succeeded in crying out, the bonds of death were separated, and I returned to life.'

Did Acid Rain Kill the Dinosaurs?

Today's acid rain is about as strong as vinegar. It may not burn holes in your clothes, but it can kill trees and fish by slowly changing the mineral concentrations in soil and water. Ronald Prinn and Bruce Fegley Jr of the Massachusetts Institute of Technology, however, have speculated that prehistoric acid rain was much stronger – about the same as strong laboratory acid – and would have attacked plants and animals, devastating life in the oceans as well as on land. So if dust clouds from an asteroid didn't wipe out the dinosaurs 65 million years ago, perhaps Prinn and Fegley's acid rain did.

Scientists almost always find high levels of the rare metal iridium in stratified layers of sediment laid down about 65 million years ago. Based on known concentrations of iridium in asteroids and comets, scientists speculate that a small asteroid or a large comet struck the Earth at that time, creating a cloud of debris that dusted the planet with iridium.

The comet, with much lower concentrations of iridium, would have had to have been about 20 times larger than the asteroid. The impact, then, would have heated up the Earth's atmosphere, turning nitrogen and oxygen into nitrous oxide. This would have combined with rain to produce nitric acid, or very acidic rain.

Dr Luis Alvarez of the Lawrence Berkeley Laboratory, California, has identified an iridium layer in rock layers of the Mesozoic era (65 million years ago). This layer has been found in various parts of the world and has been called the layer of the 'Great Dying', a cemetery marker for the enormous dinosaurs who had held dominion over the Earth for millions of years.

Wolf Children of India

The Reverend J.A.L. Singh had heard many tales about the manbeasts said to live among the wolves. And the wolves, the people said, made their den in a defunct termite mound. After Singh himself saw one of the creatures, he decided to investigate further, returning to the site with a hired crew to dig into the mound. It wasn't long before several wolves escaped their threatened den. One of them attacked the crew who shot and killed it. With the wolves gone, however, the crew continued digging until they made a shocking discovery: deep within the mound, they found two human children, one about two years old, the other approximately eight. The two little girls were curled up with two wolf cubs as if they were all siblings.

Singh took the girls, who he named Kamala and Amala, back to the orphanage he administered in Midnapore, India. The feral children walked on their hands and feet, as if they were four-legged animals. They howled and they would only eat meat. And civilized life was fatal for them: Amala, the younger child, died less than a year after they were rescued from the wolves. Nine years later, Kamala, having learned to walk upright and able to speak a few simple phrases, was also dead.

And No Time Off for Good Behaviour

It was once common practice for Mediterranean countries to use convicts to man the oars of their war ships. So in 1684, 17-year-old Jean Bapiste Mouron was convicted of arson and sentenced to 100 years and a day as a galley slave. Most of his time in the galleys, however, wasn't spent rowing since galley ships were practically obsolete by the time of Mouron's incarceration. The ships were moored as prison hulks. So Mouron was chained to a bench below the decks and left to rot along with the ship. Even so, he served his term in full, oddly enough, and finally tottered ashore a free man at the age of 117.

The Mystery of the *Joyita*

At dawn on October 3, 1955, the 70-ton vessel *Joyita* left the port of Apia in Western Samoa, bound for the Tokelau Islands, 270 miles to the north. It was found 37 days later 450 miles west of Samoa, its captain, crew and passengers mysteriously missing. The boat's provisions, logbook and instruments were gone, but on deck were a doctor's scalpel, stethoscope, and blood-stained bandages. A canvas awning had been draped over the front of the bridge.

One theory about the deserted boat suggested that the *Joyita* was rammed by a Japanese fishing vessel, its crew then looting the *Joyita* and murdering everyone on board.

Another possibility was that those on board had been kidnapped by extraterrestrials. Perhaps the most plausible idea was that the captain and a crewman had fought. The mate had fallen overboard and the injured captain had been treated by one of the passengers who happened to be a doctor. Threatened by a heavy storm and unable to navigate the ship, the crew and passengers climbed into the lifeboats, after rigging the awning above the captain who refused to abandon the boat. Then the *Joyita* was discovered by fishermen who looted it and threw the dead or dying captain overboard.

The *Joyita*, however, was not licensed to carry passengers, and it's not known if there ever were any lifeboats. Although unseaworthy, the boat held 640 cubit feet of cork in its hold during the voyage, making it unsinkable. It would not therefore, have been necessary for anyone to abandon her.

The Star of Bethlehem

Astronomers have long sought a realistic explanation for the appearance of the Star of Bethlehem that heralded the birth of Jesus Christ and led the three Magi to his manger. Now, Roger Sinnott, an associate editor at *Sky and Telescope*, explains that the appearance of the Biblical star was really the result of Jupiter's and Venus' orbits converging in the year 2 BC.

While the Jupiter and Venus convergence is well known, astronomers have discounted it as the Star of Bethlehem. They argue that if it happened in 2 BC, as Sinnott says, then it would have occurred after the death of King Herod which is thought to have happened in 4 BC. According to Bible historians, however, King Herod was still alive at the time of Christ's birth.

But Sinnott believes that the problem lies in a miscalculation of the date for Herod's death. The ancient Jewish historian Flavius Josephus reported that Herod died around the time of the lunar eclipse. To most modern astronomers, that would date his death on March 12, 4 BC. Another eclipse, however, occurred on January 9, in the year 1 BC. And if Herod died at the time of the second eclipse, he would have still been alive at the time of the Jupiter-Venus convergence, or the Biblical Star of Bethlehem.

The Left-Handed Antanalas

At least 10 per cent of the world's population is left-handed, sometimes considered as an affliction in a world dominated by right-handed people. Left-handedness was often considered as being sinister, and many children have been pressured to become right-handed, but parents' and others' efforts have usually failed.

The Antanalas, therefore, are remarkable among the world's races and cultures: the forest tribe of Madagascar is a left-handed society. In a complete reversal to the rest of the world, being right-handed is so rare that a child suspected of such a deviation from the norm would in former days have been killed.

Prehistoric Dental Floss

The common image of Neanderthal man is still one of an unattractive half-beast. But he may have been hygienic enough to clean his teeth after every meal. Neanderthal teeth found at a site near Krapina, Yugoslavia, were grooved with tiny but regular channels running from the front of the teeth to the back. Because the channels are so symmetrical, they couldn't have been formed by natural phenomena like cavities and plaque which are lumpy and irregular.

The Disappearance of Friesland

For over 100 years, from the 1550s to the 1660s the skilled craftsmen of Friesland traded with Greenland and Europe. But in the late seventeenth century, the large, well-populated island south of Greenland inexplicably disappeared from most maps. Some say the land mass sank, but if so, no one knows why. Others speculate that it was taken off the maps after being mistaken for a nearby island that did sink, which would mean that Friesland should still exist somewhere, if anyone can find it.

The Abominable Snowman on Film

Photographer Anthony Wooldridge was on an assignment in the Himalayas for the British journal *BBC Wildlife* when he spotted a large, furry animal among the snowy slopes. Of course, Wooldridge had heard all the legends about the yeti, or the Abominable Snowman, said to inhabit the mountainous region. It was a revelation to the photographer, however, to actually see a creature that could only be a mythical beast.

The creature was at least six feet tall, Wooldridge said, and 'its head was large, and the whole body appeared to be covered with dark hair'. Grateful for the once-in-a-lifetime opportunity, Wooldridge snapped several pictures of the yeti before it vanished into the Himalayan highlands.

Before *BBC Wildlife* editors would publish the photographs, of course, they submitted them to close scrutiny by two yeti experts. Both men agreed that the creature was unusual, although they differed in their opinions about what it actually was. In the opinion of Robert Martin, of University College, London, the figure could have been a 'large primate as yet undocumented by zoologists'. But anatomy expert and notorious sceptic John Napier shocked the editors by asserting his belief that the creature in the photo was definitely hominid, neither bear nor human.

Fish That Attack Sharks and Win

Sharks strike fear into most people, their great muscular jaws able to rip apart the heftiest of humans. But the little urchin fish, or Sea Hedgehog, of South America frequently attacks and destroys sharks up to 25 feet long. It has flabby speckled skin with spiky points, and can distend itself into a globular form, causing the spines to project like those of a hedgehog. When swallowed by a shark, moreover, the urchin fish eats and bores its way out, not only through the stomach wall, but completely through the side of the marine predator.

Track of the Devil

Residents in Devon, England awoke on the morning of February 8, 1855, to discover their snow-covered gardens filled with mysterious hoofprints, shaped like tiny horseshoes and covering an area of 100 miles. Oddly, the tracks ran in a completely straight line, as if whatever made them had only one foot. Found throughout 18 separate communities, the prints traipsed across fields and streams, up walls, and over rooftops.

The countryfolk were certain that they were the tracks of Satan and, for sometime thereafter, refused to venture out of doors after dark.

The Day the Sun Rose Twice

By solving an ancient Chinese mystery, scientists have been able to determine how long days were nearly 3,000 years ago. And time, it seems, does march on, because the days then weren't exactly the same as they are today.

According to the Bamboo Annals, the day dawned twice at a place called Zheng in the spring of the first year of the reign of King Yi. In fact, the sun was eclipsed just before it rose above the horizon. People in Zheng saw the sky lighten before dawn, then turn dark as the moon passed in front of the sun. The end of the solar eclipse was the 'second' dawn.

Grave robbers found the annals, written on sticks of bamboo and listing events beginning about 2,000 BC, in the tomb of King Hsiang, where they were buried in 299 BC. Modern astronomers now study them for their records of ancient events. The annals also list earlier eclipses, but in the days before clocks, none were timed accurately. The daybreak eclipse at Zheng is an exception because astronomers can calculate the time of dawn.

An eclipse on April 21, 899 BC, it turns out, matches the ancient Zheng account. But if the length of the day had remained unchanged at 24 hours, the eclipse would have been seen in the Middle East, not in China. It was seen in China, however, because the days in 899 BC were about 0.043 seconds shorter than today. Over a million days, that adds up to nearly six hours, enough to move the eclipse a quarter of the way around the Earth, where the ancient Chinese saw it as a double.

The Missing Financier and the Patient Wife

On his way home one night in 1936, financier Fred Lloyd shared a taxi with a friend. Dropping his companion off in mid-Manhattan, New York, he bid him farewell and continued uptown in the same cab. But Lloyd was never seen again.

Despite the fact that subsequent searches proved fruitless, Lloyd's wife spent the rest of her life steadfastly believing that her husband would return. When she died in 1945, Lloyd's three life insurance policies were found, still uncashed.

Monster Rats

In a bizarre twist of nature, giant rats, some weighing more than 26 pounds, were killing and eating cats in Iran. And according to the newspaper *Kayhan*, the rodents' extremely large hind legs enabled them to hop like kangaroos.

William Jackson, Professor of Biology at Bowling Green State University, believes the monster rats are similar to 'cane cutters', large rats frequently found and even eaten in West Africa. But the African rodents are vegetarians and Jackson is, therefore, baffled by the rats' taste for meat. The rats' aggressive behaviour, he says, is very strange.

The Mysterious Murder in a Locked Room

When Mrs Locklan Smith heard screaming and sounds of a struggle coming from New York City's Fifth Avenue Laundry, she called the police. When the officers arrived, however, they found the premises locked up tight – from the inside – except for an open transom window. So they lifted a small boy in through the window and he was able to open the door.

Inside, the police found the laundry's proprietor, Isidore Fink, lying on the floor. He had been shot twice in the chest and once through the left hand, powder burns surrounding the bullet holes. Strangely the cash register and Fink's pockets were full of money. But the motive for Fink's murder wasn't the only mystery.

Fink always bolted the laundry's door when he worked at night. The only way his murderer could have gained access was if Fink let him in. But, with the door locked from the inside, the only exit would have been the transom window which even a small child had had difficulty squeezing through. And the powder burns indicated that Fink was shot at close range, ruling out the theory that the gun had been fired outside the window.

After two years of speculation, New York police commissioner Edward Mulrooney was forced to conclude that the Isidore Fink homicide was 'an insoluble mystery'.

The Fatal Salute

In July of 1750, Robert Morris had a disturbing dream: he saw himself fatally wounded by cannon fire from the ship he was actually scheduled to visit the following day. When he awoke, the colonial dignitary was so petrified that he refused to board the vessel. Seeking to assuage his guest's fear, the ship's captain promised that there would be no gunfire from the ship until Morris was safely back on shore. Morris finally relented and the tour took place.

When the visit was concluded, the captain, true to his word, ordered his men to hold off firing the cannon salute until he received word that Morris was safely back on shore. While he was waiting, however, a fly landed on his nose and he raised his hand to brush it away. Taking the gesture as their cue, the crewmen fired the cannon. A fragment from the exploding cannonball struck Morris in the rowing boat not far from his destination.

So, despite the precautionary measures, his dream had come true.

The Missing Ring

In 1941, A.A. Vial of Greytown, Natal, South Africa, baked 150 cakes for the troops in war-torn Europe. After she had finished, she realized that her wedding ring was missing from her finger and concluded that it must have slipped into one of the cakes. To avoid destroying 150 cakes to find it, she sent them off to the army with a note on each one to please return her ring if found. The finder, it turned out, was her own son, who by extraordinary coincidence was handed one of the cakes and found his mother's ring in it.

Biblical Artefact Found Embedded in Massachusetts Rock?

In 1851, workmen were blasting solid rock in Dorchester, Massachusetts, USA, when they made a curious discovery: a four-and-a-half-inch-high vase, split in half by the force of the explosion. What was unusual about the object, however, was that it was made of some unknown material artfully decorated with floral inlays of silver. The editor of *Scientific American* offered the possibility that the vase had been made by Tubal-Cain, the biblical father of metallurgy.

The Woman Possessed by the Demonic Spirit of Her Father

Blasphemous voices and strange abilities began manifesting themselves in an American woman identified only as Mary when she was just 14 years old. During the ensuing 26 years, doctors diagnosed her as 'normal in the fullest sense', although they couldn't explain her bizarre personality quirks. For instance, consulting priests were spat on and cursed by some entity controlling the woman's words and actions. Finally, at the age of 40, Mary was taken to a Franciscan monastery in Earling, Iowa, to see Theophilus Reisinger, a 60-year-old monk well-versed in the ritual of exorcism.

The demon possessing Mary's body fought the monk's efforts, writhing, contorting, screeching inhumanly, and disgorging huge quantities of malodorous vomit and faeces. It spoke in strange languages and spouted profanities and blasphemies at Reisinger and the others gathered in the room. At one point, the demon even predicted the car accident that killed Father Joseph Steiger, the convent's pastor assisting Reisinger, a few days later. Yet Mary's lips never moved and, in fact, she remained unconscious throughout the ordeal.

The harrowing exorcism continued for months, and during that time Reisinger was able to identify more than one malevolent spirit inhabiting Mary's body. The leader was named Beelzebub, but he was joined by Jacob, Mary's father who instigated the possession, having cursed his daughter for refusing his incestuous advances. Jacob's mistress, Mina, was also among the demonic entities – damned, she told Reisinger, for murdering four of her own children.

The exorcism was finally completed two days before Christmas, 1928, when Reisinger was able to expel the demons as they babbled so piercingly that the room vibrated with the sounds.

The Psychosomatic Curse

Believers in the power of witch doctors and other practitioners of evil can be easily influenced by the power of suggestion. While curses in themselves may not be able to cause actual harm, the victims suffer very real psychosomatic effects that can even kill them. In the early part of the twentieth century, for example, a missionary was aided in his efforts to convert the Australian aborigines by a young converted aborigine named Rob. Rob would make frequent visits to a pocket of natives living on the outskirts of the community and led by a witch doctor named Nebo.

One day in 1919, a doctor from the International Health Division of the Rockefeller Foundation was summoned to the mission where Rob was seriously ill. Despite the obvious indications, however, there was no pain, fever or other symptoms – in fact there was no apparent organic cause for the young aborigine's sickness. But because Rob claimed that an angry Nebo had cursed him, the doctor and the missionary went to the witch doctor threatening to cut off his food supply and drive him and people from their homes if Rob died. Nebo consented to talk to Rob and told him that there had been a misunderstanding and that he had not cursed the man at all. Within moments, Rob rose from his bed, completely free of illness.

Yogi Body Heat

One of the most amazing things about Tibetan yogis is their ability to remain comfortable living in high-altitude caves, where the temperatures are well below the level tolerable for most people. And the yogis wear the thinnest of garments or nothing at all. The key is *tumo*, a mystical heat or warmth. Attaining it is a highly guarded secret among the Tibetan priests, but it is a standard part of yogi training.

A neophyte monk who believes he has the ability to warm himself from within is put through a curious ritualistic test. During the night he is taken to a frozen river or lake where he's required to sit naked on the banks. Holes are broken in the ice and a sheet is dipped into the freezing water. Then the novice is draped in the cloth and instructed to dry it using the heat generated by his body. The procedure is repeated throughout the night and, at daybreak, the dried sheets are tallied. Some dry as many as 40 sheets in one night.

Supernatural Virginia Beach

Two widely disparate organizations have been the focal points of some very powerful supernatural energy in Virginia Beach, Virginia, USA, and they have been using the vibrations for very different purposes.

In one corner is the Christian Broadcasting Network (CBN), where dramatic healings have taken place in response to the 'words of knowledge' spoken by station president Pat Robertson on his cable television show, 'The 700 Club'. He explains the healings as inspiration and gives credit to God.

On the opposite side is the Association for Research and Enlightenment (ARE), devoted to the teachings of famed medium and psychic Edgar Cayce. According to ARE president Charles Cayce, Edgar's grandson, ARE's primary work involves the investigation of ESP, reincarnation and 'the great force flowing out of Virginia Beach'. Cayce argues that CBN's healings are a result of this same spiritual force, only CBN calls it God. CBN, however, points out that references to religion are conspicuously absent from ARE's claim.

Despite the differences between the two groups, Cayce would ideally like to see the ARE and CBN combine their own forces, but he admits that it doesn't seem likely.

The Party Girl of Resurrection Cemetery

In 1931, a young girl was killed while being driven home from a dance at the O'Henry Ballroom on Chicago's Archer Avenue. Still wearing her white party dress and dancing shoes, she was buried in Resurrection Cemetery on the same street.

For years afterwards, motorists reported seeing a beautiful young woman wearing an old-fashioned white dress and hitchhiking on Archer Avenue. Mostly single males would pick her up, or she would jump into the car uninvited, asking to be driven home. Then, she'd instruct them to drop her off at Resurrection Cemetery. Some drivers claimed she would exit the car without opening the door.

One night in December 1977, a man driving past noticed a young woman in a long white gown standing behind the gate of Resurrection Cemetery. Thinking that perhaps she had been inadvertently locked inside, the driver called the police. But by the time they arrived, the woman had vanished. They noticed, however, that the bars of the cemetery's wrought-iron gate were bent slightly outward. And on either side they could see the distinct imprints of two hands.

Edgar Cayce's Psychic Gift

Famed American psychic Edgar Cayce made parapsychological history during the 1930s with his medical predictions through trance channelling, in which spiritual entities were engaged to speak through him while he remained in a sleeplike trance. Cayce said he first became aware of his considerable talents at the age of 13, while reading the Bible on the family farm in Hopkinsville, Kentucky. Suddenly sensing that he was not alone, he had looked up to see a woman standing in front of him. The bright sun behind her made it impossible to see her features clearly. But when she spoke, her voice was unnaturally soft and lyrical.

'Your prayers have been heard,' she said, telling him that he only had to ask and she would give him anything he wanted.

What he most wanted, he replied, trembling, was to be helpful to others, especially children when they're sick. With that, the woman vanished, never to be seen again. And Edgar had the feeling that he might be losing his mind.

Cayce's teachers had always complained, to his father's displeasure, that the boy, never a particularly good student, was inattentive. One evening following his vision, young Edgar was struggling with spelling, with the help of his father who was determined that his son would learn to spell. Edgar was having little success, when he suddenly heard the same magical voice again, this time telling him: 'If you can sleep a little, we can help you'. Pleading with his father, he then curled up in an armchair with his school book under his head.

After his nap, the lesson resumed and, to his father's amazement, Edgar not only spelled every word correctly on the first attempt, but went on to spell words in future lessons. He knew the page numbers for every lesson as well as being able to identify the illustrations accompanying them. From that point on, Edgar retained his ability to recall material almost photographically after he had literally slept on it.

It wasn't long after this that he may have perfomed his first psychic diagnosis – on himself. During a school holiday, young Edgar was hit with a baseball that struck him near the base of his spine. While there didn't seem to be any serious injury, the normally reserved teenager behaved strangely for the rest of the day, throwing things at his sister and being cheeky to his father. That night, his parents heard him talking in his sleep, saying that he was suffering from shock as a result of the injury to his spine and he prescribed the appropriate treatment: a poultice of cornmeal, onions, and herbs applied to the back of his head. Deciding that it couldn't do any harm, his parents followed Edgar's mysterious advice, and sure enough, Edgar was quickly back to normal, although he didn't remember a thing about the day before.

The Indestructible Grave-Digger

Grave-diggers in post-Civil War New Orleans intensely resented Samuel Dombey's low rates for preparing the final resting places of the dead. So they enlisted the reputed magical powers of a Dr Beauregard, paying US $50 for his 'supreme curse'. The next morning, as Dombey was digging in the cemetery, he heard a loud explosion and saw someone stagger from the nearby bushes. Beauregard, who was later seen heavily bandaged, had apparently overloaded a gun with buckshot, causing it to blow up.

The Beauregard incident wasn't the only attempt to kill Dombey, and soon it seemed that he was indestructible. When Beauregard bungled the job, the grave-diggers decided to take matters into their own hands. They first placed a keg of gunpowder under Dombey's cot in the tool shed and ignited it while he was asleep. The explosion destroyed the shed, but Dombey, thrown 20 feet, was unharmed.

Dombey's competitors were not easily thwarted either. Not long after the shed explosion, the grave-digger was kidnapped and, with his hands and feet bound, dropped in Lake Pontchartrain. But Dombey managed to wriggle free and make it back to shore.

Still, the attempted drowning was not the grave-diggers' last effort to rid themselves of Dombey. Next, they set fire to his house, waited for Dombey to run outside and then riddled him with buckshot. Firemen rushed to the scene and extinguished the fire, and then rushed Dombey to the hospital where he recovered.

The grave diggers were never able to kill Indestructible Sam, as the police had nicknamed Dombey. In fact, Dombey died of natural causes at the age of 98, having outlived the men who had tried to kill him.

Taking on the Burning of the Fire

The firewalking display at the summer palace in Mysore in southern India, was not a religious ceremony – or so the Maharajah told Monsignor Despartures. It was simply a spectacle the Roman Catholic bishop might enjoy. Indeed, the bishop arrived early enough to observe the preparations as well as the event itself. He watched the trench being dug to a length of 13 feet, a width of six feet and a depth of one foot, and he saw the fire lighted in the pit, giving off so much heat that the spectators had to sit at least 25 feet away.

When all was prepared, the Muslim from northern India, who hosted the event, stood at the edge of the trench, but not in it. Then he called for one of the palace servants, ordering him to step into the flaming pit. When the servant refused to comply, the Muslim forced him into the fire. As the spectators watched in amazement, the servant's look of horror quickly became one of relieved surprise. Though his legs and feet were unprotected, the man was not being burned. Seeing that their colleague was unharmed, other curious servants filed, one by one, into the flames. Soon, 10 of them were cavorting among the embers, all seemingly unaffected by the heat.

The servants were then followed into the fire by the Maharajah's band. 'The flames which rose to lick their faces bellied out round different parts of the instruments they carried, and only flickered around the sheets of music without setting them on fire,' the bishop reported.

By the end of the exhibition, some 200 people, including two visiting Englishmen, had gone into the trench, emerging unharmed. As the Maharajah rose to call an end to the proceedings, however, the Muslim suddenly fell to the ground, writhing in agonizing pain. He begged for water and drank greedily. Moments later, he was back to normal. A Brahmin standing near the Monsignor Despartures offered the only explanation for the incredible display, saying: 'He has taken upon himself the burning of the fire.'

Fainting Goats

In 1978, veterinarian Renfrow Hauser's father gave an unusual goat to his son's farm in Mount Airy, North Carolina, USA. Hauser took one look at the goat and it stiffened and fell over as if it were dead. It wasn't, but the animal was suffering from myotonia, a rare disease that blocks the uptake of neurotransmitters (a chemical substance which communicates messages through the nervous system). The goat would become as stiff as a statue whenever it was startled, falling over in a dead faint.

The swooning goat was subsequently bred with non-swooners, and there was soon a community of 25 goats inheriting the disease, the largest known population of myotonic goats in the world. Because of their affliction, the goats serve little practical purpose except as pets.

The Hauser farm is now often visited by people who go to watch the goats keel over – which they do frequently in response to low-flying planes, loud yelling or even clapping hands. Hauser often comes upon them in his pick-up truck and when he blows the horn to get them out of the road, they just fall over in a ditch. The more contact the goats have with humans, however, the less likely they are to faint.

The Phantom Battle of Buderich

The government of Westphalia collected no less than 50 eye-witness reports of a phantom battle that took place on January 22, 1854, in the village of Buderich. According to the observers, the entire army – infantry, cavalry and numerous wagons – marched in procession across the countryside. The discharges from the rifles and the colour of the uniforms could be seen clearly, and as the battalion headed towards the wood of Schafhauser, they left in their wake two burning houses and a trail of thick, black smoke. Then the army disappeared into the forest.

At sunset, the entire scene dissipated, as suddenly and inexplicably as it had appeared.

The Little Town of Bethsaida

The fishing village of Bethsaida is said to have been the home-town of the apostles Peter, Andrew and Philip, as well as the place where Jesus performed some of his greatest miracles. It is at Bethsaida that he walked on the Sea of Galilee, where he healed a blind man, and where he fed the 5,000 with a few loaves of bread and a couple of fishes. Herod the Great's son, Herod Philip, elevated Bethsaida's status to that of a city because of its large population. But despite the historical references to the city, nobody has ever been able to find it.

As early as 530 AD, scholars disagreed on the location of Bethsaida. By the nineteenth century, researchers had pinned down two possible sites – one near the mouth of the River Jordan, and the other at et-Tell, the largest mound on the northern coast of the Sea of Galilee. Now, archaeologist Rami Arav belives he has found the remains of Bethsaida about four feet beneath the 80-foot-high et-Tell.

The town beneath et-Tell, Arav says, dates from about the third century BC. For some reason, the site was abandoned suddenly, probably around 70 AD during the Jewish-Roman war.

The Mysterous Martin Bormann

Much speculation surrounds the fate of Martin Bormann, the trusted aide and confidant of Adolph Hitler. Reports suggest he was at Hitler's side when the Führer and Eva Braun committed suicide in a bunker in Berlin on April 30, 1945. After disposing of the bodies according to Hitler's own instructions, Bormann allegedly left with the rest of Hitler's staff in a convoy of tanks. But after that evening, Bormann officially became a missing person, and was subsequently sentenced to death *in absentia* by the Nuremburg War Crimes Tribunal.

But rumours continue to circulate about his fate. According to one popular theory at the time, Bormann was killed in Denmark while attempting to contact Hitler's successor, Admiral Karl Doenitz. Others said he had escaped through the Alps to Italy, or via submarine to South America. As late as 1973, he was said to have been seen in a Bolivian hospital.

Revenge of the Cactus

In 1982, David Grundman aimed his gun and fired two shots at a giant saguaro cactus in the desert outside Phoenix, Arizona. The blasts caused a 23-foot section of the cactus to fall over, landing on Grundman and crushing him to death.

The Loch Ness Bush Monster

Cryptozoologists (experts who search for proof of mythical creatures) have generally assumed that the Loch Ness monster, known endearingly as Nessie, is strictly an aquatic animal. But on at least two occasions, Nessie apparently has left the confines of the Scottish lake and walked on dry land.

In the summer of 1933, Mr and Mrs Spicer of Inverness were enjoying a leisurely holiday drive to the little town of Foyers. Suddenly, they noticed movement in the brush along the side of the road near Loch Ness. Slowing down to a full stop, they saw a huge, long-necked animal emerge from its roadside cover. It was at least six feet long and four feet high. Spicer described it as 'a terrible, dark elephant grey, of a loathsome texture, reminiscent of a snail'. It proceeded to lumber across the road and vanished into the bushes on the opposite side, returning, they suspected, to the lake.

Less than six months later, medical student Arthur Grant was riding his motorcycle on a moonlit road near Lochend when he also sighted a huge dark shape in the roadside bushes. Grant estimated its length to be about 18 to 20 feet long. The creature had an elongated neck and tail, and was eel-like, with oval eyes. And the four legs resembled flippers, definitely not designed for walking. The animal was bulky and awkward, so Grant thought he'd be able to catch it. But it was faster than he'd imagined.

Grant did manage to get a good look at the walking lake monster, however, and draw a detailed illustration when he returned home. According to Grant, it appeared to be either a prehistoric pleisosaur or a giant seal.

Painted Arson

'The Crying Boy', a popular painting sold in British stores, depicts an angel-faced child with a tear perched on his plump, rosy cheek. But the portrait may not be as innocent as the child appears, according to a retired fireman from Yorkshire.

It first struck Alan Wilkinson that there was something strange about the painting when it was found in the rubble of a house totally destroyed by fire. In the years following that first incident, Wilkinson compiled 50 similar instances in Yorkshire alone. A typical example would be a house almost completely gutted by fire. Pictures in every other room would be destroyed by the flames, but 'The Crying Boy' would be found without so much as a smudge. As the story of 'The Crying Boy' was spread by local newspapers, there was speculation that the painting was actually responsible for the fires in which it was involved.

Some owners of the painting, convinced that it was jinxed, removed it from their homes. One woman took her copy directly to Wilkinson and asked him to destroy it for her. Wilkinson left it in the fire station office, and the same day a kitchen oven overheated and burned all the firefighters' dinners.

Russian Roses from the Sky

Russian mystic and medium Madame Blavatsky had a magnetic personality. On one particular night in India, for example, she was in the company of several Indian scholars, a German professor of Sanskrit and her devoted disciple Colonel Olcott. At one point in the evening, the German professor remarked that ancient Indian sages were supposedly able to perform miracles – amazing feats like making roses fall out of the sky. Those days were gone, he lamented. No one had such powers any longer.

Madame Blavatsky took up the challenge, berating modern Hindus for no longer emulating their ancestors. But she would prove that such feats as pulling roses out of nowhere could still be done – and by a Western woman, too.

She pressed her lips together tightly and grandly swept her right hand. And with that, one dozen roses cascaded down from nowhere. Without further comment, Madame Blavatsky then resumed her previous conversation.

Incredible Monsters that Fly

Many cultures possess stories of otherwordly creatures that fly, the most common of which is probably the flying, fire-breathing dragon. Among others, however, are the Greeks' winged harpies and the Native American thunderbird. There are fossil remains, of course, of what could be the precursor of all flying monsters: the prehistoric pterodactyl, a sharp-tooth reptile with a wingspan of more than 25 feet. But there have been reports that such creatures may still be a present-day reality.

There have been occasional reports of the Jersey Devil being sighted in New Jersey, USA. The creature is said to be the size of a large crane, and described as having a long, thick neck, long hind legs, short fore legs, a wingspan of two feet, the head of a horse, or dog, or ram, and a long tail.

A frightening creative called the Kongamato resembles a flying lizard with smooth skin, a beak full of teeth and bat-like wings with a span of four- to seven-feet. And the Mothman, a man-shaped, winged creature that instils bone-chilling fear, has been sighted throughout the United States, from Texas to West Virginia.

Winds that Rock the Earth

Blustery March winds may be strong enough to knock you off your feet, but it would seem that, no matter how strong, wind couldn't possibly trigger earthquakes. Even so, Jerome Namias of the Scripps Institute of Oceanography in La Jolla, California, has studied high-pressure systems, which often spawn high winds. And two such systems may have been responsible for the earthquakes that rocked southern California in July and October 1987. During the four- to six-week period before the quakes, Namias found a recurring series of high-pressure systems over the Pacific Ocean several hundred miles off the west coast of the United States. Their unusual strength, he speculates, could exert pressure on the ocean floor, which in turn increases the stress on the inland fault lines in California.

Namias points out that other research has demonstrated that the force exerted on mountain ranges by global wind systems can alter the rate of the Earth's rotation. Therefore it is not unreasonable that winds may at times also cause earthquakes.

The Worst Nightmare

In 1924, lawyer Thornton Jones dreamt that he committed suicide. He awoke with a start, and realized that he had slit his own throat. Motioning to his wife for a pencil and paper, he wrote, 'I dreamt that I had done it. I awoke to find it true'. He died about an hour later.

Biting Poltergeists

In 1961, 13-year-old Molly Giles and her younger sister were taken to the local pharmacist by their distraught parents. The girls stated that 'something' had bitten them, but no one could explain the savage bite marks covering their arms. According to Ghost Research Society founder, Martin Riccardo, however, Molly and her sister had encountered a biting poltergeist.

Riccardo, who has documented at least half a dozen cases involving vicious ghosts, emphasizes that biting poltergeists are rare phenomena but, nonetheless, a horrible experience. In 1922, for example, the National Laboratory of Psychic Research examined Eleonora Zugon, a 13-year-old Romanian girl who had been bitten on the back and neck by some unseen attacker. While shocked researchers looked on, moreover, more teethmarks appeared on her flesh for no apparent reason.

Witnesses also observed 18-year-old Clarita Villanueva struggle with an invisible assailant in a Phillippines police station in 1953. What they thought initially to be a seizure turned out to be otherwise. When the attack subsided, Clarita's arm and legs were covered with bloody bite marks.

The Search for El Dorado

In 1492 when Christopher Columbus discovered the first of many Caribbean islands, he was on a journey to find a new route to the Orient in search of spices, jewels, gold and silver. He found none of them, and before long Europe was losing hope of unearthing great riches in the New World. In 1520, however, interest quickly blossomed again when Hernan Cortes returned with the treasures bestowed on him by the great Aztec ruler Montezuma – a finely worked duck, ornaments in the shape of native dogs, statues of tigers, lions and monkeys, all made of gold – that dazzled the Europeans. In this treasure was the germ of El Dorado, *el hombre dorado*, the man of gold. And the quest to find him has continued into the twentieth century.

Ten years after Cortes displayed the Mexican riches before the Spanish monarchs, Charles I of Spain appointed German banker Ambrosius Dalfinger the first governor of Venezuela. Dalfinger arrived and almost immediately set out to explore the territory. Reaching Lake Maracaibo, he found gold and legends of gold in abundance. The gold, they told Dalfinger, came from a people further in the interior, a people so rich that their ruler, El Dorado, painted himself gold. After repeated attempts, however, Dalfinger died in the jungle without finding El Dorado. But he had acquired another clue: the gold, he was told, came from the same place as the salt did.

The desire to find El Dorado mounted. Dalfinger's successor Georg Hohermuth, among others, also searched for El Dorado. Hohermuth was unsuccessful, although without realising it, he had come within less than 100 miles of what might have been their goal, later found by Gonzalo Jiménez de Queseda. At the southern border of the land dominated by the Chibcha Indians, salt was abundant. Here, Queseda's men tortured some of the Indians to reveal the source of their emeralds, which they then traded for gold as the expedition continued.

Then in June 1536, Queseda was led to Hunsa whose villagers were ladened with gold. There was even a real El Dorado: during the Chibcha's coronation ceremony the new king was annointed with sap and covered with gold dust. Even so, Queseda himself didn't believe that he had found the city of El Dorado, and his discovery did nothing to stem the search. Even Sir Walter Raleigh made two attempts.

Two or three times every century, someone has gone off in search of El Dorado. In the early part of this century, Colonel Percy Fawcett, following the early explorers in the search, disappeared around 1920, presumably in the dense frontier forests of Brazil and Bolivia. And the question that remains unanswered is did Fawcett find what he was looking for?

Kamikaze Birds

Suicide is almost unheard of in the animal kingdom, but in a freakish display, 400 robins perished when they flew, *en masse*, straight into a concrete wall. Some cats pursuing the dead or dying birds were then killed by late-coming, dive-bombing kamikaze birds. On the adjoining Highway 101 near Mountain View, California, a multi-car pile-up resulted when drivers attempted to avoid the mess.

Karen Fraad of the Santa Clara County Humane Society, doesn't believe the suicide was instinctive, or even planned. The robins, she suggested, were drunk. It seemed that alongside the Highway 101, the California Department of Transportation had planted pyracantha bushes, its fermented berries known to intoxicate birds. Fraad speculates that the robins had feasted on the alcoholic berries and they became disoriented. Not knowing where they were going, the birds began to fly low, and the wall just happened to be in their way.

In response to Fraad's protests about the heady plants, the California Department of Transportation has, for the most part, removed and replaced the pyracantha bushes.

Death By Insomnia

A middle-aged Italian industrial manager suddenly developed insomnia that gradually grew worse. The insomnia didn't respond to medical treatment, and by the third month of the illness, the man slept for only one hour a night and that was disrupted by vivid dreams that made him rise from his bed and perform a military salute. Other symptoms included impotence, amnesia and an incurable lung infection. Within a year of the insomnia's onset, he died from total exhaustion.

When neuropathologists autopsied the insomniac's brain after his death, they found a lesion on the thalamus as well as 85 to 95 per cent of the neurons destroyed in two parts of this region of the brain. The doctors learned that four other members of the man's family had been similarly affected, including a sister whose autopsied brain indicated that she had died from the same unidentified, strange malady.

The Green Children of Banjos

The villagers of Banjos, Spain were visited by a mysterious twosome in August, 1887. A young boy and girl emerged from a nearby mountain cave. Their skin was green, the shape of their eyes appeared Asian, they wore clothing made of an unidentifiable material, and neither spoke Spanish. The boy died shortly afterwards, but the girl eventually learned enough Spanish to explain her extraordinary origins: the children had come from a land where there was no sun, she said. One day, a great whirlwind had carried her and her companion away, depositing them in the Banjos cave. Investigators, however, were still baffled five years later when the girl died.

The Preserved Coal Miner

In 1869, miners found the body of a young man in the airless coal pits at Fort Smith, Arkansas. It caused quite a stir in the community, and a crowd quickly gathered to see who the man might be. When miners brought the perfectly preserved corpse to the surface, a grey-haired old woman slipped past the crowd and threw herself on the youthful corpse, crying and pouring out a stream of endearments. She and the dead miner, it turned out, were to have been married the day after his disappearance 40 years earlier.

The Banshee of County Monaghan

Gaelic banshees are a most benevolent sort of spirit. These female guardian ghosts will attach themselves to an individual or family for life, and will foretell the imminent death of their wards by shrieking and wailing. One of the best known was the Rossmore banshee of County Monaghan, Ireland. Her cry was first heard in

1801, at the death of General Robert Cunningham, the first Baron Rossmore.

During a stay at Cunningham's home, Sir Jonah and Lady Barrington retired early, proposing to rise early. At two in the morning, however, they were awaken from a deep sleep by a piercing wail. The voice began clearly and repeatedly to scream the name Rossmore, continuing for half an hour. When the crying finally ceased, Sir Jonah and Lady Barrington went back to sleep, still bewildered and shaken by the disturbance.

When they rose later, they discovered that their host the Baron Rossmore had died in his sleep at about half past two that morning.

On a Train to Nowhere

In September 1890, Louis Le Prince's future looked bright, having demonstrated his process for making motion pictures at the Paris Opera. Had he not disappeared, he would have received the accolades for a technique later re-invented by Thomas Edison. But the last time anyone saw him, he was boarding a train in Paris. Seven years later he was declared legally dead.

Return of the Extinct Tasmanian Tiger

The last known living Tasmanian tiger, also known as the Tasmanian wolf, or thylacine, was captured in Tasmania in 1933 and died in a zoo in 1936. But, although the animal was believed to have become extinct on the mainland of Australia 1,000 years ago, sightings have been reported during the last 55 years. And in the 1980s, the Australian government hired Kevin Cameron, an experienced aborigine tracker, to investigate the reports.

In the past, sightings have prompted numerous searches, but there has never been any proof that the creature existed. And even though Cameron reported having seen at least four separate Tasmanian tigers in the dense forest, each displaying the animals' characteristic weaving gait, the authorities remained sceptical. So Cameron went back for more concrete evidence, this time producing photographs of an animal about the size of a dog, with dark strips across its hind quarters, another distinct characteristic of the tiger. He also obtained casts of footprints – very clear forefeet with five toes and hindfeet with only four. Despite accepted scientific knowledge, some researchers believe Cameron's sightings are authentic. And Athol Douglas, retired experimental officer at the Western Australian Museum in Perth, estimates that there are at least six Tasmanian tigers living in the Australian forest.

Vanishing into Thin Air

It's one thing to disappear without a trace, but to do it in front of witnesses is bizarre, to say the least. Even so, that is exactly what happened to Orion Williamson in July 1854 before the very eyes of his wife, daughter and two neighbours in Selma, Alabama. One moment, he was walking across his pasture; the next he was gone. And a subsequent search that included the use of bloodhounds revealed no hidden holes and no sign of Williamson.

A similar incident took place in September, 1880, in Gallatin, Tennessee, when farmer David Lang took off on a tour of his fields, in full view of his wife, and simply vanished into thin air. The disappearance was also witnessed by August Peck, a local judge and his brother-in-law who had arrived at the Lang farm just moments before and had waved to the farmer.

Mysterious evidence in other similar cases includes footprints that continue for a while and then suddenly stop. One night in November, 1878, for example, 16-year-old Charles Ashmore of Quincy, Indiana, went on a simple water-gathering errand and never returned. When Charles' father and sister went out searching for him later, they found and followed his fresh tracks in the damp soil, but they ended suddenly less than halfway to the well.

In two oddly coincidental cases, also involving wells, 11-year-old boys, both named Oliver, disappeared on two Christmas Eves; 20 years apart and on different continents. Oliver Larch disappeared in 1889 on his way to the family well in South Bend, Indiana. Oliver Thomas of Rhayader, Wales, seems to have fallen victim to mysterious forces in 1909: his family heard his anguished cries of 'Help! They've got me!' But when they rushed outdoors, the boy was nowhere to be seen. They followed his footprints until they abruptly ended halfway to the well.

Biblical AIDS

Sexually transmitted diseases have been reported since the beginning of medical history, but the AIDS epidemic, some believe, is uniquely new. But British chemist John Gwilt, vice-president of the New York-based Sterling Drug Company, argues that there is evidence in the Bible that ancient Israelites suffered from an eerily similar affliction.

According to Gwilt, the twenty-fifth chapter of the Bible's Book of Numbers recounts an encounter between the Israelites and the Moabite religious prostitutes. Their 'intermingling' resulted in the illness and subsequent death of 24,000 Israelites. Although Gwilt believes that this figure may have been an error in translation – he estimates the death toll was probably 2,400 – the sexual encounters of the Israelites definitely had very deadly consequences.

The Bible, in fact, is full of medical descriptions – from heart attacks and hypothermia to epilepsy and sudden infant death syndrome – that are surprisingly accurate in terms of modern medical knowledge. The Old Testament, moreover, contains references to diseases not yet known to modern medicine. In Zachariah, Gwilt points out as an example that 'Their flesh shall rot while they stand on their feet, their eyes shall rot in their sockets, and their tongues shall rot in their mouths.' It seems to describe exactly what would happen to people in the event of a nuclear meltdown or holocaust.

Golfing Death

Michael Scaglione was playing golf with friends on April 25, 1982, in New Orleans, when he made a bad shot on the thirteenth hole. He became so angry with himself that he threw his club against the golf cart with such force that the club broke, the club-head rebounding and stabbing Scaglione in the throat, severing his jugular vein. Staggering, Staglione pulled the piece of metal from his neck, but he died from the rapid loss of blood.

Escape of the Giant Squid

The weather was perfect, and although there was a silent swell, the ocean was calm for miles around. So when the crew of the French sloop *Alecton* first sighted the monstrous sea creature on November 30, 1861, they were quite certain that it wasn't a wave or even a rock. It was, they later recounted, the legendary giant squid whose existence had been long disputed.

Sighted as the *Alecton* sailed from Cadiz, Spain, to Tenerife, the giant squid was approximately 18 feet long, with eight limbs and a huge tail. Lieutenant Bouyer, the *Alecton*'s commander, described it as 'quite appalling, brick red in colour, shapeless and slimy, its form repulsive and terrible'.

Even so, the commander set out to capture the beast, but the pitching of the vessel made it impossible for crew members to shoot it. They finally managed to harpoon the squid and even snagged its tail in a noose, but they then realized the creature was stronger than they had imagined. Waving its tentacles and rearing a head with a curious parrot-like beak, the giant squid broke free of the ropes, leaving a 40-pound portion of its tail behind.

Mysterious Geoglyphic Designs in the American South-West

About 10,000 years ago, prehistoric residents of Native American origin built vast stone alignments in present-day Panamint valley in south-eastern California. But the birds, snakes and geometrical designs of overlapping hoops and parallel lines are only recognizable from the air. Some of the 60-odd alignments are as long as a football field; others cover only 16 or 17 feet. And as many as 700 stones about six inches high were used in the designs.

The real enigma is why the hunter-gatherers would build them in such a dry, remote location, particularly when the geoglyphics could never be seen by the designers. Or could they? The alignments, as in the case of the Nazca tribes in Peru, could have been used for astronomical purposes, or they may have some religious or magical significance.

The Drunk Who Would Not Die

In 1933, Anthony Marino and four friends, experiencing financial problems, carried out an ingenious, although diabolical plan: they murdered Marino's girlfriend in order to collect on her life insurance policy. Since the scam had worked so well, they decided to try it again, setting their sights on Michael Malloy, an alcoholic who patronized Marino's speakeasy in the Bronx. Having taken out three insurance policies in his name, they worked out a plan to kill him in such a way that no one would ever suspect foul play, but Malloy proved to be a difficult victim to murder.

Thinking that Malloy, given the opportunity, would drink himself to death, Marino gave him unlimited credit at the bar. When Malloy continued to drink without even keeling over, however, the bartender, who was a partner in the scam, replaced the liquor with antifreeze. Although Malloy did finally pass out, he came to a few hours later and began drinking again, guzzling antifreeze for another week.

The bartender began filling Malloy with turpentine, and then horse liniment laced with rat poison. Yet Malloy kept returning for more. They fed him rotten oysters drenched in wood alcohol and spoiled sardines mixed with carpet tacks and Malloy would ask for second helpings. They dumped him in the snow and watered him down, leaving him to weather the night in temperatures that dropped to -14°F. But nothing would kill Michael Malloy.

Finally they hired a professional killer who, driving a car at 45 miles per hour, struck Malloy, hurling him into the air and then running over him. After three weeks in the hospital, however, Malloy returned to the speakeasy and resumed drinking.

Finally they connected a rubber hose to a gas jet and

forced the other end up Malloy's nose, leaving it there until his face turned purple. They succeeded in killing the man, but in the long run they still failed because the authorities discovered their crime. They were arrested and sentenced to the electric chair.

Champ – The Monster Inhabiting Lake Champlain

Lake Champlain is a tranquil 100-mile-long body of water linking Vermont and New York states with Canada. Beneath it, however, may lurk an extraordinary aquatic monster. The first sighting occurred on August 30, 1878, by six people enjoying a pleasure cruise on the lake. The creature had two large folds at the back of its head that had projected above the water. Another pair of folds appeared about 50 feet behind, presumably at the tail end.

Dubbed Champ, the creature has been sighted at various times since. In 1971, for example, Mrs Green, her mother and a friend were staying at a hotel overlooking Lake Champlain when they saw a snakelike creature with three humps moving smoothly through the water. Based on descriptions and the nature of its habitat, there is speculation that Champ may be a distant relative of Nessie, the Loch Ness Monster.

The Missing Judge

From 1790 to 1801, John Lansing sat on the New York State Supreme Court, serving as Chief Justice in 1798. A veteran of the American Revolution, he had served as a legislator and had also been the mayor of Albany, as well as state chancellor. In 1804, Lansing retired, keeping himself occupied as a business consultant to New York's Columbia College.

On December 12, 1829, Lansing was staying in a Manhattan hotel following a meeting with Columbia College officials. After writing some letters that evening, he went out to mail them. The 75-year-old statesman was never seen or heard of again, despite a thorough search.

Acupunctured Corn

The Chinese use the ancient art of acupuncture for much more than relieving physical ills. They also use it to ripen corn more quickly and to improve its taste. Intrigued by the idea, agricultural writer Jude Ramsey Jensen of Sandy, Oregon, decided to test the procedure, using toothpicks instead of the long, thin metal needles traditionally used on humans.

In a controlled experiment, Jensen inserted a toothpick through the base of each ear stem into the main stalk when the silk was still green. She left every other row u touched. To her amazement, the acupunctured plants matured a full week earlier and tasted very much sweeter than those that had not received the acupuncture treatment.

The procedure works by wounding the plant, which in turn sends healing sugars rushing to the injured area. The technique is a fine example of the logic of simplicity – the plant must deal with the wound – argues Jensen, who continues to use acupuncture on her corn. And she grows the sweetest and fastest maturing corn in Oregon.

The Great Ghost Maker

John Henry Pepper was an analytical chemist who became director of London's Royal Polytechnic Institute in 1852. But throughout a Victorian England equally enchanted by spiritualism as it was by science, Pepper was also known as the creator of the Ghost Show.

The Ghost Show delighted audiences by presenting eerie images that interacted with live actors on stage. The 'ghost' was actually a player below the stage. From his concealed location, a projectionist illuminated the actor, reflecting his image from a mirror on to a large pane of glass, also unseen by spectators. What appeared on stage were airy apparitions that seemed to menace actors and patrons alike.

Famed as a pre-eminent showman of science throughout Australia, Canada and the United States, as well as his native Great Britain, Pepper never claimed his ghosts were anything but illusions, something that was in stark contrast to the fraudulent but common practice at the time to present ghosts as entities that could be summoned by those who knew how to call them.

Otherworld Journeys Through The Ages

As they lay dying, ancient soldiers may have seen dead relatives beckoning them through dark tunnels leading into light. Medieval Christians probably used visions of the nether world images to reinforce images of heaven and hell. And Virgil, Dante and writers of epic underworld journeys may have based their heroes' stories on the out-of-body experiences of real-life people.

Such are a few of the possibilities posed in the book *Otherworld Journeys*, a scholarly work that analyzes near-death experiences (NDE) from ancient through to modern times. Whether science or mythology, NDEs are evidence that the soul exists apart from the body. And according to the author, Carol Zaleski, Professor of Religion at Harvard University, historical insight is the key to understanding NDEs.

Astronomy, biology and other scientific fields have progressed immeasurably during the last 1,500 years, but many aspects of the NDE are perennial. The soldier that returns from the dead in the sixth century describes a footbridge where wicked souls fall into the slimy river below, while the blessed pass over to a peaceful meadow on the other side. Twentieth-century NDE guru, Raymond Moody says that his subjects often return to their bodies with sensations of peace.

Is There More Than One Monster in Loch Ness?

Over the years, there have been numerous scientific and quasi-scientific attempts to prove the existence of the Loch Ness Monster. One of the most elaborate efforts was undertaken by Robert Rines for the Academy of Applied Science in 1972. His results were doubly surprising.

With sophisticated sonar equipment and a camera strobe light system, Rines and his team staked out the loch locations where Nessie has most often been sighted. The objective was to capture a combination of sonar and photographic evidence of Nessie.

On the night of August 8, the researchers sat in boats anchored in Urquhart Bay, a short distance from the shore. They positioned the sonar equipment on an underwater slope and the camera slightly lower, and aimed at the area detected by the sonar. Then they waited.

At around one o'clock in the morning, the sonar beam picked up a large object moving in camera's range. About forty minutes later two objects appeared on the sonar screen, which the camera photographed.

Although the water was cloudy and the photographs were, therefore, vague, several astounding computer enhancements revealed not one but two possible Nessies. Analysis of the images of flippers in some photographs estimate their length to be four to six feet long. And the two large creatures were apparently about 12 feet apart. Rines and his team had finally produced evidence of the Loch Ness Monster, but still not enough to convince sceptics.

Encouraged by the success of the 1972 expedition to Loch Ness, the Academy of Applied Science launched another search in 1975. This time, investigators used even more sophisticated and sensitive equipment, which was designed to overcome some of the technical problems that hindered the quality of the 1972 photos. Still, the more advanced camera was unable to pick up anything except the silt stirred up by the creature that eventually appeared. Fortunately, the camera used in 1972 had also been set up as an auxiliary and recorded some remarkable images during the 24-hour period of June 19 and 20 – the upper torso, extended neck, stubby appendages and the dragon-like head of a massive aquatic creature. An extensive examination of the photographs provided significant insight into Nessie's appearance. The overall length was 20 feet, its neck was about 18 inches thick, its mouth nine inches long and five inches wide, and there were two six-inch, horned appendages, 10 inches apart and protruding from the beast's head.

These and subsequent photographic images of Nessie bear a remarkable resemblance to the plesiosaur, a prehistoric water reptile presumed extinct for more than 70 million years. The Loch Ness Monster is particularly similar to one type of the plesiosaur, the elasmosaur.

Monsters of the Soviet Union

On a five-month expedition to survey mineral deposits in eastern Siberia in 1964, a team of Moscow University scientists set up camp near the shore of Lake Khaiyr. When one of the group, biologist N. Gladkikh, went to draw water from the lake he quite literally ran into a creature long reputed to abide there.

Scientists, of course, had always considered Lake Khaiyr's resident monster nothing more than a myth. But here was a reputable biologist, face to face with an animal the likes of which he had never seen before. Its small head rested atop a long, gleaming neck connected to a huge jet-black body with a vertical fin affixed along the spine. Alarmed, Gladkikh rushed back to the campsite, returning with the other scientists and their cameras and guns. By that time, however, the creature had returned to the depths.

But a few days later, the beast reappeared, this time in full view of the entire Moscow University group. According to deputy team leader G. Rokosuev, 'the creature beat the water with its long tail, producing waves on the lake'. They could no longer claim that the Lake Khsiyr monster was a myth.

The Guiding Spirit at the South Pole

The idea that spirits might guide humans is not new, but some students of spiritual lore believe that such companion or counsellor ghosts may have played a role in some of mankind's greatest adventures. Explorer Ernest Shackleton, for example, leading a brutal three-man trek across the Antarctic mountains in 1917, wrote that it often seemed there were four rather than three men in the group. His two colleagues during the 36-hour journey concurred with the sensation of having a guiding force accompanying them. And the spectral companion provided some very real support during the gruelling expedition.

A Psychic Day at the Races

While it may be true that no one has made it rich by using ESP to bet on horse races, there have been a great many reported cases of minor, isolated successes at the course achieved with the help of psychic abilities. Some of the best reports were collected during the 1930s by Dame Edith Lyttelton, a British delegate to the League of Nations with a fondness for psychic investigations.

In response to a 1934 BBC radio broadcast on the subject of precognition, Lyttelton received a flood of mail from listeners describing their own experiences with premonitions. A.W.L. Freeman of Leicester, England, for example, claimed that he had not been particularly interested in horse racing, but in November 1913, he had had a strange dream in which he was visiting the cathedral in Lincoln. Suddenly realizing the time, he ran over to the race-course, fearing he had spent so much time in the church that he had missed the Lincoln Handicap. Someone at the course informed him that the race was indeed over and that the winning horse was named Outran. The following March, Freeman learned that one of the horses scheduled to run in the 1914 Lincoln Handicap was named Outran, and despite unfavourable odds, the horse won the race.

Other cases reported to Lyttelton included an account by Phyllis Richards of London. On her way to the 1933 Grand National race in Liverpool, Richards had dreamed that the winning horse's name began with the letter 'K' and ended with 'Jack'. The horse, however, was not the first one to cross the finishing line. The winner of the actual race that day, it turned out, was Kellesboroa Jack, which came in second, preceded by a riderless horse that was disqualified.

Another premonition was experienced by a woman while she was awake, a week before the 1932 Derby. She heard a voice distinctly tell her that April the Fifth would win the race. She took a gamble and placed a small bet on the horse to win and, as she and her family then listened to the race on the radio, April the Fifth took the lead halfway through and went on to win. 'A most peculiar feeling almost made me faint,' the woman recalled. 'Almost immediately, I burst into tears.'

Competing Patriots

John Adams, the second President of the United States, and Thomas Jefferson, the country's third President, took up a spirited, if competitive friendship when the two worked together to draw up the Declaration of Independence. But it was the deaths of the two patriots that revealed an odd coincidence. Both men died on the fiftieth anniversary of the Declaration's signing, July 4, 1826. Even more curious, they seemed to have willed themselves to live until that date, partly out of a sense of patriotism, but more because neither wanted the other to die first.

On his deathbed in Virginia, in fact, Jefferson asked for confirmation of the date before expiring, while 100 miles away in New England, Adams uttered his famous last words: 'Thomas Jefferson still lives'. Adams ultimately outlived Jefferson by five hours.

The Beast of Exmoor

The legendary beast of Exmoor is said to roam the moors and hills of western England, killing hundreds of sheep and stalking unwary travellers. But naturalist Trevor Beer is certain that the creature is no myth. He has, in fact, even managed to photograph the black cat-like beast while it ravaged rabbits on a hillside.

Beer leads guided tours through the beast's habitat for the Kittiwell Hotel, which provides a unique four-day weekend package for curious tourists hoping to glimpse the beast of Exmoor. But how does Beer explain the beast's presence in the English countryside? 'I think that over the years, big cats have escaped from circuses and exotic pet situations,' he explains. 'Now we have a feral breeding population in the British Isles.'

Beer believes there is actually more than one beast of Exmoor and, he says, they are perfectly harmless. He wants to make sure, moreover, that the creature is protected. He gives the tours to attract attention and sympathy for the cats.

The Tiny Tunnels of Ancient Mexico

The Zapotec Indians flourished in south-west Mexico from 200 BC until the Spanish invasion in 1519. Like the Olmecs and the Mayans before them, the Zapotecs had a highly developed civilization, being skilled in the fields of art, astronomy and architecture. Their origins, however, are unknown, although according to Indian myth, the Zapotecs believed they were descended from trees, rocks and jaguars. But this is not the only question unanswered about the Zapotec civilization.

The remains of the Zapotec capital, known today as Monte Alban, lie seven miles from the modern Mexican city of Oaxaca, on top of an artificially levelled mountain. The ancient city is flanked on all sides by terraced steps, sunken courtyards and low-rise buildings. Archaeologists excavating the site in 1931 were impressed by the gold, jade and turquoise they found in abundance in the tombs of Zapotec leaders. But the most amazing discovery was a complex network of tiny tunnels, far too small to be used by adults or even average-sized children.

The tunnels' dimensions range from 20 inches high by 25 inches wide to even smaller ones of no more than a foot high. At first, archaeologists thought the passageways were some sort of underground drainage system. But when excavators actually entered the tunnels – with great difficulty, they could only make their way through them by lying on their backs and pulling themselves along – they found human skeletons at the end of each one, and around the bones, the same sort of riches as they had found in the tombs.

The purpose of the pygmy tunnels of Monte Alban remains unexplained.

The Flight to Nowhere

On December 5, 1945, five torpedo bombers took off from Fort Lauderdale, Florida, on a 320-mile navigational training exercise identified as Flight 19. The aircraft, believed to have been in perfect operational order at the time of take-off, were manned by experienced pilots, including Lieutenant Charles Carroll Taylor, and 12 crewmen. The route should have taken them eastward, then to the north, over Grand Bahama Island, before heading south-west on their return to base, the whole flight path being within the area designated as the Bermuda Triangle. Instead, the manoeuvres became a five-hour flight to nowhere.

Less than two hours into the flight, Taylor reported that both his compasses were inexplicably malfunctioning, and they were no longer able to determine where they were or where they were going. They assumed, for some still unknown reason, that they were somewhere over the Florida Keys, some 200 miles off their prescribed course. Fragmentary and confusing messages continued to pepper the radio waves for another three hours before Taylor announced that they would attempt to land the planes, dangerously low on fuel, together in the water.

Despite a five-day search that covered a 250,000-mile area, no trace of the five bombers was ever found. It's likely that the airmen were unable to escape before the ditched planes sank, but not even a 400-page naval enquiry could answer all the questions surrounding the bizarre circumstances leading up to the disappearance.

Among the hundreds of large and small craft and planes to go missing since Flight 19, almost 20 per cent have disappeared in the first part of December.

The Lucky and Unlucky Number

People who regularly play the horses or the lottery often bet on their lucky number: their birth dates, address or licence plate number, for example. One day in 1958, however, thousands of New Yorkers unknowingly chose a most unlucky number, but one that turned out to have a remarkable change of fortune.

A Jersey Central train plummeted from a trestle bridge into Newark Bay below. News photographers and cameramen rushed to the scene and captured a shot of the rear car as it was being lifted by crane out of the water. The following day, the picture appeared on the front page of at least one newspaper. Clearly visible on the side of the raised car was the number 932.

That same day, not only had thousands of New Yorkers placed their money on 932 in the numbers game and won, but the winning lottery number was also 932.

Canine Ghosts

For more than 40 years, Ballechin House in Perthshire, Scotland, had been the home of Major Stewart, an eccentric man with a penchant for spiritualism and a great fondness for dogs. At the time of his death in 1876, he owned 14 dogs, all living in the house. Not knowing what to do with them when the major died, unthinking relatives had all of the dogs put to sleep. One afternoon not long after the dogs' extermination, the wife of the major's nephew was in the Ballechin study when she detected the unmistakable odour of dogs. Suddenly, she felt a push, feeling oddly like a dog's nudge. And so began Ballechin's reputation as a haunted house.

After the nephew's death in a London car accident, Ballechin House passed into the hands of a relative named Captain Stewart who proceeded successfully, despite the house's reputation, to rent the estate to people wishing to use the grounds for sport hunting. But in August 1896, the occupants, so disturbed by horrible sounds in the night and mysterious nudges at their legs, forfeited their money and fled.

Soon, the house came to the attention of the Marquis of Bute, a member of the Psychical Research Society. The Marquis and his colleagues decided to throw a party at Ballechin House, by way of investigating the canine ghosts. During the course of the festivities, the 35 guests heard bizarre sounds, muffled explosions, shuffling feet and someone interminably reading aloud, which they initially attributed to owls in the attic and faulty water pipes. They later began accusing each other of fabricating the sounds. But when something began pounding on the door and a number of guests perceived a misty figure resembling a spaniel, the Marquis and his friends realized that some strong spiritual force was indeed at work in Ballechin House.

The Tie That Binds Brothers

George and Hart Northey were exceptionally close during their childhood and had never been apart for any length of time. But when George, the elder brother, joined the navy, Hart remained at home in St Eglos, Cornwall, England, where he entered the family business.

One night in February, 1840, while his ship was docked at the port in St Helena, George had a strange and disturbing dream. In it, he quite vividly saw himself at his brother's side as Hart worked in the marketplace in Trebodwina, a town not far from St Eglos. Every detail, every action was precise and clear, so much so that George believed he had travelled the miles and was actually at his brother's side. He was, however, unable to communicate with Hart in the dream – he could only accompany him and observe.

George's dream ended with Hart going home with the day's receipts. As he neared the village of Polkerrow, he was accosted by two men, familiar to George as notorious poachers. While the helpless George looked on, the two villains robbed Hart at gunpoint and fatally shot him. Setting Hart's horse loose, they dragged the corpse to a nearby stream. Then the murderers covered all traces of blood on the road and hid the pistol in the thatch of an empty hut. On waking, George was filled with such dread that during the entire trip home from St Helena, he fretted that his dream might have been more than a nocturnal fantasy.

Meanwhile, in St Eglos, the townspeople were shocked by the murder of Hart Northey, his body found in the stream where it had been dragged off the road. Two brothers named Hightwood were the primary suspects. Although a search of their home turned up clothing with tell-tale blood stains, authorities were unable to locate the gun that had killed Hart. Even so, public sentiment ran so strongly against the Hightwoods that the two men were tried and sentenced to death.

George arrived in St Eglos just before the Hightwoods' scheduled execution. Learning that his fears had been justified, the surviving brother was eager to avenge Hart's death. He went to the police and told them where they would find the murder weapon. The amazed investigators found the pistol exactly where George had said it would be. Asked how he knew where it had been concealed, George replied, 'I saw the foul deed committed in a dream'.

Mystical Masochism in the Service of Evolution

Stelio Arcadiou, who goes by the name of Stelarc, calls it obsolete body suspension, a sort of deprivation technique that symbolizes 'the physical and psychological limitations of the body'. The exercise involves placing 18 large fish hooks through his skin, attaching them to wires, and then hanging naked from trees, cranes or ceilings for as long as 30 minutes.

The suspensions, often performed before a spellbound audience, vary in design and intensity. Once Stelarc hung from the ceiling of a small, quiet room, surrounded by a circle of suspended stones. He described the session as being 'meditative and peaceful' in contrast to the 'noisy and disruptive' experience he had dangling over a New York City Street. And when he hung from a crane, 180 feet above the streets of a town in Denmark, he admitted to being frightened.

But the exercises, he says, are necessary. 'Technology has surpassed our evolutionary capability,' Stelarc explains. 'The body cannot cope with the quality or quantity of information that confronts it. Man is in a kind of evolutionary crisis – the body is obsolete. The next step in human evolution will combine technology with the body. Suspensions represent one of these evolutionary paths.'

For Stelarc and his audiences, the suspensions are a realization of the primordial desire to be suspended in space. He remains within the limits of gravitational forces, but the audience witnesses the symbolism of man overcoming the force of gravity.

Stelarc has never had any serious medical problems as a result of his meditative performances.

The Fateful Vision of Mark Twain

During one stay at his sister's home in St Louis, Samuel Clemens (better known as Mark Twain) had a disturbing dream in which he saw his brother Henry lying in a metal coffin. On the body's chest was a bouquet of white flowers with a single red rose in its centre. Twain's first thought on awaking was that Henry was indeed dead, but the feeling passed quickly, and he recounted the dream to his sister in the morning.

At that time, during the 1850s, Twain and his brother Henry worked on the riverboats that cruised the Mississippi River between St Louis and New Orleans. A few weeks after Twain's dream, the two men were returning to St Louis on separate riverboats when the boiler on one of the boats, the *Pennsylvania*, exploded killing most of the passengers, including Henry Clemens.

While most of the victims were later buried in wooden coffins, local residents contributed enough money to purchase a metal casket for Henry. Viewing the scene, Twain realized that every detail of the funeral matched his dream – except the floral bouquet. Then, as Twain stood beside his brother's body, a woman entered the parlour and placed an arrangement of white flowers on Henry's chest – and at the centre of the bouquet was a single red rose.

Doll Disease

The reproductions of the antique dolls were perfect, except for the black speckles all over their faces. Unable to stem the appearance of the spots, the young girl who had made each one by hand was distressed. Thinking that her sweating hands were responsible, she went to the surgery of British physician Conrad Harris.

The doctor decided to perform a simple test. Before firing a doll's clay head in her kiln, he instructed his patient to draw a cross on its forehead with her finger. She should then repeat the procedure with a second doll, but this time while wearing a rubber glove. Sure enough, the glove-touched doll displayed no spots.

Having determined that the girl was the source of the problem, Harris set out to discover what exactly in her perspiration caused the reaction in the dolls. Guessing that it was sulphides, his supposition was confirmed when a dietary analysis revealed that the girl regularly consumed large quantities of sulphide-rich garlic. And when she stopped eating garlic for a week, the spots ceased to appear on the dolls.

Harris's discovery, of course, has wider implications for the antique doll reproduction industry: craftspeople in Italy, Germany and France – with traditionally garlic-rich foods – regularly lose 10 per cent of their dolls to the black spot disease.

A Death-Wish Come True

While many people may have a preference for the way they die, few ever die as they wish. But American revolutionary patriot James Otis did. He had often remarked to friends and relatives that when he died he hoped it would be the result of being struck by lightning. On May 23, 1783, Otis was leaning against a doorpost of a house in Andover, Massachusetts, when a bolt of lightning struck the chimney, ripped through the frame of the house and hit the doorpost, killing Otis instantly.

Chinese Lake Monsters

Pausing on the banks of Wenbu Lake in a remote part of Tibet, a Chinese Communist Party official watched in horror as a dinosaur-like creature emerged from the water, attacking and then devouring the man's prize yak. Although the sighting by a reputable observer was reported on the country's evening news, it was not the first time that such an unidentifiable beast had been seen. While in the mountainous region of Manchuria known as Changbai, Chinese author Lei Jia twice witnessed a black, six- foot-long lake monster in 1980. The reptile-like beast, he said, had a long neck and an oval-shaped head. Three weather bureau officials, having also seen the serpent, confirmed Jia's report. When they shot at it, however, the lake monster disappeared.

At a crater lake in north-eastern Jilin province, moreover, tourists as well as the staff of a nearby weather station saw a serpent with a duck-like beak travelling through the water, creating waves in its wake like a motorboat.

The Curse of Route 55

The planned construction of a four-mile highway through New Jersey's Deptford Township was fiercely opposed by Carl Peirce, a Nanticoke Indian also known by the name of Wayandaga. At a press conference, Wayandaga publicly predicted that the Route 55 project would be doomed because its intended path would traverse an ancient Indian village and burial ground. The new highway, he protested, would desecrate the graves of the Paleo Indians, who had inhabited the area 8,000 years ago. He told officials that if they proceeded with the road, his ancestors would exact revenge.

The highway's builders, of course, didn't heed Wayandaga's warnings and went ahead with the construction. Before long, disastrous and even deadly incidents began to plague the crew. One worker was killed by an asphalt roller, while another was seriously injured when he fell from a bridge. An inspector was inexplicably struck down by a brain aneurysm. Yet another workman suffered three heart attacks during the course of the construction. The worst event, however, involved a van carrying five crewmen that suddenly and mysteriously exploded.

According to Wayandaga, deaths and injuries will continue to plague the project until the construction of Route 55 is halted or its path is diverted around the sacred ground.

Mutant Sponges

Some 25 years ago, 47,500 barrels of radioactive waste was dumped in the Pacific Ocean, just beyond San Francisco's Golden Gate Bridge. Today, the plutonium content of the sea-bed is 25 times higher than the level originally predicted by experts. Even more astounding is oceanographers' discovery, in the same area, of a new genus of sponge, mutants three to four feet tall and shaped like vases.

The Treasures of Cocos

If anyone ever manages to unearth the treasure of Cocos Island, the site of two separate illicit deposits of riches from the nineteenth century, they'd be fabulously wealthy.

In 1820, the pirate Benito Bonito captured a Spanish galleon transporting 150 tons of gold and buried the booty on Cocos, an inhospitable Pacific island 200 miles off the coast of Costa Rica. To maintain its secret location, he killed most of his crew and then sailed away. But he never returned.

Some years later, a revolution in Peru threatened the safety of invaluable state and church treasures, which authorities decided to ship to Panama. The captain of the *Mary Dier*, the vessel carrying the treasures, inexplicably altered his course and headed towards Cocos. It was the last anyone saw of the captain, crew, or the Peruvian treasures.

The Mysterious Monk

Portrait painter Joseph Aigner was often despondent and suicidal despite his admirable talent and success. He had made his first suicide attempt when he was 18 years old, but as he hung from the rafters of his family's Viennese home, he was unexpectedly visited by a Capuchin monk who somehow convinced him that life was worth living. Four years after that attempt, however, Aigner tried once more to kill himself and again the same monk mysteriously appeared out of nowhere to prevent the suicide.

During the next eight years, Aigner became a revolutionary and was eventually arrested and sentenced to death. Before the execution, however, he was reprieved – through the intervention of the very same Capuchin monk who had twice prevented Aigner's suicide.

In 1886, the 68-year-old artist finally fulfilled his death wish by shooting himself in the head. The funeral service was conducted, oddly enough, by none other than the Capuchin monk whose name Aigner never learned but who had successfully kept Aigner alive for 68 years.

Vision of a Pope's Death

A member of Renaissance Italy's Borgia family, Pope Alexander VI was a master of depravity whose reign in the Vatican was rife with murder, incest and greed. Alexander VI died in 1503, ostensibly from malaria, at the age of 73. But according to legend, his death was overshadowed by more sinister and supernatural forces.

Before his death, Alexander VI had passed an edict declaring that the estates of all deceased cardinals would become the property of the Holy See. Then, intending to murder a particularly wealthy cardinal with a gift of poisoned wine, the Pope invited himself to the cardinal's home. *En route*, however, he realized he'd forgotten an amulet purported to ward off the effects of the poison. He would need it to be able to drink the wine himself and not arouse suspicion. So he sent a travelling companion, Cardinal Caraffa, back to fetch it.

Entering the Pope's bedroom where the amulet was left, Caraffa was shocked to find a bier draped in black and lit by torches in the centre of the room. On the bier was the corpse of the man for whom he was performing his errand – Pope Alexander VI.

Meanwhile, Alexander had arrived at the banquet where a mix-up in the wine goblets resulted in the Pope drinking his own poison. A few days later, just as Caraffa had foreseen, the Borgia Pope was dead and laid out in his bedroom, on a bier draped in black.

A Fiery Death at Sea

When Mary Carpenter, her husband and children took off on their cabin cruiser for a holiday off the coast of Norfolk, England, they never imagined the tragedy that would befall them. They had been enjoying the weather on July 29, 1938, sunbathing on the boat's deck when Mary was suddenly and inexplicably engulfed in flames. As her horrified family looked on helplessly, she was reduced to ashes in a matter of minutes. Yet amazingly, nothing else on board was even touched by the fire.

The Language of Escape

During the American Civil War, a small number of Swiss nationals were soldiers in the Union Army. When they were captured by southern Confederate soldiers, the Swiss Union soldiers were transported by train to a prison camp in Salisbury, North Carolina. Under the guard of a 17-year-old named Beverley Tucker, the prisoners planned their escape, speaking in their native language to avoid detection.

When the train stopped at a station along the way to Salisbury, the prisoners made the break. But to their surprise, a Confederate regiment surrounded them, weapons aimed. Unfortunately for the Swiss, Tucker spoke their language, having gone to school in the same region of Switzerland where the prisoners were born and raised.

Poker Justice

Robert Fallon of Northumberland, England, was an avid poker player, world traveller and notorious cheat. He met his end after winning US$600 in a poker game at San Francisco's Belle Union saloon in 1858: his fellow gamblers accused him of foul play and shot and killed him on the spot. But since money obtained through cheating is considered unlucky, the callous card players needed to fill Fallon's place before they could resume their game. So they pulled in the first available passer-by, who happily accepted Fallon's winnings as his stake in the game.

Instead of losing as the murdering card players had expected, the new player increased the US$600 to US$2,200 before the police arrived on the scene. The officers ordered the stranger to turn over the original US$600 so that the money could be rightfully given to Fallon's next of kin. That, however, wasn't necessary. It turned out that the stranger was, in fact, Fallon's son and it had been seven years since he had last seen his roving, poker-playing father.

The Mystery Missile of Lakewood, California

More than 30 years after the end of World War II, a missile from that period somehow crashed into the backyard of a suburban home in Lakewood, California. The 22-pound shell hurtled out of the sunny afternoon sky and plummeted onto Fred Simons' patio, smashing a layer of concrete and creating a four-foot crater.

The local bomb squad dug the missile out and declared it was a dud containing no explosives. At first the federal Aviation Administration (FAA) investigators theorized that a prankster had dropped the missile from a plane flying in the flight path from Long Beach Airport over Lakewood. The investigators monitored flight tapes to determine if any aircraft might have opened a door and thrown something out, which would have made a screeching sound on the tape, but they didn't come up with any evidence.

The Los Angeles County Sheriff's office also launched a fruitless probe. The only thing they were able to determine was the missile had not been fired from some kind of tube or a cannon.

Lacking any clues at all, both the FAA and the Sheriff's office dropped all investigations into the mystery missile, admitting they have no idea where it came from and will probably never know what happened.

Channelled Surgery

Born in 1918 in Brazil's Belo Horizonte district, Jose Pedro de Freïtas, known simply as Arigo, was a farmer's son who rose quickly in the ranks of the iron-workers' union. At the age of 25, he was elected president of the local branch, but following a strike to protest against dangerous working conditions in the mines, he was fired and went on to manage a bar in nearby Congonhas de Campo.

During the election campaign of 1950, one of the candidates, Lucio Bittencourt, a staunch supporter of the iron workers, went to Congonhas to meet with his constituents. While there, he met with Arigo and was so impressed by the man's impassioned speech on behalf of the iron workers that he invited Arigo to continue their conversation at the Hotel Financial where Bittencourt was staying.

During the night, Bittencourt woke to find Arigo, eyes glazed over, standing over him and holding a razor. Speaking with an atypical German accent, Arigo told the stunned candidate that he required surgery, which Arigo was going to perform. Bittencourt was so shocked that he fainted. When he later regained consciousness, and found himself still very much alive, Bittencourt realized that he was covered with blood. He felt a soreness toward the back of his rib cage, where he was surprised to see a perfect, neat incision. Quickly dressing, he confronted Arigo, who had no recollection whatsoever of the experience.

Unknown to Arigo, Bittencourt had been suffering from lung cancer, but when he visited his doctor the following day, X-rays indicated that the tumour, in fact, was gone. When Bittencourt explained what had transpired, his doctor was amazed – the procedure followed by Arigo was not performed anywhere in Brazil and was generally unknown by local physicians.

It wasn't long before Arigo was besieged by sick people from all over the country seeking his miraculous medical attention. Close behind them, reporters and psychics arrived to determine the source of Arigo's powers. During the next six years, Arigo would treat as many as 300 patients a day, even performing knifeless surgery, while seemingly in a trance and having no recollection of the feats afterwards.

According to the reluctant healer, he had been having nightmares and visions since he was a child. At first, they consisted of a blinding light and a voice speaking in a language unknown to Arigo. As the episodes increased in frequency, so did their intensity, leaving Arigo with painful, lingering headaches. But they also became clearer. He was able to discern a brightly lit operating room, where a short stocky, balding man dressed in surgical garb addressed a group of colleagues – in the same strange language that Arigo had been hearing all along. Eventually, the physician revealed his identity and his purpose: he was Dr Adolpho Fritz, he told Arigo, and he had chosen the Brazilian to carry our his healing plan because of his compassionate nature.

Arigo would begin each of his treatments by saying the Lord's Prayer, during which he would go into another state of consciousness, which he described as 'a state I do not understand'. While in the trance, he'd perform surgery and write prescriptions and he achieved a phenomenal success rate.

Aware that the medical community as well as the Catholic Church were disturbed by the channelled surgery, a local priest advised Arigo to cease his practice. But Arigo refused, insisting that he was merely the intermediary between the people and the spirit of Dr Fritz. Then, in 1956, Arigo was charged with practising 'illegal medicine'.

The trial was widely publicized, and public opinion in favour of Arigo's work was overwhelming. Professor J. Herculano wrote in a Brazilian newspaper that it was 'simply ridiculous to deny that the phenomenon of Arigo exists. Medical specialists, famous journalists, intellectuals, prominent statesmen have all witnessed the phenomenon at Congonhas. We cannot possibly deny the reality of his feats'. Despite the support, however, Arigo was sentenced to prison, but granted probation on the condition that he give up his practice.

Some time later, Arigo covertly resumed his mystical surgery, an easy task since local authorities tended to look the other way where Arigo was concerned.

The Abandonment of
Marie Celeste

Navigating the waters east of the Azores on December 1872, the crew of the *Dei Gratia* sighted a brigantine bobbing on the ocean at half-sail. Moving in closer to investigate, they identified it as the *Marie Celeste*, whose captain was a close friend of David Morehouse, the *Dei Gratia's* captain. The ship was deserted, having been hastily abandoned. Its captain, Benjamin Briggs, his wife Sarah, his two-year-old daughter and the crew were gone, although the cargo appeared to be in order. Ever since the *Marie Celeste* was found, the case has been mired in legend and rumour because no one has ever been able to determine what actually happened.

The captain's last notes, written on a slate but not yet entered in to the log-book, indicated that on November 25, the vessel had been 370 miles west of where it was found. There was nothing in the log-book that might have shed light on the fate of the Briggs family and the crew.

The attorney general of Gibraltar initially proposed that the crew had broken into the ship's barrels of commercial alcohol, got drunk, killed the Briggs family and then escaped in the lifeboat. But that was improbable because the ship's alcohol would have killed anyone who drank it. Others, however, suggested that the captain had detected a leak in the flammable cargo and quickly abandoned ship. Or Briggs may have ordered the abandonment because of a waterspout: a phenomenon that causes a change in atmospheric pressure that can blow open hatch covers and force bilge water up into the ship, causing the ship to sink.

What ever happened to the passengers and crew of the *Marie Celeste* remains a nautical mystery.

Night Terror Defence

A 1987 murder trial in Britain revolved around a strange homicide with an even more bizarre defence.

According to the defendant, he had dreamed that he was being pursued by Japanese soldiers and, in self-defence, he strangled one of his attackers. When he woke up, he realized that he had strangled his wife instead, in his sleep.

Expert testimony during the trial attested to the man's suffering from a rare sleep disorder known as night terror. Unlike sleepwalking, the condition involves intense emotional disturbances that typically include sensations of falling or being attacked. The afflicted often have realistic dreams in which they physically act out what is happening in the sleeping state – as the defendant had – and they remember little or nothing when they awaken.

A similar case was reported by psychiatrist Ernest Hartmann in his book *The Nightmare: The Psychology and Biology of Terrifying Dreams*. A Massachusetts driver, under the influence of alcohol, pulled over to the side of the road to sleep off his drunkenness. While asleep, however, he started up the engine, turned the car around, and continued down the road in the wrong direction, subsequently killing three people. The man was later convicted, but only because of the alcohol level in his blood. Under Massachusetts law, the driver was able to plead insanity because he didn't know what he was doing and didn't know the difference between right and wrong.

Psychiatrists in the British case, however, argued that the night terror defence should not enable someone literally to get away with murder, as happened in the case of the man who murdered his wife. Most other violent acts, they say, carried out in an organic confusional state carry a sentence of mandatory referral to a hospital.

Beware the Twenty-First Day

For most of his life, Louis XVI of France would not see to any important business on the twenty-first of the month, all because an astrologer had warned him as a child to be wary of the date. But it wasn't always possible for the King to avoid events he couldn't control. On June 21, 1791, Louis and his Queen, Marie Antoinette, were arrested while attempting to escape the country during the French revolution. The following year, on September 21, the institution of royalty was abolished and on January 21, 1793, Louis was executed.

The Discovery of the Pygmy Hippopotamus and other Non-Existent Animals

Sir Harry Johnston first heard stories about the okapi from a group of Congolese Pygmies around the turn of the century. In 1901, he sent a whole skin, two skulls, and a detailed description of the mule-sized animal with zebra stripes to London, where it was determined that the Okapi was a close relative of the giraffe. In 1919, the first live Okapi were taken out of the Congo and placed in European zoos.

As early as 1812, palaeontologists and other scientists were proclaiming that there was little likelihood of discovering new species of animals. But even then, with the discovery of the American Tapir in 1819, the fatalists were obviously wrong. Since that time, from the tapir find up to and beyond the okapi, there has been a string of new animals found around the world.

In 1909, for example, German explorer Hans Schomburgk set out to find the giant black pig of Liberia. It took years, but finally he spotted it – big, black and shiny – but it was obviously related to the hippopotamus and not the pig. He was unable to catch it, however, and was forced to return home to face his sceptical critics. But

Schomburgk knew what he had seen and, in 1912, returned to Africa in another effort to capture the animal. This time he returned home triumphantly with not one but five pygmy hippos, each weighing about 400 pounds – one-tenth of the weight of the average adult hippopotamus.

Many unknown or extinct species have been sighted on numerous occasions before one is caught and the physical evidence is presented to sceptics. No one, for example, believed reports about Indonesia's giant monitor lizard, said to be up to 12 feet long and as much as 350 pounds in weight. The stories about the monstrous dragon eating goats, pigs, and even attacking horses, were too incredible for sceptics to take seriously. Then skins and photos were offered as proof, and eventually a live Komodo dragon was caught and exhibited.

Other so-called non-existent creatures included the mountain nyala of southern Ethiopia, the Andean wolf, the kouprey of south-east Asia. Even more interesting have been the discovery of extinct specimens. The coelacanth, a huge, large-scaled, steel-blue fish that, scientists insisted, hadn't existed for six million years, was discovered off the coast of South Africa in 1938. And as recently as 1975, the long-nosed peccary, a relative of pigs, boars and wart-hogs that supposedly died out two million years ago, was discovered in Paraguay.

Close Encounter of the Airline Kind

Eastern Airline captain C.S. Chiles and his copilot, J.B. Whitted, had expected a routine flight on July 23, 1948. Having departed Houston and bound for

Boston, the aircraft soared through the clear, moonlit night at an altitude of 5,000 feet. At a quarter to three in the morning, a few miles south of Montgomery, Alabama, Chiles noticed a red glow heading directly towards the DC-3 with alarming speed.

At first, he thought it was probably some sort of new military jet and Chiles assumed that, seeing the DC-3's red and green warning signals, the jet's pilot would veer clear. It soon became apparent, however, that this was not the case and the Eastern flight crew became increasingly alarmed as they watched the jet continue towards them. Faced with no other alternative, Chiles banked his craft sharply to the left, and as he did so he and Whitted got a good view of the oncoming craft as it passed about 100 feet off the DC-3's right wing.

What they had thought was a military jet was a cigar-shaped and wingless craft with rows of windows illuminated by a blinding white light. It went into a sudden steep climb and then, with a flash of orange flame from its rear, vanished into the sparse clouds.

The late UFO expert J. Allen Hynek believed what Chiles and Whitted saw was actually a meteor, a logical explanation except for an important point: meteors don't change direction and head back out to space.

The 'Ri' of New Guinea

Anthropologist Roy Wagner had been studying the highland natives of New Guinea for more than 20 years when, in the late 1970s, he switched his attention to the Baroks on the island of New Ireland. Living among his subjects, Wagner soon heard an intriguing tale about a 'ri', a mythical entity that had washed ashore decades earlier.

Fascinated, Wagner assumed the *ri*, recognizable by its human head and torso tapering off into the body and tail of a fish, was a member of the extensive bestiary in their legends and beliefs that featured mythical creatures. There continued to be reported sightings, however, and tribal members all insisted the ri truly existed.

Some natives told Wagner they had, on occasion, eaten the *ri* they had caught and relished the particularly tasty flesh. A young boy reported a *ri* procession through a freshwater stream on a moonlit night. One man claimed he had seen a female *ri* caught in a fishing net. Still another had captured one of the marine creatures, but by the time he arrived back at the beach with Wagner in tow, the slippery *ri* had apparently escaped.

Curious about Wagner's account of the *ri*, published after his return to the University of Virginia, cryptozoological researcher J. Richard Greenwell decided to investigate the stories first-hand. Accompanied by Wagner and two geographers, Greenwell arrived in New Ireland in 1983. It wasn't until they had travelled to an area inhabited by the Susurunga, another New Ireland tribe, that the expedition team finally saw the *ri*.

One morning just before dawn, the *ri* seekers observed a marine animal cavorting in Nokon Bay. It had a dark, sleek, slender body. It had no dorsal fin, but neither did it appear to have a human head or arms. Greenwell even managed to photograph the tail flukes as the beast dived below the surface.

Greenwell subsequently consulted numerous marine biologists, and has discounted the possibility that the offshore creature was a porpoise or a seal. At one point, he thought it might have been a dugong, a marine mammal commonly found in the coastal waters around Australia and New Guinea. The creature he observed off New Ireland, however, travelled at great speed, unlike the slow dugong. 'Dugongs, moreover, don't generally stay submerged for more than about a minute,' Greenwell adds. 'Our animal stayed down for 10 minutes.'

Deadly Cloud

According to a group of French astronomers, a giant, dense, interstellar cloud is on a direct course towards Earth and it could have drastic effects on the planet's climate. Some time during the next 10,000 years, says Alfred Vidal-Madjar, the cloud will block the sun's rays and, as a result, cause a new ice age. Alternatively, adds the head of research at France's Laboratory for Stellar and Planetary Physics, the sun could become more luminous.

Interstellar clouds are generally an astronomical mystery, but the French group speculates that the cloud approaching Earth is roughly cigar-shaped and about 10 times longer than it is wide. Estimating the cloud's rate of travel to be about 15 to 20 kilometres per second, Vidal-Madjar believes the cloud could already be as close as one tenth of a light year away.

A precise prediction is impossible but, Vidal-Madjar points out, there's a remote chance that the cloud could start displaying its devastating effects as early as the year 2001.

Prehistoric Atomic Warfare

During the first part of World War I, native officers of the British Indian Army often told their English counterparts that many of the so-called modern weapons were known and used in ancient India. These claims were accepted by the British officers with amused tolerance accompanied by the belief that these assertions were impossible.

Nevertheless some of these 'tall stories' also appeared in historical accounts by non-Indian authors. Alexander the Great received an unaccustomed setback in a war against Porus, an Indian rajah who, according to Greek records, used explosive bombs launched by special artillery troops. The Greeks (and especially their horses), were considerably affected by this phenomenon, occurring as it did more than 2,200 years before combat explosives were 'officially' invented.

Ancient Indian books such as the *Mahabharata* and the *Ramayana*, both thousands of years old, include detailed descriptions of mercury-powered aircraft, projectiles which spread poisoned air in the ranks of the enemy and explosive rockets which followed moving targets (like the sensitized rockets of today) even if they had to follow them 'through the three worlds'. In addition, a superbomb was used to wipe out enemy armies. It was called the 'Iron Thunderbolt', incredibly described as being approximately the same size as a 'Little Boy', which was the name of the first atomic bomb used in modern combat. When the 'Iron Thunderbolt' exploded, it caused great clouds to form in the sky, which were likened to gigantic opening parasols, as compared to our own description of mushroom clouds.

The *Mahabharata*, not translated into English until the middle of the nineteenth century, was long considered by Western readers solely as an interesting religious and literary work. It was not until 1945, at White Sands, New Mexico, that the *Mahabharata* was quoted in a scientific context by a famous scientist.

When the first atomic blast took place, just as the mushroom cloud was ascending, Robert Oppenheimer used a quotation from the *Mahabharata* to describe his feelings:

If the radiance of a thousand suns
Were to burst at once in the sky,

That would be like the splendour of the Mighty
One. . .
I am become Death – the destroyer of worlds.

The *Mausala Parva*, a section of the *Mahabharata*, has
more to say about the effects of the Iron Thunderbolt,
peculiarly reminiscent of the effect of nuclear bombs.

It was a single projectile charged
with all the power of the Universe.
An incandescent column of smoke and flame,
as bright as ten thousand suns,
rose in all its splendour . . .
. . . it was an unknown weapon, an iron thunderbolt,
a gigantic messenger of death
which reduced to ashes the entire race
of the Vrishnis and the Andhakas.
. . . The corpses were so burned
as to be unrecognizable
Their hair and nails fell out -
Pottery broke without apparent cause
and the birds turned white.
After a few hours, all foodstuffs were infected.
To escape from this fire,
the soldiers threw themselves in streams
to wash themselves and all their equipment.

Were these strange parallels to our own experiences
merely an example of ancient science fiction, or were
they accounts of real events that destroyed a civilization
thousands of years before our own developed?

Reunions
Visionary Encounters with Departed Loved Ones

Raymond Moody, M.D.
with Paul Perry

The loss of a loved one is one of the most distressing experiences we are ever likely to encounter. Feelings of intense grief, deprivation and anguish are familiar consequences of such a tragedy, and it is only natural that we should wish, even if only subconsciously, to regain contact with the deceased: to defy the inevitable course of nature, and reverse the irreversible.

Dr Raymond Moody was the first medical doctor to investigate the near-death experience and establish its scientific legitimacy. Now, twenty years after the publication of his ground-breaking classic Life After Life, Dr Moody presents the fruits of his latest research into the fascinating field of living people's contacts with apparitions of the dead. Using specially designed chambers to prompt visions and experimenting with such phenomena as seeing apparitions in mirrors and crystals, Dr Moody has achieved truly astonishing results in calling forth the spirits of the dead, producing visionary encounters in laboratory conditions.

Reunions explores these remarkable findings, and offers guidance on how we also can achieve a level of communication with departed relatives, friends or lovers.

The Final Prophesies of Nostradamus

Erika Cheetham

Erika Cheetham's final, long-awaited volume of
Nostradamus's prophecies, presented for the first time
since 1568 in the original text.

Since Nostradamus's predictions first appeared in
print, his reputation has grown through the centuries
and throughout the world. This French physician, seer
and astrologer foresaw the historic events of his
own and future times with remarkable clarity.

In this volume, Erika Cheetham presents fresh translations
and interpretations of Nostradamus's last prophecies - and
focuses on new and startling predictions through to
the end of this millennium, which are specifically
indicated to aid the reader.

Unlocking the Mysteries of Birth and Death:
Buddhism in the Contemporary World

Daisaku Ikeda

In *Unlocking the Mysteries of Birth and Death: Buddhism in the Contemporary World*, Daisaku Ikeda, leader of the world's largest lay Buddhist organization, the Soka Gakkai International, explores this premise and its means of realization, while charting the universal relevance of Buddhist thought and practice in today's world.

Buddhist patterns of thought can offer release from the suffering of birth, old age, sickness and death through a progressive understanding of their place in the cycle of universal existence. *Unlocking the Mysteries of Birth and Death: Buddhism in the Contemporary World* is a wide-ranging, vigorously written exposition which will challenge and absorb the interested lay reader as well as the initiate.

Warner Books now offers an exciting range of quality titles by both established and new authors. All of the books in this series are available from:

Little, Brown and Company (UK),
P.O. Box 11,
Falmouth,
Cornwall TR10 9EN.

Alternatively you may fax your order to the above address. Fax No. 01326 317444.

Payments can be made as follows: cheque, postal order (payable to Little, Brown and Company) or by credit cards, Visa/Access. Do not send cash or currency. UK customers and B.F.P.O.: please send a cheque or postal order (no currency) and allow £1.00 for postage and packing for the first book, plus 50p for the second book, plus 30p for each additional book up to a maximum charge of £3.00 (7 books plus).

Overseas customers including Ireland please allow £2.00 for postage and packing for the first book, plus £1.00 for the second book, plus 50p for each additional book.

NAME (Block Letters) ....

....

ADDRESS ....

....

....

☐ I enclose my remittance for ....

☐ I wish to pay by Access/Visa Card

Number ☐☐☐☐☐☐☐☐☐☐☐☐☐☐☐☐

Card Expiry Date ☐☐☐☐